Reports of the Research Committee of the Society of Antiquaries of London, No. 73

THE CISTERCIANS IN WALES

Tintern Abbey: fragment of a grave slab, drawn about 1820 by David ap Thomas Powell. The slab, which probably dates from c 1300, almost certainly commemorates one of the abbots of the house. Indeed, it is very tempting to associate it with the burial of Abbot Ralph, who ruled over the community from about 1294 until 1305. Importantly, Ralph was the man who oversaw the completion of Tintern's second abbey church, dedicated in 1301.
Photograph: *Central Library, Cardiff*

THE CISTERCIANS IN WALES

Architecture and Archaeology 1130–1540

David M Robinson

The Society of Antiquaries of London

DEDICATION

To Sally, Daisy and Millie

First published 2006
by
The Society of Antiquaries of London
Burlington House
Piccadilly
London W1J 0BE

www.sal.org.uk

This book is published with the generous assistance of the
following organizations:

Cadw, which is the historic environment service of the
Welsh Assembly Government
The Marc Fitch Fund
The Scouloudi Foundation in association with the Institute
of Historical Research

ISBN 0 85431 285 4
ISSN 0953-7163

726.7712 ROB

British Library Cataloguing in Publication Data
A CIP catalogue record for this book is available from the
British Library.

Original series design by Chuck Goodwin, London W2 5DA
Designed and laid out by Wenham Arts, Peterborough
Printed and bound in Great Britain by The Cromwell Press,
Trowbridge, Wiltshire

CONTENTS

ILLUSTRATIONS

Acknowledgements

Over the time I have been working on the Cistercians in Wales, and especially during the writing of this book, many friends and colleagues have provided academic advice and ideas, or have simply offered support and encouragement along the way. It is my very pleasant duty to record my thanks here. Of those to whom I owe a particularly significant debt of gratitude, I must single out Professor Peter Fergusson and Professor Roger Stalley, the doyens of English and Irish Cistercian architectural studies. It was they who encouraged me to publish, and saw to it that essential channels were opened and funding assured. They were also kind enough to read and comment on earlier drafts of the text. I can only hope the result goes some way to meeting expectations.

I am also enormously grateful to Dr F G (Fred) Cowley (my earliest Cistercian mentor); to Mr Stuart Harrison (for sharing much from his masterful reading of the surviving fabric at so many British Cistercian houses); to Dr Richard K Morris ('Morris of Warwick', generous to a fault with his accumulated knowledge); to Professor Malcolm Thurlby (wit, companion and no mean source of insight into the architecture of the Anglo-Norman realm); and to Dr David H Williams (without whom Welsh Cistercian studies would have been very much the poorer). Those who have been a source of further academic inspiration and ideas over the years include Professor Mick Aston, Mr Terry Ball, Mr James Bond, Dr Janet Burton, Dr Lawrence Butler, Dr Nicola Coldstream, Dr Thomas Coomans, Dr Glyn Coppack, Dr Richard Fawcett, Dr Alexandra Gajewski, Dr John Goodall, Dr Lindy Grant, the sadly missed Professor Lawrence (Larry) Hoey, Dr Terryl Kinder, Dr Linda Monckton and the late Sir Glanmor Williams. It is a pleasure to extend my sincere thanks to them all.

I could hardly have completed the book without the generosity of former colleagues at Cadw. In particular, Mr Richard Avent has been a source of essential support, allowing much else to fall into place. Equally, for many years, Dr Diane Williams has proved never failing in her supportiveness and encouragement, answering a whole string of requests (both small and large) along the way. Mr Rick Turner and Mr Peter Humphries are others whose encouraging words have always been much appreciated. Melanie Francis was most helpful in sorting out the scheduling and listing details appearing in the catalogue of sites, and Mrs Christine Kenyon has provided unswerving assistance in connection with photographs. Two further major debts of gratitude are owed to former colleagues:

firstly, to Mr Chris Jones-Jenkins, who has proved such a valuable sounding board with regard to architectural reconstruction and whose input underlines several of the key drawings in the volume; and secondly, to Mr Pete Lawrence, who has produced the final versions of the maps, plans and elevations with consummate skill (and rare good humour). I have long regarded them both as ex officio members of Cadw.

A number of other people, either as individuals or as representatives of corporate bodies, have offered practical help or shown some considerable kindness when needed. In this context, I should like to mention Mr Jeremy Ashbee, Professor David Austin, Mr Kevin Blockley (of Cambrian Archaeological Projects), Mr Richard Bond, Jenny Britnell and Mr Bob Silvester (of the Clwyd-Powys Archaeological Trust), Dr Jackie Hall, Mr John Kenyon, Mr J M Lewis, Mr John McNeill, Dr John Morgan-Guy, Dr Anna Keay, Mr A F Kersting, Mr Richard Lea, Mr Peter Lord, Mr Neil Ludlow, Professor Gwyn Meirion-Jones, Mr John Newman, Mr Stephen Priestly, and Mr Peter White and Patricia Moore (of the Royal Commission on the Ancient and Historical Monuments of Wales).

The staff at the Society of Antiquaries of London have been especially generous, both during the time I was working on the volume and in seeing it through the press. I am first grateful to the librarians, Bernard Nurse and Adrian James, for their unfailing assistance; the former General Secretary, David Morgan Evans, did much to ensure the success of the project, for which I thank him warmly; and I owe an immense debt to Kate Owen, Publications Manager, not only for her patience and support, but for the considerable care and attention she and her team have put into the final product.

And yet for all these many kindnesses, I could not have completed this book without the support of my family. My greatest and deepest debt belongs to them, to Sally and Daisy, and now Millie, who have seen all too little of me for far too many months. Though it can only go some way to repaying the debt, it is a joy to be able finally to dedicate the book to them, with my love and thanks.

David M Robinson
London
Feast of St Thomas of Hereford, 2004

PREFACE

For students of Cistercian history there is one plain, but all too familiar, fact of life: to turn one's back on the subject, even for a moment, is to lose the plot. No matter where our particular interests lie – be they liturgical, institutional, or architectural – the implications remain the same. Such is the universal appeal of Cistercian studies, the student is obliged to keep abreast of a constant barrage of new material appearing from almost every quarter of the world. The literature on the various early Cistercian liturgical and constitutional regulations, for example, has grown almost beyond belief. It now requires a scholar of the greatest ability to plot the history of the various recensions and present us with the framework chronology we so desperately need.[1] Similarly, the search for greater understanding of the Cistercian architectural ideal, if such ever really existed, has generated intense debate for more than half a century, with no sign of it drawing to a close.[2] Confronted by so much complexity, and by so much contradictory opinion, on occasion one may feel inclined to move away from the field altogether. And yet we are drawn back, time and again, possibly by one inspiring thought, or by a rejuvenating visit to a Cistercian ruin in its tranquil wooded valley, beneath a wide-open sky. We are soon reminded of that extraordinary quality which is the hallmark of the white monks. In the Middle Ages, it was powerful enough to mobilize the munificent patronage of kings, barons and bishops, across the whole of western Europe. For a time at least, both men and women came to see Cistercian monasticism as perhaps the most perfect way of life. Times have changed, but it is nothing if not striking testimony to the beliefs of those bread-and-water-loving ascetics of late eleventh-century Burgundy that the movement they inspired continues to exercise such widespread fascination among so many.

The Cistercians established deep roots in medieval Wales, enriching the country's religious and cultural life in a host of different ways. They caught the imagination of the native people, learning to tap the strong eremitical and heroic element in the religious traditions of the north and west, and filling the gap left by the decline of the pre-Conquest monastic centres. Yet we must remember that the Cistercians were also self-consciously international, wherever they were located. Their presence in Wales was no parochial affair, quite the contrary. The fourteen permanent white monk abbeys examined in this book, whether located in the Marcher borders or in the heart of *pura Wallia* (*see* fig 18), were to incorporate the country fully into the mainstream of European monasticism.[3] Welsh Cistercian abbots were cultured men, used to travelling abroad through attendance at the annual General Chapter held at Cîteaux, or even through the pursuit of litigation in the Roman curia.

These two themes – ongoing revision to the established literature and the need for an international perspective – may be brought together by reference to a traditional, but no less illuminating and relevant, narrative. The source is the *Vita Prima*, the life of St Bernard of Clairvaux (d 1153).[4] In particular, we should turn to the account of an event given in book two of the *Vita Prima*, written by Arnold of Bonneval. According to Arnold, the event in question took place in 1135, at a time in fact when Cistercian stone building in Wales had barely begun. Following a mission to Italy, Bernard had returned to his monastery at Clairvaux, that already highly renowned house in the Champagne region of north-eastern France.[5] Almost immediately, the saint was approached by senior members of the community who were seeking to persuade him of the desperate need to enlarge the monastery complex. The buildings were far too small, they argued, to accommodate the growing body of monks, swollen each day by further new arrivals. At first, Bernard was very far from convinced, and in an oft-quoted passage from Arnold's account we are told of his initial reply:

> See how the buildings have already been built in stone with great sweat and at great expense, and how the water-conduits have at great cost been led to the various rooms. If we throw away all this, people in the world will think badly of us, that we are either frivolous and mutable, or that excessive wealth – though we have no such thing – has made us mad.[6]

In time, nevertheless, Bernard was obliged to acknowledge the good sense of the case; he could do no other than consent to the plans. Work on a new stone church (Clairvaux II) and associated monastic buildings was begun almost immediately, and completed around ten years later.[7] It was an essential first step, probably one of the most significant, in what was to become that outstanding contribution made by the Cistercians to the architectural achievements of the Middle Ages.

What, then, is the relevance of this episode in the *Vita Prima* to the two themes I have highlighted and which are developed through the course of this book? In answering, let me begin with the need for an international perspective on the Welsh Cistercians. As it happens, Clairvaux was the source from which the white monk plantation in much of the principality took its root. Given the wide international significance of the house, coupled with the uniquely centralized structure of the Cistercian order, it would be surprising were not some strain of Clairvaux's architectural development reflected in its filiations across Wales. Furthermore, examples of expensive stone building, followed by rebuilding on a larger scale, can be found time and again throughout the order over the remainder of the Middle Ages. The degree to which this was always a matter of necessity, or became one of architectural ambition founded on increased wealth, need not be our principal concern. Here, the essential point is that the pattern was as much a feature of the Welsh foundations as it was of those anywhere else in the Cistercian world.

As to the second theme, that of frequent revision to established ideas, it may be addressed through reference to recent reviews of just how much we really know of the Cistercian buildings at Clairvaux. The closer one looks, it seems, the more it becomes clear that there is next to no consensus on any aspect of the archaeology and architecture of this fundamentally important site.[8] For example, even the precise location of Clairvaux I (the *monasterium vetus*) is not known with certainty, and authors disagree on whether the buildings recorded in 1708 were of stone or timber.[9] In particular, however, there have been several challenges to the traditional phasing of the abbey church, challenges that rock the foundations on which significant arguments in Cistercian architectural history have hitherto been based. They focus on the monumental stone church seen in the plans and drawings of 1708 (*see* figs 16 and 39). Hitherto, many scholars have accepted that the nave and transepts depicted in this material represent Clairvaux II, the church begun *c* 1135. The chevet at the east end has been considered an addition, raised after St Bernard's death in 1153, and resulting in the later church (Clairvaux III), itself dedicated in 1174. Yet it is now argued that the two buildings may well have been one and the same, part of a single build begun sometime around 1148–53, *before* St Bernard's death. It is further suggested that this single monumental building must have replaced a now-lost earlier church (perhaps of stone) raised at the time of the removal referred to by Arnold of Bonneval.[10] These points will be considered in more detail in the relevant chapters. Here, we need only grasp the fundamental implications of the argument. In sum, the Clairvaux II of the established literature has long been seen as the prototype for a plan found at Cistercian churches across Europe from the 1140s

on.[11] To successfully challenge this belief may not entirely topple a house of cards, but it comes close to it. The new debate is the more relevant in the context of this book when we realize the Clairvaux-style plan occurs at the majority of Cistercian abbeys throughout Wales.

Hence, throughout the course of the volume, I have tried to underline the European dimension to the study of Cistercian buildings in Wales, for they can be fully appreciated only when seen in that context. Equally, I have sought to alert the non-specialist Cistercian reader to areas of current debate, summarizing the arguments and highlighting the implications. I hope at the same time to have sustained a steady narrative strand that can be followed with at least some degree of confidence. It must be acknowledged, however, that any such survey of the Cistercian abbeys in Wales is likely to invite as much frustration as potential reward. Even accepting the inevitable difficulties associated with poorly documented sites, fragmentary architectural remains and diverse standards in the quality and scope of archaeological investigation, there remains yet one further disappointment. In short, despite the extent of recent scholarship on the subject of Cistercian building generally, the Welsh material has simply failed to attract sustained attention. As a consequence, in looking through the extensive body of literature which now exists on the archaeology and architecture of well over a hundred Cistercian abbeys situated throughout Great Britain and Ireland,[12] one might be forgiven for concluding that the principality has no more than a marginal contribution to make to our general understanding. With little by way of exception, the Cistercian abbeys of Wales stand as comparative Cinderellas, their above- and below-ground remains still not properly assessed, nor fully understood.

This book began as an extended essay, one in which I sought to produce a summary of the principal themes in the development of Cistercian monastic building in Wales. I was aware that the material available for study could not possibly be compared with that which exists on the English houses; nor could it rank alongside that which is available on the white monk abbeys of Ireland. I was hopeful, nonetheless, of producing something worthwhile, a contribution which might go some way towards raising the profile of this otherwise poorly appreciated group of Cistercian sites.[13] In the event, as the work progressed, and as I saw, read and understood more, it became clear there was sufficient material for something rather more extensive – if only the time and energy could be found to produce it. The result is a book of still-modest ambition, but one which I trust at last addresses an otherwise sadly neglected aspect of the white monk legacy in Wales.

The content is divided into four parts: the first three represent an overview, which is backed up by the catalogue entries in the final part. Essentially, the key chapters focus on the architectural history of the sites, though I have also drawn heavily on evidence recovered through archaeological method. In the catalogue there is rather more in the way of historical context, all of it important background for those readers wishing to follow up the details on any one particular abbey. The time-frame requires more by way of explanation. It is concentrated on the monastic centuries, beginning with the foundation of the Savigniac abbey at Neath *c* 1129–30 (Cistercian from 1147) and concluding with the final suppression of this same house in February 1539. Yet it would make little sense to launch into the Cistercian contribution to the architectural achievements of medieval Wales without first offering something on the earliest phases of Anglo-Norman church building, if only to set the scene. Moreover, the post-monastic phases of the abbeys are dealt with in two areas, first in the introduction and then more fully in each of the catalogue entries.

The perception of the extent and identity of Wales during the Middle Ages is not quite so clear-cut as one might imagine.[14] As a geographical expression, the country would have been very well recognized by the late eleventh century, but today's formal eastern border was really defined only as the shires here were given their final shape by Henry VIII's Act of Union of 1536–43. For almost two centuries after the compilation of the Domesday survey in 1086, the Anglo-Welsh frontier was in a constant state of flux. A vast sweep of border landscape, running from the Dee in the north to the mouth of the Severn, was carved into a patchwork of virtually autonomous Marcher lordships, ruled over by powerful Anglo-Norman families. The Marcher lordships were also a feature of the entire south Wales seaboard. Meanwhile, until the punitive conquests launched by Edward I, in his campaigns of 1276–7 and 1282–3, much of north and west Wales remained independent, as *pura Wallia*, governed by the native princes of Gwynedd, Deheubarth and Powys. Not surprisingly, as we shall see, these political boundaries were to exert a marked influence on the settlement and patronage of the Cistercian abbeys in Wales.

Some readers may be a little surprised to find that the book looks at fourteen 'permanent' Cistercian foundations. In truth, within what is the principality's modern border, there were no more than thirteen abbeys. Just across the north-eastern border of Monmouthshire, however, on the Welsh side of the River Wye, lies Dore Abbey. Today, one would have to consider that it belongs to Herefordshire. It was, nevertheless, founded by a Marcher, held a considerable estate in Wales and straddled the boundary between the dioceses of St Davids and Hereford, to the point of confusion and contest between several bishops. What is more, by the end of the Middle Ages, the monks of Dore were clearly perfectly content for their abbey to be identified within a definite Welsh Cistercian province, the *provincia Wallie* as it was described in a letter of 1521.[15] I have very little hesitation in including it within the discussion. Beyond these 'permanent' foundations, we must remember that some of the early communities occupied at least one temporary site before settling at their final location. In one case, a second move (from Aberconwy to Maenan) was made almost a century after the initial settlement; as a consequence there is architectural evidence for us to consider at both sites. We also know of at least two aborted attempts to found additional daughter houses. Their precise locations await definite identification and, perhaps, appropriate archaeological investigation at some time in the future.

Introduction

Despoilment and Rediscovery

Introduction

Despoilment and Rediscovery

The fourteen Cistercian abbeys that are the subject of this volume were all suppressed between 1536 and 1539. Without exception, and in common with the pattern at former monastic houses across the whole of England and Wales, an immediate and deliberate degree of despoilation took place, affecting most of the buildings.[1] Those structures condemned by the king's commissioners as superfluous were stripped of everything saleable. Items such as woodwork, iron, glass, furniture, organs, tableware, linen and vestments were very often auctioned on the spot, perhaps in the chapter house or in the cloister. The lead from the roofs was particularly valuable: it was removed, melted into pigs and its quantity carefully noted.[2] In this initial round of destruction, the abbey churches almost invariably tended to suffer to the greatest extent.[3] Meanwhile, some fragment of the monastic buildings was often pressed into new secular use, adapted or transformed to serve as a domestic residence. Such adaptations were certainly responsible for prolonging the existence of various elements of Welsh Cistercian building. Today's survivals are by no means the product of happenstance they may first appear.[4] On the whole, however, it has to be remembered, whether considering the country at large or looking specifically at the white monk abbeys of Wales, that the post-suppression history of these sites – their afterlife as it is sometimes called – is now considerably longer than that of their existence as thriving medieval monastic corporations. Even where quite significant Tudor conversions of Welsh Cistercian monasteries took place, much was for one reason or another subsequently allowed to fall into ruin. The buildings were then further ransacked for their materials. Exposed to the ravages of the weather, they fell into chronic decay, their silhouettes engulfed with a screen of brambles and ivy.

Tintern is unquestionably the best-known Cistercian abbey in Wales (fig 1). Set in the glorious lower Wye valley, it is also the site which features most frequently in general literature concerned with the afterlife of British medieval monasteries, particularly because of its association with the development of Picturesque and Romantic tourism in the late Georgian era.[5] However, notable sequences of post-suppression events also took place at a number of the other abbeys considered in this volume. To begin with, the group includes two of a mere handful of Cistercian churches in England and Wales converted for parochial worship in the mid-sixteenth century. Hence, the twelfth-century nave at Margam and the entire early Gothic east end at Dore are survivals of the greatest importance (*see* figs 42 and 62).[6] More typically, as noted above, some element of the former monastic buildings was adapted for domestic use by the new owner. The two clearest examples of such conversions come from the south, at Neath and at Margam. In the case of Neath, a substantial Tudor great house was built over the south-east corner of the claustral complex (*see* fig 177), perhaps the work of Henry Williams of Hinchingbrooke, about 1560.[7] At Margam, it was Sir Rice Mansel (d 1559) of Oxwich who acquired the site of the abbey in 1537–40, beginning work on the creation of a residence described in the 1590s as 'a faire and sumptious house' (fig 2).[8] The house itself may have been raised over the abbot's residence and the infirmary complex but, in addition to the nave of the abbey church, the chapter house and a fragment of the south transept were also to survive.

Other Tudor domestic conversions at Welsh Cistercian abbeys appear to have been somewhat less grand, or at least little evidence of a significant great house has come down to us. There is, nevertheless, documentary evidence for a 'manor house' at Whitland, perhaps formed out of the west range,[9] and it may also have been the west range which was adapted for use as a residence at Maenan.[10] In 1554, Llantarnam was acquired by William Morgan (d 1582) of Caerleon, who apparently built a house on the site, presumably making some use of the monastic buildings.[11] And at Strata Florida, where the site had passed to the Stedman family by 1567, a house was built over the area of the southern range (fig 3).[12] At Valle Crucis, which fell into the hands of a Yorkshire man, Sir William Pickering (d 1542), the east range (the abbot's residence from the fifteenth

1 Tintern Abbey: watercolour of the mid-1790s, view looking north east over the crossing towards the presbytery and north transept, by J M W Turner (1775–1851). By the time Turner produced this work, Tintern was already a magnet for visitors from across Britain. The ruins were at the height of their appeal to early tourists in search of the 'Romantic' and the 'Picturesque'.

Photograph: *Turner Bequest, Tate Britain*

2 Margam Abbey: painting of c 1700 showing the post-suppression house from the north. The surviving nave of the monastic church, together with the ruins of the polygonal chapter house, can be seen in the right foreground. The house itself was begun by Sir Rice Mansel (1487–1559) who acquired Margam after the suppression. It was described in the 1590s as 'faire and sumptious'.

Photograph: *National Museums & Galleries of Wales*

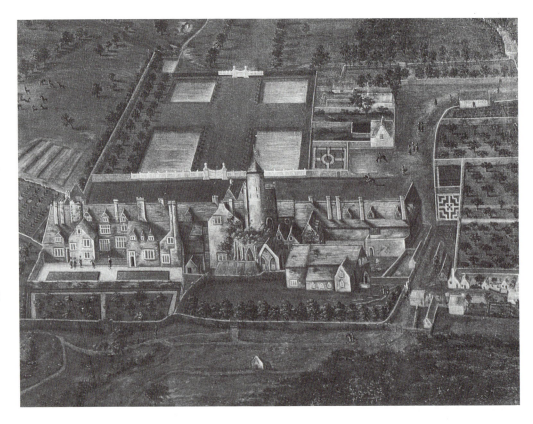

3 Strata Florida Abbey: engraving of the site from the north west, by Samuel and Nathaniel Buck, published in 1741. The house appearing to the right of the view was located over the site of the former southern claustral range. It was built by the Stedman family in the late seventeenth century.
Photograph: *National Library of Wales*

century) was to become a tenant farmhouse.[13] Likewise, at Cymer, a high-status hall located to the west of the church, now dated to the 1440s and probably representing the abbot's accommodation, has continued in use as a farm through to the present day.[14] And at Strata Marcella on the River Severn, a farm complex may have been fashioned around three sides of the former cloister.[15]

Despite these examples of sixteenth-century adaptation and reuse, much was deliberately dismantled with official authority or else the abbey buildings simply fell prey to unlicensed plunderers. It was with Crown authority, for example, that lead from Basingwerk was set aside for repairs at Holt Castle, while some was even transported to Ireland for royal works there.[16] Similarly, large quantities of stone from Maenan were taken to Caernarfon for the repair of the castle, the justice's hall and the town walls.[17] It was again lawful action, one assumes, which led to the removal of five bays from one of the nave arcades at Cwmhir to the parish church at Llanidloes, located some 16km away.[18] Though lost to its original Cistercian site, the material represents a quite remarkable survival (see fig 89). As examples of less legitimate plunder, there are three sites known to have been mercilessly ransacked for their building materials by unscrupulous Crown agents and members of the up-and-coming Elizabethan gentry. At Strata Marcella, for instance, Nicholas Purcell was accused at an inquiry of 1547 of having sold off huge quantities of stone, glass, ironwork and lead from the abbey for use in building works throughout the district.[19] Later in the century, in 1581, a special

commission was set up to investigate 'the spoliation of Whytland Abbey', such was the degree of stone robbing carried out there by Sir John Perrot (d 1592) of Laugharne and by Richard Vaughan and his son.[20] Three years afterwards, local inhabitants were accused of making severe depredations to the 'mansion house' at Valle Crucis, and of pulling down 'great and high stone walls' at the site.[21] It was no doubt these and similar actions which contributed to the severe loss of upstanding architectural features at sites such as Cwmhir, Grace Dieu, Maenan, Strata Marcella and Whitland.

By the second half of the eighteenth century, yet more of the Cistercian architectural legacy in Wales had been lost. In addition to the relentless process of depredation, the important Tudor residences at Neath and Margam were to be abandoned and allowed to fall into ruin, in turn leading to the disappearance of further medieval fabric. Meanwhile, however, there were signs of nascent antiquarian interest in the sites, notably from the brothers Samuel and Nathaniel Buck. In 1732 the Bucks captured the details of the church at Tintern (fig 4),[22] and went on to publish engravings of Neath, Strata Florida (fig 3), Basingwerk and Valle Crucis.[23] As it happens, the fortunes of Tintern were about to change at around this very time. Its setting had for two centuries become engulfed by the early iron industry in this part of the Wye valley,[24] but from the 1750s the dukes of Beaufort began to take a fresh interest in the ruins, clearing much of the debris, turfing the interior of the church and hanging locking doors and iron gates on the points of entry in

4 Tintern Abbey: view of the site from the north east by Samuel and Nathaniel Buck, produced as a preparatory field sketch for their engraving of 1732. The Bucks went on to publish engravings of several other Welsh Cistercian abbeys. At Tintern, although they omitted the north wall of the nave from the drawing, the church looks very much as it survives today.

Photograph: *National Museums & Galleries of Wales*

order to protect the good works from vandalism. By 1787 (and probably rather earlier), the duke was employing a man at Tintern 'to show it to strangers'.[25] Of course, such growing eighteenth-century pride in Gothic ruins cannot be measured in terms of any modern concept of conservation. Rather, at Tintern Abbey as elsewhere, it was stimulated by a powerful new vogue, one concerned with the emotional and pictorial qualities of natural landscape. Apart from its firm grip on artists and poets, the quest for the 'Romantic' and the 'Picturesque' also had, as a popular concept, immense appeal for the leisured classes of the late Georgian era.[26] For the Romantics, Cistercian abbey sites must have seemed the quintessential Gothic ruin, isolated in their steep-sided valleys, attractively verdant in their thick mantle of ivy and set alongside a babbling stream or river. Across the north of England, sites such as Fountains, Furness and Roche (*see* figs 56 and 57) were dramatically transformed, and their ruins were henceforth to be viewed as backdrops to picturesque garden and landscape schemes.[27]

5 *Valle Crucis Abbey: late eighteenth-century watercolour of the site from the south east, by Paul Sandby (1725–1809). For Sandby, the scene is one of a picturesque rural idyll. In the distance, the artist shows the roofless presbytery and south transept, but the buildings of the east range are shown converted for domestic use, with smoke rising from chimneys and linen hung out to dry.*

Photograph: *National Library of Wales*

In Wales, Tintern is of course the site most often associated with the Romantic movement. Indeed, following the works of restoration by the dukes of Beaufort, it continued to act as a magnet to vast droves of tourists through into the nineteenth century and beyond. Its picturesque qualities were captured in scores of drawings, paintings and engravings, by artists such as J M W Turner (fig 1), Paul Sandby, Edward Dayes and John 'Warwick' Smith.[28] Tintern apart, however, the movement was to have a significant impact on the fate of a number of other Welsh Cistercian ruins. In north Wales, for example, Valle Crucis was soon established as one of the early staging points for those tourists venturing forth from Llangollen towards Snowdonia.[29] It too was portrayed in memorable watercolours by Turner and by Sandby (fig 5) and in mass-produced printed engravings.[30] At Margam, where the post-suppression house was gradually abandoned from the 1770s and then completely dismantled in 1789–93, the former abbey chapter house and other fragments were retained as eye-catching features within a grand pleasure park, created for Thomas Mansel Talbot (d 1813).[31] Less prominent, but nonetheless attracting a degree of public notice, were Strata Florida in the south west (fig 6) and Basingwerk in the north east.

In the wake of this widespread popular interest in Cistercian ruins, antiquarian curiosity about individual sites began to grow over the first half of the nineteenth century.[32] On the one hand we might note the beginning of enquiring scholarship, found, for instance, in the careful observations made by men such as John Carter (1748–1817) at Margam (fig 7) and Tintern, or by John Chessell Buckler (1793–1894) at Dore and Valle Crucis.[33] On the other, we inevitably encounter examples of ill-judged excavation, usually carried out by an enthusiastic site-owner, with very little method and hardly any written record. In the 1820s, the new owner at Cwmhir, Thomas Wilson, cleared and excavated the site, removing great quantities of 'rubbish', and allegedly exposing the 'site of the abbot's apartments, and of the refectory, and the dormitories of the monks'.[34] Similarly, at Whitland in the 1830s, Henry Yelverton MP explored areas of the site with 'laudable zeal', uncovering 'foundations of extensive buildings'.[35] This appetite for digging and clearance continued into the middle years of the century: exploratory work took place at Strata Florida in 1847, and in 1851–2 a year-long programme of excavation was carried out on the hitherto deeply overgrown ruins of the church at Valle Crucis (fig 8).[36]

In complete contrast to this frankly destructive investigation, it is encouraging to note the meticulously measured set of drawings of Tintern prepared in the 1840s by the Lichfield architect and antiquary Joseph Potter (fig 9). A second set of Tintern

6 Strata Florida Abbey: engraving of the west front, highlighting the great west doorway, by S Sparrow, 1786. Less spectacular than Tintern or Valle Crucis, the ruins of Strata Florida were nonetheless attracting a degree of public notice by this time.

Photograph: *National Library of Wales*

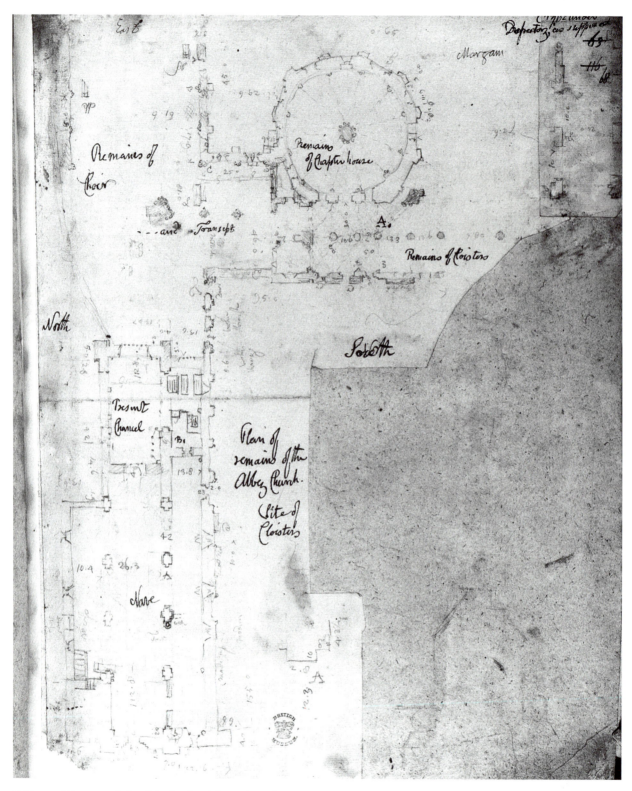

7 Margam Abbey: ground plan of the church and chapter house drawn in pencil and ink by the antiquarian illustrator John Carter (1748–1817) in 1803 (BL, Add. MS 29940, fol 68). This is one of a number of sketches Carter made of the site in the same year. His plan shows the nave of the abbey church before the extensive restorations of 1805–9. Photograph: *British Library*

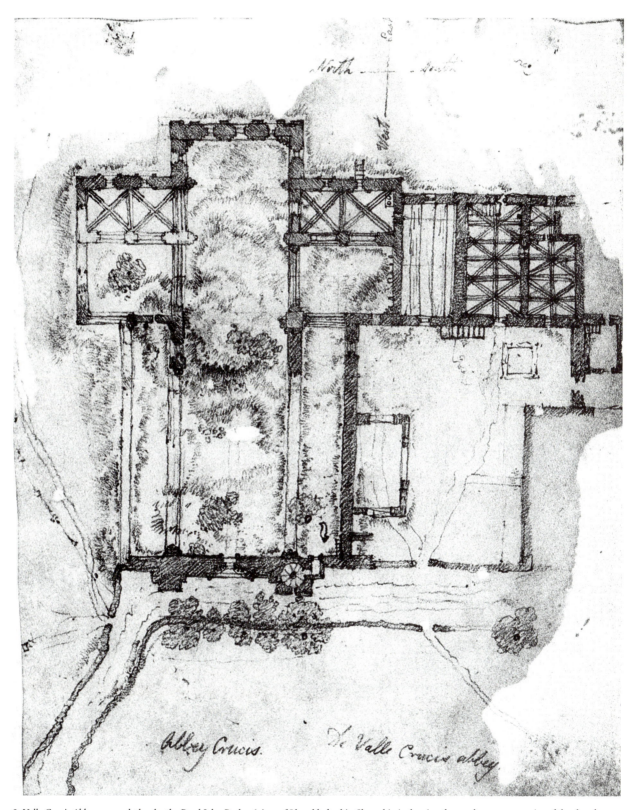

8 *Valle Crucis Abbey: ground plan by the Revd John Parker (vicar of Llanyblodwel in Shropshire), showing the much overgrown ruins of the church, c 1850. A year-long programme of exploratory excavations was carried out on the site in 1851–2.* Photograph: *National Library of Wales*

9 *Tintern Abbey:*
ground plan by Joseph
Potter, 1845. The
plan was published
together with a set of
meticulously measured
drawings of the abbey
buildings in Potter's
Remains of Ancient
Monastic Architecture
in England *(1847),*
Tintern pl i.

Photograph:
British Library

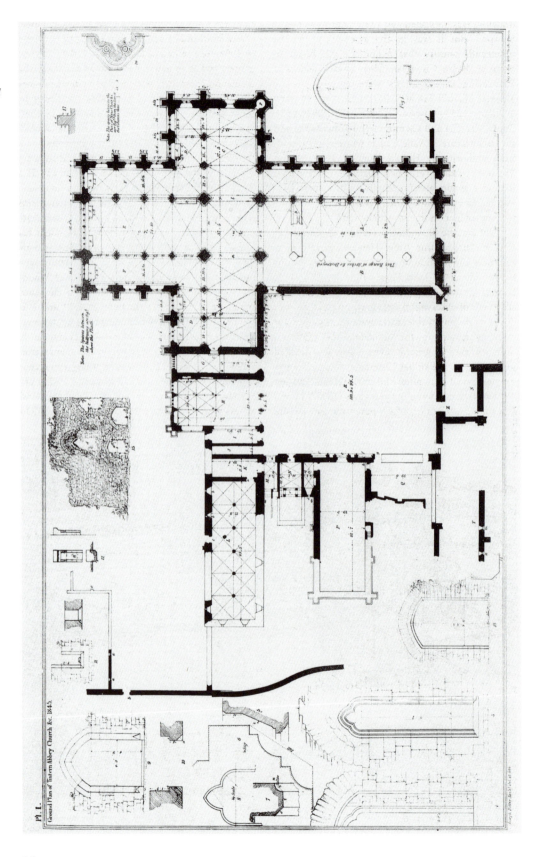

drawings was published just a year later by Edmund Sharpe.[37] But it was in the second half of the nineteenth century that major changes began to occur in Welsh Cistercian fabric studies generally. Pioneering investigations were carried out by Thomas Blashill (1850–1905) at Tintern; Stephen Williams (1837–99) excavated Strata Florida (fig 10), Strata Marcella and Cwmhir, to new standards; and the architecture at Valle Crucis was discussed with fresh authority by Harold Hughes (1864–1939).[38] The one remaining criticism might be that it is hard to find a single late nineteenth-century study of a Welsh Cistercian abbey where the author's horizons were other than in the immediate locality.

Not that the situation was very much different in England up to this time. Henceforth, however, following the publication of a series of monographs by Sir William St John Hope (1854–1919) and Sir Harold Brakspear (1870–1934), expectations for standards of observation were to be much improved. These two remarkable men were responsible for major advances in the archaeological study of monastic sites in general. Even today, our detailed knowledge of individual Cistercian plans is largely the product of excavation and interpretation carried out by them, chiefly in the years after 1900.[39] It was, too, their contribution which paved the way for the

first real work of architectural synthesis on British Cistercian monasteries. In a seminal study published in 1909, John Bilson at last addressed the European context and, in so doing, finally broke away from that insular focus which had typified late nineteenth- and early twentieth-century scholarship on Cistercian buildings.[40] Indeed, until the 1980s, Bilson's synthesis was to remain the essential basis for further scholarly understanding, both in England and in Wales.

The new chapter of developments in Britain as a whole was delayed until the years after the First World War, the time when the State began to assume increasing responsibility for ancient monuments, with Cistercian abbeys always featuring prominently on the list of acquisitions. In fact, a precedent had already been set when Tintern was taken into the nation's care in 1901 (fig 11). The ruins were purchased by the Crown, via the Office of Woods, and extensive conservation work(s) and clearances were carried out on the site between 1901 and 1928 (fig 12).[41] The pattern of State guardianship, however, was to become more widely established during the 1920s and 1930s. Over these two decades, apart from well-known remains in the north of England such as Rievaulx (1917), Byland (1921), Roche (1921) and Furness (1923), the acquisitions included the Welsh abbeys at Basingwerk (1923) (fig 13), Cymer (1930)

10 Strata Florida Abbey: the north transept chapels seen from the west during the excavations of 1887–90. The excavator, Stephen Williams (1837–99), appears as the figure to the left.

Photograph: *National Library of Wales*

11 Tintern Abbey: the west front of the abbey church in the late nineteenth century. The building had stood as an ivy-clad ruin for more than four centuries, with much of its fabric falling into an increasingly perilous condition. The full extent of the decay only became apparent in the years after the site was taken into State care in 1901.

Photograph: *Cadw, Crown Copyright*

and Strata Florida (1931). Neath was to follow somewhat later (1944) (fig 14), while Valle Crucis (1950) was the last of six Welsh houses to be so protected and conserved.[42] Over this entire period, the first priorities of the relevant government department were almost always fabric maintenance and public display. Thorough archaeological investigation and the analysis of upstanding remains took second place. Apart from official guidebooks, important enough in themselves,[43] not one programme of clearance in Wales led to the publication of a really thorough monograph on the structural history of the site, certainly not in terms of anything even remotely emulating the Bilson approach.[44] In the case of Tintern, where the works were so very extensive, this is all the more surprising and equally disappointing.

On the European stage, meanwhile, diverting our attention for a moment from those activities in England and Wales, the late 1940s and 1950s were a time when Cistercian buildings became the subject of much scholarly attention across a wide range of countries. First to appear was a major survey of the French material by Professor Marcel Aubert (1947), which, in terms of its approach and coverage, remains a source of considerable importance today.[45] Afterwards, the German houses were looked at by Henri-Paul Eydoux (1952), the Italian abbeys were discussed by L Fraccaro de Longhi (1958), those in Switzerland were considered by François Bucher (1957), and the Spanish evidence was again summarized by Eydoux (1956).[46] Of even greater significance from the full European perspective was Hanno Hahn's comprehensive overview founded on

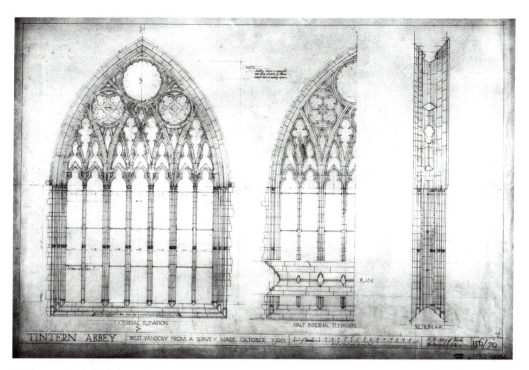

12 Tintern Abbey: HM Office of Works drawing of the west window in the abbey church, 1920. This is one of many record drawings surviving from the first round of State conservation on the site, spanning the years 1901 to 1928.

Photograph: *Ministry of Works Collection, National Monuments Record of Wales, Crown Copyright*

the German monastery at Eberbach (1957).[47] In retrospect, it seems rather surprising that nothing comparable by way of synthesis appeared on the British houses in this period, nor for that matter over the following couple of decades.

On the contrary, the years from 1960 to 1980 were marked if anything by a considerable number of individual excavations, of varying scale and duration, carried out on a wide selection of sites in most parts of the country. Of the seventy-five houses situated in England and Wales, a total of one-third was to some extent tested by the spade over these two decades.[48] It is clear that much valuable new information was recovered in this flurry of archaeological interest, but it must be said that neither the extent of investigation nor the quality of analysis was consistent in every case. In all, though the results from sites such as Boxley (Kent), Kirkstall (Leeds) and Newminster (Northumberland) remain especially useful,[49] as do those from Dr Lawrence Butler's work at Aberconwy, Maenan and Valle Crucis,[50] nothing can compare in terms of productivity or lasting value to the unique achievements made at Bordesley Abbey in the sustained programme of work which began in 1969.[51]

At long last, the 1980s were to witness a marked change in emphasis, with a revival of the European approach to Cistercian buildings pioneered by Bilson over seventy years before. The developments were heralded by an important conference on the theme of Cistercian art and architecture in the British Isles, held at Cambridge in 1983. The following year, Professor Peter Fergusson published his comprehensive and highly acclaimed account of the twelfth-century architecture of the English abbeys,[52] and in 1986 there appeared a stimulating collection of essays based on the Cambridge conference itself.[53] Twelve months after this came Professor Roger Stalley's brilliant synthesis of the Irish evidence.[54] Collectively, these works might be said to have established a major new benchmark, against which it would become much easier to assess both individual and regional elements within the corpus of British Cistercian building. The fruits can be seen, for example, reflected in two very important studies of individual Yorkshire houses: that on Fountains Abbey by Dr Glyn Coppack, and the magisterial work on Rievaulx Abbey by Peter Fergusson and Stuart Harrison.[55] Two fresh works of general synthesis have been published, meanwhile, and interest in conceptual approaches to the material has grown significantly.[56] Abroad, one of the most important landmarks of the last few years has been the publication of investigations at the Belgian abbey of Villers-en-Brabant by Dr Thomas Coomans.[57] Alongside the work by Fergusson and Harrison on Rievaulx, it sets particularly high standards for the comprehensive study of individual Cistercian sites in the future.[58]

Returning finally to the Cistercian abbeys of Wales, it has to be said that over the past few decades the material has become steadily detached from most

13 Basingwerk Abbey: HM Office of Works watercolour showing a conjectural reconstruction of the cloister arcade, 1926. Basingwerk was taken into State care in 1923, with this drawing based on ex situ fragments found during the clearance operations.

Photograph: *Ministry of Works Collection, National Monuments Record of Wales, Crown Copyright*

mainstream studies, and this in spite of the general renaissance of interest during the 1980s. Admittedly, the area lay beyond the scope of Fergusson's work on the English houses, but it is less easy to see, for example, why Wales was not thought worthy of a separate chapter in the Norton and Park volume.[59] In the case of Butler, who has since done something to redress the balance, it can be attributed to the fact that the remains are 'far less impressive or complete' when compared, say, with Yorkshire or, for that matter, with Ireland,[60] and this point does have to be conceded, at least partially, in the light of the remarks made on the quality of the surviving evidence in the preface to this volume. The destruction and loss of so much upstanding fabric is bound to hinder attempts to assess broad stylistic sources. Equally, it becomes that much more difficult to determine any wider architectural affiliations within the region. For all that, the white monk abbeys of Wales have unquestionably been victims of a particular approach to architectural history. This approach, as Roger Stalley has pointed out in his recent study of St Davids Cathedral, is one which regards style as paramount.[61] Buildings situated some distance from the so-called 'centres' of development are inevitably marginalized, with the often implicit assumption that creativity is unlikely to have occurred in such remote settings. Coupling this perceptual bias with views on the centralized nature of Cistercian authority and architectural influence, it is clear to see why Wales is so readily overlooked. Through the course of the following chapters, however, such perceptions are to some extent placed to one side, and the fourteen Cistercian abbeys in question are considered much on their own merits. In this way, a body of comparatively unexplored material is encountered, charged with all manner of possibilities for archaeological and architectural study – only some of which it is possible to cover here.

14 *Neath Abbey: view of the nave looking west in 1946. Extensive clearance excavations had been undertaken on the site by a local amateur group between 1924 and 1934. The ruins were finally placed in the guardianship of the State in 1944. In this view, a timber inspection scaffolding appears against the outer wall of the south aisle.*

Photograph: *Cadw, Crown Copyright*

Part I

Setting the Scene

Chapter 1

The Cistercians and Their Settlement of Wales

It can, in essence, be accepted that the seeds of the so-called Cistercian adventure were sown in a comparatively remote corner of north-eastern France in the spring of 1098.[1] A group of pioneering monks chose to quit the prosperous Burgundian abbey of Molesme (Côte-d'Or) and went in search of a new location where they might follow a life of true austerity and perfect solitude. They settled at a place to the south of the great ducal city of Dijon, where they established the 'New Monastery',[2] which in time was to take the name Cîteaux (fig 15). It was to become the mother house of a vast European family, eventually comprising more than seven hundred

abbeys. In all, the Cistercian achievement was quite without parallel in western monasticism and one of the most remarkable phenomena in the life of the medieval church. It would be wholly wrong, however, to present Cistercian history, especially early Cistercian history, as if all were clear-cut. The truth is very far from that.

We might take as a starting point the classic twentieth-century account of the monastic order in medieval England. In that volume, Dom David Knowles found it a comparatively straightforward task to outline the emergence of the Cistercian movement and to provide an overview of what he

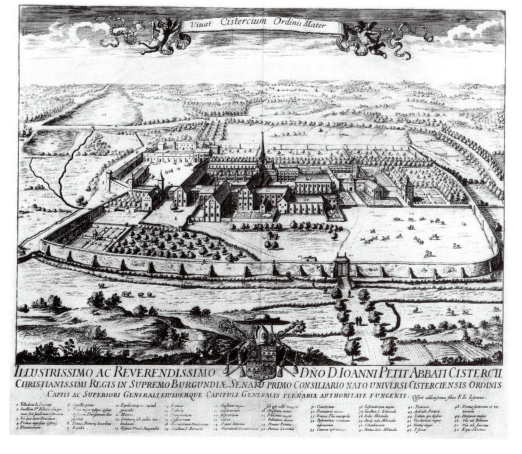

15 *Cîteaux Abbey (Côte-d'Or, France): engraving showing the site from the south by P Brissart, 1674. Founded in 1098, Cîteaux was to become the mother house of the vast European Cistercian monastic family, eventually including more than seven hundred abbeys. In this engraving the twelfth-century abbey church appears near the centre, readily identified by the flèche above the crossing. The cloister buildings are to the fore, with the whole complex surrounded by a high precinct wall.*

Photograph: *Bibliothèque Nationale de France, Paris*

19

described as the order's 'constitutional framework'.[3] Yet, as Knowles himself was aware, perceptions of the early Cistercian landscape had changed dramatically in the period between the initial appearance of his volume in 1940 and the publication of the second edition in 1963, in a large part due to the achievements of scholars such as Josef Turk and Jean Lefèvre. To underline his appreciation of this change, Knowles referred his new readers to an important work on Cistercian history, first published in 1945. J-B Mahn, a young French scholar, had claimed: 'Few religious orders possess a history of their origins as clear and simple as the Cistercian order'.[4] As Knowles was quick to point out, at the time this was written, such sweeping affirmations would have been accepted by all, whereas 'Today those words can serve only as a warning to historians that their general judgements, even when apparently based upon solid rock, may be washed away overnight'.[5]

In subsequent years, the debate between scholars concerned with the early history of the Cistercians and their literature has intensified. Time and again, the material has been shown to be complex and multi-layered, with no one universally accepted consensus emerging, or at least not until recently.[6] In particular, the dating of the key narrative accounts of the origins of Cîteaux, the *Exordium Parvum* and the *Exordium Cistercii*, has for long been problematical. Moreover, the various recensions of the fundamental constitution of the Cistercian order, the *Carta Caritatis*, have proved equally difficult to unravel, as is the case with the general body of basic regulations to be followed by the white monks, the *Capitula*. If nothing else, what has certainly become clear through all this debate is the fact that the self-identity of the Cistercians took time to develop; the process was rather slower and more gradual than was once thought. Meanwhile, almost as a consequence of the debate, some historians have been drawn to write about Cistercian history in terms of 'ideals' and 'reality'. The paradigm is one which sees everything early as a reflection of the beliefs of the founding fathers, whereas much that emerges from the late twelfth century onwards is to be interpreted as an almost inevitable process of decline from that high original position.[7] More recently, scholars have shown this was simply not the case. Indeed, the early Cistercians were never so uniform and organized as their own twelfth-century propaganda machine would have us believe.[8] This in turn brings us back to the so-called 'primitive documents'.

Father Chrysogonus Waddell has recently produced the most definitive editions yet published of three fundamental sources for our understanding and appreciation of the early Cistercians and their way of life.[9] First, he presents a critical review of the early narrative and legislative texts, offering carefully measured views on appropriate dating. Secondly, there is a solid version of the rule book in which is set out the way of life for the Cistercian lay brothers, the *Usages* as it is known. And, finally, he has published an exhaustive new edition of the twelfth-century statutes, the regulations and decisions effectively imparted to the order at the annual General Chapter meeting held at Cîteaux.[10] Controversy, however, will not go away. In particular, before proceeding note should be taken of the fresh debate about the character of the early Cistercians, triggered through a remarkable book by Professor Constance Berman, in which she asserts, principally, that the order was an 'invention' of the third quarter of the twelfth century.[11] Berman argues that the General Chapter did not appear until sometime after 1150, and that the earliest constitution belongs to the 1160s. It must be remembered, of course, that Professor Berman was not armed with Waddell's fresh assessments of the essential documents at her time of writing. Nevertheless, much of her thesis is open to question, as demonstrated in several published responses.[12]

CISTERCIAN ORIGINS

From the ninth century, the supreme guide for the monastic way of life was the Rule of St Benedict. It had originally been written sometime between AD 535 and 550 at the hilltop monastery of Monte Cassino, south of Rome, by Benedict of Nursia.[13] The Rule progressively gained currency across western Europe, and in AD 816–17 its position was ratified with imperial support at two synods held in Aachen.[14] However, the concept of the monastic life would never remain static, nor were all monks destined to make saints: standards of discipline and devotion were to vary among the Benedictine abbeys of Europe, and it was a dissatisfaction with established monastic regimes which led to periodic attempts at reform. One early centre of revival was the great French abbey of Cluny, situated near Mâcon (Saône-et-Loire). Founded in AD 909, this was a house at first insistent upon a stricter observance of the Rule of St Benedict. Its rise heralded a new dawn, and it was eventually to become the head of a vast congregation of hundreds of affiliated houses located across Europe. Yet, in time, critics were to round on Cluny's aristocratic brand of monasticism.[15]

There were, for example, men like St Romuald (d 1027), founder of the community at Camaldoli, or St John Gualberto (d 1073), who established Vallombrosa, both of whom were intent on returning to the eremitical ideals and austere simplicity of early desert monasticism.[16] By the late eleventh century, a slowly swelling tide of reform broke into open flood and Europe was to witness an unprecedented monastic renaissance, with a dramatic proliferation of new religious orders through into the early twelfth century.[17] The founding fathers of the communities born at this time were once more determined to correct abuses and to return to the simplicity of the Rule of St Benedict. Often they were inspirational dreamers, yearning for solitude, and intent upon finding a yet purer form of monastic life and observance. Many, like John of Fécamp (d 1078), again sought to dust off the beliefs of the earliest monastic fathers; theirs was a quest for the 'lovely desert … the dwelling place of lovers of God'.[18]

It was in 1098 that one such malcontent, Abbot Robert of Molesme (d 1110), decided to leave the Burgundian abbey he had founded just over two decades earlier, taking with him a group of like-minded brothers.[19] Among their motivations and intentions, Robert and his followers were determined to seek out a physically austere location, one where they might live 'more strictly and perfectly according to the Rule of the most blessed Benedict'.[20] Robert's early career as a leader of ascetics was full of restlessness, and once again he felt the need to move on. He was to lead his party of dissident monks to a marshy and forested 'desert-place' south of Dijon. At a location graphically remembered in the *Exordium Cistercii* as 'a place of horror and of vast solitude',[21] they set up the 'New Monastery' (*Novum Monasterium*). Later it took the Latin name *Cistercium*, a word derived from its marshy location. Today we know the place as Cîteaux.[22]

Robert himself was obliged to return to Molesme, and care of the fledgling community was left in the hands of his successor, Alberic (d 1109).[23] The third abbot was an Englishman, Stephen Harding (d 1133), widely acknowledged as the leader who gave the earliest legislative shape to the spiritual ideals of the Cîteaux experiment.[24] To begin with, Stephen's insistence upon a course of extreme austerity pushed the poverty-stricken house to the brink of destruction. Gradually, however, the tide began to turn. With grants of land received and new recruits arriving, Cîteaux was in a position to establish its first daughter colony, at La Ferté (Saône-et-Loire), by 1113, followed by that at Pontigny (Yonne) in 1114.[25] In the longer term, Stephen's was the rare vision and constructive genius which provided a solid platform for the expansion and success of the emerging Cistercian order.

In the same year as the foundation of La Ferté, Cîteaux's fortunes were further transformed when a young nobleman, Bernard of Fontaines, sought admittance to the novitiate with a significant group of followers.[26] Two years later, in 1115, further daughter houses were established at Morimond (Haute-Marne) and at Clairvaux (Aube) (fig 16).[27] The charismatic Bernard was appointed abbot of Clairvaux, and from there he became the movement's arch propagandist, taking a major role in the creation of the Cistercian identity.[28] A persuasive and eloquent preacher, who somehow personified the monastic ideal, Bernard was in regular correspondence with popes, kings and bishops for more than three decades.[29] Such was his universal fame and influence that by the time of his death in 1153 there were some 340 Cistercian abbeys scattered across most parts of Europe, more than 180 of which were affiliated to Clairvaux.[30] It is important to bear in mind, however, that these figures not only represent brand new colonies but also include several groups of hitherto independent congregations incorporated within the Cistercian family.[31] The abbey of Cadouin (Dordogne) in south-west France, for example, seems to have surrendered its independence to become a daughter house of Pontigny in 1119.[32] Then, in 1147, at a significant General Chapter meeting, approval was given for the absorption of the congregations of Savigny (Manche) and Obazine (Corrèze).[33]

CISTERCIAN IDEALS

As a result of the scholarly debate over recent decades, it is now widely appreciated that it would be wholly wrong to think of the creation of a fully fledged Cistercian philosophy as springing from a single mind during the events of 1098. On the contrary, the Cistercian constitution, and with it the movement's self-identity and its emergence as a distinct monastic order, was something that developed gradually over the years, partly in response to changing circumstances. Nevertheless, that all-important self-identity was clearly in evidence by the second quarter of the twelfth century. Writing about 1124, for example, the monk-chronicler William of Malmesbury described the Cistercian way of life as 'the surest road to heaven'. He concluded that the Cistercians were 'an example for all monks, a mirror for the zealous, a gadfly for the easy-going'.[34] Similarly, Orderic Vitalis, writing *c* 1135 at the Benedictine abbey of St Evroult, was impressed with the way the Cistercians had 'built monasteries with their own hands in lonely, wooded places'. His crowning accolade was his suggestion that 'by the great good they do they shine out in the world like lanterns burning in a dark place'.[35]

The spirit of the Cistercian life and the method

of its governance is set out in several recensions of the key early narrative and legislative documents.[36] Both the *Exordium Parvum* and the *Carta Caritatis* appear to date, at least in their primary form, from the abbacy of Stephen Harding (1109–33). The *Exordium Parvum*, perhaps compiled by Stephen about 1113, served as an authoritative account of the origins of Cîteaux for the benefit of a new generation of monks. Alongside it, the *Carta Caritatis*, an early version of which was confirmed by Pope Calixtus II in 1119, served as the order's constitutional manifesto. This small masterpiece of prose, clarity and good sense was the basic tool for maintaining uniformity of observance at all abbeys.[37] Both sources articulate the importance of a close adherence to the Rule of St Benedict. Indeed, as William of Malmesbury tells us, the Cistercians thought it wrong to diverge from its content 'by one letter, one iota'.[38] To underline further

their particular brand of monasticism, however, the order's founding fathers developed a series of carefully orchestrated daily organizational observances and practices, which came together in the *Ecclesiastica Officia*.[39] In addition, key decisions made by the order's governing body, the General Chapter, were formalized in a series of statutes, early codified as the *Capitula* (*c* 1136–7) and subsequently the *Instituta* (*c* 1147).[40]

Underpinned by their spiritual and legislative framework, the Cistercians came to be distinctive in almost every facet of monastic life, including such matters as vocation and recruitment, art and architecture, and estate management.[41] Fundamentally, in their garb and in their attitude, there was an uncompromising insistence upon poverty; the Cistercians rejected all sources of luxury and wealth. To ensure the seclusion essential for true

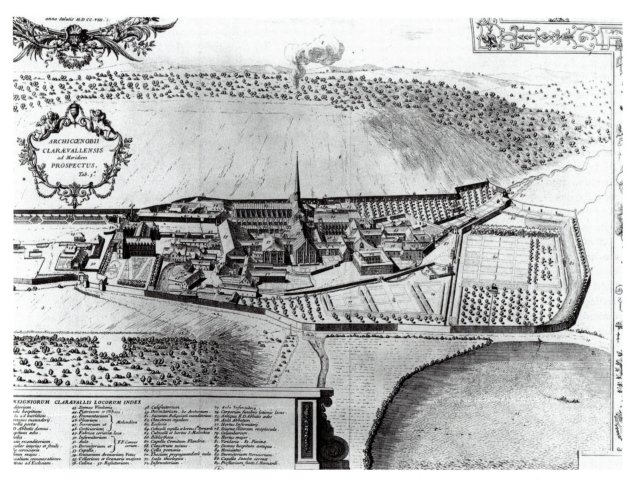

16 *Clairvaux Abbey (Aube, France): engraving by Dom Nicolas Milley showing the site from the south, 1708. Founded in 1115, Clairvaux was one of the four so-called 'elder daughters' of Cîteaux. Under its first abbot, St Bernard (1115–53), Clairvaux sent out colonies to numerous Cistercian abbeys across much of Europe, including two in Wales. The date of the abbey church (seen at the centre of this view) has become a subject of considerable debate. The three main claustral ranges lay to the south, with guest accommodation to the west and the infirmary cloister and associated buildings to the east.*
Photograph: *Bibliothèque Nationale de France, Paris*

contemplation, just as at Cîteaux, their abbeys were to be sited in isolation away from towns and villages, 'far from the concourse of men'.[42] The cult of poverty and simplicity certainly extended to their practical dress. The Cistercians turned their backs on the refined black robes of the Benedictines, forbade the wearing of woollen undershirts and breeches, and chose to dress in simple habits of coarse undyed wool – giving rise to their common identification as the 'white monks'.[43] They followed a strict rule of silence, and at first survived on a comparatively meagre vegetarian diet.[44]

Cistercian churches were to be plain and devoid of all ornament,[45] their services were to be stripped of all liturgical intricacies, and even their singing was to be kept at a discreet pitch.[46] New abbeys could be established only under carefully laid down conditions. Most were founded as colonies, or daughters, of existing houses and were to comprise at least twelve monks with an abbot.[47] Supervision was maintained across the emerging order by means of a mutual system of visitation among mother and daughter houses, even if in different countries. Moreover, all abbots were required to attend the annual General Chapter meeting at Cîteaux.[48]

The Rule of St Benedict had made time in the monastic day for manual work (*opus manuum*), but as the services in the older Benedictine and Cluniac houses had become richer and more complex, this aspect of daily life was progressively overlooked. The Cistercians chose to prune back the liturgy and to follow the offices in the basic form ordained by the saint.[49] They restored the importance of manual work to the monastic life, which was to have a profound effect on the nature of their communities. During the formative years of the twelfth and thirteenth centuries, life within a Cistercian monastery could almost be seen as falling into two halves. Where practical, the white monks chose to avoid the customary feudal sources of revenue such as church tithes, manors, mills and rents,[50] so the intensive cultivation of agricultural land was as much an economic necessity as it was an essential facet of the Cistercian monastic life.[51] But it was in the further stage of providing a labour supply to undertake this work that the order proved so revolutionary.

Although the choir monks undertook some manual work, the greater part of the heavy agricultural labour was undertaken by lay brothers, known as *conversi*. Other orders had turned to lay brethren in the past, but on nothing like the scale developed by the Cistercians from the mid-twelfth century.[52] A specific rule book, the *Usus Conversorum*, was developed in order to provide some guidance on their management.[53] Recruited largely from the illiterate classes of society,[54] the *conversi* made their contribution to religion through their labour. During the early Middle Ages they arrived in huge armies at abbey gateways, often outnumbering the choir monks by two or three to one. Some lay brothers worked in the immediate vicinity of the abbey, while others travelled to work on outlying estates, usually within a day's journey, where lands had been acquired and organized into the characteristic Cistercian farms, known as granges.[55] At the abbey, the lay brothers lived as part of the full community,[56] though they were bound by less severe rules. This division between choir monks and *conversi* had powerful influences upon the architectural arrangement of Cistercian monasteries.

When it comes to the specifics of architecture, the early narrative and legislative Cistercian texts are surprisingly vague. Apart from a single reference to bell towers,[57] as Professor Christopher Holdsworth has pointed out, there is 'not a word about the size and shape of the buildings in which the monks were to live and pray'.[58] Whatever is known about the early Cistercian attitude towards architecture has to be gleaned from other writings, such as the content of sermons, letters and the occasional treatise.[59] Here, we encounter vague words and phrases – 'grand' or 'sumptuous', 'ablaze with light and colour' – generally used in a way that might stigmatize what was considered unacceptable. Of course, information of this type can really provide only an impression of the Cistercian architectural ideal, rather than something that might be taken as a blueprint for its widespread dissemination.[60] Much has been made of St Bernard's well-publicized treatise of *c* 1125, his *Apologia* to Abbot William of St Thierry.[61] Clearly, Bernard's condemnation of 'the immense height' of certain monastic churches, 'their immoderate length, their excessive width, sumptuous decoration and finely executed pictures', has some overall bearing on the way we should interpret Cistercian architectural attitudes through to the mid-twelfth century. But it is all too easy to forget that the *Apologia* was composed at a time when the white monks had no significant monumental architecture of their own. To this point, their churches appear to have been deliberately small and especially austere, far more in the nature of simple oratories than major cruciform buildings.

From the mid-1130s onwards, however, when the Cistercians began to build on a much larger scale, a degree of similarity unquestionably emerged in the design of many of their churches. At the very least, it becomes possible to identify a distinct architectural aesthetic, hardly surprising in an order so fiercely self-conscious of its reformist image in all other areas. And yet this does not mean we have to apply a single stylistic label to Cistercian architectural forms. It may, as Roger Stalley has suggested, be more profitable to think in terms of a Cistercian 'attitude' towards architecture.[62] In this way, when we look at the Cistercian buildings of Wales, or for that matter those in any other area of Europe, we can appreciate a certain evocation of Burgundian ideals, but we are never blinded to the importance of the regional architectural style.

THE CISTERCIANS IN BRITAIN AND IRELAND

In most essentials, the order was very well established when, in 1128, William Giffard, bishop of Winchester (1107–29), brought the first Cistercian colony to England.[63] The site chosen was at Waverley in Surrey (fig 17), with the founding monks drawn from the abbey of L'Aumône (Loir-et-Cher), itself a daughter of Cîteaux and known as 'Petit-Cîteaux'.[64] It so happens, however, that a colony of the Savigniacs, that Norman congregation absorbed into the Cistercian order in 1147, had already been established. Stephen, count of Mortain and later king of England (1135–54), had settled a community at Tulketh in Lancashire in 1124, which moved to Furness in 1127; and further Savigniac colonies were to be established in the course of the 1130s.[65] Meanwhile, Waverley established its position and gradually became the mother of an important group of houses in southern and midland England. But it was Yorkshire that proved to be the true cradle-land of Cistercian success in Britain.

The systematic colonization of northern England was initiated by Clairvaux, under the direction of St Bernard himself.[66] In 1131, a group of monks appeared at the court of Henry I (1100–35) bearing a letter from Bernard, virtually ordering the king's help in the matter of the foundation of Rievaulx Abbey. It ran:

> In your land there is an outpost of my Lord and your Lord, an outpost which he has preferred to die for than lose. I have proposed to occupy it, and I am sending men from my army who will, if it is not displeasing to you, claim it, recover it, and restore it with a strong hand.[67]

Rievaulx was officially founded in March 1132.[68] Later that year came the famous secession of a group of Benedictine monks from the abbey of St Mary in York, eventually leading to the foundation of Fountains, which, having been received as a daughter of Clairvaux, was to become the largest Cistercian abbey of medieval England.[69] Between them, Rievaulx and Fountains were to become the heads of considerable families. Rievaulx alone colonized five

further daughters, and through them eventually headed a filiation of up to nineteen houses, many of them in Scotland. Fountains spawned seven daughters and four granddaughters.[70] Meanwhile, the only other first-generation Clairvaux daughter in England was the house at Boxley in Kent, founded in 1143.[71] However, Clairvaux's extensive and very important family in Ireland, which sprang from Mellifont in County Louth, founded in 1142 under the influence of Malachy, archbishop of Armagh, must not be overlooked.[72]

By 1152, the year in which the General Chapter sought to call a halt to further foundations,[73] there were almost fifty Cistercian abbeys situated across England, including eleven houses incorporated into the order from the congregation of Savigny in 1147.[74] The 1152 statute proved ineffective, but the main period of expansion in England was in any case already over. Just over a dozen further foundations were made, with the total eventually reaching sixty-two.[75]

THE WELSH FOUNDATIONS

Much as in the north of England, the Cistercians were to establish particularly deep roots in Wales, with a total of fourteen houses founded within the bounds of the modern principality, or on its immediate border (figs 17, 18 and 19). The course of their foundation and subsequent history is often seen in terms of two distinct streams.[76] On the one hand, those houses in the south and east were founded by Anglo-Norman barons (or, in one case, a Norman churchman) with their subsequent fortunes largely dependent upon later Marcher lords. In contrast, the other stream flowed through the heart of Wales, *pura Wallia* as it was sometimes called. Here, it was St Bernard's Clairvaux that was destined to be the fount of the Welsh Cistercian triumph. White monk monasticism was at home in the terrain of the north and west; its prosperity was assured by its appeal to the native dynasties of these regions.

The Cistercians made their first landfall in Wales in 1131, when a colony from L'Aumône arrived at Tintern (fig 20) in the Wye valley under the patronage of the Anglo-Norman lord of Chepstow, Walter fitz Richard de Clare (d 1138).[77] The explanation for Walter's interest in the Cistercians seems to lie in his kinship with Bishop William Giffard, who had brought the primary white monk colony to Britain just three years before.[78] Despite its early foothold in the southern March, Tintern was to play no further role in the Cistercian settlement of Wales; its only daughter houses were at Kingswood in Gloucestershire, founded in 1139, and Tintern Parva in Ireland, established in 1201–3.[79]

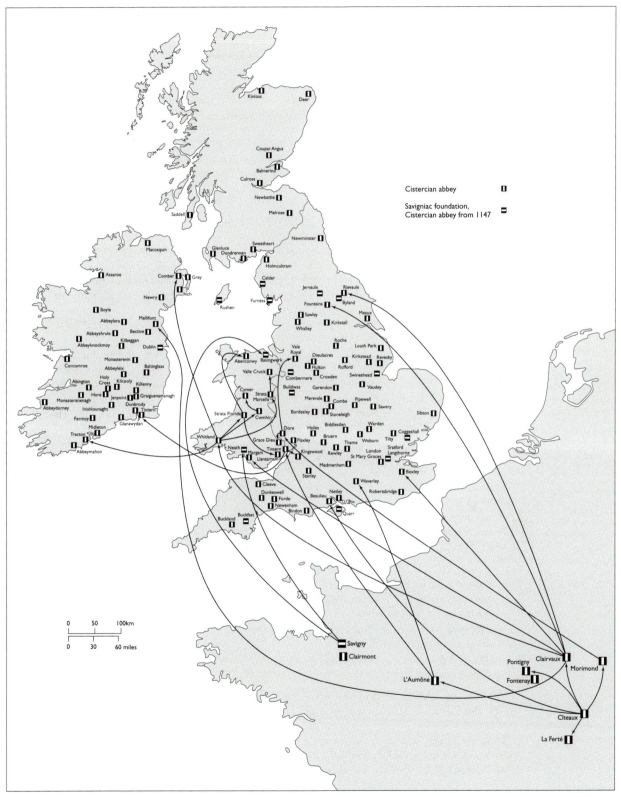

Cistercian abbey

Savigniac foundation,
Cistercian abbey from 1147

17 Cistercian abbeys in Britain and Ireland: map showing also the first-generation affiliations with French mother houses. All the family links of the Welsh houses are given. Drawing: *Pete Lawrence, for Cadw*

25

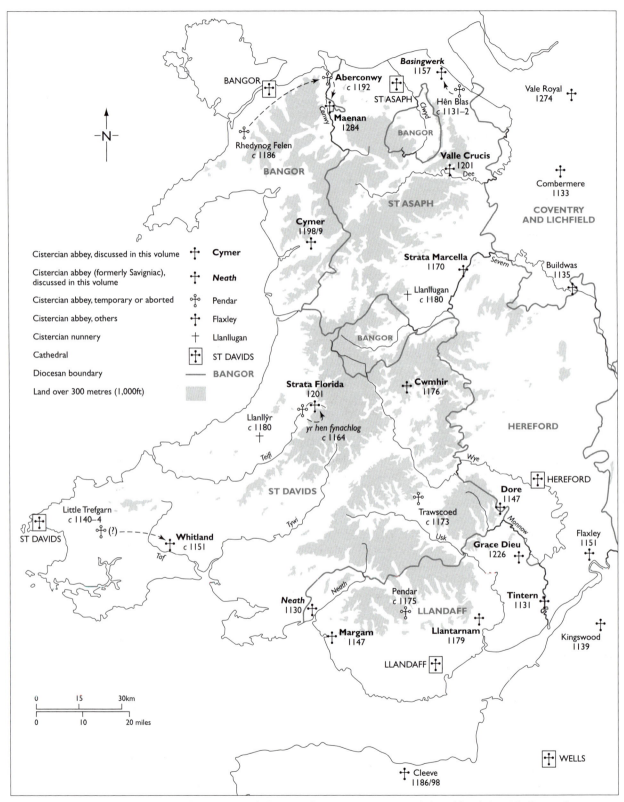

BANGOR

Basingwerk
1157

Aberconwy
c 1192

ST ASAPH

Hên Blas
c 1131–2

Vale Royal
1274

Maenan
1284

BANGOR

Rhedynog Felen
c 1186

BANGOR

Valle Crucis
1201
Dee

Combermere
1133

ST ASAPH

COVENTRY
AND LICHFIELD

Cymer
1198/9

Strata Marcella
1170

Buildwas
1135

Llanllugan
c 1180

BANGOR

Strata Florida
1201

Cwmhir
1176

HEREFORD

Llanllŷr
c 1180

yr hen fynachlog
c 1164

Teifi

ST DAVIDS

Wye

Little Trefgarn
c 1140–4

HEREFORD

Dore
1147

ST DAVIDS

Tywi

Trawscoed
c 1173

Whitland
c 1151

Taf

Usk

Monnow

Flaxley
1151

Grace Dieu
1226

Neath

Neath
1130

Pendar
c 1175

Tintern
1131

LLANDAFF

Kingswood
1139

Margam
1147

Llantarnam
1179

LLANDAFF

WELLS

Cleeve
1186/98

Cistercian abbey, discussed in this volume	✢	**Cymer**
Cistercian abbey (formerly Savigniac), discussed in this volume	✢	***Neath***
Cistercian abbey, temporary or aborted	⚲	Pendar
Cistercian abbey, others	✢	Flaxley
Cistercian nunnery	✝	Llanllugan
Cathedral	⊡	ST DAVIDS
Diocesan boundary	—	**BANGOR**
Land over 300 metres (1,000ft)		

N

0   15   30km

0   10   20 miles

18 *Cistercian abbeys in Wales and the March: map showing the locations of temporary, permanent and aborted foundations. The fourteen houses covered in the volume appear in bold type. The four medieval Welsh dioceses and their cathedrals are also shown. Drawing: Pete Lawrence, for Cadw*

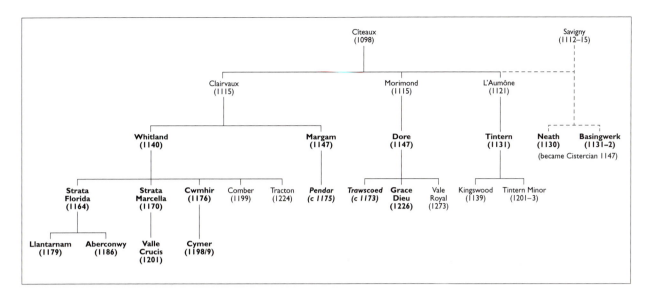

19 *Cistercian abbeys in Wales and the March: diagram showing mother, daughter and family affiliations.*

Drawing: *Pete Lawrence, for Cadw*

It is important to remember, of course, that the Cistercians were not the first of the new monastic orders to arrive in Wales.[80] Just as in England, they were preceded by the Savigniacs. Two houses of the congregation had been established in the Welsh March, staffed directly by the parent abbey of Holy Trinity, Savigny, itself situated on the borders of south-west Normandy (fig 17). In south Wales, Richard de Granville, constable to Earl Robert of Gloucester (d 1147), provided the endowments for a Savigniac monastery at Neath (fig 21), where the foundation is officially dated to 1130.[81] At much the same time, Ranulf 'de Gernon', earl of Chester (1129–53), was planning to found a further house of the congregation in an area of disputed borderland in the north east, on the western shore of the Dee estuary. The brothers arrived in 1131–2, and in the first instance may have been settled at Hên Blas, near Coleshill. With the support of Henry II, the community was moved to Basingwerk by 1157 (fig 18).[82] Neath and Basingwerk were incorporated into the Cistercian order in 1147, along with all other abbeys of the Savigniac congregation, .

The circumstances surrounding the arrival of monks from Clairvaux into south Wales are nowhere near so well documented as is the case in the north of England. Yet St Bernard would surely have been apprised of the contemporary Welsh scene through his many contacts with the nobility and distinguished ecclesiastics. In the event, 'soldiers' of the Clairvaux 'army' were first settled on Welsh soil by Bernard, the Norman bishop of St Davids (1115–48), probably in 1140. Within four years, they had been found a home at Little Trefgarn, north of Haverfordwest, but by *c* 1151 the community had moved to a more suitable site at Whitland.[83]

Meanwhile, in 1147, Clairvaux had establish its second Welsh colony, at Margam on the southern coast. The founder was Robert, earl of Gloucester and lord of Glamorgan, the bastard son of Henry I and a staunch protagonist of the Empress Matilda during the years of the Anarchy.[84] The site chosen for this house was on the western margins of Robert's lordship, at a location long occupied by a significant pre-Conquest ecclesiastical establishment, itself witnessed by an important collection of inscribed and sculpted stones.[85] In the same year that the Clairvaux monks arrived at Margam, another of the four senior houses of the order, Morimond, had despatched a colony to occupy the border monastery at Dore, its official date of foundation being given as 26 April 1147.[86] The founder here was Robert fitz Harold, lord of Ewyas, though there is no apparent explanation for his particular choice of mother house. Indeed, Morimond's main spheres of influence were in Germany and eastern Europe, and in north-east Spain.[87] Dore proved to be its only British daughter house.

Of this group of three foundations made in the 1140s, only Margam failed to establish a permanent daughter house, despite the fact it had been reasonably well endowed and with no sign that it experienced recruitment difficulties. Having said this, about 1170–5, Margam does seem to have made a quite definite attempt to colonize a site at Pendar, in the uplands of Glamorgan. Land intended for a new monastery had been granted by Gruffudd ab Ifor (d 1210), lord of the *cantref* of Senghennydd. At least two other grants were to follow, both mentioning the brethren of Pendar. Despite this clear native Welsh support, the daughter colony was to prove abortive.[88]

20 *Tintern Abbey: aerial view of the site from the south east. Set on the west bank of the River Wye, Tintern represents the Cistercians' first landfall in Wales. It was founded by Walter fitz Richard de Clare (d 1136) in 1131 and colonized by a community of monks sent from the French abbey of L'Aumône (Loir-et-Cher). The abbey church, the ruins of which are the most prominent survival, dates from the late thirteenth century. The monastic buildings lay to the north.*

Photograph: *Copyright Skyscan, for Cadw*

Similarly, Dore Abbey's first attempt to establish a daughter house ended in failure. In this case, about 1172–4, Walter de Clifford (d 1190) gave the Dore community lands and privileges at Trawscoed in Cantref Selyf, within the Marcher lordship of Brecon. The grant was intended 'to build an abbey … to increase the monastic order of the Cistercians'.[89] Again, either due to lack of recruitment, or more likely insufficient endowment, the nascent house was abandoned, possibly in the early years of the thirteenth century. The lands at Trawscoed were afterwards worked as a grange.[90] In 1226, following protracted negotiations, Dore sent out a second daughter colony to Wales, this time to Grace Dieu. Founded under the patronage of John (d 1248), lord of Monmouth, it proved to be the last Welsh Cistercian foundation.[91] Dore did, however, go on to establish yet one more daughter house. In the late thirteenth century, it was chosen by Edward I

to colonize his highly prestigious new foundation at Vale Royal in Cheshire (*see* fig 18).[92]

But it was Whitland that proved to be the most prolific of the Welsh mother houses; it was responsible, too, for the spread of Cistercian monasticism into the heart of native Wales. The key patron was undoubtedly Rhys ap Gruffudd (d 1197), the Lord Rhys, as he is generally known.[93] Rhys began to consolidate his hold over the south-western kingdom of Deheubarth in the late 1160s and willingly came to assume the patronage of the white monk community at Whitland.[94] A very few years earlier, in 1164, the Norman constable of Cardigan, Robert fitz Stephen, had drawn a colony of monks from Whitland and settled them in the *commote* of Pennardd, at a site on the Fflur brook known today as *yr hen fynachlog*, 'the old monastery'. In 1165, however, Cardigan was seized by the Lord Rhys, with fitz Stephen captured in the process. Fortunately,

21 Neath Abbey: aerial view of the site from the north east. Neath was founded by Richard de Granville in 1129–30, initially as a Savigniac monastery, and became Cistercian in 1147. The church, seen here to the right, was begun c 1280 and completed in the early fourteenth century. It is thought to have replaced a smaller twelfth-century Romanesque building. To the top of the view is the late twelfth-century west claustral range. To the left are the ruins of a Tudor great house, built over the thirteenth-century monks' day room and the late medieval abbot's lodging. Photograph: *Royal Commission on the Ancient and Historical Monuments of Wales, Crown Copyright*

Rhys took the fledgling abbey under his wing, increasing its endowments and eventually moving the community to a more suitable location on the Teifi, at Strata Florida (fig 22). In a charter of 1184 Rhys proclaimed he had 'begun to build the venerable monastery called Strata Florida, and after building it have loved and cherished it'.[95] In the meantime, in 1170, strengthened no doubt by Rhys's patronage, Whitland was able to send out a second daughter colony, to Strata Marcella on the upper reaches of the River Severn. Its founder was Owain Cyfeiliog (d 1197), poet-prince and ruler of southern Powys.[96] Six years later, monks from Whitland were settled at Cwmhir, where the necessary endowments had been provided by the Lord Rhys's cousin, Cadwallon ap Madog (d 1179), lord of the *cantref* of Maelienydd.[97] Moreover, Whitland's influence was to spread outside Wales, to Ireland, where daughter

houses were founded at Comber in County Down (1200), and at Tracton in County Cork (1224).[98]

In their turn, Whitland's three Welsh daughter houses established four more abbeys (fig 19).[99] Strata Florida led the way, sending its first colony in 1179 to south-east Wales to establish a monastery at 'Nant Teyrnon', near Caerleon. The founder was the Welsh lord of Caerleon, Hywel ab Iorwerth (d 1211). Indeed, the house was for long called Caerleon, though in due course it also came to be known as Llantarnam. A site change appears to have taken place at some point, with alas no certainty as to the original location.[100] Strata Florida's second daughter house was founded in 1184, at Rhedynog Felen in Gwynedd. Its principal early benefactor was almost certainly Rhodri ab Owain Gwynedd (d 1195), a son-in-law of the Lord Rhys. By 1192, the community had been relocated to a site near the mouth of the

22 Strata Florida Abbey: aerial view of the site from the west. Strata Florida was founded in 1164 by Robert fitz Stephen, the Norman constable of Cardigan, and was colonized by monks from Whitland. It soon fell under the patronage of Rhys ap Gruffudd (d 1197) of Deheubarth, who moved the community to a more suitable location alongside the River Teifi. The abbey church dates largely from the late twelfth century.

Photograph: Copyright Skyscan, for Cadw

23 Valle Crucis Abbey: general view of the site from the west. Founded in 1200–1 by Madog ap Gruffudd (d 1236), Valle Crucis was a daughter of Strata Marcella. It was the last house of the Clairvaux affiliation to be established in Wales. The church, to the left, dates from the thirteenth century and later. The east range, to the right, was extensively remodelled in the mid-fourteenth century.

Photograph: Cadw, Crown Copyright

River Conwy,[101] but almost a century later, in 1283–4, the abbey was closed to make way for Edward I's new fortress and town plantation at Conwy. The king made provision for a further transfer of site, offering new endowments at Maenan, several kilometres higher up the Conwy valley.[102]

Whitland's two remaining Welsh daughter houses, Cwmhir and Strata Marcella, established one more colony apiece. The circumstances surrounding the foundation of Cwmhir's daughter at Cymer have recently been re-examined. It would seem that the Cwmhir community may well have been suffering badly as a result of the ongoing border conflict between the Welsh and Anglo-Norman lords of the middle March. It is suggested that, as a consequence of these troubles, some (if not all) of the community may have taken refuge in Gwynedd, leading in turn to the foundation of Cymer in 1198–9. In any case, the chief patron was most likely to have been Gruffudd ap Cynan (d 1200).[103] As to the last house in the Whitland affiliation, this was founded from Strata Marcella at Valle Crucis (fig 23) near Llangollen in 1200–1, with Madog ap Gruffudd (d 1236), prince of northern Powys, as its patron.[104]

THE CISTERCIAN IMPACT ON WALES

Several important studies chart the detailed history of Cistercian settlement in Wales.[105] Here it is proposed to do little other than offer a basic framework to contribute towards a clearer understanding of the buildings and the context in which they were raised. As was so eloquently pointed out by the late Professor Rees Davies, the triumph of Cistercian monasticism in Wales 'had consequences out of all proportion to the number of monasteries founded'.[106] In particular, it gave the whole of Wales a degree of unity of monastic practice and religious benefaction, regardless of the divide between the native and Anglo-Norman areas. For all their differences in recruitment and political affiliation, all the houses – whether truly Welsh, such as Strata Florida and Aberconwy, or Marcher, such as Tintern and Dore – belonged to a single European family. They adhered to the same code of monastic life, guided by the successful and universal white monk constitution, and by the Rule of St Benedict.

Foremost, of course, the Cistercians gave a new dimension to Welsh religious life. Recruitment to the monastic vocation increased considerably, especially during the twelfth century. Later claims that Whitland, for example, was able to support a hundred monks were unlikely to have been exaggerated.[107] From the names of brothers which have come down to us, it seems that the houses of the

south east, notably Dore, Margam, Neath and Tintern, recruited very largely from the Anglo-Norman areas of the March or from the border English shires. In contrast, the communities at those abbeys in the north and west were as Welsh as the land in which they dwelt.[108] Similar catchment patterns were doubtless true in the case of the *conversi*,[109] though the lay brotherhood also opened up a whole new area of opportunity to men of poor means, who were to arrive at Welsh abbey gateways in even larger numbers than those seeking admission to the choir monk novitiate. Yet the call to the monastic vocation was only the beginning. The Cistercians went on from there to make huge contributions not just to the religious life of the country but to aspects of its artistic and literary culture, and especially to its economy.

The Cistercians contributed in no small measure to the literary achievements of medieval Wales.[110] Few definite books survive but there are many indications of widespread interest. In 1202, for example, Strata Florida lost no opportunity in acquiring a collection of books from Gerald of Wales,[111] and books were part of the cause of a dispute between Aberconwy and Basingwerk in 1215.[112] Margam Abbey is known to have held works by William of Malmesbury and Geoffrey of Monmouth, and Llantarnam possessed the *Homilies of St Gregory*. Moreover, from an early date, the Welsh Cistercians took upon themselves the role of compiling annals of national events. In the late thirteenth century, for instance, the monks at Strata Florida compiled the now-lost Latin chronicle that forms the basis of the *Chronicle of the Princes*. At least one translation of the chronicle into Welsh, *Brut y Tywysogyon*, was made in the scriptorium of the same house.[113] Nor should the significant role played by the Cistercians as patrons of Welsh poetry be overlooked. One of the country's greatest medieval poets, Dafydd ap Gwilym, might have been buried at Strata Florida in the fourteenth century. In the late fifteenth and early sixteenth centuries, many Welsh Cistercian abbots became generous patrons of the Welsh bardic tradition. In return, the poets heaped praise on their hospitality, as well as their cultural and artistic achievements.[114]

As a consequence of the piety of founders and benefactors, quite apart from the enterprise and acquisitiveness of the Cistercians themselves, the twelfth and early thirteenth centuries witnessed a massive transfer of wealth from secular into monastic hands. The white monks came to control vast tracts of the Welsh countryside, much of it admittedly upland pasture, but including very substantial arable holdings in river valleys and nearer the coast (fig 24).[115] The information available on

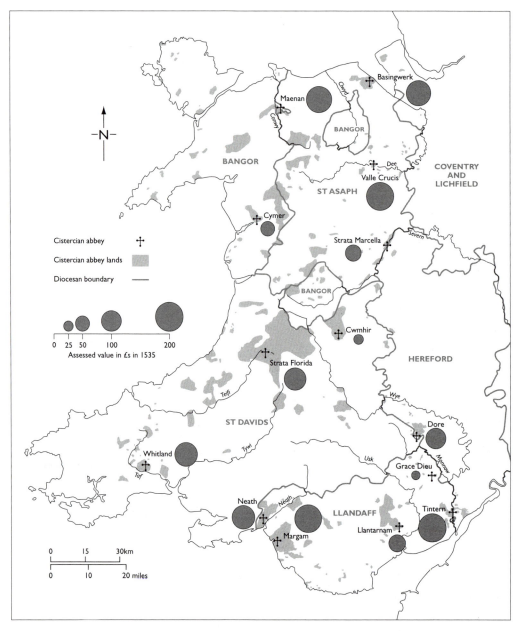

these estates gives the distinct impression of an early drive towards the creation of a grange economy, the ideal method of Cistercian land exploitation.[116] This said, specific documentation which might help illuminate case studies is largely lacking for the Welsh abbeys, and the temptation to read too much into the evidence should be avoided, especially given the degree of recent debate on the subject by Cistercian historians. Indeed, given the research which has now emerged on several European regions, it is important to question just how soon the order came to define itself in terms of a distinctive economic outlook.[117] This is the more significant in looking at Wales itself

when it is realized that many abbeys – even with such diverse patterns of patronage as Strata Florida and Tintern – were never entirely free of responsibility for serfs and tenants.[118] In sum, although the evidence suggests the grange was the preferred method of land exploitation by all the Welsh abbeys, at least through to the late thirteenth century, the inevitable generality in such a statement must be recognized. As far as the estates themselves are concerned, most is known about the historical and topographical aspects of the various landholdings, largely owing to a considerable body of work by Dr David Williams. There is much less material available, for example, on the archaeology of the grange centres, or on the character of grange buildings; and the way in which the Welsh Cistercian landscape was utilized has barely been addressed.[119]

It comes as no surprise to find that the individual fortunes of the fourteen abbeys in question varied over the course of the twelfth and thirteenth centuries.[120] For example, several of the houses were occasionally caught in the heavy crossfire between opposing English and Welsh forces. In 1212, King John threatened to destroy Strata Florida ('which harbours our enemies'), and it seems that in 1231 Henry III was poised to burn Cwmhir for its part in supporting a native action against English troops.[121] Besides this, fires as natural hazards are known to have impacted on the building programmes of at least two houses. At Valle Crucis, an undocumented fire seems to have spread throughout the church and the monastic buildings at the very time they were under construction, perhaps in the second quarter of the thirteenth century.[122] Similarly, in the 1280s, a disastrous fire brought devastation to the church at Strata Florida.[123] As to matters of a more general nature, a group of houses in the native areas of the north and west were to suffer during the two Welsh wars of Edward I, in 1276–7 and 1282–3,[124] when the estates of Basingwerk, Cymer, Strata Marcella, Strata Florida and Valle Crucis were all apparently affected. Indeed, there is strong reason to suppose that in several cases damage was inflicted on the abbey buildings themselves. In 1284, the five abbeys received compensation payments varying between £43 and £160.[125]

Some indication of the comparative prosperity of all fourteen abbeys at the end of the thirteenth century can be obtained from the papal taxation document known as the *Taxatio Ecclesiastica*, compiled in 1291. It is a source replete with problems of interpretation, and not one to be used without considerable caution. It does, nevertheless, provide a table of relative values.[126] Leading the way at the time was Margam, with an income of just under £255; Neath followed with £236; and Tintern came third with a figure of £145. At the other end of the scale, Cymer's income was given at under £29, and Grace Dieu was the smallest of the group, with a figure of less than £19.[127]

THE LATER MIDDLE AGES AND THE SUPPRESSION

There is a widely held but far too simplistic assumption that the great majority of monastic houses across England and Wales descended headlong into decline in the century or two before the suppression. Of course, it is impossible to generalize about such matters, either regionally or in looking at events within individual orders.[128] Having said this, it is difficult to escape the conclusion that Welsh Cistercian life during the later Middle Ages was rather different from that experienced by the pioneering communities of the twelfth century.[129] One very distinct change, for example, was the steady move away from the direct exploitation of landed estates, with all the Welsh abbeys adopting increasingly *rentier* economies. Whether this should be viewed as a decline from the Cistercian ideals of the earliest years is a moot point; the fact is the change definitely occurred. In Wales, as elsewhere, a number of factors lay behind the gradual process of transformation, not least the widespread economic recession of the early fourteenth century. There were, too, problems associated with labour shortages, brought about in part through the decline of the lay brotherhood.[130] These difficulties could only have been intensified by the impact of the Black Death in 1348–50.[131] In the event, the Welsh Cistercians were to lease out more and more of their former grange holdings, so that by the beginning of the sixteenth century, very little indeed was still held in demesne.

Meanwhile, war with France had made it more difficult for Cistercian abbots to attend the annual General Chapter meetings. Ultimately, this was to affect levels of observance in both English and Welsh abbeys, as links with Cîteaux and Clairvaux became more tenuous. It is no more than a snapshot, of course, but in 1352 the General Chapter observed that the Cistercian houses of England, Wales and Scotland were in urgent need of reform.[132]

In Wales, to add to the economic difficulties of the fourteenth century, most Cistercian abbeys were to experience major setbacks as a consequence of the Owain Glyn Dŵr uprising of 1400–9.[133] Up and down the land, the rebels wreaked havoc. The Cistercians, either as supporters of the cause (and therefore targets of English revenge), or simply caught up in phases of overwhelming destructiveness, took a long while to recover. And although, as pointed out by Sir Glanmor Williams, the impact of the uprising has sometimes been exaggerated,[134] we cannot entirely overlook the pleas made by various communities in the ensuing years. At Margam, for example, in 1412 it was claimed that the house had been 'utterly destroyed so that the abbot and convent are obliged to go about like vagabonds'.[135] Similarly, at Strata Marcella in 1420, the monks were given a new charter of privileges on account of 'the destruction and injury made by the Welsh rebels both to the church and the monastery and its holdings by plunder and fire'.[136] At Strata Florida, a house for

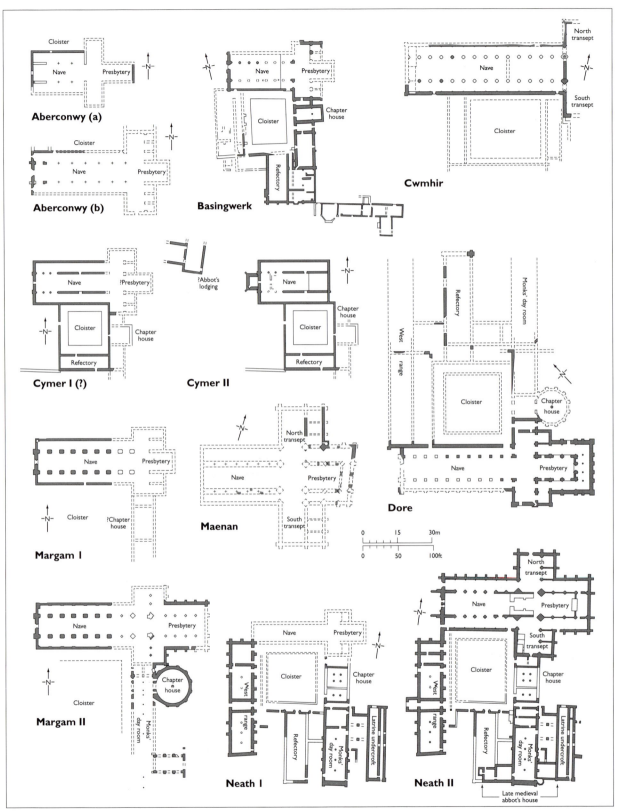

25 *Cistercian abbeys in Wales and the March, simplified comparative ground plans: Aberconwy to Neath. Drawing: Pete Lawrence, for Cadw*

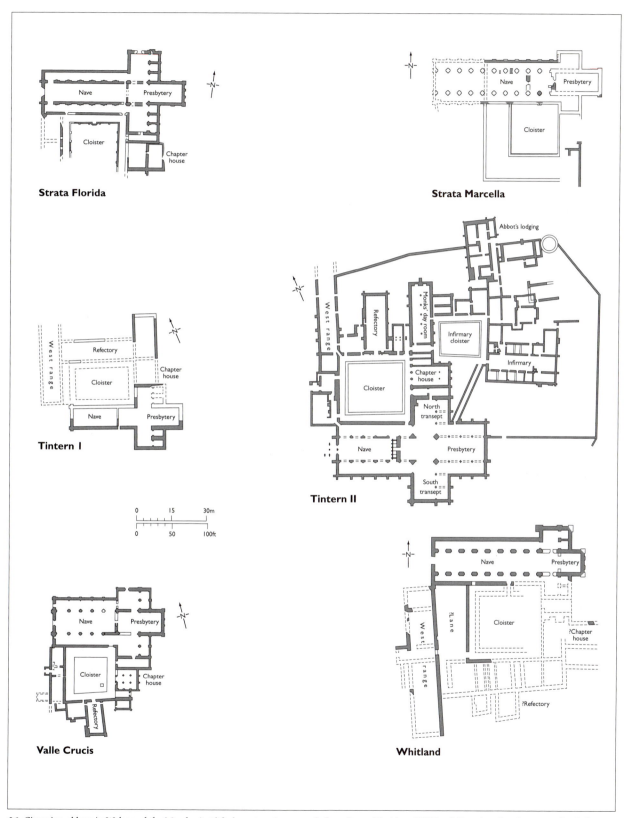

Strata Florida

Strata Marcella

Tintern I

Tintern II

Valle Crucis

Whitland

26 Cistercian abbeys in Wales and the March, simplified comparative ground plans: Strata Florida to Whitland. Drawing: Pete Lawrence, for Cadw

which we have a certain degree of first-hand knowledge of events during the revolt, it remained convenient as late as 1442 for the community to blame much of the sorry state of the house on 'Owain Glyn Dŵr and his company'.[137] Recovery was indeed a slow process. It occurred nonetheless, and there is much evidence of both spiritual and physical revival. In the surviving abbey buildings, for instance (summarized in figs 25 and 26), there is an occasional piece of fabric evidence representing a late medieval construction programme, and such indications of new works are greatly enhanced by documentary sources, especially the body of poetry by the Welsh bards of the late fifteenth and early sixteenth centuries.[138]

On the eve of the suppression, it must be said that the quality of internal spiritual life at the Welsh houses varied considerably. At Neath, Leyshon Thomas (c 1510–39), an Oxford scholar, was the foremost Welsh abbot of the Tudor age. He not only worked hard to maintain the standing of his house, but also became an influential figure within the Cistercian order at large.[139] Likewise, Richard Wyche (1521–36) at Tintern seems to have been an abbot who set a high spiritual tone.[140] In complete contrast was Robert Salusbury, abbot of Valle Crucis (1528–35), a man eventually arrested for his part in highway robbery.[141] Another of this ilk was perhaps John Glyn, who, although expelled for his poor governance at Cymer, then managed to become abbot of Dore (c 1524–8), where from 'the first day of his rule' he proceeded to squander the resources of the house. Deposed yet again, remarkably he went on to secure the abbacy of Cwmhir in its last years.[142]

Early in 1535, as a prelude to the suppression, Henry VIII commissioned a systematic valuation of church property throughout the dioceses of England and Wales, the *Valor Ecclesiasticus* as it became known.[143] In proportional terms, the annual incomes of the fourteen houses comprising the Welsh Cistercian province were rather different from the picture seen in 1291 (fig 24). The list was now in fact headed by Tintern, with an assessed revenue of £192. The sequence then ran: Valle Crucis (£188), Margam (£181), Maenan (£162), Basingwerk (£150), Whitland (£135), Neath (£132), Strata Florida (£118), Dore (£101), Llantarnam (£71), Strata Marcella (£64), Cymer (£51), Cwmhir (£28) and Grace Dieu (£19).[144] As regards the size of the monastic communities at this time, although there is no one comprehensive source of information, figures are available for most houses.[145] Again, Tintern seems to have been healthiest in these terms, with a total of twelve monks under Abbot Wyche. All the remaining houses had communities of nine or fewer, down to Cwmhir with just three or four and Grace Dieu with two.

In March 1536 an Act was passed whereby those monasteries with fewer than twelve monks, and whose possessions could not yield a benchmark valuation in excess of £200, were to be suppressed.[146] As a consequence, all fourteen abbeys were scheduled for closure later that year. The late summer saw the end of Margam (23 August), Llantarnam (27 August), Grace Dieu and Tintern (both 3 September). Two of the north Wales houses, Maenan and Cymer, survived into the spring of 1537.[147] In three instances, however (Neath, Strata Florida and Whitland), the communities successfully petitioned against immediate closure. They paid heavy fines, effectively bribes, to prolong their corporate existence. Strata Florida put up £66, Neath £150 and Whitland the enormous sum of £400.[148] Their reprieve, dearly bought, lasted but a few years. All three houses were to be finally closed in 1539.[149] Just over four centuries of Cistercian monastic life in Wales had been brought to an end.

CHAPTER 2

CHURCH BUILDING IN WALES
BEFORE THE CISTERCIANS

Initial impressions of the Welsh architectural landscape into which the Cistercians moved from the 1130s onwards are unlikely to suggest it was in any way distinguished.[1] The evidence currently available leads to the conclusion that stone churches were all but unknown in Wales before the arrival of the Norman invaders towards the end of the eleventh century, certainly churches of any monumental scale or pretension. [2]

The pre-Conquest Welsh church was essentially 'monastic' in origin, but not in a sense that might be recognized alongside those regular tenth-century Benedictine monastic foundations of south-west England or the Fens.[3] Indeed the mother, or *clas*, churches of Wales seem to have had rather more in common with Anglo-Saxon minsters. Each mother church constituted a self-contained ecclesiastical community, headed by an abbot who might also be a bishop. The clergy, or *claswyr*, were originally monks, though by the eleventh century they were to all intents and purposes secular canons, merely sharing a common income. Before the Conquest, these mother churches often claimed ecclesiastical authority over large areas, exercising parochial duties to a greater or lesser degree. Furthermore, in parts of native Wales, they were to survive well into the thirteenth century, continuing to dominate the ecclesiastical life of their respective districts.[4] Yet despite the clear importance of some of the larger *clas* churches – such as Tywyn in the north west, Llanbadarn Fawr near Aberystwyth, or Llancarfan and Llantwit Major in the vale of Glamorgan – none appears to have had a strong tradition of major stone building.[5]

Be that as it may, as the Normans pursued their advance into Wales, they immediately began to bring about widespread cultural changes, the introduction of Romanesque architecture being one of their most visible and enduring contributions.[6] The new style was to feature not only in masonry strongholds, but more especially in a flood of new church building across the entire country. Since churches are the focus of attention here, the most obvious starting place for an enquiry into the impact of Anglo-Norman innovatory architectural ideas is an examination of the four reformed episcopal centres of Bangor, Llandaff, St Asaph and St Davids. In addition, we might investigate what remains of the early fabric at those religious houses established in the lordships of the southern and border March during the late eleventh and early twelfth centuries, particularly at the black monk alien priories.[7]

THE ANGLO-NORMAN DIOCESES AND CATHEDRAL BUILDING

The Normans quickly sought to establish their authority over the Welsh church through the appointment and control of bishops. Nominees were imposed on Llandaff in 1107, on St Davids in 1115, on Bangor (following a false start in 1092) in 1120, and on the newly created or recreated see of St Asaph in 1143.[8] Alas, there is little which can be said of the twelfth-century churches at St Davids or St Asaph. At Bangor and Llandaff on the other hand, the later cathedrals do retain elements of their Romanesque fabric, and further traces have either been excavated or can be inferred from other evidence.

Bernard, the first Norman bishop of St Davids (1115–48), was a former curial cleric foisted on the see by Henry I.[9] In the request for his consecration, Bernard was described as a 'priest of the church of Hereford'.[10] He proved to be an extremely active bishop, both forceful and enterprising. Not least, he took an interest in the new monastic and canonical orders. In 1120, for example, Bernard presided over the ceremony at which the status of the Tironian priory at St Dogmaels was elevated to that of an abbey.[11] He later established an Augustinian priory at Carmarthen, *c* 1125–30,[12] and, most significantly, he brought the Cistercians to south-west Wales in 1140 – the community which eventually settled at Whitland Abbey. Unfortunately, nothing survives of the cathedral church that was (in part) built by Bishop Bernard at St Davids itself, and which is known to have been dedicated in 1131.[13] Nevertheless, when we consider Bernard's attempts to secure metropolitan authority for the see of St Davids over the whole of

Wales, it seems highly likely that he would have sought to raise a church of appropriate status. We might imagine its scale and ornament to be at least comparable to the new cathedral of his principal rival, Urban of Llandaff, on which more is said below.[14]

In north-east Wales, the creation of the Anglo-Norman diocese of St Asaph, or Llanelwy, was the last major piece in the territorial reorganization of the post-Conquest Welsh church.[15] The bishop chosen to occupy the newly created, or recreated, see in 1143 was Gilbert, though little is known of his episcopate. In 1160 he was succeeded by Bishop Godfrey, who was suspended ten years later and forced to resign in 1175.[16] Again, nothing of substance can be said about the cathedral church in this period.[17]

Despite the late creation of the diocese of St Asaph, it was in the north of Wales that the initial Norman advance had been most successful, largely because of the enterprise of Hugh of Avranches, earl of Chester (d 1101), and his cousin Robert of Rhuddlan.[18] Earl Hugh built a castle at Bangor and doubtless played some role in the nomination of one of William Rufus's chaplains, a Breton named Hervey, to the see of Bangor in 1092.[19] In the event, Hervey's career was cut short by the Welsh revolt of 1095. Thereafter, although he continued to hold the see until c 1109, it seems unlikely that he would have had any real opportunity to begin the rebuilding of the ancient *clas* church of St Deniol.[20] The recovery of native supremacy in north-west Wales meanwhile owed much to the remarkable achievements of Gruffudd ap Cynan (d 1137), the first in a new line of princes of Gwynedd. In 1120, after a lengthy vacancy, the see of Bangor was filled once more when David 'the Scot' (1120–39) was 'elected by King Gruffudd and the clergy and people of Wales'.[21]

Weight of opinion suggests that the Romanesque cathedral at Bangor was begun during the episcopate of Bishop David, coinciding with the era of relative peace and stability in Gwynedd brought about by the long rule of Gruffudd ap Cynan. The fragment of this building surviving above ground consists of little more than a single pilaster buttress and a blocked round-headed window, now occupying a position towards the western end of the south wall of the later presbytery.[22] From the evidence of excavated foundations, these features seem to have belonged to the original south wall of an apsidal eastern arm, measuring some 9.1m long by 7.9m wide. Other elements of the early cathedral uncovered by excavation include parts of the south transept, featuring a small eastern apse, together with the crossing piers.[23] A buried wall found running across the width of the nave in 1873 has been interpreted as

the west front, giving a proposed overall length of approximately 42.7m.[24] As for the chronology of the work at Bangor, it might be assumed the east end had been completed by the death of Gruffudd ap Cynan in 1137. According to a late twelfth-century biography of the prince, he was buried 'in a vault on the left side of the great altar in the church'.[25] Finally, given the fragmentary nature of the evidence, it is of course difficult to offer anything positive by way of design sources for the building. It seems likely, nonetheless, that Bishop David's cathedral owed at least some debt to the two great Romanesque churches of the northern Welsh border, those of St John and St Werburgh at Chester.[26]

At the other end of the country, Urban (1107–34), the first Anglo-Norman nominee to the bishopric of Glamorgan (Llandaff), was described as a 'priest of the church of Worcester'.[27] Urban may in fact have been at least half Welsh in origin, but there is no reason to question the probability that he was educated and received consecration at the Benedictine cathedral priory of Worcester. The documentary sources tell us little about the early years of his episcopate. In general terms the see was impoverished, and Urban was probably concerned with the reform of his chapter and the organization of a parochial system. In later years, he was much engaged in the matter of territorial disputes with the neighbouring dioceses of St Davids and Hereford.[28] As to his cathedral church, according to the *Book of Llandaff*, he inherited little more than a diminutive oratory, presumably the focus of worship for the pre-Conquest *clas* community. Urban was struck by the poverty of the building, described as 'but twenty-eight feet in length, fifteen wide and twenty high [8.5 × 4.5 × 6.1m], with two aisles on either side of but a small size and height, and with a porch twelve feet long [3.6m] and rounded in breadth'.[29] However, it appears the bishop was not in a position to begin work on a replacement until 1120. In the event, Urban's cathedral was to prove not only exotic in style but also, like Bangor, raised on a scale hitherto unimagined this deep into Wales. In the year the building programme was initiated, Archbishop Ralph of Canterbury (1114–22) offered an indulgence to all those giving alms towards the construction of the church.[30] Furthermore, to ensure the success of the enterprise, Urban arranged for the translation from Bardsey of the relics of St Dyfrig, one of the most important early saints of south Wales. They were brought to Llandaff to be interred 'in a suitable tomb in the ancient monastery before the altar of St Mary'.[31] The new cathedral was dedicated to St Peter, the apostle, and SS Dyfrig, Teilo and Oudoceus.[32]

27 Llandaff Cathedral (Cardiff): the presbytery looking east from the choir. In the distance is the highly decorated twelfth-century arch opening through into the later Lady Chapel. This arch is generally regarded as the principal survival of the church begun in 1120 by the first Anglo-Norman bishop of the see, Urban (1107–34). To the right (south) are the fragmentary remains of two contemporary round-headed windows, incorporated into later fabric.

Photograph: *Conway Library, Courtauld Institute of Art, London*

Today, the principal survival of the Norman cathedral at Llandaff is the highly decorated arch opening east from the presbytery into the Lady Chapel (fig 27).[33] It remains a focal point of the building, set immediately behind the high altar. In the adjacent south wall, there are fragmentary remains of two contemporary round-headed windows, again richly decorated. On the basis of what are admittedly limited archaeological discoveries, together with comparative analysis, it has

been suggested that the plan of the east end was designed in the not unconventional stepped fashion of the period. Here at Llandaff, both the presbytery and its shorter flanking aisles were finished with straight outer walls, each featuring an internal apse. In such an arrangement, the presbytery arch would have opened into a lower projecting chapel, in the manner employed at Hereford Cathedral.[34] More speculatively, it is suggested that the presbytery was flanked by small twin towers, intended to give

39

emphasis to the most sacred area of the church.[35] Equally conjectural are the proposals for the length of the Norman building, especially given the lack of firm evidence on the form of the nave. Nevertheless, a nave of twice the proportions of the presbytery would yield an overall length close to 45m, with the west front terminating near the point where the thirteenth-century arcades change design.[36]

Taking what is known of both the plan and the decorative details of the Romanesque cathedral at Llandaff, the work can be comfortably placed in a fairly distinctive west country architectural context.[37] Notably, very similar motifs to the distinctive beaded paterae seen around the outer order of the presbytery arch occur in a number of early twelfth-century buildings across the west of England. Their origin could be the new eastern arm at the cathedral of Old Sarum, built by Bishop Roger (1102–39) from *c* 1125,[38] but paterae are also known, for example, from Hereford Cathedral (after *c* 1107) and, marginally later, they were to be used extensively around the clerestory windows in the nave at Malmesbury Abbey.[39] Other features found at Llandaff with a good west country pedigree include the paired soffit rolls in the presbytery arch, also seen, for instance, in the nave arcades at Gloucester Cathedral (*c* 1100–30), and the beast-head label stops which occur on one of the fragmentary southern windows, again paralleled at Old Sarum and Malmesbury, and also at Leonard Stanley in Gloucestershire.[40] In sum then, although Llandaff Cathedral awaits a thorough and up-to-date assessment of its fabric, there are clear indications that the twelfth-century building was of no small architectural interest.

THE BENEDICTINE PRIORIES OF THE SOUTHERN MARCH

The first point to note when turning to the early Norman monastic houses of Wales is that in the half-century before the arrival of the Cistercians a clutch of alien priories had already been brought into being right across the newly established lordships of the southern and western seaboards.[41] Generally, though not exclusively, these alien plantations stood in the shadow of the founder's castle, on the fringes of a nascent borough; they were very much meant to serve as the spiritual arm of the Conquest strategy. Only in a few cases can much be said with confidence about the Romanesque fabric. The best survivals by far are the still comparatively little-known churches of St Michael at Ewenny (in the Vale of Glamorgan) and St Mary at Chepstow (Monmouthshire).

The priory church at Ewenny (fig 28) was established as a dependency of St Peter's Abbey,

Gloucester (now Gloucester Cathedral). It is known to have been dedicated during the time of Bishop Urban's episcopate at Llandaff, that is, before 1134. Doubtless the house began as a modest priory cell, with just a small community of resident monks. Then, in 1141, Maurice de Londres enlarged the endowment of his family's priory, on condition that it would henceforth accommodate 'a convent of at least thirteen'.[42] In matching the fabric evidence at Ewenny to the admittedly complex documentation,[43] Dr Ralegh Radford proposed that the pre-1134 church is now represented only by the nave of the existing building. He considered that this was at first extended and then heightened after the re-foundation in 1141.[44] Radford's interpretation not only contradicted earlier views on Ewenny,[45] but has since been challenged by several scholars who see no reason to attribute any of the structure to the years after 1141. On the contrary, stylistically, it seems far more likely that the entire church was raised by the time of the initial dedication.[46] On balance, then, it should be accepted that Ewenny was designed as a substantial cruciform building from the outset, with a vaulted presbytery flanked on either side by two barrel-vaulted transept chapels arranged *en échelon*. Within the church, the rib-vaulted eastern bay in the presbytery is of particular note, and in the nave the four-bay north aisle arcade is supported on stout cylindrical piers with moulded bases and scalloped capitals. As at Llandaff, the decorative detailing throughout the church links it to the putative school of west country Romanesque architecture, with particularly strong and by no means surprising stylistic links to the mother house at Gloucester, as well as to the abbey church at Tewkesbury.

Chepstow Priory was an even earlier foundation. It appears to have been established as a daughter house of the Benedictine abbey at Cormeilles (Eure) in Normandy by William fitz Osbern, earl of Hereford, before his death in 1071.[47] No more than a truncated fragment of the Romanesque six-bay nave survives today, shorn of its aisles and substantially modified as a result of several phases of restoration.[48] Nevertheless, the monumental scale of the work (fig 29) betrays considerable ambition on the part of the patron, as well as the monastic community. Construction would almost certainly have begun with the now lost eastern arm – the presbytery, crossing and transepts – presumably in the last quarter of the eleventh century.[49] The only survival is the base of the massive north-west crossing pier. It features slightly different articulation to each face: twin half-columns for the arches on the north, west and east; and triple columns to the south, representing the respond for the western crossing

28 Ewenny Priory (in the Vale of Glamorgan): view of the presbytery and south transept from the north west. Ewenny was established as a dependent cell of the Benedictine abbey of St Peter at Gloucester in the early twelfth century, with the church dedicated before 1134. In 1141 its status was raised to that of a full conventual priory. Although the stylistic links to Gloucester are not in doubt, the date of the existing church is much debated. The weight of opinion favours the view that much of the structure was in place by the time of the initial dedication.

Photograph: Cadw, Crown Copyright

arch. It is difficult to draw any firm conclusions on the basis of so little evidence, but the arrangements must have been similar, for example, to the western crossing piers at St John's in Chester.[50] Turning to the nave at Chepstow, it is clear that the elevation was of three storeys from the outset. The rather austere main arcades have sturdy rectangular piers supporting round-headed arches of two unmoulded orders.[51] For the most part, the inner order is now corbelled out from the pier, whereas in the original arrangements it was either carried on a single half-column or on paired half-shafts. Above, the triforium openings differ to either side of the nave. To the north they are single, plain round-headed arches; to the south they comprise paired, two-order shafted arches.[52] The clerestory windows, to both north and south, are deeply set round-headed openings with plain jambs. By far the most significant aspect of the Chepstow nave, however, is the fact it was covered with stone vaults.[53] On the basis of the plaster scars which can be seen today, one might envisage pilasters rising from the base of the piers to support a single-order transverse arch, between which quadripartite groins may have stood over each bay.[54] It seems likely, too, that the nave aisles were also vaulted,[55] in which case one would almost certainly expect the destroyed east end of the building to have been covered with stone vaults. Chepstow would thus rank as one of the earliest known stone-vaulted churches in Britain.[56] For the *terminus ad quem* one might look to the details at the west end of the building. Here, one of the features of note is the elongated nature of the last pair of nave piers, suggesting plans for western towers, or at least a tower over the central vessel. The richly decorated west door is of six orders, five of which are shafted. The arch orders above are variously decorated with chip-carving and chevron. As a composition, it can be related to an established west country tradition for elaborate west portals, with the more immediate connections likely to have been with Tewkesbury and Hereford.[57] A date of *c* 1120–30 might be expected.

Apart from these important survivals at Ewenny and Chepstow, the early Romanesque work which must have existed at many of the other Benedictine monasteries of the southern March should not be overlooked. Monmouth, for example, was founded between 1074 and 1086 by Wihenoc (or Gwethenoc), the Breton lord of Monmouth, as a daughter house of St Florent at Saumur (Maine-et-Loire). The church was dedicated in 1101–2.[58] Parts of the Norman west front survive within later masonry, where there is also a half-cylindrical respond marking the end of the south arcade of the nave. An *ex situ* fragment from a capital, possibly from the west portal, suggests that sculptors of the Hereford

29 Chepstow Priory (Monmouthshire): view of the nave, looking south west. Almost certainly founded by 1071, the Benedictine priory of St Mary was a cell of Cormeilles (Eure) in Normandy. The six-bay nave, in which the elevation was of three storeys, is likely to have been completed by c 1120–30. Both the main vessel and the aisles appear to have been covered with stone vaults. Photograph: *Royal Commission on the Ancient and Historical Monuments of Wales, Crown Copyright*

school may have worked on the building.[59] Rather less survives at Brecon (founded *c* 1106–10),[60] whereas the Norman churches at the likes of Abergavenny (founded *c* 1087–1100)[61] and Kidwelly (founded *c* 1114),[62] were entirely rebuilt in later centuries. The intriguing barrel-vaulted nave at Pembroke (founded *c* 1098) may be of the late twelfth century.[63]

OTHER CHURCH BUILDING

Apart from the mainstream Benedictines, other monastic congregations were responsible for colonizing a number of the new Norman religious houses of south Wales. An early community of Augustinians, for example, was established at Llanthony in *c* 1103–18, to be followed by a second group introduced at Carmarthen in *c* 1125–30.[64] Cluniacs from Montacute Priory in Somerset were settled at Malpas before *c* 1110,[65] and a priory of Tironian monks was founded at St Dogmaels in 1113–15. Here, as noted earlier, the status of the house was raised to that of an abbey in 1120.[66] Significant traces of the early twelfth-century church survive, indicating plans for a cruciform building. The presbytery was probably finished with an apse,

30 St Woolos Cathedral (Newport): view of inner west doorway, looking eastwards into the nave. In 1093/1104, the church of St Gwynllyw (Woolos) at Newport was granted to St Peter's Abbey, Gloucester, and appears to have served as a quasi-monastic dependency. The aisled nave and its west door were probably built no later than c 1140. The church was given full cathedral status in 1949.

Photograph: *Royal Commission on the Ancient and Historical Monuments of Wales, Crown Copyright*

and the transepts certainly featured apsidal eastern chapels. The nave was to have been aisled, though it may not have been completed to the initial scheme.[67]

It should not be forgotten that, aside from the four cathedrals and principal religious houses, other prominent church building was taking place at very much the same time across the wider landscape of Wales. There is, for instance, the important *clas* church at Penmon on Anglesey, with its richly decorated western and southern crossing arches, and that at Tywyn in Gwynedd, featuring an aisled nave in which the arcades rest on cylindrical piers inspired by west country types.[68] Then again there is the very intriguing quasi-priory of St Woolos at Newport (fig 30), a church given to St Peter's Abbey, Gloucester, as early as 1093. The five-bay nave arcades are especially striking and may date from about 1140, if not before.[69] Finally, in the half-century and more after the arrival of the Normans, there was an explosion in parish church building over many areas of the country. For the most part these new churches were comparatively small structures of one or two cells, yet the cumulative impact on areas previously devoid of

significant stone building must have been great. No wonder, then, the biographer of the native prince, Gruffudd ap Cynan (d 1137), felt it significant to note that the people of his time 'began to build churches in every direction'. As a consequence, he went on, Gwynedd 'came to shine with white-washed churches, like stars in the firmament'.[70]

Even from this brief review of the early Romanesque fabric to be found in the cathedrals, monasteries and other churches of Wales, it is evident that the twelfth-century architectural landscape of the country was of rather more significance than might be assumed from initial impressions. As a whole, the evidence demonstrates very clearly the existence of a fast-growing tradition of major church building in Wales before the arrival of the Cistercians. Flourishing schools of masons were already well established in workshops that had grown up around the major Norman cathedrals and monasteries of the Dee and Severnside regions. It was presumably the skills existing within and around these schools that were soon to be adapted to a new set of imported architectural ideals.

CHAPTER 3

ABBEY SITES AND
TEMPORARY BUILDINGS

Through the content of their twelfth-century narrative and legislative texts, the Cistercian fathers set out two key practical regulations for the foundation of new abbeys. The first was concerned with the appropriate geographical siting of a proposed daughter house; the second dealt with the minimum acceptable provision of initial buildings. This last of the three background chapters will look briefly at the known impact of the regulations on the siting and initial settlement of Cistercian abbeys in Wales.

THE SITING OF THE WELSH ABBEYS

In 1098, it had been a quest for a simpler and more secluded form of ascetic life that had led Robert of Molesme and his idealist followers to Cîteaux. The site they had chosen for the 'New Monastery' was in a heavily wooded and comparatively remote area, later described by the author of the *Exordium Cistercii* as 'a place of horror and of vast solitude'.[1] To ensure such seclusion was a feature of all abbeys throughout the rapidly growing Cistercian family, legislation was early introduced. In one of the statutes which probably originate from the time of Stephen Harding's abbacy at Cîteaux, it was baldly stated: 'None of our monasteries are to be built in cities, walled towns, or villages, but in places removed from human habitation'.[2] To adopt a slightly more elegant English rendering of this mandate, then, it might be said that the Cistercians sought to locate their abbeys 'far from the concourse of men'.[3] The potent attractiveness of such tranquil rural retreats, altogether removed from secular affairs, is wonderfully portrayed by Abbot Ailred of Rievaulx (1147–67) in his description of the ideal white monk life: 'Everywhere peace, everywhere serenity, and a marvellous freedom from the tumult of the world'.[4] As the Cistercian community continued to expand in the second quarter of the twelfth century, the General Chapter further enacted that daughter houses could be set up only if they were at least 'ten Burgundian leagues distant from other abbeys of our order'.[5]

There can be no question that a degree of comparative isolation characterized the setting of all the Cistercian abbeys in Wales, but many other factors played an underlying role in their general location and specific siting (figs 31, 32 and 33).[6] Of course, as Dr Robin Donkin has pointed out, the founding of a new Cistercian community was in any case a rather complicated operation, involving a number of interested parties.[7] First, a patron had to approach an existing monastery with an offer of adequate endowments. That monastery had itself to be sufficiently flourishing, with a community of at least sixty professed monks.[8] If these conditions were met, the next step may have been to secure the approval of the diocesan bishop, as stipulated in the *Cartae Caritatis*.[9] In purely practical terms, the most important initial procedure was the selection of a suitable location for the new monastery. The land offered by the patron would have to be inspected, and the precise site for the buildings chosen with care. For many years, inspections of this sort are likely to have involved a monk or a lay brother of the mother house, presumably one with appropriate surveying skills.[10] Surprisingly, in the early period, it appears that foundations could be made without the specific approval of the General Chapter. Nevertheless, for advice and support, it was decreed that a founding monastery should show the site of the proposed daughter house to the two closest neighbouring abbots.[11] From statutes of the late twelfth and early thirteenth centuries, it is clear that petitions from potential new founders tended to come by then direct to the General Chapter, as occurred when Gruffudd ap Cynan (d 1200) wished to establish Cymer Abbey in 1198. On this occasion, the petition was eventually referred to the abbot of Margam, who (together with the abbots of Buildwas and Whitland) was instructed to inspect the proposed site in Gruffudd's presence.[12] Similarly, in 1217, on learning of John of Monmouth's intention to found a new house in south-east Wales, the General Chapter ordered the abbot of Morimond to make 'diligent enquiry' into the adequacy of the proposed endowments, and to report back with the

31 *Tintern Abbey: the Wye valley setting, showing the site from the so-called Devil's Pulpit on the east side of the river. In the twelfth century, the heavily wooded slopes bordering the Wye would have provided a perfect location for a white monk foundation, 'far from the concourse of men'.*
Photograph: *Cadw, Crown Copyright*

32 Strata Florida Abbey: the site from the south east. The Strata Florida community was initially settled on the banks of the Fflur brook in 1164, at a site known today as yr hen fynachlog, 'the old monastery'. The monks moved to this permanent home on the upper reaches of the Teifi later in the century, probably in or around 1184.

Photograph: Cadw, Crown Copyright

findings in the following year.[13] In the event, five years later the abbots of Bruern (Oxfordshire) and Bordesley (Worcestershire) were acting in a supervisory capacity in connection with this same foundation, and not until 1226 was a community finally sent out from Dore Abbey to colonize the new site at Grace Dieu.[14]

In spite of the care and preparation which went into the foundation of Cistercian abbeys, as many as one-third of all the communities across Europe found it necessary to transfer to a new location, often within a decade or so of the initial settlement.[15] Of the seventy-five abbeys in England and Wales, no fewer than thirty changed their site at least once, and minor moves were almost certainly more common than can now be demonstrated.[16] Sometime after 1152, the need for such occasional migrations was formally recognized by the General Chapter: any abbot who faced 'some intolerable disadvantage' was granted permission to 'transfer his abbey to a more suitable place'.[17] For Donkin, the majority of Cistercian abbey transfers in England and Wales were to be attributed to poorly judged initial sitings, with adverse physical conditions seen as the main determinant.[18] However, while physical adversity was undoubtedly of considerable significance, a range of other practical and political factors were also of importance.

Of the fourteen Cistercian abbeys in Wales and the March, site changes are known to have taken place in at least six instances: Aberconwy, Basingwerk, Grace Dieu, Llantarnam, Strata Florida and Whitland (*see* fig 18).[19] In some cases, the first site may never have been envisaged as more than a temporary measure. This was surely true at Basingwerk, where the founding community at first seems to have been accommodated in the nearby Norman fortification at Hên Blas.[20] In other cases, adverse environmental conditions may have played some part – for example, in the moves from Little Trefgarn to Whitland, from Strata Florida's site on the Fflur brook to its permanent home on the Teifi, from Rhedynog Felen to Aberconwy, and from the first to the second location at Llantarnam. Equally, for several of these, changes in patronage or in the political landscape provide viable explanations.[21] Only in two instances are very definite motives for Welsh site changes known to us. At Grace Dieu, where the first site was colonized in 1226, the community clearly experienced a precarious early existence. In 1233, the monastery was burnt by the native Welsh, who claimed it had been built on land unfairly seized from them. Three years later, the founder was obliged to seek the General Chapter's permission to transfer the house to a more suitable location.[22] In the case of Aberconwy, a site transfer

33 Cwmhir Abbey: the site of the abbey church from the south. Set well above the 240m contour (the highest white monk abbey in Wales), in 1242 Cwmhir was said to be 'in a mountainous district remote from parish churches'.

Photograph: *author*

have been identified on the ground with any real certainty. By its very nature, a temporary monastic complex is likely to have been ephemeral, with the buildings almost certainly raised for the most part in wood. Through experience, the white monks were probably well aware that it was unwise to embark on expensive building programmes before there was absolute confidence in the suitability of the site. However, there was possibly at least one exception to this pattern in Wales, at the location initially occupied by the community of Strata Florida, a site known today as *yr hen fynachlog*, 'the old monastery', of which more is said below.[25] Before closing on this theme, another avenue for investigating the archaeological potential of temporary sites may be the two failed Welsh daughter houses. Despite their short-lived nature, Margam's aborted colony at Pendar (*c* 1175) and Dore's abandoned settlement at Trawscoed (*c* 1173) presumably both had complexes of temporary wooden buildings.[26]

In turning to consider the locations of the fourteen permanent foundations (fig 18), it is apparent that the Welsh landscape afforded ample opportunity for pioneering Cistercian communities to seek out 'places [far] removed from human habitation'. Topographically, Cwmhir was always the most isolated of the Welsh abbeys (fig 33). Landlocked and situated well above the 240m contour, it was described in 1232 as lying 'in a mountainous district remote from parish churches'.[27] No less marginal was the location chosen for Strata Florida (fig 32). Even its final site on the upper Teifi was above 185m, and as late as 1441 the house was said to be 'situated in desolate mountains'.[28] In the much lower valley locations, such as that occupied by Tintern (fig 31), heavy woodland doubtless added to the comparative isolation of the sites. Indeed, this brings to mind Bernard of Clairvaux's description of the virtues of a wooded landscape for the contemplative Cistercian life: 'Believe me who would have experience, you will find much more labouring amongst the woods than you ever will amongst books. Woods and stones will teach you what you can never hear from any master'.[29] Tintern itself lay near the head of the tidal estuary of the Wye, with similar positions occupied by Aberconwy (on the River Conwy), by Neath (close to a confluence with the tidal River Neath), and by Cymer (on the Mawddach estuary). Margam and Basingwerk were also located within striking distance of the shore, affording the advantages of both communication and marine resources, such as fish, salt and right to wreck.[30]

To further ensure the isolation they required, the Cistercians seldom balked from depopulating existing settlements. Across Europe, they acquired an

from Rhedynog Felen to the west bank of the River Conwy had already taken place between 1186 and 1192. It was almost a century afterwards, in 1283, that Edward I's decision to establish a castle and walled borough on the site of the abbey resulted in a further uprooting of the community, the monks being transferred to a location further up the Conwy valley, at Maenan.[23]

The archaeology of temporary Cistercian sites is very much an unknown quantity.[24] This is particularly true of the examples occupied for no more than one or two decades. Indeed, few such sites

unenviable reputation in this regard. As that harsh critic of monks, Walter Map (c 1140–1210), observed: 'They make a solitude that they may be solitaries'.[31] In Wales, when Valle Crucis was founded in 1200–1, it was necessary for the patron to move at least some of the inhabitants of Llanegwestl to other locations in his lordship.[32] As late as 1284, during Edward I's plans to transfer the abbey of Aberconwy to its new site at Maenan, Archbishop John Pecham (1279–92) wrote to the king on behalf of Anian, bishop of St Asaph (1268–93), seeking to prevent the move. The prospect of further Cistercians coming to the diocese of St Asaph filled Bishop Anian and the local parish priest with a degree of horror. Pecham's letter read: 'Where they plant their foot, they destroy towns, take away tithes, and curtail by their privileges all the power of the prelacy'.[33] But the archbishop's words fell on deaf ears, and the transfer to Maenan went ahead. Several former landowners were to receive compensation.[34] Meanwhile, the development of granges across Wales had also caused much settlement disruption, especially well documented on the Margam Abbey estates.[35]

Thus, for the most part, the Welsh Cistercian monasteries were, at the time of their foundation at least, located at some distance from existing centres of population. However, it should not be imagined that the early white monk communities moved into sparsely populated areas surrounded by vast tracts of previously unworked countryside. It has already been observed, for example, that Basingwerk Abbey was founded close to the Norman castle at Hên Blas. It is interesting that Neath, the other Welsh Savigniac house, also lay a short distance from a stronghold of the Conquest period,[36] while Tintern was certainly not far removed from the patron's castle at Chepstow. Nor was the proximity of castles restricted to houses of Anglo-Norman foundation. Llywelyn ab Iorwerth's patronage of Aberconwy was underlined by the presence of his fortress at Deganwy, on the opposite side of the Conwy estuary. Similarly, the lords of northern Powys overlooked Valle Crucis from the hilltop castle of Dinas Brân.

Although the evidence is slight, several of the Welsh abbeys may have been founded on or near the sites of earlier religious communities, even if none of these was active when the Cistercians arrived.[37] There is, for example, a lingering tradition that the Tintern area had been home to a hermit saint of the Welsh church.[38] Then again, Dore's location in the Golden Valley may not have been too far removed from a religious site with its origins in the early seventh century.[39] At Neath and Strata Florida the evidence of early Christian memorial stones from the vicinity of the later abbeys points, at least tentatively, to a

previous sanctity of the general locations.[40] But by far the clearest indications of an active pre-Conquest religious community come from Margam, almost certainly the site of a Welsh clas church or monastery. It is witnessed by a superb collection of sculpted crosses of the ninth to eleventh centuries, of which the tenth-century Cross of Conbelin is the most impressive example.[41]

Regardless of any pre-existing occupation in the area, and whatever the nature of the surrounding relief, there were several essential requirements for the siting of Cistercian abbeys. In the main, the most obvious necessity was a reasonably large and flat area of ground on which to lay out the church and the monastic buildings, though occasionally the strength of other factors led the Cistercians to a choice of site that might otherwise be regarded as topographically less than ideal. At Rievaulx, for instance, the abbey church had to be oriented virtually north–south, and the abbey buildings were terraced down a difficult slope.[42] Nothing quite this dramatic occurred in Wales, however, with the majority of churches following the normal east–west liturgical layout (figs 25 and 26). Dore was perhaps the main exception, its topography apparently having led to a significant shift away from the ideal orientation.

Apart from a need for level ground, the other key requirement in the siting of Cistercian abbeys was a good water supply. All the Welsh houses were adequately served in this way. The ideal site was one near a confluence, where a rapidly flowing tributary joined a gentler stream or river. Tintern, for example, lay on a broad flat bank of the Wye (fig 31), though it was the Angidy that was tapped to turn the abbey's mill wheels and flush the latrines. Similarly, Cwmhir was situated at the point where the Cwm Poeth flows into the Clywedog brook, and Whitland lay on the east bank of the Colomendy just above its confluence with the Afon Gronw (see fig 128). Fresh water supplies for washing, cooking and brewing were often drawn from springs above the sites.[43] At Dore, Maenan and Tintern, it is thought that it was water requirements which dictated the need to arrange the cloister and monastic buildings to the north of the abbey churches.

Finally, when the proposed site of a monastery was being surveyed by representatives of the mother house, some thought must also have been given to the availability of building materials.[44] From the first, timber was essential. It would be needed for the immediate construction of a temporary oratory and associated domestic accommodation, and was required in the longer term for trusses and rafters spanning major buildings such as the church, the dormitory and the refectory. Between 1235 and 1253,

Henry III granted the monks at Grace Dieu a total of twenty-six trees for just such purposes.[45] In 1289, Earl Gilbert de Clare (d 1295) gave the community at Neath 'all the timber necessary' for building work at the monastery.[46] And, from the later Middle Ages, there is no shortage of references to fine new timber constructions at many of the Welsh abbeys, notably in the various works of bardic poetry.[47] A fine fifteenth-century roof in fact survives at Cymer, probably representing the abbot's residence.[48] No less important than wood, of course, was the proximity of suitable building stone. Tintern was constructed almost entirely from a local red-green sandstone, quarried on nearby Barbadoes Hill. For specific tasks, the builders also used a certain amount of oolitic limestone, transported from the other side of the Bristol Channel. Both Neath and Margam were raised for the most part in the fairly local grey-brown Pennant sandstone, though with a plentiful supply of Sutton stone brought in from Southerndown in the Vale of Glamorgan for dressings. In much the same fashion, the builders of Strata Florida relied on local materials for the core work in the church and claustral complex, but then used a mix of purple Caerbwdy (from coastal quarries near St Davids) and oolitic limestone (transported from the Cotswolds or the Bath area) for decorative dressings. At mountainous Cwmhir, although a poor-quality local stone was available for the rubble core work, it was necessary to look much further afield for bulk quantities of good freestone. The piers, arcades and dressings of the early thirteenth-century church were built of sandstone, brought in from the Grinshill quarries near Shrewsbury.[49]

TEMPORARY BUILDINGS

As noted in the introduction to this chapter, the second piece of primary Cistercian legislation covering the practical elements in the foundation of new abbeys was concerned with the minimum acceptable provision of initial buildings. In one of the earliest statutes (*capitula*), certainly dating to Stephen Harding's abbacy at Cîteaux (1109–33) and probably in place by *c* 1113–19, it was baldly stated:

> A new abbot is not to be sent to a new place without at least twelve monks; or without these books: psalter, hymnal, collectary, antiphonary, gradual, Rule, missal; nor without having first constructed these places: oratory, refectory, dormitory, guest quarters, gatehouse – so that they may straightaway serve God there and live in keeping with the Rule.[50]

It is now widely recognized that the buildings referred to in this statute were, in the first instance, almost always constructed of wood.[51] Indeed, this was true of the French cradle-lands of the Cistercian order, where the original buildings raised by the pioneering communities were quite definitely of timber. As the *Exordium Parvum* makes clear, when Robert of Molesme and his band of dissenting monks found their way to Cîteaux in 1098 their first task was to cut down the dense thickets of thorn bushes.[52] Then, the account goes on, 'the men of God … began to construct a monastery'. Duke Odo I of Burgundy (1078–1102) was greatly impressed by their 'holy fervour', and he it was who 'completed from his own resources the wooden monastery they had begun'.[53] Remarkably, the early church seems to have survived well into the seventeenth century, when it was described in the 1640s by Angelo Manrique as 'built of sections of roughly squared trees'.[54]

The pattern may have been repeated at the foundation of Clairvaux in 1115.[55] Again, it is Manrique who provides a description of the provisional wooden buildings. He refers to a 'humble chapel' at the site, apparently 'built in a few days, and … believed to have served for the divine office for some time'.[56] However, the construction of more permanent buildings was soon put in hand. It is widely accepted that these were located in the western part of the mature abbey precinct, and were in fact described by visitors to Clairvaux in 1517 and 1667.[57] They were then recorded in an early eighteenth-century set of plans and drawings by Dom Nicolas Milley (1708), and described by him as the *capella* and *monasterium vetus*.[58] The small square church (the *capella*) seen in Milley's illustrations has been widely referred to in the literature as Clairvaux I (*see* fig 34).[59] Taking the combined evidence, J O Schaefer has argued that, on balance, the buildings were all of timber stave construction,[60] his view being subsequently supported by Fergusson, and also initially by Glyn Coppack.[61] Nevertheless, as Terryl Kinder has pointed out, a strong case can be made for suggesting that the *monasterium vetus* and its associated chapel were of stone.[62]

Whatever the nature of the developments at Clairvaux after 1115, it does seem that St Bernard's founding colony was initially accommodated in wooden buildings, just as at Cîteaux. It further seems very likely that similar patterns of development took place at the three other senior daughter houses, at La Ferté, Pontigny and Morimond. But alas, too little survives for even a useful guess at the precise details.[63] At a purely practical level, of course, wood was comparatively cheap and plentiful, yet its early use also underlined that commitment to poverty which was so strong among the founding fathers. In the longer term, wooden buildings were to serve perfectly well during the fledgling years of almost all twelfth-century Cistercian plantations, at least until some indication of permanence was assured at the site in question.

The precise extent to which lay brothers – or even choir monks – were themselves involved in erecting early timber buildings is difficult to assess. On the one hand, there is the testimony of Orderic Vitalis, a Benedictine monk writing *c* 1135, who observed that the Cistercians 'have built monasteries with their own hands in lonely, wooded places'.[64] Equally, even if the sources are ambiguous, narrative accounts do exist for several foundations in the Fountains family where there is mention of advance parties of lay brothers being sent out to raise buildings and workshops 'after our custom' or 'according to the form of the order'.[65] Perhaps the most influential early figure in this context was Geoffrey d'Ainai (d 1140), a monk sent to Fountains by Bernard of Clairvaux in the spring of 1133 to assist with the building programme.[66] Geoffrey in turn probably trained members of the Fountains community in the method of setting out new monasteries. Two monks in particular, Adam and Robert, are known to have been involved in the early construction of a number of abbeys in the Fountains family.[67]

On the other hand, there are documentary accounts demonstrating the absolutely pivotal role played by the patron in building the initial complex of structures, usually having obtained a promise from the proposed mother house to furnish a community of monks when all was ready. Such was the case, for example, in the foundation of Thame in Oxfordshire and Meaux in Yorkshire (City of Kingston upon Hull).[68] Given the available evidence, Fergusson has concluded that the most common sequence of events was indeed that in which the patron accepted responsibility for providing the initial buildings sometime in advance of the founding colony's arrival.[69]

As to the form of such early buildings, the fullest descriptive account comes in fact from the fourteenth-century *Meaux Chronicle*. Having chosen to found the abbey, William of Aumâle, earl of York (d 1179), raised 'a certain great house built with common mud and wattle ... in which the arriving lay brothers would dwell until better arrangements were made for them'. He also built 'a certain chapel next to the aforementioned house ... where all the monks used the lower storey as a dormitory and the upper to perform the divine service devoutly'.[70] As the size of the community

grew, Abbot Adam (one of the Fountains monks trained by Geoffrey d'Ainai) apparently replaced the two-storey structure with a larger wooden building of much the same form.[71] Just how representative this pattern of timber building was is difficult to say; only in recent years have archaeological discoveries helped illuminate our understanding, with at least three sites now having produced traces of substantial timber constructions, namely Bordesley, Fountains and Sawley.[72] The most telling body of evidence has come from Sawley, where as many as five temporary timber buildings have been excavated, covering the period *c* 1150–90. These were all high-quality structures, two of them fed with piped water supplies. One may have served to accommodate the lay brothers, whilst the most substantial building could have been of two storeys, following the Meaux model.[73]

Narrative sources of the kind outlined above do not exist for Wales, nor have excavations yet been undertaken on any site at a scale likely to reveal much by way of temporary wooden accommodation. This said, four of the Welsh Cistercian abbeys were founded directly from French mother houses,[74] and one might justifiably speculate on the procedures for the provision of buildings as stipulated in the relevant early statute.[75] It is possible that parties of lay brothers were sent out ahead of the monks to supervise the necessary works, or else, one assumes, it must have been the role of the patron to organize an appropriate labour force and to raise a provisional layout of acceptable timber structures. The preparations for the foundation of Margam Abbey, for example, were clearly extended over a period of many months. At one point, St Bernard sent his brother Nivard from Clairvaux to Bristol to receive the foundation endowment from Earl Robert of Gloucester. Also present at the ceremony was William of Clairvaux, the monk who was to become the first abbot of the new house.[76] Whilst it seems very likely that on a journey such as this the proposed site would have been inspected, with plans for the buildings made or confirmed, it is still impossible to be sure who was responsible for the actual construction work. Nor is there greater clarity on the procedures adopted at the second and third generations of Cistercian foundations in Wales.

Something can be said specifically of the temporary building arrangements on at least five of the Welsh sites. Though Trawscoed was eventually an aborted foundation, presumably its initial planning arrangements were no different from those at any other intended colony. The land granted to Dore Abbey at Trawscoed by Walter de Clifford (d 1190) was quite definitely intended 'to build an abbey in honour of God and St Mary, to the increase of the monastic order of Cistercians'. In his charter, Walter gave the monks 'all materials in his forest which are necessary to them for the construction of this building',[77] surely a clear indication of the proposal to raise a temporary wooden monastery.

At the two Savigniac houses, there is the intriguing possibility that the initial communities found themselves housed in a castle bailey.[78] At Basingwerk, it was Earl Ranulf of Chester (1129–53) who may have settled the founding colony in the fortification at nearby Hên Blas. It has been claimed that an early chapel excavated there in the 1950s may have been the successor to that occupied by the monks who arrived in 1131.[79] At Neath, the founder's gifts in 1130 included the chapel at his castle and, by analogy, there is a possibility that this was occupied by the first community on a temporary basis.[80] Evidence of quite a different kind was recovered from the excavations at Valle Crucis in 1970. Here, structural timbers were reused as part of the footings beneath the south range, suggesting to the excavator that they may point to temporary lodgings located elsewhere on the site.[81]

Finally there is the hearsay account related to Stephen Williams in the late nineteenth century concerning the site first occupied by the founding colony of Strata Florida.[82] At the location known today as *yr hen fynachlog*, 'the old monastery', no more than 2.4km to the south west of the permanent buildings, fragments of a modest church were said to lie beneath the turf. Measuring 'about 126 feet [38.4m] long by 42 feet [12.8m]) wide', it apparently stood on rising ground to the south side of the monastic buildings. But this takes us some way forward from any deliberate notion of temporariness there may have been in the Cistercian practice of first raising wooden buildings on the site to be occupied by a new plantation. At *yr hen fynachlog*, where the colony arrived from Whitland around 1164, the indications are that the transition to stone was well advanced within a couple of decades, and this despite the fact that a decision was soon made to move the house to an entirely fresh location.[83]

Part II

The Abbey Churches

Chapter 4

The Earliest Stone Churches

When all the available evidence, both of upstanding fabric and excavated footings, is drawn together, information exists on churches at up to thirteen Cistercian sites in Wales and the border (figs 25 and 26).[1] In some cases, notably Basingwerk, Valle Crucis and Whitland, it seems the basic ground plan of the known church was to remain essentially unmodified from the time of its initial construction in stone through to the suppression. At Strata Florida, on the other hand, the presbytery was clearly extended eastwards early in the abbey's history, while Dore and Margam underwent major rebuildings of their entire east ends during the first half of the thirteenth century. Later in the same century and on into the fourteenth, the long-outmoded Romanesque churches at Tintern and Neath were comprehensively replaced by major new buildings. At much the same time, a new abbey church of similar scale was begun at Maenan to replace that at Aberconwy. This chapter begins by looking at Tintern, the site with the clearest evidence for one of the very earliest stone Cistercian churches in Britain. Alongside this example, the speculative suggestions which have been made for similar twelfth-century churches at Dore and Neath must be examined.

By 1131, the year in which Tintern was established as the first Cistercian plantation on Welsh soil, a comparatively small stone church had been in existence at Cîteaux for some years. Apparently consecrated in 1106, it is thought to have been a simple aisleless structure, with an angled presbytery, and is generally referred to as Cîteaux I (fig 34).[2] It

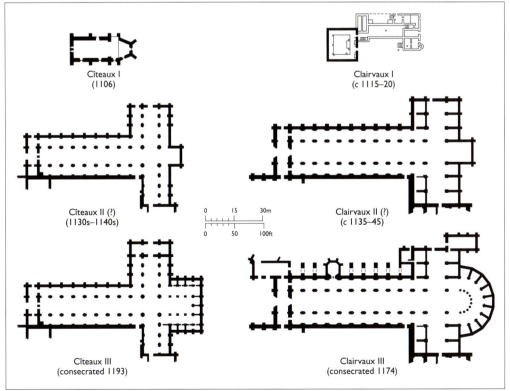

Cîteaux I
(1106)

Clairvaux I
(c 1115–20)

Cîteaux II (?)
(1130s–1140s)

Clairvaux II (?)
(c 1135–45)

0   15   30m
0   50   100ft

Cîteaux III
(consecrated 1193)

Clairvaux III
(consecrated 1174)

34 Cîteaux Abbey (Côte-d'Or, France) and Clairvaux Abbey (Aube, France): comparative ground plans showing posited stages in the development of the abbey churches. Although the first church at Cîteaux was definitely built of stone, it has been argued that Clairvaux I may have been of timber. In the mid-1130s, these diminutive early buildings were replaced by large new churches built in fresh positions on the same sites. The eastern arm of Cîteaux II has never been excavated and its form remains speculative; both the scale and form of Clairvaux II, as currently understood, are open to question. Clairvaux III was consecrated in 1174, and Cîteaux III in 1193.

Drawing: *Pete Lawrence, for Cadw*

35 Tintern Abbey, plans and details of the twelfth-century church: (1) plan of the church as first proposed by Brakspear in 1904; (2) plan of the church as modified after investigations by the Office of Works, 1919–20; (3) plinth of assumed south-west corner buttress, today covered by an inspection grille; (4) plain, trumpet-scalloped capital, a possible survival from the church.

Drawing: Pete Lawrence, for Cadw

survived into the early eighteenth century, to be described by two Benedictine visitors to the abbey in 1708.[3] Their account refers to it as a small but 'very pretty' building, no more than 4.6m wide and of proportionate length, with three windows in the sanctuary and two in the nave. It was covered, at least by this date, with a stone vault.[4] The situation at Clairvaux is less clear-cut, as noted in the previous chapter. Although the church widely known as Clairvaux I (fig 34) may have been built of stone, this view has yet to win universal approval. Were it in fact of timber, then the earliest stone construction on the site could belong to the mid-1130s.[5] Meanwhile, at Pontigny, a modest stone church, much in keeping with the scale of Cîteaux I, had been built probably very soon after the foundation of the abbey in 1114.[6] There seems little reason to doubt a similar pattern of development in the early years of both La Ferté and Morimond. As to the details of Tintern Abbey's own mother house at L'Aumône (founded from Cîteaux in 1121), they are sadly rather vague.[7] Nevertheless, it may safely be assumed that some form of stone church was begun within the first decade of its history, and presumably even before a colony was sent to Waverley in Surrey in 1128. This same sequence – with stone buildings replacing temporary

timber accommodation as the founding communities achieved stability – was soon to be repeated in Wales.[8]

THE SITE EVIDENCE

We might accordingly expect that the minimum complement of thirteen Cistercian monks who arrived in the Wye valley from L'Aumône in the spring of 1131 were greeted by the prerequisite complex of temporary wooden buildings – namely, a chapel, refectory, dormitory and guest quarters.[9] A notional precinct may also have been defined, with a gatehouse to control access. These buildings could have been erected at the expense of the founder, Walter de Clare, possibly under the direction of an advance party of lay brothers. Thereafter, within a very few years, the work of building a permanent stone monastery must have been set in hand.[10] This much can be assumed from the fact that by 1139 the strength of Tintern's economy and the numerical size of its community were such that it was able to send out the first daughter colony of its own, to Kingswood in Gloucestershire.[11]

The ghost of an aisleless Romanesque church, doubtless raised in keeping with the purity of an

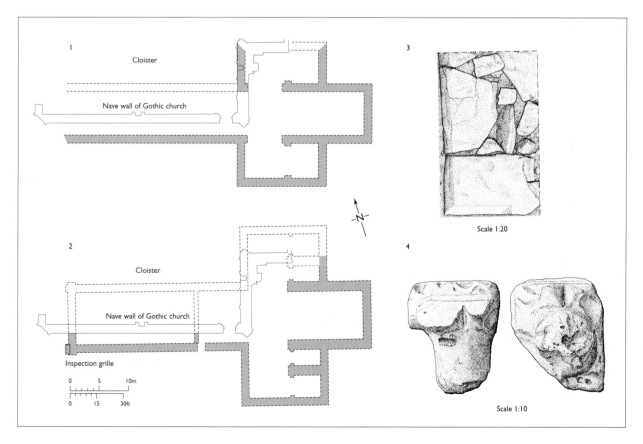

36 Tintern Abbey: conjectural reconstruction of the twelfth-century monastery. Based on little more than fragments of the ground plan, this illustration draws on knowledge of early Cistercian architecture at other sites. The east end of the church is shown with a stone vault; the nave roof was more likely to have been of timber.

Drawing: *Terry Ball, for Cadw*

early Cistercian architectural aesthetic, and which must belong to this first phase of construction, was initially proposed by Harold Brakspear in 1904–8 (fig 35, 1).[12] After further investigations by the Office of Works in 1919–20, however, the plan of Tintern I was considerably modified (fig 35, 2).[13] On the basis of the information available, this early church measured approximately 52.7m in total length. It featured a short square-ended presbytery, broad rectangular transepts, each with a pair of deep eastern chapels entered through arches of perhaps two orders, and a narrow aisleless nave.[14] It is not possible to be certain, but given the lack of evidence for arch responds on either the east or west sides, it seems unlikely the church would have had an architecturally defined crossing, and a tower is not therefore to be expected (fig 36). In such an arrangement, the nave roof would have continued uninterrupted all the way through to the presbytery arch, itself presumably corbelled out from the wall faces. In turn, we might expect the presbytery to have been stepped down in height from the nave. And, given their marginally thicker walls, both the presbytery and the deep transept chapels could have been covered with pointed barrel vaults.[15] The nave roof, on the other hand, was more likely to have been of timber.[16] Taken as a whole, the church must have been a comparatively tall building, in part confirmed by the height of the later east claustral range, which would have abutted the north transept. Almost

nothing is known of the internal details, other than the presence of a stone cross-wall part way down the length of the nave, the footings of which were found during the 1919–20 phase of clearance operations. This wall could represent the division

37 Tintern Abbey: photograph of about 1920 showing possible cross-wall in the nave of the twelfth-century church. The plan of the first church at Tintern was first reconstructed by Harold Brakspear in 1904–8. His outline was modified following investigations by the Office of Works in 1919–20. Almost certainly taken during the latter programme of work, this photograph seems to show the exposed south wall of the nave (foreground), with the cross-wall running northwards under the fabric of the later church.

Photograph: *Cadw, Crown Copyright*

between the monks' choir to the east and the lay brothers' church to the west (fig 37). Other aspects of the liturgical arrangements await further investigation.

At Neath, much as at Tintern, virtually all trace of the twelfth-century church was removed when the community finally embarked on the construction of a larger replacement building at the end of the thirteenth century (fig 25). However, the position and scale of the Romanesque church must in some way be reflected in the contours of the eventual site layout. Indeed, Lawrence Butler has put forward a not unconvincing case for a reconstruction on just this basis (fig 38).[17] There are two key pieces of evidence: the first is a section of link wall at the north-west corner of the existing cloister; and the second is the difference in the alignment between the upper and lower courses in the west wall of the rebuilt south transept. Butler takes these to mark the positions of the west front and the south transept of the early church, though his hypothesis has still to be tested by excavation or by geophysical survey.[18] It should also be borne in mind that Neath, of course, was a Savigniac foundation of 1130, becoming Cistercian only in 1147. Thus, it seems less likely that the first stone church was directly indebted to white monk precedents.

Although the details are rather difficult to determine, another aisleless twelfth-century church may have existed at Dore, where the house was founded in 1147. In particular, within the fabric of the surviving north transept, only completed in mature form in c 1175, various features point to the existence of a previous building, or at least to one designed along more primitive lines.[19] This possibility has recently been explored further by Harrison and Thurlby, to the point where they feel able to produce a ground plan, albeit an extremely tentative one (fig 38).[20] They propose a church with a rectangular presbytery, transepts in which the eastern chapels were arranged *en échelon* (possibly barrel-vaulted),[21] and a long aisleless nave. The total length of the church would have been close to 66m. As regards the reconstructed layout of the north transept, the position of the longer inner early chapel would be marked by the outer example in the mature building (fig 25), whereas the smaller outer early chapel must subsequently have been converted to serve as the book room and sacristy. It is further suggested by Harrison and Thurlby that, given the uninterrupted coursing of the masonry from the north transept arcade through into the north-east crossing pier, there is a distinct possibility that the early church would have been designed with an undifferentiated crossing, of similar form in fact to that proposed at Tintern (fig 36).[22]

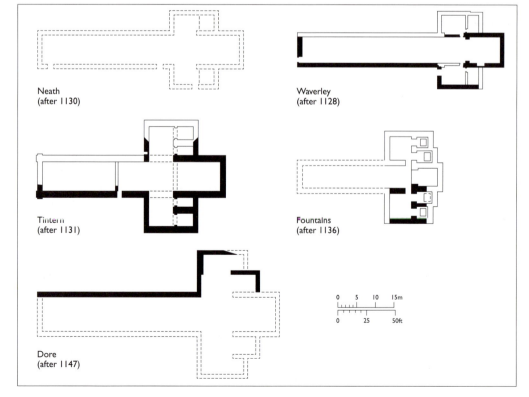

38 Aisleless Cistercian churches in Britain, comparative ground plans: Neath (after Butler 1984); Tintern (after Robinson 1996a); Dore (after Harrison and Thurlby 1997); Waverley (after Brakspear 1905); Fountains (after Gilyard-Beer and Coppack 1986).

Drawing: Pete Lawrence, for Cadw

Neath
(after 1130)

Waverley
(after 1128)

Tintern
(after 1131)

Fountains
(after 1136)

Dore
(after 1147)

0 5 10 15m

0 25 50ft

The suggestion put forward by Dr Ralegh Radford that an aisleless church similar to the Tintern model was also raised by the pioneering community at Cwmhir is much less convincing.[23] This is particularly true given the lack of any hard evidence to support an earlier notion that the site was colonized before 1176.[24] Although examples of stone churches of this form are known from late twelfth-century contexts elsewhere, it seems very unlikely that a first-generation colony in the Whitland family would have embarked on such a building at so late a date. The point is underlined when the near-contemporary arrangements known from Cwmhir's sister houses at Strata Florida and Strata Marcella are taken into account.[25]

ARCHITECTURAL CONTEXT

In so far as they are currently understood, the details of Tintern I, together with the proposals for Neath and Dore, may be compared to a small group of early Cistercian aisleless churches now recognized across Britain, and beyond.[26] It was, in fact, probably just a year or two before work started at Tintern that a church of very similar form and character was begun at the sister abbey of Waverley in Surrey (fig 38).[27] This, too, had a modest square-ended presbytery, measuring just 8.2m long by 7.6m wide, though here the aisleless nave was of distinctly elongated proportions. The transept arms were seemingly shallower than those at Tintern, each having a single diminutive eastern chapel.[28] The transepts as a whole appear to have been almost entirely screened off from the choir by narrow walls, doubtless providing the backing for the stalls of the choir monks. The entrances to the transept chapels were restricted to small doorways adjacent to the choir.

The first stone church raised at Fountains Abbey in North Yorkshire would have been marginally later than either Waverley or Tintern. It is known from excavations of 1979–80, when parts of the crossing and the south transept were exposed.[29] Building is thought to have been initiated in 1136, and the church may have been completed within a decade. It was shortly, in any case, remodelled by Abbot Henry Murdac (1144–7). In contrast to what is known of the two L'Aumône affiliations, the presbytery and flanking transept chapels at Fountains were apparently built to a stepped, *en échelon*, plan (fig 38). Like Waverley, however, the transepts were walled off from the choir so as to accommodate the backs of the choir stalls. The nave of this church has not been uncovered, though the excavator argues it was of a short unaisled form.[30]

Another of these early aisleless churches may well have been identified through geophysical survey in the area of the later cloister at Rievaulx Abbey.[31] Somewhat further afield, at the Fountains daughter house of Lysa in Norway, a similar church was raised soon after 1146.[32] Other examples in the British Isles, however, are by no means restricted to the first half of the twelfth century. Thus, although significant new developments were occurring elsewhere,[33] it would not be a total surprise if an aisleless church were being completed at Dore in the early 1150s. At Sawley in Lancashire, for instance, where the stone church was begun soon after 1150, a narrow aisleless nave was added to the new-style presbytery and transepts in 1170–80.[34] Even later, a church closer to the primitive form of Tintern and Waverley was built at the abbey of Rushen on the Isle of Man, possibly after 1196.[35] In Ireland, although a fully stressed crossing was introduced at Grey *c* 1193–1200, the nave was again built to an aisleless plan.[36] Finally, there are several examples of early thirteenth-century aisleless Cistercian churches from Scotland, notably those at Culross and Saddell.[37]

There is no doubt that the simple planning and plain architectural detailing of the earliest Cistercian churches in this widespread group would have contrasted markedly with many contemporary Anglo-Norman religious houses. The clean lines, modest scaling and unstressed crossing at Tintern I, for example, would surely have created a very different impression from the churches at Chepstow and Ewenny (figs 28 and 29), with their formalized crossings and lantern towers. Moreover, all Benedictine churches of any pretension had aisles, and the internal and external surfaces were usually articulated with wall arcading, chevron string courses, carved capitals and corbels, and richly moulded doorways.

This said, it is important to bear in mind that such simple early twelfth-century churches were by no means peculiar to the Cistercians. Apart from the secular church, other reformed monastic congregations – notably the various groups of Augustinian canons – also built them.[38] Several authors have, for example, now pointed to the aisleless early twelfth-century Augustinian churches at sites such as Haughmond (Shropshire), Kenilworth (Warwickshire), Kirkham (North Yorkshire), Merton (Surrey), Norton (Cheshire) and Portchester (Hampshire).[39] There is, too, at least a possibility that churches of a similar form were also built in Wales, at Llanthony and Carmarthen.[40] Furthermore, as the century progressed the aisleless plan remained popular, not just with the Augustinians but also with the Premonstratensians.[41] In sum, it must be acknowledged that until the appearance in Britain of more standardized Cistercian plans in the late 1140s, there is a possibility that the blueprint for churches such as Tintern I could have been derived from outside sources.[42] On the other hand, it may be too much of a coincidence to believe that Tintern and Waverley, founded within three years of one another, both as daughter houses of L'Aumône, came to build churches of such similar proportion and design without some reference to a common source.

One other intriguing Welsh monastic church worth mentioning before concluding this section is that of St Nicholas and St John at Monkton, the former Pembroke Priory.[43] As noted above (*see* chapter 2), the house was founded *c* 1098 as a cell of St Martin at Sées in Normandy.[44] Although the east end of the church was enlarged in the later Middle Ages, and very heavily restored in 1887–95, the narrow aisleless nave at Pembroke remains much as built, as perfectly austere as anything the Cistercians may have raised in the first decades of the twelfth century. The surviving pointed barrel vault over the nave runs through to the restored eastern crossing arch and the transepts were also vaulted.[45] The date is difficult to determine, though on the basis of the south doorway into the nave, which features continuous heavy roll mouldings, something towards the end of the twelfth century seems most likely.[46]

CHAPTER 5

THE ARRIVAL OF THE 'BERNADINE' PLAN

Within a few years of the earliest Cistercian stone churches going up in Britain, at least three of the senior French mother houses of the order had embarked on monumental new programmes of construction. Very much as a consequence of their own growth and success, the communities at Cîteaux, Clairvaux and Pontigny were forced to turn their backs on the small oratories and associated domestic buildings of the pioneering years. In their place, major new stone monasteries were built over the second quarter of the twelfth century (figs 15 and 16). Through the course of their development, there emerged all the principal characteristics of what was to become the standard Cistercian monastic plan.[1] Our chief concern here is with the churches of this period.

At Cîteaux itself, the church which replaced the tiny oratory of 1106 was probably in the planning stages from the early to mid-1130s, though the building work itself is generally dated to c 1140–50.[2] This church, widely known as Cîteaux II, was demolished in the 1790s and is really known only from seventeenth- and eighteenth-century antiquarian plans and illustrations (fig 15).[3] The plan of the building is usually reconstructed with a small, almost disproportionate, square-ended presbytery,[4] but this has never been confirmed by excavation (fig 34). There is much greater confidence about the four-bay transepts (that on the north having aisles to both east and west), the nine-bay nave and the full-width porch at the west end. Uncertainty returns when considering the form of the roof over the central vessel of the nave. It may have been entirely of timber, though it has been argued that a groin vault is the more plausible.[5]

The position with regard to the developments at Clairvaux at around this time is somewhat more complex. According to the traditional narrative account of the rebuilding of the monastery, as given by Arnold of Bonneval in book two of the *Vita Prima* of St Bernard, work on the new abbey began about 1135.[6] The construction programme was aided by Theobald of Blois, count of Champagne (d 1152), and it has often been accepted that the completed

church was consecrated in or before 1145.[7] Most scholars have further been prepared to accept that it is the three-bay transepts and the enormous eleven-bay nave of the c 1135–45 church which are to be seen in the plans and drawings of the site produced by Dom Nicolas Milley in 1708 (figs 16 and 39). This church, also reconstructed with a small square-ended presbytery like that of Cîteaux, has long passed into the literature as Clairvaux II (fig 34).[8] In recent decades, however, much in this conventional interpretation has come under challenge,[9] with the most comprehensive review of the evidence having been set out by Dr Alexandra Gajewski. Although Gajewski accepts that a removal from the *monasterium vetus* took place in the 1130s, and that a new church was indeed begun on the permanent site, she argues this is not the building seen in the 1708 illustrations.[10] On the contrary, she suggests that the church built from the late 1130s is likely to have been considerably smaller, and probably more akin to that at Fontenay (Côte-d'Or), a daughter house of Clairvaux founded in 1118 where the church is, again, usually dated to the late 1130s (figs 40 and 41).[11] In fact, for Gajewski, the Milley plans and illustrations represent a comprehensive rebuilding, one which is most likely to have been initiated sometime before St Bernard's death in 1153. The vast scale of this church would, she says, have been motivated by the ever-increasing number of monks attracted to the house.[12] These arguments do have much to recommend them, and matters are likely to become clearer as further research is undertaken, not least at the site itself. For the moment, however, it is difficult to reject entirely the earlier interpretations based on the Milley drawings.[13] In any case, of greatest importance to the theme explored here, it seems inconceivable that the plan of the stone church built at Clairvaux c 1135–45 could have been of a form other than that which was soon to become so widespread throughout the order.

This is further underlined by the evidence from Pontigny, where another large new church was under construction no later than the middle years of the twelfth century; unlike those at Cîteaux and

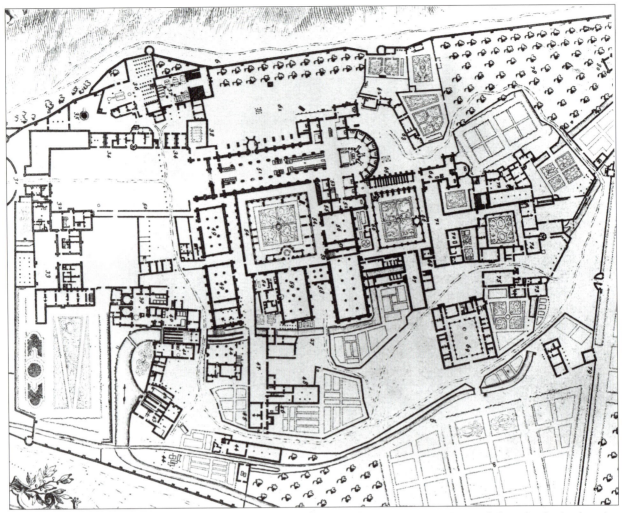

39 *Clairvaux Abbey (Aube, France): detail from a ground plan by Dom Nicolas Milley, 1708. This is the core element of a large plan showing the entire abbey precinct. The church seen here, with its eastern ambulatory and radiating chapels, was almost certainly that consecrated in 1174 – still widely known as Clairvaux III. The key monastic buildings are shown around three sides of the great cloister, with the infirmary and abbot's lodgings to the east. To the west of the church lay the inner gatehouse and the accommodation set aside for guests. Photograph: Bibliothèque Nationale de France, Paris*

Clairvaux, it survives virtually complete. Moreover, despite the later rebuilding of the east end, the likely form of the original presbytery at Pontigny has been recovered through excavation.[14] Dr Terryl Kinder has argued that the construction programme was begun significantly earlier than has been allowed by most previous commentators.[15] She suggests that work on the church was started at the east end in the late 1130s, with the nave completed 'around or shortly after 1150'.[16] More recently, Gajewski has reasserted the arguments for a commencement sometime in the 1140s.[17] The completed church featured a square-ended aisleless presbytery, two-bay transepts (with aisles to both east and west) and a nave of seven bays preceded by a western porch or narthex.[18] The transepts and the nave aisles have groin vaults set

between transverse arches; the main vessel of the nave is covered with rib vaults.[19]

In spite of the disappearance of Cîteaux II and Clairvaux II, authorities remain widely agreed that it must have been these great churches – together with Pontigny and others soon modelled upon them – which were responsible for quickly introducing a marked degree of uniformity into the Cistercian architectural aesthetic.

DEFINING THE 'BERNARDINE' PLAN

In the early 1950s the German scholar Karl-Heinz Esser considered the resemblances within the Clairvaux family of houses in particular, coining the label 'Bernardine' to sum up the principal

40 *Fontenay Abbey (Côte-d'Or, France): interior of the abbey church, looking east. Fontenay was founded in 1118 as the second daughter house of St Bernard's Clairvaux. The church, which stands as the earliest surviving representation of the so-called 'Bernardine' plan, is thought to have been constructed c 1139–47. Its comparatively austere style has often been taken to represent the very embodiment of early Cistercian architectural practice.*

Photograph: *author*

characteristics.[20] A few years later, Esser's thesis was substantially developed by Hanno Hahn in his major investigation of the European evidence founded on the Rhineland house of Eberbach (Hesse).[21] In the same influential book, Hahn developed the thesis that Cistercian builders employed a modular or proportional system in setting out their churches, based on two squares used to determine key points of the plan.[22] At much the same time, François Bucher published a similar study based on Bonmont and the

other early abbeys of the order in Switzerland.[23] Through these and other contributions, the concept of a specific 'Bernardine' style became entrenched in the literature. At times, moreover, this has been linked – almost as an article of faith – to the notion that a specific architectural ideal had been developed by the saint himself.[24] Despite certain convincing aspects seen in the various modular theories, more recent scholarship has tended to reject any blanket proposition of a single architectural model derived from Clairvaux. Much more rigorous qualification is needed, certainly in so far as any aspect of the planning or uniformity should be directly connected with Bernard's name.[25] Nevertheless, the extraordinarily widespread occurrence of the so-called 'Bernardine' plan throughout the Clairvaux filiation of houses is undeniable. For at least two decades from the later 1140s, this highly distinctive church plan was almost universally employed at Cistercian abbeys across Europe (fig 41). Furthermore, isolated examples were to appear in Britain, as elsewhere, right through into the early thirteenth century.[26]

Although definitive information is lacking because of the loss of the actual building, there cannot really be much doubt that the genesis of the plan itself is to be traced back to the new church built

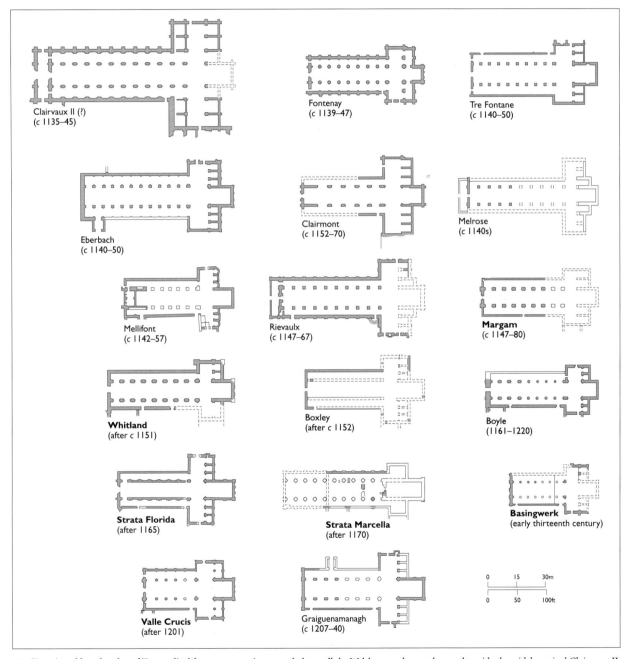

41 *Cistercian abbey churches of 'Bernardine' form, comparative ground plans: all the Welsh examples are shown alongside the widely posited Clairvaux II, with others from Europe, Britain and Ireland included for further comparison. Drawing: Pete Lawrence, for Cadw*

at Clairvaux *c* 1135–45 (figs 16, 34 and 41).[27] It is believed that the construction of this church was entrusted to Geoffrey d'Ainai, at the very least something of a practical organizer within the abbey community and possibly one with considerable architectural skill and experience.[28] He was assisted in the task of setting out the new church by Achard (or Archardus), master of the novices at Clairvaux.[29] As we have seen, the building generally thought to have been raised at this time featured a short, projecting, rectangular presbytery, transepts with three square-ended chapels on their east and west sides, and a long aisled nave of eleven bays. Because of its destruction, we are unable to say much with any confidence about the superstructure of this important church.[30] Scholars have turned instead to several of Clairvaux's well-known early daughter houses as a basis for a broader understanding of the new type of architecture represented by the 'Bernardine' plan, with Fontenay, in Burgundy's Côte-d'Or, far and away the most frequently cited example.

Fontenay was founded as the second daughter house of Clairvaux in 1118. Although the community is known to have transferred to the existing site in 1130, it has long been suggested that construction of the permanent church only began in 1139, with the building supposedly consecrated eight years later.[31] In plan, the completed church at Fontenay bears all the essential hallmarks of what is still recognized as the classic 'Bernardine' form (fig 41): a short square-ended presbytery; transepts with squared eastern chapels; a long aisled nave (in this case of eight bays); and a porch at the west end. More significantly, it has been argued on the basis of this standing church that the distinctive style identified in the 'Bernardine' plan extended also into the elevation of such new Cistercian buildings (fig 40). At Fontenay, for example, it is immediately striking that there is no clerestory above what are already rather plain pointed arcades. The surface decoration, meanwhile, extends little beyond the modest foliage capitals. Despite this, there are several quite distinct characteristics within the church, especially the emphatic bay divisions and the pointed barrel vaults which cover all the spaces. It is notable, too, that the whole interior is suffused in a soft clear light which complements the simple forms and fine proportions.[32] Another of the more prominent features is the way that the nave vault carries through in an unbroken line to the presbytery arch, with the result that there is no marked crossing nor any capacity to carry a central crossing tower. The presbytery and transepts are then set at a lower level, with a consequent stepping down of the roofs at the east end of the building.[33] In point of fact, it was largely the so-called 'Fontenay style', marked by the absence of a crossing tower and a diminutive east end, which was to set the Cistercian churches of the 1140s and 1150s apart from many other Romanesque forms of the same period.[34]

All in all, as Stalley points out, in the past Fontenay has always been regarded as 'the very embodiment of Cistercian architectural practice'.[35] Yet despite its widespread fame, it is now well recognized that this one Burgundian church may not necessarily be the most representative example in the very widespread 'Bernardine' group.[36] The absence, for example, of a clerestory level in the Fontenay nave (fig 40) has been noted, though in fact many churches of the Clairvaux affiliation built from the 1140s onwards featured quite definite two-storey elevations. In turn, without examining the primary evidence with care, this has tended to colour the general consensus on the likely arrangements at the mother house itself.[37] In reality, of course, it must be recognized that away from the French heartlands of the order, in Italy, the Rhineland, in north-west Spain, in Scandinavia, or, for that matter, in Yorkshire, somewhat different elevations – employing a mixture of both imported elements and indigenous local characteristics – were soon to be built on basically the same 'Bernardine' plan. This is not something that should cause any great surprise. For the Cistercians themselves, the most important aspect in the planning of any new church was the disposition of liturgical space. For this purpose, a ground plan setting out the essential parameters might easily be transmitted over very long distances, especially when guidance was available through experienced monks such as Geoffrey d'Ainai. Beyond the plan, established according to the new orthodoxy, the overall massing of churches, their elevation and general proportions, and the degree of appropriateness in their architectural detailing, all followed in some ways as secondary elements.

THE 'BERNARDINE' PLAN IN BRITAIN

In the event, it seems clear that the plan was transmitted to Britain soon after its emergence in the cradle-lands of the order.[38] It might well have appeared first at Rievaulx in North Yorkshire, founded in 1132 as Clairvaux's primary British colony.[39] The founding abbot, William (1132–46), was himself an Englishman, though he had joined the Cistercians at Clairvaux around 1118, and had served as Bernard's secretary. There is some evidence to suggest that Abbot William's first stone church at Rievaulx was of the aisleless form.[40] It has recently been argued, however, that within a few years the rapid growth of the house led to the construction of a second church, perhaps no later than the mid-1130s. It is further argued that this church adhered very closely to the 'Bernardine' plan.[41] Such a view gains support when the evidence from Melrose in Scotland, a daughter house of Rievaulx founded in 1136, is examined.[42] The church here was dedicated in 1146, and there is clear evidence to show that its presbytery and transepts were essentially of the 'Bernardine' form, even if the transept chapels were arranged in a variant *en échelon* fashion (fig 41).[43] Meanwhile, at Fountains, which had been adopted into the Clairvaux family, Abbot Henry Murdac had been responsible for the completion of a similar church. In this case it is presumed that the design was partially indebted to Henry's previous abbey at Vauclair (Aisne), though it may also have been influenced by Abbot William's developments at Rievaulx.[44]

Clairvaux's next plantation in the British Isles was made at Mellifont in Ireland (fig 17), where the founding colony arrived in 1142, largely through the influence of Malachy, archbishop of Armagh (d 1148).[45] Of particular interest, Bernard sent one of his monks, Robert, to assist Malachy with 'the buildings and other things necessary for the well-being of [the] house'.[46] It is not known how long Robert remained at Mellifont, though it is generally assumed that the church laid out there in the 1140s and consecrated in 1157 was the result of his influence (fig 41).[47] Certainly, in broad terms, the plan of this church conformed to 'Bernardine' principles, its dimensions in keeping with the proportional system proposed by Hahn.[48] Yet there are also one or two anomalies, especially the design of the transept chapels with their alternation of square and semicircular forms, for which there is no really satisfactory explanation.

In 1143, the year after the foundation of Mellifont, Clairvaux decided to establish what was effectively only its second directly affiliated English colony. With the support of William of Ypres, a son of the count of Flanders, monks were sent to occupy a site at Boxley in Kent (fig 17).[49] Very little of the abbey survives above ground, though from excavations carried out there between 1953 and 1972 it seems that the plan was again based on the 'Bernardine' model (fig 41).[50] Given the marginally deeper proportions of the presbytery, together with what few architectural details have been recovered, it is suggested that the church shows minor advances on the earliest 'Bernardine' forms, moving towards what might be considered a mature version of the plan.[51] The church may have belonged to the time of Abbot Thomas (*c* 1152–62), who had previously been a monk at Fontenay.[52] Were this the case, it would come as no surprise to find the presbytery was initially covered by a barrel vault.[53] Again, the solid walls between the transept chapels suggest that these spaces too were barrel-vaulted.

Back up at Rievaulx, it was probably the ongoing success of the monastery which led Abbot Ailred (1147–67) to pull down substantial parts of his predecessor's buildings, constructing afresh on a rather larger scale.[54] In particular, shortly after assuming the abbacy, Ailred began work on a substantial new church (fig 41). Once more, this was a building imbued with all the significant qualities, of the 'Bernardine' form despite the *en échelon* arrangement of the transept chapels. The long, nine-bay nave featured a two-storey elevation (fig 43), and there was a galilee porch at the west end, similar to those appearing at Clairvaux and Fontenay.[55] Finally, it cannot have been too long after the work was started at Rievaulx that a monumental new 'Bernardine' church was begun at Fountains by Abbot Richard (1151–70), who had been a monk at Clairvaux before serving as abbot of Vauclair.[56]

THE EVIDENCE FROM MARGAM AND WHITLAND

Building on this already substantial body of evidence for the influence of Clairvaux and its immediate French family on early Cistercian church planning in Britain, the evidence from Wales should now be examined. As it happens, the next two communities to arrive in the Anglo-Norman lordships of the south had been given their marching orders by St Bernard himself. In other words, like those at Mellifont and Boxley, the brothers who arrived to colonize Whitland in 1140 (early settled at Little Trefgarn), followed by those who occupied Margam in 1147, were presumably familiar with the new church at Clairvaux, built *c* 1135–45. And, although their initial accommodation needs were doubtless met by temporary wooden buildings, to judge from the standing remains at Margam and from the excavated evidence on the final site of Whitland, there can have been no great delay before stone churches of 'Bernardine' plan were under construction (fig 41).

The survival of the greater part of the mid-twelfth-century nave at Margam is truly quite remarkable (fig 42), though its full significance has too often been overlooked.[57] Nowhere else in Britain is there now more eloquent testimony of that severe and often desolate simplicity so typical of the early Cistercian architectural aesthetic. Although the aisles appear to have been largely rebuilt in the restoration of 1805–9, it is the original six west bays (from a total of eight) which now serve as St Mary's parish church (fig 25).[58]

42 *Margam Abbey: view of the nave, looking north west. Six bays of the two-storey Cistercian nave survive as St Mary's parish church. Nowhere else in Britain is there now more eloquent testimony of that severe and often desolate simplicity so typical of the early Cistercian architectural aesthetic. Note the blocked clerestory windows above the two north-western bays.*

Photograph: *Cadw, Crown Copyright*

The two-storey internal elevations of the nave could scarcely be any plainer (fig 43), with a complete lack of any bay articulation along the entire length of the building. The ashlar piers are essentially rectangular, and rise from plain chamfered plinths to round-headed arcades springing from simple chamfered imposts. In detail, coursed pilasters on the east and west faces of the piers create what is in effect a cruciform profile (fig 44). In turn, this is followed by the two square orders in the arches above.[59] Over the arcades and their spandrels, the walls were always of rubble build, even if the elevation is now somewhat reduced in height. On the north side, where the later plaster covering has been removed, it is possible to see the base and splays of several of the blocked clerestory windows, sitting directly over the apex of the arches to the arcade (fig 42). The absence of any convincing evidence for responds or shafts indicates that the roof over the central vessel was always of timber, though this could well have been boarded to resemble a barrel vault.[60] This would certainly have sprung from a higher point than the existing roof, allowing for an additional window, or

perhaps windows, in the original gable of the west front.[61] In the aisles, the medieval arrangements are masked as a result of the early nineteenth-century restoration work, but it is perfectly possible that the plaster groin vaults reflect the pattern of stone originals.[62]

At the west front of the church (fig 45), in spite of the modified roof pitch and the extended buttresses with their top-heavy arcaded terminals (both features introduced during the restorations of the nineteenth century), there is much which survives of the original Romanesque fabric. The central doorway is of three, shafted orders. The shafts carry two rows of doughnut-like shaft-rings, and the capitals are carved with foliate and scalloped designs. Above, the three round-headed windows have two shafted orders to the jambs, again featuring multiple shaft-rings.[63] As noted, although the original gable is lost, one might speculate that it perhaps contained a simple oculus, as proposed for, say, Rievaulx.[64] In any case, taken as a whole, the Margam composition seems to echo near-contemporary Burgundian Cistercian forms. The combination of a relatively

43 Cistercian churches of the mid-twelfth century, comparative nave elevations: Margam (reconstructed, David Robinson); Clairmont (Mayenne, France) (Chris Jones-Jenkins / David Robinson); Rievaulx (North Yorkshire) (reconstructed, after Fergusson and Harrison 1999); Tre Fontane, Rome (Latium, Italy) (based on Romanini 1994).

Drawing: Pete Lawrence, for Cadw

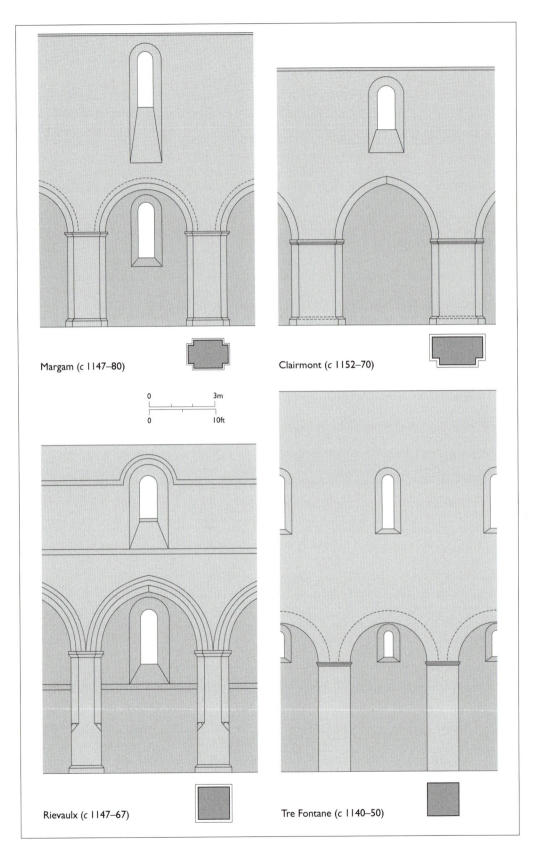

Margam (c 1147–80)

Clairmont (c 1152–70)

0   3m
0   10ft

Rievaulx (c 1147–67)

Tre Fontane (c 1140–50)

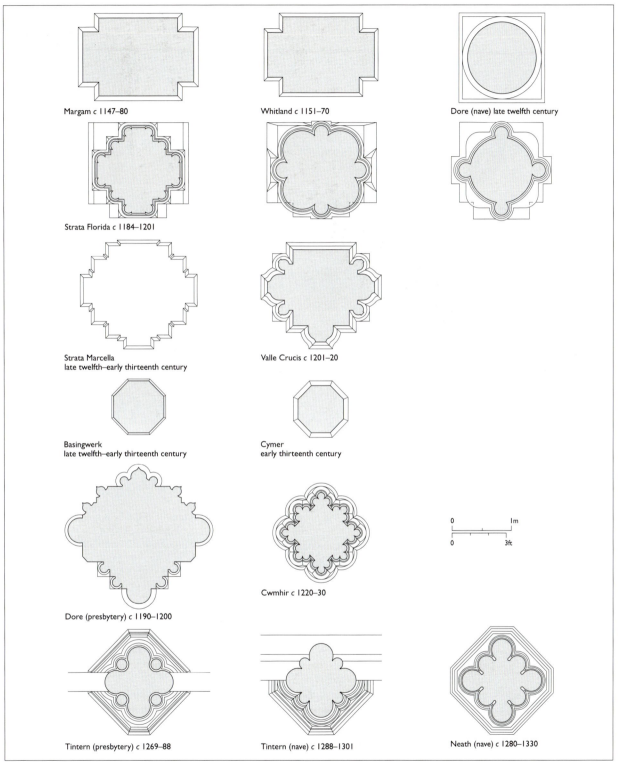

Margam *c* 1147–80

Whitland *c* 1151–70

Dore (nave) late twelfth century

Strata Florida *c* 1184–1201

Strata Marcella
late twelfth–early thirteenth century

Valle Crucis *c* 1201–20

Basingwerk
late twelfth–early thirteenth century

Cymer
early thirteenth century

Dore (presbytery) *c* 1190–1200

Cwmhir *c* 1220–30

Tintern (presbytery) *c* 1269–88

Tintern (nave) *c* 1288–1301

Neath (nave) *c* 1280–1330

44 *Cistercian abbeys in Wales and the March, comparative pier profiles: Margam (David Robinson); Whitland (after Ludlow 2002); Dore (David Robinson); Strata Florida (after Williams 1889a/Stuart Harrison); Strata Marcella (after [Jones] and Williams 1891); Valle Crucis (David Robinson); Basingwerk (David Robinson); Cymer (David Robinson); Dore (David Robinson); Cwmhir (after Williams 1894–5); Tintern (David Robinson); Neath (David Robinson). Drawing: Pete Lawrence, for Cadw*

45 *Margam Abbey: view of the west front. Although restored in 1805–9, when the roof pitch was modified and the buttresses extended with their Italianate terminals, the west front still conveys much of the character of the twelfth-century building. It bears comparison, for example, with the appearance of the near-contemporary west fronts at Clairvaux's French daughter houses of Fontenay and Trois-Fontaines.*

Photograph: *Cadw, Crown Copyright*

modest doorway with a tight register of three round-headed windows above is reminiscent at least of the marginally more elaborate scheme at Fontenay Abbey (fig 46), and bears comparison too with that at Trois-Fontaines (Marne).[65] Like the French sites, there was also a porch at the west front of Margam.

Given the rather primitive qualities seen in the nave design at Margam, it seems very likely that the entire 'Bernardine' church was well advanced by the mid-1150s. The general form is certainly close to that of the nave at Rievaulx (fig 43), now believed to date from the early years of Ailred's abbacy (1147–67).[66] In these circumstances, it is difficult to know just what to make of the consecration of an 'altar of the

Holy Trinity' at Margam Abbey by William of Saltmarsh, bishop of Llandaff, in 1187.[67] If this nave altar was in the lay brothers' area of the church, one might be tempted to link the consecration with the completion of the west front, yet the stylistic details, including the keel moulding applied to the continuous angle rolls around the inner splays of the three large windows, together with the trumpet-scalloped capitals which feature in the exterior jambs of both the doorway and the windows, all indicate a more likely *terminus ad quem* of about 1175–80.[68]

In this same context, mention should also be made of the late twelfth-century doorway apparently

46 *Fontenay Abbey (Côte-d'Or, France): the west front of the abbey church, perhaps completed by c 1147. The row of corbels set beneath the string course originally supported a lean-to roof over a so-called galilee porch.*

Photograph: *author*

removed from Margam in 1849 to the parish church of St Brides-super-Ely, where it continues to serve as the entrance to the south porch (fig 47).[69] The shafts of the outer order again feature trumpet-scalloped capitals, whereas the round-headed arch above is framed by a continuous moulding of lily-like flowers, an ornament known from a number of other west country sites of *c* 1175–1200.[70] The inner arch order has gaping chevrons. In trying to place this doorway in Margam's late twelfth-century arrangements, it is tempting to see it as the processional entrance from the east walk of the cloister into the nave, in which case it would add much to our understanding of the full character of the early church.

In sad contrast to the striking remains seen at Margam, the surviving medieval masonry at Whitland now stands no more than a few courses high (fig 48). Our understanding comes chiefly from partial excavations undertaken in the 1920s, and from a further programme of excavation and archaeological survey carried out in more recent years.[71] In sum, given the unsettled early history of the community, it seems reasonable to suggest that

47 *St Brides-super-Ely (Vale of Glamorgan): south porch doorway, late twelfth century. Said to have been located in a stable to the west of the abbey church at Margam in 1840, it was removed to St Brides-super-Ely nine years later. If its Cistercian pedigree can be accepted, it is tempting to identify the doorway as the original processional entrance into the nave from the east cloister walk.*

Photograph: *author*

48 Whitland Abbey: the landscaped remains of the abbey church, looking west. Founded in 1140, Whitland was a first-generation daughter house of St Bernard's Clairvaux. Having experienced at least one change of site, the community began the construction of its permanent stone church in or before 1151. Following the classic 'Bernardine' model, the building was designed with a short rectangular presbytery, unsegregated crossing and an eight-bay nave.

Photograph: *author*

work on construction of the abbey church was probably begun marginally later than at Margam. The monks first arrived in south-west Wales in 1140, under the patronage of Bishop Bernard of St Davids. Within four years, it appears they were settled on episcopal land at Little Trefgarn near Haverfordwest, where they may have remained until 1151, or thereabouts, when they finally took possession of the permanent site.[72] There is a distinct chance that the building of the presbytery and transepts could already have been in hand; the whole church was presumably completed over the next decade or two.

The two main programmes of excavation at the site have confirmed that, in terms of the plan at least, the nave was based on very much the same blueprint as that employed by the builders at Margam (figs 26 and 41). The Whitland nave was also of eight bays,[73] though here the piers of the arcades were apparently of two different sizes. They all seem to have featured the chamfered base plinth and cruciform profile seen at the sister house (fig 44), but the three eastern pairs were marginally longer along the principal axis than those to the west.[74] The bay spacings between

the piers also varied in accordance with the two groupings, the combined evidence suggesting a break or pause in the construction programme. As at Margam, one suspects the main vessel of the nave was most likely covered with a timber roof, though the comparatively narrow width of the aisles suggests there was at least an intention to cover these with stone vaults. In the south aisle, where the outer wall was partially rebuilt in the nineteenth century, there are indications of two doorways. That to the west may be original, in which case it presumably connected with the west walk of the cloister. The dressings of the main west door into the church had been entirely robbed out before the excavations of the 1920s, though Collier reported finding what he interpreted as a length of one of the jamb shafts near the centre of the entrance itself.[75] He speculated as to whether Whitland might in fact have had a west doorway of a similar character to that of its daughter house at Strata Florida (*see* fig 73).[76] In this context it is particularly interesting to try and place the features seen in an 1838 drawing of the site by Charles Norris (fig 49).[76] Though ill-defined, Norris's illustration seems to depict the jambs of a multi-shafted doorway, its scale and character in keeping with what might be expected at the western entrance to the nave.[77]

Turning to consider the eastern arms of the mid-twelfth-century churches at Margam and Whitland, it must be acknowledged that the precise details are difficult to establish. At Margam virtually everything was swept away when the presbytery and transepts were rebuilt in the early thirteenth century (fig 25), while at Whitland it is once again only the excavated outline that has been recovered. By analogy, however, and on the strength of various clues, tentative reconstructions might be posited.

Beginning at Whitland, it is very clear that the ground plan of the church was based on the now familiar 'Bernardine' model (figs 26 and 41). The two-bay, box-like presbytery was flanked by somewhat narrow transepts, each with two virtually square eastern chapels divided from each other by solid walls.[78] Foundations for significant buttressing, seen against the end wall of the presbytery and the north wall of the north transept, indicate that these eastern spaces were vaulted in stone, probably as part of the original design. And, if building were indeed under way by the early 1150s, barrel vaults might be expected to have been employed.[79] The substantial dimensions of the buttress at the north-west corner of the north transept suggest it may have accommodated a spiral stair, providing access to the roof spaces.[80] Internally, as revealed by the most recent programme of excavations, there are distinct

49 *Whitland Abbey: drawing by Charles Norris showing a doorway with multi-shafted jambs, 1838. The scale and character of the features suggest they could represent a mid- to late twelfth-century west portal, though the evidence is far from conclusive.*

Photograph: *Central Library, Cardiff*

50 *Fontenay Abbey (Côte-d'Or, France): presbytery and transepts from the south east. The unstressed crossing (bearing no tower), with the distinctive stepping down in the height of the presbytery roof to the east, appears to have been one of the hallmarks of Cistercian church design in the mid-twelfth century.*

Photograph: *author*

73

indications that the floor levels of the church rose from west to east. A step or steps must have led from the nave up into the crossing, and from the crossing up into the presbytery.[81] Of further and possibly greater significance is Ernest Collier's report, dating from when Whitland was first excavated on a large scale in the 1920s, that there 'do not seem to have ever been any large piers at the crossing, at any rate strong enough to carry a tower'.[82] This observation has been confirmed by the fresh investigations at the site. In other words, as far as can be seen, in a church reaching a total length of some 67m, the clues suggest it would have featured an unstressed crossing in the Fontenay style (fig 50). If this were the case, the nave ceiling would have been carried through uninterrupted all the way to the eastern crossing arch, and presumably both the transepts and the presbytery would then have been roofed at a marginally lower level.[83]

There is every indication that a similar arrangement existed at Margam, until, that is, the east end of the Romanesque church was entirely rebuilt in the first half of the thirteenth century (figs 25 and 41). To begin with, it is certain that the twelfth-century nave extended a further two bays beyond the east gable of the present church. It is likely, too, that the position of the original south transept is more or less fixed by the alignment of the east range of claustral buildings, despite the subsequent rebuilding of both. Beyond this, the standard two-bay projecting presbytery, again set at a lower level than the nave, might be postulated, while on the basis of the later arrangements there were very probably two eastern chapels to each of the transepts.[84]

In sum, even though definitive proof may be lacking, there are strong grounds for believing that the organization of the crossing, presbytery and transepts at both Margam and Whitland followed the common pattern seen throughout the Clairvaux family at this time, not to mention its occurrence more widely across the Cistercian order at large. By way of further support, in addition to those well-known surviving examples in France, such as Fontenay (figs 41 and 50) and Noirlac (Cher),[85] there is now good evidence to show that the general form was far from uncommon in mid-twelfth-century Britain. Compelling arguments for the existence of an unstressed crossing and a stepped east end have been made in the case of the early churches at Fountains, Rievaulx and Melrose.[86] In addition, such arrangements are known to have been favoured well into the second half of the twelfth century at several of the Cistercian houses in Ireland, notably at Baltinglass, Boyle and Jerpoint.[87]

THE WIDER ARCHITECTURAL CONTEXT

Having considered the surviving evidence for the plans and elevations of the churches at Margam and Whitland, we might well conclude that many elements certainly conform to the classic 'Bernardine' principles established in Burgundy and neighbouring Champagne during the 1130s and 1140s, just as has been observed at Clairvaux's first-generation daughter houses in England and Ireland. At the same time, there were significant differences, especially when the details are compared to the familiar Fontenay model with its use of compound piers, foliage capitals and strong bay divisions, not to mention the stone vaulting over all spaces (fig 40). Indeed, the almost total absence of interior articulation which characterizes the Margam nave, and which was almost certainly repeated at Whitland, seems to be representative of a very distinct early Cistercian architectural aesthetic.

To appreciate the broader context for this, one needs to look well beyond Burgundy, taking into account a widely dispersed group of generally early churches, both within and outside the Clairvaux affiliation. At the very simplest level we might, for example, consider the church at Bonmont in Switzerland.[88] From there, we might go on to look at churches such as Boquen (Côtes d'Armor),[89] L'Escaladieu (Hautes-Pyrénées),[90] Melleray (Loire-Atlantique)[91] and the excavated Vauclair,[92] all in France; Amelungsborn[93] and Maulbronn in Germany;[94] Alvastra in Sweden;[95] and Monasteranenagh in Ireland.[96] In some of these, including Bonmont and L'Escaladieu, there was no clerestory over the main arcades. Others featured a two-storey elevation, though in these instances the detailing could scarcely have been reduced any further. Then again, despite the fact that several of the churches were closed with high masonry vaults, at others there was a clear preference for timber, even if this may have been boarded to imitate barrel vaulting.

In the Burgundian heartlands of the order, Cistercian churches were undoubtedly indebted to local architectural traditions.[97] Prominent bay divisions and stone vaulting, like those at Fontenay, clearly belong to those traditions. For Jean Bony, the subsequent development of Romanesque Cistercian church forms across Europe was to be considered practically, and seen in terms of two main movements. In the northern regions (in which he included Boquen and Melleray and various churches in England), Bony referred to an unvaulted and non bay-divided 'first Cistercian architecture'. In contrast, he argued that in the more southerly regions, where vaulting was generally more common, a sequence

51 *Tre Fontane, Rome (Latium, Italy): interior view looking east towards the unstressed crossing and the presbytery. A daughter house of Clairvaux, Tre Fontane was founded in 1138. The church was probably raised in the 1140s. The austere style of the building, with its bare walls and lack of bay articulation, may owe something to the monastic reform culture pervading the papal city at this time.*

Photograph: *author*

could be followed through increasingly prominent bay articulation as it gradually moved from just the vault storey (as at L'Escaladieu) to encompass the whole elevation.[98] Other models have, however, been put forward to explain these variations. Bucher, for example, felt that in its 'simple austerity' the church of Bonmont should be 'counted as the best representative of early Cistercian architecture'.[99] It was a building very much reduced to an essential architectural framework, cleared of all excessive decorative elements, and with the emphasis on the importance of liturgical spaces. These same basic characteristics reappear throughout the broad grouping of churches cited above. And it is this pronounced appearance of 'stripped austerity' which has been taken by many to encapsulate the essence of the white monk approach to the architecture of the monastic church.[100]

Rievaulx is generally thought to be the prime example of this Cistercian church type in England, where it is the stumps of the piers, the lower courses of the outer nave walls and sections of the transepts that have survived. In the first reassessment of the evidence for many years, Richard Halsey argued that this was a work of about 1140, possibly replacing an earlier stone church on the site.[101] As noted above, in the most recent study of Rievaulx, Fergusson and Harrison attribute the standing fragments to a church built by Abbot Ailred, begun soon after 1147 (figs 41 and 43).[102] In assessing the context for this church, the authors are content to acknowledge a degree of debt to Burgundian precedents, as well as to contemporary work in the north of England. But in a new twist they go on to demonstrate that other elements in the design could well have been inspired by the ongoing reform culture surrounding the papal court in Rome. Ailred had visited that city in 1142, perhaps staying at the newly founded Cistercian house of Tre Fontane.[103] It is therefore of particular interest to note the close similarities between Rievaulx and this Italian church (figs 41, 43 and 51), with the common occurrence of squared piers, a two-storey elevation, an absence of vertical bay articulation, gabled roofs over the transept chapels and a stuccoed finish to the exterior.

No such direct historical link to the reform architecture of Rome can be demonstrated for the communities at Margam and Whitland, although – as pointed out by Fergusson and Harrison – the Roman element which may underlie certain aspects of Cistercian church design has generally received very little attention compared to the well-known Burgundian connection. For the moment, however, there is still much to recommend further comparison with other first-generation daughter houses of Clairvaux in many regions.

52 *Clairmont Abbey (Mayenne, France): interior view looking eastwards along the nave towards the presbytery. Founded in 1152, Clairmont was another daughter house of St Bernard's Clairvaux. The austere style of this two-storey unvaulted church, completed by c 1170, bears comparison with mid-twelfth-century Cistercian examples in Britain, notably Rievaulx and Margam.*

Photograph: *author*

For example, Clairmont (Mayenne) in north-western France remains one of the more intriguing sites for drawing many general parallels with the details observed at Margam (figs 41, 43 and 52).[104] Founded in 1152, it seems that the church at Clairmont was completed by about 1170. Admittedly, the nave arcades at the French site are slightly pointed and there are variations east to west in both the pier length and bay width, something not encountered at Margam. Other resemblances to the Welsh house are particularly close, however, including the essential pier form and the two square orders of the arches, springing from almost identical moulded impost blocks,[105] while the way the clerestory windows are positioned in blank fields of masonry directly over the apex to the arches is very similar. Finally, although the transept chapels were barrel-vaulted, the Clairmont community was also content to accept a timber ceiling over the nave.

When the mid-twelfth-century 'Bernardine' churches at Margam and Whitland are considered in the context of the existing Anglo-Norman Romanesque architecture that had taken root in south Wales, it is clear they represented something quite new. In Ireland, as Stalley reminds us, it is important to bear in mind that the pure stylistic aesthetic imported with the earliest Cistercian churches was effectively the country's first acquaintance with European Romanesque architecture.[106] The same cannot really be said about south-east Wales. Enough is known of Llandaff, for instance, or of the Benedictine priories at Chepstow and Ewenny, to show that Margam represented a rather different approach.[107] The same was almost certainly true at Whitland, despite so little being known of the first Norman cathedral at St Davids. As with many of their sister foundations across Europe, the churches at Margam and Whitland do appear to have been the product of a deliberate and carefully considered approach to architecture.[108] Through it the Cistercians were attempting to set themselves further apart from existing monasticism. Harking back to the simplicity of the antique past, and with a confident and fierce sense of individual identity, they were in effect setting out a new definition for the appropriate physical surroundings of monastic worship.

CHAPTER 6

THE TRANSITION TO REGIONAL GOTHIC FORMS

There is a long-held view, stretching back to the middle years of the nineteenth century, that the Cistercians played a fundamental role in the dissemination of Gothic architecture, to such an extent that they have been hailed 'missionaries of Gothic'. This view has always been based on wide general agreement that the white monks were indeed responsible for the transmission of a rudimentary version of Burgundian Gothic forms to many parts of Europe hitherto unfamiliar with the new style.[1] In identifying Cistercian acceptance of the Gothic vocabulary in Burgundy itself, the nave at Pontigny – with its consistent use of pointed arches and rib vaulting – is the building around which discussion has tended to focus (fig 53). For Robert Branner, the Pontigny nave was little more than 'rib-vaulted Romanesque'. Dominant solid wall surfaces and the occurrence of groins in the aisles were hardly consistent, he felt, with nascent Gothic influences.[2] Others have been rather more willing to accept Pontigny's early Gothic credentials, suggesting it points the way to a wider Cistercian acceptance of the emerging vocabulary. Like the Burgundian Cluniacs, the white monks seem to have engaged in an architectural dialogue with the powerhouse of early Gothic development in northern France. Hence elements of the new repertoire were to become standard features in Cistercian building.[3] The use of ribs, for example, was to proliferate, not just in churches but also in monastic buildings. Thus we find them employed in the west range at Clairvaux by about 1140–60.[4] They appear again in the chapter house at Fontenay, usually dated to *c* 1150–5, where they spring from elegant clustered piers in an altogether more convincing early Gothic composition (fig 54).[5] The process of further dissemination was undoubtedly multi-faceted, yet the speed by which the new style was transmitted to, say, Germany or Italy, or to northern Spain, must surely have owed much to the order's highly centralized structure.

Despite the all but inevitable chronological uncertainties, together with differences of opinion over precise definitions, the 'missionary' image first

53 *Pontigny Abbey (Yonne, France): view of nave, looking east. There are different opinions concerning the precise start date of the 'Bernardine' church at Pontigny, but it seems likely the nave was under active construction c 1140–50. The aisles feature groin vaults set between transverse arches, though it may be argued that it was always intended to cover the main vessel with rib vaults. For many, the church at Pontigny points the way towards the rapid Cistercian acceptance of the emerging Gothic style.* Photograph: *Conway Library, Courtauld Institute of Art, London*

54 Fontenay Abbey (Côte-d'Or, France): interior of chapter house, looking north east. The building is usually dated c 1150–5, with its clustered piers and rib vaults seen as a clear reflection of early Cistercian interest in the new Gothic architectural repertoire.

Photograph: *author*

given to the Cistercians almost a century-and-a-half ago has continued to find its supporters. In the early twentieth century it was underlined in the work of John Bilson,[6] and gained new currency through its adoption by Marcel Aubert.[7] In more recent years, the appropriateness of the image has won fresh support in a number of important studies. Primacy must go to the highly influential work of Dr Christopher Wilson on the north of England,[8] though Stalley's views on Ireland should also be considered,[9] as well as those of José Carlos Valle Pérez on Spain.[10] As we shall see when examining the evidence from northern Britain, the great significance of Wilson's work, in particular, has been to demonstrate that the Cistercians were occasionally responsible for the promotion – perhaps even the introduction – of a rather more evolved strain of early French Gothic architecture, its form virtually unknown in the Burgundian mother houses themselves.

EARLY GOTHIC THEMES

The beginnings of Gothic as a new and distinct style of architecture are to be traced to the region around Paris, the Île-de-France, in the years after *c* 1135.[11] As long ago as 1806, it was recognized that the key building was the abbey church of St-Denis, and most

art historians would still agree.[12] Here, in 1140–3, Abbot Suger (1122–51) was responsible for the construction of a colossal new ambulatory or shrine-choir, described by Bony as 'the first articulate manifestation of the new ideal in art'.[13] The immediate and specific impact of Suger's work might be debated, but it was surely the great prestige and royal associations of St-Denis which ensured that the Gothic style was soon taken up by other masons in the Île-de-France, and by those working throughout northern France more generally.[14] In a building boom which gathered pace from the 1150s, the region extending from the Pas-de-Calais to northern Burgundy – embracing the Paris environs, French Flanders, Picardy and Champagne – was to acquire a large number of new cathedrals and monastic churches, not least those raised by the Cistercians and by their close allies the Premonstratensian canons.[15] Interestingly, these were also the very lands regularly traversed by English and Welsh Cistercian abbots on their journeys to and from the annual General Chapter at Cîteaux.[16] It is especially unfortunate, therefore, that so little survives of the order's churches. One thinks, for example, of those at Foigny (Aisne), begun about 1150,[17] or Clairmarais (Pas-de-Calais), apparently started in 1152,[18] and particularly that at Vaucelles (Nord), since the house was reprimanded by the General Chapter in 1192 for the overly sumptuous qualities of its church.[19] Despite the many losses, it is scarcely surprising, given the known general circumstances, that north-eastern France is thought to have contributed significantly to the formation of Cistercian early Gothic architecture in Britain, most notably in the north of England.[20]

In practice, of course, the situation surrounding Gothic architectural innovations across the various British regions was somewhat more complicated than this and was neither a single event, nor a sustained process.[21] Influential Cistercian abbots will surely have played some role, but only in so far as building opportunities were open to them in any particular part of the country at just this formative point in time. New ideas would in any case have been circulating without discrimination among masons working for great church patrons of all kinds on both sides of the English Channel. The dynamics were such that when the British Cistercians first became involved, perhaps from about 1150–5 onwards, the new constructional repertoire – based on pointed arches, piers of clustered shafts, rib vaults and lighter masses of masonry – was assembled in rather different and sometimes quite novel ways. In sum, although the resulting buildings may not have looked entirely French, or for that matter exclusively Cistercian, they certainly embraced the spirit of the emerging Gothic style.[22]

The customary starting point when looking at the surviving remains is Kirkstall Abbey on the outskirts of Leeds.[23] The church here (c 1152–78) was one of the last raised by the northern Cistercians in that distinctive blend of Burgundian and Anglo-Norman Romanesque traditions.[24] At the same time, it may well have been one of the earliest examples in England designed with a crossing tower from the outset. Furthermore, the fasciculated or clustered piers at the west end of the nave, together with the two piers supporting the chapter house vault (fig 55), are clear signs that Kirkstall was not an entirely conservative building.[25] One interpretation of the piers at Kirkstall is to see them as precocious examples of the rather more developed forms soon to be introduced by masons working on Cistercian and non-Cistercian building projects throughout the region.[26] In looking for the probable source, we might remember that piers of a broadly similar character had been used in both England and France during the eleventh century, but had fallen out of use.[27] They reappeared, as several writers have pointed out, in north-eastern France a little before 1150, occurring for instance at Pogny (Aube), Berteaucourt-les-Dames (Somme), and at the Premonstratensian churches of Dommartin (Pas-de-Calais) and Selincourt (Somme).[28] At much the same time, as noted above, clustered piers were to feature in Cistercian claustral contexts in Burgundy (fig 54).[29]

55 *Kirkstall Abbey (Leeds): clustered piers in the chapter house. Dating from c 1160–5, these are among the first examples of a pier form to be much favoured in both Cistercian and non-Cistercian early Gothic building in the north of England.*

Photograph: *English Heritage, National Monuments Record, Crown Copyright*

56 *Furness Abbey (Cumbria): north transept, east elevation. Possibly dating from the late 1150s or the 1160s, the elevation was of three storeys and featured clustered pier forms to the arcade. The rebuilt 'Bernardine' church at Furness was undoubtedly influential in the formulation of northern Gothic architecture.*

Photograph: *author*

collegiate church at Ripon.[32] It is Ripon which survives best, though both were clearly innovatory structures, with the use of clustered piers just one element in new skeletal forms of design.[33] Alongside these two highly important episcopal works, four principal white monk churches are generally cited as having influenced the formulation of northern Gothic architecture, namely Furness in Cumbria (fig 56),[34] Byland and Roche in Yorkshire (fig 57) and Kirkstead in Lincolnshire.[35] In point of fact, the absence of firm dating evidence from both the episcopal and the monastic sites means it is now virtually impossible to determine the precise relative chronologies, but this should in no way devalue the early Gothic characteristics which might be observed in the Cistercian churches, nor should it obscure their place in our understanding of wider developments within the order. At the very least, the fragmentary remains demonstrate that, by the third quarter of the twelfth century, Cistercian communities in Britain were content to allow masons the freedom to experiment with new forms of detailing, and especially with the introduction of greater vertical emphasis into the overall proportions of their buildings (fig 56).

To focus on what is perhaps the most obvious demonstration of the changes brought about, it is of particular interest to note how quickly the Fontenay style was firmly abandoned as the exemplar for appropriate design in white monk churches. The crossings at Roche and Byland, for instance, were certainly designed to carry towers from the outset, and the same was very likely the case at Kirkstead.[36] No less significant was the fact that all four churches employed three-storey elevations (figs 56 and 57), the first in British Cistercian architecture to do so.[37] In terms of detailing, the clustered pier forms, often going on to feature keeled shafts, were of far greater elaboration than the simple rectangles which existed at Rievaulx, or at Margam and Whitland.[38] An increasingly systematic use was made of the pointed arch, and stone rib vaulting was to occur much more widely,[39] as in the transepts at Kirkstead, in the transept chapels and in the nave aisles at Furness, and throughout the entire church at Roche (fig 57). Taking the evidence as a whole, one might conclude that although individual ideas may have been borrowed from full-dress early Gothic almost at random, there can be no doubt that the northern Cistercians of the later twelfth century were ultimately heavily indebted to the building stock of north-eastern France, specifically Picardy and the Aisne valley.[40]

Switching our attention to the west country, and to Wales in particular, it must first be recognized that

There are, moreover, grounds for thinking that similar pier forms existed in at least one important early Gothic Cistercian building much closer to the English Channel.[30] Here, the relevance of the lost churches at Clairmarais, Foigny and Vauclair – all constructed at this formative period – becomes especially clear. Within a decade or so, clustered piers had reached the north of England, with the nave at Kirkstall merely the typological starting point.[31] Clustered piers went on to enjoy considerable and sustained popularity in Gothic churches across much of northern England and Scotland.

Outside the purely Cistercian milieu, there seems little doubt it was Archbishop Roger de Pont l'Evêque (1154–81) who played the really decisive role in the promotion of the French Gothic style in the north of England, through his choir programme at York Minster and in his subsequent rebuilding of the great

any contribution the Cistercians may have made to the introduction of Gothic architecture in the region is less well evidenced, and consequently less well understood, than is perhaps the case in the north of England.[41] Indeed, the destruction and loss of so many key white monk churches of the mid-twelfth century robs us of the opportunity to draw any really firm conclusions on the importance of their role in this regard. Of the material which does survive, or which has been carefully excavated and appraised, the common observation is that of its dependence upon the traditions of west country Romanesque building. At Buildwas, for example, the squat two-storey nave elevation with its columnar piers (under way by c 1160–5) was a simplification of regional forms going back to the eleventh century (figs 58 and 59).[42] A nave of similar character has been suggested on the basis of the excavated material at Bordesley,[43] and the longevity of the tradition is witnessed by Cleeve, in north Somerset, where a nave with cylindrical piers was constructed in the first half of the thirteenth century.[44] If, on the other hand, there were mid-twelfth-century Cistercian churches in the west of England which served to promote the

eventual regional Gothic manner then we might look, for instance, to Flaxley in the Forest of Dean in Gloucestershire (founded 1151),[45] or to Stanley in Wiltshire (where the permanent site was occupied from 1154),[46] or perhaps to Tintern's daughter at Kingswood in Gloucestershire (founded 1139, with the final site settled c 1164–70).[47] Yet these are unfortunately three of the very sites where so little survives above ground, and where excavations have barely recovered enough to enable us to make informed judgements. At the same time, even if the churches at these various sites were built along traditional lines, there is the distinct possibility that Gothic elements made an early appearance in some of the monastic buildings. At Buildwas, for example, the rib-vaulted chapter house has none of the ponderous tendencies seen in the nave (fig 60).[48]

There are, in any case, clear indications that any contribution made by the white monks in the south-west region must set alongside the role of other reformed religious orders, together of course with the inevitable local diocesan influences. Thus, as Wilson has argued (his views since endorsed by Thurlby), the abbey of Victorine canons at

57 Roche Abbey (Yorkshire): view of church from the north west. The generally accepted date for the construction of the early Gothic church at Roche is c 1170–80. The builders employed three-storey elevations, clustered piers, and made consistent use of pointed arches.

Photograph: *English Heritage, Crown Copyright*

58 Buildwas Abbey (Shropshire): the church, looking west from the presbytery. Located at no great distance from the Welsh border, Buildwas was founded as a Savigniac house in 1135, becoming Cistercian in 1147. Work on the permanent stone church may have begun about 1150, moving on to the nave, with its columnar piers and squat two-storey elevation, by the 1160s. The low tower or lantern over the crossing represents a modification to the original design. Photograph: *English Heritage, Crown Copyright*

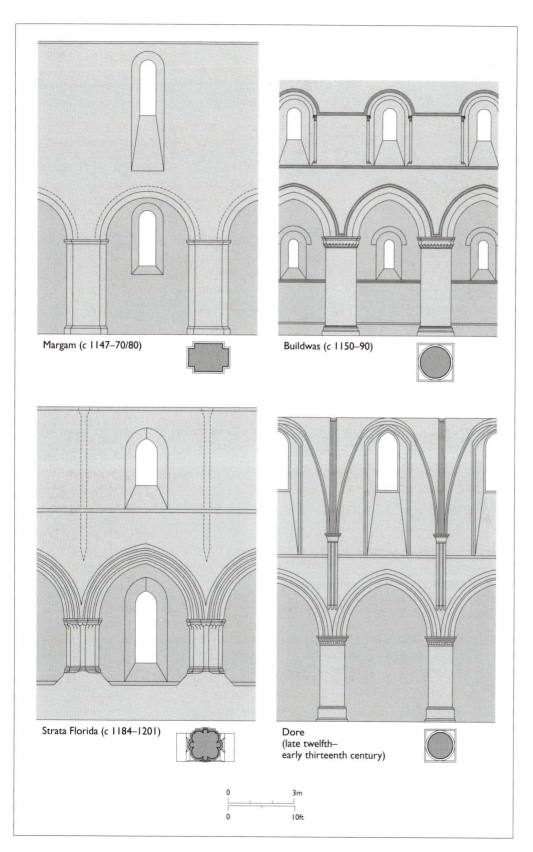

Margam (c 1147–70/80)

Buildwas (c 1150–90)

Strata Florida (c 1184–1201)

Dore
(late twelfth–
early thirteenth century)

0   3m

0   10ft

59 *Cistercian abbeys in Wales and the border, comparative nave elevations: Margam (David Robinson); Buildwas (after Potter 1847); Strata Florida (after Williams 1889a / Stuart Harrison); Dore (after Harrison and Thurlby 1997).*

Drawing: Pete Lawrence, for Cadw

60 Buildwas Abbey (Shropshire): interior of the chapter house, looking north east. The building dates from c 1170, and, unlike the church, the features reveal a growing interest in early Gothic tendencies.

Photograph: *English Heritage, Crown Copyright*

Keynsham near Bristol (begun *c* 1169) might lay claim to being one of the earliest examples of south-western Gothic, even if the conclusion is drawn on the basis of no more than the excavated courses of the church walls and a large quantity of *ex situ* fragments.[49] Related to Keynsham are the west bays in the nave of Worcester Cathedral (fig 61), a connection explained by the fact that one of the co-founders of the Victorine house was Roger of Gloucester, bishop of Worcester (1163–79). Initiated soon after 1175, it is broadly recognized that the Worcester scheme represents the first large-scale and unequivocal early Gothic design in the west of England.[50] Following this, about 1180, rebuilding began at St Andrew's in Wells, the church which was to become Wells Cathedral.[51] Wilson suggests that the purism of Wells – almost completely devoid of the inherited Romanesque ornament which is such a prominent characteristic of both Worcester and Keynsham – may owe something to Cistercian precedents in the region.[52] Then again, by way of

contrast, the ruins of the Lady Chapel at Glastonbury Abbey (*c* 1184–9) demonstrate the way 'antique' Romanesque elements could be given fresh vigour in what is otherwise a progressive early Gothic design.[53] The same might be said of St Davids Cathedral (begun *c* 1182), another building that owes a certain debt to Worcester, even though other progressive influences were involved too (*see* fig 74).[54] Finally, one last site which ought to be mentioned in connection with contemporary Cistercian developments is Llanthony Priory in Monmouthshire (*see* fig 72). The date generally given for the start of work on the east end of the Augustinian church here is *c* 1175, in which case several of its features may still have appeared quite novel in the region. This would have been true, for instance, of the triple-shaft wall responds with their nibbed or keeled central shaft and trumpet-scalloped capitals. In this instance the shafts were reflected – in perfectly conventional manner – as the transverse and diagonal ribs of the presbytery vault.[55]

61 Worcester Cathedral (Worcestershire): west bays of the nave arcade, north side. Begun soon after 1175, the rebuilt west end of Worcester Cathedral was probably the first large-scale early Gothic design scheme in the west of England. Its influence was to spread further westwards, and can be traced at several Cistercian abbeys in Wales and the March.

Photograph: *Conway Library, Courtauld Institute of Art, London*

THE EARLY GOTHIC TRANSEPTS AND THE NAVE AT DORE

The one Cistercian building on the Welsh borderland which can be accepted with confidence as an early example of French Gothic influences is Dore (fig 62).[56] Founded in 1147, it was to prove the only British abbey colonized by Cîteaux's elder daughter at Morimond.[57] There are, as we have seen, indications that the initial church may have been planned along pre-'Bernardine' lines, but it is the

ensuing campaign of work which is of interest in this early Gothic context. In a rebuilding thought to have been initiated no later than the 1170s, Dore was to adopt a formal 'Bernardine' plan. Unpicking the building sequence is no easy matter.[58] The complexity stems in part from the piecemeal replacement of an apparently earlier scheme in the area of the north transept.[59] The 'Bernardine' presbytery was itself superseded in turn by an altogether enlarged eastern arm, and consequently much of its detail was either lost or masked. Nevertheless, in so far as we can

62 Dore Abbey: general view of east end and south transept from the south west. Although founded as early as 1147, the remains of the abbey church at Dore date largely from the early Gothic rebuilding initiated in the 1170s. In turn, the 'Bernardine' presbytery was quickly superseded by a much enlarged eastern arm of ambulatory form.

Photograph: Cadw, Crown Copyright

judge, the new church featured a square-ended, aisleless presbytery of two storeys, a fully stressed crossing (with tower above) and two-storey transepts, each with a pair of eastern chapels. As the work on these areas progressed, it cannot have been too long before the builders also turned their attention to the substantial aisled nave.

The first (western) bay of the 'Bernardine' presbytery was to survive the later remodelling, with both the north and south sides featuring three-order arches through into what would have been the adjacent transept chapels (fig 25).[60] On the east side

of each arch there is a triple-shaft group rising from floor level, indicating the intention of a high vault, and also offering some confirmation that the presbytery would have projected by no less than another full bay.[61] It is clear from the ground plan that the transepts were both eventually of broadly similar design (fig 25), with the paired eastern chapels arranged in fairly typical 'Bernardine' manner. What is less obvious is the fact that the northern chapels were originally covered by separate gabled roofs, each running back to the main wall of the transept.[62] This has led to the suggestion that the inner chapel on both sides of the presbytery was deeper than its neighbour, resulting in a stepped, or *en échelon*, plan.[63] Indeed, on the north side, the arch which connects the former inner chapel with the subsequent ambulatory aisle to the east is of a simple chamfered style, very similar to that connecting the chapel with the presbytery. The most obvious conclusion is that they are contemporary, in which case the eastern arch would have opened to an extended chapel, whereas the arch through to the presbytery may well have served as the upper choir entrance.[64]

As one begins to look more closely at the form of the Dore transepts, it is soon evident that there are a number of significant differences in detail between the two. It further seems clear that the programme of construction must have begun on the northern side.[65] For example, the walls here are comparatively thin, with no sign of an external plinth or buttressing. There was also a solid wall between the two eastern chapels, a generally earlier characteristic in Cistercian churches and already abandoned by this time in several of the progressive northern buildings.[66] The Dore northern chapels were, nevertheless, covered with rib vaults springing from angled corbel capitals.[67] Much more innovative was the prominent bay articulation at the centre of the transept main vessel, created by opposing groupings of five high vault shafts.[68] It was this, together with various traits in the sculptural detail of capitals and other features, which quite definitely heralded the arrival of the early Gothic style. Over on the opposite side of the crossing (fig 63), the walls in the south transept tended to be thicker and were supported externally by broad angle buttresses. It was, for instance, the greater thickness of the chapel arcade which allowed for the inner order of the arches to be set, more conventionally, at the centre of the wall. Again, unlike the north transept, the chapels on this side were not formally separated, but were left to communicate through a large chamfered arch, and here the vaults were carried on shafts rising from the floor. The main body of the south transept would have been flooded with light from the two large lancets in the end elevation, and by a third in the west wall, all featuring continuous inner angle rolls.

Both transepts were clearly intended to support quadripartite high vaults. The transverse and diagonal ribs were to be carried on the five-shaft responds at the centre of the east and west walls, and on the cone-like terminals which can be seen in the corners. The arrangements also included wall arches, which survive to both north and south. Whether or not these high vaults were actually constructed in stone has in the past been doubted, especially given

63 Dore Abbey: the south transept, looking south east. The work here is one of the clearest unequivocal examples of white monk early Gothic architecture in Wales and the March.

Photograph: *author*

the relative thinness of the walls on the north side. Yet a strong case has recently been made for the likelihood of timber ribs, a feature now recognized with increasing frequency at early Gothic sites across Britain.[69]

At the centre of the church, the crossing piers and their uniform arches seem to indicate that the new scheme allowed for a low tower or lantern. As noted above, towers had been introduced at a number of northern Cistercian churches by this time. Similarly, in the west of England a lantern tower may have been raised over the period one church at Bordesley, while another had been built as part of a modified scheme at Buildwas, perhaps in the early 1160s (fig 58).[70] Here at Dore, on the nave side of the crossing, the responds of the western arch are stopped short of the floor, essentially to accommodate the backs of the choir stalls which ran into the first bay of the nave.

In sum, the Dore eastern arm of about 1170–80 certainly included elements of new and exotic detailing, even if we must guard against interpreting isolated traits and sculptural motifs as indicative of a coherent and full-blown early Gothic design. It was Jean Bony who first drew attention to the potential significance of the Herefordshire church in this regard.[71] He argued that the design of the transepts bore a strong resemblance to buildings of the 1160s and 1170s in eastern Normandy and the Vexin, notably the transepts of Cistercian Mortemer (Eure) and the churches at Chars (Val d'Oise) and Le Bourg-Dun (Seine-Maritime).[72] In particular, Bony felt the prominent bay articulation seen in the Dore transepts (arising from the tall vault shaft groupings) could be paralleled at the French sites he identified. Bony's ideas were subsequently developed by Dr Carolyn Malone, who considered Dore to be 'the most extensive early example of French gothic design that remains in the west of England'.[73] This hypothesis was very broadly supported by Fergusson, who also considered the parallels between Dore and Le Bourg-Dun to be particularly striking.[74] More

recently, however, the notion of any direct contact between the Dore masons and early Gothic buildings in France has been challenged. The vault shaft groups at Dore, for instance, are in effect set up against blank transept walls, whereas at Le Bourg-Dun they are part of a large compound pier.[75] If anything, it is the arrangement in the west bays of the nave at Worcester (fig 61) which is somewhat closer to that in the French church, and then only in a very general way. Brian O'Callaghan concludes that the French influences at Dore were of no more than a general nature.[76] Similarly, although Harrison and Thurlby acknowledge that certain features are typically French, such as the detail in the profile of the inner order of the south transept arches, their overall conclusion on the early Gothic work at Dore is to see it as 'a local and not very sophisticated interpretation of the style'.[77]

Work on the construction of the 'Bernardine' east end cannot have advanced all that far before it was necessary for the builders to contemplate the laying out of the nave. At the very least, the eastern bay would have been required to lend support to the crossing and perhaps a low lantern tower (fig 64). It is unfortunate, therefore, that little more than fragments of the Dore nave survive above ground, and for the most part our knowledge of its extent is

64 Dore Abbey: the ruined nave, looking east towards the crossing and transepts. Presumably begun at much the same time as the early Gothic eastern arm, the piers in the nave at Dore were of columnar form, reflecting the lingering influence of west country regional architectural traditions.

Photograph: *author*

based upon minor excavations and observations made over a period of almost forty years by Mr Roland Paul.[78] In all, Paul published no fewer than six different ground plans of the abbey, some showing only minor modification. To begin with, he thought the nave had eleven bays, later revising this to nine, and finally, after further excavation, opting for ten (fig 25).[79] If a nave of this scale was planned from the outset, it represents a scheme of very considerable ambition, one which may have taken many years to bring to complete fruition.[80]

On the basis of the surviving fragments of the eastern bay (fig 64) – which include both piers – together with Paul's excavated evidence, it is possible to make a reasonably well-informed reconstruction of the elevation (fig 59). Comparing this elevation with those of the transept arcades, its generally conservative nature is striking. The cylindrical piers echo the squat examples of perhaps the 1160s at Buildwas (fig 58), and in turn reflect west country types going back to the eleventh century. Here, though, they are comparatively slender, and in turn support arches of moulded orders showing greater sophistication than the extremely plain forms seen at Buildwas. In the upper stage of the elevation there was but a single additional storey, featuring clerestory lancet windows with steeply raking sills.[81] Along the length of the nave, as well as from side to side, it seems that the masons were allowed to introduce conscious decorative variety. The two surviving piers, for example, were of different coloured stone: red to the south, grey to the north.[82] The pier capitals may have been of several different forms, thus fitting with the rich variety of capital sculpture seen throughout the eastern arm of the church. Hence the north pier capital is of trumpet scallops, whilst that to the south is of a flat-leaf type. Another example from the south arcade is known to have had regularly spaced crockets with small flat trilobes beneath.[83] This same decorative variety also extended to the moulding profiles of the arcades.

The nave aisles were definitely vaulted, with the ribs springing in part from somewhat unusual corbels situated at the back of the piers, again featuring various designs. There is clear evidence for the form of these aisle vaults above the blocked arches into the transept arms (fig 64). Paul in fact reported finding two bosses from the north aisle vault.[84] As to the main vessel of the nave, we cannot be certain, but there may have been an intention to build high vaults from the outset.[85] In any case, there is some evidence to suggest that a scheme could have been initiated in the early thirteenth century, though it was perhaps up to a century before it could be seen through to completion. The most prominent

survival of the eventual vault is a selection of its handsome bosses (see fig 170).[86] The nature of this vault and the character of the bosses are considered further in the following chapter.

STRATA FLORIDA IN THE LATE TWELFTH CENTURY

In the heart of Wales, the first traces of these new stylistic impulses in Cistercian church design are to be found at Strata Florida, that greatly celebrated abbey established under the patronage of Rhys ap Gruffudd, prince of Deheubarth (fig 32).[87] The best-known survival at the site is the impressive west doorway to the nave (fig 65), though the entire layout of the church has been recovered through excavation and is exposed to view.[88] Construction work at Strata Florida was not only very nearly contemporary with the early Gothic introductions at Dore, it was also under way at much the same time as the rebuilding of St Davids Cathedral.[89]

Strata Florida was first established on the banks of the Fflur brook in 1164 by Robert fitz Stephen. At a site still known today as *yr hen fynachlog*, 'the old monastery', the colony which had been sent out from Whitland began to erect a stone church and associated monastic buildings.[90] Then, within a year of the foundation, the area was seized by the Lord Rhys, who happily embraced the role of defender and patron of the infant community. In his charter of endowments of 1184, Rhys proclaimed to all that he had 'begun to build the venerable monastery called Strata Florida, and after building it have loved and cherished it'.[91] This surely indicates that the plan to remove the monks to a new location had been finalized, and that the arrangements for the stone buildings on the present site were well in hand, a view broadly confirmed by the most recent reassessment of the Strata Florida evidence.[92]

Although the constructional history at Strata Florida was undeniably complex, making it difficult to clarify every last point of detail, the principal conclusion to be drawn from the surviving material is that this is a building which combined elements of ultimately Burgundian Cistercian origin with others in the distinct regional early Gothic manner. In attempting to analyse the various elements it should be noted, first of all, that the ground plan is of the classic 'Bernardine' form (figs 26 and 41): an aisleless rectangular presbytery, transepts with three chapels to each arm and a long seven-bay nave.[93] If, moreover, we piece together the various clues, a very strong case can be made for suggesting that the original east end of the building was based on the Fontenay-style model, with an unstressed crossing

65 Strata Florida Abbey: west doorway to the nave. Originally featuring six continuous roll-moulded orders without capitals or bases, this doorway stands as the most prominent survival of the early Gothic abbey church.

Photograph: *Cadw, Crown Copyright*

and a short presbytery set at a lower level (fig 66). The work of construction began with the south transept, in which we might observe that the south respond of the chapel arcade is no more than a simple pilaster. The early work also took in the crossing, where the eastern responds of the nave arcades (that is, on the west side of the western crossing piers) are again just plain stepped pilasters (fig 67), in this case taking no account of the much more elaborate profile used in the eventual nave piers themselves. In other words, these features appear to indicate plans for a church of that same austere style employed at Margam, not to mention Strata Florida's own mother house at Whitland. As building continued, however, taking in the presbytery and the north transept, stylistic changes were to be introduced. In particular, a decision was made to alter the design of the early piers. Even in their

remodelled compound form, they were still outmoded by progressive English standards of the 1160s – certainly in terms of their non-water-holding base profiles – but they nonetheless indicate a significant departure from the initial concept.

This pattern of progressive development from the south to the north transept was rendered even more pronounced by the sculptural details found in the capitals. At first rather tentative, but gradually becoming bolder and more elaborate, the work as a whole reflects the growing prominence in Wales of masons whose skills seem to have been derived from the larger west country architectural lodges. To take just one example of a capital from the south transept, we might note the trumpet-scalloped design with trilobe leaves recorded by Stephen Williams in the nineteenth century (fig 68).[94] In terms of its general form, it might easily be paralleled by examples of

66 *Strata Florida Abbey: tentative reconstruction of proposed east end of the early church. This is to suggest that the initial design of the building featured an unstressed crossing and a Fontenay-style stepping down in the presbytery roof height. The scheme was modified as work on the nave progressed.*

Drawing: *Terry Ball, for Cadw*

around 1170 from across the west of England, with analogues for its specific components also occurring quite widely. Furthermore, Stalley has drawn attention to this same fragment, suggesting it is comparable to the work of the so-called 'Baltinglass Master' (*c* 1160–80), which introduces the much wider concept of the interplay and exchange of ideas within an Irish Sea province.[95] Turning to the north transept, several examples of the capitals from the main arcade, again located by Williams in the late 1880s, are of a markedly different form (fig 68).[96] Here they were executed in deep purple Caerbwdy stone, featuring large palmette leaves with developed stems all carved to a very high standard (fig 69).[97]

67 *Strata Florida Abbey: east respond of the nave south arcade. The form of this primary feature is no more than a plain stepped pilaster, and takes no account of the more elaborate profiles subsequently used in the nave piers themselves.*

Photograph: *author*

68 *Strata Florida Abbey: illustrations of excavated stonework by Worthington G Smith, published by Stephen Williams in* The Cistercian Abbey of Strata Florida *(1889). The contrast in style between the single south transept fragment of c 1170 (bottom left) and the marginally later pieces from the north transept with their generally larger leaf forms is very clear.*

Photograph: *Society of Antiquaries of London*

In the transepts as completed, the six chapels were covered with four-part rib vaults, the profiles of the individual ribs showing considerable variety in design.[98] Within the web of each vault there was a foliate boss with an iron pin on its underside, presumably used to suspend a lamp over the altar.[99] As in the Dore north transept, solid walls were again used to separate the chapels one from another,[100] and it is known that the arcades were of slightly pointed form.[101] In terms of their full elevation, the transepts were almost certainly of two storeys, with deeply splayed clerestory windows above the arcades (fig 66). Adding somewhat more to our overall impression of the appearance of the upper level, the recent investigations of *ex situ* stonework at the site have recovered sufficient material to suggest that bay dividing shafts may have been employed between the window splays. To speculate still further, it is possible that these shafts could have risen to support a high vault.[102]

69 *Strata Florida Abbey: capital from the north transept with large palmette leaf decoration, carved in red Caerbwdy stone. The workmanship is generally more developed and of higher quality than that found on the carved stones recovered from the south transept.*

Photograph: *author*

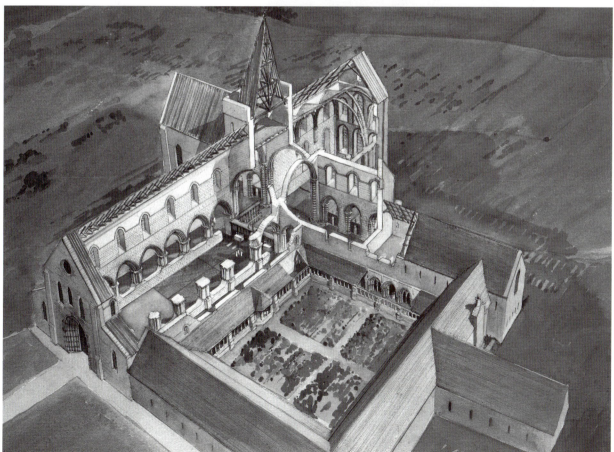

70 *Strata Florida Abbey: speculative reconstruction of the church and cloister as they may have appeared at the end of the fifteenth century. The cutaway of the church shows the variety in the form of the late twelfth-century nave piers. In line with the modified programme for the building, the crossing is regularized and the stone vault is depicted over the extended presbytery. The full extent of the east and west claustral ranges is unknown; the form of the proposed north–south refectory is entirely conjectural. Drawing: Terry Ball, for Cadw*

71 Strata Florida Abbey: west respond of the nave south arcade. As was the case with the arcade pier forms along either side of the nave, the clustered shafts of the respond stood on a low wall. Effectively, the arrangements seen here confirm the height of the screen walls and pier bases along the full length of the nave.

Photograph: *Cadw, Crown Copyright*

72 Llanthony Priory (Monmouthshire): view of nave looking north west from the western crossing arch. The Augustinian priory was founded c 1103–18, with the church rebuilt from c 1175. The nave was completed in the early thirteenth century. This view shows what survives of the integrated clerestory-cum-triforium arrangement above the north arcade. The curved mouldings seen at the far end, against the north-west tower, probably represent supports for a timber vault. Photograph: Royal Commission on the Ancient and Historical Monuments of Wales, Crown Copyright

73 Strata Florida Abbey: west doorway, detail of spiral terminals. Each of the thirteen cross-bands which run over the roll-moulded orders of the doorway terminate with similar scroll-like ornament. Photograph: author

Assigning a precise date to the initial construction of the east end is difficult, though on the basis of the stylistic evidence it is by no means unreasonable to propose that the Lord Rhys's charter of 1184 actually marked the completion of a significant phase in the building. The pilaster form of the east nave responds quite definitely indicates a pause in the construction at this point, giving time for the work in the choir area and the transepts to reach a stage at which they might be occupied by the community.[103] Thereafter, although the church was unfinished when Rhys died in 1197, a key date is recorded in the Welsh chronicle, *Brut y Tywysogyon*, just four years later. In 1201, the chronicler noted, 'the community of Strata Florida went to the new church on the eve of Whit Sunday, after it had been nobly and handsomely built'.[104] By this stage, whether the Fontenay-style arrangement at the east end had been fully completed or not, the scheme seems to have been modified. Again, a number of clues survive to suggest the course of events. In particular, the presbytery was extended eastwards, as marked by a chamfered base plinth around the exterior walls. More notably, the walls were heightened, with a most unusual three-bay stone rib vault inserted (fig 70). The form of this vault, with ribs of squared section bearing a 'domino' or pellet motif along the exposed sides, has only recently been determined.[105] From what is known of the details of the western crossing arch, we can interpret this as a secondary feature, especially since one of the corbels on which it was supported had been reused from elsewhere.[106] Taken as a whole, the evidence indicates a deliberate transition to a formal crossing (fig 70), with plans for a squat tower or belfry above.

The construction of the greater part of the nave and the west front presumably followed, with the church reaching an overall length of about 65m. As in the transepts, the nave elevation was probably of two storeys (figs 59 and 70), in which the spacing of the piers, the pointed arches and the reconstructed height all show a progression towards the early Gothic manner. The piers seem to have been of three different profiles (fig 44), all with well-developed water-holding bases, quite unlike those of the transepts.[107] In fact, one of the profiles, in which the four large corner shafts are separated by smaller examples at the cardinal directions, might be said to be the closest we find to the clustered piers of northern England.[108] Another is of the so-called *pilier cantonné* form, with a single shaft applied to the four sides of a circular core, as used in the near-contemporary nave at St Davids Cathedral.[109] Unlike the effect seen in the Dore transepts, however, there was no attempt at Strata Florida, or the cathedral, to extend the pier shafting as a means of introducing a vertical connection with the elevation above. In somewhat unconventional fashion, the Strata Florida piers were designed to stand on low continuous walls, about 1.5m high (figs 70 and 71), allowing for the backs of the lay brothers' choir stalls to be arranged along each side of the central vessel of the nave.[110] From the fragments which survive, the pier capitals appear to have been rather more restrained than those of the transepts. Williams was able to produce a composite drawing of a single capital, which we can probably accept as a fairly representative example. Devoid of neck mouldings, it is of pointed broad-leaf design, with tied palmettes at the angles.[111] Over the piers and their capitals, the builders introduced still further diversity by using three quite different profiles for the arches of the arcades.[112] Above, at clerestory level, just as in the transepts, there may well have been bay dividing shafts between the window splays (fig 59). Far more conjecturally, the possibility of some form of integrated clerestory-cum-triforium arrangement, as for example in the naves at Llanthony (fig 72) and St Davids, cannot be entirely ruled out.[113]

Finally, although there is too little evidence to support the idea that the nave or its aisles were ever vaulted in stone, there is a chance timber may have been used, with the high vaults in the nave at Llanthony and the transepts at Dore serving as good regional models.[114]

Of the upstanding fabric that survives at Strata Florida, the striking west door is by far the most memorable feature (fig 65). Originally, there were six orders of continuous roll mouldings, without capitals or bases, divided at regular intervals by thirteen cross-bands, each one terminating with a scroll-like or spiral ornament (fig 73).[115] It is a design which manages, without figure sculpture, to achieve a remarkably rich effect.[116] True, in the use of continuous multiple orders, the work may be seen in the broad framework of the west country regional school. It is tempting, in fact, to trace its pedigree back to the form of the great monumental arch at the west front of Tewkesbury Abbey.[117] However, it remains a stunning composition in its own right, clearly the product of a mason of considerable ingenuity, and all the more extraordinary for its occurrence at this comparatively remote site, located far from the recognized centres of twelfth-century architectural invention.[118] Over the west doorway, there were at least two tall lancet windows, flanked internally by a blind lancet arch at each end. The mouldings to the back of the deeply splayed jambs carried distinctive fillets. There was probably a third window at the centre of the group, though its sill stood marginally above those of its neighbours (fig 70).

To summarize, the balance of probability suggests that the church at Strata Florida was completed by 1201. In the process of construction, it is clear that those Burgundian Cistercian elements that had been part of the initial design concept had become increasingly submerged by traits more characteristic of the regional early Gothic manner. Consequently, there are distinct similarities between the features at this church and those at other buildings emanating (at least in part) from the Worcester and border workshops, including Dore Abbey and St Davids Cathedral, to name but two. One small but very distinct motif which links Strata Florida to a number of other west country sites is the fragment of hood mould bearing a chain of lily-like flowers which Williams found near the north transept doorway.[119] The very same pattern occurs at the churches of Bredon in Worcestershire, St Mary's in Shrewsbury, and St Brides-super-Ely in the Vale of Glamorgan (fig 47), as well as at St Davids, and further afield at Christ Church Cathedral in Dublin.[120]

74 *St Davids Cathedral (Pembrokeshire): view of nave, looking east. The rebuilding of the cathedral church was initiated c 1182 by Bishop Peter de Leia,
with the nave completed by c 1200. A number of clear borrowings between the masons working on the near-contemporary Cistercian church at Strata
Florida are to be observed.* Photograph: Cadw, Crown Copyright

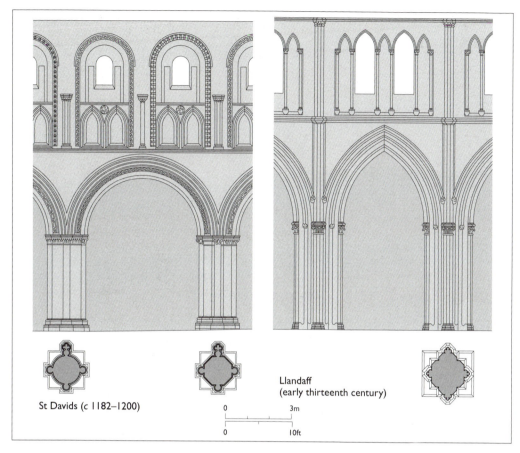

St Davids (c 1182–1200)

Llandaff
(early thirteenth century)

0   3m

0   10ft

75 *St Davids Cathedral (Pembrokeshire) and Llandaff Cathedral (Cardiff), comparative nave elevations: St Davids (after* The Builder*); Llandaff (after Freeman 1850b and James 1929).*

Drawing: *Pete Lawrence, for Cadw*

PATRONAL LINKS WITH STRATA FLORIDA

Of rather more general importance and interest are the very clear architectural affinities between Strata Florida Abbey and its episcopal neighbour, St Davids Cathedral, which was also rebuilt in that settled and prosperous era during which the Lord Rhys ruled over Deheubarth.[121] According to one version of the native Latin chronicle, the Norman building was destroyed in 1182 and the cathedral begun anew.[122] We are not told how the old church came to this fate, whether through accident or design, though the bishop at the time was definitely Peter de Leia (1176–98), a man who had been imposed on the see by Henry II, having previously served as prior of the Cluniac house at Much Wenlock in Shropshire.[123] In 1188, mass was said at the high altar by Baldwin, archbishop of Canterbury (1184–90),[124] and in 1197 the Lord Rhys was buried in the new church.[125] As to the actual fabric of the building, its complexity means that various sequential and chronological uncertainties have still not been entirely ironed out.[126]

Though the nave (figs 74 and 75) and crossing (and the eastern arm) may have been well advanced

by the close of the twelfth century, we know that a major set-back occurred when the new tower collapsed suddenly in 1220.[127] It has always been assumed that the presbytery was modified and completed after this date.[128] Among the borrowings between the masons working at St Davids and Strata Florida, we can definitely cite similarities in pier design,[129] the common use of chevron ornament (even if much more prevalent at the cathedral),[130] and the way in which bands of purple Caerbwdy stone were interspersed with a cream oolitic limestone to create a decorative effect in arches.[131] On the other hand, the design of the nave arcades at the cathedral seems consciously Romanesque in its approach, with an average bay span of some 6.7m and with outmoded half-round arches (fig 75).[132] At Strata Florida the average bay span was closer to 4.3m, and the arcade arches took on a quite definite pointed profile (fig 59). The broad comparisons are, nonetheless, of considerable interest, and it is unfortunate that on their own they do not allow us to decide in which direction the influences were moving at any one time. Just as in the north of England, the various chronological uncertainties prevent us from concluding whether the pace was

76 *Talley Abbey (Carmarthenshire): view of church, looking east. Founded for Premonstratensian canons in 1184–9, it was, like Strata Florida, initially under the patronage of Rhys ap Gruffudd. The remains of the church are severely plain when compared with the evidence from its Cistercian neighbour. The transept chapels were covered with pointed barrel vaults, probably derived from Cistercian precedents.*

Photograph: *Cadw, Crown Copyright*

being set by the Cistercians or by the cathedral authorities. Yet there can be no doubt that the affinities of style and workmanship provide what is the strongest evidence for a conscious interplay of ideas between the two buildings.[133] In closing on this point, it is well worth remembering the long-term metropolitan aspirations held by the canons at St Davids, pressed in particular at this time by Gerald of Wales. Both Peter Draper and Roger Stalley emphasize the importance of the claim in driving forward the ambitious rebuilding programme,[134] just as similar efforts to achieve increased status led to major rebuildings elsewhere. Draper argues that it was the Welsh canons within the chapter, rather than Canterbury-appointed Bishop Peter de Leia, who drove the scheme forward.[135] However, the potential role played by the Lord Rhys should not be overlooked. As Dr Huw Pryce points out, Rhys's relationship with Bishop Peter could never have been easy, but it was in the new cathedral rather than his own Cistercian house at Strata Florida that he eventually chose to be buried.[136] It is surely not improbable that this exceptional man was somehow the catalyst for the strong architectural links between the two buildings.

At this point it is worth remembering that from the late 1160s the patronage of Strata Florida's mother house at Whitland had again been in the hands of the Lord Rhys.[137] Although, as observed, the ground plan of the church and the nave pier form were of that early and distinctly austere variety, the *ex situ* material recently excavated from the site, together with various fragments dispersed locally, indicates that elements within the upper fabric must have been of a rather more developed character. In so far as can be judged, construction must have continued for quite a few decades after the community settled here in 1151. Among the fragments that have come to light are one or two vault ribs similar to those from the Strata Florida transept chapels, along with a collection of moulded arch voussoirs again comparable to examples at the daughter house. Of even greater significance is the discovery of at least one fragment of 'domino' pattern vault rib, such as existed in the remodelled presbytery at Strata Florida.[138] Also, it is worth noting that in a secondary phase of work at Whitland screen walls were introduced to the north, south and east of the crossing (fig 26). In the north wall, the excavations have located a doorway, the jambs of which were framed with dog-tooth ornament rising from developed water-holding bases, features which suggest an early thirteenth-century date. We might remember that one of the most notable abbots of the early thirteenth century was Cadwgan (1203–15), 'an extraordinarily eloquent and wise man', and it is especially interesting to note he had arrived here from Strata Florida, familiar with all of the recent developments.[139]

Before leaving the south west, mention should be made of the remains of the Lord Rhys's nearby Premonstratensian foundation at Talley (fig 76).[140] Founded in 1184–9 as a daughter house of St-Jean at Amiens (Somme), its community arrived in Wales from that very region in north-eastern France which had been at the forefront of early Gothic developments.[141] Whatever early aspirations the Talley canons may have cherished, however, their church was to be one of extreme austerity. The late twelfth-century ruins show few signs of Gothic influences, other than the consistent use of pointed arches. Although some elements may have been imported, it seems far more likely that the Burgundian-style pointed barrel vaults used in the transept chapels were transmitted locally through neighbouring Cistercian houses, perhaps Whitland or even Strata Florida.[142]

Moving on to the other late twelfth- and early thirteenth-century Welsh Cistercian churches in the Whitland family, we shall begin with those where construction works almost certainly overlapped with the building of Strata Florida, namely those at Strata Marcella, Cwmhir and probably Llantarnam. Soon afterwards came Aberconwy, Cymer and Basingwerk, with Valle Crucis perhaps the last church in what might be considered the Welsh 'Bernardine' group (figs 25, 26 and 41). Where the material survives, it shows further integration with west country architectural traits, culminating with the enormously ambitious nave scheme at Cwmhir.

STRATA MARCELLA

Strata Marcella was founded as a daughter of Whitland Abbey in 1170. It thus stood directly alongside Strata Florida in the family hierarchy (fig 19), and there is every indication that its church was begun within a few years of that at its sister house. Alas, the buildings at Strata Marcella are only really known from excavations undertaken by Stephen Williams in the late nineteenth century, and today the site is represented by little more than prominent earthworks (fig 77).[143] Very few positive traces of the presbytery and transepts were recovered in the 1890s, although it seems likely that the design of the eastern arm was of 'Bernardine' form (fig 26).[144] On the east side of the crossing there may have been several steps rising up into the presbytery, the floor of which stood around 0.41m higher.[145] However, there is simply too

77 Strata Marcella Abbey: aerial view of site from the south east. Almost nothing of the buildings survives above ground, though excavations were undertaken by Stephen Williams at the end of the nineteenth century. His clearance work on the church accounts for the distinct rectangular depression seen to the right of centre in this view. The pattern of the cloister can be distinguished to the left (south). The northern and western perimeters of the complex appear to be marked by an enclosing boundary bank and ditch.

Photograph: *Clwyd-Powys Archaeological Trust, Welshpool*

78 *Strata Marcella Abbey: illustrations of excavated stonework by Worthington G Smith, published by M C Jones and Stephen Williams (Montgomeryshire Collect, 1891). Several pieces bear close comparison with the near-contemporary late twelfth-century work at Strata Florida.*

Photograph: *Society of Antiquaries of London*

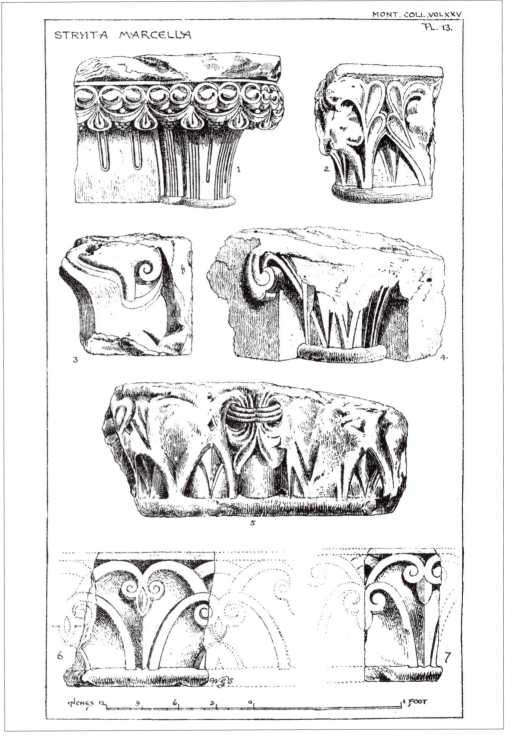

little evidence from the excavations to determine whether a formal crossing may have existed in the original layout of the building. As to the long eleven-bay nave proposed by Williams, this is almost certainly open to question. Were his plan accurate, it would have meant a church somewhere in the region of 83.2m in overall length. In more recent years, the evidence has been re-examined by Dr Christopher Arnold, who makes a strong case for the nave having been of seven bays, giving a church with a total length closer to 61m.[146] His proposal seems to fit rather better with what evidence is available on the layout of the cloister. Of further speculative interest, we should note the suggestion that the fine south doorway at the nearby parish church of Llanfair Caereinion may have come from Strata Marcella, in which case one of the more likely locations for its original position is as the processional doorway from the east cloister alley into the nave.[147]

Regardless of any firm conclusion on the overall scale of Strata Marcella, several of the architectural fragments recovered from the nineteenth-century excavations do demonstrate clear links to the masons engaged in the contemporary works at the sister house of Strata Florida.[148] Among these, we might observe the fragmentary capitals with palmettes set in tied rings, and those bearing fleshy leaves with curled tips (fig 78).[149] Other features at Strata Marcella, on the other hand, show that it was a more fashionable and up-to-date church than was the case at Strata Florida. The nave piers, for instance, were bundled-shaft compositions standing on sub-bases not at all unlike those found at its daughter house at Valle Crucis (fig 44). The excavators also recovered fragments of arch mouldings with filleted rolls, and two even more developed bases for multiple shafts, one of which was interpreted as the south jamb of the entrance into the choir.[150] Finally, although not mentioned in the original report, wall responds of triple shafts are known from the site. They presumably derive from the nave aisles, indicating stone vaulting.[151]

CWMHIR IN THE LATE TWELFTH CENTURY

Cwmhir is one of the most intriguing of all the Welsh Cistercian abbeys (figs 25 and 33). It was founded as the third daughter house of Whitland in 1176 by the lord of Maelienydd, Cadwallon ap Madog (d 1179), a cousin of Rhys ap Gruffudd. None of the fabric which survives today can be assigned to the late twelfth century.[152] Nevertheless, in his review of the available evidence from the site, Ralegh Radford suggested the Cwmhir community first constructed a stone church c 1176–95, further arguing that this was likely to have been of a simple aisleless plan, similar to the early churches at Waverley and Tintern.[153] In Radford's view, this building was replaced in the early thirteenth century by one of far more ambitious design, the construction programme beginning with the nave and moving from west to east. In the event, although the nave may have been set out in its entirety, there was much too little provision available for the work. Such was the enormously extravagant scale of the scheme that

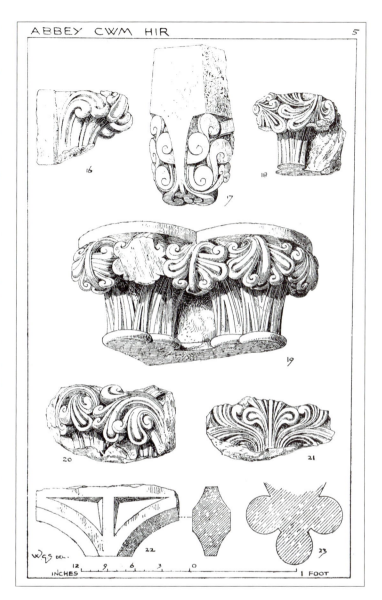

the east end of the church was never brought to completion.[154]

However, as argued earlier (see chapter 4), the balance of probability suggests it is rather unlikely that a church of aisleless form would have been built here in the last quarter of the twelfth century. Given other developments in the Whitland family of houses, it seems much more likely that the presbytery and transepts would have been laid out along 'Bernardine' lines, with plans for an aisled nave included from the outset of the programme. Indeed, as it happens, although Stephen Williams thought he had failed to find any trace of the east end during his 'trifling excavations' of the 1890s, his published drawings depict a few fragments of ex situ stonework which hint that transept chapels did indeed exist and

79 Cwmhir Abbey: illustrations of excavated stonework by Worthington G Smith, published by Stephen Williams (Trans Hon Soc Cymmrodorion, 1894–5). Most pieces date from the late twelfth and early thirteenth centuries.

Photograph: *Society of Antiquaries of London*

80 Devannor (Ty Faenor) (Powys): stone corbel, a possible fragment of the late twelfth-century church at Cwmhir. The piece was unearthed in the late 1960s, though it is very likely that it was imported to Devannor from Cwmhir during levelling works in the nineteenth century.

Photograph: *Royal Commission on the Ancient and Historical Monuments of Wales, Crown Copyright*

that they might well have been of a similar form to those at Strata Florida. Included amongst the capitals, for instance, one or two of the drawings show examples carved with foliate designs not unlike those from the south transept arcade at Strata Florida. Even more interesting is the illustration of a vault boss, very like those Williams had found in the transept chapels at the sister house, and doubtless intended to support a lamp above an altar in the same way (fig 79).[155] Moreover, a recent geophysical survey on the site of the presbytery appears to have located traces of buried features, which could well be the late twelfth-century building.[156] One further strand of evidence may shed light on the possible character of the early church at Cwmhir, namely the head corbel unearthed at nearby Devannor (Ty Faenor) in the late 1960s (fig 80).[157] Fashioned as a male head with a curly beard, deeply set almond-shaped eyes, prominent ears and a long neck, it can probably be understood as part of an eaves table. The piece is unlikely to have originated at Devannor itself, and the explanation that it was taken there from Cwmhir in the late seventeenth century, among rubble that was used to level a platform during the construction of the Fowlers' family house, seems plausible.[158]

If the early community at Cwmhir had indeed begun work on the presbytery and transepts of a 'Bernardine' abbey church in the late twelfth century, it is intriguing to speculate on whether the

building sequence was brought to an abrupt halt by the disturbed political situation in the middle March during the late 1190s. It has recently been suggested that some, if not all, of the monks were in fact forced to abandon their house in 1198, owing largely to the aggressive and expansionist policies of Roger Mortimer (d 1214).[159] He had already expelled the Welsh patrons of the abbey from Maelienydd, obliging them to take refuge in the Gwynedd of Gruffudd ap Cynan (d 1200). It is possible that the Cwmhir monks had little option but to follow, and this may have presented the opportunity for the foundation of the daughter house at Cymer.[160] Meanwhile, in 1199 Mortimer was to offer a significant charter of endowments to the mother house. It virtually amounted to a 're-foundation', perhaps giving the necessary assurances to encourage the bulk of the exiled community to return.[161] When the building programme was resumed, it was with a much needed boost of resources. The subsequent developments at Cwmhir will be considered below.

LLANTARNAM AND ABERCONWY

Next, in order to retain something of a chronological progression, and remaining with those sites where the construction of the abbey church seems to have spanned the late twelfth to early thirteenth centuries, we shall look at the two daughter houses colonized from Strata Florida, namely Llantarnam in the borders of the south-eastern March and Aberconwy in Gwynedd (figs 18 and 19).

Llantarnam Abbey was founded in 1179 by the Welsh lord of Caerleon, Hywel ab Iorwerth (d 1211).[162] A transfer of site almost certainly took place, and it is regrettable that the date cannot be determined with accuracy.[163] Nevertheless, if, as might be expected, the move occurred within a decade or two of the foundation, it is reasonable to assume that when the community arrived at the permanent site it would have determined upon a church in much the same style as the mother house. Our knowledge is unfortunately hampered by the fact that virtually all trace of the Cistercian monastic complex has been lost because of a sequence of post-suppression building.[164] The only evidence for the church yet to have been recovered comes from a series of excavations carried out in 1977–82. It is thought that this work located 'the east end of the presbytery [and] the east front of the south transept',[165] but all we currently have to go on is a sketch plan produced by the excavator, A G Mein.[166] It shows a church of somewhat unusual proportions, with a surprisingly broad presbytery projecting from formal transepts, and with a nave of perhaps six or seven bays. Until the evidence is published in full, however, it would be unwise to draw any firm conclusions.[167]

As for Strata Florida's second daughter house, Aberconwy, the details of both the design and the structural history of the church are, sad to say, again unclear. We do know that in 1186 the monks were initially settled at Rhedynog Felen (fig 18), and that they had moved from this temporary location to a site on the west bank of the River Conwy by 1192.[168] In the 1890s, it was Harold Hughes who was one of the first to realize that fragments of the monastic church survived in the fabric of the parish church of St Mary, notably at the west front with its triplet of lancet windows (fig 81).[169] Subsequently, however, there have been several different views concerning the way the remaining evidence at St Mary's should be interpreted. In the 1950s it was argued that the existing church – measuring approximately 41m in length, and with fabric thought to date to c 1190–1220 in the east and west ends – represents merely the nave of a more extensive but ultimately incomplete monastic scheme. Implicit in this view was the presumption that although the church may have been laid out along 'Bernardine' lines, it was the nave which became the focus of the early building programme.[170] However, when Lawrence Butler came to piece together the archaeological and architectural clues in the mid-1960s, he put forward a case for a church of full cruciform design. He too followed Hughes in accepting that the eastern and western limits of the Cistercian building were determined by the length of St Mary's. Consequently, his reconstructed plan of that time depicts a very small church with a nave of perhaps just four bays (figs 25 and 158), the whole a long way removed from ideal 'Bernardine' proportions.[171]

On balance, it does in fact seem more likely that St Mary's cannot represent more than the nave of the Cistercian abbey church. Indeed, given the relative importance of Aberconwy as a Welsh royal foundation, coupled with its role as the tomb-church of Prince Llywelyn ab Iorwerth, Llywelyn 'the Great' (d 1240) and other members of the Gwynedd dynasty, it would be very surprising if the community had not managed to build a church of mature 'Bernardine' plan by the mid-thirteenth century. What became of the presbytery and transepts when Edward I removed the community to Maenan in 1283–4 it is difficult to say. Nonetheless, we are left today with a structure of similar proportions not only to the nave at Strata Florida, but also to that at the head of Clairvaux's Welsh family, Whitland.[172]

81 *St Mary's Church, Conwy (Conwy): west front. Below the tower stage, much of the masonry, including the graduated lancets, may well survive from the thirteenth-century Cistercian church of Aberconwy. The doorway was probably moved here from the abbey's chapter house.*

Photograph: *Cadw, Crown Copyright*

CYMER IN THE THIRTEENTH CENTURY

Cymer is yet another of the houses in the Whitland family group where there are uncertainties about the original plan form. Effectively, as noted above, the abbey was founded in 1198–9 as a daughter house of Cwmhir. The principal early patrons were Gruffudd ap Cynan and his brother Maredudd (d 1212).[173] The surviving remains are those of a very simple, rectangular early thirteenth-century church, measuring approximately 33.5m long by 18.2m wide, with the addition of a fourteenth-century tower at the west end (figs 25 and 82).[174] There are no transepts, though aisles do run along the full length of the building, in part separated from the central vessel by solid walls rather than open arcades. We might remember that the Cymer monks were almost

*82 Cymer Abbey:
west end of nave and
western tower, from
the south west. In
origin, the nave
dates from the early
thirteenth century,
with the tower added
in the mid- to later
fourteenth century.*

Photograph: *Cadw,
Crown Copyright*

always in a pitiable state of poverty, suffering badly during the Welsh wars of Edward I, which took place in the last quarter of the thirteenth century.[175] Taking these circumstances into account, together with the very significant fact that the east wall of the building is not bonded to the lateral walls of the presbytery and its aisles, the eventual layout of the church is perhaps best interpreted as a necessarily curtailed version of a somewhat more ambitious early scheme. In other words, there is a distinct chance that the church was at first designed along 'Bernardine' lines, making greater sense of the dispositions – so far as they are known – of the chapter house and the east cloister alley (fig 25).[176]

It is not easy to determine the date of the changes, though in the revised programme of construction the builders clearly made use of earlier carved details. In its own way, the final composition of the east end would not have appeared unattractive (*see* fig 166). It was based on two tiers of graduated early Gothic lancets, with the inner splay of the principal window decorated by a continuous roll moulding.[177] Set into the wall on the south side of the presbytery there is a triple sedilia, again of early thirteenth-century date, and originally fronted by an arcade with mini clustered piers and foliated capitals.[178] The solid walls which replace open arcades for much of the eastern half of the church can be

paralleled, for example, at several Cistercian sites in the west of Ireland.[179] Butler has recently argued that the walls here at Cymer at first extended through to the west front. For him, the surviving three-bay north arcade is an insertion of the fourteenth century.[180] Compared to most of the Welsh sites (figs 59 and 83), it is a diminutive composition based on octagonal piers with moulded bases and capitals (fig 44), above which are pointed arches of two plain chamfered orders. In support of Butler's view, there is the irregular alignment of the clerestory windows with the main arcade (fig 83),[181] but at the same time the features are no guarantee of a fourteenth-century date in themselves. There are indeed several comparable examples of thirteenth-century arcades featuring similar piers and capitals, again with simple chamfered arcades.[182]

THE THIRTEENTH-CENTURY
CHURCH AT BASINGWERK

Over on the Marcher border at the north-east corner of the country, Basingwerk Abbey had been founded for a community of Savigniac monks as early as 1131–2.[183] In 1157, Henry II granted the house a charter of endowments which could well have amounted to a re-foundation. At the very least, the king's charter served to restore the flagging fortunes

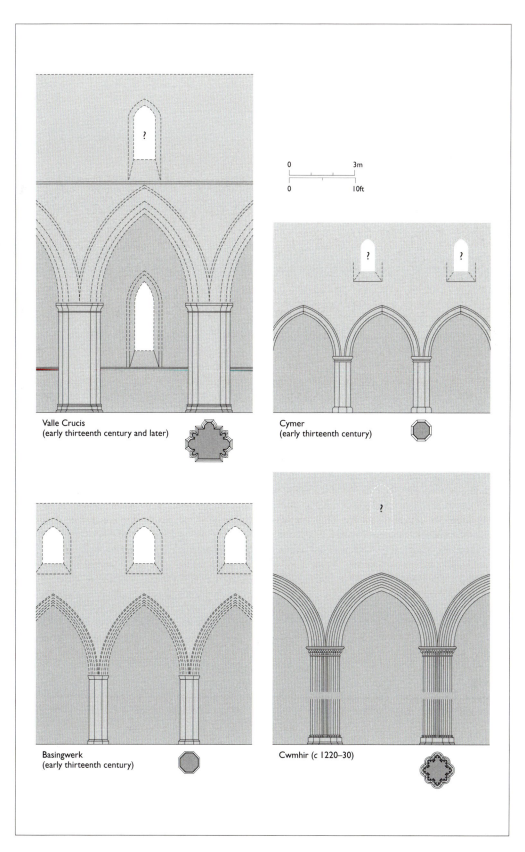

Valle Crucis
(early thirteenth century and later)

Cymer
(early thirteenth century)

Basingwerk
(early thirteenth century)

Cwmhir (c 1220–30)

0   3m

0   10ft

83 Cistercian abbeys in Wales, comparative nave elevations: Valle Crucis (Chris Jones-Jenkins/David Robinson); Cymer (David Robinson); Basingwerk (Chris Jones-Jenkins/David Robinson); Cwmhir (now at Llanidloes parish church, after Hamer 1873).

Drawing: Pete Lawrence, for Cadw

84 *Basingwerk Abbey: drawing of the south transept and east claustral range from the south west, 1800. The drawing shows several features now lost, notably the gable wall of the transept (which collapsed in 1901) and, to the left, the head of the east processional doorway.*

Photograph: *Royal Commission on the Ancient and Historical Monuments of Wales, Crown Copyright*

of the early community, the timing of the grant possibly coinciding with the removal of the house to its permanent location on the south bank of the Greenfield stream (fig 18).[184] In the same year, the General Chapter placed the Basingwerk community under the authority of Buildwas Abbey in Shropshire, another former Savigniac house.[185]

It seems reasonable to assume that a stone church was built at the permanent site in the mid-twelfth century, but all trace has been lost, and exploratory trenches dug in 1937 failed to locate any sign of the foundations.[186] As for the surviving building, although its construction may have been started a little before 1200, on stylistic grounds it probably sits more comfortably in the first years of the thirteenth century.[187] Once again the builders adopted the standard 'Bernardine' plan (figs 25 and 41), by now becoming very conservative when compared with the most ambitious Cistercian developments elsewhere. Here at Basingwerk, however, resources were limited, a point underlined by the fact that the total length of the completed church was no more than about 51.2m.

On either side of the two-bay presbytery was a pair of deep eastern chapels to each of the transepts.[188] The buttressing around the whole of the eastern arm indicates the likelihood of stone vaulting. However, at the centre of the church, the lack of full-height responds raises questions over the nature of the crossing and whether the piers would have supported a low tower or lantern.[189] The corbelled springing for the western and southern arches survives on the south-west crossing pier, indicating similar height openings towards the nave and the south transept. From drawings and photographs showing the south transept before the collapse of its end wall in 1901, we know that in the gable there were three lancets linked with a continuous hood mould (fig 84).[190] The nave was of seven bays, in which the arcades were supported for the most part on plain octagonal piers (fig 44). The eastern responds, however, were of half-round columns. Enough fabric survives over that on the south side to show that the arcades themselves were of two chamfered orders, their profile of steeply pointed early Gothic form (figs 83 and 85). At clerestory level, the windows were presumably lancets with wide splays, similar no doubt to that in the west wall of the south transept.[191] It is of interest to note that there was no door into the west front of

85 Basingwerk Abbey: remains of east processional doorway into the south aisle of the nave, early thirteenth century. Enough survives to show that the jambs of the doorway featured moulded orders fronted by detached shafts. Beyond, to the right, is the arch which linked the south aisle to the south transept, and to the left the springing of the first bay of the nave arcade. The church as a whole was probably built in the early years of the thirteenth century.

Photograph: *author*

the thirteenth-century church, something Basingwerk had in common with its Savigniac family mother house at Buildwas.[192] Yet the processional doorway linking the east cloister alley with the south aisle of the nave was particularly elaborate. Its jambs were of three richly decorated orders, featuring both attached and detached shafts (fig 85). The rounded outer head seems to have framed a trefoiled inner order (fig 84).

VALLE CRUCIS IN THE EARLY THIRTEENTH CENTURY

Perhaps the last of the Welsh Cistercian churches to be raised on the traditional Cistercian plan was that at Valle Crucis (fig 86). Located just north of the

pretty little eisteddfod town of Llangollen, the abbey was founded in 1200–1 by Madog ap Gruffudd (d 1236), ruler of northern Powys, and colonized by monks from Strata Marcella.[193] The compact version of the otherwise standard 'Bernardine' layout must have been determined within a very few years of the foundation (figs 26 and 41). Though the church had a two-bay, box-like presbytery, flanked by transepts with two chapels in each arm, and a comparatively short nave of just five bays, it is clear that, compared with the churches at Cymer or Basingwerk, it was conceived on an altogether more substantial scale, with greater height, more elaborate piers and richer sculptural detail.[194]

Hence, we find that provision was made for a fully articulated crossing tower from the outset, its

86 *Valle Crucis Abbey: general view of church, looking south east along nave. Begun in the early thirteenth century, the layout of the church followed the by-then outmoded 'Bernardine' plan. It featured a box-like two-bay presbytery, flanked by transepts with two chapels in each arm, and a comparatively short nave of five bays.* Photograph: *Cadw, Crown Copyright*

87 Valle Crucis Abbey: detail of nave pier, aisle side. The design featured broad-filleted shafts around three sides of a rectangular core. Towards the central vessel of the nave, the face was left flat, presumably to allow for the back of the lay brothers' choir stalls. The design was closely related to the piers at the mother house, Strata Marcella.

Photograph: *Cadw, Crown Copyright*

piers fashioned with moulded responds of varying profile.[195] The most common pattern is to be seen in the east and west responds of the northern crossing arch, the east respond of the southern arch and the responds leading from both of the eastern piers into the adjacent transept arcades. It features a broad central roll with a particularly wide frontal fillet, flanked by bold angle rolls with fillets. In the lower half of the presbytery, the focal point above the high altar would have been the well-proportioned composition of three graduated lancets. The central window has more elaborate jamb mouldings than its neighbours, with the shafts rising to support foliage capitals; it is also both marginally wider and taller than the two flanking windows. Clearly, there was an intention to provide a rib vault over the presbytery, as witnessed by the angled corner shafts, and by the central triple-shaft respond which articulates the bay division in the side walls (*see* fig 188).

The transept chapel arcades were of two broad orders, and it is of interest to note that the profile of the central pier is remarkably similar to that of the piers in the north aisle arcade at the nearby Augustinian abbey of Haughmond in Shropshire.[196] In both transepts, the two chapels were separated one from another by narrow screen walls, though not of

88 *Valle Crucis Abbey: east processional doorway in the south aisle of the nave, early thirteenth century.*

Photograph: *Royal Commission on the Ancient and Historical Monuments of Wales, Crown Copyright*

full height. All four chapels were vaulted, probably with heavy, plain chamfered ribs. In each chapel, there was a single lancet above the altar, those in the north transept featuring moulded rere-arches.[197] In the western half of the church, the piers of the nave arcades were of multiple shafts (fig 87), which must have been closely related in scale and form to those at the mother house at Strata Marcella (fig 44). At Valle Crucis, in particular, the piers were flattened towards the central vessel of the nave, doubtless so as to accommodate the backs of the lay brothers' choir stalls. The nave elevation was of two storeys, here apparently divided by a string course running at the base of the clerestory (fig 83). Too much of the upper level has been lost to say if there was any form of vertical bay articulation. In the nave aisles, on the other hand, the original design does seem to have included bay-dividing shafts, presumably intended to carry quadripartite vaults.[198] Finally, in the east bay of the south aisle, there survives the early thirteenth-century processional doorway from the cloister (fig 88). Both the jambs and the pointed head are of three orders of clustered shafts, and the capitals are adorned with a version of stiff-leaf foliage.

Taken as a whole, despite the very traditional plan of the church at Valle Crucis, its internal features were rather more up to date and in some ways show considerable novelty and originality.[199] In any case, the construction programme appears to have been fairly well advanced by the mid-thirteenth century, at about which time progress was severely checked by an extensive fire which seems to have swept throughout the entire monastery complex.[200] Soon afterwards, Valle Crucis was hit by a further round of misfortune in Edward I's Welsh wars of 1276–7 and 1282–3. It was in the wake of these episodes that the original design of the church was at first modified, and the whole in due course completed.[201]

THE EARLY THIRTEENTH-CENTURY NAVE AT CWMHIR

The prime candidate for the culmination of early Gothic developments in the Cistercian churches of Wales is the nave at Cwmhir.[202] At some point within the first three decades of the thirteenth century, and for reasons we may never fully appreciate, the otherwise poverty-stricken community at this remote house was able to embark upon a construction of quite astonishing overall conception (fig 25).[203] Although it is far from clear whether the monks were ever able to complete the scheme to the original design, as first laid out the Cwmhir nave was a staggering fourteen bays in length. Stretching to a total of approximately 78m, it would have been larger

than any other example known from a British Cistercian church. Everything about it seems to betray a patron with major connections and high ambition.

Today, the only substantial remains at the site are the greatly reduced outer walls of the north and south aisles, along with fragments of the west walls of the north and south transepts (fig 33). The masonry, other than a few tall isolated sections, stands little more than 0.9 to 2.4m high; when the site was first excavated in the 1820s rather more of the original detail could be seen. Two or three of the arcade piers, for example, remained standing to a height of up to 1.2m.[204] Also, in the south wall, elaborate doorways were found near the east and west ends, presumably intended to serve as the processional entrances from the east and west walks of an extended cloister. The western example was the better preserved. It featured jambs of three orders, the first with a single shaft, the second and third with triple-shaft groups, all set on water-holding bases, and with capitals apparently ornamented with 'palm leaves'.[205] We might note, however, that there is no trace of a main doorway into the west front of the nave, despite several attempts to locate it in the past.[206]

By great good fortune, the site evidence at Cwmhir itself can be augmented very significantly by the remarkable survival of five bays from one of the nave arcades, removed to the parish church at Llanidloes, probably during a phase of reconstruction there about 1540–1 (fig 89).[207] The average centre-to-centre spacing in the four eastern bays at the parish church is virtually identical to the pattern known from the abbey site, although the piers themselves have almost certainly been shortened.[208] In all, the combined evidence suggests that each of the free-standing piers in the original Cwmhir nave was designed with eight triple-shaft groups set around a square core, the axial shaft in each group bearing a prominent fillet (fig 44). But, as the remains of the south-west crossing pier at the abbey demonstrate, as well as both the responds at Llanidloes, there was a variation on this theme, in which several single shafts were set along the side faces.[209] The capital sculpture at the parish church ranges from comparatively simple trilobe leaf-and-scallop forms, carved with very little relief, through to far more luxuriant and deeply undercut foliage in rich overhanging and windblown patterns.[210] Above, the arch mouldings consist of a sequence of consistently proportioned and mostly filleted rolls towards the nave, replaced with two plain chamfered orders towards the aisles.[211] In the westernmost bay, heavy rolls take the place of the plain chamfers on the aisle side.[212]

89 Llanidloes parish church (Powys): view of north aisle arcade looking east. The material for the construction of this arcade was transferred here from the suppressed abbey of Cwmhir, c 1540–1. Given a range of historical and stylistic evidence, on balance the date of its original construction in the nave at Cwmhir is to be placed c 1218–31. All trace of the clerestory level has been lost.

Photograph: *Royal Commission on the Ancient and Historical Monuments of Wales, Crown Copyright*

Turning to consider the full thirteenth-century elevations at Cwmhir, it seems likely they were of that characteristic two-storey form which seems to have been generally preferred by the Cistercians in Wales and the west of England (figs 59 and 83).[213] Yet once again we cannot be certain whether the clerestory level featured anything by way of vertical bay articulation, nor do we have any evidence of a vault over the central vessel of the nave. In the aisles, though, each bay was to be covered with a four-part rib vault, the ribs springing from wall responds of triple shafts rising from low benches. As with the main piers, the axial shaft in each group was filleted.[214]

All the essential ingredients for the Cwmhir nave design had been assembled in the west of England during the last quarter of the twelfth century, with much undoubtedly emanating from the workshops centred on the church of St Andrew at Wells.[215] The general pattern of the pier form was firmly established in this highly influential new church by *c* 1180–90, and a modified version of the pier type also appeared in the great church at Glastonbury, begun in 1185.[216] Interestingly, as long ago as the 1890s, Stephen Williams linked the general character of the work at Cwmhir to the nave at Llandaff Cathedral (fig 90), a building with unequivocal links to Glastonbury.[217] Here, the early Gothic programme was probably pushed forward during the time of the reforming Bishop Henry of Abergavenny (1193–1218) and his successor, Bishop William of Goldcliff (1219–29).[218] The broad comparison is now well known and remains perfectly valid, especially in terms of the pier form, the triple-shaft groupings

111

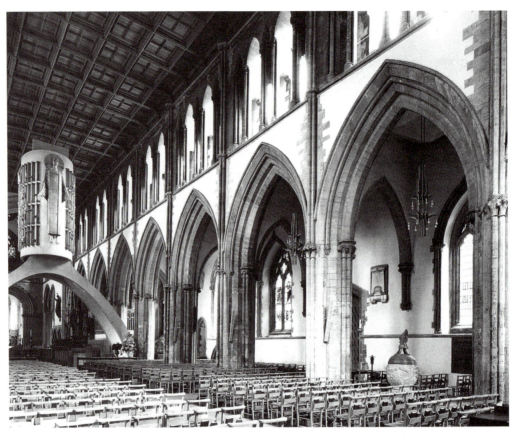

(and their purpose) and the elaborate stiff-leaf foliage. Of course, it should also be admitted that there are significant differences between the two buildings. The abaci at Llandaff, for example, are polygonal – as at Wells and Glastonbury – whereas those at Cwmhir (now at Llanidloes) were semi-circular forms. Again, the arch mouldings at the Cistercian site were clearly more ornate than those at the cathedral. But of greatest note is the fact that the Llandaff scheme involved a combination of pier and wall shafts to create full-height bay articulation (fig 90), a traditional west of England form.[219] For the Cwmhir master, pier autonomy may have been of greater importance.

In the same general 'west country' milieu, we should certainly include the extended presbytery at Dore Abbey, the Lady Chapel at Hereford Cathedral, the former presbytery at Pershore Abbey in Worcestershire (fig 91), the church of Augustinian canons at Chirbury in Shropshire, the nave arcade at St Mary's church, Haverfordwest, the nave at Llanthony Priory (a smaller and plainer cousin in the group), and (further afield) the choir and transepts at Lichfield Cathedral.[220] Nonetheless, it remains very difficult to assign a precise date to the Cwmhir programme, not least because of the complexity of

the political background in the middle March during the late twelfth and early thirteenth centuries. On the basis of the development in the capital sculpture to be seen at Llanidloes, Richard Haslam suggests the work could span the period *c* 1190 to *c* 1215.[221] Radford noted the same sequence of change and thought the building programme might have been 'spread over a generation', proposing a date in the second quarter of the thirteenth century, though allowing for 'a possible extension back for a few years'.[222]

Taken as a whole, although some elements of the design may have been a touch precocious, a case could tentatively be made to support a start date for the new nave scheme *c* 1200, coinciding with Roger Mortimer's patronage of the house and the grant of his important charter of endowments in 1199. The chief focus of Mortimer family patronage seems to have been the house of Victorine canons at Wigmore, where the church was dedicated in 1179,[223] but Roger was undoubtedly a man of vast ambition, who might well have had links to the centres of architectural innovation.[224] On balance, however, the evidence still just about weighs in favour of the view that the main building programme was at least completed in the period of stability during which Llywelyn ab

Iorwerth exercised supremacy over the region, that is, from about 1218 until his death in 1240. In fact, a great deal must have been achieved by 1231, when the chronicler Roger of Wendover referred to the 'sumptuous buildings' at Cwmhir, built at considerable expense and labour.[225] To underline this, the closest stylistic parallels for the form of the Cwmhir piers, their developed capital foliage and their arch mouldings, are to be found in buildings which can be more securely dated to around 1220–40. In particular, there are strikingly similar parallels to be drawn with the presbytery arcades at Pershore Abbey (fig 91), begun after 1223 and probably consecrated in 1239,[226] and also with features in the Lady Chapel at the Augustinian priory of St Frideswide in Oxford, where the work is thought marginally to post-date the beginnings of the Pershore scheme.[227]

In concluding, we might consider the low mass of the Cwmhir piers as rebuilt at Llanidloes (figs 83 and 89), and speculate a little further on the nature of the original upper elevation. This is the more intriguing when we consider the illusion of verticality introduced to the upper stages of the elevation at Pershore, with its well-known linkage of triforium and clerestory (fig 91).[228] As we shall see below, low piers were again a feature of the extended presbytery at Dore, where the master was able to create a similar effect of height through the use of tall lancets with deep raking sills (*see* fig 97). Given that the Cwmhir nave was designed in much the same milieu, it seems reasonable to assume that the master's total concept included a desire for much greater verticality than is apparent today.

91 Pershore Abbey (Worcestershire): former presbytery arcade, c 1230–9, looking south west. The rebuilding of the eastern arm of the Benedictine abbey church may well have been inaugurated about 1220. It has been argued that the four principal bays of the arcades, running west through to the crossing, date from a second phase of work, consecrated in 1239. The features of the arcades and their piers are strikingly similar to what we know of those at Cwmhir Abbey.

Photograph: *author*

CHAPTER 7

THE WELSH CISTERCIAN CHURCH TRANSFORMED

Despite the examples of the late and persistent use of the 'Bernardine' plan in Wales, we have already observed that by the close of the twelfth century it was no longer typical of the more progressive architectural developments within the Cistercian order. Indeed, all the principal French mother houses had abandoned the form by this time. In the main, the change was brought about through the construction of a much enlarged eastern arm, based on a fully developed ambulatory with encircling chapels, and following one of two principal models.[1]

The first community to transform its church in this way was probably that at Clairvaux. On the basis of what is an equivocal written source, the rebuilding has most often been dated to the years immediately after the death of St Bernard in 1153, with the

programme almost certainly begun in anticipation of his canonization and prompted by a desire to create a more fitting setting for the eventual shrine.[2] For early scholars, including Aubert, Esser and Hahn, the new presbytery at Clairvaux could only be interpreted as a relaxation of early Cistercian principles of modesty and simplicity, a landmark departure from the orthodoxy of the 'Bernardine' church. Of course, this could not have happened before the death of the saint himself.[3] In more recent years, however, the view that the work could well have been initiated marginally earlier than 1153 has won greater credence.[4] In particular, Gajewski, building on her arguments that it was the entire abbey church which was reconstructed in the mid-twelfth century, claims Bernard himself could have

92 Pontigny Abbey (Yonne, France): the rebuilt presbytery, perhaps c 1180–1200. In its original form, the church featured a 'Bernardine' eastern arm. This was remodelled in the late twelfth century, with the plan of the new apse and ambulatory based on Clairvaux III. In comparison to Clairvaux, however, the presbytery as a whole was lengthened, allowing for eleven radiating chapels around the ambulatory instead of nine.

Photograph: *author*

93 *Byland Abbey, North Yorkshire: aerial view of church and cloister, from the west. Begun c 1170, the church at Byland undoubtedly stood at the forefront of early Gothic architectural developments in the north of England. The presbytery was of rectangular ambulatory form, and the elevations were of three storeys throughout.*

Photograph:
Copyright Skyscan, for English Heritage

played the pivotal role. She suggests that one of the key motives, apart from the need to accommodate an ever-growing body of monks, may have been to provide an appropriate mausoleum for Bernard's great friend Malachy, archbishop of Armagh, who is known to have been buried in the church at Clairvaux on 2 November 1148.[5] To test the legitimacy of these interesting new ideas, of course, it is clear that we require a fuller archaeological and architectural study of the fabric history at Clairvaux. Be that as it may, it is generally agreed that the church still widely known as Clairvaux III (figs 16 and 34) was eventually consecrated in 1174 – the very year of Bernard's canonization. As completed, the presbytery terminated in an apse and ambulatory, with a circuit of nine radiating chapels housed within an unbroken, but apparently faceted, outer wall.[6] Such was the

atmosphere of celebrity and belief surrounding the new building, it is hardly surprising that others were soon modelled upon it. Near the end of the century, a similar but somewhat larger apsidal scheme was put in hand at Pontigny. Opinions vary over the date of this surviving work (fig 92), though construction must surely have centred on the years *c* 1180–1200.[7] Meanwhile, a comparable east end may have been under construction at Savigny from *c* 1173,[8] and derivatives were beginning to appear further afield.[9]

Although the community at Cîteaux would have been well aware of the rebuilding programme at Clairvaux, there is no evidence to suggest a rapid move to follow suit. Indeed, it seems, based on documentary evidence, that the new presbytery at the order's Burgundian mother house may not have been under construction until as late as *c* 1180–90,

*94 Cistercian abbeys
in Britain, comparative
ground plans of
churches with aisled
rectangular eastern
arms: Byland (North
Yorkshire), Jervaulx
(North Yorkshire),
Dore, Rievaulx (North
Yorkshire), Waverley
(Surrey), Netley
(Hampshire), Margam,
Tintern, Neath.*

Drawing: *Pete
Lawrence, for Cadw*

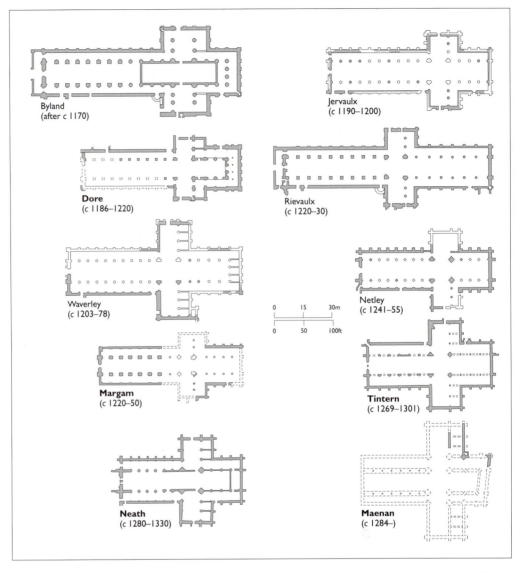

Byland
(after c 1170)

Jervaulx
(c 1190–1200)

Dore
(c 1186–1220)

Rievaulx
(c 1220–30)

Waverley
(c 1203–78)

Netley
(c 1241–55)

Margam
(c 1220–50)

Tintern
(c 1269–1301)

Neath
(c 1280–1330)

Maenan
(c 1284–)

with a consecration recorded in October 1193. In contrast to the radiating design adopted at Clairvaux, the extended presbytery at Cîteaux was to be of the so-called rectangular ambulatory form, resulting in the church widely known as Cîteaux III (figs 16 and 34).[10] This same rectangular pattern may already have existed in prototype at another of the important mother houses of the order, Morimond, although the evidence from this site is especially complex and the chronology remains confused.[11]

There is no single explanation to be offered for what were undoubtedly major transformations of the 'Bernardine' churches at these senior French mother houses. On the one hand, there may well have been an element of architectural rivalry, as well as a desire to provide additional altar space. On the other hand, there are definite grounds for suggesting

that the extended eastern arms were intended to serve as appropriate mausoleums for a growing cult of abbot-saints.[12] Regardless of any one interpretation, the new buildings certainly offered fresh models for appropriate design in Cistercian churches, models that were quickly disseminated through the entire order.

ENGLISH DEVELOPMENTS OF THE LATE TWELFTH AND THIRTEENTH CENTURIES

In England, the first signs of the new departures to come appeared at Byland, one of the buildings which stood at the very forefront of northern Gothic architecture and which dates, it has been argued, from as early as the 1170s.[13] Aisled throughout, with elevations of three storeys and a nave of eleven bays,

it is generally considered to be the most ambitious twelfth-century Cistercian church in Europe (figs 93 and 94).[14] It was also the first example of the order in Britain to incorporate a rectangular ambulatory. In much the same fashion as Cîteaux, the presbytery aisles were effectively continued around the end of the building, with the further provision of space for five additional chapels in a lower straight-ended eastern extension.[15] The same basic plan was soon interpreted on a rather smaller scale at Dore, a building discussed in more detail below. In addition to these two prominent surviving examples, evidence from archaeological excavations suggests similar arrangements existed on several other British Cistercian sites. The clearest indications come from Waverley, where a new six-bay presbytery was built between 1203 and 1214, presumably derived directly from the Cîteaux model (fig 94).[16] There are signs, too, that the form may have appeared at Meaux in Yorkshire, Newbattle in Scotland, Stratford Langthorne in Essex and Hailes I in Gloucestershire.[17]

The more popular British alternative to the fully aisled rectangular presbytery made its first Cistercian appearance at Jervaulx, c 1190–1200 (fig 94). Unlike the pattern which existed at Cîteaux, or for that matter at neighbouring Byland, the four-bay eastern arm at this Yorkshire site terminated in a flat, full-height wall, without a projecting aisle or chapels, giving the whole composition a rather box-like profile.[18] Often described as a 'cliff' east end, this same design was taken up very widely across the entire country during the thirteenth century, as much outside the Cistercian order as within it, although significantly it is very rarely found on the Continent.[19] After Jervaulx, the most striking white monk example in England is that of Rievaulx, where a seven-bay presbytery of cathedral-like splendour was built about 1220–30 (figs 94 and 95).[20] In the south of the country, a broadly comparable surviving layout can be seen at Netley (c 1241–55) in Hampshire (fig 94).[21] Others are known merely from their foundations, or from excavated evidence, as at Stanley in Wiltshire, Pipewell in Northamptonshire, and Sawley and Whalley in Lancashire.[22]

In addition to the surviving architectural and archaeological evidence, further proof of the widespread Cistercian use of the rectangular ambulatory plan in the early decades of the thirteenth century comes from the well-known portfolio of drawings by the Picard draughtsman Villard de Honnecourt. In a plan of about 1230, Villard depicted a building with a four-bay presbytery of precisely this layout, bearing the

95 Rievaulx Abbey (North Yorkshire): remodelled presbytery and south transept, c 1220–30, viewed from liturgical south west. As completed, the new rectangular presbytery at Rievaulx featured a flat, cliff-like wall at the east end, a form found very rarely outside Britain. It was, however, taken up at several Cistercian sites in Wales, notably at Tintern and Neath.

Photograph: *English Heritage, Crown Copyright*

caption: 'This is a church made of squares for the Cistercian order'.[23] The case for the overall prominence of the form, then, is hardly in doubt. However, it should not be forgotten that the hemicycle design, first seen at Clairvaux III, had also spread much further afield by this time, even if not as extensively. A variation on the theme – in which the chapels of the chevet projected outwards in 'bubble-like' fashion – had also emerged.[24] In England, although apsidal presbyteries were never greatly taken up by the Cistercians, the basic model was introduced at King John's abbey of Beaulieu in Hampshire after 1204, very probably via Bonport (Eure) in Normandy.[25] Later on, a grander scheme with projecting chapels appeared as Hailes II in Gloucestershire (begun *c* 1270) and another was built at Vale Royal in Cheshire (begun *c* 1277), both of which were again royal foundations.[26]

The Cistercian abbeys of Wales and the March shared in these new Cistercian architectural developments in no small measure. Indeed, it seems the community at Dore chose to abandon its 'Bernardine' presbytery as early as the 1180s, with the construction of a much-expanded eastern arm continuing into the first quarter of the thirteenth century. Then, within a few decades, the monks at Margam had determined upon the complete rebuilding of the presbytery, choir and transepts of their mid-twelfth-century Romanesque church. In the second half of the thirteenth century, totally new abbey churches were begun at both Tintern and Neath. Finally, in the 1280s, it was Edward I's decision to remove the abbey at Aberconwy that led to the construction of a further new church on a fresh site at Maenan. At Dore, Margam, Tintern and Neath the new presbyteries were certainly of the rectangular ambulatory form and, on the basis of excavation, the same has been suggested for Maenan (figs 25, 26 and 94).

THE NEW PRESBYTERY AT DORE

About the year 1186, possibly just a little earlier, Adam I became abbot of Dore.[27] Gerald of Wales paints a picture of a grasping and avaricious man, one whose ambition would stop at little if it served to improve the prosperity of his house.[28] Nevertheless, there are also grounds for seeing Adam as something of an intellectual,[29] and he was without doubt a builder of considerable note. Indeed, soon after taking up the abbatial office at Dore, Adam embarked on a grandiose and highly up-to-date remodelling of his predecessor's barely completed 'Bernardine' church.[30]

In essence, the overall plan of the late twelfth-century Dore scheme was an interpretation of that found in the new church at Byland, and likewise featured a rectangular ambulatory encircling the now fully arcaded presbytery (fig 96). Perhaps the most significant difference from the Byland arrangement was that the end ambulatory aisle was not accommodated within the full-height elevation of the building. Instead, it was positioned beyond the gable wall and therefore contained, along with the eastern chapels, in the lower two-bay extension.[31] There is no evidence for any direct connection between the Herefordshire abbey and Byland, and in any case it seems far more likely that the sources for Abbot Adam's new work were Continental. Fergusson was prepared to consider that the near-contemporary Cîteaux III scheme might have provided the model (fig 34), arguing that the architecture at the Burgundian abbey would have been familiar from Adam's repeated visits to the General Chapter.[32] Equally plausible, however, if not more so, is the possibility that the really decisive influence came from Dore's own mother house. As noted above, a presbytery of rectangular ambulatory plan could well have been introduced at Morimond in the second half of the twelfth century, perhaps even before that at Cîteaux.[33] After all, the Champenois abbey of Morimond was extremely influential, with a total filiation in excess of 200 houses, chiefly located in central and eastern Europe,[34] and it is of particular interest to note the proliferation of straight-ended, aisled presbyteries among, for instance, the houses of its German family.[35] There again, a comparison of the Dore presbytery plan with that excavated at Morimond in the early 1950s reveals several notable differences.

Turning to the details, Abbot Adam's extended eastern arm at Dore was based on an outwards expansion of the 'Bernardine' building. In part, therefore, the design of the new programme was constrained by the need to incorporate much of the fabric of the existing presbytery and transepts. In the process, the inner transept chapels were to be sacrificed, now becoming the first bays in the rib-vaulted aisles flanking an enriched three-bay central vessel (figs 94 and 96). Within the completed presbytery itself, the first (west) bay was retained from the older scheme. On the north side, this is represented by a plain arch of three continuous chamfered orders.[36] To the east, the main arcades of the two added bays were also of three orders, though here they are all moulded (fig 44): the two outer orders in each case are continuous, whereas the inner order is carried on demi-shafts with foliate capitals and rounded abaci. At the far end, the composition terminates just behind the high altar in a grouping of

96 *Dore Abbey: presbytery and ambulatory aisle, from the south east. The rebuilding of the eastern arm at Dore, a scheme which was to include a fully arcaded presbytery and rectangular ambulatory aisle, was begun by Abbot Adam I soon after 1186. A similar, if larger, eastern arm had been raised at Byland up to a decade earlier, yet it is likely that the really decisive influence behind the Dore scheme came from its mother house at Morimond in eastern France.*

Photograph: *author*

three comparatively narrow but richly moulded arches (fig 97). The heads rise to the same point as those in the lateral arcades, but they spring from a higher level. The bundled central piers feature triple-shaft groups to the cardinal angles, an earlier occurrence of that distinctive west country motif seen at Cwmhir. Here at Dore the groupings carry the inner and outer orders of the arches, whereas the middle order springs from a single shaft. The responds also feature a triple-shaft group to carry the inner arch order.

Throughout the extended presbytery, the lower storey has a rather conservative, almost ponderous feel, whereas in the upper level a lighter, more sophisticated quality was introduced, with a greater emphasis on verticality. Whether this represents a change of workshop is a moot point.[37] In any case, above the continuous string course surrounding the two eastern bays, the clerestory windows all have steeply raking sills and the same copious use of continuous mouldings around the jambs. When it comes to the graduated lancets at the east end, the arrangement of attached and detached shafts is slightly more elaborate, the two outer orders featuring stiff-leaf capitals (fig 97). It seems that the entire central vessel scheme would have been completed with a high vault, though on balance this is most likely to have been of timber rather than stone.[38]

The rectangular ambulatory aisle was lit with a single lancet to each bay. Externally, a horizontal billet string course is carried over each of these

97 *Dore Abbey: interior view towards east end of presbytery. The narrow bays of the arcade are carried on squat bundled piers with triple shaft groups to the cardinal angles. Some authors have argued that the clerestory level has a more sophisticated quality, with a greater emphasis on verticality, possibly representing a change of master mason. In any case, the whole scheme may have been completed as early as 1208, and certainly no later than 1220.*

Photograph: *author*

lancets as a decorative gable-like ornament (fig 96). Today, the gables appear partially truncated, and it has been argued in the past that in the original arrangements they may have formed a series of transverse gable roofs running around the three sides of the building.[39] Fresh studies, however, have shown that this could not have been the case and that the billet moulding was indeed no more than decorative.[40] For reasons not entirely apparent, the floor level of the ambulatory aisle is set lower than

that in the main vessel of the presbytery. As we have seen, the ambulatory was continued around the straight end of the building, to be combined at that point with the eastern chapels in an especially attractive two-bay 'hall'-like treatment (fig 98). Of particular interest, the overall form of this combined eastern aisle at Dore is very close to that found in the church at Morimond's daughter house of Lilienfeld in Austria, apparently begun *c* 1202–6.[41] The similarity is so strong that it would be surprising if it

98 *Dore Abbey: east ambulatory aisle, looking south. The aisle was combined at this point with a row of five eastern chapels in an attractive 'hall'-like arrangement. The four-part vaults are carried on delicate bundled piers of four coursed and four detached shafts.*

Photograph: *author*

had occurred by mere chance. At the Herefordshire abbey, the four-part rib vaults in this part of the ambulatory are carried on delicate bundled piers of four coursed and four detached shafts, with the latter set on the cardinal points. The capitals all feature stiff-leaf foliage. Screen walls ran between the piers and the outer wall of the aisle to create five individual chapels. It seems likely that further chapels were also accommodated in the north and south aisles,[42] again echoing what is known of the liturgical arrangements at other Cistercian houses of rectangular ambulatory plan.

Stylistically, art historians have been inclined to date the completion of the Dore eastern arm to around 1210–20.[43] However, Joe Hillaby reminds us that this is to underestimate the widespread impact of the Interdict of 1208–13. He argues very forcibly

that any such programme of construction is likely to have been broken over these years, and he suggests that Abbot Adam's contributions at Dore are more likely to have been completed by 1208.[44]

THE THIRTEENTH-CENTURY EASTERN ARM AT MARGAM

There is much evidence to attest to the economic well-being of Margam Abbey in the first quarter of the thirteenth century, as well as the influential position occupied by its community.[45] Indeed, everything points to its strength and influence being reflected in at least two major programmes of rebuilding during the time of Abbot Gilbert (1203–13) and his immediate successors.[46] It is intriguing to note that Gilbert was installed at

Margam by 'foreign visitors', presumably monks sent from the mother house at Clairvaux.[47] He was doubtless appointed with a view to reform and improvement, and it is the more interesting to reflect that Gilbert arrived in south Wales from Kirkstead Abbey in Lincolnshire, where he would have been familiar with the important early Gothic church believed to have stood at that site.[48] In due course, Abbot Gilbert enjoyed especially cordial relations with King John, and there can be little question of his well-intended ambitions for the economic and architectural aggrandisement of Margam. He was, nevertheless, to make an enemy of Gerald of Wales in the process, in much the same way as Adam of Dore.[49] Gilbert was followed by two of Margam's most highly regarded abbots, John of Goldcliff (1213–36/7) and John de la Warre (1237–50). Both men must have pushed forward the ongoing building programme at the house.[50]

The outstanding survival of the early thirteenth-century Gothic work at Margam is the gorgeous polygonal chapter house, discussed in more detail in Chapter 10. But the qualities and significance of the new east end should not be underestimated, despite the rather poorer preservation of its fabric (fig 94). As we shall see, on the basis of the stylistic evidence its construction cannot have followed too long after

the completion of the chapter house and associated works. In the scheme as devised, the posited Fontenay-style presbytery, transepts and choir all had to be sacrificed to make way for a much larger and now more fashionable structure which would suit the changing liturgical needs of the community. The master mason was undoubtedly constrained by the twelfth-century arrangements, most noticeably in the area of the remodelled south transept, which itself had to align with the existing east range of claustral buildings. In the event, there was a rather clumsy relationship between the corner of the southern chapel in the south transept and the northern side of the chapter house (fig 25).

In impressive fashion, the new presbytery was laid out in a total of five bays. Given that no trace of the north and south arcade piers survives above ground, the bay width is now determined by the external buttresses. The aisles were definitely covered with quadripartite rib vaults, springing from *en délit* wall shafts. The occasional fragment of rib which can be found scattered around the site indicates that the main vessel of the presbytery was also vaulted in stone. Indeed, what is thought to have been a high vault boss bearing the arms of de Clare was discovered among the ruins in 1836.[51] In the south aisle, a single two-light window survives at the west

99 Margam Abbey: windows in south transept chapels (left) and presbytery south aisle (right). Although these two-light plate tracery openings show signs of Victorian restoration, they are similar to Cistercian examples known from Netley (Hampshire) (after 1241) and Hailes (Glos) (after 1246). They may well date from the 1230s or early 1240s.

Photograph: *author*

end (fig 99), and two bays to the east of this there is a doorway with detached and belted shafts, moulded capitals and a moulded head. As part of the overall process of reconstruction, the crossing was regularized with large central piers introduced to support a tower. In turn, this would have demanded a design solution that married the comparatively low elevation of the nave on one side of the crossing with that of the new presbytery scheme on the other. In a similar sequence of events at Fountains, for example, the early thirteenth-century choir was kept to two storeys, thereby maintaining at least a measure of continuity on either side of the crossing.[52] At Rievaulx, on the other hand, all such idea was entirely rejected. There, the eastern arm of the 1220s was higher than the nave, with the remodelled transepts and new presbytery designed with consciously grand elevations of three storeys.[53] In looking at the Margam evidence, a single pier base which can be seen on the north side of the nave, situated at the point where the first pier west of the crossing might be expected, must be taken into account. The core is of lozenge plan, surrounded by evidence of eight shafts sitting on non-water-holding bases. It is difficult to know whether this should be considered at face value, but it does beg questions of the revised arrangements at this end of the nave.[54] As for the remodelled transepts, for the reasons outlined above they were of necessity rather shallow, with two eastern chapels to each arm.[55] The south transept is the best-preserved area, even if the chapel windows do show signs of late Victorian restoration (fig 99).[56] The chapel arcade featured piers with rather unusual two-tier bases (fig 100), of similar general plan to that single example found in the nave.[57] When the work as a whole was complete, the overall length of the abbey church had been increased to around 80m.

As for the liturgical arrangements within the enlarged Margam presbytery, it seems likely there were at least four chapels against the end wall. However, neither of the two broad types of rectangular ambulatory plan within the five-bay layout can be easily discounted. On the one hand, the arcades may have continued through at one level to meet a 'cliff' east end, in which case the chapels would have been accommodated within the easternmost bay, as at Jervaulx and Rievaulx.[58] Alternatively, there is a chance the chapels were placed in a projecting aisle, like those at Byland and Waverley, a possibility further underlined by the close proximity of the similar scheme at Dore.[59] The doorway in the second bay of the south aisle, positioned not unlike those at Byland, Jervaulx and Rievaulx, must have led to and from the ambulatory. It would not be unreasonable, therefore, to suggest

that the high altar was positioned in the third bay from the east, presumably beyond some form of screen or parclose.

The remains of the south-east crossing pier may be of assistance in ascribing a closer date to this Margam work (fig 101). Towards the eastern and southern arches of the crossing itself, this is severely plain, but the responds towards both the presbytery and transept arcades are far richer. Here, around polygonal cores, the way in which coursed shafts rising directly from the plinth were used to frame *en délit* shafts set on water-holding bases is particularly noticeable. The basic design concept had existed in west country early Gothic architecture from at least the late 1180s and is found, for example, in the crossing piers at Glastonbury Abbey. The motif seems to have become far more common in the first quarter of the thirteenth century, occurring for instance in the richly moulded rere-arches of the three large lancets in the west front of Llandaff Cathedral and in the eastern arm of Worcester Cathedral (begun 1224).[60] But an even closer analogue for the style of work found in the Margam

100 Margam Abbey: base of south transept arcade pier. The rather unusual two-tier bases to the individual coursed shafts have a polygonal middle stage. The arcade itself must have formed part of the entire eastern arm, almost certainly completed sometime in the second quarter of the thirteenth century.

Photograph: *author*

101 *Margam Abbey: base of south-east crossing pier. As part of the early thirteenth-century rebuilding of the eastern arm at Margam, the crossing was regularized in readiness to support a tower above. Towards the eastern and southern arches of the crossing the south-east pier was left severely plain. However, towards both the presbytery and the south transept arcade (in the foreground of this view) the responds were much richer. The combination of coursed, attached shafts and en délit shafts set on water-holding bases suggests a date of around 1220–30.*

Photograph: author

crossing pier might be the Lady Chapel responds at Pershore Abbey (*c* 1220–3), even though these feature triple-shaft groups not seen at the south Wales site.[61] Unfortunately, almost nothing is known of the free-standing piers in the rebuilt Margam presbytery. The polygonal core to the surviving west respond of the south arcade (fig 101) might suggest some links with the nave at Llandaff (fig 90), but this is very tentative. The single shafts surrounding the core in the Margam respond are quite unlike anything seen at the cathedral. In sum, if a date of around 1220–30 for the south-east crossing pier is accepted, this would certainly not be far out of step with the characteristics of the south presbytery doorway.[62]

At first glance, the same might be said of the window in the south presbytery aisle and its companions in the south transept chapels (fig 99). These are of two-light plate tracery form with multiple mouldings to the external jambs, a quatrefoil piercing the spandrel and rere-arches featuring shafts with plain capitals and steeply pitched heads. They might be compared very broadly to both secular and ecclesiastical work of the 1220s and 1230s in west and south-west England.[63] Nevertheless, the better (and Cistercian) parallels are to be found in the presbytery and chapter house at Netley (begun *c* 1241) and probably

in the nave aisles at Hailes (after 1246).[64]

Thus, analysis of the early thirteenth-century presbytery at Margam reveals certain paradoxes. In the crossing piers, for example, the prominent surface articulation was deliberately rich in its conception and thoroughly in keeping with the best of contemporary west country early Gothic design. Far removed from the austerity of the nave, it echoes an era of new-found abbatial confidence, one which presumably began with the construction of the highly elaborate chapter house a decade or so earlier. Even in its fragmentary state, however, there are hints that the purity of the work – with its clean lines, good proportions and greater illumination – continued to evoke the earlier Cistercian aesthetic ideal while at the same time giving a new spiritual emphasis to that part of the building which remained at the heart of the monastic life.

THE NEW CHURCH AT TINTERN

Compared with the rebuilt eastern arms at Dore and Margam, the existing churches at Tintern and Neath must have appeared positively outmoded. Hitherto, despite any tensions that may have arisen over the need for additional liturgical space, the communities at both houses had apparently resisted all temptation to modernize or to expand the Romanesque

102 Tintern Abbey: view of church, from the north east. Begun c 1269 and completed in the early part of the fourteenth century, it stands as one of the best-known and best-preserved Cistercian churches in the British Isles.

Photograph: *Cadw, Crown Copyright*

structures of their pioneering years. The pre-'Bernardine' aisleless churches of the 1130s (or thereabouts) had remained essentially unaltered – and this despite the fact that the principal monastic buildings at the two abbeys had been greatly expanded in the first half of the thirteenth century. Moreover, beyond the Cistercian order, church building had been progressing across the whole of the southern Welsh March. Apart from ongoing works at St Davids and Llandaff,[65] the mendicants had begun to arrive in some of the larger towns. Construction of the Franciscan churches at Cardiff and Carmarthen, and those of the Dominicans at Brecon and Haverfordwest, had presumably helped maintain the pool of skilled masons operating across the region.[66] In the event, it was not until the later decades of the thirteenth century that Tintern and Neath were finally ready to match, and to exceed, the earlier ambitions of their various ecclesiastical neighbours. Each community was to commission a brand new church, designed in the emerging Decorated style (fig 94).[67] At Tintern the work was put in hand about 1269. The start of construction at Neath was to follow a decade or so later. The two programmes were finished in the early years of the fourteenth century, with the completed churches marking the apogee of Cistercian church building in Wales.

Tintern is of course one of the best-known and best-preserved white monk churches in the whole of the British Isles (fig 102).[68] Its construction can, fortunately, be placed within a broad chronological framework provided by two documentary sources.

The first, a chronicle probably compiled at Neath Abbey *c* 1300, provides us with a start date. The entry for 1269 reads: *Incepta est nova ecclesia de Tinterne.*[69] The second source, a sixteenth-century transcript by Thomas Talbot of an earlier Tintern chronicle, provides not only a date for the commencement of the church, but also one which appears to mark its formal dedication. The entry for 1301 reads: 'The new church of Tintern abbay, 32 yeres in building, was finished by Roger Bygod, and at his request was halowed the.5. kalends of August'.[70] In so far as these two pieces of evidence are reliable, the decision to begin work on the new church (Tintern II) must have been taken by Abbot John (*c* 1267–77), a man whose Crown and Cistercian duties certainly took him to Westminster, as well as providing him with chances to view the new building programmes at both Netley and Waverley.[71] As to the question of patronage by Roger Bigod, fifth earl of Norfolk (1270–1306) and lord of Chepstow, there are some aspects of its

chronology and extent which remain rather vexed. The first signs of his active support do seem to date from before 1290, though not it seems as early as the very beginning of the new church programme.[72] Proof positive of Bigod's benevolence towards the Tintern community can be dated to 1302, when he granted the monks 'all his manor of Acle' in Norfolk. The circumstances surrounding the future of his estates at this time are of interest, but there is no doubt this was a particularly generous gift. Acle was to become Tintern's single most profitable asset, accounting for up to a quarter of the community's annual income on the eve of the suppression.[73]

Taken in general terms, the comprehensive unity of the initial Tintern master's original design is evident from a glance at the ruins. He was, after all, given the opportunity to plan a brand-new church from scratch, though it is also clear that his builders had to work within certain restrictions. Specifically, Tintern II had to be laid out slightly to the south and

104 Tintern Abbey: *presbytery and south transept, from the north west. The vast east window in the presbytery was of eight tall lights surmounted by Geometrical oculi in the head. The elevations were of two storeys throughout, the triforium stage filled for the most part with a blank field of masonry.*
Photograph: *Royal Commission on the Ancient and Historical Monuments of Wales, Crown Copyright*

105 Tintern Abbey, moulding profiles of selected window jambs, heads and arcades in the abbey church (after Potter 1847 and Sharpe 1848): (1) west window; (2) east window; (3) presbytery aisles; (4) presbytery arcade; (5) nave arcade.

Drawing: *Pete Lawrence, for Cadw*

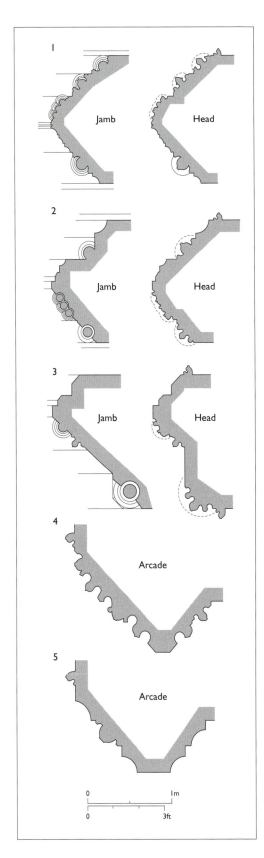

east of the twelfth-century church, with construction advancing in such a way as to allow the monks to occupy the older building for as long as possible. In effect, the Gothic church grew in the fashion of an envelope, surrounding its much smaller and more humble predecessor (fig 103). According to the traveller and antiquary William Worcestre, who was at Tintern in the 1470s, enough progress had been made by April 1287 to permit a mass within the rising building. Eighteen months later, in October 1288, the first mass was celebrated at the high altar and the choir monks were able to transfer their full daily round into the completed presbytery.[74] It can be inferred that by this stage the south transept of the old church had probably been dismantled, thereby providing clear access into the new choir from the monks' dormitory to the north. As the programme on the western bays of the nave continued, the remainder of the Romanesque church would have been gradually pulled down, its stone probably salvaged for use as core-work in the fresh construction.[75]

On the basis of the fabric evidence, both stylistic and archaeological, at least one break in the construction programme is to be identified in the south aisle of the nave and the south clerestory. Before the posited break, in the rere-arches of those windows in the eastern bays, detached shafts were set in hollows along the inner jambs of each splay. After the break (which occurs between bay two and bay three in the clerestory, and within bay four in the aisle) these detached shafts were replaced by a roll moulding. There are, furthermore, a number of other aspects of the design details that seem to underline the significance placed on this structural break.

The most prominent of these, by a long way, is the evidence seen in the greater window tracery. This progresses from the Geometrical oculi in the presbytery (fig 104) and south transept through to the intersecting pattern filled with daggers and pointed trilobes in the west front. It seems very likely, too, that the contrast between the form of the minor tracery in the south and north aisles of the nave was related to structural phasing. As in the presbytery aisles, the windows in the four eastern bays of the south aisle were of two lights with sexfoil heads featuring crisp, squared terminals to the cusps, and with the glazing set in external rebates (fig 105). The windows in the two west bays probably belong to a later phase of work, and are smaller with higher sills and quatrefoil heads.[76] Similarly, in the north aisle, where construction would have been delayed until the removal of the Romanesque nave, the windows in the five western bays all have quatrefoil heads, and

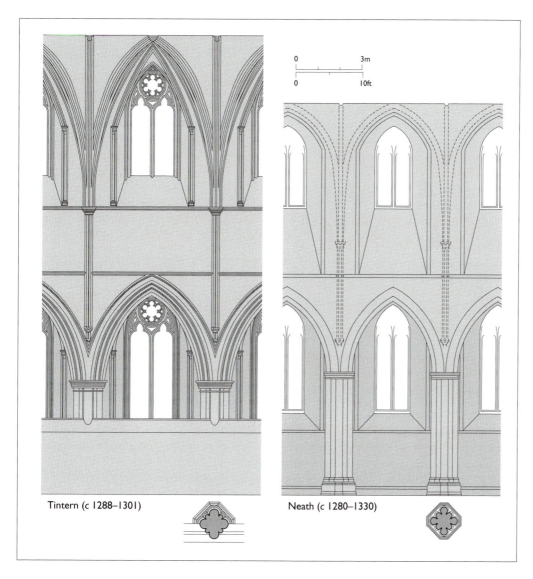

Tintern (c 1288–1301)   Neath (c 1280–1330)

106 *Cistercian abbeys in Wales, comparative nave elevations: Tintern (after Sharpe 1848); Neath (Chris Jones-Jenkins/David Robinson).*

Drawing: *Pete Lawrence, for Cadw*

here the glazing was set in grooves along the centre of the jambs. Before concluding on these differences in window design, it should be noted that the form of the major tracery in the north transept may well be misleading in terms of chronology. Structurally, this must have been one of the last areas of the new church to be completed, in which case the Geometrical oculi may well have been retained for the sake of aesthetic uniformity within the eastern arm as a whole. Indeed, the inner splays of this principal window were clearly treated differently from those in the presbytery and the south transept.[77]

Other broad stylistic differences between the eastern and western arms of the church can be seen in the form of the piers and arch mouldings of the arcades (figs 44 and 105). In the presbytery and transepts, each of the great clustered piers comprised

a quatrefoil core with a detached and belted shaft to each angle. Here, the arch mouldings are particularly rich, and include a distinctive roll and fillet flanked to one side by a prominent angle fillet.[78] In the nave, on the other hand, above integral screen walls, all eight shafts in the piers were raised as coursed stonework (fig 44), and the arch mouldings were of a much simpler pattern with a predominance of hollow chamfers. Of course, it might well be argued that these particular differences may have been related to the varying liturgical status of the presbytery and the nave. Yet there is one specific design detail where the alternate forms almost certainly have a chronological link. Specifically, in the presbytery and the south transept the detached shafts to the piers were deliberately 'broken' midway by a solid belt or band, itself coursed with the quatrefoil core. In contrast, in

129

107 Hereford
Cathedral
(Herefordshire):
north window of
north transept,
c 1255–68. Built by
the Savoyard bishop,
Peter of Aigueblanche
(1240–68), this great
window introduced
the new design
possibilities offered
by bar tracery to the
west of England. In
addition to the tracery,
however, other aspects
in the design of the
Hereford transept can
also be found in the
late thirteenth-century
church at Tintern.

Photograph:
Conway Library,
Courtauld Institute
of Art, London

the later north transept, these belts were hollowed
out, allowing the shaft (or at least part of it) to run
right through.

Taken as a whole, these many differences in both
general form and design detail confirm that Tintern
II was by no means the uniform building projected
through its initial appearance. In turn, this raises the
distinct possibility that the community engaged
more than one master mason over the thirty-year
period of construction, with the works consequently
falling into several broad phases.[79]

In assessing the overall characteristics of the
completed church, with its four-bay presbytery (fig
104), strongly defined crossing and six-bay nave, the
impression is one of a building straddling the ideals
of early Cistercian austerity and sumptuous
cathedral splendour. The architecture, for example,
of clustered piers, moulded capitals and bases, plain
string courses and uncomplicated quadripartite
vaults with simple rib profiles, is all very much in
keeping with earlier white monk preferences.[80] Of
particular note, we can be reasonably confident that
the Tintern community was content to reject any
idea of a large tower crowning the silhouette of its
new church (fig 102). Instead, the roofs are likely to
have met above the crossing in the manner of many
contemporary French Gothic churches. The central
point, nonetheless, may well have carried an

108 *Tintern Abbey: the west front. The tracery in the great seven-light window contrasts markedly with that seen at the east end of the church and may well reflect a hiatus in the building programme. The pattern reflects new trends in tracery design at the end of the thirteenth century, ultimately derived from London work of the 1270s and 1280s. However, the lower part of the elevation is likely to belong to an earlier phase of construction.*
Photograph: *Cadw, Crown Copyright*

109 Tintern Abbey: doorway from cloister to book room. Fashioned in connection with the completion of Tintern II, the doorway was located between the new north transept and the early thirteenth-century chapter house. The continuous orders of the deeply moulded splays fade into the chamfered bases, in a style which was to become fairly widespread in the south west during the first half of the fourteenth century. The composition here, with its central trumeau and open traceried head, is unlikely to be much later than c 1300.

Photograph: *Royal Commission on the Ancient and Historical Monuments of Wales, Crown Copyright*

octagonal spired flèche, large enough to have housed bells.[81]

The internal elevations in both the presbytery and the nave were of the two-storey form still very much favoured by the order in Britain (figs 104 and 106).[82] The triforium stage at Tintern was occupied by a blank field of masonry, defined horizontally by string courses above and below, and given vertical bay articulation by vault shafts rising from sculpted corbels set in the arcade spandrels.[83] There is a notable exception to this pattern in the transepts,

where the need to accommodate wall-passages (allowing access to the roof spaces) led the designer to create big open rere-arches to the clerestory windows. The windows themselves were then placed high up into the head of the arch, with the wall-passages running along at sill level. Seeming to imply a third storey without there actually being one, it was an arrangement that had earlier been introduced in a Cistercian context at Netley (c 1241–51). At Tintern, although the pattern occurs on both sides of the north transept and in the west wall of the south

110 Tintern Abbey: reconstruction of the pulpitum, c 1325–30 (after Harrison et al 1998). The last remains of this elaborate liturgical fitting were swept away from the nave in the late nineteenth century. The reconstruction is based on extensive ex situ fragments preserved at the site. There is a strong case to suggest that the designer of the screen was the west country master mason, William Joy. Drawing: Chris Jones-Jenkins, for Cadw

transept, it does not wholly interrupt the deliberate rhythm of the otherwise plainer elevations along the main axis of the church.

Where Tintern II seems radically to turn its back on Cistercian architecture of the earlier thirteenth century is in the form of its windows. In other words, the effect of the eastwards view in the new church is strikingly different from, for instance, the two banks of lancets above the high altar at Rievaulx (fig 95).[84] Then again, it must be borne in mind that few great church designers in the second half of the thirteenth century could have easily ignored the influence of Westminster Abbey, rebuilt on a magnificent scale

from 1245 by Henry III. In particular, this was the building which focused national attention upon the latest French addition to the vocabulary of Gothic architecture: bar tracery.[85] It was, incidentally, Henry's contemporary patronage of Netley which presumably led to an early Cistercian use of the form there.[86] In any case, within a few decades this novel and highly fashionable court innovation had been taken up in a new generation of buildings throughout the country.[87] Admittedly, whilst Tintern may not have been able to compete in the first league in terms of quantity, the individual scale and quality of its principal windows was quite astonishing.

111 *Tintern Abbey: details of* ex situ *pulpitum fragments. To the right is a section of the blind Geometrical tracery which ran along the west face of the solid backing wall. From this the vault ribs (left) sprang forward to the ogee arcade facing the nave.*

Photograph: *Cadw, Crown Copyright*

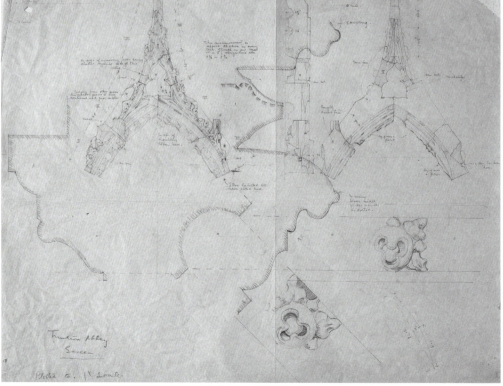

112 *Tintern Abbey: drawing of pulpitum details, c 1920. Together with moulding profiles, this Office of Works record illustration shows the front and back of one of the seven ogee-headed arches known to have fronted the screen. The ballflower fleurons (bottom right) studded the underside hollow of the arch mouldings.*

Photograph: *Cadw, Crown Copyright*

134

113 Tintern Abbey: cut-away reconstruction, showing liturgical divisions within the church. As designed, solid screen walls ran between the arcade piers along the full length of both the nave and presbytery. The monks' choir and the presbytery were enclosed by the pulpitum to the west and by a further screen or parclose behind the high altar to the east. An arcaded porch is known to have been introduced outside the west door, probably in the 1320s. The form of the superstructure shown here is necessarily conjectural.

Drawing: *Terry Ball, for Cadw*

At the time work began on Tintern's new abbey church, an exemplar for huge bar tracery window patterns already existed in the west of England, in the rebuilt north transept at Hereford Cathedral, *c* 1255–68 (fig 107).[88] However, at first glance, it may not be immediately obvious whether the first Tintern master borrowed anything beyond the general manner of this important west country scheme. The use of a comparatively heavy central mullion at the cathedral, for example, was certainly disregarded in the breathtakingly daring and slender design of Tintern's vast eight-light east window (*c* 1269–88).[89] We shall return to potential architectural links with Hereford below, but for the moment there is more to say on the tracery patterns. In fact, a closer comparison for the general form and proportions of

Tintern's extraordinary presbytery opening is the east window in the Angel Choir at Lincoln Cathedral (begun 1256).[90] Meanwhile, the six-light window in the south transept at Tintern was probably planned at much the same time as its eastern counterpart, and can hardly have appeared much less impressive when complete. Then, as observed above, in contrast to these Geometrical forms at the east end of the church, the tracery in the west front of Tintern II clearly marks a fresh stylistic impulse, one which we might reasonably infer followed some hiatus in the building programme (fig 108). The form appears to reflect fashionable new trends in tracery design in the 1280s, emanating once again from London and rapidly disseminated to various regional centres of construction.[91] Ultimately, it was the new work of the

135

1270s and early 1280s at Old St Paul's Cathedral which had probably led the way, and – further underlining the notion of metropolitan dominance – a good analogue for Tintern's west window is provided by St Etheldreda's, Ely Place (*c* 1284–6), formerly the chapel at the London residence of the bishops of Ely.[92] The appearance of such a fashionable feature at this south Wales Cistercian house may be explained by the influence of the well-travelled and highly regarded Abbot Ralph (*c* 1294–1305), the man who must have negotiated with Earl Roger Bigod over his patronage and who presumably officiated in some capacity at the dedication ceremony of 1301 (*see* frontispiece).[93] Yet, while admitting the undoubted influence of London fashion, we also have to remember that a number of major workshops in the south west of England were bustling with activity around this time, notably those centred on Wells and Exeter. Indeed, the closest parallels for the combination of forms seen in the Tintern west window are to be found in the Lady Chapel and presbytery at Exeter Cathedral (*c* 1282–97).[94]

Clearly, from what has been said so far, there are several directions we might take in tracking down the architectural context and stylistic affiliations of Tintern II. The north transept at Hereford Cathedral cannot be overlooked, regardless of what has been said on the bar tracery patterns above. If nothing else, the timing of its completion (*c* 1268) would have meant that a pool of masons now familiar with the court-inspired style was available to move on to a new project. Given that the Tintern programme is believed to have been started in 1269, and that the site is located less than 44km to the south of Hereford (fig 18), we begin with a degree of circumstantial evidence. Stylistic comparisons take us a good deal further. Hence, beyond the vast sheets of glass made possible by the tracery, we might note the similarity between the piers in the Tintern presbytery and transepts and that in the transept arcade at the cathedral church: both have lozenge-shaped bases and a quatrefoil core with detached and belted shafts to the angles. In addition, the steep, pointed pitch of the clerestory lights at the abbey finds an antecedent in the triforium openings at Hereford. The same might be said of the lavish diaper work seen in the spandrel panelling and blind tracery at Tintern's west front, again found earlier in the spandrels of the triforium openings at the cathedral.[95]

Towards the later stages in the completion of Tintern II, workshops on the other side of the Bristol Channel may have begun to exert greater influence on the craft skills based at the abbey lodge. The

potential role of the masons involved with the Exeter Cathedral window tracery has been mentioned above, and this same flow in the traffic of craftsmen can again be demonstrated in the case of several of the comparatively minor tasks associated with the completion of the new church. For instance, the moulding profiles of the replacement book room doorway (fig 109) and the sacristy vault ribs (*c* 1300), both introduced in connection with the final stages of construction on the north transept, seem very close to the style of work at the palace of Bishop Robert Burnell (1275–92) in Wells.[96]

On balance, there is probably enough evidence to suggest that all the main components of the new abbey church were completed in time for the monks to take part in the dedication ceremony recorded in the Tintern chronicle for 1301, a ceremony at which Earl Roger Bigod himself is likely to have been present.[97] There can, nevertheless, be no doubt that the liturgical furnishing and fitting out of the building continued into the early decades of the fourteenth century. The clearest indication of this comes from an analysis of the now fragmentary pulpitum (fig 110), an essential feature within any monastic church, but one, in this case, which cannot have been installed until the late 1320s.

In the case of most of the Welsh Cistercian abbey churches, little more can be done than guess at the nature of liturgical furnishings such as screens, altars, portable altarpieces and so on.[98] Indeed the recent 'rediscovery' of the Tintern pulpitum serves to highlight just how much may have been lost elsewhere.[99] Specifically, as reconstructed on paper from *ex situ* stonework fragments (fig 111), the Tintern screen is revealed as a sumptuous piece of micro-architecture, drawing extensively on the rich vocabulary of contemporary themes and ornamental motifs within the English Decorated style. In what was a five-bay design, the decorative work fronted a solid screen wall running between two of the nave piers. Applied to the west face of the wall was a pattern of blind Geometrical tracery, in which the enclosing arch in each bay had an octofoil in the head, set above a pair of ogee-cusped arches (fig 111). One bay forward of this, and connected by an ingenious mini-vault, stood an elaborate arcade of seven ogee arches: five to the front and one at each side. The whole was decorated with ballflowers and naturalistic foliage (fig 112), and finished with a bold embossed cornice. The stylistic context for this glamorous fitting has been traced to the architectural lodges of the south west. In fact, there are strong grounds for suggesting that its designer was William Joy, whose best-known later work is the choir at Wells Cathedral.[100] If this attribution is correct, the commission is probably to be dated to the late 1320s, and perhaps no later than *c* 1330. For the Tintern monks of the late medieval period, entering the church from the west door during feast days processions, the screen would have served as a highly dramatic focus, adding to the spectacle and solemnity of their return into the ritual choir for high mass.[101]

Staying with the theme of the liturgical usage of Tintern II, it should be noted that when the plans for the church were originally drawn up, the community had settled upon a layout that allowed for the then characteristic Cistercian needs (fig 113). Four altars were placed against the 'cliff' east wall of the presbytery, and the aisles at this end of the church were cut off from the main vessel by stone walls integrated with the pier construction. A transverse wall or parclose separated the eastern ambulatory from the high altar, which itself stood in the second bay. The choir monks were to be accommodated in stalls extending from the crossing, through into at least the first bay of the nave. The inner mouldings of the western crossing piers were corbelled out at a higher level to allow for the backs of the stalls. To the west again, beyond the eventual position of the pulpitum, the central area of the nave was separated from its aisles by even thicker screen walls than those in the presbytery. Traditionally, these would have formed the backing for the lay brothers' choir stalls. In the event, over the half-century from the start of building on the church through to the installation of the pulpitum in the 1320s, with the gradual demise of the lay brotherhood, the community might well have come to the realization that such traditional liturgical arrangements were no longer necessary. In spite of the provision made for them, the lateral screen walls in the nave were probably soon removed, with the individual bay spaces perhaps used for further chapel and burial accommodation.[102] But this is to progress to those changes which took place in the later Middle Ages, when we have yet to consider Tintern II's contemporary church at Neath Abbey.

THE NEW CHURCH AT NEATH

On stylistic grounds, it appears that the decision to replace the twelfth-century church at Neath was taken during the abbacy of Adam of Carmarthen (*c* 1266–89).[103] The date generally given is about 1280,[104] in which case the programme must have been well in hand when the site was visited by Edward I in 1284. During his visit, Edward presented the community with 'a very beautiful baldachin', perhaps a *baldacchino*, or canopy, intended for the high altar.[105] Some five years later, in 1289, it was Abbot Adam

who entered into an agreement with Gilbert de Clare (d 1295), earl of Gloucester and lord of Glamorgan, whereby the abbot surrendered considerable tracts of the abbey's lands in return for annual rents worth £100 deriving from a number of local boroughs and manorial holdings. It has been suggested that one of the reasons which could well have prompted such a major step was the need to realize ready cash for the building operations.[106] Indeed, on the same day as the agreement was reached, de Clare granted the Neath community 'all the timber necessary' for the building of the monastery, and for the construction of one of its granges.[107] Whatever the truth in this particular episode, it seems fairly certain that the construction of Neath II itself extended well into the early years of the fourteenth century.

As at Tintern, it may be assumed that the work progressed in such a way that the monks were able to use their existing building for as long as possible (fig 25).[108] Hence, the programme must have started with the east end of the new church, progressing to the north transept, the north wall and north arcade of the nave, and gradually on around to the west front. The south side of the nave and the south transept can only have been completed when the Romanesque church was at last dismantled. One break in the sequence may be posited on the basis of the surviving details of the relatively tall, two-light windows in the north nave aisle (fig 114). Moving from east to west, the fabric in bays one and two does not survive to sufficient height to draw any firm conclusions, but in bays three and four the rere-arches of the windows were quite definitely carried on shafts with moulded capitals. Then, in the last three bays, for no apparent reason, the form of the jamb mouldings changes.[109] Staying with the tracery theme there is in the porch or narthex, set centrally between the two major buttresses at the west front of the church, a blind fragment which seems to follow London patterns of the later 1280s. It could, as observed at Tintern, be rather later in this regional context.[110] Another clue on dating, as well as on stylistic context, is provided by the jambs of the processional doorway at the east end of the south nave aisle (figs 115 and 116). The intricate profile of the vertical mouldings, and the way they die into a simple angled plinth at the base, is not unlike the pattern seen in the book room doorway at Tintern (fig 109). The Neath work belongs perhaps to the very earliest years of the fourteenth century, and is another example of those architectural links between the south Wales seaboard and the major lodges in the Bristol and Wells region.[111]

Two other pieces of evidence provide grounds for pushing the final stages in the construction and fitting out of Neath II into the first half of the fourteenth century. To begin with, there are the two bosses from the high vault recovered during the clearance excavations of 1924–35. One of these is a particularly fine piece carved with the figure of Christ in Majesty (fig 117). The figure is surrounded by an undercut quatrefoil studded with ballflower pellets, from which foliage turns back towards the rib articulation. It cannot be earlier than the first quarter of the fourteenth century, and indicates that some areas of the church were vaulted around this time.[112] The second strand of evidence comes from the extensive areas of tile pavement known to have existed in the choir and east end of the church (fig 118). Although several factors do have to be taken into account before determining the probable date, a prominent heraldic sequence in the overall patterns suggests the tiles were laid around 1340.[113]

The completed church was approximately 62m long internally and, in plan at least, of a similar scale to Tintern II. The east end was laid out in very much the same fashion, with a four-bay presbytery, a substantial crossing and transepts with two eastern chapels to each arm. The nave, however, was of seven bays, compared to the six built over much the same length at Tintern (fig 114). Further comparison might be drawn with Tintern when we consider that,

despite the loss of so much of the fabric, we can be reasonably confident that all four gable walls at Neath were also filled with elaborate tracery designs.[114] Broadly speaking, there must have been a fairly strong vertical emphasis in the church, created by the comparatively slender piers and narrow bay spacing, and by the vault wall shafts in the aisles and those which presumably existed at clerestory level.[115] The pier profile in the nave comprised large rounded shafts set in the cardinal directions, with rather smaller shafts in the angles between them (fig 44). Foundations show there were screen walls between the piers surrounding the presbytery and choir, though there is no clear evidence in the four central bays of the nave.

For reasons that are not understood, the nave arcades appear to have stopped one bay short of the west front, with the final bay filled instead with solid walls. Taking the evidence as a whole, there is just enough to show that the nave elevations were again of two storeys, though not of the Tintern pattern (fig 106). In the surviving west bay, the jambs at the inner edges of the clerestory windows indicate tall rere-arches rising from a moulded string course set just above the apex of the arcade arches. A deep splay then projected from string-course level to the base of the windows themselves, a feature substituting for

114 Neath Abbey: view of church, looking north west along the nave, towards the west front. On stylistic grounds, building is thought to have been initiated c 1280, and may have progressed into the first decades of the fourteenth century. In plan, the new church was of a very similar form to that at Tintern, though the nave elevations were of smaller proportion.

Photograph: *Royal Commission on the Ancient and Historical Monuments of Wales, Crown Copyright*

the vertical 'triforium' wall between two strings which occur in the Tintern elevations. On the face of it, this Neath pattern is close to the form of the proposed elevations of the presbytery at Exeter Cathedral (under way *c* 1288–91), and provides another potential link with the traffic in craft skills from south-west England.[116] The entire church at Neath, both in its aisles and main vessels, was covered with quadripartite rib vaults.

The liturgical arrangements within Neath II were again similar to the pattern observed at Tintern. Hence, along the inner face of the vertical east wall of the presbytery there were four new chapels. The high altar was set west of an ambulatory passage in the next bay,[117] and the monks' choir extended from beneath the crossing into the first bay of the nave. The stone foundations for the support of the choir stalls still survive (fig 114). Given the very obvious significance attached to the pulpitum by the community at Tintern, it would be surprising were not something of comparative scale and quality to have been commissioned by the monks at Neath. Given also the decline in the number of lay brothers, the use to which the nave was put from the mid-fourteenth century was doubtless akin to those suggestions made above for the Monmouthshire house.

EDWARD I AND MAENAN

In addition to the well-known churches at Tintern and Neath, a third new and very important Welsh

Cistercian church was begun during the last quarter of the thirteenth century. Hitherto quite unexpected by the community concerned, its construction was consequent upon an unusual set of circumstances. In the spring of 1283, having determined upon building a castle and walled town near the mouth of the Conwy river, Edward I was obliged to consider the removal and rehousing of the white monk community at Aberconwy.[118] By September of that year, the General Chapter had given its consent to the scheme, subject to the monks not being disturbed until a new location was sufficiently ready for them to observe the regular life.[119] In March 1284, Edward may well have been present to see the inauguration of 'his' new abbey at Maenan, and a further visit by both the king and his queen in October of that year was possibly the occasion for a ceremony of dedication.[120] Edward undoubtedly contributed handsomely to the fabric fund. For example, a gift of some £53 for finishing certain works in the abbey church (and for building a bakehouse and brewhouse) coincided with his visit of October 1284. Again, at some point in 1284–6, the king paid for the making, probably at Chester, of glass windows and their ironwork, destined for Maenan.[121] One last indication of Edward's generosity to the community comes from

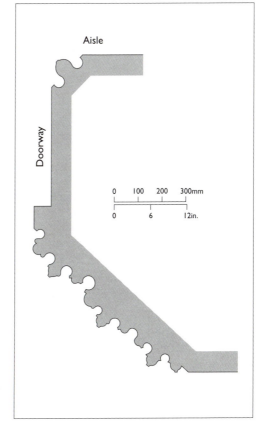

115 Neath Abbey: jambs of east processional doorway in south aisle. This early fourteenth-century doorway must have been one of the last features to have been completed in the new abbey church. The nature of the mouldings suggests links with craftsmen working at the major architectural lodges on the opposite side of the Bristol Channel, especially at Bristol and Wells.

Photograph: *author*

116 Neath Abbey: moulding profile of east jamb of processional doorway in south aisle.

Drawing: *Pete Lawrence, for Cadw*

the abbey's own 'Register and Chronicle', where it is recorded that he gave 'large funds for new building'.[122] Meanwhile, he was also pouring vast sums into the construction of another new Cistercian abbey church, that at Vale Royal in Cheshire.[123] Here, the works were under the direction of that highly significant royal mason, Walter of Hereford (d 1309).[124] Indeed, there arises the intriguing possibility that Walter, in connection with James of St George (Master of the King's Works in Wales), was responsible for some aspect of the initial building programme at Maenan Abbey.[125]

It is especially unfortunate, then, that so little is known about the fabric of this potentially very important building. Nothing of the church can now be seen above ground, and virtually all our information comes from exploratory trenching in 1924 and from two seasons of limited excavation by Butler in 1963–8.[126] In the main, this work appears to have uncovered the east wall of the north transept chapels, together with a newel stair located in the junction with the north presbytery aisle (fig 25). On the basis of a few additional scattered clues, a conjectural overall ground plan has been pieced together. Not surprisingly, perhaps, the form and proportions seen in this plan bear a strong resemblance to those at Tintern and Neath (figs 25 and 26). It is suggested that the Maenan presbytery was three bays in length and of rectangular ambulatory form. The transepts may have featured three eastern chapels and the nave was possibly of seven bays. On the basis of Butler's excavations, it seems construction work on the church may well have extended into the fourteenth century.[127]

LATER WELSH CHURCH WORKS

Setting aside any reservations there may be about the specific form of Maenan, what is particularly interesting about all three late thirteenth-century Cistercian churches in Wales is the comprehensive nature of the building programmes. Although, as we have seen, Vale Royal was under construction at much the same time, as was Sweetheart (or New Abbey) in Scotland (begun c 1273),[128] very few other totally new white monk churches were raised in Britain after 1300. The exceptions were at Whalley in Lancashire (c 1330–80), St Mary Graces in London (begun c 1350) and Melrose in Scotland (rebuilt following war damage in 1385).[129] On the other hand, there are numerous examples of additions or modifications to existing fabrics from sites across the whole of the British Isles.[130]

In picking up this thread in Wales, it may be instructive to begin with documentary references for two sites. At Margam Abbey, for instance, where all the surviving fabric evidence suggests the extended presbytery was complete by about 1250, there is

117 Neath Abbey: high vault roof boss of the early fourteenth century. Found during clearance work at the site in 1928, the boss bears the figure of Christ in Majesty surrounded by a quatrefoil studded with ballflower pellets.

Photograph: *Royal Commission on the Ancient and Historical Monuments of Wales, Crown Copyright*

mention of a 'master of the works of the new church' as late as 1307.[131] One possible explanation for this is the construction of a substantial tower over the new crossing. There is some support for this suggestion in a bardic description of Margam in the early sixteenth century, which says that the abbey was 'a perfect paradise, comparable with Gloucester's fane – a crystal rock crowned by its battlemented tower'.[132]

In south-east Wales, and in much the same vein, there are several references to 'the Keeper of the Work of the church of Tintern' up to fifty years after the dedication of Tintern II (1301).[133] In part, this role may have been related to the furnishing and fitting out of the new building, but it is not possible to be specific. The construction of the pulpitum between the monks' choir and the nave in the late 1320s has already been noted, and there has also been reference to the likely removal of the screen walls linking the nave piers at a later date.[134] Another Tintern work which appears to date from the early years of the fourteenth century is the addition of a porch, situated immediately outside the west door of the church (figs 108 and 113).[135] Today, this is represented by no more than four fragments of masonry, probably the bases which carried a delicate arcaded construction, partially masking the main portal. Whether this porch in turn carried an elevated chapel, housing the revered statue of St Mary the Virgin which led to Tintern becoming something of a place of pilgrimage in the early fifteenth century, is questionable.[136]

Among the houses of the north and west, a range of remedial works and new construction was almost certainly made necessary by damage inflicted during the two Welsh wars of Edward I, in 1276–7 and 1282–3.[137] Valle Crucis was one of the houses we may be sure was affected in this way. As noted earlier, the church was begun to a 'Bernardine' plan soon after the foundation in 1200–1. The work may have been

reasonably well advanced by the mid-thirteenth century, at which point a disastrous fire apparently swept across the entire site.[138] With barely time to recover, the community was undoubtedly severely hit during the Edwardian years of conflict. In December 1283, the king possibly had the opportunity to see war-damaged Valle Crucis first hand; he offered a gift of some £26 to the abbey at the time.[139] A year later, Valle Crucis received £160 by way of compensation, by far the largest sum given to any of the Welsh Cistercian houses for their losses during the wars.[140] In assessing the fabric evidence itself, there are considerable problems in trying to disentangle the chronology, especially when dealing with the extraordinary buttressing at the east end of the church (fig 119) and when looking at the detail of the west front (fig 120). On first appearance, the composition of the west front – with its three two-light windows featuring cusped circles to the heads and a single enclosing arch above – might easily belong to the third quarter of the century. It is equally possible that the work here and at the east end may have followed war damage of the early 1280s, with the chance that it could have been undertaken by masons otherwise involved in Edward I's castle building in north Wales.[141] In any case, before the middle of the fourteenth century, the Valle Crucis community was obliged to make further changes to its church, notably in the area of the west gable (fig 121). Completed in fine ashlar, with an attractive eight-light rose window, the new work stands out very clearly from the rubble construction below. A rare inscription running across the stonework dates it quite closely to c 1330–40.[142]

Strata Florida was another house to suffer a sequence of misfortunes at the end of the thirteenth century. It, too, received compensation for war damage in 1284,[143] though very much worse was to come. Almost immediately, in fact, the belfry was

118 Neath Abbey: tiles representing the legendary combat between King Richard I and Saladin. These measure c 200mm by 130mm and were included in a series of elaborately designed pavements laid in the choir and east end of the new abbey church, c 1340.

Photograph: *National Museums & Galleries of Wales*

struck by lightning, causing a fire which was said to
have 'devoured the whole church'.[144] As if the monks
had not endured enough, their abbey was deliberately
put to flames by a royalist force during the violent
Welsh uprising of 1294–5. In 1300, Edward I granted
the abbot and convent permission 'to construct
afresh, and rebuild their house'.[145] In the main, the
works seem to have been of a remedial nature. They
included the reroofing of the church in stone rather
than in lead, and a degree of liturgical reordering
accompanying a probable reduction in the size of the
monks' choir.[146]

Meanwhile, the communities at the abbeys of
Basingwerk, Cymer and Strata Marcella had also
been awarded compensation payments in 1284.[147]
Again, it is difficult to be certain of the precise
damage inflicted during the wars, or to be sure that
significant rebuilding programmes followed as a
result. Indeed, at Cymer, as noted earlier, it seems far
more likely that the early thirteenth-century church
had to be reduced in size at some point (fig 25). The
best that could be achieved by a later generation of
monks was the construction of a small tower, added
to the west end of the nave in the mid- to later
fourteenth century.[148] At Strata Marcella, on the
other hand, the 1890 discovery of a large number
of worked stones near the crossing, carved with a
distinctive wave moulding, suggests an important
new build in the early fourteenth century. The

excavator, Stephen Williams, felt sure the stones must
have come from the 'piers of the tower'.[149]

Although the border abbey at Dore escaped the
direct impact of the late thirteenth-century Welsh
wars, the community had in any case been struggling
to finish work on its ambitious building programme
for some time. In 1260, Peter of Aigueblanche,
bishop of Hereford, had granted an indulgence to all
those who contributed to the building of 'the
sumptuous church of Dore'.[150] At the time, although
vault springers had probably been in place within the
nave for some decades, the high vault itself remained
incomplete. A substantial amount of liturgical fitting
out was also being undertaken within the nave at
about this time.[151] Nevertheless, a consecration was
carried out at Dore sometime during the episcopate
of Bishop Thomas Cantilupe (1275–82).[152] In this
context, there is a significant point of controversy,
namely the date of the wonderful group of figurated
bosses which has survived from the nave vault (*see*
fig 170). For some scholars, these cannot be earlier
than the first quarter of the fourteenth century, which
suggests the nave remained incomplete at the time of
the dedication.[153] More recently, the sculpture has
been reassessed and an argument made to suggest the
bosses could well have been in place before 1282.[154]

Very little survives by way of fabric evidence for
Welsh Cistercian church building during the late
Middle Ages, but a number of documentary sources

CHAPTER 8

THE CLAUSTRAL LAYOUT

If the Rule of St Benedict was the bedrock for the Cistercian way of life, it was the cloister which served as the physical centre of the world for each and every monk.[1] It follows that in any regional survey of white monk abbeys, in spite of the overriding importance of the church, we must also consider the qualities and significance of the cloister and its surrounding conventual buildings. We know something of the disposition of the principal claustral layout at up to thirteen of the abbeys considered in this volume. Moreover, standing remains exist at as many as nine separate locations, with the most complete survivals to be seen at Tintern and Neath (figs 25, 26, 122 and 123). Almost all the principal structures are represented. In terms of dating, the building works extend from the earliest permanent stone constructions raised at Tintern, probably before 1150, all the way through to the various additions and remodellings made at a number of sites up to the eve of the suppression in the sixteenth century.

No one has yet produced a truly comprehensive overview of Cistercian monastic buildings, at least not one that draws upon the extensive body of European evidence at large. The sheer scale of the subject is unquestionably daunting, but in any case there has been a widespread failure to recognize the value of these structures in their own right. On the whole, architectural historians and archaeologists have tended to show little more than marginal interest, certainly when compared to the attention lavished on the order's churches.[2] This is the more surprising when we appreciate that the corpus of buildings includes a very large number of highly impressive Gothic spaces, all of them significant architectural compositions in their own right. Of course, there are exceptions to this across-the-board observation. In terms of individual countries, for instance, the French material was very well covered by the standards of the mid-twentieth century by Marcel Aubert.[3] More recently, Roger Stalley has reviewed the surviving evidence for white monk cloisters and domestic buildings in Ireland.[4] Then again, for Europe as a whole, Wolfgang Braunfels

published a useful introduction to the architecture of Cistercian claustral buildings in the early 1970s.[5] More recently, this has been surpassed in a wide-ranging synthesis of white monk architecture produced by Terryl Kinder.[6] In the meantime, as regards the order's approach to specific elements within the monastic plan, it was Peter Fergusson who opened our eyes to fresh research possibilities in his stimulating assessment of the twelfth-century refectories at Byland and Rievaulx,[7] following this up with an account of the architectural and iconographical significances of the chapter house at Rievaulx.[8] Encouragingly, his lead has since been taken up in a collection of essays which include introductory accounts on both dormitories and infirmaries, again covering the meaning as well as the form of their architecture.[9]

However, for summary accounts of the vast majority of individual monastic buildings at British Cistercian houses in general, we are still obliged to turn to sources such as official guidebooks, some of which draw on pioneer studies made in the late nineteenth and early twentieth centuries.[10] Looking to the future, remarkable new standards have been set by Fergusson and Harrison in their volume on Rievaulx,[11] and by Thomas Coomans in his study of the Belgian abbey of Villers.[12] These two modern works represent by far the fullest and most comprehensive accounts yet available on the development of Cistercian monastic buildings anywhere in Europe.[13] Not surprisingly, their content is of immense value for comparative study.

Here, our investigation begins with a general consideration of the Cistercian abbey plan, moving on to look at the disposition of the rooms within the key individual ranges, and offering an overview of the material which survives or has been excavated at the Welsh sites. In the ensuing chapters, four particular elements will then be singled out for somewhat closer investigation in Wales: the cloister and its surrounding arcades; the chapter house; the monks' refectory; and finally the area to the east of the cloister, looking mainly at the abbot's accommodation and the infirmary.

122 Tintern Abbey: reconstruction drawing showing the church and claustral layout in the later Middle Ages. At Tintern, somewhat unusually, the great cloister stood on the north, rather than the south, side of the nave. Other than this, however, the disposition of the monastic buildings followed a common Cistercian pattern. Around the cloister were the three principal ranges, including (in origin) accommodation for both the choir monks and the lay brothers. Grouped around a lesser cloister to the north east (right) were the monks' infirmary and the abbot's lodging. West of the church, within the inner court area, lay guest accommodation and a number of service buildings. Drawing: Terry Ball, for Cadw

THE CISTERCIAN PLAN

There is an understandable reluctance now to refer to any form of 'standard' Cistercian plan – that idealized layout of a white monk monastery as presented some decades ago by Aubert and by Dimier.[14] Useful though this concept of a standard plan may be for introductory purposes, it does tend to obscure the many spatial and temporal differences which were so commonplace. It is important, for example, not to overlook the subtle and sometimes contemporary differences that existed in the layouts of houses of similar status, perhaps even of the same filiation, and

often located no great distance apart. Then again, the extent to which radical changes were introduced at individual sites over the course of time is now appreciated with greater clarity. In the British Isles at least, the vast communal chambers raised by the swelling bodies of monks in the twelfth and early thirteenth centuries were frequently reduced or altered to suit the needs of the very much smaller communities occupying the sites during the later Middle Ages. After the mid-fourteenth century, for instance, there can only have been a reduction in the accommodation set aside for the lay brothers. Another significant change seems to have been the

148

123 *Neath Abbey: east range undercroft, the monks' day room, looking north. Introduced as part of the early to mid-thirteenth-century remodelling of the east and south cloister ranges at Neath, this five-bay rib-vaulted chamber stands as one of the most complete examples of white monk claustral building in Wales.*

Photograph: *Royal Commission on the Ancient and Historical Monuments of Wales, Crown Copyright*

growth in the extent of the complex given over to the use of the abbot and his guests.[15]

There was, even so, little of striking originality in the eventual planning of Cistercian monasteries. From the mid-1130s, the order began to adopt a layout based upon the already long-established European model. At the heart of this model was the cloister (*claustrum* or *claustra*), a square (or rectangular) open courtyard around which were positioned the church and the three principal ranges of conventual buildings. As a concept, the claustral layout itself appears to have emerged during the Carolingian monastic reforms of the late eighth and early ninth centuries. What is more, it is clear from the celebrated St Gall plan of *c* 820–30 that virtually all the key elements seen in the layout of later medieval monasteries had already found their place by this time.[16] Stylistic development apart, little by way of fundamental change was introduced over succeeding years. Hence, by the end of the eleventh century, the arrangements seen in the St Gall plan had become more or less standard practice for all major Cluniac and Benedictine abbeys.[17]

The Cistercians were initially reluctant to follow the established model. In line with their radical approach to the religious life and their single-minded insistence upon poverty and humility, the order's founding fathers seem to have experimented with new forms of monastic planning, as is witnessed by the early layout recorded at St Bernard's Clairvaux (fig 34), and by documentary descriptions of the timber buildings raised at various sites across Europe.[18] In due course, however, the white monk community at large was obliged to accept the practical good sense behind the 'standard' claustral layout.[19] From there it was merely a question of adapting specific elements to suit their own particular requirements. As can be seen from the mature plan of Clairvaux (fig 39), they soon came to favour the cloister as much as any of the other mainstream religious orders. Usually, though far from exclusively, it stood to the south side of the church, tucked into the angle of the nave and its adjoining transept. Around its periphery lay the three most important ranges of monastic buildings.

THE EAST RANGE

In the most common pattern, where the cloister indeed stood on the south side of the nave, the east range of monastic buildings abutted immediately on to the gable wall of the south transept (figs 15, 16, 39 and 50). Alternatively, if the cloister was positioned on the opposite side of the abbey church, then the range adjoined the north transept. Either way, the building itself was always the exclusive preserve of the choir monks. It was of two storeys, often running out for some distance beyond the cloister proper.[20] In the Welsh group of houses, standing east-range fabric survives at Basingwerk, Dore, Margam, Neath (fig 123), Strata Florida, Tintern (fig 124) and Valle Crucis (fig 125).[21] Minor traces have also been recovered by excavation or clearance at Cwmhir, Cymer and Strata Marcella, and there is recent geophysical evidence for some features of the range at Whitland (figs 25 and 26).[22]

Beginning with the ground floor, there was a narrow rectangular bay adjoining the transept, most often accommodating two separate chambers. Towards the cloister was the book room (*armarium*), and to the east lay the sacristy or vestry (*vestiarium*). Examples can be found at sites across the whole of Europe. Although there is no one universal model, the book room was generally reached from the east walk of the cloister, whereas the sacristy tended to feature a doorway opening directly into the adjacent transept.[23] This is the pattern found, for instance, at Fontfroide, Fontenay and Noirlac in France;[24] at Casamari in Italy; and at Alcobaça in Portugal.[25] Interestingly, at Tintern there are indications of a somewhat earlier arrangement. Here, the original east range must have been laid out in stone before *c* 1150, with no sign of a book room and sacristy adjacent to the north transept (fig 26). It seems likely that the small collection of books held by the community over the first few decades of its history could be readily accommodated in the two stone cupboards set into the wall of the transept in the east cloister walk.[26] The same appears to have been true at Villers in Belgium.[27] Indeed, Kinder now argues this was the commonplace early pattern, with book rooms becoming a distinct element within the east range plan only as Cistercian libraries began to expand later in the century.[28]

Examples of what might be considered the mature pattern are to be seen at Basingwerk, Dore, Neath, Strata Florida and Valle Crucis, all dating from the late twelfth or early thirteenth centuries. In each case, the doorway arrangements indicate the existence of an internal division between the book room and the sacristy, though nowhere is there any clear extant fabric evidence. At Valle Crucis, where the room(s) survive particularly well, the entire space is covered with a single unbroken barrel vault. The doorway from the sacristy into the transept is plain, whereas that leading from the cloister to the book room features moulded jambs, stiff-leaf capitals and three rounded orders to the head (fig 125).[29] Back at Tintern, when the completion of the new abbey church allowed the community to introduce a

124 Tintern Abbey: east range, monks' day room, looking south. The range was probably built in stone for the first time before c 1150, and was extended northwards by about 1200. The whole was largely rebuilt in the first half of the thirteenth century. The octagonal columns seen here in the day room supported a stone rib vault introduced as part of the thirteenth-century remodelling. The upper floor of the range was occupied by the monks' dormitory, with the crease of the roof appearing in the distance against the north transept.

Photograph: *Cadw, Crown Copyright*

similar layout *c* 1300, the book room was likewise given an elaborate cloister doorway (fig 109). In this case, too, traces of the internal stone division with the sacristy survive. Indeed, the different functions of the two rooms were also given clear architectural expression: the book room was covered with a plain barrel vault, whereas the sacristy was given a quadripartite rib vault.[30]

The next room within the east range was the chapter house. Typically, this was quite a large and imposing chamber of considerable architectural pretension, befitting its role as one of the most important liturgical spaces in the entire abbey complex. Its detailed characteristics will be examined in the context of the Welsh examples later; here only the barest of information is required.[31] Entrance from the cloister was by way of a symmetrical facade, most often featuring a central doorway flanked by a pair of unglazed windows.[32] At several English sites, notably at the northern houses of Fountains and Furness, the facade took the form of a richer triple-arched arcade.[33] Internally, Cistercian chapter houses almost invariably featured ribbed stone vaults.[34] It might be argued that 'universal' preference was for a nine-bay (three by three) arrangement, in which the central bay was framed by the four slender piers carrying the quadripartite vaulting, as seen in the ground plan of Clairvaux (fig 39).[35] In such an arrangement, the tripartite division of the entrance facade was neatly reflected in the three north–south bays.[36] It was also an arrangement which (on the Continent at least) could quite readily be contained within the width of the range. In the British Isles, however, a definite preference emerged for chapter houses set out on an east–west axis.[37] Although the three north–south bays were frequently retained, they were now developed along the length of the building as 'aisles', with anything up to four bays projecting beyond the outer wall of the range itself. The result was often the creation of a very attractive early Gothic space, the architectural qualities of which were no doubt seen as an appropriate backdrop for the importance of the daily chapter meeting.[38]

Immediately to the south of the chapter house, again contained at ground level, was the inner parlour. Traditionally, this narrow rectangular chamber is seen as the place where the monks were allowed to converse on matters of importance without breaking the cloister rule of silence.[39] Yet in recent years there has been a growing appreciation that the primary purpose of the parlour may have been that of an office for the prior.[40] It is also possible that the room was the place where essential business might be conducted with lay outsiders, otherwise excluded from chapter meetings. In Wales, evidence for the parlour comes from Basingwerk, Neath and Tintern. At Basingwerk there were doors on both the east and west sides of the room (fig 84), as found also, for instance, in the twelfth-century ranges at Buildwas, Fountains, Rievaulx and Roche.[41] It might be concluded from this that the parlour served as much as a passage through the range as it did a discrete room. In contrast, at Neath and Tintern – where the east ranges were remodelled in the second quarter of the thirteenth century – the only access to the parlour seems to have been from a doorway on the cloister side. Clear traces of this doorway may be seen at Tintern, where the jambs were adorned with clustered shaft groups. There is rather less to go on at Neath, but the suggestion that the parlour was vaulted in two aisles must be viewed with some caution, given the rarity of such an arrangement.[42]

The narrow bay often found next to the parlour contained the day stair to the monks' dormitory. This was the position of the original mid-twelfth-century day stair at Fountains and at Rievaulx, and the same arrangement may well have occurred at Tintern, and possibly at Neath.[43] Later, the preferred position for this stairway, at least among the majority of Cistercian houses in England and Wales, was apparently in the south-east corner of the cloister, effectively in the angle between the east and south ranges. It usually climbed in a single flight alongside the inner wall of the east range, a pattern known from Beaulieu, Buildwas, Fountains (as rebuilt), Hailes, Jervaulx and Netley.[44] In Wales, there is a good example of the arrangement at Basingwerk, where the surviving lower steps may be seen extending out into the east walk of the cloister.[45] A similar design was to feature at Neath after the rebuilding of the eastern and southern claustral ranges in the early thirteenth century. Here, too, there are traces of a stone handrail rising against the wall of the east range.[46] At Tintern Abbey, where the eastern and northern ranges were again rebuilt in the early thirteenth century, the approach to the day stair from the north-east corner of the cloister was by way of a large recessed archway with plain chamfered jambs. Inside, the singe bay with a quadripartite rib vault served as a lobby. From this point, two further archways opened northwards. The smaller example on the west side, rebated for a door, led to an outside yard. The taller arch to the east gave access to the day stair itself. The roof beyond was graduated so as to accommodate the rise in the stair.[47]

In spite of this eventual preference for the position of the day stair among the majority of British Cistercians abbeys, in mainland Europe the popularity of the older design was to continue. Examples of stairs rising within the width of the east range to a point near the centre of the dormitory floor are to be found, for instance, in the early thirteenth-century east ranges at Villers and Val-Saint-Lambert in Belgium, at Eberbach in Germany and Casamari in Italy.[48] It is interesting, too, that after the fourteenth-century rebuilding of the east range at Valle Crucis Abbey, access to the day stair was once more from a doorway in the cloister facade (fig 125).[49]

Returning to the general layout of the east range, the next element was a transverse passage running through the width of the building, known as a slype. Rarely treated in other than a utilitarian fashion, it served to connect the great cloister with the infirmary and other buildings to the east. Occasionally, as at Neath and Tintern, there was a doorway in the south (or north) wall of this passage, connecting with the long single chamber which completed the ground-floor arrangements within the range. The final chamber itself was usually vaulted in two parallel 'aisles',[50] and frequently extended to five, six, or even more bays, thus projecting well outside the confines of the cloister

proper. Among the longer examples known from England, one might think of Fountains (seven bays), Beaulieu (eight), Sawtry (eight), Forde (twelve), Stanley (twelve) and Furness (thirteen).[51] At many sites, of course, it is clear that the fabric represents more than one phase of construction.

At Tintern, for example, when the east range was first built in the mid-twelfth-century, its comparatively thin walls ran for a total length of no more than 32m from the north transept (figs 26 and 124). The room at the northern end (unvaulted at this stage) probably included the warming house, with traces of an early hearth uncovered in a later window embrasure (fig 126).[52] Between the late twelfth and mid-thirteenth centuries, however, the range was at first extended by around 15.2m and then remodelled, with the walls thickened and vaults introduced to the main ground-floor chambers. The now extended northern room was of six bays, in which the plain chamfered quadripartite rib vaults sprang from moulded corbels set into the walls, and were supported centrally on a row of octagonal columns with moulded bases (fig 124).[53] Also of mid-thirteenth-century date, though rather better preserved, is the southern end of the east range at Neath (fig 123).[54] The room here was five bays in

length, and again featured four-part rib vaults, this time supported on four circular columns with moulded bases and capitals and, again, on moulded corbels set into the walls. There is a further example of the same room to be seen at Basingwerk Abbey in north-east Wales (fig 25). Marginally smaller in scale than those at either Tintern or Neath, it was never aisled or vaulted. A row of beam holes survives in the east wall, showing the position of the timber floor to the room above.[55] Lastly, although considerably more ruinous, there are indications of a long vaulted chamber at the southern end of the east range at Margam Abbey. Here, two isolated pier bases which seem to be *in situ* indicate that the range as a whole extended for at least 61m from the south transept (fig 25).[56]

At all these sites, both within and beyond Wales, the essential architectural character of the room was that of an undercroft, though there have been different views on the precise use to which it was put by Cistercian communities. In older British literature, particularly in the works of Hope and Brakspear, the most common explanation given to the space is that of accommodation for the novices. As pointed out by Brakspear in his account of the east range at Stanley, this view was largely 'a result of argument by

125 *Valle Crucis Abbey: east range, cloister facade. The rubble construction around the doorway to the book room (left) dates from the original thirteenth-century range. The ashlar to the south (right) belongs to the extensive phase of rebuilding in the early to mid-fourteenth century. The pointed doorway at the centre of the composition is the entrance to the chapter house.*

Photograph: *Cadw, Crown Copyright*

126 Tintern Abbey: east range, early fireplace in east wall of the monks' day room. The first stone claustral ranges at Tintern were probably raised in the middle years of the twelfth century. Much of the east range fabric was to survive, heavily encased in thirteenth-century masonry. Today, towards the southern end of the later day room, at the base of a lancet window embrasure, are the exposed remains of a twelfth-century fireplace, almost certainly indicating the position of the original warming house.

Photograph: Cadw, Crown Copyright

exhaustion', though supported by the queen of Sicily's description of Clairvaux in 1517, when the novices were certainly located in this area.[57] Nonetheless, during the twelfth and thirteenth centuries, it seems just as likely that the east range undercroft was multi-purpose in character. If any one specific use were to be sought, then the space might best be seen as a day or common room for the choir monks.[58] Surely, then, it would have been here that the brothers carried out some of the manual tasks prescribed for the monastic life in the Rule of St Benedict, allocated to them on a daily basis by the prior.[59]

Almost the entire upper floor of the east range was occupied by the monks' dormitory, very often the largest single conventual space in the abbey complex.[60] For the Cistercians (as for other orders), the great size of the chamber was determined by the Rule of St Benedict, which stated that wherever possible the monastic community should sleep in one place.[61] From the first, in fact, a common dormitory was seen as an essential element in the white monk abbey plan, as revealed by the statute of *c* 1113–19 stipulating those buildings which had to be in place before a community could be sent out to colonize a new location.[62] By the mid-twelfth century, the order had begun to raise particularly impressive examples, their scale in turn determined by the length of the east range itself. At Clairvaux, for instance, the twelfth-century dormitory was of three vaulted aisles, extending to over 79m in length.[63] At Eberbach in Germany the highly impressive mid-thirteenth-century dormitory remains in its entirety, measuring approximately 73m from north to south. Another vast white monk dormitory survives at Poblet in Spain, here up to 87m long.[64] On at least one occasion, the scale and sumptuousness of the chamber appear to have gone too far. Hence, in 1192, the General Chapter ordered the community at Longpont to rebuild its dormitory 'according to the form and custom of the order'.[65] In the meantime, across much of Europe, the Cistercians often chose to cover their dormitories with stone vaults.[66] In Provence, for instance, the comparatively small late twelfth-century examples at Sénanque (Vaucluse), Silvacane (Bouches-du-Rhône) and Le Thoronet (Var) all featured barrel vaults.[67] Elsewhere, rib vaults supported by a central row, or rows, of relatively squat piers were widespread and commonplace. There are handsome thirteenth-century survivals at Le Val (Val-d'Oise) in France, at Eberbach in Germany and at Alcobaça in Portugal.[68] Many more can be traced as ruins, including a massive structure at Chaalis (Oise) to the north east of Paris, four bays in width.[69]

On the basis of the surviving evidence, it seems unlikely that any British Cistercian abbey featured a dormitory with the level of opulence seen in some of the grander European examples. Often, where the east range as a whole was designed for a rather smaller community, the dormitory could be less than 46m long, as at Bindon, Buildwas and Cleeve, and at Grey and Jerpoint in Ireland.[70] In Wales, a comparatively modest dormitory of just this type was built at Basingwerk Abbey in the early thirteenth century. Measuring 32m long by 7.9m wide internally, the creases of its roof can be seen in early illustrations depicting the south transept wall before its collapse (fig 84). A section of the east wall still survives almost to eaves level, featuring three broadly splayed lancets.[71] Elsewhere across England and Wales, it was far from unusual for one of the more successful houses to build a dormitory on a considerably more ambitious scale. At Roche the room was around 49m long, at Fountains it was 54m, at Forde no less than 64m, at Rievaulx 75m, and at Furness as much as 79m.[72] Among the larger Welsh examples were those at Tintern, Neath and Margam. Despite the lack of extensive fabric evidence, it is clear that the dormitory at Tintern must have been approximately 50m long internally. The crease of its high-pitched roof is still preserved against the outer face of the north transept (fig 124).[73] At Neath the dormitory was closer to 56m long,[74] and at Margam the room reached at least 61m.[75] There is even less to go on at Dore, but there are certainly two phases of roof line to be seen against the north transept wall, and it has been suggested the dormitory itself may again have exceeded 61m in length.[76] All these English and Welsh examples were covered with wooden roofs. In fact, the absence of stone vaulting was probably the most striking difference between British Cistercian dormitories and those on the Continent.

As noted earlier, one means of access to the dormitory was by way of the day stair, usually accommodated within or alongside the east range itself. Yet during the night the monks filed in and out of the room through a doorway in the adjacent transept arm, with the best Welsh survivals to be found at Tintern (fig 124) and Valle Crucis. This doorway connected with the night stair, which ran down into the body of the church. There is a good example of this stair to be seen in the south transept at Neath, where there is also a carved handrail set into the west wall.[77] As to the internal arrangements within Cistercian dormitories, these are unlikely to have varied in any significant way from those of the mainstream Benedictine communities.[78] A typical layout would see the beds set out in two long rows against the outer walls, with perhaps some 1.2m of space allocated to each bed.[79] On this basis, the dormitory at Basingwerk might have housed up to about fifty monks, and those at Tintern and Neath may have accommodated around eighty and ninety respectively. At all sites, there were probably clothing chests and other storage lockers along the centre of the room. Following the Rule of St Benedict, the monks were expected to sleep fully clothed, their conduct governed by a strict sense of order and decorum.[80]

It is important to bear in mind that in the later Middle Ages significant changes were often made to these once vast open chambers. In particular, as the size of communities fell, and as demands for privacy increased, partitions were introduced into the dormitory at many Cistercian houses across Europe. Despite efforts by the General Chapter to contain the trend, white monks as individuals came to expect the private space afforded by a small room or cell.[81] Just how soon this began to happen in Britain is uncertain. It is interesting to note, however, that the English Benedictines found it necessary to condemn the introduction of partitions into dormitories from the late thirteenth century onwards – 'a sure sign', says Barbara Harvey, 'that the innovation was already becoming popular'.[82] Indeed, this was probably no less true of the white monks. One Welsh site where this can definitely be expected is Valle Crucis. The full extent of the thirteenth-century dormitory is unknown, although excavations suggest that the east range itself may have extended for at least another 12.2m to the south of the surviving building.[83] During the mid-fourteenth century the range was comprehensively rebuilt, the masons employing a good-quality ashlar throughout (fig 125).[84] As completed, the dormitory space was much reduced from earlier Cistercian expectations, measuring just 20m in length. It was lit by a series of small glazed windows with trefoil heads in each of the side walls, and it seems likely that the room was soon, if not from the first, divided up into a small number of private 'apartments'.[85] The actual partitions might have taken the form of curtains hanging on bars, or might have been more substantial timber screens attached to the walls.[86] The practice was almost certainly more common than can now be demonstrated at virtually all the Welsh abbeys.

The final element within the overall layout of the east range was the monks' latrine. This was generally sited well away from the church, often projecting eastwards from a point near the far end of the range, and ideally located over a channel which could be flushed by running water.[87] Invariably, the latrine facilities themselves were reached directly from the dormitory. In France, good examples of such arrangements may be seen at L'Escaladieu, Royaumont (Val-d'Oise) and Sénanque, to name but three.[88] Among the better survivals in England are those at Cleeve, Fountains, Hailes, Jervaulx, Rievaulx, Roche and Sawley.[89] As for the evidence from Wales, at Tintern the two-storey latrine block projected at right angles from the north-east side of the dormitory. Located on the upper floor, the privies were positioned over the stone-lined drain, which can still be seen.[90] The basic arrangements were very similar at Valle Crucis, though here the latrine was set against the gable end of the rebuilt east range, accessed by a central doorway in the south wall of the dormitory.[91] A more unusual pattern is found at Neath, where a seven-bay latrine block with a vaulted undercroft was positioned a short distance away from the range proper (fig 25). It was built on a parallel alignment, standing above a drain running north–south. The link between the dormitory and the latrine block was carried on a two-bay arcaded bridge with quadripartite rib vaults.[92] Interestingly, latrines running similarly parallel to the range are found at two other houses which began their existence as Savigniac communities, those at Byland and Furness.[93] The trait was not, however, exclusive to this group. Back in south Wales, at Margam – Cistercian from its foundation – three vaulted undercroft bays extend outwards from a point near the southern end of the east range, an indication of another bridge link from the monks' dormitory to the latrine.[94]

THE SOUTH (OR NORTH) RANGE

The range of buildings running parallel to the nave of the abbey church was always dominated by the choir monks' refectory. Of particular interest, and in contrast with most other mainstream monastic orders, the Cistercians generally constructed their refectories at right angles to the alignment of the range. This arrangement became one of the key hallmarks of their developed abbey plan (fig 122). It allowed for both the warming house and the main kitchen to be included within the body of the range itself, one to the east of the refectory and the other to the west.[95] In Wales and the March (figs 25 and 26), some evidence for the buildings within the south (or north) range as a whole survives or has been excavated at Basingwerk (south), Cymer (south), Dore (north), Neath (south), Tintern (north) and Valle Crucis (south), with recent geophysical evidence for the layout also recovered at Whitland (south).[96]

The refectory is to be considered in more detail in a later chapter.[97] Here, one of the key points to note

is that it was another of those buildings which, for the early Cistercians, had to be in place before a founding colony could be sent out to a new location.[98] To begin with, it may well have been some form of temporary wooden structure, with examples possibly represented among the growing number of timber buildings which have now been recognized through excavation at several British sites, notably at Fountains and Sawley.[99] Interestingly, as individual communities then began to build in stone, they initially chose to follow the common east–west monastic arrangement for their refectories.[100] The decision to swing the orientation of the building through 90 degrees may well have emerged during the rebuilding of St Bernard's Clairvaux, perhaps about 1150.[101] In any case, from the third quarter of the twelfth century, Cistercian refectories set out on a north–south axis began to appear in growing numbers across Europe. The earliest British examples are known from the 1160s and 1170s, at Byland, Fountains, Kirkstall and Rievaulx.[102] Nothing quite this early is to be found at any of the Welsh sites, though, as will be seen when picking up the theme later, several north–south examples of the thirteenth century do survive.

In the revised plan of the south (or north) range, as noted earlier, the warming house (*calefactorium*) was positioned in the gap created between the refectory and the east range.[103] Other than the kitchen, this was the only room in the abbey with a fireplace. The fire was kept burning over the winter months,[104] and here amid the daily round the brothers were allowed to warm themselves in their moments of rest and leisure. Another significant use of the room was that of periodic blood-letting (the *seyney*), something which each monk might expect to go through up to four times a year.[105] Occasionally, the Cistercians also used the warming house for the shaving of the tonsure, as well as for mundane tasks such as greasing winter boots and drying clothes.[106] In general terms, the room was close to square in plan, with the fireplace(s) frequently set into one of the lateral walls. This is the type found, for instance, at Burgundian Fontenay,[107] at Fossanova in Italy,[108] and at Byland, Croxden, Fountains, Furness, Hailes, Kirkstall, Rievaulx and Waverley in England.[109] At Clairvaux, by contrast, if the early eighteenth-century ground plan is taken as a clear representation, the warming house had a central hearth surrounded by four small piers, presumably supporting a cowl above the fire itself (fig 39). One of the best survivals of this arrangement can be seen at the French abbey of Longpont, dating from the early thirteenth century.[110]

There is another good example of the type at Tintern. It has already been noted that in the twelfth-century layout at Tintern the warming house was probably located within the east range (fig 126). Its relocation to the north range coincided with the general reconstruction of the abbey's claustral buildings during the first half of the thirteenth century.[111] In its newly completed form, the warming house was entered from the north cloister alley through a doorway of two enriched orders. Inside, the first part of the room was of two rib-vaulted bays, towards the end of which stood the fireplace. The great hooded cowl was carried on four square piers, with arched passageways to the left and right allowing for access on all sides. North of the fireplace, the room continued beyond the range proper, at this point covered by a simple projecting gabled roof.

As for the other abbeys in this survey, the approximate positions of the warming house at Dore, Neath and Valle Crucis are known, even if very little of the fabric survives at any of these sites (figs 25 and 26).[112] At Basingwerk, on the other hand, the evidence, although more extensive, is rather puzzling. As laid out in the twelfth century, the south range at Basingwerk probably housed an east–west refectory. The warming house at this time may well have been located towards the southern end of the east range. When, in the mid-thirteenth century, the refectory was rebuilt on a north–south alignment, there was definitely no room to accommodate a warming house on its east side (fig 25). Instead, it has been suggested that it may have been located in an extension to the east range. This extension was of four vaulted bays, divided into aisles of equal width by a row of three piers with water-holding bases. The location of the fireplace is uncertain, and in any case the room as a whole was extensively remodelled in the later Middle Ages.[113]

Understandably, in order to avoid the risk of fire, Cistercian warming houses everywhere tended to be covered with stone vaults. An additional chamber sometimes existed above the vault, presumably accessed by way of the day stair. Clear signs of such a room are to be seen at Fountains, where its dry and secure nature suggest it may well have served as the muniment store.[114] A similar room at Rievaulx was known as 'the house for evidence' at the time of the suppression,[115] and further possibilities have been identified at Byland and Croxden.[116] The same explanation seems every bit as plausible for a small vaulted chamber above the warming house at Tintern.[117]

On the opposite side of the refectory, the last chamber in this range was the principal abbey kitchen. It was positioned so that meals could be served directly not only to the choir monks, but also to the lay brothers, whose refectory was situated in the adjacent west range.[118] Taking their lead from the Rule of St Benedict, on Sunday mornings Cistercian communities appointed several of their number to act as kitchen helpers and refectory servers for the week.[119] Sadly, few of the kitchens in which they worked stand today in a very complete state, though there are good examples at Chorin in Germany, Poblet in Spain and Bonport in France.[120] Others of a more ruinous but nonetheless informative nature may be seen at Villers in Belgium, and at Byland and Fountains.[121] None of the Welsh sites retains much evidence in this regard, although the basic form of the kitchen may be seen at Basingwerk, Tintern and Valle Crucis (figs 25 and 26). The Tintern kitchen retains the hatch through which food was passed to the monks' refectory.[122]

THE WEST RANGE

The St Gall plan suggests that in the ideal Benedictine monastery the range on the west side of the cloister should be given over to storage, with cellarage on the ground floor and a larder above.[123] In the eleventh and twelfth centuries, this suited the majority of Cluniac and Benedictine communities well, at least up to a point. Almost invariably, the monastery's great storehouse was indeed located on the ground floor of the west range, where it was under the charge of the cellarer, that 'universal provider of all foodstuffs' for monks, guests and servants alike.[124] The pattern was followed at the abbeys and priories built by the newer Augustinian congregations over the course of the twelfth century.[125] It is less easy to define a single general usage for the arrangements made on the upper floor of the range by these various groups. In time, two principal patterns seem to have emerged: either the space served as a private apartment for the abbot or prior, or it was given over to accommodation for important guests.[126]

The Cistercians also developed a two-storey range on the west side of the cloister, but for them it had to be tailored to a very specific need. Given the nature of white monk communities during the twelfth and thirteenth centuries, in which an often very large body of lay brothers (conversi) required discrete accommodation,[127] the architectural solution was to adapt almost the entire west range in such a way that it might serve this purpose. At ground-floor level, although a storage element was retained in one section of the range, much of the space was taken up by the lay brothers' refectory. The whole of the upper floor served as their dormitory.[128] In similar fashion to the Benedictines, a cellarer was appointed to take charge of the monastery stores, but the Cistercians also gave him the responsibility of overseeing the work and conduct of the lay brothers.[129] To this end, he generally had a small office located within the west range.

Far and away the most significant survival of a Cistercian west range is the recently restored example at St Bernard's Clairvaux (figs 16 and 39). Built *c* 1140–60, it was originally fourteen bays long. Both the ground and first floors were divided into three aisles by two rows of octagonal piers supporting the stone vaults.[130] Other good examples may be seen, for instance, at Longuay (Haute-Marne) and Noirlac in France, at Chorin and Maulbronn in Germany, and at Alcobaça in Portugal.[131] As it happens, though, the largest twelfth-century lay brothers' quarters to be found anywhere in Europe are located at Fountains.[132] At this well-known Yorkshire site, the range in question was initially laid out during the abbacy of Henry Murdac (1144–7). It was conceived on a singularly impressive scale, the building reaching some 76.2m in length, with a dormitory large enough to have accommodated up to 140 lay brothers. It is a surprise, then, to see that within three decades, Murdac's early range was to be replaced by an even larger building, raised in the time of Abbot Robert of Pipewell (1170–80). As completed, the new range was of truly colossal proportions, this time extending to approximately 91.4m. The ground floor was rib-vaulted in twenty-two double bays, the ribs springing from a single row of central piers without capitals.[133] Beginning at the northern end, the first

two bays were walled off to form the outer parlour. This was where the cellarer was authorized to speak with up to two *conversi* at a time, and where he might meet visitors to discuss matters of estate, trade, or other business.[134] The next six bays provided storage space, followed by two more serving as the entrance to the cloister. The remaining twelve bays were occupied as the lay brothers' refectory. A hatch in the east wall of one of these bays connected directly to the kitchen. Again, the whole of the upper floor served as the lay brothers' dormitory. Near the southern end, positioned above the River Skell, the brothers' latrine projected westwards out of the range.[135] Elsewhere there are ruins of other substantial west ranges across England at Byland (eighteen bays), Furness (sixteen), Jervaulx (thirteen), Kirkstall (eleven) and Waverley, and at Melrose in Scotland.[136] At Beaulieu the restored northern half of the range stands in a very complete state, and at Rufford in Nottinghamshire the entire ground floor survives more or less intact.[137]

In Wales and its immediate border, there is some evidence for the west ranges at Basingwerk, Dore, Strata Florida, Valle Crucis and Whitland (figs 25 and 26), but the best-preserved examples are to be seen at Neath and at Tintern.[138] The Neath range dates from the late twelfth to early thirteenth centuries and in places stands to roof height (figs 21 and 127). Like the rest of the abbey, it is built of local Pennant sandstone, with dressings of imported creamy white

127 Neath Abbey: west range, from the south west. With its origins in the late twelfth century, this is the best surviving example of Cistercian lay brother accommodation in Wales. Much of the ground floor was occupied by the brothers' refectory, with their dormitory above. After the demise of the lay brotherhood in the fourteenth century, the building would have been given over to other uses.

Photograph: *author*

Sutton stone.[139] Externally, it measures approximately 53m from north to south, and is divided into ten bays by once prominent buttresses (now much robbed out). The ground floor was lit by a single large lancet set into the west wall of each bay. The upper floor had smaller lancets in both the east and west walls, together with a triplet in the south gable. Internally, the four southern bays on the ground floor are likely to have served as the lay brothers' refectory. This area was covered with quadripartite rib vaults, as demonstrated by the bases of the central octagonal piers and by several corbels which remain in the side walls. Some of the corbels were decorative, with that in the north-west angle featuring a trumpet-scalloped capital. Moving northwards, the next bay was cut off from the remainder of the range by solid walls to either side. Tunnel-vaulted, and with doorways at the east and west ends, it was essentially a passageway through the range, thus forming the main entrance to the cloister. A two-storey porch was added to the front of this passage in the fourteenth century. Beyond this bay, much of the northern half of the ground floor was probably given over to cellarage. First, there were three more rib-vaulted bays, the last of which could be accessed from both the cloister and from a porch on the west side, suggesting it may have served as the outer parlour. The final two bays were enclosed by a partition wall across the range, with another subdividing wall apparently introduced during the fourteenth century. As built, the entire upper floor of the range was presumably taken up by the lay brothers' dormitory. There are indications that their latrine opened off the south-west corner, while a stair down into the cloister, and thence to the church, might be expected somewhere in the northernmost bay.

At Tintern Abbey, the structural history of the west range is clearly complex, and archaeological excavation might be required if there is to be any chance of unpicking the full sequence of events.[140] One of the more puzzling elements, for example, is the base of a twelfth-century doorway now standing isolated near the centre of the building. It is set at a distinct angle, and seems to bear little if any relationship to anything in the subsequent fabric history. In its current form, the range dates largely from the first half of the thirteenth century. At the southern end, aligning with a point near the middle of the west cloister alley, was the outer parlour. The next four bays all seem to have been vaulted in single spans, without any central support. Initially, these bays may well have served as the lay brothers' refectory, with a doorway in the east wall providing direct access to and from the kitchen. A change in the character of the masonry beyond this point suggests

more than one phase of construction, and further modifications were to be introduced during the second half of the thirteenth century, possibly coinciding with a fall in the number of lay brothers within the abbey community. The southern part of their refectory, for example, was cut off by a partition wall, and at much the same time a porch was added to the outer parlour.

At the other Welsh abbeys where there is evidence for the form of the west range, there is much less fabric to be observed above ground. Beginning with Strata Florida, although some of the wall faces lie exposed near the northern end of the range, the full extent of the building has never been investigated.[141] The most notable feature is the small turning staircase located in the north-west angle, connecting with the south-west corner of the nave. This may well represent the route followed by the lay brothers when entering the church from their dormitory. Similarly, at Whitland, despite one or two prominent upstanding fragments, the full layout of the west range is difficult to interpret with any confidence. This said, an outline has been put together based on the recent programme of investigations at the site, one which includes the suggestion of a porch on the west side of the cloister entrance (fig 26).[142]

The west range at Valle Crucis Abbey was excavated by Lawrence Butler in 1970, and its low walls later laid out for public display (fig 26).[143] Built in the early years of the thirteenth century, and measuring approximately 33.5m in length, it was definitely something of a modest structure when compared to the lay brothers' quarters at many English sites. Of particular interest, the excavations revealed that the range could well have been one of the first stone buildings to be erected at Valle Crucis: its north-west corner apparently pre-dates the angle of the abbey church at this point.[144] On the basis of the fabric uncovered, Butler suggested that the northern end of the range was used as the cellar and felt that the southern part of the building may have included a day room for the lay brothers in addition to their refectory.[145] Centrally placed in relation to the cloister, a passage ran through the middle of the range, presumably serving as the outer parlour. As at Neath, a porch was added to the west face of this passage, perhaps in the fourteenth century. At much the same time, the southern end of the range seems to have been reduced in length. Instead, a small new room was introduced at the south-west corner of the cloister, interpreted by Butler as the cellarer's office.[146]

Finally, at Dore and at Basingwerk, no more than minor wall fragments now remain to view. The southern end of the eventual west range at Dore was correctly identified by Roland Paul in his various works on the abbey.[147] Recently, however, Harrison has put forward the possibility of a two-phase sequence, positing an earlier and somewhat narrower west range sitting alongside a smaller twelfth-century cloister.[148] At Basingwerk, the equally scant remains appear to mark the general positions of the eastern and southern walls.[149] In fact, given the extent of loss here, and taking into account the building traditions of this part of the Welsh border, it is of interest to speculate whether the range may have included an element of timber framing.[150] The same could have been true at Strata Marcella, where there is nothing to be seen above ground, but where there is documentary evidence for the removal of framing from the site soon after the suppression.[151] Again, if the west range was ever fully completed at Cymer in the north west, then it was probably a timber-framed structure sitting on low sill walls.[152]

One further characteristic of Cistercian west ranges which has not hitherto been mentioned is the occasional presence of a so-called 'lane', described by Aubert as the 'ruelle des convers'.[153] Where it occurred, this rectangular open space separated the range proper from the back of the west cloister walk. Both for Aubert and for Dimier, the lane was sufficiently commonplace for it to be included as an element within their 'standard' Cistercian plans.[154] Indeed, as one very clear mark of its significance, a lane most definitely featured in the mature mid-twelfth-century claustral layouts at both Cîteaux and Clairvaux (fig 39).[155]

Such lanes were often relatively narrow spaces, appearing (in plan at least) as no more than passages. Clairvaux is the best French example of the form, though it also appeared at twelfth-century Aiguebelle and Fontfroide, and again at the great thirteenth-century royal abbey of Royaumont.[156] Much the same pattern featured at Fossanova in Italy and at Alcobaça in Portugal.[157] British examples of the type are known from Beaulieu, Boxley, Buildwas, Byland, Rufford and Sawley in England,[158] and from Mellifont in Ireland.[159] In Wales, the best example of a lane in the form of a comparatively narrow passage is that at Neath,[160] though one might argue for something similar having existed at Basingwerk,[161] and perhaps in the mid-twelfth-century layout at Tintern (figs 25 and 26).[162] In strong contrast to this pattern, the width of the lane at Cîteaux was such that it could almost be described as a courtyard. The same could be said of the arrangements at Clairmont in France, Villers in Belgium, Eberbach in Germany,[163] and Kirkstall and Stanley in England.[164] There is the possibility that similar courtyard forms also existed at the Welsh abbey of Whitland and

at Dore in Herefordshire.[165]

The exact purpose of the lane, together with the reasons for its occurrence at some sites and absence at others, has been much debated over the years. At the end of the nineteenth century, there was a rather vague suggestion that it was intended merely to cut off the sound of the 'noisy trades' carried out by the lay brothers within the west range itself. But as Hope pointed out, 'this will not do'.[166] A more plausible proposal was put forward as early as the 1880s by J T Micklethwaite, who wondered whether the lane may in fact have served as the lay brothers' cloister.[167] This particular view has continued to find its supporters,[168] who further point out that when a lane is absent from a site, there is sometimes a separate cloister court or yard for the conversi, as identified against the outer face of the west range at Fountains.[169] More recently, Fergusson has sought to explain the differences by reference to the changing nature of the relationship between choir monks and lay brothers in the second half of the twelfth century. The absence of lanes and enclosing walls at Fountains and Rievaulx may, he says, reflect 'the more egalitarian values associated with the earlier period'. But as tensions between the two groups grew later in the century, there was an ever increasing need for more formal segregation.[170]

BUILDINGS TO THE EAST AND WEST OF THE CLOISTER

Apart from the church and the three main ranges of claustral buildings, two other significant structural complexes were located close to the centre of the Cistercian abbey plan. Broadly speaking, one of these lay to the east and south east of the cloister, the other to the west. There was greater diversity in these areas than has been seen so far, and it is consequently more difficult to refer to any form of 'standard' arrangement. Basically, however, the buildings which eventually came to be grouped immediately beyond the east claustral range included the monks' infirmary and the abbot's private lodging. Over on the west and south-west sides of the cloister, there was sometimes a lay brothers' infirmary, and virtually all Cistercian communities made sufficient provision here for the housing of guests of differing status.[171]

The best place to consider those buildings found to the east of the cloister is in the chapter which examines the Welsh material in more detail; only the basic characteristics need be introduced at this point.[172] To begin with the infirmary complex, the general position and planning of the buildings raised by the Cistercians was in essence little different from those earlier adopted by other monastic orders. Hence, from the late eleventh century the infirmary area within Cluniac and Benedictine monasteries had come to be dominated by a large open hall, with associated structures such as the infirmarer's lodging, a chapel, kitchen, latrines and a bath-house all grouped around it.[173] In time, a second or lesser cloister emerged between these buildings and the main east claustral range. From the middle years of the twelfth century, elements of this same pattern began to appear at white monk houses across Europe. Once again, the predominant feature in the complex was a large hall, although the small infirmary cloister which took shape outside the east range was equally characteristic.[174] By way of summing up Cistercian developments, one might look for example at the expansive nature of the infirmary complex at Clairvaux, as depicted in Milley's 1708 ground plan and views of the site (figs 16 and 39).[175] In addition, fairly typical Cistercian infirmary arrangements can be observed in a late sixteenth-century drawing of the abbey of Dunes in Belgium.[176]

The Cistercian decision to locate the abbot's private accommodation somewhere adjacent to the infirmary complex was in marked contrast to the position adopted by Benedictines, Cluniacs and Augustinians, who all tended to house their abbots within or beyond the west claustral range.[177] Moreover, it should be remembered that the provision of such a discrete abbatial lodging conflicted with early Cistercian custom, which decreed that the abbot should sleep in common with his monks in the main dormitory.[178] This, however, was a position the order found very difficult to maintain. As early as the 1150s, a precedent for the change was set at Rievaulx, when a separate apartment was built at right angles to the east claustral range for Abbot Ailred, on account of his acute illnesses.[179] Within a very few years, probably before 1170, the abbot of neighbouring Fountains had built himself a private lodging in a block adjoining the monks' latrine.[180] The same trend was to increase substantially over the course of the thirteenth century, as witnessed by the remains identified, for instance, at Buildwas, Byland, Furness, Jervaulx, Kirkstall, Roche and Waverley.[181] By the middle of the fourteenth century, separate abbatial residences – often of considerable architectural pretension – had become commonplace throughout the entire order,[182] a trend which will be picked up again in Wales.

Turning, for the moment, to those buildings located broadly around the west and south-west periphery of the cloister, the first structure to consider is the lay brothers' infirmary.[183] The existence of a separate facility for the *conversi* is implied in a statute of 1189.[184] Examples are certainly known from a number of larger abbey sites across Europe, though the exact position may not have been rigidly fixed. At Clairvaux, for instance, it is clear from Milley's plan and drawings of 1708 that the lay brothers' infirmary complex was located south east of the west range. The buildings included a hall, a separate dormitory, a chapel and an infirmarer's lodging.[185] At Villers, by contrast, there was a six-bay infirmary hall for the use of the *conversi* running parallel with the main west range, linked to it by a latrine building.[186] In England, examples of lay brothers' infirmaries are known from Fountains, Jervaulx and Waverley (each at the south-west corner of the west range), and at Roche (to the south of the range). All were substantial aisled halls, of between three and eight bays.[187] No such building has yet been uncovered at any of the Welsh abbeys.

Also situated somewhere to the west of the cloister, in the area known as the inner court, was the accommodation set aside for guests of different standing.[188] The Rule of St Benedict had enjoined that all guests should be welcomed 'as Christ himself',[189] a duty willingly embraced by the early Cistercians. Indeed, for the order's founding fathers, a guest house was one of the essential buildings which had to be erected before a colony could be sent out to occupy a new location.[190] In due course, specific charge of the guest house was given to one of the monks, assisted by at least one lay brother.[191] At Margam Abbey, for example, the names of several possible guest house monks are known from their appearance as witnesses to charters around the turn of the twelfth century, where they are identified as *hospitati* or *hospitales*.[192] At much the same time, Gerald of Wales freely acknowledged the Cistercian reputation for generosity to guests: 'The monks of this order', he wrote, 'incessantly exercise, more than any others, the acts of charity and beneficence towards the poor and strangers'.[193]

Although guests of widely varying social standing might expect to find food and accommodation at any Cistercian abbey, there is clear evidence to show that they were segregated according to status. Again, it was Gerald of Wales who was quick to complain when the monks at Strata Florida placed him 'in the public hall among the common guests and the noise of the people'.[194] He was, after all, very much aware that such halls could be rowdy places, having earlier encountered a brawl in the common guest house at Margam, during which a young man had lost his life.[195] In the late thirteenth century, the guests at Beaulieu Abbey were effectively graded as they arrived at the gatehouse. Those of sufficient rank were given preferential treatment, not only in terms of lodging, but also in the quality of the food at their table.[196]

At monastic sites, generally, an architectural distinction in the provision of accommodation made for high- and low-status guests may go back to the early ninth century, as witnessed by the two separate complexes shown on the St Gall plan.[197] However, determining the extent to which such a pattern may have occurred at Cistercian houses across Europe is hampered by a lack of surviving evidence, and by too few modern studies of this element in the white monk plan.[198] Hence, despite the survival of a late twelfth-century guest building to the west of the church and cloister at Clairvaux (fig 39), the full nature of the accommodation offered to the abbey's numerous contemporary visitors is unclear.[199] Elsewhere in France, other isolated examples of early Cistercian guest accommodation may be seen at Fontenay and at Quincy (Yonne),[200] and foundations of buildings have also been uncovered through excavation at Silvacane and at Vauclair.[201] In Belgium, a surviving thirteenth-century guest house at Villers has recently been studied in detail by Coomans, who also examines the function of the building within a broader complex of structures.[202]

Among the English houses of the order, it is possible to point to several clear examples of social distinction in the provision of guest accommodation. The arrangements at Fountains Abbey, in particular, are of considerable interest. Here, in the 1160s, a pair of guest houses was constructed close to the River Skell, just to the north west of the lay brothers' infirmary.[203] Both of these were two-storey buildings, vaulted at the lower level, and having a self-contained apartment (comprised of hall, chamber and latrine) situated on either floor. Although each suite of rooms was evidently intended for the abbey's higher-status guests, the differences in quality between the east and the west buildings and between the upper and lower floors meant the monks could offer four separate grades of accommodation. Moreover, within a decade, the Fountains monks were to extend their guest facilities still further, with the addition of a large seven-bay aisled building to the north of the existing apartments.[204] This building is known only from a plan, but it looks much more like the sort of open communal guest hall in which a reluctant Gerald of Wales found himself lodged when staying at Strata Florida (c 1200).

On the basis of excavations in 1902, something comparable to the Fountains arrangements seems to have existed at Waverley. Brakspear identified what

he called a superior guest house, of c 1200, located immediately to the west of the abbey church. A little way to the north west of this he also found a larger hall, of marginally later date, intended 'for those of inferior position'.[205] Again, at Kirkstall in Yorkshire, a more recent programme of excavations has uncovered a long sequence of development in the abbey's guest accommodation.[206] In the early thirteenth century, a four-bay timber-framed hall, equipped with its own service wing, was raised to the west of the church. This was rebuilt in stone before the end of the century and further improved with the addition of a two-storey chamber block at the north end, the whole clearly intended for guests of higher status. The abbey's poorer visitors would have been housed in a second guest hall, newly built on the western side. The whole complex was further modified through into the fifteenth century, by which time the west hall had been adapted for other purposes. Elsewhere in England, where indications of the guest accommodation survive at all, it tends to be the higher-status element.[207] This is true of Buckfast, for example, where the remains of the early fourteenth-century guest house represent one of the largest medieval halls known from Devon and Cornwall.[208] Similarly, at Stoneleigh Abbey in Warwickshire there is a fine two-storey guest range, completed c 1349–50, set alongside the inner gatehouse.[209] And at Furness, it is again the foundations of a high-quality fourteenth-century guest house which may be seen to the north east of the abbey church.[210]

As for the evidence from Wales, there are, as already noted above, documentary references of c 1200 to communal guest halls at both Margam and Strata Florida. Moreover, when considering the importance of many of the known visitors to the Welsh abbeys – King John, for example, stayed at Margam on a number of occasions during the early thirteenth century – it seems perfectly reasonable to assume that higher-grade guest accommodation would have been available at the majority of sites.[211] It is unfortunate, then, that so little remains to be seen today. The best evidence comes from Tintern, where beyond the west front of the abbey church the guest house area was first uncovered as part of the clearance works in the early twentieth century. The site was further explored in the early 1970s and more fully excavated by Dr Paul Courtney in 1979–81 (figs 122 and 128).[212]

Furthest away from the church, the most prominent survival is that of a large two-storey rectangular building, its western end hidden under the modern road which bisects the abbey precinct at this point. The walls are of high-quality masonry, featuring a deep outer plinth. Within, traces of several octagonal piers show that the basement was stone-vaulted. The building was presumably constructed in the late twelfth or early thirteenth century, and might tentatively be interpreted as a higher-status guest house.[213] To the east, Courtney's excavations were focused upon a large four-bay aisled guest hall, measuring some 21m long by 15.5m wide, dated by comparison with that at Kirkstall to the thirteenth century. There was an open hearth at the centre of the hall proper, whereas the northernmost bay seems to have been screened off from the remainder, either forming a service area, or possibly a chamber block. Other structures lay around the northern, western and southern peripheries of the hall, and are likely to have included a kitchen and possibly a brewhouse. The hall itself had probably fallen out of use by the mid-fifteenth century, as indicated by the signs of metalliferous industrial activity over the former floor area. Nevertheless, the range immediately along its western side was refurbished, and a new block raised further to the south. Both of these were residential structures and may still have been intended for guests, or possibly for 'corrodians', those long-term secular guests or inmates who came to feature at a large number of monasteries during the later Middle Ages.[214]

A rather different perspective on the Cistercian approach to hospitality comes from what is known of a considerable number of the Welsh abbots in the late fifteenth and early sixteenth centuries. In particular, these men were highly praised for their generous attitude towards guests, most notably in an extensive body of poetry produced by grateful native bards.[215] In one work addressed to Abbot Dafydd ab Ieuan (c 1480–1503), for example, Guto'r Glyn wrote: 'Of Valle Crucis Abbot good, Whose full-stocked tables ever groan'.[216] Again, Lewis Morgannwg's picture of Neath in the time of Abbot Leyshon Thomas (c 1510–39) ran in very much the same vein: 'In this compact retreat will be found warmth of hospitality, And welcome banquets'.[217] As for Basingwerk under Abbot Thomas Pennant (c 1481–1522), Tudur Aled tells us: 'Besides the cells of the monks there are new houses for guests who are said to be so numerous they have to be accommodated for meals in two sittings'.[218]

Alas, at these and other Welsh abbeys where the bards provide similar indications of late medieval hospitality, it is far from easy to identify specific buildings set aside for the accommodation of the guests themselves. One suggestion which has sometimes been put forward is the farmhouse sitting to the west of the abbey church at Cymer (fig 25).

This clearly incorporates a once grand four-bay hall featuring a cusped arch-brace roof, now dated through dendrochronology to the mid-fifteenth century, but it may be better interpreted as the abbot's private lodging.[219] Another possibility arises at Valle Crucis, where around the turn of the fifteenth century the northern half of the monks' dormitory, on the upper floor of the east range, seems to have been converted to serve as a set of apartments for the abbot's private use (see fig 157).[220] In such circumstances, it is perfectly possible that the remainder of the former dormitory space was given over as guest accommodation. Indeed, the poet Guto'r Glyn spent his last years as a resident guest of Abbot Dafydd ab Ieuan. He died at the monastery in 1493, 'aged, lame, blind and deaf', and was buried there by his great patron.[221]

The situation at Basingwerk in the early sixteenth century is even more intriguing. Today, it must be said that at first sight there is nothing obvious among the surviving buildings that might be interpreted as either guest accommodation, or lodgings for the abbot himself. One possible candidate, however, is the long rectangular range that extends for more than 42.7m east from the south-east corner of the main complex (fig 25). Much reduced from its original form, the building has sometimes been dismissed as post-medieval, probably overlying the site of the former monastic infirmary.[222] Only the stone-built ground-floor level now survives, though early photographs show that it was in fact half-timbered and of conventional box-frame construction.[223] The frames in the side walls featured large curving braces, clearly intended for architectural display, and the roof was supported on both crown-post and arch-braced trusses. In sum, there can be no doubting the medieval origin of the range. And, although stylistically earlier than the abbacy of Thomas Pennant, there is at least a possibility it served as guest accommodation in this period.

THE WIDER ABBEY PRECINCT

Although the church and main claustral buildings were at the heart of any Cistercian abbey plan, they covered a relatively small percentage of the total ground area. The monastic precinct as a whole was a very much larger entity.[224] Indeed, at many of the wealthier British houses, the precinct often extended to more than 20.2ha,[225] its limits usually determined by a high stone wall through which access was gained by one or more gatehouses. The walls and gates ensured a high degree of seclusion and tranquillity, representing a physical and conceptual boundary

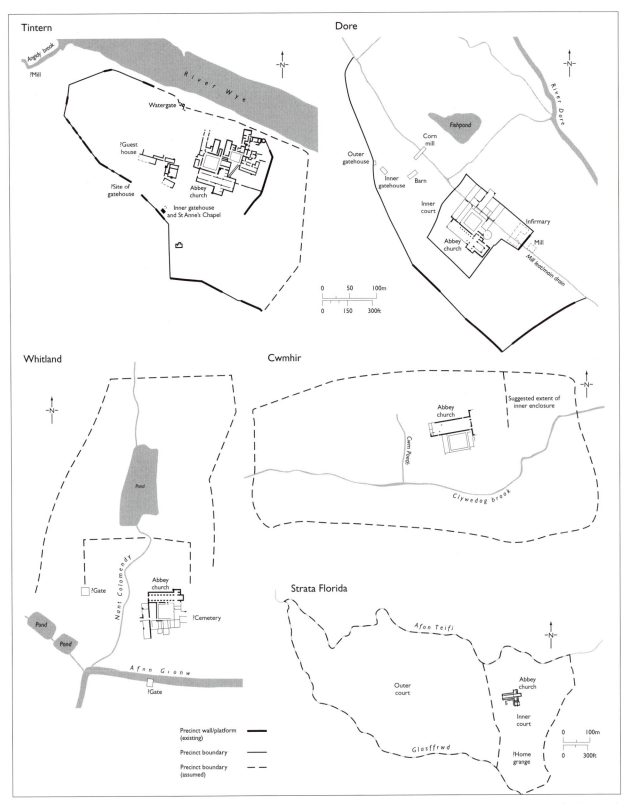

128 *Cistercian abbeys in Wales, precinct plans: Tintern (after Robinson 2002a); Dore (after Stone 1997); Whitland (after Ludlow 2002); Cwmhir (Sian Rees); Strata Florida, at half the scale of the others (David Austin).* Drawing: Pete Lawrence, for Cadw

between the commitment to the monastic life within and the affairs of the secular world outside.[226] In this, as with much else of course, there is very little practical difference from most other religious orders. Nonetheless, it is of interest to note that the creation of a clearly demarcated boundary was an early priority for the Cistercian founding fathers, as witnessed by the statute of *c* 1113–19 stipulating the buildings necessary for a new plantation.[227] A gatehouse or porter's lodge is given as one of the few indispensable elements in the complex, which in turn implies the need for at least some kind of formal boundary enclosure from the outset of the foundation. Thereafter, given the symbolic role of the gatehouse as the entry point to the abbey, the duties of its keeper were always to remain a high priority within the daily life of the house.[228]

The great precinct at Clairvaux makes a good starting point, for we are fortunate in having, from an anonymous early thirteenth-century writer, a delightful description in which the literary device of following the river course flowing through the monastery is used as a way of presenting its various elements.[229] In fact, the precinct wall at Clairvaux was raised as part of that general enlargement of the abbey buildings which began in the 1130s. It was completed, as Arnold of Bonneval tells us in book two of the *Vita Prima* of St Bernard, 'with unlooked-for speed, embracing in a great sweep the whole extent of the monastery'.[230] The wall, which is well depicted in Milley's 1708 plans and drawings (figs 16 and 39), enclosed an area of around 30ha.[231] The buttressed walls surrounding the full abbey complex at Burgundian Cîteaux made for another substantial enclosure, as seen in the late seventeenth-century engraving of the site by Brissart (fig 15).[232] Other early illustrations revealing elements of the medieval precinct in France exist, for instance, for La Ferté, Le Val (Val-d'Oise), Pontigny, Vaucelles and Vauluisant (Yonne),[233] but there can be no finer early depiction of a mature Cistercian precinct than the late sixteenth-century drawing of Dunes in Belgium by Pierre Pourbus.[234]

In England, it is estimated that up to two-thirds of all white monk precincts are today represented, at least in part, by earthworks.[235] Rarely, however, do such earthworks depict a single phase in the development of the abbey in question: they are much more likely to be an archaeological palimpsest, in which post-suppression features are sometimes just as significant as those of the monastic centuries. With this in mind, one of the largest English Cistercian precincts was undoubtedly that at Rievaulx, developed in three main stages and calculated to have covered as much as 37.2ha in its

final form.[236] The complete circuit of the enclosure can be traced in the present landscape, with a considerable length of its wall surviving on the north-east side of the complex. Another massive example is to be found at Bordesley (Worcestershire), where two principal phases of development have been identified.[237] Here, to judge from the magnificent series of earthworks which mark the site, the eventual precinct extended to some 36ha.[238] Only marginally less imposing were the enclosures at Fountains (where a development sequence has again been untangled) and at Furness. Both occupied about 28.3ha, and in each case stretches of the surrounding walls continue to stand up to 3.3m high.[239] Lower in the scale, at around 17.7ha in extent, the precinct at Beaulieu might be said to represent the middling rank of houses.[240] Below this, there is no shortage of examples of a somewhat smaller scale.[241] At the Wiltshire abbey of Stanley, for instance, the full enclosure is unlikely to have exceeded 15.7ha;[242] at Cleeve (where it was surrounded by wet moats) it was closer to 11.3ha;[243] at Kirkstead it covered 8.5ha;[244] and at Boxley in Kent it was apparently just 6.9ha.[245]

Scholars have long been in agreement that the main entrance to English Cistercian precincts was generally by way of a paired arrangement of gatehouses.[246] The precinct wall itself was broken by the outer gate, leading to a small enclosed court or lane. At the far end of the court stood the great or inner gatehouse, with further passage controlled at this point by the abbey's porter. Such a pairing of gates has been traced, for example, at Beaulieu, Byland, Cleeve, Croxden, Fountains, Furness, Kirkstall, Roche and Tilty.[247] This said, little survives to attest to the actual form of outer gatehouses from any period, leading to the suggestion that they must have been rather ephemeral structures of no great architectural pretension. As for inner gatehouses, at least twenty-five examples survive in varying states of completeness,[248] the earliest dating from the 1170s.[249] All were clearly quite significant buildings, usually arranged over two storeys. And, as Fergusson has shown,[250] the model adopted in the north of England at the end of the twelfth century involved a degree of sophisticated planning, with the form devised so as to allow for discrete access to the two main areas of the precinct. On the one hand, any traffic making for the agricultural and industrial areas of the outer court would have entered an open bay or lobby at the end of the gate-passage, and from there moved on towards the relevant enclosure via an archway in one of the side walls.[251] On the other hand, a visitor heading for the inner court, towards the guest house area and the west front of the abbey church, would have passed directly through the middle of the gate-passage. In this direction, traffic was controlled by one of two gates operated by the porter: a wider example with double doors for vehicles, a smaller one for pedestrians. The porter himself was usually accommodated in a chamber to one side of the gate-passage. The upper floor of the gatehouse was often used as the abbey's court house and exchequer, a place where business with the outside world might be conducted.[252]

One building very closely associated with the entrance to Cistercian precincts was the gatehouse chapel, the *capella extra portas*. Although such chapels were not specified in the Rule of St Benedict, or in the early statutes, they occurred at white monk houses right across Europe.[253] Just over twenty examples are known from England, either through documentary or surviving fabric evidence.[254] They were often free-standing buildings, located in the walled lane somewhere between the outer and inner gatehouses. As to purpose, traditionally it has been assumed these chapels were used by abbey dependants, by guests and wayfarers, or by women and other groups who were for some reason not allowed within the inner court.[255] Recently, Dr Jackie Hall has challenged such blanket assumptions, and has pointed to rather more varied patterns of usage over time, including quasi-parochial functions, as pilgrimage centres, and as burial chantries for certain patrons.[256] One of the very best English survivals can be seen at Kirkstead in Lincolnshire, dating from *c* 1230–40. Others are to be found at Coggeshall, Furness, Hailes, Merevale, Thame and Tilty.[257] As one interesting variation, at some abbeys there was a chapel on the upper floor of the main gatehouse, as at Beaulieu and Whalley, and possibly at Cleeve.[258]

Before moving on to consider what may be said of the wider precinct elements at the Cistercian abbeys in Wales and the March, it is worth summarizing general opinion on the three key internal components. By now, it should be abundantly clear that at the heart of the whole complex lay the abbey church and main cloister buildings, accessed through the outer parlour in the west range. As part of the same central zone, most scholars would also include the infirmary and the abbot's lodging, both positioned on the secluded eastern side of the great cloister. The second component was the inner court, the area to the immediate west of the abbey church. Among the principal buildings to be found here would have been those for guest accommodation, together with a range of service structures such as the brewhouse, the bakehouse, granaries, stables and probably a smithy.[259] To reach the inner court enclosure,

pedestrians and vehicles would have needed to pass through one of the gates in the main passage of the inner gatehouse, under the control of the abbey's porter. The third and final component of the precinct was the outer court, most often the largest single area in the complex. Here one would expect to find various agricultural and industrial buildings linked to the well being of the abbey's economy at large. At most sites, for example, a mill or mills would have featured within its bounds. In addition, the outer court usually contained a selection of storage and processing structures, such as a tannery, and perhaps something akin to the great wool house known from Fountains.[260] The spatial arrangements and scaling between these three precinct components were rarely fixed, being largely determined by the natural topography in which the community was obliged to operate. The Cistercians, of course, are well known for the scale of their water-engineering works, one of the principal characteristics of their abbey sites.[261] It seems, too, that the presence of large open areas of pasture and water meadow was another distinctive feature of the order's precinct topography.[262]

Almost all the Welsh sites retain at least some element of their wider precinct topography, though this is not an area that has received much detailed attention in terms of modern landscape archaeology. Indeed, the quality of survey information lying behind the existing group of precinct plans is variable (fig 128). The work on Tintern, for example, dates back to Brakspear's initial investigations at the site, though much has since been refined (figs 20 and 31). In all, it is calculated that the enclosure covered approximately 10.9ha.[263] At Cymer, whilst no overall plan has been compiled, Williams has shown that some aspects of the precinct layout can be reconstructed using a survey of 1794.[264] More recently, work on the precinct at Dore Abbey indicates that its overall extent was about 19.4ha.[265] As regards the other recent investigations at Cwmhir, Whitland and Strata Florida (fig 32), only the Whitland findings have yet been published in full. In this case, a combination of landscape, antiquarian and cartographic sources leads to the suggestion that an inner enclosure of some 4ha was in turn surrounded by an outer precinct boundary encompassing approximately 15ha.[266] Similarly, the proposed boundary limits at Cwmhir are put forward largely on the basis of topographical features in the present landscape.[267]

As in England, it seems very likely that many of the Welsh Cistercian precinct boundaries were of stone. Much if not all of the enclosure at Tintern was definitely surrounded by stone walls, with substantial sections surviving on the southern and western sides. At Dore some fragments can still be seen, though it is unclear if the wall continued along the banks of the Dore river (fig 128).[268] Once again, stone walls are to be suspected at the Glamorgan houses of Neath and Margam,[269] with confirmation in the latter case coming from post-suppression documentation: in 1543 lands at Margam were described as being 'within and without the walls' of the former monastery.[270] At Basingwerk, too, if one can rely on a literary source, walls apparently existed.[271] At Strata Marcella, a boundary of some form can be seen today as an earthwork, though it is less clear if this definitely represents a wall.[272]

Among the earliest references to the existence of gatehouses at the Welsh abbeys, Gerald of Wales observed in 1188 the large numbers of poor who daily congregated outside the 'monastery gate' at Margam.[273] Half a century later, in a charter of about 1240, there is mention of the 'abbey gate' at Basingwerk.[274] More specifically, it is known from documents dating to the years immediately before the suppression that the movement of traffic through the precincts of at least three of the Welsh houses was still controlled by a 'great gate'. At Margam, for instance, the reference to the great (or inner) gatehouse is known from 1532.[275] Likewise, two years later, a great gate was noted at Llantarnam. This example continued to stand through to the late eighteenth century, when it was described by William Coxe as 'a beautiful gothic gateway … still called Magna Porta'.[276] The reference to the great gate at Tintern dates from February 1536, at which time Abbot Richard Wyche appointed a lay servant to the 'office of our porter and keeper of our gaol and garrett'. The porter's duties were to include the closing of the great gate at night, and he was to have sufficient timber, stone and iron railing in order to maintain in good repair the gate and the gaol.[277] Other, less precise, documentary references to Welsh gatehouses are also known from later medieval centuries. In the fifteenth century, the poet Guto'r Glyn referred to the food and charity offered to both rich and poor at Strata Florida's 'southern gate'. For the same site, there is a post-suppression reference to a 'chamber on the gate' called Penny Perth.[278] It is tempting to link this with the building which can be seen to the immediate west of the church in the 1741 Buck engraving of the abbey (fig 3). Finally, at Grace Dieu, a gatehouse is known to have been occupied by corrodians at the time of the suppression.[279]

In terms of fabric evidence, the only sites where the remains of precinct gatehouses can now be found are Tintern and Neath. At Tintern, in fact, there are fragments of two gatehouses (fig 128). First, on the River Wye frontage – and once approached from boats up a cobbled ramp – there is a broad segmental archway, with double-chamfered jambs and head. The rebate with a drawbar hole on the landward side shows that the doors opened inwards. The gate structure as a whole was once substantially larger, with the east side much reduced, and the western half incorporated in a later building.[280] Secondly, the abbey's 'great gate', referred to in 1536, may survive in part as St Anne's, a private house situated on the rising ground to the south west of the church and cloister. On the north side of the house there are traces of a thirteenth-century two-bay vaulted gate hall, featuring moulded capitals and the springers for chamfered ribs. A chamfered doorway at ground level may have led to the porter's chamber.[281] At Neath, some distance to the north west of the main abbey complex, are what are probably the remains of the inner or great gatehouse, now standing isolated alongside a main road.[282] These would have been the rooms to the northern side of the gate-passage. The room on the west side, with doorways on the south and east, may have been the porter's lodge. The room to the east features a twelfth-century eastern doorway and open arches flanking the gate-passage to the south. The gate-passage itself ran where the pavement and road now lie. Entering from the west, all traffic would have passed under an outer arch. Carts would then have progressed through a large gate near the middle of the passage and pedestrians through a smaller gate alongside. The Sutton stone jamb of one of these central gates may still be seen.

Loosely defined, there is evidence for gatehouse chapels, or *capellae extra portas*, at three sites: Margam, Tintern and Strata Florida. At Margam, on the edge of the hill overlooking the north-west side of the abbey church, there is a ruinous chapel, known as Hen Eglwys, or Cryke chapel. Measuring about 20.4 by 7.3m, it is single-cell structure with a two-light traceried west window and a fine Perpendicular east window with moulded jambs.[283] There is one doorway on the south side and another under the west window. Thomas Gray thought it might have been built about 1470, in which case the west window was almost certainly reused.[284] Given the topography, the chapel is unlikely to have sat within the precinct boundary, but Evans was in little doubt that it served as the abbey's *capella extra portas*.[285] Yet more intriguing is the situation at Tintern, where the gatehouse chapel appears to have been located above the south side of the gate-passage and today survives incorporated within the fabric of St Anne's house (fig 128).[286] Dating from the thirteenth century, the most prominent survival of this chapel is the three-light plate tracery east window. Internally, the otherwise rather plain appearance of this window is enhanced by applied shafts, on which the capitals bear stiff-leaf foliage. In the head, quatrefoils are set within moulded circles. There is also one original lancet surviving in the north wall. Not long after the suppression, and certainly by 1568, the chapel was converted to a dwelling house. The name St Anne's goes back to at least this time.[287] For the third site, Strata Florida, there is documentary evidence to show that a chapel for the local population had been built 'in the monastery' by the time of the suppression. There were two priests to serve the people as chaplains.[288]

Other than the already mentioned guest accommodation at Tintern, there is little of substance that can be said about the nature of the inner or outer courts and their buildings at any of the Welsh sites, though it is true that elements of water engineering are not uncommon. At Whitland Abbey, for example, the extensive earthworks defining the precinct area at large include evidence for watercourses, fishponds and several dams (fig 128).[289] At Dore, the course of a mill leat can be traced, and the positions of two mills in the outer court have been suggested (fig 128).[290] Again, to the north of the main complex at Margam there is a large pond, for long thought to have been a medieval feature. On the west side of this are the remains of a mill, known as Cryke mill, which may well have been monastic in origin.[291] At Tintern, the most likely position for the abbey's home mill lies just outside the known precinct boundary, near the point where the Angidy brook flows into the Wye (fig 128).[292] Elsewhere, one of the more puzzling precinct features is the great eleven-bay stone barn to the north of the site of the church and cloister at Llantarnam Abbey. It is usually ascribed to the Middle Ages, though this view does not go unchallenged.[293] By way of conclusion, it is of interest to note that when John Leland saw Strata Florida in the late 1530s, he observed that the 'base court or camp afore the abbay is veri fair and large'. This may have been a reference to the inner court (fig 128), or perhaps to the precinct as a whole.[294]

CHAPTER 9

CLOISTERS AND CLOISTER ARCADES

Such was the dominance of the cloister (*claustrum*) in all medieval monastic planning that the very significance of this fact can be easily overlooked. Remarkably, its four-square architectural form was adopted by virtually every religious order across Europe, almost without question and regardless of any specific ideals. In sum, the cloister is rightly seen as the single most inventive and 'enduring achievement' of monastic building.[1] The central open court or garth served as a haven of tranquillity at the heart of the abbey complex, entirely cut off from the outside world.[2] On all four sides there were covered passages, known as cloister walks or alleys. Fronted by handsome rhythmic arcades of a generally uniform character, these walks served the practical function of linking church to chapter house, chapter house to refectory, and so on. They also provided an ideal backdrop to processions and other ritual events.

PHYSICAL AND CONCEPTUAL QUALITIES OF THE CLOISTER

The basic principles behind the form of the monastic cloister were already well established by the early ninth century, as witnessed by the plan of the Carolingian abbey of St Gall.[3] In particular, the St Gall plan shows the cloister on the south side of the church, tucked into the angle of the nave and its adjoining transept. This turned out to be the pattern followed by the vast majority of all medieval religious houses, and, as already noted, it was far and away the most common arrangement among abbeys of the Cistercian order. It was true, for example, of Cîteaux and Clairvaux (figs 15, 16 and 39), and also seems to have been the case at most of the early foundations in Burgundy and neighbouring Champagne.[4] On occasion, however, certain factors led to the abandonment of the preferred norm. Either through choice, or the lack of it, communities were sometimes prepared to opt for a cloister to the north of the church. This occurred quite early at Cîteaux's elder daughter at Pontigny, for instance.[5] Even so, were one to speculate that fewer than

20 per cent of all white monk houses followed this pattern, it may not be too far from accurate. Northern cloisters were certainly unusual among the Cistercian abbeys of England, with those at Buildwas, Forde and Stanley, and likewise at Melrose in Scotland, very much exceptions.[6]

In Wales and its border, the cloister was positioned to the south side of the abbey church in up to nine of the eleven recorded instances (figs 25 and 26), with some evidence to suggest that Llantarnam should be added to the list.[7] The two best-known exceptions are Tintern (figs 20 and 122) and Dore, where it is generally assumed that topographical factors underlay the decision to place the cloister to the north of the nave. There are indications to suggest the same was true at Aberconwy, and again at its replacement site at Maenan.[8] As to the proportions of the cloister garths themselves, it can be seen from the ground plans that they varied as much in Wales as elsewhere, though with something close to a four-square layout predominating (figs 25 and 26). In any case, the proportions were occasionally modified over time, in line with rebuilding programmes on the churches and monastic buildings.

Although far from specific to the order, the character of an individual Cistercian cloister was to a great extent determined by the nature of its arcades. In Wales attempts to envisage this have to be made from only a few disarticulated fragments, but it is much more apparent when looking at better-surviving examples on the Continent. It was the arcades in particular which gave a constant rhythm to the layout of the court. In visual terms they tended to conceal the structure of the ranges behind, giving the impression of a unified architectural ensemble, sometimes to buildings of varying date and design.[9] The general point is very well made when one looks at the surviving arcades in the cloister at Fontenay.[10] By the time permanent stone buildings were under construction here, we can be confident that well-proportioned cloisters had become essential components within the Cistercian plan. As discussed earlier (*see* chapter 5), the church at Fontenay was probably completed in the late 1140s, with the east range usually dated to *c* 1150–5. One assumes the cloister walks and arcades followed. The basic framework of the arcades was determined by the buttressed piers marking the principal bay divisions. On all four sides of the garth, each of the eight bays was then subdivided into paired arches, carried centrally on coupled free-standing columns. It was a formula that occurred widely across late twelfth- and early thirteenth-century Europe.[11] At Fontenay, as elsewhere, the strength of the buttressing to the arcades was required to support the internal vaults. Here they took the form of pointed barrels, though with the precise detail varying from one side of the garth to another. Fontenay also serves to remind us that for many Cistercian communities the original cloister layout, complete with its arcades, was deemed perfectly acceptable for the entire Middle Ages.[12]

One other notable physical characteristic of Cistercian cloister arcades is the comparative rarity, especially in the twelfth and thirteenth centuries, of figure sculpture.[13] On the one hand, considering the architectural aesthetic which seems to have defined white monk buildings in general, this is almost to be expected. Then again, we might remember that just when the order was finding its feet, Romanesque cloister sculpture had begun to flourish, not least in Burgundy. In this context, one simply cannot overlook Bernard of Clairvaux's *Apologia* of *c* 1125, that hard-hitting satire addressed to his Cluniac friend, William of St Thierry.[14] Having condemned the 'immense height' and 'immoderate length' of certain monastic churches, Bernard went on:

> What is more, what can justify that ridiculous array of grotesques in the cloister where the brothers do their reading – I mean those extraordinary deformed beauties and beautiful deformities? What place have obscene monkeys, savage lions … what is the meaning of fighting soldiers or hunters sounding horns? You can see a head with many bodies and a multi-bodied head. Here is a quadruped with a dragon's tail, there an animal's head stuck on a fish. There is a creature beginning as a horse and ending as a goat … With such a bewildering array of shapes and forms on show, one would sooner read the sculptures than the books … Ah, Lord! If the folly of it all does not shame us, surely the expense might stick in our throats.[15]

The *Apologia*, and this passage in particular, is much debated. Yet one is hard pressed to underplay its long-term significance on Cistercian cloister design, or at least the significance of the stance it might be taken to represent. The message was further underlined in one of the order's earliest statutes, which decreed:

> Sculptures are never permitted; and the only paintings allowed are on the crosses, which must themselves be only of wood.[16]

Moving on from the purely practical attributes of the four cloister walks, there is no doubt that, for all Cistercian communities, the entire space was charged with symbolic meaning. Indeed, throughout the order's literature it is not unusual to find the courtyard and its central garden associated with the heavenly paradise, though it should be borne in mind that the metaphor of cloister as paradise could be further extended to the entire abbey site, as well as to the monastic life itself.[17] Nevertheless, seen in this broad context, the cloister served not only as a physical entity, but also as an imagined or abstract space, the meaning of which might be enhanced by the symbolism of processions and by various other liturgical rites carried out within its confines. It would be impossible to argue that there was anything exclusively Cistercian in such ideas; they are no less applicable to the Benedictine cloister or even to the cloister of the Augustinian canons. Yet at the same time, the importance of white monk cloister liturgy should not be underestimated.

Processions were quite definitely one element of this, even if their occurrence was always minimal, especially when compared with Benedictine or Cluniac liturgy. In so far as can be judged, by the second half of the twelfth century there were just three major annual processions in a Cistercian monastery. One was held on Palm Sunday, the second at Candlemas and the third on Ascension Day.[18] On each of these occasions, the procession began in the church. From the presbytery, the entire abbey community moved out into the cloister, walking around the east, south and west walks, before returning into the church at the west end. The symbolism of the Palm Sunday procession, for example, is very clear, imitating as it did Christ's triumphal entry into Jerusalem.[19]

Aside from these three annual processions, the cloister also featured in the weekly Sunday rite known as the *benedictio aquae*, which took place before high mass.[20] As part of this rite, one of the monks aspersed the cloister and the principal monastic buildings with water blessed immediately for the purpose. Cassidy-Welch sees this as another example of the Cistercian attitude towards the 'sacred nature of the claustral landscape'.[21]

CLOISTER ARCADES OF THE TWELFTH
AND THIRTEENTH CENTURIES

Little can be said of British Cistercian cloisters before about 1170. At sites such as Fountains, Rievaulx and Waverley in England, or Margam and Tintern in Wales, a fair amount is known about the disposition of the surrounding buildings, but the precise character of the cloister garth and its arcades escapes us. Archaeologists and architectural historians tend to fall back on an assumed temporary arrangement, with the not unreasonable suggestion that the arcades themselves may have been of timber, if they existed at all.[22] It is with the last three decades of the twelfth century that our knowledge begins to increase, particularly in the case of houses in the north of England, though several southern examples are also recorded.

At Byland, Furness, Newminster, Rievaulx and Roche, for example, stone cloister arcades seem to have been erected in the 1170s or soon after.[23] Typically, in the by then ubiquitous monastic design, all of these northern arcades were set out as rows of paired colonnettes supporting a sequence of round-headed or pointed arches. At Rievaulx, a small section of the arcade (c 1170–5) was rebuilt in the north-west corner of the cloister in the early twentieth century.[24] It reveals a pattern of alternating circular and octagonal coupled columns, with a four-shaft grouping at the corner angle. The capitals feature a variety of waterleaf and scalloped designs, and the arches themselves are round-headed. The moulded cornice presumably took a wall plate carrying the timbers of a lean-to roof.[25] Similarly, the Roche arcades again featured paired columns with waterleaf capitals, though in this case the arch heads were of pointed form.[26] Of particular interest, the *ex situ* fragments from Roche indicate a change in the design of one of the arcades part of the way along its length, presumably a reflection of a slightly prolonged constructional sequence. Yet there is no sign of any concern on the part of the abbey community, and it is certainly a pattern encountered elsewhere. The most elaborate of these late twelfth-century northern arcades occurred at Fountains, where the work is thought to have been completed during the abbacy of Robert of Pipewell (1170–80).[27] In this case, the twined colonnettes were of black Nidderdale marble, supported on moulded bases, and with capitals bearing leaf decoration. There were particularly rich mouldings to the outer face of the trefoil-headed arches, in turn surmounted by a prominent hood mould. Away from Yorkshire, in southern England, a late twelfth-century arcade of a somewhat different design was discovered by Brakspear at Waverley Abbey. Interestingly, in this case Purbeck marble bases supported an alternate arrangement of coupled circular columns and single octagonal ones.[28]

Hitherto, nothing to compare with this late twelfth-century English cloister material has been identified at any of the Welsh Cistercian sites. Nevertheless, setting aside the possibility that wood may have been used on occasion, it seems logical to accept that the earliest arcades are likely to have followed the prevailing general pattern, that is with paired columns, arches with rounded heads, and lean-to roofs.[29] In support of this, it may be noted that both coupled capitals and bases are known from an early cloister arcade at Whitland Abbey, even if its precise date is uncertain.[30] Further, in 1889 Stephen Williams recorded finding evidence of twined capitals and bases from the cloister arcades at Strata Florida.[31] Here, however, the description of the capitals (as well as the accompanying illustration) indicates that they carried a narrow band of dog-tooth decoration, suggesting that it is just as likely to be a work of the early thirteenth century.

Twin-columned cloister arcades were, in any case, to remain very popular with the British Cistercians well into the thirteenth century, despite the inevitable stylistic advances made in line with early Gothic taste. There is evidence for one such arcade a little way beyond the Welsh border, at Buildwas in Shropshire (fig 18). The only specific remains on the site today are the narrow dwarf walls surrounding the garth, but a few *ex situ* capitals and other fragments reveal the character of the early thirteenth-century detail.[32] Among other examples known from across England, it will be sufficient to mention Beaulieu in Hampshire and Stanley in Wiltshire. At Beaulieu, Hope and Brakspear found evidence of open arches and coupled columns featuring moulded capitals and bases, all standing on dwarf walls 0.48m wide.[33] The arrangements identified by Brakspear at Stanley Abbey were again very similar.[34] There is no close date for the work at either site, yet it is unlikely these cloisters were finished much before 1250.

When it comes to thirteenth-century developments in cloister design in Wales and the March, we are on significantly firmer ground regarding the mature early Gothic arcades at Tintern and Dore, both of which have been carefully drawn from *ex situ* fragments (fig 129). The details of these two reconstructions demonstrate that the Cistercians of this south-eastern border region (fig 18) were by now content to give their cloister masons a great deal of free rein, allowing them to experiment with increasingly inventive forms for the arcades.

129 *Cistercian abbeys in Wales, comparative cloister arcade elevations: Dore (after Harrison 1997a); two of the identified forms at Tintern (Stuart Harrison).*

Drawing: *Pete Lawrence, for Cadw*

Dore (thirteenth century)

a)

b)

Tintern (thirteenth century)

At Dore, the thirteenth-century eastern arm of the abbey church was itself a significant early Gothic composition. On its completion, the monks presumably pressed on with the enlargement of their principal cloister buildings, all of which must have been finished by the middle years of the thirteenth century.[35] In other words, during the time of Abbot Stephen of Worcester (*c* 1236–57), the community must have been ready to begin work on new cloister walks and arcades.[36] On the eastern side of the garth, the wall footings for these arcades were identified early on by Roland Paul, though his work makes no

mention of the form of the arcades themselves.[37] In his more recent investigations on the site, however, Harrison has located just enough *ex situ* material to posit the reconstruction of a single bay.[38] This can be projected, albeit tentatively, to give us the overall form of the completed Dore arcades (fig 129). Arch heads of unusual cinquefoil design are envisaged, with mouldings facing the garth, but with plainer work to the rear. A prominent rebate beneath the outer stones was intended to accommodate a second inset layer of arcading, again moulded towards the garth. Each bay may then have been subdivided by tracery, but there is no firm evidence for this. The arcades were carried on groups of three detached shafts whose height is undetermined, although examples of both the trefoil bases and the stiff-leaf capitals survive.[39] Harrison has further identified one other detail relating to these arcades, suggesting that a fragmentary capital, which must have been supported on a cluster of five detached shafts, could well represent the arrangements at the corner angles of the arcades (fig 129).

The new cloister arcades introduced at Tintern Abbey, probably in the mid- to later thirteenth century, proved to be more inventive still. Over much of the previous three to four decades, the Tintern monks had been busy extending and rebuilding their three main ranges of claustral buildings.[40] So extensive was the programme on the east and north ranges in particular that it was probably necessary for the builders to sweep away any existing twelfth-century cloister arrangements. Whether the monks had been prepared to lose the use of their enclosed walks for an extended period is perhaps a moot point, but in any case the arcades on all four sides of the garth were now to be laid out completely afresh. From a close investigation of the *ex situ* stonework representing this new Tintern arcading it can be

seen that in essence the design was based upon two separate rows of elegant trefoil-headed arches (figs 129 and 130).[41] These were set out in a somewhat unusual 'syncopated' pattern, in which both the inner and outer rows were independently carried upon free-standing colonnettes, all of which probably featured plain moulded capitals and bases.[42] Although the height of the colonnettes can only be estimated, it was their staggered spacing which highlighted the syncopated rhythm to the composition at large.

Taken as a whole, one cannot deny that the completed thirteenth-century cloister layout at Tintern included a degree of eccentricity. Looking in detail at the *ex situ* fabric, for example, it is clear that the form of the arch heads must have varied around the four sides of the garth, and very probably on the internal and external faces. Indeed, at least five different moulding profiles have been identified, some featuring a semicircular enclosing arch (fig 129b), others not (fig 129a). It is also clear that the builders used at least two different stone types. Yet at the same time, the generally accomplished form of the arcades indicates that the community had chosen to engage a mason capable of producing precisely such a novel design. His confident use of

130 Tintern Abbey: reconstruction of thirteenth-century cloister arcade, looking north west. Despite variations in the precise form around the four sides of the garth, in essence the design of Tintern's thirteenth-century cloister arcade was based on two rows of trefoil-headed arches set out in a staggered, or syncopated, pattern. Here we see the north arcade, probably dating from c 1245–50, or soon after, with the refectory façade behind.

Drawing: *Terry Ball, for Cadw*

micro-vaulting linking the two rows of arches, for instance, may well reflect the fact he had already worked on a similar cloister arcade elsewhere. In common with such potentially earlier examples,[43] the Tintern vault ribs projected diagonally from the rear spandrel of each springer in the inner and outer arcades, thus forming a series of small pointed arches of zigzag plan. Carefully jointed ashlar was then used to form tiny intervening vault webs. At one of the corners, identified from the *ex situ* material, the springer of the internal arcade was supported on a triple-shaft group (fig 129a). From the springer, two richly moulded diagonal vault ribs, set side by side, spanned the gap to the outer arcade.[44] Other than the vaults, one more element of sophistication which occurred in the Tintern design was the clever use of pointed arches in half-bay widths at some point along at least one side of the cloister. This allowed for an alignment in the inner and outer bays of the arcading, thus creating a doorway out into the centre of the garth.

Very few examples of syncopated cloister arcades have so far been identified, although it is reasonably certain that the form originated before the 1220s. The only extant instance of the design does not occur in Britain, but is to be found in the very beautiful cloister garth at the Benedictine abbey of Mont-Saint-Michel (Manche) in Normandy, apparently completed by 1228.[45] There is also a second Norman example, long destroyed, known from an early illustration of the cloister at Saint-Pierre-sur-Dives (Calvados).[46] It is generally agreed that the elegant Mont-Saint-Michel arcades, with their shafts of dark polished stone, moulded bases and capitals, and rich spandrel sculpture, owe something to English architectural influence in Normandy,[47] even if the precise source of inspiration for the layout remains uncertain. As Dr Lindy Grant has suggested, one of the possible routes may well have begun at Lincoln, where it is to be traced to the well-known syncopated wall arcades in the aisles of St Hugh's choir (*c* 1192–1200).[48] In this case, the staggered rows of arches both rest on free-standing colonnettes but are aligned side by side, with no space for an intervening vault. Closer to what is known of later cloister developments are the arcades inside the west porch at Ely Cathedral (*c* 1235), which not only follow a syncopated rhythm but are also linked together by a very small stone vault.[49] Another work recently added to the list of related designs is the probable nave screen arcade recovered from fragments at Keynsham Abbey.[50] Finally, from the Cluniac priory of Monk Bretton in Yorkshire comes one definite English syncopated cloister arcade to set alongside Mont-Saint-Michel and Tintern. With a posited date

of *c* 1230–50, it has again been reconstructed from *ex situ* fragments.[51] These recent discoveries indicate that syncopated cloister designs were almost certainly more common than previously imagined.

At Tintern, considering the comprehensive reworking of the claustral ranges in the first half of the thirteenth century (as noted above), the possibility of the monks being obliged to make do without their covered cloister walks for several decades must at least be acknowledged. In any case, one suspects that the beginnings of the new scheme cannot be pushed back much before 1250. Against this proposal, one may cite the somewhat earlier thirteenth-century date preferred for a Cistercian cloister arcade of similar character at Croxden in Staffordshire. Admittedly this was not of syncopated form, instead featuring a standard arrangement of trefoil-headed arches supported on paired columns with moulded capitals and bases. Even so, the detailing can certainly be compared in broad terms with that at Tintern.[52] There again, among the earliest moulding profiles in the Tintern assemblage, one can pick out quite definite similarities with those of the Salisbury Cathedral workshop of the 1260s.[53] Moreover, other elements in the Tintern design find close parallels in works of the last years of the thirteenth century, and even later.

In sum, by way of a working hypothesis, it may be suggested that Tintern's syncopated cloister arcades were begun no earlier than *c* 1245–50, with probably all four sides of the garth included in the original scheme. This would mean that the southern arcade and its walk must initially have been placed alongside the north wall of the Romanesque abbey church (figs 26 and 103). The key differences in the moulding profiles and other detailing were doubtless related, at least in part, to the complexities within the subsequent constructional history. For instance, with the removal of the old church, and its eventual replacement by Tintern II,[54] the north–south cloister axis was deepened, presumably making it necessary to reposition the southern arcade and to insert linking sections into the east and west sides, perhaps *c* 1300.[55] Finally, we cannot discount the possibility of further intricacy in the layout of the arcades. There may, for example, have been a Collation porch that extended out into the garth, either before or after the construction of Tintern II.[56]

Before moving on, we must recognize that despite the degree of novelty seen in the thirteenth-century cloister arcades at Dore and Tintern, by the standards of contemporary white monk developments on the Continent their basic design was beginning to look old-fashioned. In particular, they were still covered with timber lean-to roofs, whereas the open arcades would have meant the actual cloister walks were left exposed to the winter elements. Meanwhile, in parts of France and elsewhere, the Cistercians had been willing to take part in new experiments in cloister arcading and vaulting. At Heiligenkreuz in Austria, for instance, the vaulted cloister walks had apparently been glazed at the time of their original construction, c 1220–50.[57] Later in the century, as bar tracery came to the fore, yet further possibilities for arcade design were opened up. At the 'Bernardine' house of Noirlac, for example, although the disposition of the late twelfth-century buildings remained unchanged, around 1270 the community decided to update the entire cloister court, a programme which extended well into the fourteenth century. The phasing of the work is reflected in the various tracery patterns around the garth, some of which show evidence of glazing.[58] At much the same time, the monks at Maulbronn in Germany were busy constructing vaulted walks on three sides of their cloister garth. Each bay featured quadripartite ribs, with French-inspired tracery to the arcades.[59]

Across the whole of England, let alone Wales, there is precious little one can discover of Cistercian cloisters of the late thirteenth century to compare with these impressive Continental examples. Netley and Hailes are two sites which, given their dates and royal connections, present themselves as possibilities, but too little evidence has survived to make any informed judgement.[60] It is, then, of especial interest to note the record of a possible traceried cloister arcade at Strata Marcella. The suggestion was made by the excavators of 1890, based on the recovery of fragments of Geometrical tracery showing no sign of glazing, with the cloister seen as the most likely source.[61]

DEVELOPMENTS IN THE LATER MIDDLE AGES

The next group of Welsh Cistercian cloister developments about which anything can be said probably dates from the fourteenth century. First, there is some indication that the cloister walks at Margam were refashioned during the early part of the century, though it is difficult to be sure of the full extent of the programme. From the surviving remains, it is clear that the processional doorway from the east cloister walk into the nave was definitely remodelled around this time. Towards the cloister, the doorway features continuous mouldings rising through to its arched head, the whole set in a rectangular panel with a heavy roll-moulded frame. The spandrels are occupied by beaded trefoils. To the west, and therefore in the south wall of the nave,

there is a second panel, here with quatrefoil tracery to the spandrels. This second panel housed an arched niche or recess, originally divided by a central column with a quatrefoil at the head. Traces of a further panel fragment beyond suggests that similar niches may have run along the entire south wall of the nave.[62] Some confirmation comes from a plan of the abbey made in 1736 (see fig 174),[63] showing an arrangement of eleven such niches set into the wall face. The plan also shows four additional recesses along the wall of the south transept. Although individual seating replacing communal benches would have been unusual, this is what appears to have been introduced, at least in this part of the cloister. Moreover, it may not be pushing the realms of possibility too far were we to assume a near-contemporary refashioning of the surrounding arcades.[64]

It may have been towards the very end of the fourteenth century that new cloister arcades were introduced at the abbeys of Basingwerk and Valle Crucis. Although the fragments on which the Basingwerk reconstruction presented here was based have been lost since the 1920s, they seem to reflect a new and stylish twist on the paired colonnette arrangement of the twelfth century (figs 13, 131 and 132).[65] Instead of the free-standing columns employed in earlier arcades, the Basingwerk masons seem to have carved twin shafts from the same block of masonry, linking them together with a thinner plate or web of stone.[66] In outline at least, the form of the shafts and their bases was octagonal, whereas the mouldings to the capitals ran through in combined unbroken fashion (fig 132). Each bay of the arcade was approximately 0.9m wide, with crisp trefoil-headed arches separated by sunken spandrels. The arrangements in the later medieval cloister arcades at nearby Valle Crucis, first identified from ex situ fragments by Harold Hughes in the 1890s, appear to have been very similar (fig 131).[67] No capitals have been recorded here, however, and the bay spacings were somewhat narrower than at Basingwerk.[68]

Although this new style of cloister arcading retained the slim elegance of the earlier coupled shaft arrangement, it had the advantage of greater strength. Generally known as a 'dumb-bell' pier form, it was particularly characteristic of Irish Cistercian cloisters in the later Middle Ages.[69] Interestingly, there are also numerous ex situ fragments of plain 'dumb-bell' profile piers based on linked polygonal colonnettes surviving among the ruins at Tintern Abbey. These are unlikely to represent replacement arcades for the main cloister, though they could well have come from a late medieval reworking of the infirmary garth

131 *Cistercian abbeys in Wales, comparative cloister elevations: Basingwerk (based on Office of Works drawing); Valle Crucis (after Hughes 1895a).*

Drawing: *Pete Lawrence, for Cadw*

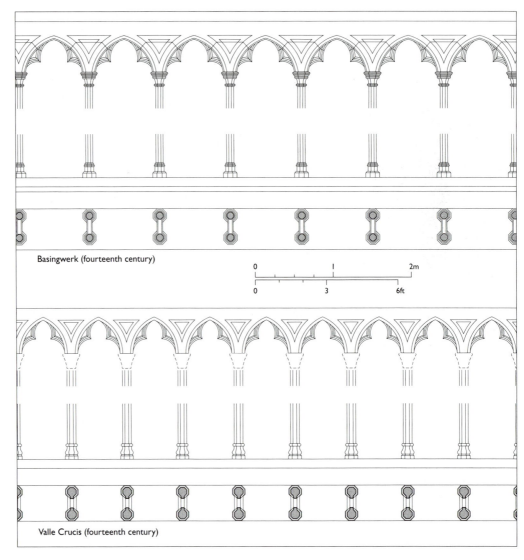

Basingwerk (fourteenth century)

Valle Crucis (fourteenth century)

(*see* figs 122 and 156).[70]

To place these Welsh developments in context, we must remember that in England the pace of change in cathedral and monastic cloister design in general had increased dramatically over the fourteenth century, forefronted by the new works at places such as Westminster, Gloucester and Worcester.[71] Even so, for much of the period the Cistercians appear to have been no more than bit players. At Stanley, for instance, although the cloister arcades were apparently rebuilt in the fourteenth century, the excavated material showed no positive signs of glazing or of vaulting.[72] Rather more advanced were the new arcades built at Bordesley Abbey *c* 1400, the form of which has been reconstructed based on fragments excavated at the north-east corner of the garth.[73] Externally, the bay divisions were marked by prominent buttresses set at

regular intervals, and internally by engaged respond shafts set on polygonal bases. In each bay, above a lower tier of wall panelling, there was a three-light window with fine Perpendicular-style tracery to the head. As Professor David Walsh points out, although one might expect the internal shafts to have carried up to stone vaults, nothing resembling rib fragments or webbing was located during the excavation, and a timber roof is again more likely.[74]

Cloisters were to continue to feature among the rebuilding programmes at a number of English Cistercian houses during the fifteenth and early sixteenth centuries. At Byland, for instance, all four cloister walks were reconstructed with glazed tracery windows, perhaps about 1450.[75] At Hailes, it was possibly Abbot William Whitchurch who began the rebuilding of the cloister with glazed and vaulted walks around 1460, a programme which may well

132 Basingwerk Abbey: fragments of cloister arcade, fourteenth century. The fragments were recovered during clearance work in the 1920s, but they are no longer at the site. The arches and their capitals were probably supported by small piers of the so-called 'dumb-bell' form.

Photograph: *Cadw, Crown Copyright*

have continued through to the early sixteenth century.[76] Considerably more elaborate than either of these two schemes was that begun at Forde in Devon by Abbot Thomas Chard (1521–39) just before the suppression. There can be no doubt it was one of the most ambitious Cistercian cloister designs ever attempted in the country.[77]

In the meantime, Strata Florida had been one of the Welsh abbeys which had definitely chosen to upgrade its cloister alleys as best it could in the fifteenth century (figs 70 and 133), and the same may have been true of its mother house at Whitland. Though not as grand as the work seen on some British sites, in the new Strata Florida design the north and east alley walls were divided into five bays by regularly spaced buttresses.[78] There were five lights to each bay, with iron glazing bars set near the springing of the slightly pointed heads. It is possible, in fact, that only the heads of the lights were glazed.[79] Much less survives at Whitland, yet it is not unreasonable to suggest that the cloister was upgraded at this time, based on a number of *ex situ* fragments recovered through excavation.[80]

Finally, by far the most sophisticated of all the Welsh Cistercian cloister schemes was begun in the third quarter of the fifteenth century at Tintern. Some decades earlier, in 1411–12, the community had been concerned merely to repair the roofs of the existing walks.[81] Now, however, it was probably Abbot Thomas Colston (*c* 1460–86) who chose to embark on a complete rebuilding programme. The prompt

may have come from William Herbert, earl of Pembroke (d 1469), who had been the abbey's lay steward and patron since the 1450s. In his will, Herbert made provision for his funerary monument in the abbey church, offering any surplus in the endowment 'to build new cloisters'.[82] As is evident from the thickened wall foundations around the edges of the garth, a degree of progress was definitely made. Moreover, in the south-east corner of the court, there are traces of the intended design against the north transept wall, including evidence of construction on at least four lavish stone-vaulted bays. Thus, just as at Hailes and later at Forde, there was nothing distinctly Cistercian in this new Tintern scheme. In ambition, it clearly matched many similar monastic cloister programmes in the south west around this time. It is unfortunate that the full extent of progress before the suppression is uncertain.

FEATURES OF THE WALKS AND THE GARTH

Although archaeology has so far told us very little, it seems likely that for much of the twelfth and early thirteenth centuries the alleys surrounding the cloister garths at most (if not all) Welsh Cistercian abbeys were at best paved with stone slabs.[83] Across Britain as a whole, tile pavements were probably introduced sparingly over the course of the later thirteenth century,[84] though they were undoubtedly to become more common in the later Middle Ages. When Stanley in Wiltshire was excavated in 1905, for

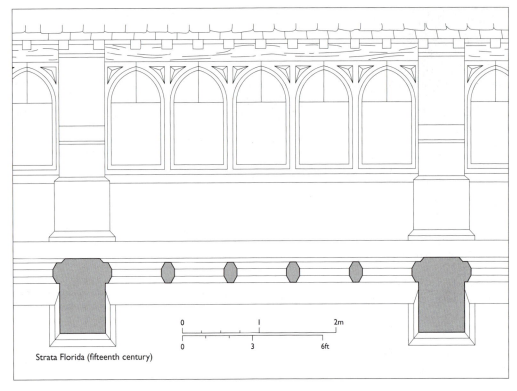

Strata Florida (fifteenth century)

example, the fourteenth-century paving in the west cloister walk 'was found in a very perfect state' for over 12.2m.[85] Today, more commonly, we encounter just occasional fragments, as is the case at the border abbey of Buildwas.[86] In Wales, the most recently excavated monastic cloister is that of the moderately wealthy Augustinian priory at Haverfordwest, where three of the alleys were found to have been completely paved with plain green and buff chequered tiling, probably dating from the late fifteenth century.[87] It seems probable, therefore, that later medieval tile pavements would have featured in the majority of Welsh Cistercian cloister alleys, though definite evidence is recorded only from Basingwerk and Neath.[88] Again, there have been no modern excavations on the central garths at any of the Welsh sites so there is little that can be said with confidence about their layout, though from what has been recovered elsewhere, the presumption has to be that garden beds, filled with flowers, herbs and perhaps fruit trees, were divided by a series of paths leading out from the cloister alleys.[89]

One of the more prominent features known from Cistercian cloister garths on the Continent is some form of centrally planned fountain pavilion, a small but distinctive building usually found projecting from the alley adjacent to the refectory.[90] It was here that the monks washed themselves before meals, and where the important weekly rite known as

the *mandatum* took place.[91] The structure might be square, circular, or polygonal; within it the *lavatorium* basin itself was fed with a constant flow of running water. Such pavilions appear on early plans of Cîteaux and Clairvaux (fig 39),[92] with other good French examples known from Fontenay, Le Thoronet (reconstructed) and Valmagne (Hérault).[93] Elsewhere there are fine survivals at Alcobaça in Portugal, Santes Creus and Poblet in Spain, Bebenhausen and Maulbronn in Germany, and Heiligenkreuz and Zwettl in Austria.[94]

It has been argued that such free-standing *lavatoria* are to be expected at a number of early Cistercian foundations in Britain, with claims having been made for Byland, Fountains, Kirkstall and Rievaulx.[95] Indeed, the foundations of one such twelfth-century structure are to be seen in the cloister garth at Melrose in Scotland.[96] It seems, however, they were less favoured after about 1170, their decline apparently coinciding with the rebuilding of south ranges generally, and with the reorganization of refectories on a north–south axis.[97] From this point on, British Cistercian *lavatoria* were more commonly placed in a recess positioned within the facade of the south refectory wall.[98] Yet it may be misleading to think the move was universal, as witnessed by the remains of the very handsome, and once vaulted, octagonal fountain pavilion of *c* 1200–10 still to be seen in the cloister garth at

134 *Strata Florida Abbey: Collation bay in north cloister alley. The cloister alleys at Strata Florida were rebuilt in the fifteenth century, at which time this formal bay was incorporated into the design of the northern walk. It represents the position of a reader's lectern.*

Photograph: *Cadw, Crown Copyright*

Mellifont in Ireland.[99] Were one to speculate on where such free-standing *lavatoria* may have existed in Wales, Tintern surely has to be one possibility, with an equal chance of such an arrangement existing in the twelfth-century claustral layout at Margam.

One last feature of the cloister which deserves mention is generally to be found in the alley adjacent to the church, and is linked with the Cistercian custom of holding the evening ceremony known as Collation in this spot.[100] At least two of the Welsh houses preserve architectural evidence connected to the Collation ceremony. In origin, it goes back to the Rule of St Benedict, which decreed that after Vespers the community should sit together to listen to a reading before going to the church for Compline.[101] The ceremony took its name from the *Collationes* of St John Cassian (d 435), one of the books recommended for reading.[102] We might look for three structural indications of a connection with the Collation. First, there might be a stone bench, running along the wall of the church, on which the monks would sit during the reading.[103] Secondly, given that the abbot would have presided at the centre, there may be signs that his seat was distinguished by a prominent architectural frame. Finally, there was sometimes a specific bay created in the cloister arcade opposite, where the lectern was accommodated and where the reader took up his

position. The most elaborate surviving abbot's seat and associated benching is to be found at the French abbey of Cadouin, where the work dates to the second half of the fifteenth century.[104] In Britain, striking evidence (documentary as well as archaeological) for the construction of a late fourteenth-century Collation bay comes from Boxley Abbey in Kent.[105] There are, in addition, structural indications of one kind or another from Byland, Cleeve and Fountains in England,[106] Melrose in Scotland,[107] and Graiguenamanagh, Grey and Jerpoint in Ireland.[108]

As to the Welsh evidence for the Collation ceremony, at Tintern not only does stone benching run along the north wall of the nave of the second abbey church, but at the centre of this benching there is also a recess with a pointed arch representing the position of the abbot's seat.[109] Over at Strata Florida, slight traces of stone benching exist at the east end of the nave wall. More impressively, there is a canted bay projecting out from the middle of the north cloister alley, undoubtedly representing the position of the reader's lectern (fig 134).[110] Further possible evidence for a Collation bay has recently been revealed through geophysical survey at Whitland.[111] In Wales, as in the rest of the Cistercian world, however, architectural evidence for the abbot's seat, for example, is so rare that it might be assumed that such permanence was not always considered necessary, and that wood may have sufficed in most instances.

CHAPTER 10

THE CHAPTER HOUSE

After the conventual church, the chapter house undoubtedly ranked as the most important building in any medieval monastic complex. By the late eleventh century, for the majority of old-established black monk communities of Europe, the room had acquired great practical and ritual significance. Indeed, the chapter meeting itself had become a multi-functional assembly, partly liturgical, partly disciplinary, partly commemorative and partly administrative.[1] For the Cistercians, over the course of the twelfth century, the daily chapter meeting came to occupy no less a symbolic position in the corporate and spiritual life of individual communities. And, from the occasional surviving text, we gain some impression of the order's deep regard for the sacred character of the room in which the meeting took place. Writing in the late twelfth century, for example, the noted white monk preacher Hélinand of Froidmont (d 1237) felt sufficiently moved to claim: '… no place is holier than the chapter house, no place more worthy of reverence; in no place is the devil farther away, in no place is God closer; for there the devil loses whatever he might gain elsewhere and there God regains obedience whatever he might lose elsewhere through negligence or contempt'.[2]

The carefully orchestrated form of the Cistercian chapter house ritual can be reconstructed, at least in a prescribed sense, from the order's customary, the *Ecclesiastica Officia*.[3] Each morning, after mass, the monks filed into the chamber to the sound of a ringing bell. When the abbot had taken his seat, the business of the assembly could begin. It was in the chapter house that the monastic body corporate celebrated the ideals of communal life, especially through the reading of a chapter which signified the monks' total obedience to the Rule of St Benedict.[4] It was in chapter, too, that saints and benefactors were commemorated, faults were confessed and penances assigned. Again, on certain feast days, the choir monks were joined by the lay brothers to listen to a formal sermon delivered by the abbot.[5] The daily chapter meeting was also the occasion when secular matters concerned with the business and administration of the monastery might be discussed.[6] In sum, the chapter house should be regarded as the primary gathering place for the whole abbey community.[7] Furthermore, it seems clear that from the last quarter of the twelfth century, the chapter house was the prescribed burial space for former abbots, as well as for kings, queens and bishops, should they so choose.[8]

In keeping with the spiritual and administrative significance of the building, from the middle years of the twelfth century white monk chapter houses began to be singled out for elaborate architectural treatment. In many cases, the importance of the room was at once emphasized by a comparatively elaborate entrance facade. Inside, the conceptual qualities of the chamber were nearly always handled carefully, especially through the judicious use of space, light and proportion. In this context, we may note the not infrequent claim that it was in the chapter house (rather than in the abbey church) that Gothic architectural forms sometimes made their earliest Cistercian appearance. This is often said of Fontenay (fig 54),[9] for example, and also of Buildwas in Shropshire (fig 60).[10]

Among the Cistercian abbeys of Wales and the March, the sites with the best-surviving chapter houses are Basingwerk (fig 135), Margam and Valle Crucis.[11] Other details have been recorded at Cymer, Dore, Neath, Strata Florida and Tintern, with certain elements at several of these sites accurately reconstructed on paper.[12] In addition, the findings of late nineteenth-century excavations provide intriguing clues on the nature of the buildings at Cwmhir and Strata Marcella, and, finally, some information has recently been derived from geophysical survey at Whitland (figs 25 and 26).[13]

On the whole, it is the striking example at Margam (*see* figs 137–139), probably dating from *c* 1203–13, which has tended to excite greatest interest in the scholarly literature.[14] Of course, it must be recognized at once that its centrally planned polygonal form is unusual in both monastic and secular chapter house design,[15] and a structure of such a plan and form seems altogether unknown

135 *Basingwerk Abbey: general view of chapter house, looking east. The initial twelfth-century chapter house at Basingwerk may well have been housed within the width of the east range. The room was expanded in the early thirteenth century, with the new eastern extension entered by way of paired round-headed arches.*

Photograph: *author*

among white monk communities on the Continent.[16] At the same time, in the conceptual qualities of its architecture – including the elaborate stellar vault pattern – the Margam chapter house would surely have resonated with the importance of the daily ritual once carried out within. From the ruins at Dore, Tintern and Strata Florida, on the other hand, one may be less immediately drawn to the qualities of the original building. Nevertheless, as completed in the first years of the thirteenth century, these were all attractive and significant early Gothic architectural spaces in their own right, as was true of several other Welsh Cistercian chapter houses.

EARLY CISTERCIAN CHAPTER HOUSES

The earliest appearance of the chapter house in the monastic plan is of interest in itself, though this is not a subject that can be dealt with in any great detail here. Suffice it to say, there is no sign of such a discrete building in the well-known plan of Carolingian St Gall, dating from *c* 820–30.[17] There again, just such a construction was ordered to be built by Abbot Ansegis, the contemporary head of the Frankish monastery of Fontenelle near Rouen (822–33). As the abbey's own chronicler recorded, it was called 'the assembly or court house … because the brethren are wont to gather there to take counsel over anything whatsoever'. Daily readings were conducted from a pulpit, and the authority of the Rule of St Benedict was underlined. Ansegis also left instruction that he should be buried in the chamber, establishing a precedent which in time came to be followed by abbots throughout the Christian world.[18] Firm evidence for the introduction of dedicated chapter rooms begins to increase from the early eleventh century, with that built at Cluny around 1030 undoubtedly one of the key examples.[19]

By the third quarter of the eleventh century (that is, before the foundation of Cîteaux in 1098), the chapter house had emerged as a structure of considerable significance in the lives of monks and canons of all mainstream religious orders.[20] Given this importance, it is surprising that no such chamber has been identified in what is known of the very earliest Cistercian buildings.[21] It is the more surprising to find no specific mention of a chapter house in the statute of c 1113–19, which stipulated the basic complement of buildings required in a new white monk foundation.[22] Be that as it may, by c 1135–60, or, in other words, when new claustral ranges were under construction at Cîteaux and Clairvaux (fig 39), the chapter house had assumed its long-term position within the east range. At these two particular abbeys, the range itself was three bays in width, allowing for the accommodation of a quite spacious independent chamber.[23] It is estimated that the completed twelfth-century chapter house at Cîteaux had a ground area of approximately 360 square metres, sufficient to accommodate up to 300 monks.[24] At both sites, the chapter house was separated from the south transept by the narrow space used as the book room and sacristy and was confined to a single storey so as to accommodate the monks' dormitory on the floor above. Internally, the room was subdivided into nine square bays or cells, with the four piers surrounding the middle bay giving the architecture a distinctly centralized character.[25]

The more typical Cistercian east range was two bays in width, as was the case with Fontenay (c 1150–5), a daughter of Clairvaux. Once again, all the ground-floor chambers were kept to a single storey. Here, though, the chapter house was designed with a third 'free-standing' bay projecting beyond the east wall of the range, thereby allowing for another centralized chamber with the space required for the whole community (fig 54).[26] In contrast, at another of Clairvaux's daughter houses, Noirlac, and similarly at Cîteaux's daughter of Pontigny, where the east ranges were also two bays wide, the chapter house was fully contained within the lateral walls of the building. To achieve the necessary space, the room was extended southwards along the length of the range. Two median piers were then set out on this longer axis, giving a six-bay plan.[27]

Across Europe as a whole, it appears to have been the latter rectangular form – with the room usually contained within the depth of the east range – which predominated among Cistercian chapter houses of the twelfth century.[28] Often, as at Noirlac and Pontigny, just two median piers were used to create six quadripartite vaulted bays, though four piers framing a central bay (of nine) may have been the more common pattern.[29] Indeed, there is now a suggestion that the square, four-pier, three-bay by three-bay plan may well have originated with the Cistercians in France in the late 1130s and 1140s, though it would be stretching the point too far to speak of any highly regularized form.[30] Continental examples of the twelfth and thirteenth centuries include L'Escaladieu, Flaran (Gers), Fontfroide and Vaucelles in France, Alcobaça in Portugal, Santes Creus in Spain, Casamari and Staffarda in Italy, Heiligenkreuz in Austria, and Val-Saint-Lambert in Belgium. As for examples of six-bay chapter houses with only the two median piers, we might cite Preuilly (Seine-et-Marne), Sénanque and Silvacane in France, Ossegg in Bohemia, and Fossanova and San Galgano in Italy.[31]

THE EARLIEST CISTERCIAN CHAPTER HOUSES IN BRITAIN

At the majority of English Benedictine and Cluniac monasteries of the late eleventh and early twelfth centuries, we can perhaps trace a clear preference for an east–west axial arrangement in chapter house design, not infrequently coupled with an apsidal east end to the building. One might think, for instance, of those at the early Norman foundations such as Battle, Durham, Castle Acre, Reading, St Albans or Wenlock.[32] In the meantime, the white monks began to arrive from the late 1120s onwards. Not for the first time, it is of interest to note that the growth and expansion of the order across the British Isles took place at much the same time as the senior Burgundian abbeys of the order were engaged in their major rebuilding programmes.

At Waverley Abbey, founded from L'Aumône in 1128, the first stone church and associated claustral buildings were laid out in the 1130s,[33] that is before the new works at Cîteaux and Clairvaux could have progressed very far. It has recently been suggested that the chapter house at Waverley was arranged on a north–south axis, positioned immediately adjacent to the south transept, with its rectangular form contained within the width of the east range.[34] At

Rievaulx, founded from Clairvaux in 1132, the initial chapter house of *c* 1135–55 was likewise contained wholly within the lateral walls of the east range. Here, though, it is argued that the plan was even closer to the near-contemporary French models, probably with two median 'piers' set out on the longer north–south axis.[35] Again, much the same probably existed at Fountains (where the first stone chapter house was built by Abbot Henry Murdac in 1144–6),[36] and perhaps at Jervaulx.[37] All these examples are thought to have been fairly low single-storey chambers, their only light coming from windows located in the east wall. There is no indication of vaulting from any of the sites, and it is thought more likely that the rooms were covered by relatively low wooden roofs. A chapter house of similar form – with median piers – could well have been built at Melrose (*c* 1145) in Scotland, in which case it was doubtless derived from its mother house at Rievaulx.[38] Again, at Mellifont in Ireland, the earliest chapter house of the 1150s was once more housed within the walls of the east range, though here it was perhaps vaulted over two median piers, with French prototypes seen as the likely source of the design.[39]

The earliest Welsh Cistercian chapter house of which we have any knowledge is that at Tintern

(fig 136). The ruins of the building as they stand today are very much as consolidated during the first round of conservation works in the initial years of the twentieth century, with the antiquity of the basic arrangements confirmed by Joseph Potter's 1845 ground plan of the site (fig 9). In sum, these ruins reflect the mature thirteenth-century layout within the east range as a whole.[40] However, Tintern was founded within two years of Waverley, again from L'Aumône, and in these circumstances it seems highly plausible that the mid-twelfth-century claustral arrangements included a chapter house fully contained within the width of the range, closely analogous to the pattern posited for its sister house. In turn, it would be surprising if the Tintern details were very far removed from those suggested for Rievaulx and Fountains.

Admittedly, the evidence is by no means extensive, but there are strong indications that Tintern's first stone-built church and claustral ranges would have been fairly well advanced by about 1150.[41] In this early phase of planning, the cloister was set out along comparatively modest lines, with the east range measuring some 8.8m wide internally (fig 26). In seeking to reconstruct the precise layout of the chapter house within the range, we are obliged to draw on a

136 Tintern Abbey: general view of chapter house, looking east. The ruins belie what must have been a particularly handsome early Gothic composition, itself representing an extensive remodelling of a much smaller and plainer mid-twelfth-century building.

Photograph: *Cadw, Crown Copyright*

few clues in the conserved fabric of the later building.[42] It seems that the core of the southern wall – which was shared with the north transept of the twelfth-century church (fig 26) – must lie fossilized within the surviving masonry at this point. In contrast, the east wall has effectively been lost altogether. In so far as one can tell, it would have returned in line with the east wall of the range as a whole, a conclusion supported by the suggestions made for the three key comparative sites in England.[43] If we can accept the form of the masonry as consolidated, the only surviving indication of the twelfth-century east wall is a slight stub of footing projecting from the northern wall of the later building.

This leads us to consider the position of the original north wall. One possibility is that it lay on the same line as the thirteenth-century division with the inner parlour (fig 26), which would have resulted in a room of virtually square plan, measuring approximately 8.5m wide by 8.8m deep, with around 75 square metres of internal space.[44] On the other hand, considering the predominance of the rectangular north–south layout among the early Cistercian chapter houses of France, and of the comparable proposals made for the British layouts at Waverley, Rievaulx, Fountains and Melrose, it seems far more likely the Tintern community would have determined upon a room of similar plan. In other words, it may be that the original northern wall was positioned a little further out in the east range. In fact, the line of the north (rather than the south) wall of the thirteenth-century inner parlour becomes a more attractive option (fig 26).[45] In this revised reconstruction, the early chapter house would still have been 8.8m deep, but its width would have been almost 12.2m, thereby giving a total ground area of approximately 108 square metres.

As to the overall character of Tintern's twelfth-century chapter house, although nothing survives to indicate the form of the entrance facade, it is reasonable to infer a central doorway flanked by two small window openings. This arrangement was to prove by far the most common across the order at large.[46] Internally, it is unlikely to have been a room of any great architectural pretension. Fully housed within the width of the east range, it must have been a relatively low and dark space, lit only by comparatively small windows in the eastern wall. If the layout was indeed of the preferred early Cistercian rectangular form, the possibility of a median 'pier' (or 'piers') on the longer north–south axis cannot be discounted. A stone vault seems rather unlikely, and a flat wooden roof is more probable.

Elsewhere in Wales and its immediate border, although even less direct evidence has survived,

twelfth-century chapter houses of a similar character, probably contained within the width of the east range, may well have existed at Basingwerk, Dore, Margam, Neath and Whitland. At Basingwerk (figs 25 and 135), if one can rely on the Office of Works consolidation programme of the 1920s, there is some trace of the jambs of the doorway from the cloister, but very little else.[47] In the case of Dore, given the limited nature of his excavations, Paul suggested that the original chapter house may have been about 9 square metres.[48] The details of the buildings at Margam and Whitland would be of particular interest were anything to survive archaeologically, since both abbeys were first-generation daughter houses of Clairvaux, founded at precisely the time the new claustral ranges were under reconstruction at that house. At Margam, it is very tempting to equate the arrangement of the remodelled thirteenth-century chapter house vestibule with the extent of the original building (fig 25).[49]

A NEW GENERATION OF BRITISH CISTERCIAN CHAPTER HOUSES

This rather restricted and generally enclosed design for British Cistercian chapter houses fell rapidly out of favour. New and very different models were introduced in a fresh generation of buildings begun during the 1150s and 1160s. The first sign of those changes was provided in no uncertain manner by the striking new chapter house raised at Rievaulx in the 1150s, during the time of Abbot Ailred.[50] In specific terms, the characteristics of this tall free-standing building, with its apsidal east end and lower flanking aisle running around all sides, rendered it unique. The precise design was never adopted by any other Cistercian house in Britain or on the Continent. Even so, certain basic qualities in the structure were to become common traits in the years ahead. Above all, in architectural terms, the Rievaulx chapter house shifted the main axial direction of the building. It was now set at right angles to the east range, effectively embracing the consistent and widespread predilection among English monastic houses for an east–west orientation. In turn, this allowed for new experiments in lighting and roofing, especially beyond the width of the range. The generous provision of space within the Rievaulx building, including that in the vestibule and the adjacent east cloister walk, also gives us something to think about when considering the planning at other sites. As argued by Fergusson and Harrison, the amount of room within Ailred's new chapter house may be explained, at least in part, by the inclusive nature of his abbacy. One of his main concerns may have been the occasional

137 Margam Abbey: view of the chapter house, from the south east. The building has generally been dated to c 1200, though it may have been introduced during the time of Abbot Gilbert (1203–13), who came to Margam from the abbey of Kirkstead in Lincolnshire.

Photograph: *author*

need to accommodate the entire community, including the abbey's many lay brothers.[51]

In building on this theme, it may be worth considering whether the vestibules found in many subsequent white monk chapter houses were originally intended for the accommodation of lay brothers,[52] with the developments at Fountains in the 1160s of particular interest in this regard. Here, as part of a busy ongoing building programme, it was Abbot Richard of Clairvaux (1151–70) who oversaw the construction of the vast new chapter house. At six bays long and three wide, and with an internal floor area of approximately 320 square metres, it was one of the largest chapter houses ever raised in England.[53] As with Rievaulx, Richard's chapter house was orientated at right angles to the east range, and was again based on quite a different model from that adopted by the Cistercians in Burgundy just a few decades earlier. The completed room featured a western vestibule three bays wide and two deep, in which the vaults, supported on monolithic marble columns, were fully contained below the floor of the dormitory.[54] In the twelve (three by four) free-standing bays projecting beyond the range proper, the vaults were raised in height, giving a space with a lighter, less cramped general character. The Fountains chapter house was also the first example in England to employ an entrance facade comprised of triple arches, a rare Cistercian feature outside this country.[55] One of the most remarkable aspects of the design is the scale of its ambition, especially when seen in the context of the chapter house at Abbot Richard's previous abbey of Vauclair.[56]

In the wake of these new buildings at northern England's two most influential Cistercian abbeys, the same basic chapter house layout was to become commonplace across the whole of the British Isles. A range of influences doubtless underlay the changes, and the proportions and precise design of the buildings were to vary, determined not least by the resources available to the house and the size of its community. Nevertheless, the general trend can be detected wherever we look. Staying in the north, something of this nature must have existed in the revised layout of the chapter house at Kirkstall (c 1165) (fig 55),[57] and it was probably towards the end of the twelfth century that the pattern was taken up at Jervaulx and Roche (fig 57).[58] In the south and south west of England, one might think of the chapter houses at Buildwas (c 1160–70) (fig 60), Combe (c 1170), Forde (c 1160–70) and especially Waverley (c 1180–93).[59] Although not always architecturally well defined, each one featured a western vestibule element and a partially free-standing east end projecting beyond the width of the range.

THE POLYGONAL CHAPTER HOUSES AT MARGAM AND DORE

In Wales and the March, the trend for building chapter houses of greater architectural and liturgical distinction can be picked up around the turn of the twelfth century. Remarkably, two of the earliest examples are also among the most impressive and extraordinary structures ever raised by the British

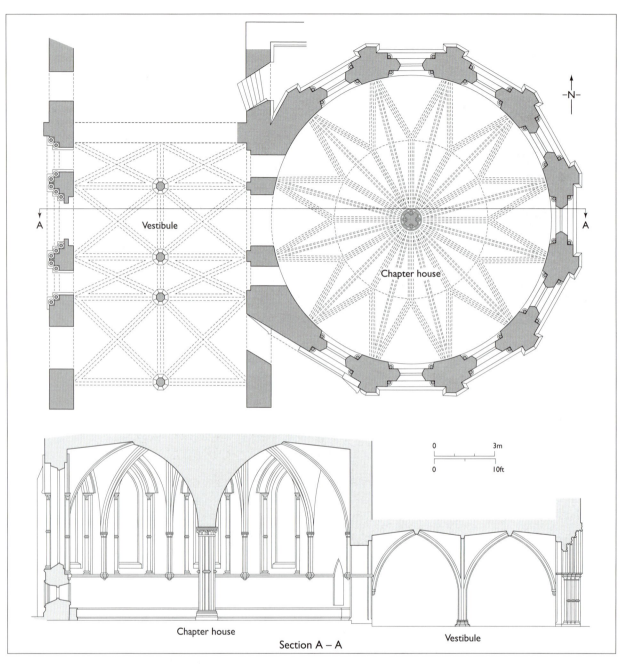

138 *Margam Abbey:
chapter house, ground
plan and reconstructed
cross section (Chris
Jones-Jenkins/David
Robinson; plan after
Paul 1896 appearing
in Birch 1897, with
modifications).*

Drawing: *Pete
Lawrence, for Cadw*

Cistercians. In their way, the polygonal chapter
houses at Margam and Dore were no less exceptional
than the structure put up at Ailred's Rievaulx half a
century before.[60] On stylistic grounds, the Margam
chapter house has generally been considered the
earlier of the two buildings,[61] almost always dated to
the very last years of the twelfth century, or perhaps
c 1200. Not everyone agrees, however, with several
writers claiming that primacy belongs to Dore.[62]
Most recently the case has been argued by Hillaby,
who believes that the Dore chapter house was

completed by 1208, during the abbacy of Adam I
(*c* 1186–1213). He considers the Margam design to be
derivative, awkward in detailing, and of marginally
later date.[63] We shall return to questions of chronology
below, after first considering the characteristics of
the structures themselves.

For some reason unknown to us, the Margam
chapter house escaped deliberate demolition at the
time of the suppression and was incorporated as an
outbuilding into the new Mansel dwelling on the site
(fig 2). Thereafter, it survived with its vault completely

186

139 *Margam Abbey: engraving of the chapter house interior by Francis Chesham, from a painting by Samuel H Grimm, 1780. This important illustration shows the building before the final collapse of the vault in 1799.*

Photograph: *National Library of Wales*

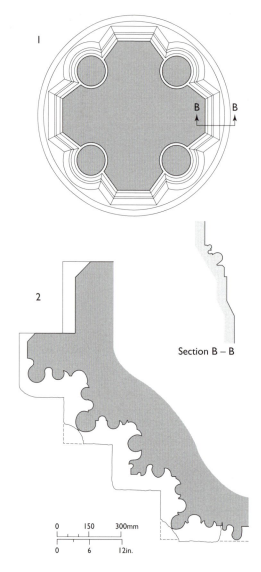

Section B – B

0   150   300mm
0   6   12in.

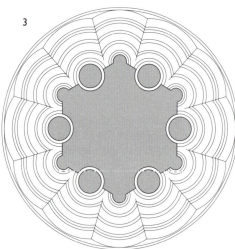

*140 Margam Abbey and Dore Abbey: chapter house pier plans and selective moulding details.
(1) Margam pier base plan and section (David Robinson);
(2) Dore pier plan (after Harrison 1997a); (3) Margam vestibule, jamb of central doorway (David Robinson).*

Drawing: *Pete Lawrence, for Cadw*

141 Margam Abbey: central pier, detail of the capital and vault springing. The compound capital features deeply undercut stiff-leaf foliage, above which a moulded abacus carries the springing for twenty-four individual vault ribs. Photograph: *author*

intact through into the last years of the eighteenth century.[64] Even in its present ruinous condition, the architectural qualities of this handsome polygonal structure are readily evident (figs 137 and 138). Before its construction, as suggested above, the community probably held its daily chapter meeting in a mid-twelfth-century room accommodated within the width of the initial east range. This may well have lain undisturbed whilst the bulk of the ambitious early Gothic composition was erected immediately adjacent to the outer wall. Interestingly, in terms of the overall plan of the new chapter house, although the vaulting arrangements were based on a regular dodecagon, with the full transverse ribs creating twelve equally spaced bays, only eight of the external facets were of like-for-like proportion. Indeed, the lengths of the three sides about the entrance varied quite considerably (fig 138).[65]

142 *Margam Abbey: chapter house vestibule, looking east. In the original twelfth-century east range, this area may well have served as the chapter house proper. It was remodelled as a vestibule to the new polygonal chapter house in the early thirteenth century, at which time the vault was inserted.*

Photograph: *Royal Commission on the Ancient and Historical Monuments of Wales, Crown Copyright*

At each of the external angles is a broad, if rather shallow, clasping buttress in ashlar (fig 137). Above the uncoursed rubble of the lower walls, each of the nine exposed faces was lit by a tall lancet window, all featuring plain chamfered jambs set back from the wall face in the form of a second order. The jambs are framed externally (and internally) by slender detached shafts, banded at mid-height and with moulded bases. The capitals bear a range of scalloped, foliate and stiff-leaf designs, on top of which squared abaci were used consistently. The hood moulds above the lancets, both outside and in, terminate with foliate stops.

Internally, the chapter house is perfectly circular, and measures a full 15.2m in diameter. The restrained beauty of the original design seldom fails to impress. Fortunately, our appreciation of the surviving details can be supplemented by a very good engraving of 1780, showing the room before the final collapse of the vault in 1799 (fig 139).[66] Centrally, the vault ribs were supported on a single pier consisting of four chamfered arms, with a detached and belted shaft worked into a hollow in each of the angles. The pier sits on a moulded base (fig 140) and is crowned with

a compound capital featuring deeply cut and brittle-looking stiff-leaf foliage (fig 141). From the moulded abacus – the form of which mirrors the profile of the pier itself – spring the broken ends of the twenty-four individual vault ribs. Originally, as these ribs spread out and thickened, they were of triple roll-and-fillet section. Twelve of them were full transverse ribs, forming a single pointed arch spanning from the central pier to the outer wall (fig 138). Between these, the second set of twelve ribs rose from the pier to the circular crown ridge within the vault, at which point they split into two diagonal ribs spanning the remaining distance to the walls. At least one of the Y-shaped 'triradial' rib junctions from this arrangement survives at the site. Against the walls, the vault ribs were carried on triple-shaft responds, featuring plain chalice capitals. In turn, the responds sat on corbels, of varying design, set in a bold string course at sill level. When the monks were assembled in the room for chapter meetings, they presumably sat on benching arranged around the walls. Nothing survives today to suggest the character of this seating, though Birch thought it likely there were panelled wooden stalls.[67] To emphasize the importance of the

189

abbot's position, which lay directly beneath the most eastern lancet, the inner arch head of the window was treated differently from all the others, enriched with elaborate mouldings.[68]

As work on the construction of the new building drew close to completion, the community may have been able to transfer its chapter meetings, thereby freeing up the space formerly occupied within the east range. The older area was then remodelled as a vestibule, in addition to providing a section of the undercroft for the monks' dormitory above (figs 138 and 142). The two-bay quadripartite vaults sprang from octagonal central columns with no capitals, and were brought down to wall-mounted corbels. The doorway and window openings from the vestibule into the chapter house proper have simple, plain chamfered jambs. The lay brothers may have gathered before these openings to listen to sermons on the prescribed feast days. To the west, the triple doorways opening into the vestibule from the adjacent east cloister walk together made for a particularly stylish early Gothic composition. Here, the central doorway is of four orders. The jambs of the three outer orders all feature detached and banded shafts, which in this case are nibbed or keeled. The shafts have moulded bases, and the capitals were prepared (though perhaps not completed) with foliage carving in mind. The marginally thinner shafts of the innermost jamb order have no central banding, but they carry a fillet. Above, the arch head is greatly enriched with multiple mouldings, both keeled and filleted. A slender band of dog-tooth ornament sits in the central arch (fig 140). The two flanking doorways are of rather plainer design.

In turning to the evidence from Dore Abbey, we find that the fabric of its polygonal chapter house has suffered to a much greater extent since the suppression. In fact, there is only a relatively small fragment of surviving in situ masonry, to be seen at the south-west side.[69] Standing about 3m high, the fragment in question includes one of the internal angles of the chapter house proper. Immediately to the west, effectively within the vestibule area, there are traces of a small triangular-shaped compartment in which there is a single trumpet-scalloped capital supporting a vault springer.[70] The first person to have identified the polygonal form of the building was Thomas Blashill, whose ideas were published in the early 1880s.[71] Then, in 1892–3, the foundations were partially excavated by Roland Paul. He was able to determine the precise overall dimensions and produced a reasonably accurate ground plan.[72] More recently, the qualities of the Dore chapter house have been reassessed by Hillaby and the fabric considered in greater detail by Harrison.[73]

Following the Margam suggestion, we can assume that the Dore monks initially attended their daily chapter meeting in a room located within the width of the twelfth-century east range. Similarly, it is likely that their new building would have been constructed in such a way as to minimize disturbance for as long as possible. Unlike the arrangements at Margam, however, the walls of Dore's completed thirteenth-century chapter house came much closer to a regular dodecagon, in which the polygonal form was used inside as well as out (see fig 169). However, with an internal dimension of approximately 13.1m across, the scale of the Dore building was significantly smaller than the structure at Margam.

As to the upstanding form of Dore's new chapter house, it seems reasonably certain that, above what appears to have been a substantial external base plinth, there was a lancet in each of the nine exposed faces. Inside, Paul found traces of the stone wall bench on which the monks sat during their chapter meetings.[74] At the centre of the room, just as at Margam, there was a single pier supporting the weight of the vault. As Blashill noted in his early investigations, this was a clustered composition featuring six large shafts and six smaller intermediate shafts.[75] Further details of the pier and its base have recently been elucidated by Harrison, who confirms that around a hexagonal core the twelve shafts definitely alternated between major and minor (fig 140).[76] He suggests, in fact, that the major shafts sat in hollows worked into the surface of the core, and were themselves detached and banded. Against the walls, triple-shaft vault responds were probably positioned in each of the angles. In contrast with those at Margam, these began at the level of the wall bench, from there rising uninterrupted to the springing point. The middle shaft in each group was detached, with several examples of the associated stiff-leaf capitals recently identified. The two outer shafts, meanwhile, rose above the level of the capitals to form wall ribs. Harrison has made a very convincing case for the form of the vault pattern having been almost identical to that at Margam.[77] He has, for instance, identified one of the tri-radial rib junctions, which (unlike the Margam example) is decorated with a foliate boss.

The details of the remodelled vestibule area, contained within the width of the existing east range, were perfectly in keeping with the design of the new chapter house, suggesting the work formed part of the same overall building campaign. The vault, probably springing from two central piers comprised of clustered shafts, would have been kept comparatively low so as to allow for the floor of the monks' dormitory above. The vault ribs were apparently of the same profile as those in the main body of the new building.[78] Entrance into the vestibule from the east cloister walk was by way of a triple-arched facade, not unlike the basic form used at Margam. Here, though, to judge from what is known of the southern respond, the detailing was rather more elaborate. The two central piers were probably treated in what was a favoured west country early Gothic fashion, with alternating coursed and detached shafts employed in richly clustered compositions. Of course, the triple-arched facades at both Dore and Margam repeated the pattern first seen at Fountains in the 1160s.

Before turning to the question of possible archetypes for the Margam and Dore buildings, it is worth mentioning the intriguing possibility that a third polygonal chapter house may at least have been planned at Cwmhir Abbey, at very much the same time. The evidence admittedly is slight, but consists of a number of capitals found during the excavations of the early 1890s. These capitals and their abaci look as though they could have been positioned around a free-standing octagonal pier of substantial proportions (fig 143). For Stephen Williams, the most likely location for such a pier was in a polygonal chapter house, though he acknowledged that it may never have been completed.[79]

Now, as noted earlier, centrally planned chapter houses of polygonal design appear to have been a peculiarly British tradition, and it surely cannot have been coincidence which led to the construction of the two definite early thirteenth-century Cistercian examples in the south west. The architectural significance of the buildings at Margam and Dore is immediately heightened when it is realized that they were probably the first of their type, effectively establishing the basic pattern followed in all other polygonal forms over the following two centuries.[80] This said, at least one earlier regional archetype, or model, is known, namely the large, centrally planned chapter house built at the cathedral priory of Worcester c 1100–15,[81] and in general terms there is no denying the architectural influence of the Worcester workshops in south-west England and southern Wales during the late twelfth and early thirteenth centuries.[82] In support of the notion that the Cistercians of Margam and Dore were seeking to emulate the Worcester chapter room in the design of their new buildings, it should be noted that it may have influenced an earlier regional imitation at the Benedictine Pershore Abbey.[83] Yet not only were these two black monk structures circular in plan, they were also contained on the line of the east range, with no separate vestibule.[84] It may, in any case, be worth considering a second possible model, for

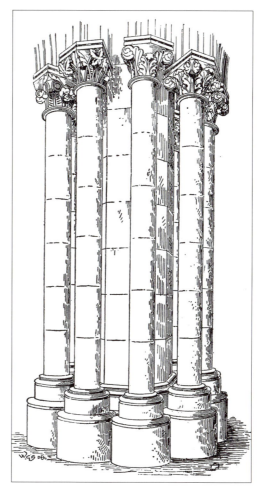

143 Cwmhir Abbey: speculative reconstruction of free-standing octagonal pier by Worthington G Smith, published by M C Jones and Stephen Williams (Montgomeryshire Collect, *1894–5*). *Williams argued that such a pier may have featured in a centrally planned chapter house.*

Photograph: *Society of Antiquaries of London*

instance those circular and polygonal fountain pavilions built out into the cloister garths at a number of European Cistercian houses, not least at Cîteaux and Clairvaux.[85] One example which may well have been known to several white monk abbots in Wales is that at Mellifont, dated to c 1200–10.[86] The pavilion there was octagonal in plan, about 7.3m across internally, and with the ribs of the vault springing from a single central pier.[87]

At root, a number of symbolic conceptions may have lain behind the basic centrally planned chapter house design. Hence, in searching for an iconographical explanation, authors have looked, for example, to baptisteries and mausoleums, to centrally planned buildings associated with the Virgin, and to the cenacle (or *cenaculum*, the room of the Last Supper).[88] However, a fuller account of the way such archetypes were incorporated in the conceptual qualities which lay behind the design of the Margam and Dore buildings must await further art-historical investigation.[89] For the present, it is not unreasonable to interpret the completed arrangements along those lines discussed earlier. At each site, the vestibules could well have served as the occasional gathering point for the lay brothers, with the polygonal extension reserved for the choir monks.

Finally, we should return to the question of chronology, and try to establish the absolute and relative dates of the two buildings. On the whole, as noted above, the Margam chapter house has been seen as the primary structure.[90] This was challenged some years ago by Stratford,[91] and more recently by Hillaby. For Hillaby, such were the limitations imposed by the Interdict (1208–13) during the reign of King John that it would be difficult to imagine work at Dore progressing after 1208. On the other hand, the Margam community was in a more favoured position during the years of the Interdict, receiving special privileges from the king. In such circumstances, Hillaby implies, building may have continued for longer.[92]

In looking for the potential parentage of the specific architectural ingredients used by the Margam chapter house master, the majority seem to have made their appearance in buildings of no later than *c* 1200 across much of the west country region. This includes detached and belted shafts, scalloped, foliate and chalice capitals, triple-shafted wall responds and keeled and filleted mouldings. Antecedents for many can be found in, say, the west bays at Worcester Cathedral (fig 61), the nave at Wells Cathedral and in the great church at Glastonbury Abbey, all dating from the last quarter of the twelfth century. At the same time, it must be recognized that most of the features retained their currency into the first quarter of the thirteenth century, hence their occurrence in the naves at Llanthony Priory (fig 72) and Llandaff Cathedral (fig 90), both probably begun around 1200 or soon after.[93] The most inventive new element in the Margam design was undoubtedly the stellar vault pattern, for which a convincing genealogy has yet to be advanced.[94] Historically, a very good case can be made for the Margam building having been initiated in the time of Abbot Gilbert, who took office in 1203.[95] A former monk of Kirkstead, his appointment was made by 'foreign visitors', probably with a view to the reform of the house.[96] Moreover, as Hillaby observes, Gilbert does indeed seem to have been on good terms with King John. It was a relationship that secured for Margam those same privileges the king afforded his own Cistercian foundation at Beaulieu.[97] There is, moreover, every indication that the economy of the house was steadily buoyant in this period. In short, the circumstances for fashionable architectural patronage were all in place. Despite vehement attacks on the character of Abbot Gilbert by Gerald of

Wales,[98] following his enforced retirement in 1213 and his death at Kirkstead a year later, the Margam annalist described him as 'a man of honoured memory'.[99] Thus, although we may never arrive at a definitive date for the Margam chapter house, a bracket of *c* 1203 to 1213 seems highly plausible.

At Dore, on the other hand, although the main phase in the construction of the extended eastern arm of the abbey church clearly belongs to the time of Adam I (*c* 1186–1213),[100] the extent of progress on the early Gothic chapter house during his abbacy is much less certain. Regardless of any architectural rivalry there may have been between Adam and his contemporary at Margam,[101] the Dore chapter house most definitely looks the later building. Advances in design are evident from the fully polygonal plan, the more progressive character of its decoration and various points of detailing in both the vault and the entrance to the vestibule.[102] Indeed, if it is accepted that the Interdict brought a general hiatus to the construction programmes at Dore, it seems more likely that the chapter house was completed during the abbacy of Adam II (*c* 1213–27), despite the epitaph from Gerald of Wales describing him as no more than 'modest in a mediocre way'.[103]

EXTENDED CHAPTER HOUSES AT STRATA FLORIDA, BASINGWERK, TINTERN AND NEATH

The impressive polygonal chapter houses at Margam and Dore were, as we have seen, exceptional buildings. The more common development in the design of Welsh Cistercian chapter houses during the early thirteenth century followed the growing preference among English abbeys for a rectangular eastwards extension. This appears to have occurred at Strata Florida, for example, even if the full structural sequence of the building is rather complex to unravel (fig 26). In trying to unpick the sequence, it seems reasonable to assume that the primary chapter house foundations were laid out in the late twelfth century, at much the same time as the abbey church, and it is equally feasible that the building was initially contained within the width of the east range. Were this the case, the layout would probably have been much as uncovered by Williams in the 1880s: a room on a north–south axis measuring some 11.3m wide by 8.5m deep.[104] Next, given the evidence of *ex situ* stonework fragments recovered in the late nineteenth-century excavations, it is clear that the entire cloister facade was refashioned about 1220–30. As completed, the central doorway and flanking openings featured stepped jambs, heavily moulded and filleted arches, and capitals with bulbous stiff-

144 *Strata Florida Abbey: reconstruction of cloister and east range, showing chapter house facade from the south west. The chapter house as a whole was probably remodelled* c *1220–30, at which time it was given an elaborate facade towards the cloister. The central doorway featured stepped jambs, stiff-leaf capitals and a heavily moulded arch head. Conjecturally, the composition is shown here as a triple-arched entrance, though the possibility that the flanking openings were simply unglazed windows on low walls cannot be discounted. Drawing:* Terry Ball, for Cadw

leaf foliage. In the most recent reconstruction of this facade (fig 144), it has been decided to show a triple-arched entrance arrangement, though the possibility that the flanking openings were simply unglazed windows cannot be discounted.[105] This aside, when the extent of the remodelling represented by the facade is taken into consideration, it seems likely that a significant eastwards extension of the building, known only in plan, dates from the same period (fig 145).[106]

After its transformation, the chapter house at Strata Florida still measured close to 11.3m wide, but was now as much as 16.5m deep (fig 26), giving a very substantial overall ground area of up to 186 square metres. The older western half may have served as a vestibule, with the chapter house proper located beyond a cross-wall in the new eastern extension. The whole was presumably finished in time for the recorded burial within the building of the Deheubarth prince, Maelgwyn ap Rhys, in 1231.[107] Thereafter, a number of other princes of the dynasty were to be interred in the room through into the late thirteenth century.[108] In looking to reconstruct other features of the remodelled building, one imagines the east wall of the extension was pierced by a triplet of lancet windows. Internally, a stone bench ran along the lateral walls, traces of which still survive (fig 145). We cannot be certain whether the room was initially covered with a stone vault, though it would have been unusual were this not the case. At a later date, perhaps following the many troubles which beset the house at the end of the thirteenth century,[109] the Strata Florida chapter house was reduced in size. The cross-wall, which

193

145 Strata Florida Abbey: south-east corner of chapter house during clearance excavations of the mid-twentieth century. The evidence is by no means conclusive, but the southern and eastern walls (to the left and in the foreground) are likely to represent an eastwards extension to the original layout of the building.

Photograph: *Royal Commission on the Ancient and Historical Monuments of Wales, Crown Copyright*

hitherto may have served as the division between the vestibule and the chapter house proper, was blocked to form a new east wall. The area formerly occupied by the free-standing projection seems to have been given over to burial, with at least two graves cutting the earlier foundations.[110]

It is certainly worth mentioning, if only in passing, the probable upgrading of the chapter house facilities at Aberconwy in the first years of the thirteenth century. Like Strata Florida, this was another house under the patronage of the native princes. Although very little can be said of the scheme as a whole, the evidence comes from what is now the west doorway in the parish church of St Mary (fig 81). This has a two-centred arch with roll-and-fillet mouldings springing from moulded abaci, in turn set on capitals with stiff-leaf foliage. As noted by Hughes and others,[111] the arch is clearly reused and cannot have accommodated a door in its original position. It seems very likely that both the arch and its capitals formerly stood on the jambs of the chapter house doorway, to be removed here in the works of conversion following the closure of the abbey by Edward I in 1283–4.[112]

Considerably more survives of the early thirteenth-century extension made to the chapter house at Basingwerk Abbey on the north-eastern border (figs 18, 25 and 135). The initial room, which was probably low and dark, and contained within the width of the east range, was now expanded eastwards as part of a general remodelling of the entire range.[113] The new extension was entered by way of a pair of round-headed arches, each with a chamfered inner order and springing from a central octagonal column. The space was covered with a quadripartite rib vault. A lancet window survives in the north wall, and the splay of another can be seen to the south. There were probably three such lancets in the east wall. Meanwhile, as shown by the row of beam holes (fig 135), the older area contained within the lateral walls of the range itself was covered with a lower wooden roof, thus allowing for the dormitory above. Presumably, it would have functioned from this time as a vestibule.

Architecturally, the most significant thirteenth-century rectangular extension to a Welsh Cistercian chapter house was probably that at Tintern. Following the rebuildings at Margam and Dore, not to mention the new scheme at the sister house of Waverley,[114] the conditions in their now antiquated and seriously cramped chapter house of *c* 1150 must have seemed, to the monks of Tintern, to be crying out for improvement.[115] In fact, a start had been made on the expansion of the initial layout of monastic buildings around the turn of the twelfth century, but it was perhaps the 1220s before the community was in a position to begin work apace. In 1223–4, William Marshal the younger (d 1231), earl of Pembroke, granted the abbey a particularly generous endowment which may have been ear-marked to finance the rebuilding of all three main claustral ranges, a programme which was to continue on into the third quarter of the century.[116] It is tempting to associate some of the progress on this scheme with Abbot Ralph (*c* 1232–45), a man 'gifted in no small way with sobriety of habits, and splendour of wisdom'.[117] In any case, one of the most prominent indications of the extent and quality of the work is to be found in the rich detailing of the greatly improved and extended chapter house (fig 136).

Although the building is much reduced, it is now possible, following careful investigation of both the consolidated *in situ* material and a large number of dispersed *ex situ* architectural fragments scattered across the site, to present a reasonably accurate reconstruction of Tintern's early thirteenth-century chapter house, at least on paper (figs 146 and 147).[118] Like the example at Strata Florida, by this time the plan form would have been very familiar to Cistercian communities throughout the whole of England. In essence it was a scaled-down version of the 1160s chapter house at Fountains. The Tintern building, which was five bays long, measured some 17.1m by 8.5m, giving around 145 square metres of internal space. Three of the main axial bays were contained beneath the dormitory, that is, within the width of the east range itself. The remaining two projected beyond the line of the outer wall (figs 26 and 146). To assess the character of the overall composition, it will be helpful to consider the various individual elements, several of which were measured and drawn by Joseph Potter in the 1840s (fig 148).[119]

Towards the cloister, the new chapter house facade featured a stunning group of three richly clustered archways, which must have appeared particularly impressive. Something of the original quality of this composition may be discerned from the north and south responds, and especially from the two central piers (figs 136 and 148). Around what was essentially an eye-shaped core, the piers comprised no less than fourteen shafts, six of which were coursed and filleted, with the remaining eight detached, all of them sitting on linked water-holding moulded bases. The form of the arch mouldings supported by these piers is unknown, but it seems likely the profile was an intricate roll-and-fillet form, as depicted in conjectural outline in the reconstructed section (fig 146).

Beyond the facade, the full plan of the chapter house interior was broken into fifteen bays or cells, in the five-by-three arrangement preserved in outline today. The form of the bays was determined by the

two rows of four slender piers supporting the vault. The nine bays (three by three) occupying the range proper were virtually square in plan. However, the six to the east (three by three) were elongated on the east–west axis (fig 146). Originally, it is possible that the two outer bays at the westernmost end were partitioned off from the remainder. They may have been intended to serve as book cupboards, entered from the cloister by the northern and southern arches of the entrance facade. Such an arrangement occurred, for instance, in the chapter house at Fountains and in the near-contemporary building at Furness.[120]

One of the key elements of the Tintern chapter house recorded by Potter was the form of the piers, including the mouldings of the bases and capitals. The four pier bases located today towards the east end of the building were also in place in the 1840s (fig 9), with Potter's drawing confirming much of the current detail (figs 148 and 149).[121] Above a chamfered plinth, the profile of the true base is essentially of three tiered rolls. Rising from this composition, there is a short length of plain 'pier', which is as much as now survives *in situ*. However, Potter was able to show a form of sub-base with a richly moulded profile sitting on top of these lower fragments (fig 149). It is difficult to be certain whether he located just such a piece, but we might further observe that his drawing shows a second profile to the side and it so happens that a circular stone with just this simple profile exists at the site.[122] Moreover, on its underside it carries a distinct rim, of precisely the diameter to sit neatly on the base 'pier'. On its upper surface, this same fragment provides the width of the pier proper. Finally, Potter's plate of chapter house drawings gives us the form of a capital, featuring a prominent neck-ring. It seems almost certain that several of the chapter house capitals are represented by the moulded fragments currently marking the positions of the four western piers, though as yet no positive evidence has been located to confirm the neck-rings. In sum, the authenticity of the four *in situ* pier bases at the east end can be accepted, though caution must be exercised with regard to the form of those to the west.[123]

Fortunately, the components which allow us to be reasonably confident about the form and detail of the vault survive quite well. To begin with, the springers remain in position in both the north-east and south-east corners (fig 136) and their characteristics point the way to a significant collection of *ex situ* springer fragments, mainly derived from the eight free-standing piers.[124] It is clear that three different forms are represented. In the first of these, the developing ribs look as if they

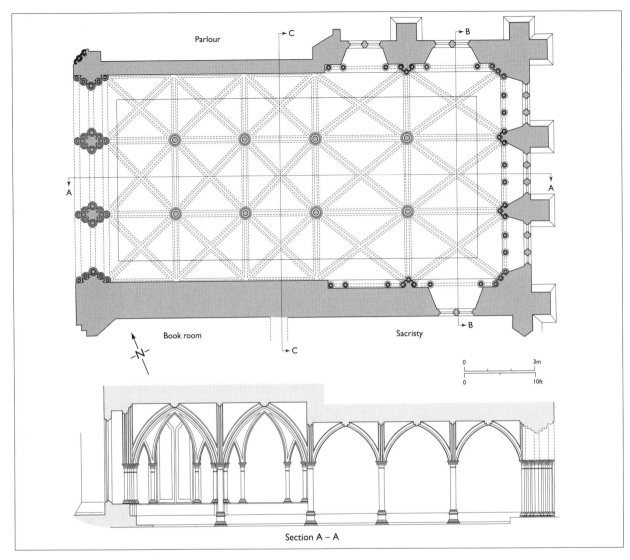

Parlour

Book room

Sacristy

0   3m
0   10ft

Section A – A

146 Tintern Abbey: chapter house, ground plan and reconstructed cross section, looking south (Chris Jones-Jenkins/David Robinson).

Drawing: *Pete Lawrence, for Cadw*

are intended to follow a comparatively steep angle, and therefore belong to the taller eastern bays. The second reveals a less acute angle to the ribs, a pattern to be expected in the lower bays to the west. The third form indicates a mix of the two profiles, and is to be associated with those middle piers bridging the change in the height of the vault (fig 146). Additionally, the springers in turn give us the profile of the individual vault ribs. The triple roll-and-fillet section was in fact drawn by Potter (fig 148), and a large stock of loose rib fragments remains at the site. At least six cross-rib pieces also survive. Several have a small foliate boss, and from the angle of the ribs it can be seen that these sat over the square western bays. Two examples carry a fuller swirling stiff-leaf pattern, and here the angle of the ribs suggests they sat over the elongated eastern bays, adding further to the enhanced decoration at this end.[125] As the plan of

the building illustrates (fig 146), apart from the surviving springers in the corners, in the east bays the outer ends of the vault ribs were generally carried on shafted responds. To the west, no such responds appear to have existed, and it is therefore assumed the ribs were supported on corbels in the upper walls.

Perhaps the most difficult element of the Tintern chapter house to reconstruct with certainty is the form of the windows, both in the eastern facade and in the side walls of the end bays. However, just enough evidence survives of the sill in the southern bay at the east end to recover the basic window divisions. This confirms Potter's assessment that we are dealing here with plate tracery forms. As shown by him (fig 148), there were indeed three lights to each bay, and therefore nine lights in all. The central light in each case was about 0.7m wide, whereas the side lights were closer to 0.4m. One or two *ex situ*

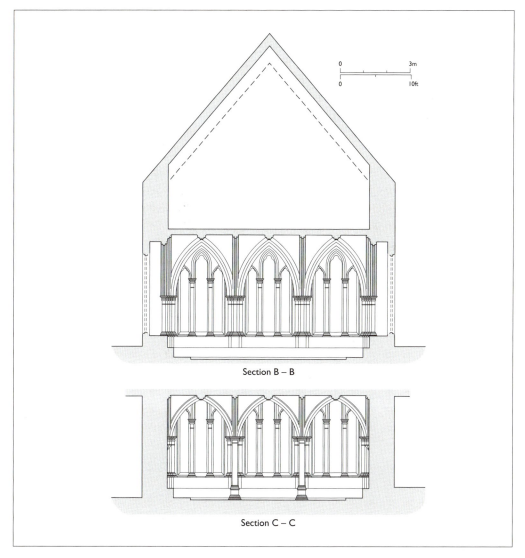

0   3m
0   10ft

Section B – B

Section C – C

147 *Tintern Abbey: chapter house, reconstructed cross sections, looking east (Chris Jones-Jenkins/Davis Robinson).*

Drawing: *Pete Lawrence, for Cadw*

fragments of the mullions are to be found at the site, and the profile is perfectly matched by further stones representing the trefoil heads of the narrower side lights.[126] It seems almost certain that the centre light of each triplet also featured a trefoil head. As for the additional windows in the side walls of the eastern bays (two on the north and one on the south), apart from the splays virtually all evidence has been lost.[127] As reconstructed here, the south window is shown with mullions of the same form as those in the east facade, and with similar trefoil-headed lancets adapted to the scale of the opening.

All of these rather plain plate tracery outer lights were almost certainly given a more decorative inner arcade, in much the same fashion as the windows in the monks' refectory.[128] One of the key pieces of evidence comes from the remains of two very worn shaft bases on the sill in the blind fourth bay

(counting from the west) on the south side of the room (fig 146). The height of the shafts themselves is uncertain, but comparison with other contemporary architectural works of a similar nature allows for an informed reconstruction. Alas, all sign of the original inner sill of the eastern facade has been lost, though the arcade is again to be expected. In the reconstructed sections offered here, shafts have been placed in line with the plate mullions (figs 146 and 147). It must be acknowledged, however, that the height of the capitals and the form of the arch heads are of necessity conjectural. There is no shortage of other contemporary west country examples with a comparable approach to enhancing the appearance of otherwise rather dull plate tracery windows. We might think, for instance, of the manner in which the eastern lancets in the Lady Chapel at Hereford Cathedral (*c* 1217–35) were treated. Similarly, one

148 *Tintern Abbey: details of the chapter house drawn by Joseph Potter, 1845, published 1847. At the top left Potter reconstructs the plan of the east windows, and at the top right he shows the general form of the vault piers. There is a plan of one of the multi-shafted entrance piers towards the bottom left, with the profile of a standard vault rib to the right.*

Photograph: *British Library*

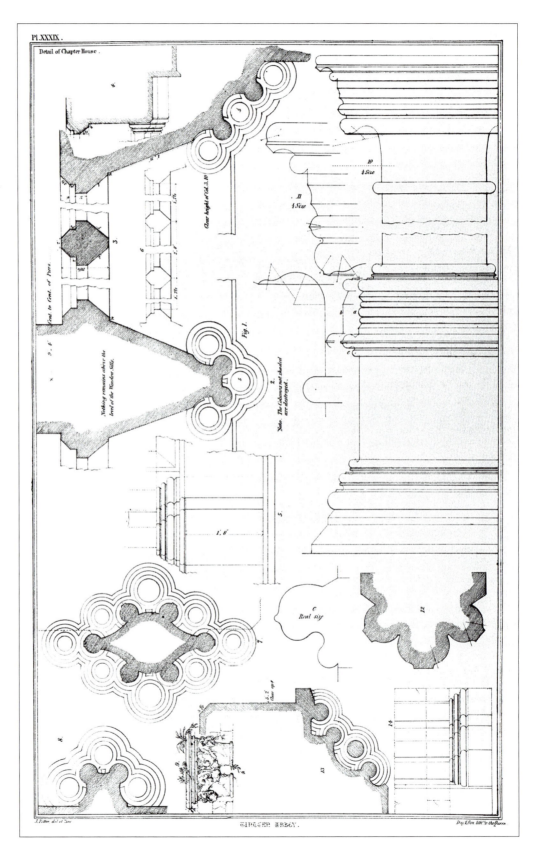

might look at the treatment visible in the chapter house at the Augustinian priory of St Frideswide in Oxford (*c* 1230–50), now Christchurch Cathedral, in the chapter house at Lacock Abbey in Wiltshire (*c* 1230–40), or again, more locally, in the presbytery at Brecon Priory (*c* 1230), now the cathedral.[129]

The reconfigured chapter house at Tintern was, as stated, part of a general upgrading of the abbey's three main ranges of claustral buildings. As it happens, the work was paralleled by a campaign of a similar period and nature at Neath (fig 21). Sadly, the Neath work is once again undocumented, though stylistically it must belong to the two or three decades before *c* 1250.[130] Without question, the chapter house would have been one of the main features of the programme. One imagines the monks at Neath would have envied the striking new chapter room at neighbouring Margam, especially considering the intense rivalry between the two houses in the first half of the thirteenth century.[131] Yet whether they attempted to emulate the qualities of the Margam structure in their own building it is impossible to say, such is the extreme paucity of the present remains.[132] As seen, the layout of the Neath chapter house presumably dates from the consolidations begun soon after 1949.[133] If the evidence is accepted at face value, the thirteenth-century room was entirely retained within the width of the range (fig 25). It would have measured a rather modest 9.8m deep by 8.8m wide, with no more than 86 square metres of floor space. A nine-bay (three by three) plan has been proposed, with a stone vault carried on four central piers. The positions of the two western pier bases are located in the turf.[134] Nevertheless, given what is known of the size and wealth of the Neath community at the time, it seems much more likely that a chapter house of the extended rectangular form would have been preferred.[135] For the moment, the question must be left open.

Summing up at this point, one suspects that all these early thirteenth-century Welsh Cistercian chapter house schemes may be explained, at least in part, by a genuine need on the part of each individual community to provide sufficient space for its daily chapter meeting. In addition, the creation of formal vestibules may have originated in the desire to provide an appropriate architectural setting for the accommodation of the lay brothers on prescribed feast days. Indeed, across Britain as a whole, many other Cistercian communities were clearly proceeding along very similar lines in much the same period. At Furness, for instance, a fifteen-bay (three by five) chapter house was built *c* 1220–30, with others introduced at Dundrennan in Scotland (three bays by four) and Stanley in Wiltshire (three bays by six)

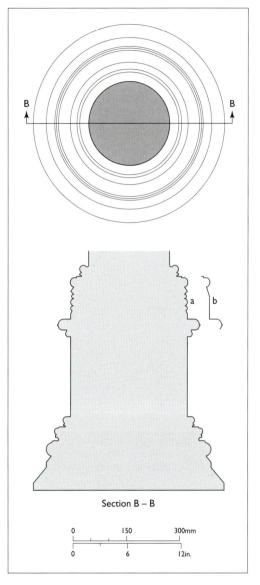

149 Tintern Abbey: chapter house, plan and profile of the base mouldings of the four eastern piers. The two alternate sub-base profiles ('a' and 'b') are those identified by Joseph Potter in the 1840s. An example of the 'b' profile survives on the site today.

Drawing: Pete Lawrence, for Cadw

Section B – B

0   150   300mm

0   6   12in.

around the mid-thirteenth century.[136] But somehow this does not go all the way to explaining the greatly increased elaboration and sophistication of the buildings. No less significant may have been a growing emphasis upon the importance of the chapter house ritual within the daily life of Cistercian communities. The room had become imbued with a deep sense of corporate and communal memory, underlined not least by the commemoration of the dead and by the burial of former abbots beneath the floor.[137]

A LATE REBUILDING AT VALLE CRUCIS

There is only one Cistercian chapter house in Wales with evidence of construction later than the thirteenth century, and that is at Valle Crucis (fig 26).[138] By remarkable good fortune, the room continues to stand virtually complete (fig 150), its clean lines and bold proportions making for an arresting if simple elegance. Nothing can be said about the form and scale of the building it replaced, but the new chapter house was clearly part of a comprehensive remodelling of the east range during the later Middle Ages. One of the more obvious features of this programme is the extensive use of good quality ashlar both inside and out. The pointed doorway from the cloister into the chapter house itself has two wave-moulded orders without capitals (fig 125). To the north (left) of this doorway, in what otherwise might be an undistinguished facade, there is a flamboyant – not to say bizarre – traceried screen fronting a small book cupboard.

The virtually square interior of the room measures close to 9.1m by 9.1m. The space is subdivided by four squat piers, bringing us back to the Burgundian nine-bay, centrally planned chapter house forms of the mid-twelfth century. Effectively, the piers themselves have double bases (fig 150), the lower of which are chamfered, the higher wave-moulded. Intriguingly, each base is of a different height and section from its fellow, for no readily apparent reason.[139] The broad ribs of the quadripartite vaults spring direct from the piers, with no capitals, and die into the side walls without corbels or responds. To

the east, the room is lit by three windows, each with flowing tracery to the head. The tracery in the three-light side windows is original, whereas that in the marginally wider four-light central opening is a replacement of 1884.[140] Unusually, certainly in terms of earlier chapter houses, the south wall contains three large recesses, perhaps intended for tombs. Some mention has already been made of wave mouldings. On closer examination it becomes clear that the entire design is totally overrun with this distinctive stylistic trait, including the window frames, the pier profile and the vault ribs.[141]

Stylistically, especially given the wave mouldings,[142] it is reasonable to suggest that construction of the new Valle Crucis chapter house took place around the second quarter of the fourteenth century,[143] but on historical grounds the architectural evidence does not go unchallenged. In particular, it seems the abbey may well have suffered extensive damage during the Glyn Dŵr uprising of the early fifteenth century.[144] Indeed, in 1419, Robert of Lancaster (1409–33) was permitted to hold the abbacy of Valle Crucis in addition to the bishopric of St Asaph on account of his having 'repaired the monastery on its destruction by fire'.[145] Though the full truth escapes us, the possibility that some elements of the rebuilt east range were completed during the early fifteenth century cannot be overlooked.

150 *Valle Crucis Abbey: chapter house interior, looking north east. The design is completely overrun with wave mouldings, suggesting a date of c 1325–50. The nine-bay (three by three) centrally planned layout goes back to the preferred Cistercian chapter house form of the mid-twelfth century.*

Photograph: *Cadw, Crown Copyright*

CHAPTER 11

THE MONKS' REFECTORY

Medieval monastic refectories were often buildings of considerable scale. Tall open halls of wide span and extensive floor space, they could also be especially fine pieces of architecture, comparable indeed to many secular great halls.[1] The splendour of the building is associated by many with the importance of the main meal in daily monastic life,[2] particularly through its links to one of the defining moments in the relationship between Christ and the Apostles.[3] The connection could sometimes be made in overt fashion, with a picture of the Last Supper painted on the wall at the high end of the building. This is found, for example, in any number of late medieval Italian refectories, although the tradition itself is older.[4] The liturgical significance of the meal was further emphasized by the reading of an appropriate holy text from a pulpit set into one of the walls, as meanwhile the brothers otherwise ate in silence.[5]

Broadly speaking, such features of remembrance and liturgy were just as important in the Cistercian approach to refectory architecture as was the case with any of the other mainstream medieval religious orders.[6] Specifically, the way in which the white monks were to use the room was set out in minutely choreographed detail in the *Ecclesiastica Officia*.[7] In similar fashion to the chapter meeting, the monks gathered together at their refectory to the sounding of a bell, washing their hands before entering the room itself. On arriving at their seats they were to bow towards the high table and wait for the arrival of the prior.[8] A psalm and several prayers were recited, followed by grace. Then, as the appointed brother began to read from the pulpit, it signalled the beginning of the meal proper. Taking their lead from the prior, each monk removed the napkin covering his bread. From that point, a rigid etiquette was prescribed: no one was to leave the refectory during the meal; if a brother wished to wipe his hands or a knife on his napkin, he was first to wipe them on a piece of bread; monks were to hold their cup in both hands; and salt was only to be taken on the end of a knife. When the meal had finished, at the appropriate moment the prior signalled to the reader to end.

Rising to their feet, the monks then processed out of the refectory chanting the Miserere.[9]

Of the buildings in which this daily performance was carried out in the Cistercian abbeys of Wales and the March, fabric evidence survives at Basingwerk, Cymer, Dore, Neath, Tintern and Valle Crucis, with geophysical survey also contributing something on the possible form of the structure at Whitland (figs 25 and 26).[10] For the most part, the Welsh refectories were arranged in the standard Cistercian pattern, that is, at right angles to the cloister. The kitchen was positioned on the west side, with the warming house to the east.[11]

THE EMERGENCE OF THE PREFERRED CISTERCIAN REFECTORY FORM

In the idealized Carolingian monastery, as depicted in the early ninth-century St Gall plan, the monks' refectory was orientated east to west, effectively occupying the whole of the south claustral range. The kitchen was positioned as a more or less free-standing building, outside the immediate confines of the cloister. As for the warming house, this appears to have been located on the ground floor of the east range.[12] By the end of the eleventh century, these general dispositions were being followed at the majority of Benedictine and Cluniac monasteries across Europe. Furthermore, the east–west refectory arrangement was also taken up by many of the new monastic congregations established over the late eleventh and early twelfth centuries, especially the Augustinian canons and the closely related groups of Premonstratensian and Gilbertine canons. It should be said, however, that the canons often favoured the construction of a two-storey south range, in which the refectory was located on the upper floor above an undercroft.[13]

As noted earlier, in that central early statute on buildings (*c* 1113–19) the Cistercian fathers stipulated that a refectory was one of the structures which had to be in place before a founding colony could be sent out to a new location.[14] It was also observed that in the pioneering years the refectory was likely to have been constructed of wood, with possible examples identified among the timber buildings now excavated at several British sites, notably at Fountains and Sawley.[15] It is particularly interesting that in the next stage of development, that is, when the budding communities began to achieve a degree of stability and embarked on stone construction for the first time, they chose to build their refectories in accordance with customary monastic preference. In other words, the earliest stone refectories were arranged on an east–west axis, parallel to the church and adjacent to the south walk of the cloister. In so far as the structural and archaeological evidence allows, this was precisely what occurred in the primary stone layouts in Britain.[16]

At Waverley, for instance, a stone-built refectory was laid out in this manner perhaps as early as the 1130s.[17] Others have been identified from the 1140s through to the late 1150s at Byland (fig 93), Fountains, Furness, Kirkstall and Rievaulx in the north of England,[18] with another possibility at Boxley in the south.[19] In Wales, the early twentieth-century clearance work at Tintern Abbey uncovered the footings of a similar east–west orientated refectory, measuring 7m wide. It was probably built in the later 1130s or 1140s (figs 26 and 36).[20] The same arrangement may well have existed by the mid-twelfth century (or soon after) at Basingwerk,[21] Dore,[22] Neath, Margam[23] and Whitland. In all cases, confirmation must await future archaeological investigation.

The decision by the Cistercians to swing the orientation of their refectories through 90 degrees, aligning them north to south, most probably emerged during the rebuilding of Clairvaux, perhaps about 1140–50.[24] In much of the literature, this change in alignment tends to be explained merely by its practical benefits, allowing as it undoubtedly did for a greatly enlarged dining area suitable for rapidly expanding communities.[25] But, as Fergusson has said, there were almost definitely other reasons for the change, not least the growing standardization of monastery planning within the order, coupled with a desire for an even closer adherence to the Rule of St Benedict. With the position of the refectory altered, it made it possible for the warming house and the kitchen to be drawn into the heart of the claustral complex. Consequently, all the buildings essential to the monastic life could now be reached directly from one or other of the four cloister walks.[26]

Even though a date of c 1140–50 for the new Clairvaux refectory is perfectly plausible, attempting to chart the subsequent progress of change through the order as a whole is fraught with difficulty. At Clairvaux's own daughter of Fontenay, no less, where the monastic buildings were under construction c 1150–60, it seems the original refectory was built parallel with the south walk of the cloister, and was only rebuilt on a north–south axis in the thirteenth century.[27] It must be remembered, too, that the abandonment of the traditional orientation was by no means universal, with examples of refectories running alongside the cloister to be found at Obazine, Sénanque and Silvacane in France, at Heiligenkreuz in Austria, at Staffarda in Italy, and also at Boyle, Dunbrody, Hore and Monasteranenagh in Ireland.[28] Notwithstanding either point, the undoubted Cistercian preference for a north–south refectory arrangement from the mid- to late twelfth century onwards is unequivocal. Of course, in the development of this trend, it would have been highly significant that a building of the form was soon introduced at Cîteaux, certainly no later than the beginning of the thirteenth century.[29] Although lost, the scale of this great refectory, as well as that at Clairvaux, can be seen in later plans and views of the two sites (figs 15, 16 and 39). Rib-vaulted buildings divided into three aisles by two rows of central columns, each was likely to have been an important example of the early Gothic style. The Clairvaux refectory was five bays in length; that at Cîteaux was a bay longer.

Across much of Europe, the number of tall, well-lit Cistercian refectories covered with stone vaults was to increase markedly through the first half of the thirteenth century. Apart from anything else, as noted by way of introduction, these buildings bear striking testimony to the growing liturgical significance of the daily meal. At Alcobaça in Portugal, for instance, there is a superb rib-vaulted example set out in three aisles, similar to those at Clairvaux and Cîteaux. Rather more common were the two-aisle layouts, with a single row of central columns, as at Noirlac (four bays in length), Reigny (six bays) and Royaumont (six bays) in France, or at Maulbronn in Germany (eight bays), and again at Villers in Belgium (six bays). Barrel vaults were also favoured in some regions, with surviving examples to be seen at Aiguebelle (Drôme) in France, and at Poblet and Rueda in Spain.[30]

THE PROCESS OF TRANSITION IN ENGLAND

On present evidence, the earliest of the English Cistercian communities to have made the transition from an east–west to a north–south refectory arrangement were those at Kirkstall and Byland. At Kirkstall,[31] both archaeological and architectural evidence suggests that when the south range was first laid out in the 1150s or early 1160s,[32] a refectory of about 21.3m long by 9.1m wide was set out parallel with the south walk of the cloister. Incredibly, the major decision to switch the axis of the building completely seems to have been taken during the course of construction. Though the evidence at Byland is less clear cut (fig 93), a similar process may well have occurred at much the same time.[33] In both cases, given the logistical and financial implications of opting for such a revised building programme in mid-stream, one imagines the communities were wholly convinced of the need to adhere to the revised orthodoxy.

Alongside the Kirkstall and Byland schemes, it was probably in the mid-1170s that Abbot Robert of Pipewell (1170–80) began the construction of a brand new refectory in the remodelled south range at Fountains. The result was a decidedly impressive structure divided into two aisles by a five-bay arcade carried on tall slender piers, the whole measuring approximately 33.5m long by 14m wide.[34] Subsequently, a new refectory was begun at Rievaulx, late in the time of Abbot Sylvanus (1167–88). In this case, because of the fall in the ground, the building had to be carried on a substantial undercroft. As completed in the 1190s, it stood as 'one of the most magnificent' examples ever raised by the British Cistercians, reaching up to 38.4m long by 11.6m wide.[35] In the meantime, in the south of the country, the monks at Waverley had also chosen to rebuild their refectory on a north–south alignment.[36] Moreover, in line with the new convention, at almost all major abbeys where the work on the south claustral range began after c 1170, the refectory was built in this fashion from the start. Examples from the last quarter of the twelfth century are to be found at Roche, Jervaulx and Sawley, and possibly at Bindon.[37] Of the many thirteenth-century examples, there is good evidence of one kind or another from Beaulieu (where the refectory now serves as the parish church), Cleeve (fig 151) and Hailes, and also from Melrose in Scotland.[38]

As in mainland Europe, however, we must remember that a number of British white monk communities were content to retain the older east–west refectory arrangement throughout their history. This appears to have been the case at Buckfast, Sibton and Robertsbridge, for example, and at Culross in Scotland.[39] Then again at Cleeve, where the refectory was first constructed at right angles to the cloister in the thirteenth century, the entire south range was rebuilt with a brand new first-floor refectory on an east–west axis in the late fifteenth century. This building continues to stand, complete with its fine arch-braced timber roof intact (fig 151).[40]

Before moving on to look at the Welsh material, it is worth considering two broad contrasts between British Cistercian refectories and those on the Continent. First, despite the widespread tendency at many larger European houses to cover these buildings with stone vaults, this did not win favour with masons working for white monk communities in Britain. Indeed, every known example of a Cistercian refectory across the whole of England, Wales and Scotland was covered with a wooden roof, even if on occasion the trusses may have been boarded so as to resemble barrel vaulting.[41] Secondly, as noted in a previous chapter, there appear to have been contrasting preferences for the position of *lavatoria*, the place where the monks washed their hands before entering the refectory for meals.[42] In mainland Europe, a definite preference for free-standing fountain pavilions can perhaps be detected. Almost invariably, these projected out into the cloister garth from the alley adjacent to the refectory entrance,[43] as may be seen on the ground plans of Cîteaux and Clairvaux (fig 39).[44] Something comparable may have existed alongside the early east–west refectories in England, with specific claims made for Byland, Fountains, Kirkstall and Rievaulx.[45] Moreover, the surviving foundations of one such structure can be seen further north, in the cloister garth at Melrose.[46] However, from the 1170s, when the British Cistercians began to reorganize their refectories on a north–south axis, it became more common for the *lavatorium* to be placed within a recess in the entrance facade to the building.[47] Good examples of the arrangement survive at Fountains, Rievaulx, Cleeve, Hailes and Netley.[48]

THIRTEENTH-CENTURY REFECTORIES IN WALES

In the wake of the late twelfth-century refectory rebuildings at several of England's most influential Cistercian abbeys, the communities in Wales and the March began to follow suit as soon as they were able. It is especially unfortunate, therefore, that so little is known of the south ranges at Margam and Whitland (figs 25 and 26). Given their direct filial relationship to Clairvaux (figs 18 and 19), one suspects they may well have been among the first houses in Wales to conform to the newly approved model. Be that as it may, on the basis of the evidence which survives, the earliest and most ambitious updated refectory programmes were initiated c 1220–40 at Tintern, Neath and Dore. The work at these sites was followed soon afterwards by a similar scheme at Basingwerk. Meanwhile, the first stone refectory raised by monks at Valle Crucis (only founded in 1200–1) was built at

151 Cleeve Abbey (North Somerset): general view of refectory, from the south west. In the foreground, the rubble foundations and tile pavement represent the thirteenth-century north–south refectory. This was replaced by a brand new first-floor refectory on an east–west axis in the fifteenth century, the building which survives to the rear. Photograph: *English Heritage, Crown Copyright*

right angles to the cloister from the outset. At Tintern and Basingwerk, enough of the thirteenth-century fabric survives to provide a very good indication of the original form of the structures. The walls of the refectory at Valle Crucis stand up to about 0.9m high, but at Neath and Dore there are sadly little more than ground plans to go on.

At Tintern, the new refectory was one of the main elements in the comprehensive remodelling of both the east and north claustral ranges during the first half of the thirteenth century.[49] Construction of the building began at the north, and was pushed forward in such a way that the monks were able to occupy their older east–west refectory for as long as possible. Indeed, tell-tale joints in the side walls of the standing building show that it was erected up to the outer face of the twelfth-century range before its final removal.[50] As completed, the doorway to the thirteenth-century refectory opened off the centre of the north cloister walk (figs 26 and 130). In turn, this doorway stood at the middle of an elaborate composition of five richly moulded archways, all springing from multiple clusters of attached and detached shafts, doubtless burnished or painted to add to the decorative effect. A close inspection of the fabric reveals that the jambs of the doorway alone featured five en délit shafts sitting on moulded bases, between which a further five attached and filleted shafts were set slightly back.[51] The arched recesses to either side of the doorway comprised the *lavatorium* or washing place, an arrangement not unlike the earlier examples found at Fountains and Rievaulx. At Tintern, the larger outer recesses probably housed sizeable troughs lined with lead or pewter, in which the monks would wash their hands before going into the refectory to eat. The smaller inner arches may have been used for holding towels, though this is more speculative. The troughs would have been supplied with fresh running water from lead pipes, which by analogy with other sites were presumably fitted with taps.[52]

Aside from its use by the monks for washing their hands, we can be confident that the Tintern *lavatorium* would also have been designed in such a way that it could accommodate the liturgy associated with the weekly rite known as the *mandatum*.[53] This important cloister rite, hitherto mentioned only in passing,[54] would have been carried out at both pavilion and recessed versions of white monk *lavatoria*, probably with very little distinction. The rite had originally been prescribed by St Benedict,[55] and involved a symbolic washing of the brethren's feet. This action – carrying with it definite meanings of humility and exemplary charity – was clearly done in imitation of Christ washing the feet of

the Apostles before the Last Supper. Such was the importance of the *mandatum* to the early Cistercians, St Bernard suggested it should be made the eighth sacrament.[56] The basic rite was carried out every Saturday, when the washing was performed by those monks appointed to serve as the kitchen helpers for the week.[57] On Maundy Thursday, as part of an expanded *mandatum* liturgy, the abbot himself washed the feet of twelve members of the community: four monks, four novices and four lay brothers.[58] To facilitate the procedures in both these ceremonies, *lavatoria* set into the refectory facade sometimes featured a bench positioned above the washing trough, allowing the monks to sit with their feet close to the water. Traces of such benches have been identified, for example, at Fountains and Rievaulx, and also at Vaux-de-Cernay in France.[59] The same cannot be recorded positively at Tintern, though the richness of the architectural treatment around the *lavatorium* certainly encourages us to look for explanations other than pure utility.

Beyond the cloister facade, in terms of its true scale and original architectural qualities, the remains of the Tintern refectory can be somewhat misleading (figs 152 and 153). In point of fact, measuring approximately 26m long by 9m wide, it was a room of sizeable proportions and sophisticated decorative splendour.[60] Structurally, the building comprised four double bays, clearly demarcated by stepped external buttresses. In the southern bay, given the positioning of the kitchen to the west and the warming house to the east, the side elevations were denied windows of any form. Northwards of this point, however, the free-standing bays were flooded with as much natural light as possible by large four-light plate tracery windows, arranged two to each bay.[61] As shown by the four examples which survive on the east side of the building (fig 152), the individual windows featured two pairs of tall trefoil-headed lancets, with a small oculus set between the heads of each pair. In some of the bays, a larger oculus was positioned in the arch head above, giving unity to the composition as a whole.[62] Although the evidence has entirely disappeared, potentially there was space for a further three windows of identical design in the north gable wall of the building.[63] Then, greatly enhancing the decorative effect of the plate tracery pattern as a whole, a far more delicate and ornate arcade ran along the inner edge of the sills. In essence, the arrangements were not unlike those adopted for the east windows of the chapter house in much the same period.[64] Here in the refectory, arches with rich roll-and-hollow mouldings were carried on slender shafts with moulded bases and capitals, all repeating the basic eight-light pattern of the bays. To

152 Tintern Abbey:
refectory east wall,
looking south. The
twelfth-century
community at Tintern
built its first stone
refectory on an
east–west axis. This
was replaced during
the second quarter of
the thirteenth century
by a handsome new
structure set at right
angles to the cloister.
The decorative effect of
the large plate tracery
windows was enhanced
by a far more delicate
arcade carried on
slender shafts along
the inner sill.

Photograph: *Royal*
Commission on the
Ancient and Historical
Monuments of Wales,
Crown Copyright

strengthen the otherwise free-standing shafts out at the centre of the windows, small masonry bridges were used to link them to the plate tracery. In the blind southern bay, this decorative arcade was carried through as wall panelling (figs 152 and 153).

Below the windows, the lower walls of the Tintern refectory were almost entirely plain, effectively forming a blind dado against which the monks would have sat looking outwards to the centre of the room (fig 153). The prior and other senior monks would have sat at a table on a raised dais at the northern end of the building. In the middle of the west wall, a doorway with a moulded head gave access to a flight of stairs housed within the thickness of the masonry. They led to what must have been a projecting pulpit from which one of the brothers would have read during the meal.[65] In the south-west corner of the building, there is a rectangular serving hatch from the kitchen. Next to it, in the southern wall, a shallow rectangular recess probably housed a drop-down table on which dishes of food could be momentarily rested. On the opposite side of the entrance, there are two trefoil-headed recesses. One of these, equipped with a drain and a shelf, may have been for washing dishes. The other, rebated for a door, must have been a cupboard. A doorway in this same south-east corner of the refectory leads into a small vaulted

chamber, which presumably served as some form of pantry or storeroom. Finally, in common with the preferred pattern among the British Cistercians, there is no indication of a stone vault covering the building. On the contrary, it seems far more likely a boarded wooden ceiling was used, possibly of barrel form, in which the rhythm of the bay divisions could easily have been picked out with simple cross ribs (fig 153).[66]

The north–south refectory at Neath Abbey was similarly raised as part of an extensive refurbishment of the principal claustral ranges, a programme which seems to have been centred on the second quarter of the thirteenth century.[67] Earlier, just as at Tintern, the Neath monks had probably taken their meals in a refectory aligned parallel with the south walk of the cloister. As it happens, the basic arrangements within their new building may also have been analogous to those found at Tintern (fig 25).[68] The jambs of the doorway which opened into the room from the south cloister walk were certainly embellished with a similar array of attached and detached shafts, though the doorway itself looks to have been narrower.[69] The wide recesses which survive to either side of this doorway would likewise have housed the troughs or basins of the monks' *lavatorium*. As for the scale of the refectory hall itself, although it has almost

153 *Tintern Abbey: conjectural reconstruction of refectory, c 1250, looking north. In common with the preferred British pattern for monastic refectories and secular halls, the roof of this great building was covered with wood.*

Drawing: *Terry Ball, for Cadw*

entirely disappeared, it was clearly somewhat larger than the Tintern structure, measuring approximately 30.8m long by 8.8m wide. The only fragment of original fabric is in the south-east corner, and includes traces of windows incorporated within the layouts of the late medieval abbot's house and post-suppression mansion.[70]

The date of the new refectory at Dore Abbey is less certain than is the case at either Tintern or Neath. Nevertheless, given what is known of the development of the site in general, it seems likely it was constructed in the first half of the thirteenth century.[71] The scanty remains were investigated by Roland Paul at the turn of the nineteenth century. To begin with, although Paul identified the north–south plan, he thought the refectory was no more than 7.9m in width.[72] After further excavation, he revised his ideas and produced a fresh annotated sketch plan, showing indications of wall benching along the northern and western sides.[73] Recently, this evidence has been reassessed by Harrison. He concludes that the refectory measured almost 37.8m long by 10.4m wide (fig 25), making it by far the largest example known from Wales and the March.[74]

Now, at much the same time as the communities at Tintern, Neath and Dore were engaged with building new refectories on north–south alignments,

the monks at Valle Crucis were constructing theirs in stone for the first time.[75] From the findings of his excavations in 1970, Butler has suggested there may have been a short-lived timber-framed range running parallel with the adjacent cloister walk. Before long, however, any such early southern range was replaced by a stone-built north–south refectory hall, measuring a modest 15.2m long by 6.4m wide. Of particular note, the axis of the building was not quite at true right angles to the cloister (fig 26). Within the thickness of the lateral walls, Butler found a series of regularly spaced cavities at intervals of about 4m. He interpreted these as the positions of vertical wooden posts, left over from the primary timber-framed phase and utilized within the structure of the stone refectory as a form of strengthening for the wall plate and roof frame.[76] Butler also recorded slight traces of white plaster on the inner faces of the walls. At the south-west corner of the refectory, the walls were thickened to accommodate a curving flight of stairs leading up to the reader's pulpit. The lower jambs of the doorway to these stairs survive, with two vertical bands of dog-tooth ornament flanking a roll moulding. Hereabouts, during the excavations of 1970, a remarkable thirteenth-century carved stone head was uncovered.[77] This life-sized fragment is one of

154 *Valle Crucis Abbey: sculpted stone head, found during excavations in the refectory. One of the most striking pieces of white monk figure sculpture known from Wales, this thirteenth-century head was found close to the position of the refectory pulpit in 1970. The crown-like inscription above the brow reads ⼁MORUS (430mm by 365mm).*

Photograph: *National Museums & Galleries of Wales*

the most striking pieces of white monk figure sculpture known from Wales (fig 154), and has been linked to a posited northern school of carving.[78] The features include a deeply furrowed brow, wide-set eyes and a long beard. On the band above the brow there is a crown-like inscription reading +MORVS, presumably intended to name the figure, though Butler was unable to identify the individual with any certainty.[79] Recently, however, it has been claimed that the head represents Rabanus Maurus (d 856), theologian and sometime abbot of the Carolingian abbey of Fulda, with the suggestion that his commentaries on biblical texts may have been appropriate subjects for readings from the pulpit during meals.[80]

The last of the definite thirteenth-century north–south refectories in Wales is to be found at Basingwerk Abbey, where the standing fabric suggests it was built marginally later than any of the examples considered so far (fig 155).[81] Once more, this is a site where it seems certain that the twelfth-century community ate in a refectory hall running parallel with the south walk of the cloister. In fact, traces of the early building may well have survived within the north wall of the remodelled range.[82]

Interestingly, there was perhaps a passage running through the east end of the early building, not unlike the example known from Abbot Ailred's Rievaulx.[83] The reconstruction of the claustral ranges at Basingwerk was apparently initiated in the early thirteenth century, progressing to the refectory in the years around or soon after 1250. In what is now a familiar pattern, the hall was laid out at right angles to the cloister, though not springing from a central point as was so often the case, but much closer to the existing monks' day room (fig 25). Consequently, unlike the majority of known layouts, there was no room for a warming house within the width of the reorganized southern range.[84]

As completed, the Basingwerk community's new refectory was approximately 20.1m long by 8.2m wide. Although virtually all of the north and much of the south gable ends have been lost, in places the lateral walls still stand close to the level of the wall plates (fig 155). There is enough evidence to show that the interior of the building was chiefly lit from windows on the south and west sides. Hence, in the surviving corners of the south wall, tall splays with a roll moulding to the outer edge reveal the scale of the original thirteenth-century openings, and it is clear from several early illustrations made before the collapse of this gable end that the wall as a whole contained a total of four lancets, the middle two graduated above the outer pair.[85] The evidence for the window arrangements in the west wall survives rather better. On this side, the features were combined with those of the refectory pulpit. As a whole, the composition was effectively given the unity of a continuous arcade, with moulded shaft groups banded at mid-height, moulded capitals and bases, and a boldly projecting hood running throughout. There are four lancets at the northern end (one of which is blocked), and a single lancet of different proportions in the southern corner. Between these, there are four remaining bays, all of them now blocked.[86] The doorway at the south end gave access to the stair leading to the reader's pulpit. The outer face of the wall at this point was originally thickened to accommodate the stair. The next two narrower lancets lit the stair, and the position of the final bay reflects the location of the pulpit itself. Stylistically, the composition may be compared in very broad terms with the refectory pulpit at the Benedictine abbey of Chester, and is not too far removed from the lancet arrangement in the presbytery of the Dominican friars at Brecon.[87] As to the remaining features here at Basingwerk, there is a hatch which led through to the kitchen at the northern end of the west wall, and opposite this a cupboard with a pointed head, rebated for a door. On

155 Basingwerk Abbey: view of refectory, looking north west. It is almost certain that this mid-thirteenth-century building replaced an older refectory on an east–west axis. From early illustrations it is known that the southern gable wall was pierced by four tall lancets. The roof structure was of seven bays.

Photograph: *author*

the basis of several surviving corbels, the refectory appears to have been covered with a timber roof of seven bays.[88]

In addition to the confirmed examples of Welsh white monk refectories newly built on a north–south axis in the thirteenth century, fresh evidence has recently come to light at Whitland. Practically nothing of the abbey's south claustral range survives above ground, but a geophysical survey now appears to have confirmed its general position, including some indication of the refectory layout (fig 26).[89] If the earliest stone monastic buildings at the site were laid out in the 1150s and 1160s, then the refectory might again be expected to have been positioned alongside the cloister, parallel with the nave of the church. However, a distinct central projection picked up in the recent survey suggests a subsequent remodelling, in which the building followed the revised Cistercian orthodoxy for refectory planning. Although the work is so far undated, it would not be entirely unsurprising if it went back to the late twelfth century.

One final Welsh Cistercian refectory for which some structural evidence survives is that at Cymer. Given that the house was founded in 1198–9, and that the claustral buildings were probably built in the first half of the thirteenth century, it is notable that the design of the refectory followed the by-then-outmoded east–west model.[90] Only foundation courses survive, but the jambs of doorways in both the north and south walls may be seen (fig 25). The point has already been made above, but Cymer serves to remind us that refectories arranged on a north–south axis were by no means universal among the later Cistercians.

In conclusion, we might note that at least one of the Cistercian refectories in Wales had probably already fallen into disrepair sometime before the suppression. Writing of Strata Florida around 1539, John Leland noted 'the fratry … be now mere ruines'.[91] Indeed, unless a refectory was modified for fresh use by the very much smaller communities of the later Middle Ages, it must have been difficult for some of the impoverished Welsh houses to have maintained it alongside those other large open chambers of earlier centuries.[92]

CHAPTER 12

INFIRMARY PROVISION AND THE ABBOT'S ACCOMMODATION

In this final chapter we shall return to look in more detail at the nature of the buildings situated east of the main claustral complex, and in particular at the evidence known from Wales.[1] Essentially, there were two groups of structures in this area: the choir monks' infirmary and the lodgings set aside for the private use of the abbot. For the most part, scholars have tended to consider the groupings as almost entirely separate entities, although recognizing the fact they shared certain facilities, notably kitchens. This is hardly surprising when we appreciate that by the mid-thirteenth century, possibly even earlier, the abbot's lodging and the infirmary had come to occupy semi-formal and quite distinct positions around a secondary or lesser cloister. In the past decade, however, several studies have argued the need for a more subtle appreciation of the ways in which the two complexes were adapted in response to changing circumstances. It is now suggested that Cistercian communities were more flexible in their use of the buildings, with a degree of interchange occurring in both early and later medieval centuries.

Most recently, the issues surrounding the buildings to the east of the cloister have been examined in some detail by Hall. Having surveyed both the structural and historical evidence from a number of white monk houses across England, she puts forward various thought-provoking ideas. Among her arguments for the multiple use of infirmary halls, for example, Hall makes a good case for their having served as locations for conducting abbatial business, including entertainment, in the decades before the construction of a separate abbot's lodging. Then again, she also encourages us to think about the presence of several sets of high-status chambers somewhere within this general vicinity of the precinct. We certainly know from documentary sources that such rooms were occasionally required for the accommodation of retired abbots, as well as for honoured guests sent from other houses.[2] All in all, by the late Middle Ages, as Coppack and others have demonstrated, for instance at Fountains, Rievaulx and Waverley, the physical distinction

between the infirmary complex and the abbot's lodging had grown increasingly ill-defined.[3]

THE CISTERCIAN INFIRMARY

The main reasons – practical, medical and spiritual – for the location of white monk infirmaries to the east of the main claustral complex have been carefully considered by Professor David Bell.[4] There is also a stimulating general discussion of the subject by Fergusson and Harrison in their account of the infirmary complex at Rievaulx.[5] As pointed out in both these studies, the arrangements followed by the Cistercians were little different from those of other orders. Fundamentally, it was the Rule of St Benedict that determined the provision made for the sick by all monastic communities. Care of the sick, the Rule enjoined, 'must rank above and before all else, so they may truly be served as Christ'. The instruction went on: 'Let a separate room be designated for the sick, and let them be served by an attendant who is God-fearing, attentive, and concerned'.[6]

Not surprisingly, a clear architectural response to St Benedict's instruction was built into the layout of the idealized Carolingian monastery. Hence, in the early ninth-century St Gall plan, a discrete and clearly defined infirmary complex is depicted immediately to the north east of the abbey church.[7] Subsequently, new ideas on infirmary design appear to have surfaced during the monastic revival of the late eleventh and early twelfth centuries, with developments at Burgundian Cluny from *c* 1040 onwards likely to have been of particular significance in this regard.[8] By and large, the typical Cluniac or Benedictine infirmary complex came to be dominated by a substantial open hall or ward, around which were gathered a series of associated structures such as a chapel, the infirmarer's lodging, a kitchen, latrines and a bath-house. In due course, these buildings were commonly separated from the main east claustral range by a secondary cloister.[9]

In spite of this emerging pattern among the older monastic orders, the early Cistercian fathers do not appear to have regarded an infirmary as one of the essential buildings for a new foundation, at least in so far as can be judged from the statute of *c* 1113–19 listing the minimum complement of structures.[10] Nevertheless, as once fledgling communities began to mature, and as numbers of both sick and infirm monks grew, the provision of infirmary facilities would doubtless have become a greater priority. Henceforth, one imagines such provision would have been made in strict accordance with the instruction given in the Rule of St Benedict. Indeed, no later than the mid-twelfth century, the appropriate conduct of a Cistercian infirmary patient, together with the duties of the infirmarer and his helpers, were articulated in the order's customary.[11]

The earliest surviving architectural evidence of a white monk infirmary anywhere in Europe is to be found at Rievaulx, and probably dates from *c* 1155–7.[12] At much the same time, however, as this building was under construction by Abbot Ailred, influential models for a new formality in Cistercian infirmary design were probably being introduced during the comprehensive rebuildings at Cîteaux and Clairvaux. Sadly, the twelfth-century infirmaries at both these sites were modified after 1300, although it is suggested that the later halls could well have stood over the footprints of the original stone buildings.[13] Arranged on an east–west axis, the main infirmary hall at Cîteaux may be seen in Brissart's engraving of 1674 (fig 15).[14] Records and plans made before its destruction show that it was a tall, three-aisled structure measuring as much as 59m long by 21m wide, with quadripartite ribs over the twenty-four individual bays (three by eight).[15] At Clairvaux, the infirmary hall was again orientated east–west, though here it was of two aisles, seven bays in length. Of particular interest, Milley's 1708 ground plan and views of the site reveal the full extent of the greater infirmary complex, showing something very like the old-established Benedictine pattern (figs 16 and 39).[16] And, as noted earlier in the volume, the same basic arrangements are very well depicted in an imaginary drawing (1580) of the abbey of Dunes in Belgium, though here the infirmary hall appears to have been orientated north–south.[17] Today, among the best survivals of infirmary halls found on the Continent are those at Ourscamp (c 1210–20) in France, Eberbach (c 1220) and Maulbronn in Germany, and Fossanova in Italy.[18]

As for Cistercian infirmaries in England, the first point to note about the fabric evidence is that it comes almost entirely from buried or substantially ruinous buildings, in many cases excavated or cleared when archaeology was in its infancy.[19] Bearing this in mind, it can be assumed that the earliest structures were generally raised in timber, presumably echoing the pattern established in France. Indeed, when Brakspear excavated the site of the infirmary at Waverley Abbey in the early twentieth century, he found traces of wooden structures buried beneath the later stone complex. Though undated, these were probably put up in the second quarter of the twelfth century.[20] Evidence for another timber infirmary has been excavated at Kirkstall Abbey, in this case orientated north–south and thought to date from the 1170s.[21] Meanwhile, as pointed out above, a remarkably early stone infirmary hall had been built in the mid-1150s by Abbot Ailred at Rievaulx. This ten-bay structure ran parallel with the east claustral range and featured a single aisle on the outer site.[22] Within a very few years, it is possible that a hall of similar scale and design was constructed at Fountains.[23] And, once again, when the infirmary complex at Waverley was rebuilt in stone *c* 1190–1200, the hall was similarly arranged on a north–south axis with a single aisle on the east side, though here with the addition of a small rectangular chapel opening off the north-east corner.[24]

Apart from this small early group, the majority of white monk infirmaries known from across England date from the thirteenth century. Although much ruined, the largest and at one time most impressive complex was almost certainly that built at Fountains during the abbacy of John of Kent (1220–47).[25] Measuring 55m long by 23.8m wide, and more or less orientated north–south, Kent's great infirmary hall is described by Coppack as 'one of the largest aisled halls ever built in medieval England'.[26] Smaller but no less significant thirteenth-century halls of varying form are known from, for instance, Beaulieu, Buildwas, Croxden, Jervaulx and Kirkstall.[27] In addition, there is documentary evidence for the construction of new infirmaries at Meaux in the time of Abbot Richard of Ottringham (1221–35), and at Louth Park in the time of Abbot Richard de Dunham (1227–46).[28] The last great Cistercian infirmary hall built in England was that raised at Furness *c* 1300, measuring a massive 38.7m long by 14.3m wide.[29]

THE EVIDENCE FOR WELSH INFIRMARIES

The surviving evidence for Cistercian infirmaries in Wales and the March is very disappointing. With one notable exception, hardly anything is to be seen above ground, and the buried remains have so far attracted little attention from archaeologists. Nothing at all is known of the primary arrangements at any of the sites, although it is perfectly possible that timber, if not stone, infirmary buildings had been erected before the end of the twelfth century at, say, Dore, Margam, Neath, Tintern and Whitland.

156 *Tintern Abbey:*
infirmary and abbot's
lodgings, from the
south west. In the
right foreground is
the great thirteenth-
century infirmary
hall, and to the left
of this the infirmary
cloister. Northwards,
at the far left, are the
foundations of the
fourteenth-century
abbot's hall. By the
end of the Middle Ages,
extensive kitchens were
positioned between the
infirmary hall and
the abbot's hall.

Photograph: *Cadw,*
Crown Copyright

The one Welsh abbey site where infirmary structures have been exposed to view is Tintern.[30] Here, allowing for the northern claustral arrangement, the mid-thirteenth-century hall was located in accordance with the accepted pattern. It lay to the north east of the abbey church, and due east of the east range, from which it was eventually separated by a formal cloister (figs 20, 26, 122 and 156). When the complex was observed by the antiquary William Worcestre during his visit to Tintern in 1478, he noted: 'The infirmary chapel is 34 yards long, that is 60 of my steps, and 8 yards wide; and the Infirmary is 60 of my steps long, that is 34 yards, and 8 yards wide.'[31] However, long before the end of the nineteenth century, all trace of any buildings had been lost. The recovery process began in 1907, when Brakspear was commissioned to produce a ground plan of the whole abbey. As his correspondence reveals, he was particularly keen to uncover what remained of the infirmary. Men were put at Brakspear's disposal, and over a few weeks they cleared the hall and also determined the outline of the infirmary cloister.[32] In subsequent years, the Office of Works uncovered an area of kitchens to the north of the hall.[33] Today, the consolidated walls of Tintern's infirmary stand up to 1.5m high.

The Tintern community did not follow the north–south pattern of its sister house at Waverley, but chose to align its new infirmary hall on an east–west axis. The building comprised a tall central 'nave' aisle, with a lower flanking aisle to either side, the whole measuring approximately 33m long by 16m wide. At the far ends of the hall, the three aisles were always separated one from another by solid walls. In contrast, the main middle section featured arcades, probably of five bays, resting on compound piers. From the surviving north-west and south-east responds, it seems that the free-standing piers had a central column on a moulded base, with a detached shaft at each of the cardinal points. There were external buttresses in line with the arcades at the east end, and an angle buttress on a chamfered plinth at the south-east corner. But the lack of any convincing buttressing along the lateral walls argues for open or boarded wooden roofs rather than stone vaults. The aisles were lit by coupled lancets, of which traces of several sills may still be seen. Light was probably brought into the central part of the hall through clerestory windows and via a substantial opening in the east gable wall. In fact, soon after Brakspear's clearance of the building, James Wood reported: 'A large part of the tracery of the great window of the hall lies outside the east wall and appears to have been thrown bodily outwards.'[34] The infirmary hall was entered from the adjacent cloister by a doorway leading into its main central aisle, and traces of two other doorways are to be found opening northwards from the north aisle. Finally, at the northern corners of the building there were two further substantial rectangular rooms. The north-west example projects over a drain at its far end, indicating that this area probably served as the infirmary latrine. The chamber at the north-east corner was marginally bigger, and possibly served as the infirmarer's lodging.[35]

General sick care was regarded early on as important not only by the Tintern community, but also by the abbey's patrons. About 1240, for example, Gilbert Marshal, earl of Pembroke, granted the monks 'both shoulders of all wild animals of the wood, to wit, stag and hind, deer and doe, taken in Trelleck Park' for the use of the sick brethren dwelling in the house.[36] The nature of the infirmary structures at this time is unclear, though it is possible they were still of timber. The lavish scale of the subsequent stone hall says much about the growing emphasis given to infirmary facilities by the Cistercians generally. It also reflects the importance of spaciousness and generous lighting in medieval medicinal theory, in which corrupted air was seen as a major contributing factor to illness.[37] A further explanation for the great size of the Tintern hall, equally applicable to those at Fountains, Kirkstall and elsewhere, may have been the periodic need to accommodate those monks recovering from blood-letting. In the twelfth century, the order's customary made it clear that all monks were to remain in the cloister both during and after the process.[38] Yet in time the instruction seems to have been relaxed, and four times a year the entire community may well have retired to the infirmary in groups, there to recover for several days from the significant trauma of this medieval medicinal ordeal.[39]

In the later Middle Ages, beginning as early as the fourteenth century, it was not unusual for Cistercian infirmary halls to be substantially modified, often being internally subdivided by stone or wooden partitions in order to create a number of individual cells or apartments. Structural evidence for this pattern is known from Fountains, Kirkstall and Waverley, among others, and it is documented for Meaux.[40] In the fifteenth century (specifically in the years 1449 and 1460), probably when it was already too late, the General Chapter condemned the practice of dividing communal infirmary spaces into private rooms.[41]

At Tintern, the first sign of any modification appears in the main west door, as indicated by the one surviving fourteenth-century wave-moulded jamb. This new work was probably connected to the construction of a covered passage or gallery, linking the infirmary (and the abbot's lodging) with the north aisle of the presbytery (figs 26, 122 and 156).

Then, probably in the fifteenth century, it appears the arcades in the centre bays were taken down, with the outer aisles now separated from the main central area by solid partition walls. Private cells were created in the walled-off bays, each fitted with a fireplace and a small bedside cupboard or locker. A larger fireplace was introduced to the east wall of the putative infirmarer's lodging, and another substantial fireplace was built at the eastern corner of the south aisle. In referring to these fireplaces in his account of the building, Wood mentioned that 'numerous parts of the chimney stacks and tops with cleverly cut openings to induce updraughts' were to be found among the remains.[42] One final but important element of these fifteenth-century modifications was the addition of a new kitchen to the north of the infirmary hall.

One of the more puzzling aspects of the Tintern infirmary complex is the location of the chapel mentioned by William Worcestre in his description of the abbey buildings.[43] In a somewhat unconvincing analysis of the point, Wood used the order's customary, the *Ecclesiastica Officia*, to argue that a chapel would not in any case have been required in Cistercian infirmaries. He then sought to convince his readers that Worcestre's account was obviously confused and inaccurate.[44] Brakspear, on the other hand, felt sure that a chapel would have been an indispensable element of the complex, suggesting that it merely remained to be found.[45] Nothing further has come to light over the last century. It is possible, however, that the chapel was not in fact a free-standing structure, and may for instance have been contained within the east end of the infirmary hall itself.

At most if not all of the remaining white monk abbeys in Wales and the March, we might expect to find the infirmary complex located in much the same general position within the claustral layout. The topography would suggest this was the case at Valle Crucis for instance,[46] and a series of archaeological earthworks border a similar location at Strata Florida.[47] We can be a little more certain at Dore, where it appears that Paul may have come across several walls connected to the infirmary at some distance to the east of the east range (fig 128).[48] In fact, 'the great infirmary' at Dore is known from a documentary source of 1330. Next to the building there was 'a certain chamber with a porch', in which the abbot conducted formal business transactions.[49] It is from documents, too, that we know the infirmary at Strata Florida was probably in ruins before the suppression,[50] whereas that at Valle Crucis appears to have been still in use in 1528, and that at Margam was mentioned in 1531.[51]

THE ACCOMMODATION OF
CISTERCIAN ABBOTS

Following the instruction given in the Rule of St Benedict, twelfth-century Cistercian abbots slept in common with their monks in the main dormitory range.[52] At several sites in France, there is evidence to indicate the presence of a small chamber set aside for the abbot at the inner end of the range, close to the transept of the abbey church.[53] As Martha Newman argues, the literal interpretation of the Rule's prescription in this regard suited a deliberate policy on the part of the founding fathers, lessening the distance between the abbot and his community at large.[54] In the event, it was a position the order found very difficult to maintain. In time, the majority of white monk abbots came to occupy a set of private lodgings, usually located somewhere adjacent to the infirmary complex.[55] As noted in an earlier chapter, this pattern was in marked contrast to the position adopted by, among others, the Benedictines, the Cluniacs and the Augustinian canons, who all tended to house their abbots within or beyond the west claustral range.[56]

As late as the 1180s, the abbot's accommodation at Clairvaux may still have been located somewhere within the main dormitory range.[57] Yet, as it happens, the way for subsequent change had already been prepared some thirty years earlier, at Rievaulx in the north of England. In the 1150s, Abbot Ailred had been granted permission to build a separate block of rooms projecting at right angles to the east claustral range, probably on account of his extreme illnesses. Given both the documentary and fabric evidence, it seems the features of the building included a principal chamber, or hall, a two-storey antechamber and a chapel.[58] Within a very few years, and probably before 1170, the abbot at neighbouring Fountains, Richard of Clairvaux, had built himself a private lodging in a block adjoining the monks' latrine, technically under the same roof as the dormitory.[59] Indeed, such extensions to the communal latrine may well have become an accepted way for the abbot to remain in close physical proximity to the dormitory, thereby adhering to the spirit (if not the letter) of the clear instruction now set out in the *Ecclesiastica Officia*.[60] Other examples have been identified at Kirkstall and Waverley,[61] and possibly at Croxden, Roche and Jervaulx.[62] Over the course of the thirteenth and fourteenth centuries, the trend towards larger and more comfortable suites of abbatial accommodation, often of considerable architectural pretension, was to increase across the entire order. In England, this is witnessed by the remains identified to the east and south east of the main claustral complexes at Buildwas, Byland, Croxden and Furness, to name but four.[63]

English Cistercian abbots continued both to expand and to improve the quality of their accommodation during the late Middle Ages. At Fountains and Rievaulx, for instance, houses of remarkable scale and complexity were created through the conversion and extension of earlier structures, not least those of the infirmary.[64] Again, around 1500, one of the last abbots of Thame in Oxfordshire began a very comfortable new lodging in the traditional location to the east of the cloister. A further sumptuous addition was made to this block in the years immediately before the suppression.[65] In the meantime, however, the number of exceptions to this particular aspect of Cistercian planning had begun to grow. It was no longer unusual to find an abbot's apartment situated elsewhere in the claustral complex. A favoured new location seems to have been the west range, where considerable space became available after the demise of the lay brothers in the fourteenth century. The abbot of Sawley, for example, may have moved his household there before 1400, and the west ranges at Rufford, Hailes and probably Stoneleigh were all later converted to serve in a similar fashion.[66] Far and away the best survival of a late Cistercian abbot's house in England is to be found at Forde, projecting westwards from the former west range.[67] The work of Abbot Thomas Chard (1521–39), it includes not only a private lodging with an impressive great chamber, but also a palatial hall entered by way of a showy three-storey towered porch, all fully comparable with anything which might have been built by a secular lord of similar standing around this time.

THE DEVELOPMENT OF THE
ABBOT'S LODGING AT TINTERN

In Wales, Tintern Abbey provides a particularly good example of the sequential development in Cistercian abbatial accommodation.[68] Remembering once again that the cloister here was located to the north side of the church, we find the buildings associated with the abbot's residence at the far north-east corner of the site (figs 20, 26, 122 and 156).[69] To begin with, throughout the second half of the twelfth century, Tintern's abbots were presumably content to sleep in the common dormitory, perhaps conducting formal business in a room near the southern end. Then, during the second quarter of the thirteenth century, the expansion of the east and north claustral ranges appears to have prompted the move towards a 'separate' residence. Before 1250, the abbot had moved into an L-shaped hall and chamber block built against the gable end of the monks' latrine (fig 26), a pattern also observed at Fountains, Kirkstall and Croxden.[70] Here, at Tintern, the north-west angle buttress with its ashlar chamfer is one indication of the two-storey arrangement, whereas it was probably always envisaged that the southern facade of the building would have been fronted by the infirmary cloister. At first-floor level, intercommunication between the new lodging and the monks' dormitory would have been possible via the latrine chamber. Once again, it is tempting to link the programme with the energetic Abbot Ralph (c 1232–45), though this may be pushing the evidence too far.[71]

Interestingly, this was not the only residential accommodation to be erected at Tintern around this time. On the contrary, a completely free-standing two-storey block was also built a short distance to the north east (fig 26). Following suggestions made for similarly placed structures of varying date at, for example, Fountains, Kirkstall and Waverley,[72] this has sometimes been identified as the accommodation set aside for the abbot of Tintern's French mother house, L'Aumône, during his prescribed annual visitation.[73] Although the ubiquitous application of this historic model has been rightly challenged by Hall,[74] it remains difficult to attribute a specific alternative use to the mid-thirteenth-century building in question at Tintern.

In any case, towards the middle of the fourteenth century, probably c 1330–45, one of Tintern's abbots, clearly concerned with matters of architectural prestige, chose to make significant improvements to his domestic accommodation.[75] In the first place, an imposing new five-bay hall was built at right angles to the earlier free-standing building at the north-east corner of the site (figs 26 and 156). Measuring some 26.8m long by 14.6m wide, the hall itself lay on the upper floor above passages and storerooms at ground level. The exterior bays were punctuated with large buttresses sitting on a prominent plinth moulding. At the level of the hall, the buttresses doubtless framed large traceried windows. The building was entered by way of a handsome doorway and lobby facing east, presumably approached via an independent landing stage on the River Wye. The jambs of the doorway feature wave-and-chamfer mouldings on pyramidal stops. Henceforth, the now-adjacent thirteenth-century building was attached in some way to the eastern side of the new hall. The upper floor may well have served as the abbot's camera, with a latrine built to communicate with its east end. Next to this, the foundations of a circular dovecote are known from excavation. A two-storey block was added to the south side of the camera, housing a private chapel on the upper floor.

A Cistercian comparison for the fourteenth-century abbatial great hall at Tintern can be found in the west of England at Croxden, where Abbot Richard of Shepshead raised a somewhat smaller two-storey construction of four bays in 1335.[76] Seen in a rather wider context, however, the Tintern building reflects a growing fashion during the early fourteenth century for impressive aisleless halls, raised for both secular and ecclesiastical patrons. In the Severnside region alone, it stands comparison with Henry de Gower's hall in the bishop's palace at St Davids, with the so-called Guesten Hall at the cathedral priory of Worcester, with the abbot's hall at the Augustinian abbey of Haughmond, and with the great halls in the castles at Berkeley and Caerphilly.[77] Like all these, the Tintern building was presumably spanned with a fine open timber roof.

DECLINE AND RECOVERY: THE PRELUDE TO NEW BUILDING BY THE WELSH ABBOTS

On the basis of fabric evidence alone, the early fourteenth-century abbot's hall at Tintern might be said to represent one of the last major, and unequivocal, white monk building programmes known from anywhere in Wales and the March. At first glance, apart from the near-contemporary work on the east claustral range at Valle Crucis, there is little else of prominence one can place alongside it.[78] However, it would be wholly wrong to overlook the many references to buildings found in that large corpus of poetry written by grateful native Welsh bards over the late fifteenth and early sixteenth centuries in tribute to their bountiful Cistercian patrons.[79]

The poets were frequently prone towards flattery and exaggeration. The livelihood of many depended upon just this. Moreover, a poem is by its nature a work of art, and it would be a mistake to take descriptions of buildings too literally.[80] For all this, the content is unlikely to have been fabricated in its entirety. On the contrary, it seems to provide us with valuable insights into the architectural interests of quite a number of the late medieval Welsh Cistercian abbots. The focus is upon churches and their ornament, especially works in wood, but there is also frequent reference to abbatial accommodation and, in particular, to the sumptuous hospitality offered within. When we return to a closer scrutiny of the fabric on the sites themselves, there are at least a few telling indications that this bardic praise was more than merely hot air.

At the beginning of the fifteenth century, as is widely agreed by historians, the Cistercian monasteries of Wales and the March were at an exceptionally low ebb.[81] Having struggled through the economic difficulties of the fourteenth century, compounded by the specific impact of the Black Death in 1348–50, virtually all houses had now been calamitously affected during the Owain Glyn Dŵr rebellion of 1400–9.[82] It was as a direct consequence of the rebellion that in 1412 it was claimed Margam Abbey, for example, had been 'utterly destroyed so that the abbot and convent are obliged to go about like vagabonds'.[83] Similarly, in 1420, the community at Strata Marcella was given a new charter of privileges on account of 'the destruction and injury made by the Welsh rebels both to the church and monastery … by plunder and fire'.[84] Even as late as 1442, the monks at Strata Florida Abbey continued to lay the blame for the tragic state of their house on 'Owain Glyn Dŵr and his company'. The monastery was so damaged, it was said, 'the walls of the church excepted', it could not easily be repaired.[85] And yet, despite the grave and lasting damage inflicted by the rebellion, this must not be allowed to obscure clear signs of Cistercian recovery during the second half of the fifteenth century.

It so happens that one of the first white monk abbots to offer his patronage to the native poets was Abbot Rhys (c 1436–41) at Strata Florida. Guto'r Glyn, for instance, rewarded him with praise for his lavish hospitality and for his attempts to improve the monastery buildings. According to Guto ap Siencyn, Rhys laid plans for work on the refectory, and built another fine room 'with glass windows' and 'with flowery ornament'.[86] Even greater stability was brought to Strata Florida during the abbacy of Morgan ap Rhys (1444–86). If the poet Dafydd Nanmor is to be believed, Morgan's reputation as a restorer extended to Burgundian Cîteaux itself.[87] It is unfortunate, then, that so few traces of the abbot's accommodation of this period, or any other, can be seen at Strata Florida today.[88]

There is a similar story at Strata Marcella Abbey. Here, for a brief period in the last quarter of the fifteenth century, probably c 1485–90, the house was led by that most able of late Welsh Cistercian abbots, Dafydd ab Owain. He subsequently became head of Strata Florida, and from there returned north to Maenan, in a period when he also served as bishop of St Asaph (1503–13).[89] Whether Dafydd chose to improve his accommodation at Strata Marcella is unclear, but he was certainly praised by a number of the Welsh bards during his period of office. It was Tudur Aled, for instance, who produced this splendid description of Dafydd's hospitality:

In Dafydd's hall … the tables bent beneath
the weight of great masses of prime venison,

wild game, and sea fish, with all manner of vegetables and fruits, including oranges and grapes. And exotic wines that washed it all down! – wines from Germany … the vintages of the fragrant vineyards of Burgundy. All these and the home-brewed cider, mead, and bragget, too.[90]

Again, sadly, all upstanding trace of the buildings in which such feasts were held is entirely lost to us (fig 77).

As bishop of St Asaph, Dafydd ab Owain is remembered for his rebuilding of the episcopal palace, and possibly the west tower at the church of St Giles in Wrexham.[91] Meanwhile, according to the bards, he had found the buildings at Maenan Abbey in something of a ruinous condition. He devoted much energy to their rehabilitation, with several poems, notably from the pens of Tudur Aled and Gruffudd ab Ieuan ap Llywelyn Fychan, recording the impressiveness of his work.[92] Dafydd's lodging at the abbey may well have been located in the west range, at least to judge from what is known of the post-monastic history of the site.[93]

FIFTEENTH-CENTURY BUILDING AT CYMER

In turning more specifically to surviving examples of fifteenth- and early sixteenth-century fabric evidence, we might take as our starting point Cymer Abbey. Although it was not one of the houses to have attracted extensive praise from the native bards, Cymer does nonetheless preserve one of the most telling buildings of the period. The structure in question is the more remarkable for having been erected during a particularly unsettled period in the abbey's history. Indeed, during the early 1440s, ill-governance by two rival claimants to the abbacy was pushing the house ever closer to the brink of destruction.[94] In spite of this, one of the two men apparently found the resources to build a not insubstantial domestic residence a short distance to the north west of the abbey church, now represented by Y Faner (Vanner), or Abbey Farmhouse.

As it survives, the building incorporates a very fine four-bay late medieval hall, originally open to the roof.[95] At 7.6m wide, it represents one of the most ambitious medieval hall houses in this part of Wales.[96] There is some indication of an inner room at the dais end of the hall; the possibility of an outer room at the opposite end cannot be discounted. A wing projecting at right angles from the west side of the hall is interpreted as a possible parlour. A detached kitchen is likely to have existed somewhere in the immediate vicinity. Both the hall and the putative parlour wing feature ornate arch-braced collar-beam trusses, between which run decorative cusped wind braces. The hall must have been heated by an open hearth at the centre, as evidenced by the heavily smoke-blackened timbers, and by traces of a louver opening. The estimated felling date of the timber used in the roof of the hall is 1441.[97] Given the general location of the building in the abbey precinct, it is possible it was intended to serve as a communal guest hall. There again, its architectural qualities suggest it was more likely to have been built by one of Cymer's ambitious mid-fifteenth-century abbots as a block of high-status accommodation for himself (fig 25).

THE DORMITORY CONVERSION AT VALLE CRUCIS

At Valle Crucis Abbey, regardless of its position in the wake of the Glyn Dŵr rebellion,[98] the community was to experience a quite remarkable revival of fortunes under the three very notable abbots who ruled the house during the late fifteenth and early sixteenth centuries. Siôn ap Rhisiart (c 1455–61/80), Dafydd ab Ieuan (c 1480–1503) and Siôn Llwyd (c 1503–27) earned for themselves reputations as scholars, bardic patrons, collectors of Welsh literary manuscripts and builders of considerable note.[99] Indeed, they were to give their abbey greater standing in north-east Wales than it had enjoyed for quite some time. Once again, however, it was in the roles of patronage and the provision of bountiful hospitality that these men truly excelled, as witnessed by the many ecstatic verses produced by grateful bards.

Siôn ap Rhisiart's favourite poet seems to have been Gutun Owain, whose works leave us in no doubt as to the mouth-watering qualities of the abbot's table. In a wry comparison of Siôn's bardic reputation with the Cistercian ideals of the early twelfth century, Sir Glanmor Williams wrote: 'anything less like those bread-and-water-loving ascetics than this *bon vivant* whose "wines and viands made a heaven of earth" it would be hard to find'.[100] Gutun frequently suggested that Siôn ought to have been elected to the see of St Asaph. That aside, in a typical work of praise he wrote: 'Siôn, of the saintly host, whose name for lavish gifts is known to fame ... Nor Kings nor Barons can excel, the wine thou dost bestow so well'.[101]

Siôn's successor, Abbot Dafydd ab Ieuan, was no less popular with the poets. He was a particular patron of Guto'r Glyn, who spent his last years at Valle Crucis, 'aged, lame and deaf'.[102] In one work seeking to compare Dafydd with a prominent

member of a Welsh gentry family, Guto'r wrote: 'Our land boasts lord of like mood, Of Valle Crucis Abbot good, Whose full-stocked tables ever groan, With wine and meat free as your own. Like is he to your nobleness, Save for his tonsure and his dress'.[103] In another poem dedicated to Dafydd, Guto'r refers to features of the monastery itself. He calls it 'the palace of Peter' and speaks of 'the holy altars, where Dafydd said the prayers', and mentions how 'he gilt and foliated the images, the choir, the chalices, and books'.[104] And, in much the same vein, one of Gutun Owain's eulogies in praise of Dafydd runs: 'A place where gold is freely current is the monastery, and its choir excels that of Sarum, and rich are the carvings of the leaves, and of the statues ... It is equal to Sheen or the renowned St Paul's'. In the same poem, Gutun apparently refers to the abbot's fine dwelling house, 'with its skilfully wrought roof', all of which 'he [Dafydd] has walled about'.[105]

From the architectural point of view, the most intriguing aspect of the bardic accolades loaded on the three early Tudor abbots of Valle Crucis is the way they have been directed back to the buildings surviving on the site. For more than half a century, in fact, scholars have accepted that one of these abbots, most probably Dafydd ab Ieuan, chose to transfer his household into the upper floor of the east range.[106] In considering the few structural pieces of evidence for this, perhaps the first point to recognize is that the number of monks in the community had probably fallen to fewer than ten.[107] Even so, the decision to take over the northern half of the communal dormitory would surely not have been a step taken lightly.

In any case, as reconstructed, although the resulting lodgings might be described as well appointed, they can hardly have been luxurious by some English standards (figs 5, 125 and 157). At the northern end of the range, in what is thought to have served as the abbot's hall, a large new fireplace was built into the east wall, its hood carried on projecting quadrant corbels. Opposite this there was a doorway, presumably opening onto a wooden staircase leading down into the cloister.[108] In turn, this suggests that the cloister arcades, or at least the eastern arcade, had been removed by this time (fig 157). The new arrangements were completed, it is believed, with the addition of a new private chamber fashioned in an extension built over the east half of the thirteenth-century sacristy. In the meantime, the southern end of the former dormitory may have been set aside for guest accommodation, in which case it must be assumed that the few remaining monks had moved into some other part of the claustral complex. But perhaps the most surprising aspect of this posited

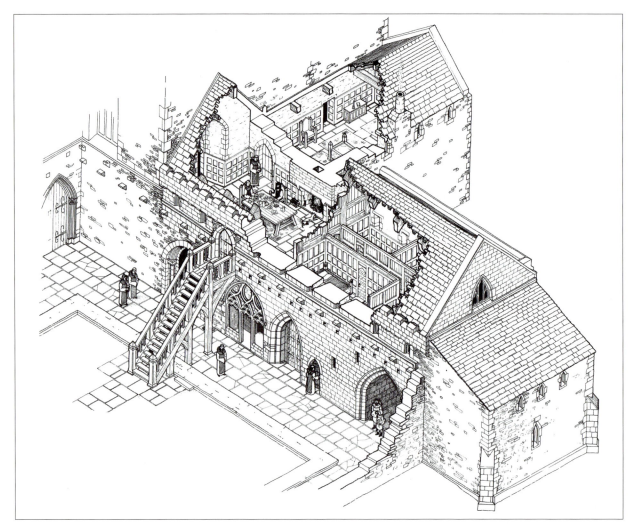

Drawing: Chris Jones-Jenkins, for Cadw

157 Valle Crucis Abbey: reconstruction of east range, early sixteenth century. The conversion of the former monks' dormitory as a private lodging for the abbot may well have been the work of Dafydd ab Ieuan, who ruled over the house from about 1480 to 1503. A great chamber was fashioned for his use in a new extension over the eastern part of the twelfth-century sacristy.

conversion is the absence of any new fenestration in any of the chambers. It is difficult to imagine Abbot Dafydd and his successors being entirely happy with the meagre amount of light coming in through the small fourteenth-century openings in the lateral walls.[109]

THE LATE ARRANGEMENTS AT BASINGWERK

After a long period of misrule running through the second and third quarters of the fifteenth century, much was done to shore up the fortunes of Basingwerk Abbey in the time of Thomas Pennant (1481–1522).[110] The poet Tudur Aled described Thomas as a 'godly man with a fine taste for minstrelsy and a generous patron of the bards'.[111] Tudur was further moved to write of the abbey's lovely situation 'on a haven within sight of the waters'. 'It is roofed with lead', he noted, 'and ornamented with glass windows'. We are also told of

Abbot Thomas's new buildings: 'besides the cells of the monks there are new houses for guests who are said to be so numerous that they have to be accommodated for meals at two sittings, when they have a choice of wines from Aragon, Spain, and Brittany'.[112] In another account of the abbey at this time, written in very much the same vein by Gutun Owain, the verse runs: 'It is a part of heaven … Excellent are the buildings … Of faultless freestone'.[113]

Interestingly, there is a very definite candidate for the late medieval abbot's lodging at Basingwerk, located at the southern end of the east range (fig 25). The archaeological sequence in this area is complex, and understanding is not helped by the absence of records from the Office of Works' clearance programme.[114] Nonetheless, it seems a four-bay vaulted chamber was initially added to the existing range around the middle years of the thirteenth century.[115] In the later Middle Ages, probably in the time of Abbot Thomas Pennant himself, the west wall of this thirteenth-century chamber was taken down, and the building as a whole extended up to the east wall of the refectory. New partition walls were inserted and the floor level raised. A projecting fireplace was added on the south side, and there appears to have been a second floor, at least above the extended western half of the block. The character of the spaces is very much domestic and private, far more suited to the accommodation of an individual than to any form of communal usage.[116]

THE NEW ABBOT'S LODGING AT NEATH

In the aftermath of the Glyn Dŵr rebellion, even as late as 1423, the community at Neath Abbey was said to be suffering grievously from indiscriminate pillaging. The house had been violated and robbed of its books, chalices and ornaments.[117] The initial steps on the long road to recovery were taken by the very able Thomas Franklin (1424–41), a reformer of considerable stature who went on to become abbot of Margam (1441–60), and also carried out duties on behalf of the General Chapter in Wales and further afield.[118] By the end of the fifteenth century, Neath had emerged in a decidedly healthier condition than most other Cistercian abbeys in Wales, both spiritually and financially. In particular, its position of relatively high standing in the years immediately before the suppression owed much to the qualities of Abbot Leyshon Thomas (c 1510–39). An Oxford graduate and a man of considerable learning, he worked hard to maintain the standing of his house, becoming also an influential figure within the order at large. He was, for example, one of five abbots appointed by the General Chapter to visit Cistercian houses in England and Wales.[119] Abbot Leyshon's eminent reputation for scholarship and hospitality encouraged a particularly glowing tribute from the local poet Lewis Morgannwg. 'The convent of Neath', Lewis wrote, 'how much talked of in England! The lamp of France and Ireland! A school much resorted to by scholars … In this compact retreat will be found the warmth of hospitality and welcome banquets'. Lewis's eulogy also describes certain features of the abbey church, including crystal windows of every colour, the 'gold-adorned choir, the nave, the gilded tabernacle work, the pinnacles', and the 'vast and lofty roof … like the sparkling heavens on high'.[120]

Surprisingly, perhaps, it was not Leyshon Thomas himself who initiated the building of a new abbot's lodging at Neath. In fact, if the stylistic evidence is accepted, the work is far more likely to have been carried out by one of his immediate predecessors, probably around 1500.[121] Either way, the abbot in question must surely have been a man of considerable character since, by any standards, the decision to appropriate to his own use parts of the former communal buildings running along the south side of the site was remarkably bold (figs 21 and 25).[122] In essence, the programme of conversion focused on the ends of the main east claustral range and the adjacent parallel latrine block, taking in both a large section of the monks' dormitory and its rib-vaulted undercroft (the former day room). To the west, the new building further projected over the southern end of the monks' refectory, which may in any case have been reduced in scale by this time. Linking units were built between the three thirteenth-century ranges, thereby creating a highly comfortable suite of rooms with a continuous south-facing aspect, all set out over two and three storeys, and reaching approximately 39.6m in length.

The importance of this conversion is all too rarely identified, largely because many of the details were to be disguised by the construction of the Tudor mansion over this same corner of the site (*see* fig 177). The features of the abbot's lodging are perhaps most readily identified by the windows and dressings executed in Bath stone. The jamb of one such window, located in the upper level of the block linking the former dormitory with the latrine, indicates hollow-chamfered transomed lights with arched heads and sunk spandrels set in a squared frame. Next to this particular window, a polygonal stair turret may be seen projecting beyond the south-east angle of the dormitory. It was presumably introduced to improve access between the two main floors. As to the specifics of the internal arrangements, these are almost entirely lost to us. Nevertheless, we might speculate that the southern end of the dormitory served as the abbot's hall, with a series of private chambers opening to both east and west. The inner rooms were probably located on the west side of the lodgings. Here, the outer block was serviced by a latrine tower with entrances at each floor level.

In sum then, even if much of the late medieval poetry written in praise of Welsh Cistercian abbots was coloured with a liberal dose of hyperbole, it clearly provides telling insights into the overall character of their monasteries in the fifteenth and early sixteenth centuries. In particular, we must appreciate that men such as Guto'r Glyn and Gutun Owain in the north, or Lewis Morgannwg in the south, were undoubtedly the leading poets of their generation, to whom many of the finest homes of Wales offered an open door. As Sir Glanmor Williams once pointed out, although these bards had probably seen more buildings than most, the abbots of Maenan, Valle Crucis, Neath and Basingwerk clearly 'ranked as high as any on their list of builders of enterprise and good taste'.[123]

The Welsh Cistercians had by now come a very long way from those timber buildings raised by their pioneering predecessors during the early twelfth century. For just over four hundred years, the fourteen abbeys examined in this study had exercised considerable architectural patronage. Their building programmes had drawn in masons and influences not just from western and southern England, but also from France and Ireland. White monk church building in Wales had begun with the aisleless prototypes found, for example, at Tintern and Neath. There followed a new 'Bernardine' regularity, first introduced at Margam and Whitland. Thereafter, the culmination of Welsh Cistercian church building is undoubtedly represented by the late thirteenth-century works at Tintern, Neath and Maenan. Equally significant was the effort invested by the white monks of Wales in their claustral buildings, notably in the superb early Gothic constructions at Dore, Margam, Neath and Tintern. Of course, these were raised in periods of immense prosperity and in the expectation of accommodating communities of monks and lay brothers quite unimaginable by the standards of the fifteenth century.

The abbatial conversions which occurred at Valle Crucis, Neath and elsewhere reflect a national trend. With fewer than ten monks maintaining the Opus Dei at most of the Welsh houses, for example, the vast communal buildings of earlier centuries had effectively lost their purpose. In the revised Cistercian planning of the late fifteenth and early sixteenth centuries, a new emphasis was given to the place of the abbot and his household within the monastery complex.[124] At Tintern, although a satisfactory position had been reached by the mid-fourteenth century, the expansion of the infirmary kitchens to the point where their main purpose was surely that of serving the abbot's lodging reveals yet further changes in lifestyle.[125] In the early decades of the sixteenth century, the complex of buildings at this north-east corner of the site (fig 156) housed 'the abbot's table', where sat the 'members and gentlemen' of his household. They were attended by six servants in 1535, each wearing a tunic of the abbot's livery.[126]

At the time of the suppression, the situation was doubtless very similar at many of the other Cistercian abbeys of Wales, and, after the closure of certain houses, it was doubtless the comfort already offered by the abbot's accommodation which led to its incorporation into some form of post-monastic residence on the site. This pattern has already been observed at Neath Abbey, and the same was certainly true at Valle Crucis.[127] Similarly, at Margam, the Mansel family house was so positioned that it might easily have been developed out of the former abbot's lodging (fig 2).[128] Again, the same may have been true of the houses of the Wynns at Maenan and the Morgans at Llantarnam,[129] thus bringing us back full circle to the introduction of the volume, where the process of despoilment and rediscovery of the Cistercian buildings of Wales is first broached.

PART IV

CATALOGUE OF CISTERCIAN SITES IN WALES AND THE BORDER

THE CATALOGUE

INTRODUCTION

This catalogue aims to provide a concise summary of the historical, archaeological and architectural information on each of the thirteen 'permanent' Cistercian foundations of medieval Wales. Considering the lengthy occupation of the site at Aberconwy, and then the replacement abbey of Maenan, it seems appropriate to provide separate entries for each. For consistency throughout the volume, an entry is also included on the border abbey at Dore in Herefordshire. In all, then, the catalogue includes fifteen individual entries. They are intended to supplement the largely thematic (and chronological) account of the buildings given in the preceding parts of the volume, and to assist readers seeking the principal sources on any particular house.

In each entry, the site name is followed first by the present local authority administrative area and the medieval diocese in which the abbey lay, and then by a six-figure national grid reference. Although the entries themselves do not follow a rigid formula, the emphasis is upon the archaeology and architecture of the site. By and large, the material breaks down into some five principal themes. First, the basic historical framework of the house is outlined. Any documentary evidence for building work, or an indication of it, is noted. Secondly, there is a general consideration of the siting of the abbey, with details (where known or recorded) of any temporary locations occupied by the community. Thirdly, in so far as the excavated and upstanding fabric allows, an outline structural history of the medieval buildings is provided. For any key points of interpretation, or for different views in the published accounts, the relevant sources are given in note form. Next, there is mention of the post-monastic fate of the site, with events followed through to the beginnings of scholarly enquiry and more recent investigation. Finally, the entries close with a note on the current status and condition of the buildings and archaeological remains, with mention of any statutory protection as scheduled ancient monuments or listed buildings (with the reference or record numbers).

In all but two cases, the entries are accompanied by a ground plan, each drawn to the same scale, and phased where possible. As will be appreciated from earlier parts of the volume, the degree of completeness and accuracy in these plans depends on the quality of investigation at the site to date.

The catalogue entries conclude with full bibliographies, giving all known works with specific coverage on the abbey in question. Two lists are offered: one including items concerned primarily with archaeological, architectural and art historical aspects of the site; the other citing material chiefly concerned with aspects of the abbey's history. Full details are given in the bibliography at the end of the volume.

Beyond those works of a specific nature, it is as well to remember that a number of general titles, providing both Welsh and national overviews, include material of direct relevance to individual houses. All these have already been cited earlier in the volume.[1]

ABERCONWY ABBEY, Conwy, Bangor, SH 781776

According to the 'Register and Chronicle' compiled by one of its own monks, Aberconwy Abbey was founded on 24 July 1186 as a daughter house of Strata Florida (fig 19).[1] From *Brut y Tywysogyon* ('Chronicle of the Princes'), we further learn that the community was initially settled at Rhedynog Felen, 4.4km to the south west of Caernarfon, in the *cantref* or lordship of Arfon (fig 18).[2] Although there is no extant foundation charter, all indications suggest the abbey's principal early benefactor was almost certainly Rhodri ab Owain Gwynedd (d 1195), then lord of Arfon and a son-in-law of the Lord Rhys, patron of Strata Florida.[3] Another early patron was Gruffudd ap Cynan (d 1200), Rhodri's nephew and likewise a member of the expansive dynasty of Gwynedd princes.[4]

The relocation of the community to its more permanent home at the mouth of the River Conwy, in the *cantref* of Arllechwedd, was probably effected by 1192.[5] Here, in due course, the monks were to receive new support from Llywelyn ab Iorwerth, Llywelyn 'the Great' (d 1240). Even though the date and authenticity of 'his' two charters – usually attributed to 1199 – have been questioned, there can be little doubt Llywelyn bestowed extensive gifts and privileges upon the community.[6] Within a generation of its uncertain beginnings, Aberconwy Abbey had accumulated an estate estimated to be in excess of 15,384ha. Much of this land was upland pasture, though several important arable granges were held on the island of Anglesey.[7] The abbey church, meanwhile, became the burial place of a significant grouping of princes of the Gwynedd dynasty, most notably Gruffudd ap Cynan and Llywelyn ab Iorwerth, together with Gruffudd's son Hywel (d 1216) and Llywelyn's sons Dafydd (d 1246) and Gruffudd (d 1244).[8] In the later thirteenth century Aberconwy enjoyed friendly relations with Prince Llywelyn ap Gruffudd, Llywelyn 'the Last' (d 1282). From time to time, for example, the prince based his court at one of the abbey's granges[9] and, among other privileges, he granted the community the royal chapel at Llanbadrig in Anglesey.[10]

In November 1277 Aberconwy was the scene of Llywelyn ap Gruffudd's capitulation to Edward I, sealed in fact as the Treaty of Aberconwy.[11] In 1283–4, it was Edward who brought monastic life at Aberconwy to a close, when he transferred the community to Maenan to make way for his new castle of Conwy.[12]

No trace of the temporary site occupied by the monks in 1186 has been identified with certainty, despite the fact that Rhedynog Felen served as a grange throughout the abbey's subsequent history.[13] At Aberconwy itself, the monastery lay at the extreme north-east corner of Arllechwedd, hemmed in by the estuary of the Conwy, by the coast and by mountains.[14] The buildings were laid out on a relatively flat shelf of land to the north of a tidal creek formed by the mouth of the River Gyffin, possibly the most level area within the monastery's entire Aberconwy holding. There is no obvious source for the medieval water supply to the monastic buildings.[15] The abbey is now represented by St Mary's parish church, in which various elements of Cistercian work survive.

The monastic origins of St Mary's went unrecognized by antiquarian authors. Writing in the early nineteenth century, for example, the Revd Robert Williams felt sure that, 'Of the original abbey in Aberconwy there are now no remains'.[16] Some sixty years later, it was Harold Hughes who first highlighted the upstanding fragments of the abbey church. In particular, he identified the early thirteenth-century work surviving as thin slabs of uncoursed rubble in the west front, where in fact three plain graduated lancets with chamfered jambs remain *in situ* (fig 81). He also drew attention to what he felt was work of a similar character in the lower parts of the present chancel east wall. Here, below the restored Perpendicular window, there is a simple string course which Hughes thought was 'of an early section'; it certainly runs behind the two corner buttresses. Finally, he pointed out the reused voussoirs of monastic date set in the entrance to the south porch.[17] Hughes was also aware that the Cistercian church was almost entirely rebuilt following the events of 1283–4, thereafter serving a parochial function within the new royal borough.

In the survey of St Mary's by the Royal Commission on Ancient and Historical Monuments in Wales and Monmouthshire (RCAHMW), it is suggested that the whole length of the existing structure represents merely the nave of an uncompleted conventual Cistercian church, its limits determined by the fabric thought to be of *c* 1190–1220 in the east and west ends.[18] However, following his excavations adjacent to the south-west side of the main site in 1961, coupled with a review of the architectural and archaeological remains, Dr Lawrence Butler proposed an alternative arrangement.[19] Employing the evidence of wall foundations further observed by Hughes,[20] Butler pieced together the ground plan of a full cruciform church, though one (as he noted) of especially small and rather unusual proportions, difficult to parallel among the permanent houses of the order (fig 158).[21]

The overall length of the existing church is some 41m, with its original width estimated at about 16.8m. In fact, these figures bear comparison with just the nave of the church at Aberconwy's mother house, Strata Florida, itself measuring approximately 40.1m long by 18.6m wide. Likewise, at Cymer, where the surviving remains probably represent the nave of the initial design concept, the external dimensions are about 36.6m by 18.3m.[22] The nave at Whitland is marginally longer, though again the comparison is justified. In sum, then, there is a chance that the later parish church at Aberconwy began life as the nave of the Cistercian monastery. Indeed, given its relative wealth and its importance as a Welsh royal foundation, it would be surprising if the community had not managed to build a church of full 'Bernardine' plan.[23]

In 1245 the abbey was sacked by the forces of Henry III, its goods looted and outbuildings burnt.[24] Hughes suggested the present south chancel wall was built following damage inflicted during this episode, whereas the RCAHMW argue it is a later construction.[25] It is clear, nevertheless, that in the

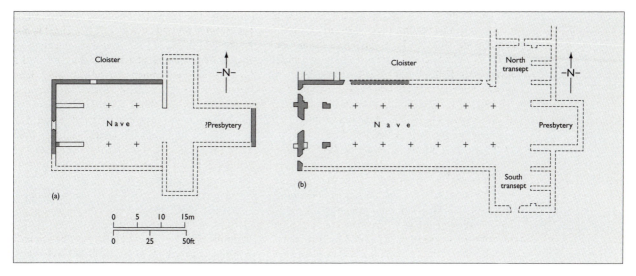

158 *Aberconwy Abbey, conjectural ground plans:* (a) on the basis that St Mary's represents the full abbey church (after Butler 1964); (b) based on the layout of Strata Florida.

Drawing: *Pete Lawrence, for Cadw*

half-century following Edward I's conquest – with his new castle and borough established at Conwy – the Cistercian abbey church was comprehensively remodelled to serve its new purpose. It featured an aisleless chancel, a four-bay nave and a spacious south transept. A tower was also fashioned over the central west bay of the monastic nave.[26] Among the modifications in the later Middle Ages, a large five-light window was installed in the east wall of the chancel.[27] The church was restored by Gilbert Scott in 1872, when all the roofs were renewed.[28]

There is little trace, if any, of the conventual buildings above ground, though records of chance finds and the existing topography suggest very strongly that the cloister lay to the north of the church. On his visit to Aberconwy in 1773, the antiquarian and topographer Thomas Pennant (1726–98) saw: 'A long vaulted room of good masonry, worked with clay, but plaistered with lime', together with what he described as a 'Saxon door'.[29] Moses Griffith (1747–1819), who illustrated Pennant's tour, shows parts of two buildings then standing on the north-east side of the church.[30] It is presumably Pennant's 'long vaulted room' which appears as a thatched two-storey structure, with the 'Saxon' door near its west end.[31] According to the Revd Robert Williams, these remains were taken down before the end of the eighteenth century. He further noted that in 1832 various wall foundations, regarded as different parts of the abbey, together with a sepulchral slab, were unearthed in the rear yard of the Castle Hotel.[32] There is also a suggestion that the arch and capitals of the chapter house doorway were reused to form the west door of the parish church.[33]

The parish church of St Mary is a Grade I listed building (record number 3353), with no other statutory protection afforded to the site.

BIBLIOGRAPHY

Architectural: Butler 1964; Butler 2004, 118–20; Elias 1898, 35–8; Gresham 1968, 255–6; Hughes 1895b and 1937; RCAHMW 1956, 39–46; Robinson 1998, 64–5; Ward 1994; Williams 1835.

Historical: Gresham 1939 and 1982–3; Hays 1963; Insley 1999; Knowles and Hadcock 1971, 112, 118; Lowe 1912–28, I, 266–78; O'Sullivan 1947, 17–18; *Register Aberconwy*; Richards 1966; Williams 1990, 36–8; Williams 1835, 70–5.

BASINGWERK ABBEY, Flintshire, St Asaph, sj 195774

Basingwerk Abbey was initially founded for a community of Savigniac monks by Ranulf 'de Gernon', earl of Chester (1129–53), one of the most powerful barons of the English kingdom (fig 19). The precise chronology surrounding the foundation is uncertain, though the settling colony probably arrived on the shore of the Dee estuary in 1131, and almost certainly no later than 1132.[1] The monks were to find themselves in the *cantref* or district of Tegeingl, part of a wider region of disputed borderland in north-east Wales.[2] In common with all other Savigniac houses, Basingwerk was absorbed into the Cistercian order through the merger of 1147.[3]

For a time at least, the monastery appears to have been sited somewhere other than its eventual Greenfield location. Thus Henry II's confirmation charter, granted in 1157, refers to 'the chapel of Basingwerk in which they [the monks] first dwelt'.[4] A clue as to the possible siting of this chapel emerged in the 1950s, following discoveries at the Norman fortification of Hên Blas, situated at Coleshill some 4.8km to the south east (fig 18). Excavating in the outer bailey, G B Leach uncovered the surviving walls of a late twelfth- or early thirteenth-century chapel. Considering the documentary and archaeological evidence as a whole, Arnold Taylor put forward a well-reasoned argument to suggest that this building was the successor to that occupied by the founding colony in the 1130s.[5] However, the interpretation does not go entirely unchallenged, with David Williams preferring to allow for the possibility that the temporary site may have lain rather closer to the final one.[6]

In any case, Henry II's charter of 1157 seems to have amounted to a re-foundation of the monastery – or perhaps the restoration of its flagging early fortunes.[7] It is likely, too, that the timing of the grant may have coincided with the community's move to the permanent location at Greenfield. As a further sign of the new order, in the same year Basingwerk was placed under the authority of Buildwas Abbey in Shropshire, another former Savigniac house.[8] Three decades later, in 1188, Gerald of Wales and Baldwin, archbishop of Canterbury (1184–90), spent a night at Basingwerk near the end of their celebrated journey through Wales. Gerald's only reference to the abbey was as a 'small cell', or priory.[9]

Over the twelfth and thirteenth centuries, Basingwerk's border position meant that the monks would benefit from the patronage of both Welsh princes and Anglo-Norman, or English, nobles.[10] Earl Ranulf's grants to the founding community included the lordship of Fulbrook-Greenfield, eventually encompassing three granges, together with lands at West Kirby on the Wirral. Through his charter of 1157, Henry II added to the monastery's endowments with his own gift of the manor and church at Glossop in Derbyshire. The monks continued to build up this distant estate to such an extent that it emerged as their single most valuable possession.[11] Property at Gelli to the west of Basingwerk was the gift of Prince Llywelyn ab Iorwerth (d 1240), and the monks had extensive grazing rights in the upland Welsh district of Penllyn, where they also possessed Lake Bala.[12] In 1240 Prince Dafydd ap Llywelyn (d 1246) granted the community patronage of Holywell church, together with the pilgrimage shrine-chapel of St Winifred.[13] Thirteen years later, in 1253, the abbots of Basingwerk and Buildwas gained the approval of the General Chapter for the saint's feast day (3 November) to be kept as a Feast of Twelve Lessons in their monasteries.[14]

There can be no doubt Basingwerk suffered extensive damages across its estates during Edward I's Welsh war of 1282–3.[15] In 1284 the community was awarded £100 by way of compensation for its losses.[16] Edward subsequently extended his patronage to the abbey, confirming eleven earlier charters in 1285,[17] and then in the first years of the 1290s granting permission for the monks to hold weekly markets and annual fairs at Holywell and Glossop.[18] In the *Taxatio Ecclesiastica* of 1291, the annual income from the abbey's temporalities was assessed at £68 8s 0d.[19] As a further indication of Edward's interest in Basingwerk, it might be noted that its abbot was one of four among the Welsh Cistercian houses to be summoned to Parliament during his reign. The first known summons occurred in 1295, with five subsequent instances recorded. The abbot of Basingwerk was the only Welsh superior to be so summoned during the reign of Edward II.[20]

Although there were still some twenty monks at the house in 1347,[21] for much of the fourteenth century the community was beset by a series of economic and political difficulties.[22] The situation was compounded in the fifteenth century by several disputed elections. Abbot Henry Wirral (*c* 1430–54), a man of particularly dubious character, assumed his position at Basingwerk without legitimate authority. Only after his arrest for various felonies in the county of Flint was he finally removed from office. Similarly, the abbacy was claimed by Richard Kirby in 1465, who continued to resist attempts to oust him until at least 1476.[23]

Against this background of troubles, it is of considerable interest to note that the fifteenth century witnessed the increasing popularity and importance of the shrine of St Winifred.[24] Henry V (1413–22) made the pilgrimage on foot from Shrewsbury in 1416, and the shrine was later visited by Edward IV (d 1483). In a construction programme apparently dating from the turn of the fifteenth century, the chapel and well chamber were rebuilt to a sophisticated design, generally thought to have been supported by Lady Margaret Beaufort (d 1509), countess of Richmond and Derby. Basingwerk's abbot at this time was Thomas Pennant (*c* 1481–1522), who appears to have done much to transform the fortunes of his house. He was described by the poet Tudur Aled as a 'godly man with a fine taste for minstrelsy and a generous patron on the bards'.[25] Tudur was in fact rewarded by Abbot Thomas for his eulogy of St Winifred and her well.[26] Moreover, his work praises Basingwerk's lovely situation 'on a haven within sight of the waters and the beauty of the country of Dinas Basi'. 'It is roofed with lead', he wrote, 'and ornamented with glass windows'. We are also told of Abbot Thomas's new buildings: 'Besides the cells of the monks there are new houses for guests who are said to be so numerous that they have to be accommodated for meals at two sittings, when they have a choice of wines from Aragon, Spain and Brittany'.[27] In much the same vein runs Gutun Owain's description of Basingwerk: 'It is a part of heaven … Excellent are the buildings'.[28]

The last abbot of Basingwerk was Thomas Pennant's third son, Nicholas (1525–36), who headed a community of perhaps just three monks at this time. Nicholas increased the tendency for the abbey's property to be hived off on long leases in return for fixed cash rents – notably to members of his family.[29] In 1535 the net income of the house was given as £150 7s 3d, with £10 derived from offerings at St Winifred's shrine.[30] Monastic life at Basingwerk may have been brought to an end in the autumn of 1536, and certainly no later than the spring of 1537.[31]

In turning to the abbey buildings, and first considering the temporary site, it seems most unlikely that the outer bailey of the Norman castle at Hên Blas could have been intended, if at all, as other than a short-term refuge. The excavations of the 1950s do not appear to have uncovered anything specific to suggest definite occupation by Basingwerk's founding Savigniac colony. The chapel – thought by Taylor to be the successor of an earlier building – was a single-cell structure, built of stone, and measuring some 13.1m long by 6.4m wide. A water-holding base to one of the surviving door jambs points to a date sometime after Henry II's charter of 1157.[32]

At Greenfield itself, the abbey stood near to a natural routeway. The buildings were placed on the south bank of the Greenfield stream, close to where it enters the Dee estuary.[33] Today, the principal remains comprise parts of the nave and south transept, much of the east range and the lateral walls of a fine north–south refectory (figs 159 and 160). On the south-east side of the complex there is a long, narrow range of buildings, known to have been half-timbered, running eastwards for over 42.7m.[34] There is now no trace of the west range, and the possibility that this too was of timber-framed construction, above sill walls, cannot be discounted.

The earliest masonry on the site is to be seen in the cloister facade of the east range (including the jambs of the chapter house doorway), and is thought to date from the middle to second half of the twelfth century.[35] Exploratory trenches dug in 1937 failed to locate any evidence of a contemporary church.[36] The surviving church is among the smallest raised by the Cistercians in Wales. It was of 'Bernardine' plan, with two chapels to each transept and a seven-bay nave. The nave arcades, carried on diminutive octagonal piers, can have been of no great height (fig 83). Construction could have been put in hand before 1200, although the work must have continued into the early years of the thirteenth century. A mid-thirteenth-century mosaic tile group – comprised of circles with surrounding borders broken by roundels (fig 161) – feasibly comes from the completed building.[37] The east range was rebuilt in the early

thirteenth century, with the now extended chapter house and buttressed dormitory block constructed of large rectangular stones laid in regular courses. Towards the middle years of the same century, a grand new refectory was raised at right angles to the cloister, allowing no room for a warming house in the angle with the east range.

As noted above, Basingwerk received £100 by way of compensation for its losses during Edward I's Welsh war of 1282–3, but there is no indication of the extent of any specific damage to the abbey itself. Indeed, there is little archaeological or architectural evidence for any major stone building programmes throughout the later Middle Ages. This said, tile groups from the site indicate refurbishments in various areas during the mid- to late fourteenth century (figs 162 and 163).[38] In addition, fragments of cusped arcading recovered during the conservation works of the 1920s suggest the cloister alleys must have been refashioned in the second half of the fourteenth century (fig 132). In the late fifteenth or early sixteenth century, probably therefore in the time of Abbot Thomas Pennant, a domestic apartment was fashioned at the southern end of the east range. As for Pennant's other building works referred to by the Welsh bards, there is now no positive trace, unless one considers the once half-timbered range running eastwards from the south corner of the east claustral range.[39]

On 10 May 1537 the site of Basingwerk Abbey was leased to Hugh Starkey, but three years later the property was sold to Henry ap Harry of Llanasa and Peter Mutton of Meliden. Subsequently, it passed through marriage to the Mostyns of Talacre, in whose hands it remained to the twentieth century.[40] Meanwhile, in the immediate wake of the suppression, liturgical furnishings were removed from the church and lead was taken from the roofs of the buildings. There is, for example, good evidence to show that the choir stalls were taken to the church of St Mary on the Hill in Chester. An entry in the churchwardens' accounts for 1536 reads: 'In there tyme the quere was boght at basenwerke, and sette uppe with all costs and chargis belonging to the same'.[41] There is also a suggestion that the nave roof at the parish church of St Mary, Cilcain (Flint), came from the abbey.[42] In 1538 lead from Basingwerk was probably used in the repair of Holt Castle, and in 1546 a greater quantity of lead was transported to Ireland 'for the covering of Dublin castle and for other of the King's castles and houses'.[43] Even so, about 1550, three abbey bells were still at the abbey site.[44] More than two centuries later, some of the buildings apparently remained in use as a dwelling house,[45] but by the end of the eighteenth century the majority of the former monastic

159 Basingwerk Abbey: south transept and chapter house, from the west. In the foreground is the west front of the abbey church. The cloister appears to the right.

Photograph: *Cadw, Crown Copyright*

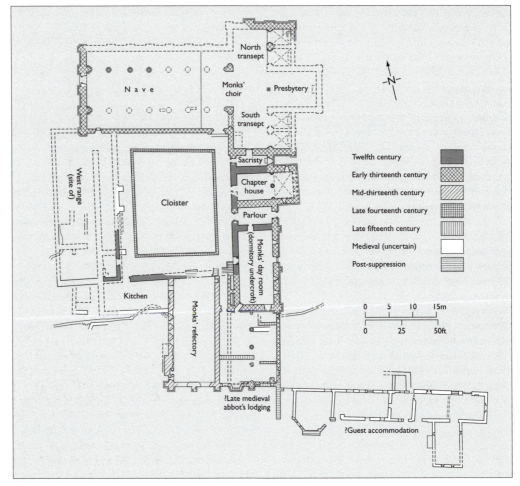

160 Basingwerk Abbey: ground plan (after Taylor 1971/Robinson 2006a, with modifications).

Drawing: *Pete Lawrence, for Cadw*

complex had fallen into disuse, with much of the stone used to build mills in the valley.

One of the earliest accounts of the surviving buildings at Basingwerk appeared in 1846, at which time all trace of the presbytery was lost.[46] The author was somewhat confused as to the layout of the site, failing to identify the chapter house and mistaking the east range for the refectory. A rather more assured survey of the remains was produced by Loftus Brock in the 1870s, to be followed by those of Edward Hodkinson and the RCAHMCW.[47] A poorly conducted and apparently unpublished excavation was carried out by Vaughan Hughes in 1890.[48] Fortunately, there are both drawings and photographs showing the gable of the south transept before its fall in 1901 (fig 84).[49] There are also illustrations which show the south gable of the refectory with its composition of four lancet windows before its collapse, including the Buck view of 1742 and a drawing of 1800.[50]

In the 1920s Abbey Farm (adjacent to the site) was worked by Peter Williams, who is said to have traced the greater part of the channel which supplied the monastery with water and formed the main drain in its lowest part.[51] The site was placed in State care in 1923. Following a programme of conservation works,[52] an official opening took place in 1927. A guide was published by Taylor in 1939,[53] since supplemented by the official Cadw guide.[54] A geophysical survey carried out in 1991 recorded several anomalies of possible archaeological significance, though no firm conclusions were drawn.[55]

The site lies in a country park. The abbey church, monastic buildings and core of the precinct are together scheduled as an ancient monument, with some 1.2ha covered (FL1).[56]

BIBLIOGRAPHY

Architectural: Brock 1878b, 468–76; [Brock] 1891; Davies 1924; Gresham 1968, 255; Hodkinson 1905; Hubbard 1986, 353–5; Jones and Williams 1846; Knowles and St Joseph 1952, 108–9; Leach 1960; Lewis 1999, 227; [Lovegrove] 1921; RCAHMCW 1912, 40–1; Robinson 1996b; Robinson 1998, 66–7; Robinson 2006a; Taylor 1946a; [Taylor] 1947; Taylor 1971; W[illiams] 1846, 99–102.
Historical: Jones 1933; Knowles and Hadcock 1971, 112, 115; O'Sullivan 1947, 25–7, Owen 1919–20; Williams 1978 and 1981a; Williams 1990, 38–40; W[illiams] 1846.

161 Basingwerk Abbey: mosaic floor tiles, mid-thirteenth century. Large areas of the floor at the east end of the completed thirteenth-century abbey church may well have been decorated with patterns of these mosaic roundels. Photograph: *National Museums & Galleries of Wales*

162 Basingwerk Abbey: decorated mosaic tiles, second half of fourteenth century. The central element of this mosaic pattern was a pointed quatrefoil tile impressed with the design of a winged creature bearing a human head.

Photograph: *National Museums & Galleries of Wales*

163 Basingwerk Abbey: line-impressed tile, fourteenth century. This tile, inscribed DEUS, would have been part of a border around a large mosaic carpet pattern, presumably laid in a refurbishment of some area of the abbey church. Photograph: *National Museums & Galleries of Wales*

CWMHIR ABBEY, Powys, St Davids, SO 055711

It is likely that Cwmhir, the abbey 'of the long valley', was established as a daughter house of Whitland in 1176 (fig 19).[1] The founding colony of monks was settled on land given by Cadwallon ap Madog (d 1179), lord of the *cantref* of Maelienydd and a cousin of Rhys ap Gruffudd (d 1197) of Deheubarth – himself an enthusiastic supporter of the Cistercians and by then patron of Whitland.[2] Writing in the late 1530s, apart from noting that the first foundation was made by Cadwallon, the Tudor antiquary John Leland (d 1552) stated that the abbey was intended for sixty monks.[3] The suggestion that Cwmhir was originally established in 1143 by Cadwallon's elder brother, Maredudd (d 1146), rests on the flimsiest of evidence and should not be given credence. Apart from any other consideration, the community at Whitland itself had still to find a permanent home at this date.[4] Equally questionable is the theory that a site change may have taken place. In fact, there is very little to support the notion of an aborted early foundation at Devannor (once Ty Faenor), the site of a late seventeenth-century house built by the Fowler family, 1.6km or so to the east of the abbey ruins.[5]

Cwmhir's border position was to cause its community great difficulty, certainly in the late twelfth and early thirteenth centuries. The middle March of Wales remained an area of intense conflict between Anglo-Norman and Welsh lords.[6] The founder, Cadwallon ap Madog, was assassinated by men of Roger Mortimer (d 1214) in 1179, and – certainly after the death of Henry II in 1189 – all hope of a peaceable accord in the region was lost. From the mid-1190s, with the support of new royal ministers, Mortimer was once more on the offensive. In 1195, or soon after, he expelled Cadwallon's sons Maelgwn (d 1197) and Hywel (d 1212) from Maelienydd.[7] Thereafter, in spite of a major defeat at the hands of Rhys ap Gruffudd in the late 1190s, he managed to maintain a firm grip over the district. In 1199 Mortimer issued a significant charter to the monks of Cwmhir, doing so in memory of his forebears, and in honour of 'our men who died in the conquest' (*et eorum qui in conquesta de Melenid mortui sunt*).[8] Meanwhile, following their expulsion from the March, the princes of Maelienydd had very probably looked to Gruffudd ap Cynan (d 1200) of Gwynedd for protection.[9] Professor Beverley Smith argues that it was possibly in the wake of these events that some, if not all, of the Cwmhir monks actually transferred to north-west Wales, leading to the creation of a new daughter colony at Cymer in 1198–9. If this were the case, it is just conceivable that Mortimer's extensive charter of 1199 amounted to a 're-foundation', or at

least a deliberate attempt to encourage the return of the exiled community to the mother house. Meanwhile, the new abbey at Cymer survived with the support of the Gwynedd dynasty of princes.[10]

As for the early community at Cwmhir itself, little is known apart from the likelihood that the first abbot was named Meurig, a Welshman who died in 1184.[11] In 1195 the General Chapter was told that lay brothers of Cwmhir had stolen their abbot's horses because he had forbidden them to drink beer.[12] After the death of Roger Mortimer, in 1214 King John placed the abbey under his protection. His charter was in turn confirmed by Henry III in 1232. It is from these two important royal confirmations that we derive most of our knowledge of the original grants and privileges given to the monks of Cwmhir.[13]

The bulk of Cwmhir's landed estate lay in hilly and mountainous country, by and large over 228m high, especially that property in the immediate vicinity of the monastery itself.[14] The home estate (the largest single property) came to be administered as the manor of Golon,[15] and was largely devoted to sheep-rearing and the production of oats. Another significant pastoral property was the grange of Nant yr Arian, situated further to the west in what is now Ceredigion. Also to the west was the grange of Dolhelfa, where the property was initially the gift of Roger Mortimer.[16] One of the abbey's leading mixed economy granges lay on the Shropshire border to the north east, at Gwernegof (earlier Gwernygo).[17] The community also held low-lying arable granges in the upper Lugg and Teme valleys to the east and at its Cabalfa-Carnaf complex by the River Wye to the south east.[18]

In the years 1212–18, Prince Llywelyn ab Iorwerth (d 1240) of Gwynedd made dramatic gains in the Marcher areas of Wales. From 1218 onwards, much of his expansionist effort was concentrated on the eastern and south-eastern borderlands, buttressing the position of the native Welsh rulers and curbing the ambitions of Anglo-Norman barons. In Maelienydd, earlier Mortimer successes were to some degree reversed as the area fell once more under the orbit of Welsh control.[19] To further meet his strategic ends, Llywelyn arranged the marriage of one of his daughters to Ralph Mortimer (d 1248), described as 'a warlike and vigorous man', who succeeded to the family estates from his half-brother, Hugh (d 1227). The sequence of these events, as we shall see below, may have considerable significance for our understanding of the construction of the abbey church at Cwmhir. They also remind us of ongoing border tensions, giving a broad context for an episode which seems to have taken place in 1231.[20] During a royal campaign launched on the central border of Wales in that year, a troop of English soldiers was apparently tricked into an ambush, the blame being placed on a monk or lay brother of Cwmhir, presumably of Welsh sympathies. Outraged, Henry III retaliated by burning 'a certain grange of the abbey, which had been plundered of all its goods'. Henry was further poised to burn the abbey itself, 'which had likewise been plundered'. In the event, the abbot paid a massive fine of 300 marks, in order 'to save the buildings [which had been] constructed with very lavish expenditure'.[21]

Whatever the truth in this story, the king did not entirely turn his back on the Cwmhir community. He granted the monks certain privileges in 1231, followed by his confirmation charter in 1232. Yet it may be telling that both grants were effectively subject to an agreement not to support the king's enemies in Wales.[22] Further royal support for the abbey followed in 1252–4, when the bailiffs of Montgomery were instructed not to permit the men of Montgomery to waste or destroy the woods of the abbot and monks of Cwmhir within their bailiwick.[23] Even so, the community never loosened its ties entirely with the native princes. In 1234, for instance, Cadwallon ap Maelgwn (a descendant of the founder) was buried at the abbey.[24] Later in the century, when charges were brought against Llywelyn ap Gruffudd (d 1282) by Bishop Anian II of St Asaph (1268–93), the abbot of Cwmhir was one of those Cistercian heads in Wales who rallied to the prince's defence, writing on his behalf to the pope,[25] and it was probably Abbot Cadwgan ab Yeva (c 1279–97) who received Llywelyn's body for burial at Cwmhir following his death within a few kilometres of Builth in December 1282.[26]

Evidently, Cwmhir was never a cash-rich house. Its income in 1291 was assessed at the comparatively low sum of £35 12s 0d,[27] with no sign of any significant improvement during the later Middle Ages. Little is in any case known about the history of the house over the entire fourteenth and fifteenth centuries.[28] This said, by the later fourteenth century (if not a good deal before), the community was leasing out grange property formerly worked by the lay brothers, as was the case at its Cabalfa-Carnaf holding in 1397.[29] A slightly earlier record (1387–9) notes there were some eight monks in residence around this time.[30] Within a few years, disaster struck during the Welsh uprising of the early fifteenth century, if John Leland's testimony of the 1530s is accepted: 'Al the howse was spoilid and defacid by Owen Glindour'.[31] At the very least this must have added to the abbey's economic difficulties. Whether it ever really recovered, financially or architecturally, after this date is something of a moot point.[32]

William Jones (alias Johns) was abbot in the early sixteenth century, resigning his office by 1516.[33] He was succeeded by Richard Vayn (alias Vaughan), who seems to have ruled the house through to c 1532, heading a community of just three other monks. About 1535, John Glyn managed to secure the abbacy, despite the fact he had already been expelled for misrule at Cymer and had also been subsequently deposed for squandering the finances at Dore.[34] In his short time at Cwmhir, the income of the house was assessed in the Valor Ecclesiasticus at the small sum of £28 17s 4d.[35] By this date, in common with the pattern across the country, almost all the abbey's landed estate had been demised. The home manor of Golon, for example, was administered by a lay bailiff and had been split up into at least seventy-five separate holdings.[36] As for Glyn, his office lasted through to the formal suppression of the abbey on 2 March 1537.[37]

The site chosen for the construction of the church and monastery buildings in 1176 lay on the north bank of the Clywedog brook, near the point where it is fed by the Cwm Hir. The Clywedog runs eastwards out of that 'long valley' from which the abbey name was derived (fig 128). Immediately west of the site, the Cwm Poeth flows southwards into the principal stream. It was probably diverted to provide the necessary water supply to the monastic complex. At approximately 250m above sea level, Cwmhir is the highest and now most isolated of all the Cistercian sites in Wales. When it was seen by John Leland in the late 1530s, he described it thus:

Comehere an abbay of White Monkes stondith betwixt ii great hilles in Melennith in a botom, wher rennith a litle brooke … No chirch in Wales is seene of such lenght as the fundation of walles ther begon doth show; but the third part of this worke was never finisched.[38]

As noted above, neither an initial foundation date of 1143, nor the suggestion of the community having occupied a temporary site at nearby Devannor (Ty Faenor), is to be taken seriously. We should, nevertheless, bear in mind the corbel unearthed during building works at Devannor in the late 1960s (fig 80). Fashioned as a male head, with a long neck, it would originally have projected about 0.3m from a wall face, and can probably be interpreted as part of an eaves table. The head itself is crudely modelled, with a long blunt nose, deeply set almond-shaped eyes, prominent ears and a curly beard. The mouth is now ill defined. As Harry Brooksby has pointed out, the piece is unlikely to have come from a building on the Devannor site. Rather, it seems probable that it was brought here from Cwmhir itself, among rubble used to level a platform during the construction of the Fowler house in the late seventeenth century.[39]

In reviewing the archaeological and architectural evidence at Cwmhir in 1982, Ralegh Radford suggested that the early community began construction of a permanent stone monastery in the period c 1176–95, first raising an aisleless cruciform church and perhaps the chapter house.[40] However, if there is general agreement on a primary colonization of the house in 1176, as now seems most likely, then it must be acknowledged that an aisleless church of this 'primitive' form begins to look rather spurious. Of course, aisleless naves continued to be employed by white monk communities through the late twelfth century and on into the early thirteenth, notably at Grey in Ireland, at Culross and Saddell in Scotland, and at Rushen on the Isle of Man,[41] yet more often than not such a plan was a feature of houses with limited resources. Although such a possibility at Cwmhir cannot be entirely discounted, a church of the full 'Bernardine' plan – with similarities to others in the Whitland family – seems far more likely.

If this were indeed the case, the programme of construction might be expected to have begun with the presbytery, crossing and transepts, probably before the close of the twelfth century. Alas, it is impossible to be certain since almost all upstanding

trace of the east end has long disappeared, and two phases of clearance-cum-excavation in the nineteenth century failed to recover much by way of buried material.[42] As it appears today, the site remains very much as landscaped in the nineteenth century (fig 33).[43] The only substantial remains are the gnarled and much reduced outer walls of the once enormous fourteen-bay nave, for the most part standing no more than 0.9m to 2.4m high, though with a few isolated sections rising close to 6.1m. Of the east end, there are just fragments of the west walls of the north and south transepts. Internally, there is little other than the sub-bases of three piers of the nave arcades, the base of the south-west crossing pier (clearly worked on all four sides), together with a few pieces of the vault responds in the aisles and of engaged shafts in the north transept (fig 164). The rubble used in the construction was local siltstone and sandstone, but for the dressings – including piers, capitals and doorways – a good-quality sandstone was brought in from the Grinshill quarries near Shrewsbury, some 88km away.[44]

Fortunately, to further our appreciation of the scale and quality of the church, the fragmentary material which exists at Cwmhir itself may be supplemented by the remarkable survival of five bays from one of the nave arcades, now to be seen in the parish church at Llanidloes (fig 89).[45] The centre-to-

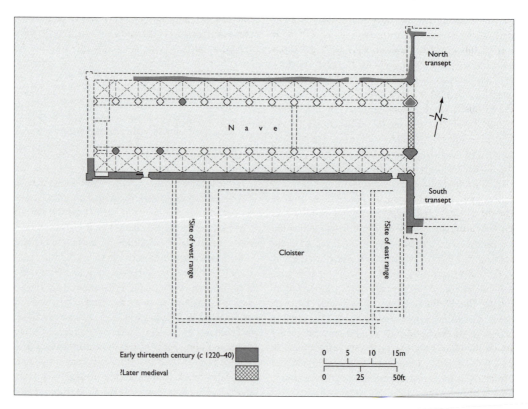

164 Cwmhir Abbey: ground plan (after Williams 1890b/ Jones 2000b, with modifications).

Drawing: *Pete Lawrence, for Cadw*

centre spacing of the four eastern bays in the Llanidloes arcade is virtually identical to what is known of the original Cwmhir arrangement, though the piers themselves have almost certainly been shortened, perhaps by more than a metre.[46] No clue survives as to the form of the original clerestory. Radford suggested that the Llanidloes material was probably removed from the east end of the north arcade, so as to involve a minimum of disturbance to the abbey fabric.[47]

In attempting to provide a close date for the Cwmhir nave, one is hindered by the unsettled nature of the abbey's patronage during the late twelfth and early thirteenth centuries,[48] especially in so far as the Mortimers retained any interest after the death of Roger in 1214. However, as far back as the 1890s, Stephen Williams linked the general character of the work to that in the nave at Llandaff Cathedral (fig 90). He was content to accept Edward Freeman's view that Llandaff could be no earlier than the 1220s.[49] In fact, the Llandaff nave is probably to be attributed to the episcopates of the reforming Henry of Abergavenny (1193–1218) and his successor William of Goldcliff (1219–29).[50] The comparison with Cwmhir is, nonetheless, well known and perfectly valid, especially when we consider the essential pier form, the triple-shaft groupings (and their purpose) and the elaborate stiff-leaf foliage. On the other hand, the arch mouldings at Cwmhir were more ornate than at Llandaff, and the abaci at the cathedral are polygonal whereas those at Llanidloes are of circular form. In broad terms, the creative genius lying behind both buildings emanated from the south-western workshops centred on Wells Cathedral and the great church at Glastonbury, both under construction from the 1180s.[51] In the same general milieu, other buildings to be considered include Dore, the Lady Chapel at Hereford Cathedral, Pershore Abbey, the nave arcade in St Mary's church, Haverfordwest, and the smaller and somewhat plainer Welsh cousin in the group, the nave at Llanthony Priory.[52]

In looking at the detail of the capitals used at Llanidloes, Richard Haslam felt the evidence could provide a degree of 'inferential information' on the progress of the Cwmhir nave. Observing that the forms move from flattish leaves with virtually no undercutting, through to luxuriant overhanging stiff-leaf foliage, he suggested the range could span the period c 1190 to c 1215.[53] The sequence was also noted by Radford, and for him the whole series 'should perhaps be spread over a generation, during which the more elaborate style was developing'. He proposed a date in the second quarter of the thirteenth century, though 'with a possible extension back for a few years'.[54]

Even if never fully realized, the conception behind this nave scheme at Cwmhir was nothing short of astonishing. It is the more remarkable when one remembers the small scale of the direct annual income available to the community. All in all, at least on historical grounds, a case could be made to support a start date for the building programme c 1200, that is, coinciding with Roger Mortimer's patronage of the house and the grant of his significant charter in 1199.[55] There are, though, very close stylistic comparisons to be drawn with several major west country buildings more securely dated to around 1220–40, notably the presbytery at Pershore Abbey in Worcestershire and the Lady Chapel at the priory of St Frideswide in Oxford, now the cathedral.[56] This would suggest that the Cwmhir nave was under construction during the period when Llywelyn ab Iorwerth exercised supremacy over the region (c 1218–40). It is therefore especially interesting to note the reference of 1231 in the chronicle of Roger of Wendover to the 'sumptuous buildings' at Cwmhir, built at considerable expense and labour.[57]

The cloister and monastic buildings lay to the south of the church. Shortly before Stephen Williams became involved at Cwmhir, a drain was cut across the area of the cloister, revealing traces of foundations and the lines of two lead pipes which supplied the conventual buildings with water.[58] As to the form of the surrounding buildings, very little can be added to the plan produced by Williams in the 1890s.[59] Williams himself pointed out the line of what he thought to be the eastern wall of the east range, its position pointing to the possibility of an earlier church. Radford felt the masonry in question 'must represent the east side of the chapter house and of the passage'.[60] Of far greater interest is the reconstruction by Williams of a free-standing octagonal pier of 'considerable size', surrounded by detached shafts at the angles, surmounted by capitals of quite a different character to those from the nave arcades. His observations were based on the recovery of five of the capitals, each with a tapering abacus (fig 143). Williams went so far as to suggest such a pier in a central position could have supported the vault in a polygonal chapter house.[61]

In the recent programme of conservation at the site, the remains of the wall at the east end of the nave, linking the two western crossing piers, has been investigated. Butting against the piers, it was found to be no more than clay-bonded. It is suggested it must be an addition to the thirteenth-century work.[62] The foundations of a second cross-wall were located in the 1820s, five bays west of the crossing. This work has now gone altogether, though it too was no more than clay-bonded.[63] One assumes the walls were related to the liturgical use of the church, though whether they reflect an early compromise or actions after the posited Glyn Dŵr destruction, it is difficult to say.[64] We can be sure, though, that the church continued in use. In 1524, Rhys ap Thomas bequeathed £8 in order 'to bye a paire of Organs to honour God within the said Abbey'.[65] And from the time of the suppression it is known the monks possessed a famed 'picture of Jesus', presumably displayed at some point in the church.[66]

Shortly after the suppression in 1537, the site and many of the abbey's former possessions were leased to William Turner, subsequently passing to Sir John Williams of Oxfordshire and then, in 1565, to the Fowlers of Grange in Shropshire.[67] As we saw above, fabric was soon removed from the church, with five bays of one of the nave arcades removed to the parish church at Llanidloes, 16km to the north west, probably during a phase of reconstruction there about 1540–1.[68] The jambs of the south door at Llanidloes could also have come from Cwmhir.[69] There have been claims, too, that the fine roof over the nave at Llanidloes, together with the east window and a screen removed from the church in 1816, as well as a screen at Llananno church, all came from the abbey.[70] None can really be substantiated.[71]

During the Civil War of the mid-seventeenth century, Cwmhir was still held by the Fowlers, who garrisoned the site for the king. They must have occupied a substantial house, which in 1644 was taken by storm and then wrecked by a parliamentarian force led by Sir Thomas Myddleton. Sir Thomas described the place as 'a very strong house, and built with stone of the greatest thickness, and the walls and outworks all very strong, the house in former times an Abbey of the Papists'.[72] After the war Sir Richard Fowler (1618–86) served as sheriff of Radnorshire in 1655 and was apparently the builder of the family's new seat at Devannor (Ty Faenor), c 1670, doubtless employing further stone from the abbey site.[73]

Writing about 1818, the historian of the county, Jonathan Williams, observed of the former abbey that 'neither door or window, or arch, or column' remained.[74] A few years later, in 1822, the estate was purchased by Thomas Wilson. A terrier prepared for him records the presence of a large house near the abbey ruins, and also 'a garden' in the precincts. In c 1822–4 Wilson built a 'small, but elegant' house to the north west of the abbey, executed in an 'Elizabethan style' and using stone from the site.[75] Then, in 1837, he sold the property to Francis Phillips. The house, to be named 'The Hall', was rebuilt by George Phillips from 1867, to a design by Poundley & Walker. In 1919 the Phillips family sold the property to a Mr Fowler.[76]

Exploration of the church and monastic buildings was begun in the early 1820s by Thomas Wilson, with the only report of the discoveries made by W Jenkin Rees in 1849.[77] Rees tells us that great quantities of 'rubbish' were cleared and removed:

> In removing the rubbish to the original floor of the building, great quantities of freestone, as well as stone of the district, were met with. The workmen also turned up a great many human bones, ironwork that had been in the windows, pieces of painted glass, ornamental lead-work … and many other curious and interesting articles.

Rees further reported that Wilson's work had uncovered the 'site of the abbot's apartments, and of the refectory, and dormitories of the monks … with portions of two magnificent pillars'. He also referred to earthworks defining the monastic precinct on the east and west sides, enclosing an area of about 4ha. At the south-west corner of this defined precinct was:

> the great oven of the monastery, the remains of which were removed in 1831, which shewed that, when complete, it was 12 feet in diameter, and 3 feet in depth, and was built 3 feet from the ground, from which large dimensions it may be inferred that the inmates of the place were, at one time, no inconsiderable number.[78]

Rubble and dressed stone fragments were subsequently used both functionally and decoratively in a variety of buildings in the neighbourhood, notably in Wilson's own house and in its extension as The Hall in the late 1860s.[79] Alas, there is no authoritative provenance for one significant piece which seems, nevertheless, very likely to have been derived from the ruins, namely a trefoil-headed tympanum, bearing a figure-carved scene of the Ascension, now built into a garden wall in the village (fig 165).[80] Much had already been lost when the site was further investigated by Stephen Williams in the 1890s. The owner at this time, Mrs Philips, had begun further clearances, locating the jambs of the east and west doorways from the nave into the cloister and recovering several carved capitals. Williams posed fresh questions over the existence of the east end and wondered whether the nave was a replacement work. He was later able to dig, carrying out what he described as 'some trifling excavations', the results of which have already been noted above.[81]

By the late 1980s, the condition of the fabric at

Cwmhir had become a matter of great concern. A survey of the standing remains was carried out by the Clwyd-Powys Archaeological Trust in 1988. Subsequently (1994–8), a comprehensive programme of conservation and consolidation was carried out by Cadw, with an accompanying three-stage re-survey of the consolidated ruins.[82] The precinct topography has also been surveyed by the Clwyd-Powys Archaeological Trust, the survey programme including a geophysical investigation of the cloister and east end of the church.[83] The results of the geophysical survey provided further evidence to support the existence of the hitherto poorly appreciated presbytery and transepts.

Various topographical features associated with the surrounding abbey precinct seem to survive, enough to propose a possible outline (fig 128). One is tempted to suggest that Home Farm, situated to the immediate north west of the nave, may represent the home grange. The freshly conserved masonry of the nave, together with small areas to the south, west and east – a total of approximately 1.2ha – are scheduled as an ancient monument (RD12). The garden of The Hall, along with its associated pleasure grounds (encompassing the abbey), have been included in the register of parks and gardens of historic interest in Wales, at Grade II.[84]

BIBLIOGRAPHY

Architectural: Blockley 1998b; Brooksby 1970; Butler 2004, 120–3; [Davies] 1934; Davies 1992; Day 1911, 19–25; [Evans] 1999, 118–22; Grigson 1959; Hamer 1873, 163–76; Haslam 1979, 140–2, 215–16; Jones 2000a and 2000b; Jones and Thomas 1997; [Lovegrove] 1932, 434–5; Radford 1982; RCAHMCW 1913, 3–7; [Rees] 1849, 244–55; Robinson 1998, 94–6; Williams 1905, 338–40; Williams 1890a, 1890b, and Williams 1894–5.

Historical: Banks 1888; Charles 1970; Davies 1946; Knowles and Hadcock 1971, 112, 115; O'Sullivan 1947, 10–11; Percival 1993; [Rees] 1849, 233–44; Remfry 1994; Rowley-Morris 1893; Williams 1976b; Williams 1990, 40–1.

CYMER ABBEY, Gwynedd, Bangor, SH 722195

In 1198 a petition came before the Cistercian General Chapter from 'Grifini', prince of north Wales, who wished to build a new abbey. Unresolved, the matter was broached for a second time in the General Chapter meeting of 1199, with the result that the abbot of Margam was instructed to visit the proposed site in the presence of the founder.[1] The prince in question was Gruffudd ap Cynan (d 1200),

165 Cwmhir Abbey: tympanum carved with Ascension scene, early thirteenth century. The robed figure of Christ is framed against a mandala; with his left arm he gestures towards a group of disciples. The low kneeling figure in the right group is probably the Virgin Mary. If the piece indeed comes from the abbey site, it is a rare example of white monk figure sculpture of this date. The most likely location would have been a tympanum above the east processional door in the nave.

Photograph: author

and the abbey he wished to build was Cymer. In the event, the house was to be colonized by a community of monks from Cwmhir in Maelienydd (fig 18).[2] Confirmation of Gruffudd's early benefactions, together with those of his brother Maredudd ap Cynan (d 1212), and his son Hywel ap Gruffudd (d 1216), comes from an important charter granted to the community at Cymer by Llywelyn ab Iorwerth (d 1240) in 1209.[3]

In his recent account of the abbey's early history, Beverley Smith has argued that the motives behind its foundation may not match the classic model of Cistercian expansion – or 'apostolic gestation' – with Cwmhir seeking to establish a daughter colony in a further remote corner of unexploited countryside.[4] To begin with, our attention is drawn to one of the versions of *Brut y Tywysogyon*, where it is recorded that in 1198 'the community of Cwmhir went to reside at Cymer'.[5] We should then bear in mind the difficult circumstances in which the Cwmhir monks found themselves at the time of the migration. Their founder had been killed in 1179 by the men of Roger Mortimer (d 1214)[6] and by the mid-1190s Mortimer was engaged in a fresh campaign of warfare and aggression against his Marcher adversaries in Maelienydd. The founder's sons were expelled from the district, apparently seeking refuge in Gwynedd, where they would probably have been received by Gruffudd ap Cynan. It seems highly likely that these events would have caused serious disturbance to the Cistercian convent at Cwmhir. Thus, as a consequence of the same difficulties encountered by their Welsh patrons, some, if not all, of the monks may have transferred to Gwynedd. In due course, Mortimer presumably enticed a number of the brothers to return to their mother house,[7] though not before the new abbey at Cymer had taken root.

After 1199, Llywelyn ab Iorwerth exercised complete supremacy over the whole of Gwynedd.[8] When he came to give his support to the monks of Cymer in 1209, apparently at their request, he did so wholeheartedly. His charter of that year became one of the monastery's prized possessions, confirming the grants and privileges of previous benefactors 'lest what has been justly given may be taken away by unjust presumption in the future'.[9]

The bulk of the landed possessions held by Cymer lay close to the site of the monastery itself.[10] In particular, the community held large mountainous tracts rising above the valleys of the Mawddach and Wnion around Llanelltyd and Llanfachreth. There were granges, for example, at Abereiddon and Esgaireiddon, both in the parish of Llanfachreth,[11] at Brynbedwyn in Brithdir, and at Cwmcadian in Pennal. Given the predominance of upland holdings, it is no surprise to find that the abbey's early economy was based on pastoralism, though it was dairying rather than sheep-rearing which seems to have proved its mainstay.[12] A number of Cymer's granges must be seen, therefore, as serving as large cattle farms, supplemented in turn by several important arable holdings, notably those at Gellisarog in Llanegryn to the south west, and at Neigwl on the Lleyn peninsula (the abbey's most valuable early property). In addition to farming, the monks were able to exploit the resources of the sea and rivers to complement their economy. Somewhat surprisingly for such a small community, mining and metallurgy also appear to have been a source of some wealth.[13]

Despite these assets, Cymer was always destined to be something of a poor house, barely achieving that stability required for the regular round of observance. As early as 1241, certain difficulties encountered by the abbey seem to have led to an instruction from the General Chapter for the monks to be dispersed, an action resisted by the abbot at that time.[14] However, later in the century – in the years before Edward I's conquests – the monks were to enjoy a close relationship with Prince Llywelyn ap Gruffudd (d 1282).[15] In 1274, for example, he loaned Abbot Llywelyn £12 to enable him to attend the General Chapter meeting at Cîteaux[16] and, on several occasions, the prince based his court at Cymer's grange of Abereiddon, writing letters and transacting business there.[17]

Cymer certainly did not escape the impact of Edward I's Welsh wars, though the precise nature of the damage to its property and buildings is unclear. Towards the end of his second campaign, in May 1283, the king used the abbey as the centre of his operations in the region.[18] In October 1284, *en route* from Harlech to Castell y Bere, the king visited Cymer once again, on which occasion he granted the monks £5 for building work, presumably then in hand.[19] The following month, the community received £80 by way of compensation for war damages.[20]

In 1291 the abbey's modest annual income was recorded as £28 8s 3d[21] and financial matters showed no vast improvement over the next two centuries. By the end of the fourteenth century there were just five monks at the house.[22] There is no specific evidence to suggest how Cymer fared during the Glyn Dŵr uprising at the beginning of the fifteenth century,[23] though by the early 1440s ill-governance by its abbots appears to have been setting the house on the very brink of destruction. In particular, the actions of rival claimants to the abbacy weakened Cymer's economic position even further, not to mention the impact on the spiritual life of the community.[24] One of the claimants, John Cobbe, urged Henry VI to transfer the abbey's lands into the care of keepers.[25] His petition, or another, secured the desired result, and in 1443 Cymer and its abbot (now given as Richard Kirby) were placed under the protection of Sir Thomas Stanley (d 1459), controller of the royal household.[26] Ten years later, in 1453, Cymer was once again placed in royal custody. By now, the income of the house was said to have been reduced from some £60 to less than £15, and it was further reported that 'divine worship and other works of piety are discontinued and the dispersion of the monks is feared'.[27]

Somehow Cymer survived, even if question marks must be raised over the nature of the monastic daily round. In the 1520s there were once again rival claimants to the abbacy, with both John (occurs 1521–5) and Lewis ap Thomas (c 1517–37) responsible for a sequence of late leases of monastic demesne.[28] Nevertheless, in the context of the time, Abbot Lewis gained something of a reputation for good management.[29] In 1535 Cymer's net income was assessed at £51 13s 4d,[30] though at the time its monastic community may have comprised no more than Abbot Lewis and a single monk. The house was probably suppressed in March 1537.[31]

Cymer Abbey was built on the wide east bank of the River Mawddach, a short distance above its confluence (its *cymer*) with the Wnion. It lay close to the earlier motte of Uchdryd ab Edwin. The principal remains are those of the church (figs 82, 166 and 167), which seems to date from the early thirteenth century. The tower at the west end was probably added in the second half of the fourteenth century.[32] South of the church there are slight traces of the

166 *Cymer Abbey: view of the presbytery, looking east. The end wall was pierced by two tiers of graduated lancets. To the right, in the south wall, are the remains of a triple sedilia. Structurally, the end wall was not bonded to the lateral walls of the church, clearly representing a compromise solution to an earlier plan.* Photograph: *Cadw, Crown Copyright*

cloister and surrounding monastic buildings, and to the west what was probably the late medieval abbot's lodging survives within the fabric of the present farmhouse. The structures were built of a variety of local slate and dolerite, irregularly coursed, and using glacial boulders. A pale, fine-grained sandstone was used for dressings in the church.[33]

It is difficult to offer any firm conclusions on what stands as a rather unorthodox Cistercian church. Apart from the tower, the surviving building is little more than a plain rectangle, measuring some 33.5m by 18.2m internally. There are no transepts, though aisles run along its entire length, in part cut off from the central vessel by solid screen walls. In the east wall of the presbytery there were two tiers of three graduated lancets, and the full clerestory seems to have been lit on either side by six windows with deeply splayed sills.[34] Of particular note, the entire east wall – closing off both the presbytery and its

aisles – is clearly not bonded to the lateral walls. Construction in this fashion almost certainly represents a compromise solution to an earlier, and perhaps unfinished, 'Bernardine' design (fig 25). If we accept this model, rather than envisaging a sequence in which the nave was built first,[35] it seems far more likely (as at Cwmhir) that the arrangement represents a contraction in the overall scale of the church. Determining the date is problematic, though in the revised scheme the masons certainly made use of earlier carved details. This may, for example, make better sense of a fragment of chevron moulding found on one of the jambs of the central east window. It would, furthermore, help to explain the ground plan in terms of the dispositions, so far as they are known, of the east cloister alley and the chapter house (fig 167). That building work of some kind was in hand in 1284 is evident from Edward I's gift of £5 towards the costs, but it is not certain that the £80 paid to the community a month later was directly related to structural damage sustained during the king's second Welsh war.[36] Indeed, the only addition which definitely post-dates the 1280s is the western tower. Built in the mid- to later fourteenth century, it featured angle buttresses and a

167 Cymer Abbey: ground plan (after Radford 1946/ Robinson 1995a, with modifications).

Drawing: *Pete Lawrence, for Cadw*

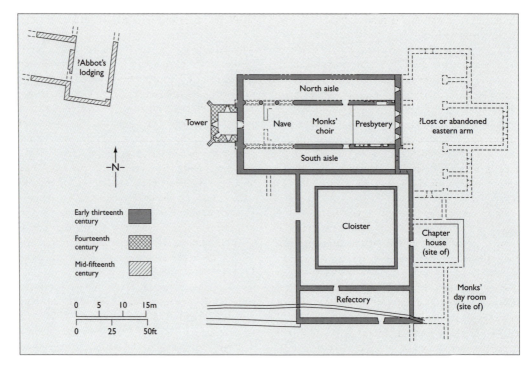

circular stair in the internal south-west corner.

Of the cloister and its surrounding monastic buildings to the south, no more than foundations survive. The position of the chapter house has been identified, and in the south range the refectory appears to have been set out on an east–west alignment. The west range may never have been completed in stone. Just westwards of the church is Y Faner (Vanner), or Abbey Farmhouse. The present building incorporates a very fine four-bay late-medieval hall, some 7.6m wide, originally open to the roof, and with evidence of a louvre opening. On its west side is an adjoining parlour wing. There is some evidence for a cross-wing (now lost) at the dais (north) end of the hall, and possibly an outer room at the opposite end of the building. Both the hall and the parlour have ornate arch-braced collar-beam trusses, with the hall recently dated through dendrochronology to about 1441.[37] The building could have served as a guest house, though it may be better interpreted as high-status accommodation for the abbot himself (fig 25). There was presumably a detached kitchen somewhere in the vicinity. The evidence suggests that, despite the difficulties of the early 1440s, either Abbot John ap Rhys or Abbot John Cobbe chose to upgrade their accommodation at this time. Alternatively, the house may have been constructed when the abbey was placed in the custody of Sir Thomas Stanley in 1443.[38]

In May 1538 the site of Cymer, 'convent and precincts', was granted to John Powes, a servant of

the royal household, upon a lease of twenty-one years. Though his possession was subsequently attested, it would seem that Y Faner in any case became the centre of an estate based on the former monastic lands in the immediate vicinity. One bell still remained on the site in 1556.[39] By the mid-seventeenth century the property was in the hands of Hywel Vaughan, whose family – the Vaughans of Nannau – continued to hold Cymer into the twentieth century.[40] A survey of 1794 survives, giving a description and plan of Y Faner, from which elements of the monastic precinct and home farm can be reconstructed.[41]

The buildings at Cymer were first described by H L Jones in the mid-nineteenth century, at which time there were plans to prevent the 'venerable pile from falling into further decay'.[42] In the early 1870s, Loftus Brock published a fresh account of the ruins, accompanied by a plan showing the fifteenth-century hall as well as the abbey church. Brock was of the opinion that the church represented a single build, with nothing that could be ascribed to a period before 'the end of the thirteenth century or the beginning of the fourteenth'. Nevertheless, he was aware that the north and south walls of the presbytery were not bonded to the east end of the building, which (together with the lancets at its centre) suggested it might be the earliest part.[43] A further description of the ruins was given in the Merioneth inventory by the RCAHMCW, who revised the dating to the late twelfth and early thirteenth century.[44] At the time of these accounts, the western arcade of three bays on the north side of the nave was filled with blocking walls. The north aisle was roofed over and was used for farm purposes. One of the trusses – a medieval survival (though not necessarily in its original position) – was illustrated by the RCAHMCW.[45] The site was placed in State care in 1930, but there is no published record of the works and clearance which subsequently took place. An official guide was published by Ralegh Radford,[46] which, having passed through several reprintings, is now supplemented by the official Cadw guide.[47]

In two recent reviews of the evidence, Lawrence Butler now seems drawn to the view that the Cymer community indeed began building with the expectation of achieving a regular 'Bernardine' plan.[48] He argues that, given the use of the early thirteenth-century triple sedilia and other features in the south wall of the eventual presbytery, the change of design must have been decided at an early stage.[49] Butler also claims that the three-bay arcade at the west end of the church 'is clearly fourteenth-century in date'. In support of this view, one may note the uncomfortable alignment of the clerestory windows above the arcade (fig 83). However, the evidence is by no means as conclusive as Butler claims, with little clear indication of insertion within the fabric, and with several examples of comparable thirteenth-century octagonal piers, with moulded capitals, bases and simple chamfered arcades.[50]

An arbitrary area of some 0.35ha at Cymer is scheduled as an ancient monument (ME1), though this covers but a small part of the monastic precinct, even omitting Y Faner. The house and associated buildings are, nevertheless, listed as a group, all at Grade II* (record number 4739).

BIBLIOGRAPHY

Architectural: Brock 1878b, 463–7; Butler 2004, 116–18; Ellis 1927, 1–7; [Jones] 1846, 446–50; Knowles and St Joseph 1952, 112–15; Radford 1946; RCAHMCW 1921, 96–7; Robinson 1995b; Robinson 1998, 97–8; Smith and Butler 2001, 317–25; Smith 2001, 447, 469–71; Smith and Suggett 2002, 58–62; Suggett 1996, 28, 107, 109.

Historical: Gresham 1984; [Jones] 1846; Knowles and Hadcock 1971, 112, 118; O'Sullivan 1947, 16–17; Pryce 2001, 273–87; Richards 1957–60, 240–9; Smith 1999; Smith and Butler 2001, 297–317; Williams 1981b; Williams 1990, 41–3; Williams-Jones 1957–60.

DORE ABBEY, Herefordshire, Hereford, so 387303

In the strict sense, of course, Dore does not lie in Wales. Nestling in the picturesque landscape of the Golden Valley, just a few kilometres beyond Monmouthshire's northern border, it belongs to the county of Hereford. In the Middle Ages, however, the situation was not quite so clear cut. The bounds of the diocese of St Davids, for example, ran particularly close to the western margins of the abbey precinct (fig 18).[1] We should remember, too, that the monks of Dore possessed considerable landholdings in Wales, both in the modern county of Monmouthshire and in the medieval Marcher lordship of Brecon. There is also the testimony of the Dore community to consider. In 1281, for example, the abbot petitioned the General Chapter for his house to be considered among the Welsh abbeys for taxation purposes.[2] Moreover, by the early sixteenth century, the monks were perfectly content for their house to be included in a fully recognized Welsh province, the 'provincia Wallie' as it was described in a letter of 1521.[3]

Dore was founded by Robert fitz Harold, lord of Ewyas, in 1147.[4] It was unique in Britain as the only house to have been colonized by the great abbey of Morimond, located in the Champagne region of north-eastern France, and one of the four so-called 'elder daughters' of Cîteaux (figs 17 and 19).[5] In turn, however, Dore was to send out three colonies of its own. First, in the mid-1170s, an attempt was made to establish a daughter at Trawscoed, on the upper stretches of the River Dulas in Cantref Selyf.[6] Hereabouts, in 1172–4, Walter de Clifford (d 1190) granted the Dore monks various lands and privileges 'to build an abbey … to the increase of the monastic order of the Cistercians'. Walter's gifts also included 'all materials in his forest which are necessary to them for the construction of this building'. The grant was made on the condition 'that the abbey shall remain in Cantref Selyf, with the abbot and convent for ever'.[7] In the event, the plantation proved abortive, possibly because of a lack of recruits or of sufficient additional endowment to make it a going concern. For Gerald of Wales, the fault was that of Abbot Adam I, who did not flinch from reducing the status of the fledgling house to that of a grange, perhaps in the early years of the thirteenth century.[8]

In 1226, after protracted negotiations, Dore sent out a second daughter colony, this time to Grace Dieu in Wales. It, too, had something of an unsettled beginning, including a site change, though the community did eventually take root.[9] Some four decades later, in the 1260s, Dore was chosen to be the mother house of a prestigious new royal foundation. It was planned by the future Edward I as the largest

Cistercian house in Britain. Had his scheme been brought to full fruition, Vale Royal Abbey might well have become one of the greatest works of piety ever undertaken by a medieval English king.[10] The foundation represented the fulfilment of a vow made by Edward in 1263–4. With the authority of the General Chapter, an inspection of the proposed site – at Darnhall in the royal forest of Delamere in Cheshire – took place in 1266.[11] A foundation charter was at last issued in August 1270,[12] though it was to be another four years before the colonizing monks arrived from Dore, and then only to find that the site was less than ideal. In 1277 Edward laid the foundation stone for the high altar on a fresh site, to be named Vale Royal. The monks finally moved there in 1281.

By then, the community at Dore itself had long established its economic base.[13] From the first, the monks held extensive lands in the Golden Valley, where they controlled up to nine granges. In an effort to establish consolidated holdings, they had bought up and exchanged various parcels of land, and in this way had managed to create an unbroken block of territory between the Dore and the Wye, encompassing six of the granges.[14] By 1213 they held more than 486ha in the royal forest of Treville, much of which they had sought to assart and cultivate. Again, it is Gerald of Wales who best characterizes the activity, telling us how the monks managed to 'turn an oak wood into a wheat field'. He describes how they bought 122ha in the forest from Richard I. The purchase price of 300 marks was easily recovered when the timber, 'sold in Hereford for building purposes', yielded more than three times the amount.[15] Beyond the Golden Valley, the community expanded into what is now northern Monmouthshire, where the lands were organized around four grange centres, at Llyncoed, Llanfair, Cold grange and Morlais grange. Most is known about Llanfair, situated to the south west of Grosmont, and granted to Dore in the early thirteenth century by Hubert de Burgh (d 1243). Its significance is emphasized by the fact it was to house a cell of monks (later replaced by secular chaplains) who were to say mass in the chapel for the souls of de Burgh and other benefactors of the abbey.[16] Elsewhere, Dore's third major block of properties was situated beyond the Black Mountains in the district of Cantref Selyf, where there were a further three granges. The core of these lands was initially granted by Walter de Clifford, expressly with the intention of establishing the daughter house at Trawscoed.[17] The rights and privileges of the community to all these gifts were underlined in two important confirmatory charters, the first given in the 1230s by Henry III, and the second granted almost a century later by Edward III.[18]

The first abbot of Dore about whom anything is known is Adam I. He was in office by 1186 and can be traced to at least 1213.[19] Much of our knowledge is drawn from the writings of Gerald of Wales, whose antipathy towards Adam can be explained by the fact they were rivals for the vacant see of St Davids in 1198.[20] Gerald presents us with a picture of a grasping and avaricious man, one who would stop at little to bolster his own position or to extend the prosperity of his house.[21] Yet there are grounds for seeing Adam as a significant intellectual. As we shall see below, he was also a builder of considerable note, ranking alongside his near-contemporary at Margam, Abbot Gilbert (1203–13), whose purposeful and no less commercially orientated style of leadership came in for similar criticism from the embittered Gerald.[22] By 1216, at the latest, Adam had been succeeded by Abbot Adam II. Gerald of Wales reports that he had earlier been a Cluniac, but thought him no more than 'modest in a mediocre way'. He went on to criticize Adam for falling under the bad influence of the Dore community.[23]

Stephen of Worcester served as abbot from about 1236 until 1257.[24] The period is best remembered as that when the scholarly bishop, Cadwgan, resided at Dore. A noted writer, Cadwgan had been professed as a monk at Strata Florida, and later became abbot of Whitland (1203–15).[25] He was appointed to the see of Bangor in 1215, retiring to the Cistercian cloister at Dore in 1236, where he was 'honourably received'. It appears that Cadwgan was then granted special privileges at Dore, and it was perhaps these which were the cause of a rebuke from the General Chapter in 1239. Cadwgan was accused of neglecting to keep the observance of the order, by breaking silence and by the mode of his living. His actions were said to be fomenting dissension and scandal.[26] But this cannot diminish his reputation as a theologian, nor should we underestimate the significance of the gift of 'his store of books' to the library at Dore. Cadwgan died at the abbey and was buried there in 1241.[27]

The third quarter of the thirteenth century brought rather mixed fortunes to the Dore community. Abbot Henry (c 1257–73) found himself engaged in various costly litigation disputes, all of which must have placed a strain on the finances of his house.[28] Of particular note, building work on the abbey church itself had still to be completed. On 3 July 1260 Peter of Aigueblanche, bishop of Hereford (1240–68), granted an indulgence of twenty days to all those who contributed to the building of 'the sumptuous church of Dore'.[29] Within a few years, the plans for the foundation of Vale Royal had emerged, surely placing additional demands on Dore's resources. In sum, in 1273, the General Chapter noted the house was 'deficient in temporalities', and consequently the abbot of Morimond was ordered to visit his daughter community.[30]

At the time of the *Taxatio Ecclesiastica* in 1291, the annual income of the house stood at around £100, a figure exceeded at several of the larger Welsh abbeys.[31] There were, nevertheless, some 3,000 sheep recorded on the community's pastures. An almost contemporary source indicates that its wool was of the very best quality; the monks were certainly trading this wool with Italian merchants by the very early years of the fourteenth century.[32] By this time, however, there are signs of increasing financial difficulty. As early as 1295, Dore was obliged to acknowledge a debt of £100 owed to Edmund, earl of Cornwall.[33] Of greater significance, it can be assumed that as the general economic recession of the fourteenth century progressed, the community began to lease out more and more of its grange property in return for fixed annual rents. By the time of the suppression in 1537 very little was left in demesne.[34] In a quest for new endowments, Dore turned to the appropriation of parish churches. The process could be both lengthy and costly, yet could reap significant rewards.[35] In 1328–30, for example, the monks were given the church of Duntisbourne Rouse in Gloucestershire by Sir John le Rous (d 1346), on account of a range of difficulties, including 'sterility of lands … murrain of animals … wars and other external disturbances'. As rector, Dore was held responsible for the upkeep of the chancel.[36] Wigtoft church in Lincolnshire was given to the monks by John de la Warre in 1330. Papal confirmation of its appropriation was granted in 1345 on account of Dore's sufferance from 'the wars between the English and Welsh'.[37] In all, on the eve of the suppression, Dore was deriving up to a quarter of its annual income from spiritualities.

At the time of these appropriations, and indeed over much of the first half of the fourteenth century, Dore was headed by Abbot Richard of Madeley *alias* Straddel (1305–46), a man of considerable scholarship, widely respected in both Cistercian and royal circles.[38] In 1321, for instance, on behalf of the General Chapter and the Crown, Richard was requested to accompany the abbot of Margam on a visitation of Cistercian houses in Ireland.[39] In 1327 he journeyed to Scotland with William Melton, archbishop of York, to treat for peace between the English and the Scots, and later he went to France on royal business on at least three separate occasions. Edward III was certainly appreciative of Abbot Richard's 'great labours', and in return granted special privileges to the monastery of Dore.[40] As a

further mark of Richard's standing, we should note that in October 1321 William de Grandson (d 1335) presented the house with 'a fragment of the wood of the Holy Cross, very beautifully adorned with gold and precious stones … in return for the grace and favour of the lord Straddel, abbot'. This significant relic was presumably housed in some appropriate setting.[41] Grandson and his wife were eventually buried at Dore.

The years at the turn of the fourteenth century were particularly troublesome for the community. In the late 1390s there was a bitter and divisive election dispute between John Holand of Dore and Jordon Bykeleswade of St Mary Graces in London.[42] Although Bykeleswade seems to have received both papal and episcopal backing in 1398, the dispute dragged on, made worse by interference and even armed raids perpetrated by outsiders, doubtless taking advantage of the power struggle.[43] The next abbot, Richard Grisby (*c* 1405–14), had barely taken over when the community became fearful of the Glyn Dŵr uprising. Permission was granted for the monks of Dore 'to treat with the rebels for the safety of the abbey, which is in great peril of destruction and burning'.[44]

At times over the later fifteenth and early sixteenth centuries, the daily round of monastic life at Dore must have seemed difficult to maintain, with documentary sources revealing a catalogue of ongoing troubles.[45] The rule of Abbot Richard Rochester (*c* 1441–72), for example, appears to have been broken for several years by the claims of a rival candidate. In 1453 the abbey was said to have been 'oppressed by sons of iniquity', and was entrusted for a while to secular guardians.[46] Further mismanagement followed during the abbacy of Richard Dorston (1495–1500), who had earlier been abbot of the daughter house at Grace Dieu (*c* 1486–95). He was eventually deposed from office at Dore, with his 'inordinate Rule and governance' later cited as the main reason the house stood 'gretly in ruyn and decay'.[47] Abbot Thomas Cleubery (*c* 1516 to 1523), on the other hand, was a rather different man, a scholar and a bibliophile. And yet his time, too, ended in difficulties. The background is obscure, but in the second half of 1523 Cleubery was increasingly harassed by a Thomas ap Richard and his followers. In September ap Richard led a heavily armed band into the monastery, entering 'the quire and chancel of the church' at the time of High Mass, determined to assault the abbot. In this way, Cleubery was eventually evicted from his office altogether. Within a few years, however, matters were sufficiently settled at Dore for him to be given a reasonable corrody. He occupied a complex of three rooms called 'the new

168 *Dore Abbey: view of the presbytery, looking south east. The Dore community began work on a presbytery of 'Bernardine' form in the 1170s. This was barely completed when, c 1186, the whole eastern arm of the church was extended in rectangular ambulatory form. After the suppression, the presbytery remained in use as a parish church. The great wooden screen between the eastern crossing piers dates from the restoration of the church in the 1630s.* Photograph: *Cadw, Crown Copyright*

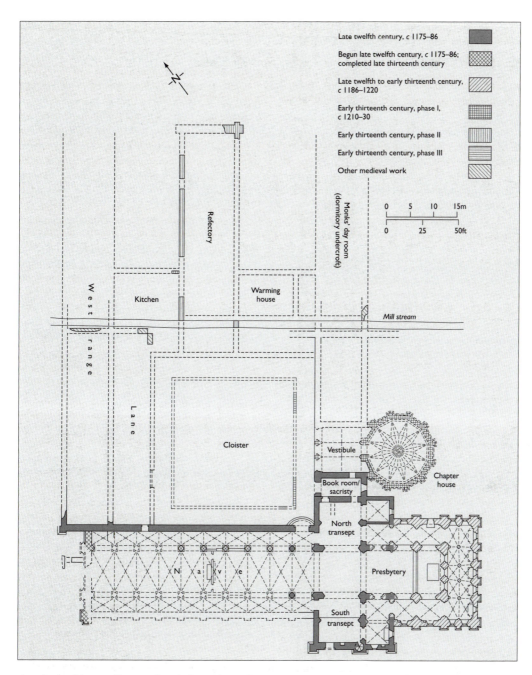

Late twelfth century, c 1175–86

Begun late twelfth century, c 1175–86; completed late thirteenth century

Late twelfth to early thirteenth century, c 1186–1220

Early thirteenth century, phase I, c 1210–30

Early thirteenth century, phase II

Early thirteenth century, phase III

Other medieval work

169 Dore Abbey: *ground plan (after* RCHME 1934/ Harrison 1997a, *with modifications).*

Drawing: *Pete Lawrence, for Cadw*

chamber', with an adjacent chapel, located on the north side of the monastery.[48]

Abbot John Glyn (*c* 1524–8), Cleubery's successor, had in fact already been expelled from Cymer in north-west Wales for poor governance. At Dore, from 'the first day of his rule', he proceeded to squander the resources of the house. Although once again deposed, he still managed to become abbot of Cwmhir about 1535.[49] The last abbot of Dore was John Redborne (1529–37).[50] He it was who provided the required information to the *Valor Ecclesiasticus*

commissioners in 1535, at which time the net annual income of the house was recorded as £101 5s 2d.[51] The suppression came on 1 March 1537, when nine monks and sixteen or more servants surrendered the house to the king's visitors.[52]

The choice of site for Dore Abbey was presumably made in agreement with visitors from Morimond. It was to be located close to the south-west border of Herefordshire, in the lordship of Ewyas Harold, with the necessary land perhaps carved out of the parish of Bacton. The abbey complex was placed on the west bank of the River Dore, a few kilometres above its confluence with the Monnow. Topographical considerations led the builders to position the church along a north-west to south-east axis. The cloister, surrounded by the three main claustral ranges, effectively lay on the north-east side of the nave, that is to site north. A part-canalized leat was drawn from the Dore upstream, to run through a mill complex, and then on to service the claustral buildings, before tracking south east to rejoin the river. In total, the precinct is estimated to have enclosed around 19.4ha, not all of which was necessarily surrounded by a wall (fig 128).[53]

The surviving remains are enormously impressive (figs 62, 168 and 169). It so happens that the site retains perhaps the best-preserved and most complete fragment of an early Gothic Cistercian church to be found anywhere in Britain. At Dore, all too often overlooked in favour of the more celebrated ruins in northern England, one is able to see the entire liturgical east end of the building, including its transepts and ambulatory aisle, all with roofs, and long since serving a parochial function. In addition, outside the blocked western crossing arch, there are traces of the ruinous nave, notably the two cylindrical drum piers of the eastern bay, together with the first arch of the south arcade. To the north of the church, there are various indications of the claustral layout. In particular, attached to the north transept are the remains of the twelfth-century book room and sacristy, and beyond this the fragmentary remains of the early thirteenth-century polygonal chapter house (fig 169). Against the facade of the north transept are two high roof creases, representing two phases in the roof over the monks' dormitory.

There is a large and sometimes confusing body of literature on the site, reflecting an undoubtedly complex building history. The earliest significant scholarly interest in Dore is to be traced to the 1880s, to the contributions made by the late Victorian architect Thomas Blashill.[54] His work encouraged further interest from Roland Paul, who first explored elements of the archaeology and architecture of the abbey buildings in 1892–3. Thereafter, over a period of almost forty years, Paul produced no fewer than six different published ground plans of the abbey, some with only minor modification. His findings were published, however, in something of a random fashion, with, alas, no single complete synthesis to which we may now turn for any general conclusions. Paul's final contribution appeared in 1931.[55] This last brief article was written in response to the account of Dore published that same year by the Royal Commission on the Historical Monuments of England (RCHME) in its inventory of south-west

Herefordshire.[56] Paul was particularly critical of the Commission's work, so much so that it felt obliged to produce a note of correction with a fresh ground plan, published three years later.[57]

Wider interest in the possible international significance of the abbey might be said to have been triggered by Jean Bony. In a footnote to an influential article of 1947, he drew attention to the resemblance of some of the features at Dore to those found in early Gothic churches in eastern Normandy and the Vexin.[58] Although this point was not directly taken up by Nikolaus Pevsner, his 1963 account is nonetheless perceptive and provides more of the regional and Continental contexts needed for a fuller appreciation of the building.[59] Bony's ideas were eventually to be developed by Carolyn Malone, beginning with her thesis of 1973 and then in an essay published in 1984. For her, the Dore transepts represent 'the most extensive early example of French gothic design' remaining in the west of England.[60] Also in 1984 Peter Fergusson produced his seminal study of twelfth-century Cistercian architecture in England. In this work, the Herefordshire abbey was at last firmly placed in the context of European developments as a whole. Broadly, Fergusson supports Malone's hypothesis, arguing that the style of the Dore transepts was 'remarkable for the purity of the Early Gothic ideas imported from France'. On the other hand, he is in no doubt that the nave and the extended presbytery reflect 'an unequivocal assimilation of local west country influences'.[61] More recently, Brian O'Callaghan has challenged the precise nature of the design sources for Dore. For him, it is certainly not necessary to make a case for specific French antecedents. The similarities with the early Gothic of France are, he says, of no more than 'a general nature'.[62] Likewise, in the most recent account of the building, although Stuart Harrison and Malcolm Thurlby acknowledge that some features appear typically French, their overall conclusion on the early Gothic work at Dore is to see it as a regionalized and unsophisticated manifestation of the style.[63] This last essay is one of the contributions to a comprehensive overview of the history, fabric and contents of the abbey published in 1997.[64]

In beginning to unravel the development of the abbey buildings as revealed through this body of work, it seems reasonable to assume that in 1147 the monks were greeted by an arrangement of temporary wooden structures.[65] Thereafter, although the evidence is slight, there are indications that a small and probably austere stone monastery was laid out over the first two or three decades of the community's history. Notably, within the upstanding fabric of the modified north transept, a number of features point to the existence of an earlier building, or at least to one designed along more primitive lines.[66] This possibility has been explored in more detail by Harrison and Thurlby, to the extent that they feel able to produce a tentative ground plan (fig 38). They show an aisleless church, in which the transepts are arranged *en échelon*, and in which the outer bay of the north transept is now represented by the book room and sacristy.[67]

A distinct change of style, marked by elements of exotic detailing, suggests that a rebuilding of the church was initiated no later than the 1170s.[68] In this scheme, the east end was planned along typically 'Bernardine' lines, but with a fully stressed crossing. The aisleless rectangular presbytery, featuring at least one projecting bay, appears to have been prepared with a stone vault in mind.[69] The two-storey north and south transepts were clearly covered with vaults, in timber if not in stone. There were two rib-vaulted eastern chapels to each transept; the inner chapel on either side was possibly deeper than its neighbour, resulting in an *en échelon* plan.

This new programme of works must have begun with the northern transept where there is a solid wall between the two chapels, a generally earlier Cistercian characteristic.[70] However, in the same part of the building, the prominent bay articulation created by the grouping of five high vault shafts, along with various traits in the sculptural detail, herald the arrival of the early Gothic style. Precisely what kind of Gothic the Dore master had encountered beforehand is unclear, but in any case as the work progressed through the crossing and on into the south transept, sources from the west of England become ever more prevalent.[71] Indeed, taken as a whole, the south transept reveals quite considerable differences from its northern counterpart. The arcade wall, for instance, is noticeably thicker here; the high vault was supported externally by broad angle buttresses; two large lancets, with continuous inner angle rolls, pierced the principal south elevation; and the eastern chapels were left to communicate through a large chamfered arch in the later Cistercian style.

By this stage of building, some headway must also have been made with the laying out of the nave. At the very least, the eastern bay would have been required to support the crossing and perhaps a modest tower. Even so, at ten bays in length, it was a particularly ambitious undertaking, and it may have been close to a full century before the community was able to bring it to a successful conclusion.[72] Designed with cylindrical piers, not unlike those at Buildwas (fig 59), the elevation was of two storeys, in which the clerestory windows had steeply raking

sills.[73] Both the form of the capitals and the arcade mouldings are likely to have varied, perhaps over the full ten bays. Almost certainly, from the outset of the work, there was an intention to vault both the central vessel and the aisles in stone.

It cannot have been too long after the ambitious Adam I became abbot of Dore, *c* 1186, that he chose to embark on a grandiose and up-to-date remodelling of the barely completed 'Bernardine' east end.[74] Effectively, the scheme was an interpretation of that seen in the new church at Byland, and was likewise to feature a rectangular ambulatory encircling a now aisled presbytery.[75] There is no evidence for any direct connection between Dore and Byland, and it seems more likely that the sources for Abbot Adam's new work were Continental. At Burgundian Cîteaux, for example, a rectangular ambulatory was under construction in 1188 and the completed church (Cîteaux III) was consecrated in 1193 (fig 34).[76] If the idea for the Dore scheme was indeed borrowed from Cîteaux, it may well have emerged from repeated visits to the General Chapter by Abbot Adam, or even his predecessor. Equally, however, the decisive influence could well have been Dore's mother house at Morimond, which also adopted a rectangular ambulatory plan, arguably in the second half of the twelfth century.[77]

In the Dore scheme of works, the existing inner transept chapels had to be sacrificed in favour of rib-vaulted aisles flanking the enriched presbytery. These single-storey aisles were continued around the end of the eastern arm as a straight ambulatory. Here, the vaults were carried on delicate bundled piers of eight shafts (fig 98). The presbytery itself was of three bays,

170 Dore Abbey: vault boss, late thirteenth or early fourteenth century. On stylistic grounds, this and several other figurated high vault bosses from the site have generally been dated to the early fourteenth century. Given that a consecration of the abbey church is known to have taken place in 1275–82, however, there is a case to suggest they may be of marginally earlier date.

Photograph: *Cadw, Crown Copyright*

terminating just behind the high altar in a richly moulded arcade supported on piers of sixteen shafts (fig 97). The lower storey has a conservative, almost ponderous feel, whereas the upper level (much like the east ambulatory aisle) takes on a lighter, more sophisticated quality. The three eastern lancets have deep raking sills, and are framed by both attached and detached shafts, the two outer orders featuring stiff-leaf capitals. On balance, it seems likely the high vault was constructed of timber, and the entire programme was probably completed in the first decade or so of the thirteenth century.[78]

The evidence of the 1260 indulgence offered by Bishop Peter of Aigueblanche in favour of Dore's building programme suggests that, elsewhere in the church, work of one kind or another was continuing well into the second half of the thirteenth century. At the time, although the springers had probably been in place for some decades, the nave vault was possibly one of the main elements still requiring attention. In addition, Harrison's investigation of *ex situ* fragments has shown that a substantial amount of liturgical fitting out was being undertaken in the nave around this time.[79] It may, nevertheless, have been the fully completed church which was consecrated by Thomas Cantilupe, bishop of Hereford (1275–82), at some point during his episcopate.[80] In this context there is one significant item of controversy, namely the figurated bosses from the high vault in the nave. Several of these pieces survive (fig 170), and have generally been dated to the early fourteenth century, indicating later works. More recently, Harrison and Thurlby have suggested they could well be earlier, installed in time for the Cantilupe consecration.[81]

Turning to the claustral buildings, it may have been Abbot Adam I who instigated at least some reconstruction of the initial stone ranges, with the work presumably continuing under his successors. As noted, little survives above ground, though the plan of a north–south refectory has been recovered. The most outstanding feature of Dore's claustral layout must surely have been its impressive polygonal chapter house. The details have recently been reconstructed on paper, and it is now argued that the building should be dated marginally later than the comparable example at Margam.[82] The design of the mid-thirteenth-century cloister arcade featured unusual arches of cinquefoil design, the bays supported on clusters of three detached shafts (fig 129).[83] The abbot's lodging and the infirmary were most likely situated at some distance to the north east of the church.[84] There is a documentary reference to 'the great infirmary' (1330), next to which there was 'a certain chamber with a porch', in which the abbot conducted formal business transactions.[85]

On the very day marking its suppression, 1 March 1537, a sale of goods was held at the abbey. The chief buyer was John Scudamore (d 1571), a local gentleman who had been appointed Crown receiver at Dore, as well as at several other Herefordshire religious houses.[86] In addition to almost all the household items, for £2 Scudamore acquired the roof, the slate and the timber of the refectory; an 'old house by the wayside next to the bridge'; and the organs from the monks' choir. Along with two other buyers, for a further £3 3s 0d, he shared in the spoils of the 'old infirmary', together with all the glass and iron of the windows of the dormitory, refectory and chapter house. As Crown receiver, Scudamore also had responsibility for the custody of the lead from the abbey roofs, including that on the spire, 'le Steple'. It was soon melted down, and up to 2,540kg are recorded. Meanwhile, four of the bells were retained by the Crown, but two others were purchased by the churchwardens for parochial use.[87]

By 1545 Scudamore had acquired the site of the abbey with some of the surrounding property. The nave, together with most of the cloister buildings, were probably allowed to fall into ruin, though the east end of the church was retained to serve the parish. In 1632, almost a century after the suppression, it was John, the first Viscount Scudamore (d 1671), who began the restoration and refurbishing of the building.[88] The arches into the nave and nave aisles were blocked up, new roofs and ceilings erected, and a tower was built over the inner chapel of the south transept. A service of reconsecration took place in March 1634. The roofs and the bell frame in the tower were the work of John Abel (d 1675), who presumably fashioned the handsome if rather bulky screen now dominating the entrance to the presbytery. In 1727 Matthew Gibson noted that Lord Scudamore had rescued the medieval stone altar, ordering it 'to be restored, and set upon three Pilasters of stone'.[89]

Gibson's work might be said to mark the beginnings of antiquarian interest in Dore. In the early nineteenth century, some of its features were first recorded in detail by John Chessell Buckler (d 1894). He it was, for example, who produced the first accurate ground plan of the church.[90] In 1877 the Royal Archaeological Institute met in Hereford. Fairless Barber drew the attention of the members to 'a small excavation recently made at the entrance of the vestibule to the chapter house which has disclosed the base of the shafts by which the portal was decorated'. There was little doubt, he felt, 'that a careful and not very expensive exploration of the other remains would yield mouldings and details of very considerable interest'.[91] Further excavations were carried out by Thomas Blashill, apparently accompanied by the Revd Alfred Phillipps, in advance of a visit by the Woolhope Naturalists' Field Club in 1882.[92] Ten years later, Roland Paul began his investigations at Dore, first digging on the site of the nave, and then following this up with a series of excavations through to 1907.[93] Meanwhile, the church was in need of repair and restoration. An appeal was first launched in 1898, with Paul writing an accompanying booklet.[94] Following a second appeal in 1901, the works were carried out by Paul in 1901–9, allowing him further opportunities for investigation, including beneath the floors of the east end.[95] Recently, in advance of a new programme of restoration, the timbers of the ambulatory roof have been dated by dendrochronology.[96]

The area surrounding the church and cloister, and much of the wider monastic precinct, are together scheduled as an ancient monument, reference 30011. The surviving east end of the abbey church is a Grade I listed building.

BIBLIOGRAPHY

Architectural: [Blashill] 1882; Blashill 1883–5, 1885 and 1901–2; Colvin 1946–8; Fergusson 1984a, 94–100, 111; Gibson 1727; Harrison 1997a and 1997b; Harrison and Thurlby 1997; Hillaby 1988–90 and 1997a–d; Malone 1973, 44–59; Malone 1984; Morgan 1973; NRS 1829; O'Callaghan 1995; Paul 1893, 1896 and 1898b; [Paul] 1899b, 1902a, 1902b and 1903; Paul 1904, 1927 and 1931; Pevsner 1963, 57–62; RCHME 1931, 1–9, and 1934, 227; Shoesmith 1979–81; Shoesmith and Richardson 1997; Sledmere 1914; Tyers and Boswijk 1998; Vince 1997; Wathen 1792.
Historical: Bannister 1902; Knowles and Hadcock 1971, 112, 115; Talbot 1943 and 1959; Shoesmith and Richardson 1997; Williams 1965–8b and 1970–8b; Williams 1976a, 1–57; Williams 1990, 43–4; Williams 1997a and 1997b.

GRACE DIEU ABBEY, Monmouthshire, Llandaff, SO 452131

At the General Chapter meeting of 1217, the assembled body considered a petition from John (d 1248), lord of Monmouth, announcing his intention to establish an abbey in the border country of south-east Wales. The abbot of Morimond was instructed to appoint 'discreet men to diligently enquire' into the matter, with a report of the findings to be presented to the Chapter in the following year.[1] In the event, the prolonged, even troubled, negotiations were to drag on for almost a decade. Not until 24 April 1226 was a convent of monks finally sent from Morimond's daughter house at Dore in Herefordshire to colonize the new foundation, christened Grace Dieu (fig 19).[2]

Just seven years later, in 1233, the fledgling monastery was said to have been 'completely overthrown' by the Welsh, who alleged that it had been built on land unfairly seized from them.[3] Amid further attacks and depredations, in 1235 Henry III granted the community twenty trees from the Forest of Dean to rebuild their house, 'which had recently been burnt'.[4] In the following year, however, John of Monmouth sought permission from the General Chapter to transfer the house to an altogether more acceptable location. The abbot of Buildwas in Shropshire was charged with instructing him to proceed with the move without further delay.[5] Henry subsequently made two further grants of timber for building work: four oaks from Grosmont Forest in 1240, and two from Seinfrenny Wood in 1253.[6] Even so, the community's troubles were still not at an end. It was perhaps a renewed phase of border violence which, in 1276, led to yet another proposal for a change of site, this time under the patronage of Edmund (d 1296), earl of Lancaster and lord of Monmouth.[7] Whether the move actually took place cannot be determined with certainty.

As it turned out, Grace Dieu remained always a small and poorly endowed house of no great importance. Its few granges were largely located in the immediate vicinity, though the monks also held a significant property at Stowe in the Forest of Dean.[8] As early as 1267, it was perhaps financial difficulties which led the abbey to lease its manor at Penyard Regis (Herefordshire) in return for a one-off cash payment and a small annual rent.[9] In 1291, although the community had some 729ha of arable under the plough, the net annual income of the house was given as just £18 5s 8d.[10] Despite the appropriation of the church of Skenfrith,[11] and one or two minor fresh land acquisitions in the 1330s,[12] there was little by way of significant financial improvement during the later Middle Ages.

In 1356/7, Henry, duke of Lancaster (d 1361) and lord of Monmouth, granted the monks of Grace Dieu a chapel in the castle of Monmouth, to serve as a chantry.[13] In the early fifteenth century, the monks apparently suffered from the 'ill-governance of Richard Moyne of Morgan [Margam] and his adherents',[14] whilst two subsequent fifteenth-century abbots felt forced to resign. First, in 1451, 'not without bitter sorrow', Roger of Chepstow resigned his post to the abbots of Dore and Llantarnam, on account of the 'several misfortunes of his monastery, the ill-will of the world and the pressure put on him by neighbours'. Roger remained at Grace Dieu, and was given 'his own chamber with one or more servants'.[15] Then, in 1484, Abbot John Mitulton, 'a good man of honest conversation', resigned because of harassment 'by his enemies'. He was succeeded by Richard Dorston (c 1486–95), who went on to become abbot of the mother house at Dore.

In the great survey of 1535, the annual income of Grace Dieu stood at £19 4s 4d, by then the lowest assessment for any Cistercian abbey in the whole of England and Wales.[16] The house was suppressed on 3 September 1536. At the time, the community consisted of no more than the abbot and a single monk. They were attended by three servants, with several corrodians also in residence. In addition, two former abbots were maintained from the abbey's revenues.[17] The following year, the site of the house and its adjacent property were leased to Dr John Vaughan,[18] one of Cromwell's local agents. In 1545 ownership passed to Sir Thomas Herbert (d 1588) of Wonastow and William Brett.[19]

Documentary sources show that by the time of the suppression a 'gate house' within the abbey precinct had been given over to apartments for corrodians.[20] Again, it is written sources which suggest that neither the church nor any of the monastic buildings were covered with lead roofs in the 1530s. There were nevertheless three bells at the abbey, valued at £5 10s 0d.[21] In the later sixteenth century stone from the site may well have been used to build Parc Grace Dieu.[22] Indeed, it was probably extensive stone robbing – from a site that may in any case have lacked truly substantial medieval structures – which resulted in the removal of all significant trace of the monastery by the early eighteenth century.[23]

Various documentary and topographical clues indicate that the first site of Grace Dieu Abbey was most likely situated on the west bank of the River Trothy, possibly at a field or close identified in 1535–6 as 'le Old Abbey', adjacent to 'lands of the lordship of Ragland'.[24] John Leland described the site as 'stonding in a wood and having a rille running by hit'.[25] Some authorities have also looked to the west side of the river for the final location settled by the community. As early as 1801, however, the Revd William Coxe placed the site on the east bank, in what he described as 'a sequestered situation, in the midst of fertile meadows'. The ruins, he pointed out, 'are extremely insignificant, consisting only of part of a barn and a few detached fragments of walls'.[26] Today, the spot is known as Abbey Meadow.

Small-scale exploratory excavations were carried out in Abbey Meadow by David Williams in 1970–1. The work appears to have confirmed the general location of the monastery, even if no convincing trace of the principal buildings was recovered.[27] A geophysical survey undertaken early in 2000 – in less than ideal conditions – broadly confirms this view. Multi-phase occupation at the site is suggested, though the results are again inconclusive as regards the positioning of the church and principal monastic ranges.[28] Deep alluvial deposits may account for why there are no obvious archaeological earthworks in the immediate vicinity. Otherwise, a single *ex situ* carved fragment said to derive from the abbey has recently been identified at Hendre Farm.[29]

The whole of Abbey Meadow, a total of some 3.6ha, is scheduled as an ancient monument (MM158).

BIBLIOGRAPHY
Architectural: Mein 2000a and 2000b; Newman 2000, 235; Phillips and Hamilton 2000; Robinson 1998, 121–2; Williams 1961–4, 1970–8a and 1971a; Williams and Jenkins 1970.
Historical: Bradney 1904–32, II, pt 1, 122–7; Harrison 1998; Knowles and Hadcock 1971, 113, 120; O'Sullivan 1947, 33–5; Owen 1950; Williams 1961–4, 1970–8a and 1971a; Williams 1976a, 59–75; Williams 1990, 44–5; Williams and Jenkins 1970.

LLANTARNAM ABBEY, Torfaen, Llandaff, ST 312929

According to the chronicle compiled at its mother house, Llantarnam Abbey was established by the Welsh lord of Caerleon, Hywel ab Iorwerth (d 1211), in 1179.[1] There can be no doubt that it was indeed Strata Florida which sent out a founding colony of monks to this corner of south-east Wales (figs 18 and 19), but there is much less certainty about the site they initially occupied, and on the name given to the new monastery.

That the community was for a time settled at a temporary location is accepted by most authorities. A key indication comes from the papal *Taxatio Ecclesiastica* of 1291, where there is a reference to a Llantarnam landholding '*apud veterem Abbathiam*'.[2] As for the name of the house, the problem is highlighted in *Brenhinedd y Saeson*, one version of the native Welsh chronicle. There, for the year 1179, we read: 'And a community was established at Nant Teyrnon; – others call it the monastery of Dewma, others the monastery of Caerleon-on-Usk'.[3] Such has been the degree of confusion over the nomenclature that in the past some historians have assumed the existence of two separate houses.[4] In reality, until

1239 the abbey seems to have been known principally as Caerleon (if in a variety of transcriptions), but from 1266 the name Llantarnam begins to appear in the sources.[5] And, although the General Chapter sought to regularize matters in 1273 with a decree stipulating that the name *Lanterna* rather than *Vallium* was to be entered on official lists, both Caerleon and Llantarnam continued to be used throughout the later Middle Ages.[6]

Very little early information on Llantarnam's estates survives, though by the end of the thirteenth century the monks appear to have been farming in excess of 1,725ha of arable holdings.[7] Large blocks of land were held to the north and west of the abbey, between the Afon Llwyd and the Ebbw river, with other property in the uplands further west, including that at Penrhys high above the valley of the Rhondda. Upland granges were complemented by important arable units on the coastal lowlands, with the most significant property located at Pwl-pan (now Pwll-Pen), itself contributing nearly half the value of the abbey's landed property in 1291. The total net income of the house in that year was given as £44 15s 0d.[8]

In the first quarter of the fourteenth century, the Llantarnam community appears to have been in some difficulty with regard to its landed possessions. The impact of an unfavourable exchange agreement with Gilbert de Clare (d 1295), coupled with the effects of the local Welsh uprising led by Llywelyn Bren in 1316, led to a direct appeal to the king. In a petition of 1317, the abbot claimed his house was 'now so impoverished that only 20 monks can be maintained there with difficulty; and they live in great discomfort where there were formerly wont to be 60 monks and [more] … serving god'.[9]

Although nothing is really heard of it until the later fifteenth century, when coming to prominence in the work of Welsh poets, Llantarnam was responsible for a very notable pilgrimage centre on its estate at Penrhys. In the chapel was to be found what Professor Glanmor Williams described as 'the pre-eminent Welsh shrine' dedicated to the Virgin.[10]

On the eve of the suppression, in the *Valor Ecclesiasticus* of 1535, Llantarnam's net annual income was given as £71 3s 2d, of which £6 was derived from oblations at the chapel of Penrhys.[11] The following June there were still six monks in the community, headed by the last abbot, Jasper ap Roger. The closure of the house was brought about on 27 August, as part of the first round of suppressions. At the time, there were just four monks together with seventeen servants in residence.[12]

Neither the site occupied by the founding colony, nor the length of time the monks remained there, can be determined with any degree of certainty. In the 1840s Thomas Wakeman was of the opinion that the community at first settled in Caerleon itself, the location marked by the house known as the Priory.[13] This is wholly rejected by David Williams, who instead favours the possibility of a site in the vicinity of Pentre-bach, formerly Llantarnam's grange of Cefn-mynach.[14] In any case, the abbey was eventually removed, presumably to what must have been a more suitable site, between the Afon Llwyd and the Dowlais brook. Williams wonders whether the transfer might have taken place around 1272, the year in which the General Chapter instructed the abbots of Dore and Tintern 'to go personally to Llantarnam, to inquire diligently concerning the said house, and to order and dispose all things as they shall see fit'.[15] It must be said, however, rarely would one expect such a long period of occupation at a 'temporary' site. Moreover, were the Llantarnam monks really obliged to move almost a century after the foundation of their house, it would certainly have been the result of an exceptional set of circumstances.[16] The point is the more significant when considering the likely form of the monastic church and claustral buildings.

The site of Llantarnam Abbey is now occupied by an early nineteenth-century house, with nothing of obvious medieval origin surviving above ground.[17] Limited excavations (as yet unpublished) were carried out on the site in 1977–82 by A G Mein. Although the medieval foundations were badly disturbed, the work is thought to have recovered 'the east end of the presbytery, the east front of the south transept and probably a portion of the sacristy'.[18] A sketch plan by Mein, recently published by Williams,[19] shows a church of somewhat curious dimensions, in which the eastern arm of the building lies beneath the north-west corner of the house and its enclosed courtyard. A short but proportionately wide presbytery is seen projecting from formal transepts, and there is an aisled nave of perhaps six or seven bays.[20] As reconstructed, the overall length of the church would have been approximately 58m, with a width of about 42m across the transepts. The cloister is shown to the south of the nave, but the position is queried.

It is known from documentary sources that towards the end of the fourteenth century the abbey was seriously damaged by a fire. Abbot John ap Gruffudd (*c* 1377–1400) is credited with pushing forward the work of restoration. In 1398 his agent managed to secure the papal privilege of an indulgence, offered to all those penitents who 'give alms for the repair of the Cistercian abbey of St Mary, Caerleon, *alias* Llantarnam … the books, buildings and other ornaments of whose church have been enormously devastated by fire'.[21]

In 1504 David Mathew made a bequest of £10 to the community, for glazing the west window of the abbey church.[22] And, in his will of 1532, Morgan Jones gave 10 marks sterling to buy a vestment for the Lady Chapel in the building, and a further £10 towards the 'making [of] an arch at the entre of the church out of the cloisters', and for the construction 'of an arch in the body of the church'.[23] At the time of the suppression (1536) the bell tower housed four bells.[24]

Within months of the closure of the house, the receiver's accounts show that plumbers, carpenters and various labourers were at work on the site, cutting down the bells and removing the lead from the roofs. Yet there were still four bells at Llantarnam as late as 1555.[25] Meanwhile, the abbey was at first leased to John Parker, a man who enjoyed links with court,[26] then bought by William Morgan (d 1582) of Caerleon in 1554. He apparently constructed a house on the site, presumably making some use of the former monastic buildings. His son, Edward (d 1634), added to this house.[27] When it was seen by the Revd William Coxe in the late 1790s, he described it thus:

> The present mansion appears to have been finished in the time of queen Elisabeth, from the old materials of the abbey. The only remains of the ancient structure are the stone cells, converted into stables, the walls of the garden, and a beautiful gothic gateway, which is still called Magna Porta, and was the grand entrance.[28]

In 1834–5 the house was rebuilt for the Morgan heir, Reginald James Blewitt. His architect was the young T H Wyatt (1807–80), who adhered to a largely Elizabethan design.[29] In 1895 the estate was bought by Sir Clifford Cory, of the Cardiff shipping family. He lived at Llantarnam as a recluse until his death in 1940, with the only significant alterations of this period being in the garden.

To the north of the house are the roofless remains of a great eleven-bay stone barn, usually attributed to the medieval period. This view does not go unchallenged, and Mein argues that it should be redated to the eighteenth century.[30]

The barn alone is scheduled as an ancient monument (MM137). The house, together with Wyatt's entrance lodge, known as Magna Porta, are together listed as Grade II (record number 3127). The garden and the surrounding nineteenth-century park have been included on the register of parks and gardens of historic interest in Wales, at Grade II.[31]

BIBLIOGRAPHY
Architectural: Lewis 1999, 238; Mein and Lewis 1990–1; Newman 2000, 336–8; Robinson 1998, 135–6; [Whittle] 1994, 80–2.
Historical: Allgood 1907; Bradney 1904–32, III, pt 2, 224–40; Knowles and Hadcock 1971, 113, 121; Mahoney [1979]; O'Sullivan 1947, 35–8; Williams 1965–8c; Williams 1976a, 77–93; Williams 1990, 46–8.

MAENAN ABBEY, Conwy, St Asaph, SH 790657

On 13 March 1283, during his second Welsh campaign (1282–3), Edward I moved his headquarters to Aberconwy, where the abbey precinct and buildings were immediately pressed into royal use.[1] The campaign itself had already led to the death of Prince Llywelyn ap Gruffudd in December 1282, and the complete conquest of north-west Wales was all but achieved.[2] As it turned out, Edward was to remain at Aberconwy more or less until the end of the war, finally leaving on 9 May 1283. His decision, meanwhile, to establish a castle and walled borough near the mouth of the River Conwy showed that there could be no room for sentiment in the heart of the victor – it was to lead to the entire uprooting of the existing Cistercian community, the monastery most closely connected with the Gwynedd dynasty of princes. A 'new' abbey was created instead, with Edward determined upon his role as its royal patron.[3]

Inevitably, the removal was a protracted episode, but one which appears to have been carefully planned from the outset.[4] As early as April 1283, the abbot of the Cistercian Vale Royal was at Aberconwy,[5] and it is tempting to see his presence connected with some discussion of the king's scheme. In September of that year, the General Chapter gave its consent to the move, subject to the approval of the new site by its inspectors, and so long as sufficient buildings were in place before the monks were disturbed at their Aberconwy home.[6] On 11 September James of St George, Edward's celebrated master mason in north Wales, was instructed to go in person to Maenan, some 11.3km higher up the Conwy valley (fig 18). His task was to take formal possession of the manorial estate there and then to convey it in the king's name to the abbot and convent.[7]

Just over six months later, on 26 March 1284, it is likely that the king journeyed to Maenan for a very specific purpose. It was a visit that may well have been timed to coincide with the inauguration of his new abbey on the Conwy. Edward and his queen were once again at the site on 8 October, this time quite possibly in connection with the dedication and occupation of the initial buildings.[8]

Between the two visits, Edward had given short shrift to an appeal made by Archbishop John Pecham

(1279–92) on behalf of Anian, bishop of St Asaph (1268–93). Anian wished to prevent the Cistercian community's move away from the diocese of Bangor – where most of its lands were also situated – and into his own diocese on the east side of the River Conwy. In his letter to the king, Pecham was expressing the fears of both the bishop and those of the local parish priest when he wrote: 'where they [the Cistercians] plant their foot, they destroy towns, take away tithes, and curtail by their privileges all the power of prelacy'.[9] Although the king sought to assure Bishop Anian and his priest that they would not suffer as a result of the move, he had no intention of changing his plans at this late stage. Finally, after a year and more of much activity, on 23 October 1284, in a long and detailed charter, Edward formally granted the new site and surrounding lands to the abbey.[10]

In sum, the transfer of the Aberconwy community to its new site in the Conwy valley may well have been completed in all essentials by October of 1284. Thereafter, the abbey was known by various names in documentary sources, with Aberconwy, Conwy and Maenan in most common usage.[11] In this account, to avoid confusion, the name Maenan is used in all references to the new location.

In November 1284 Maenan was one of six Welsh Cistercian abbeys to receive payments for war damages resulting from Edward's campaigns. The comparatively large sum of £100 was awarded, with only one house receiving more.[12] Before the end of the century, a picture of the abbey's economy and the relative importance of its estates comes from the *Taxatio Ecclesiastica* of 1291.[13] The total annual income of the house is given as £76 15s 8d. Dr Rhys Hays looked in some detail at the figures given for individual properties in this source, comparing them with the sums given in a second valuation of the abbey's property dating from *c* 1350. He argued that they were consistently rather smaller, and gives the overall figure for the later date as £111 5s 4d.[14]

In the fourteenth century, various financial difficulties hint at a degree of mismanagement in Maenan's affairs, though it is important to recognize that the community was far from alone in what was something of a widespread situation at the time. Nevertheless, in 1344, for example, the abbot was obliged to acknowledge a debt of £200 owed to Italian merchants of Florence. Two years later, 'a great sum' was also due to Edward, the Black Prince.[15]

At the beginning of the fifteenth century, during the Welsh uprising led by Owain Glyn Dŵr, Abbot Hywel ap Gwilym of Maenan eventually sided with the rebel cause. Although he made his peace with Henry IV in 1409,[16] his support for Glyn Dŵr may already have cost his house dear. In the late 1420s

Maenan suffered the further misfortune of a brief rule under Abbot John ap Rhys. If the allegations of Strata Florida are to be believed, the man was little short of a desperado. The monks of the south Wales mother house claimed that he had come there in the Lent of 1428, 'with a great troop of armed people and archers', holding the monastery by force for forty days and carrying away much of its property.[17] Two decades later, in 1448, the Maenan community claimed that it was still suffering from the effects of the Glyn Dŵr rebellion. The abbot and monks declared that 'the house was burned in the time of the war in Wales, and all their books, vestments, chalices and other ornaments spoiled and carried away, and that they have since repaired a great part of their house'.[18]

The tide had turned somewhat by the beginning of the sixteenth century, when Maenan was headed by two notable abbots, Dafydd ab Owain (*c* 1503–13) and his successor, Geoffrey Kyffin (*c* 1514–26). Dafydd had been abbot successively of Strata Marcella and Strata Florida. In his time at Maenan he was also bishop of St Asaph, and there he is remembered for the rebuilding of the episcopal palace. Both men were in fact notable builders, eulogized by Welsh bards for their works at Maenan.[19]

In 1535, on the eve of the suppression, the net annual income of the house was given as £162 15s 0d.[20] The last abbot, Richard ap Rhys (1535–7), himself elected under dubious circumstances, did his utmost to try and prolong the life of the house, going so far as to send Cromwell £40. His pleas, and bribes, were to no avail, and by March 1537 monastic life at Maenan had been brought to an end.[21] At the time, the community may have comprised no more than five monks.[22]

The site occupied by Maenan Abbey lay just above the flood plain of the River Conwy, about 550m from its east bank. To the immediate north there is a small tributary stream, the Nant Llechog, flowing west into the Conwy. The site is now occupied by a house built for the Elias family in 1848–52, which has served as an hotel since the 1960s. Nothing of obvious monastic origin survives above ground, at least not *in situ*. It seems, however, that the church and monastic buildings were situated to the east of the hotel, that is, closer to the modern main road (A470).

Given Edward I's undoubted early interest in the new abbey, it is unfortunate that so little is known of the completed buildings. The loss is the greater considering the tantalizing hints of important royal masons connected with the initial programme of works. Master James of St George's involvement with

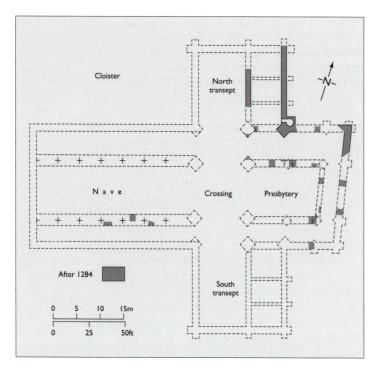

Cloister

North
transept

N

Nave

Crossing

Presbytery

After 1284

0   5   10   15m

0   25   50ft

South
transept

171 Maenan Abbey:
conjectural ground
plan (after Butler and
Evans 1980).

Drawing: *Pete*
Lawrence, for Cadw

the land transfer at Maenan raises the possibility that he at least took some part in the overall planning.[23] Furthermore, Master Walter of Hereford was in charge of the king's works on Vale Royal Abbey at this very time, and again there is a chance he played some role in the earliest phase of Maenan's construction.[24]

The attendance of the king and queen at Maenan on 8 October 1284, possibly (as suggested above) for the dedication ceremony, was also the occasion for making a payment of £53 6s 8d for finishing certain works in the new abbey church and for the construction of a bakehouse and a brewhouse. A further £6 17s 10d was given for the purchase of such necessities as boards, shingles, nails and iron.[25] At much the same time, the king gave the abbey a set of glass windows, which, together with their ironwork, had probably been made in Chester.[26] One last indication of Edward's generosity to the Maenan community comes from the abbey's own 'Register and Chronicle', where it is said that he gave 'large funds for new building'.[27]

The only positive information so far recovered on the actual form of the buildings at Maenan comes from three minor excavations. Exploratory work was first undertaken by the owner in 1924. In the main, it revealed a section of medieval walling, some 14.6m long and 1.1m wide, terminating at a newel stair at its southern end. It was interpreted as the east wall of the north transept chapels, with the stair located at the junction with the north presbytery aisle.[28] Following minor excavations in 1963, Lawrence

Butler rejected this interpretation, choosing instead to see the length of masonry as the east wall of the eastern range of monastic buildings.[29] In the light of a further phase of work undertaken in 1968, Butler (with Dave Evans) cautiously reverted to the earlier interpretation, as perhaps the 'best fit' solution.[30] Piecing various fragments of information together, the authors produced a conjectural ground plan of the church (fig 171). For the east end of this church, there is at least a tentative terminal point for the presbytery wall, whereas the length of the nave is less certain. Not surprisingly, perhaps, the plan bears a strong resemblance to those known from the contemporary rebuildings at Neath and Tintern. The nave is shown with seven bays. As for the cloister and monastic buildings, these may well have been positioned to the north of the abbey church.[31]

From the small assemblage of material recovered during the excavations, Butler and Evans suggest that building work on the church extended throughout the fourteenth century.[32] Some indication of later construction phases comes from documentary sources. There may have been some remodelling of the site following the Glyn Dŵr episode of the early fifteenth century and there can be little doubt that Abbot Dafydd ab Owain and Abbot Geoffrey Kyffin were improving certain elements of the complex in the early sixteenth century.[33]

Soon after Maenan's closure in 1537, the evidence suggests the church was comprehensively demolished. Stone and timber from the site were certainly used for the repair of the castle, justice's hall and town walls at Caernarfon.[34] Further use of both rubble and dressings – including Perpendicular window tracery – was made by John Wynn (d 1559) in the building of nearby Gwydir house.[35] Some twenty years after the suppression, a great lead ingot, derived from the roofs of the buildings, was still on the site of the abbey.[36]

The abbey site and its adjacent property changed hands several times between 1538 and 1580.[37] It was first granted to Sir John Puleston in 1537, and sold *c* 1565 to Sir Richard Clough. In 1599 Thomas Middleton was residing there.[38] In 1610 the Wynn family of Melai acquired Maenan through marriage to a Clough heiress. In 1654 it seems it was John and Dorothy Wynn who built a new house on the site, as witnessed by a date-stone bearing their initials.[39] In 1736 the Wynn heiress married Sir John Wynn of Bodvean and Glynllifon. Their son was created Lord Newborough, his family remaining owners of Maenan until the early years of the twentieth century.[40]

When Thomas Pennant saw the Wynn building in the 1780s, he described it as 'a large old house, built from the materials of the abbey'.[41] An eighteenth-century drawing has also long been known.[42] In 1987 Butler published a newly located ground plan (1799), together with a view (1809) of the mansion from the east. In all, the evidence suggests to him that the house was most likely raised over the west range of monastic buildings, possibly indicating that the late medieval abbots had chosen to convert this for their own use.[43] The new evidence also leads him to reject the idea that the Victorian house, built by the Elias family in 1848–52, incorporates any element of the Wynn mansion.

A few fragments of masonry exposed during the various excavations were earlier (1977) visible above ground, though nothing of any great significance can now be seen. Part of the site remains scheduled as an ancient monument (CN82), with some 1.14ha included.

BIBLIOGRAPHY

Architectural: Brown *et al* 1963, 337–41; Butler 1963 and 1987; Butler and Evans 1980; Elias 1898, 39–45; Owen 1917; RCAHMW 1956, 1–2, 185–9; Robinson 1998, 64–5; White 1987.
Historical: Butler 1981; Hays 1963; Insley 1999; Knowles and Hadcock 1971, 112, 118; Lowe 1912–28, I, 266–84; Owen 1917; *Register Aberconwy*; Williams 1990, 36–8.

MARGAM ABBEY, Neath Port Talbot, Llandaff, ss 802863

By common consent, Margam stands as one of the more significant white monk abbeys in Wales, both architecturally and historically. Of particular note, it was a first-generation plantation of Clairvaux, and therefore one of a mere handful of British sites colonized by the great French mother house during the abbacy of St Bernard (figs 17 and 19).[1] The founder was Robert, earl of Gloucester (d 1147), the illegitimate eldest son of Henry I (1100–35), and lord of Glamorgan since 1113.[2] In fact, Robert was close to the end of his life when, in the summer of 1147, he set in motion the procedures for the founding of a Cistercian monastery on the western margins of his south Wales lordship. At a prestigious ceremony of endowment held in Bristol, the earl made over the necessary gifts of land for the abbey to Nivard, a brother of St Bernard. The settling colony is said to have arrived at Margam under its first abbot, William of Clairvaux, on 23 November 1147.[3]

In his foundation charter, Robert gave the monks 'all the land between the Kenfig and Afan rivers from the brow of the mountains to the sea'.[4] However, it was left to his son, Earl William (1147–83), to carry through the plans and to strengthen the footing of the early community. In a charter granted sometime before his own son's death in 1166, William granted the Margam monks further land between the higher and lower brow of the mountains, an area until then in dispute.[5] The grant effectively consolidated the abbey's position in this area. Patronage from the Gloucester dynasty continued, with important confirmations of all donations to the monastery coming from both William and from his heiress, Countess Isabel of Gloucester (d 1217).[6]

Unlike the Cistercian foundations in the west and north of Wales, Margam was to remain a predominantly Anglo-Norman house, a fact reflected in what is known of its abbots and its community through to the end of the thirteenth century.[7] Despite this, however, in the years before about 1230 the monks received a string of gifts from native Welsh families, both in the uplands between the Afan and Taff rivers and in various pockets across the Vale of Glamorgan and its border.[8] As it happens, just several decades after the foundation, and perhaps about 1170–5, Margam gave serious consideration to establishing a daughter house at Pendar in the uplands of Glamorgan (figs 18 and 19), where land for the purpose was first granted by Gruffudd ab Ifor (d 1210), lord of the *cantref* of Senghennydd. At least two other grants from native Welsh freemen were to follow in the nearby area of Llanwynno, both mentioning the brethren of Pendar.[9] Yet despite this clear Welsh support, Margam's nascent daughter colony in the Glamorgan hills was to prove an abortive one. Later, after a protracted dispute, the lands passed to Llantarnam Abbey.[10]

Towards the end of the twelfth century, Abbot Conan (*c* 1156–93) found himself in trouble with the General Chapter over the matter of excessive beer drinking by the lay brothers at the abbey's granges.[11] In 1190 he was reprimanded for not having done penance, and the following year he was ordered to surrender his abbatial functions for forty days, 'because of the enormities which were committed in his house'. The apparent ringleaders, the lay brothers Jordon and Ralph, were to report to Clairvaux to perform a penance designated by the Chapter.[12] Fifteen years later, a more serious revolt by the *conversi* broke out at Margam. The brothers formed a conspiracy, threw the cellarer from his horse, drove off the abbot, and then barricaded themselves in their dormitory and withheld food from the choir monks.[13] The beer-drinking issue may again have played some part, though Gerald of Wales laid the blame for the disorder squarely on the shoulders of Abbot Gilbert (1203–13), whom he accused of 'flagrant injustices'.[14]

In an unusual step, Gilbert had been installed as abbot of Margam in 1203 by 'foreign visitors', who must have been sent from Clairvaux. He had been a monk of Kirkstead and was doubtless appointed head of the Welsh house with a view to reform and improvement.[15] Gilbert's early administration augured well. In his first year in office he managed to obtain a very comprehensive bull from Pope Innocent III (1198–1216), confirming all the major gifts and privileges granted to the community.[16] Indeed, there can be no question of his well-intended ambitions for the aggrandizement of Margam, both economically and architecturally, even if he did make an enemy of Gerald of Wales in the process.[17] Exceptionally, Gilbert seems to have enjoyed cordial relations with King John (1199–1216), who granted the abbey a significant confirmation charter in 1205; further privileges were to follow. In 1210, on his way to and from Ireland, the king stayed at Margam twice, and it was apparently as a result of his warm affection for the house that John placed it under his special protection, exempting it from the general extortion to which he was subjecting the Cistercians at this time.[18] In 1213, visitors sent by the abbot of Clairvaux were once again at Margam. They accepted the resignation of Abbot Gilbert, who then retired back to the Lincolnshire monastery of his first profession.[19]

Gilbert was succeeded by two of Margam's most highly regarded abbots, John of Goldcliff (1213–36/7) and John de la Warre (1237–50),[20] both apparently pushing forward the ongoing building programme at the house. In due course, John of Goldcliff became involved in the affairs of the Irish Cistercians. In 1228, in the wake of the so-called 'conspiracy of Mellifont', he journeyed to Ireland with Stephen of Lexington, abbot of Stanley (1223–9) in Wiltshire, on a mission to correct the internal affairs of a group of overtly nationalist monasteries.[21] In the measures taken to break up the Mellifont affiliation, Margam was appointed mother house of no less than four Irish abbeys: Abbeydorney, Holy Cross, Midleton and Monasteranenagh.[22] Despite the fact that the original affiliations of these houses were restored in 1278, the abbot of Clairvaux was still recognizing Margam's jurisdiction over them as late as 1445.[23] As for John de la Warre, he has the distinction of being one of the few Welsh Cistercians to graduate to the episcopate, coming out of retirement to become bishop of Llandaff (1254–6).[24]

In 1236 Henry III confirmed his father's grant of protection to Margam,[25] by which time the final pattern of the abbey's estates had all but been delineated. It is estimated that Robert of Gloucester's

initial grant between the Afan and Kenfig rivers amounted to a block of some 72sq km of territory. From this consolidated base the monks worked tirelessly to expand their holdings, through purchase, exchange and rental.[26] They were obliged, too, to deal with the consequences of a bitterly fought land dispute with the neighbouring house at Neath.[27] Yet in all, by 1250, the abbey was operating a thriving grange economy based on a chain of estates across the Vale of Glamorgan and its hinterland, notably at Stormy, Llangewydd, Laleston, Bonvilston and Llanvithyn, and also at Moor near Cardiff. Of further interest, the abbey administration, in forging the creation of its granges, had not infrequently proved ruthless in a systematic policy of clearing the tenants and freeholders who may have occupied areas of the original endowment. In the process, several churches were made redundant, being either destroyed (as at Llangewydd) or incorporated into grange buildings.[28]

More is known about the granges of Margam Abbey than about those of any other white monk house in Wales.[29] A great deal of information was brought together in the late nineteenth century by G T Clark and Walter de Grey Birch, their work encouraging several pioneering studies of individual granges by the local antiquarian Thomas Gray.[30] In more recent decades, as well as the work of Leslie Evans, a collection of studies by F G Cowley, and the mapping of the abbey's lands by David Williams, the RCAHMW has gathered together all the key historical detail on Margam's granges in its coverage of Glamorgan. Moreover, there is now, for the first time, a valuable record of all known archaeological and architectural remains.[31]

At the end of the thirteenth century, Margam was actively farming somewhere between thirteen and two dozen granges.[32] A number of these fell within the bounds of Robert of Gloucester's initial grant, including Meles, Hafod-y-Porth, New Grange and Theodoric's Grange.[33] One of the largest and most valuable properties was that at Llangewydd, where tenants had been removed, the church abandoned, and even an early castle dismantled.[34] In all, it is estimated from the figures given in the *Taxatio Ecclesiastica* of 1291 that the monks were working close to 2,630ha of arable, with upwards of 5,000 sheep grazing on their pastures.[35] The total income of the house was given as £255 17s 4d, making Margam the wealthiest Cistercian abbey in Wales and ranking it alongside some of the more successful English houses.[36]

There were, however, already signs of the many crises and economic difficulties that were to dog all monastic communities in the fourteenth and fifteenth centuries. Margam's troubles may be said to have begun in 1285, when several of its granges in west Glamorgan were seized on behalf of Earl Gilbert de Clare (d 1295), the abbey's patron.[37] Six years later, in 1291, the community appears to have been forced into a somewhat one-sided agreement with the earl.[38] A good deal of mountain pasture had to be given up, the monks receiving very little in return. Within a year, the injustice of the agreement was all too clear: in 1292 the abbot of Cîteaux was obliged to write to Edward I with the complaint that Gilbert de Clare 'troubles the abbey of Margam without reasonable cause'.[39] In 1329 the abbot and convent, their grievance still unresolved, petitioned William, Lord Zouche, the new lord of Glamorgan, claiming their house was in dire straits and that it had already been necessary to reduce the community by ten monks. At a sympathetic hearing, the jurors upheld Margam's case and the lands in question were finally restored to the abbey.[40]

Seven years afterwards, in 1336, the abbot drew up a full survey and valuation of the community's property in response to an instruction from Clairvaux.[41] In comparing the evidence provided in this survey with that of the 1291 valuation, Dr Cowley has pointed to a marked decline in the arable acreage under the plough.[42] Indeed, in a postscript to the survey itself, we read a rather all-round gloomy report of the monastery's affairs. Although the community consisted of thirty-eight monks and forty lay brothers, the abbot insisted that they were impoverished and unable to pay pressing debts, let alone the taxes imposed on them by the king and pope. Among the difficulties they had to face was the flooding of coastal lands, diseases among livestock, and even war and hostile attacks. Furthermore, the abbey's position 'on the high road, far distant from any place of common refuge', meant it had become overrun by guests of all kinds.[43]

Though direct evidence may be lacking, there is strong reason to suppose that as the fourteenth century progressed Margam moved ever closer towards a *rentier* economy, its granges becoming less and less distinguishable from manorial holdings.[44] The falling profitability of direct estate exploitation, and growing difficulties with labour shortages, can only have been compounded by the effects of the Black Death in 1348–50, and then by its recurrence in the 1360s. Meanwhile, some financial relief must have been provided through the appropriation of a number of churches, beginning with that of Llangynwyd shortly before 1353,[45] but especially in the last quarter of the century, when St Fagans (1377), Aberafan (1383) and Penllyn (1384) were all acquired.[46] In 1383 the abbot and convent claimed their income did not exceed £266 per annum. Two

years later, it was said that a hundred persons were maintained from an income not exceeding £366.[47]

The calamitous effects of the Glyn Dŵr uprising on Glamorgan during the first decade of the fifteenth century can scarcely be exaggerated. There can be no doubt Margam suffered significant financial setbacks across its estates. In 1412 it was alleged that the house had been 'utterly destroyed so that the abbot and convent are obliged to go about like vagabonds'.[48] The claim was surely overstated, but further proof of the long-term impact of the rebellion on the abbey's economy is supplied by a deed of 1440. Through this document, certain lands were restored to the community by Henry VI (d 1471), on account of the losses to its coastal property by incursions of the sea, and particularly in consideration of the injury to the church, granges and houses pertaining to them, sustained at the hands of Glyn Dŵr and his followers.[49]

The principal architect of Margam's later revival was perhaps Thomas Franklin (1441–60), the abbot who had earlier (1424–41) transformed the fortunes of Neath Abbey.[50] He won the support of Richard Neville (d 1471), earl of Warwick and lord of Glamorgan, being commended for having repaired and restored the house, for increasing the number of monks and ministers, and for improving its worship and possessions.[51] In addition to his duties at Margam, Abbot Thomas was responsible for a degree of reform of the Cistercian order in Wales.

In the late fifteenth and early sixteenth centuries, Margam could afford to become a centre of patronage for Welsh poets and literature. Lewis Glyn Cothi, for example, paid testimony to the wisdom of Abbot William Corntown (c 1468–87).[52] Even greater praise was heaped on Abbot David ap Thomas ap Hywel (1500–17). Richard ap Rhys wrote of the celebration of mass within the abbey, and of the 'beautiful belfry' and vestments. On occasions, he claimed, a hundred guests would pass through the cloister of 'David's house'. All this, despite the fact that Abbot David openly acknowledged concubines, by whom he had at least one son and four daughters.[53]

The last abbot of Margam was Lewis Thomas (1529–36), whose virtues were once again extolled by the bards. For one poet, 'no fitter person had donned the white habit since St Benedict had died'. The abbey, 'wherin the sweet sounds of bells and organ commingled in perfect harmony', was 'a perfect paradise, comparable with Gloucester's fane – a crystal rock crowned by its battlemented tower'.[54] Yet such praise would soon count for very little. In the *Valor Ecclesiasticus* of 1535, Margam's net annual income was given as £181 7s 4d.[55] Now with just nine monks remaining, the house was suppressed on 23 August 1536.[56]

Margam Abbey was very deliberately planted at a location long occupied by a significant pre-Conquest ecclesiastical establishment. This shadowy Welsh religious community is itself witnessed by an important group of surviving early Christian memorial stones.[57] The precise site chosen for the medieval abbey was at the highest point of the flat coastal platform, just below the rising slopes of Margam mountain. Hereabouts, two streams converge in a deep ravine breaking the mountain escarpment. The waters appear to have been tapped to create a fishpond, and must also have supplied the monastery buildings. To the west of the ravine, occupying a circular platform, there is a late medieval chapel. The summit of the hill to the east of the ravine is the site of a large univallate hill fort, Mynydd y Castell.

By immense good fortune, six bays of Margam's twelfth-century nave survive as the parish church of St Mary (figs 42 and 45). Internally, it is the most striking example of that deliberate Cistercian austerity – so typical of the order's early architectural ideal – to be found anywhere in the British Isles.[58] The simple piers and plain, round-headed arcades are executed in whitish grey Sutton freestone, quarried near Southerndown. On the basis of its style, we might expect the church to have been completed by around 1180. It was almost certainly of 'Bernardine' plan, featuring an unsegregated crossing in the so-called 'Fontenay style' (fig 25). However, there is a definite reference to the dedication of an 'altar of the Holy Trinity' in 1187 by William of Saltmarsh, bishop of Llandaff (1184–91).[59] Meanwhile, the monastic buildings were set out on the south side of the nave. These, too, were presumably well advanced before the close of the twelfth century. Traces of the east range lie fossilized in a later rebuilding. A doorway with a flat, segmental head (leading from the cloister to the usual position of the book room and sacristy) may date from this early period.[60] The adjacent twelfth-century chapter house would have been housed within the range. It may have been rectangular in plan, arranged on a north–south axis.[61]

In connection with the twelfth-century buildings, there is reliable evidence for the removal of a fine Romanesque doorway from Margam to the parish church of St Brides-super-Ely in 1849 (fig 47).[62] It seems the doorway in question was found by chance when a stable to the west of the abbey was taken down in 1840. Its appearance at St Brides can be attributed to Mrs Charlotte Traherne, wife of the then rector and sister to Christopher Rice Mansel

Talbot (1803–90) of Margam. Considering the form and stylistic detail, one is inclined to suggest it originally served as the processional doorway from the east walk of the cloister into the nave. Otherwise it is difficult to place such a feature in a Cistercian context.

From about 1200, or soon afterwards, a sequence of major rebuilding programmes at Margam extended well into the thirteenth century (fig 172). It is virtually certain that the remodelling of the east range and the construction of the abbey's magnificent polygonal chapter house belong to the earliest years of the century, the work very likely initiated by Abbot Gilbert (figs 137, 138 and 173).[63] In turn, the mid-twelfth-century 'Bernardine' east end was replaced by an aisled presbytery of five bays, a scheme which surely spanned the abbacies of John of Goldcliff and John de la Warre and was probably completed no later than c 1240–50. As part of the process, the crossing was regularized. New piers were introduced and the reconstruction extended at least one bay into the nave. As late as 1307, there is a mention of the 'master of the works of the new church'.[64] It seems reasonable to infer that one of the last works of the thirteenth century, and one which may well have continued through to 1307, was the construction of a substantial tower over the now formalized crossing. There is some support for this suggestion in the bardic descriptions of just such a structure on the eve of the suppression.

Among other work of the later Middle Ages was the rebuilding of the processional doorway from the east cloister alley into the nave. Externally, this doorway is set in a rectangular panel framed by a heavy moulding, the spandrels decorated with beaded trefoils. The jambs feature continuous orders (outside and in) and a casement moulding, all dying into a plain base. To the west, and therefore in the south wall of the nave, there is a second panel, again featuring a square moulded frame, though here with quatrefoil tracery to the spandrels. This panel housed an arched recess, originally divided by a central column with a quatrefoil at the head, now broken. Traces of a further fragment beyond suggest that similar recesses may have run along the full north walk of the cloister. Some confirmation of such an arrangement comes from a plan of Margam dated 1736 (fig 174), in which recesses are not only shown along the north cloister walk but also against the west wall of the south transept.[65] It is not unlikely that the cloister alleys were entirely refashioned at some point during the later Middle Ages.

The floor tile assemblage known from Margam is by no means large, but there is certainly enough material to show that in the mid-fourteenth century parts of the church would have been finished with handsome pavements of a similar pattern to the better-recorded examples at Neath.[66] Overhead, the high vault covering the east end of the church seems to have featured decorative roof bosses. One of these, discovered in 1836, featured a central shield bearing the arms of de Clare.[67]

One or two further insights into the nature of the buildings at Margam in the later Middle Ages come from documentary sources. In a grant of 1349, for example, Thomas of Afan referred to 'the noble and magnificent structure of the walls continually made in the said monastery'.[68] In the early 1530s, although parts of the abbey were in need of substantial repair, the monks' infirmary was apparently still in use.[69] At the time of the suppression, there were six bells hanging in the church, and – to judge from a valuation of £372 – the roofs of many of the abbey buildings must have been covered with lead.[70] Finally, in the late 1530s, John Leland wrote: 'Morgan an abbay of White Monkes wher was a veri large and fair church'.[71]

Apart from topographical indications nothing remains of the precinct boundary, though there is a reference of 1532 to the 'great gate'.[72] South east of the church, a medieval gatehouse (probably the inner gate) survived as part of the post-suppression house at Margam. It was destroyed in 1744.[73] To the north of the site, on the western side of the pond, are the remains of a mill (known as Cryke mill) which may be monastic in origin.[74] On the edge of the hill overlooking the abbey church stands a ruinous chapel (Hen Eglwys, or Cryke chapel). This single-cell structure had a two-light traceried west window and a fine Perpendicular east window with moulded jambs. It might well have served as the *capella extra portas*.[75]

On 29 February 1537 the site and demesne of Margam Abbey were leased for twenty-one years to Sir Rice Mansel (1487–1559) of Oxwich. In 1540 he was allowed to make an outright purchase of the abbey church, bell tower, cemetery and a number of granges. In all, over a period of seventeen years, Sir Rice managed to buy the greater part of the entire monastic estate, for which he was obliged to raise enormous sums totalling almost £2,500.[76] In the meantime, a decision had been made to retain the nave of the abbey church for parochial use. Repairs 'to the chancel' were carried out *c* 1537–9, and again perhaps around 1552.[77]

It was certainly from 1552 that Sir Rice began building himself a dwelling over the south and south-eastern parts of the former monastic complex. In the 1590s, when Margam was held by Sir Thomas Mansel (d 1631), the family dwelling was described

by the historian Rice Lewis as a 'faire and sumptious house'.[78] It is especially fortunate therefore that two remarkable topographical paintings of the late seventeenth or early eighteenth century survive to show us the general character and layout of this building (fig 2).[79] It is believed the two works, one looking at the house from the north and the other from the south, must have been commissioned either by Sir Edward Mansel (1636–1706) or by his son Sir Thomas Mansel (1667–1723). The paintings reveal a long building, evidently of several constructional phases, with the much reduced abbey church and chapter house clearly depicted in the northern view. The eastern half of the house was of older origin, and was possibly raised over the abbot's lodging and infirmary complex. The western part was of more recent seventeenth-century date, and is revealed as a very important piece of classicism. At the centre of the house, a tall prospect tower seems to have been positioned over part of the east monastic range.

In the second half of the eighteenth century, the Margam estate passed to Thomas Mansel Talbot (1747–1813), who proceeded to create a new residence at Penrice on the Gower peninsula. From as early as 1770, there is evidence of a gradual dismantling of the old family seat, a process largely completed in the years 1787 to 1793.[80] Margam became instead a 'pleasure park', dominated by a vast orangery of 1787–90. Built to a design by Anthony Keck, this magnificent building was intended to house the family's notable collection of citrus trees.[81] From the 1820s, Christopher Rice Mansel Talbot (1803–90) began to contemplate building a new house at Margam. His plans were eventually realized by the architect Thomas Hopper, the Tudor Gothic mansion rising on the higher ground to the east of the abbey site in 1830–5. It has long been known as Margam Castle. All that survives of the earlier Mansel house is the 'Temple of the Four Seasons', the facade of a late seventeenth-century summer banqueting house re-erected to the north of the orangery in 1837.[82]

As regards the survival of the abbey church and the various monastic structures over these centuries, to begin with there is a record of part of the church (presumably the nave) having been covered and the belfry 're-edified' by 1612.[83] From the plan of the abbey made in 1736 (fig 174), however, it would seem the chapter house was by then used as a coal store, with the vestibule within the east range serving as a brewhouse. The process of decay was accelerated when the lead from the chapter house roof was stripped to cover the summer banqueting house. In 1760 Thomas Mansel Talbot obtained an estimate for arresting the decay, though nothing was actually

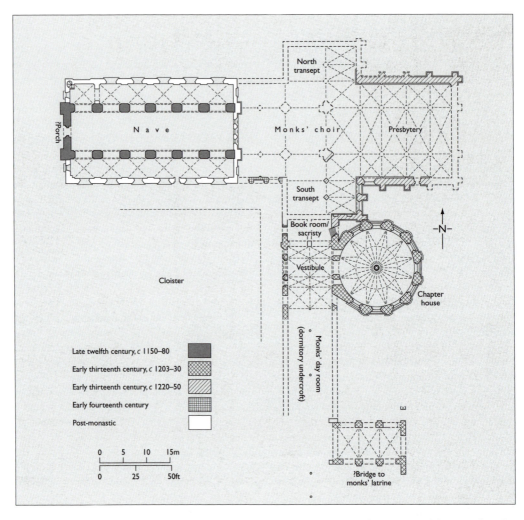

done.[84] When the chapter house was seen by Henry Wyndham on one of his tours of Wales in the late 1770s, the vault remained largely intact, though the roof was covered by no more than 'thick oiled paper'. The details are captured in an engraving of 1780, published a year later in the second edition of Wyndham's tour volume (fig 139).[85] Part of the ruins adjoining the chapter house was taken down by Talbot in 1788, and – within five years – two of the windows and 'the entire column had given way'. Whatever remained of the chapter house vault finally collapsed in 1799.[86]

At the same time, the general condition of the church had become lamentable. In the late 1760s, the parishioners were desperately petitioning Thomas Mansel Talbot to effect repairs, but to no avail. In 1787 the church was described as being 'in a very slovenly state', and by the close of the century a dilapidated roof over the south aisle had been removed and some of the nave arcades filled with brick as a temporary measure.[87] In 1803 some of the

details were captured in a series of drawings by John Carter.[88] His ground plan (fig 7) and general view of the west front show that a belfry chamber had been built over the west bay of the north aisle, whereas the two eastern bays of the north aisle had been excluded from the post-suppression chancel altogether. Finally, about 1803–4, Talbot was stirred out of his apathy. Plans were made for a major programme of repair and restoration, largely through the efforts of the then incumbent, Dr John Hunt. Under the direction of the Swansea architect Charles Wallis, the work began in 1805. The aisles were rebuilt with lath and plaster groins, the west front remodelled, the clerestory windows blocked up, new windows and furnishings introduced, and almost the entire interior of the church plastered over. Largely completed by 1809, the total cost of the works amounted to £6,490.[89]

Early fears concerning the poor standard of workmanship in some of the scheme were to prove justified: the chancel roof was already in a state of

173 *Margam Abbey: interior of chapter house, looking north west. Although the exterior of the building was of polygonal form, the inside was designed to be perfectly circular. The vault ribs sprang from a single central pier, supported in the surrounding walls by triple-shaft responds rising from dado level between the lancets.*

Photograph: *author*

advanced decay by 1831. A second major programme of renovation was eventually carried out in 1872–3. This was in the time of Christopher Rice Mansel Talbot, though the inspiration and drive came largely from his son, Theodore (d 1876). A wood-panelled ceiling replaced the lath and plaster effort of 1805–9, high pews were removed in favour of new seating, and much of the plaster and whitewash was removed from the internal walls.[90] Theodore's sister, Emily Charlotte Talbot (d 1918), inherited Margam in 1890. She soon embarked on a comprehensive set of improvements across the estate, spending up to £11,000. She was responsible for the further development of the gardens and parkland, and seems

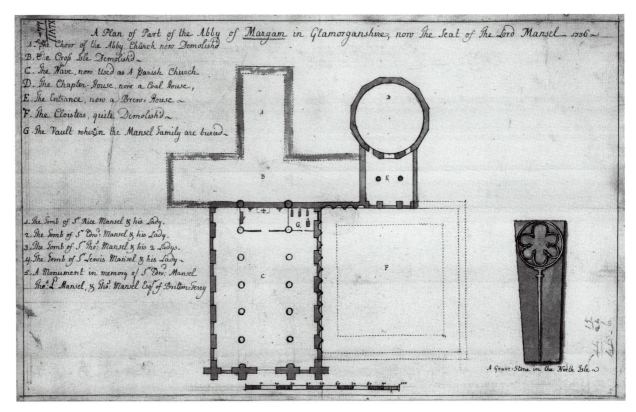

A Plan of Part of the Abby of Margam in Glamorganshire, now the Seat of the Lord Mansel. 1736

A. The Choir of the Abby Church now Demolished

B. The Cross Isle Demolished

C. The Nave, now used as a Parish Church

D. The Chapter-House, now a Coal House,

E. The Entrance, now a Brew-House

F. The Cloisters, quite Demolished

G. The Vault wherein the Mansel Family are buried.

1. The Tomb of Sr Rice Mansel & his Lady.

2. The Tomb of Sr Edwd Mansel & his Lady.

3. The Tomb of Sr Thos Mansel & his 2 Ladys.

4. The Tomb of Sr Lewis Mansel & his Lady.

5. A Monument in memory of Sr Edwd Mansel
   Thos L Mansel, & Thos Mansel Esqr of Briitton-Ferry.

A Grave-Stone in the North Isle

174 Margam Abbey: ground plan, 1736 (BL, K. Top. XLVII, 44.3A). At the time this plan was produced, the chapter house (marked D) served as a 'coal house' and its vestibule (E) was in use as a 'brew house'. The conjectural form shown for the east end of the church is incorrect. The niches seen running along the south wall of the nave and the south transept may well have been introduced in the fourteenth century.

Photograph: *British Library*

to have paid some attention to the monastic ruins.[91]

Little by way of formal archaeological excavation has ever been undertaken at Margam. One of the earliest descriptions of the upstanding remains is that by G T Clark,[92] supplemented by those of John Prichard, S C Gamwell and Walter de Gray Birch.[93] Fresh accounts were given by H E David, Leslie Evans and Lawrence Butler.[94] A summary of the evidence with additional analysis was published in 1993.[95] Evans mentions an excavation of about 1930, when various foundations of the post-suppression Mansel house were uncovered. He also refers to a series of works in 1951, when a patch of tiles was found in the presbytery. In the same year, much of the restored sandstone walling above the original ashlar in the chapter house was removed to leave the rubble core, and a gap which existed on the south side was filled in.[96] Minor excavations were carried out on the north side of the orangery in 1974–5, revealing traces of monastic-period walls.[97] In 1984 the stonework of the chapter house and adjoining vestibule received attention.[98] Most recently, in advance of proposed landscaping works, an archaeological evaluation of the presbytery and east range was carried out by the Glamorgan-Gwent Archaeological Trust in 2001.[99]

The site is today inappropriately separated into two parts. The nave (the parish church) is approached from the west, whereas the ruins of the east end and the chapter house are managed from the adjacent country park, the responsibility of Neath Port Talbot County Borough Council. An area of around 0.7ha is scheduled as an ancient monument (GM5), though this represents far too little of the monastic precinct. The chapel on the hill to the north, Hen Eglwys, is also scheduled (GM163). St Mary's church is currently a Grade A listed building (record number 14148); the ruins of the chapter house are Grade I; the east range ruins, Grade I; the orangery (record number 14152), Grade I; Margam Castle, Grade II*; and the remains of the monastic mill, Grade II. The park and garden are now included on the register of parks and gardens of historic interest in Wales, at Grade I.[100]

BIBLIOGRAPHY

Architectural: Adams 1981 and 1984; Birch 1897, 82–101; Butler 1971; Clark 1867–8, 324–34; David 1929; Evans 1996, 21–36; Gamwell 1887, 10–12; Jones 1981; Lewis 1999, 239; Locock 2001a and 2001b; Knowles and St Joseph 1952, 120–1; Moore and Moore 1974; Newman 1995, 424–9; Prichard 1881; RCAHMW 1981, 323–31; Robinson 1993a; Robinson 1998, 138–41; Tavener 1998; [Whittle] 2000, 102–13.

Historical: Birch 1897; Clark 1867, 1868; Cowley 1963, 1967a, 1967b, 1992 and 1998; Evans 1996; Gamwell

1887; Gray 1903a, 1903b and 1905; Griffiths 1988; Hughes 1998; Knowles and Hadcock 1971, 113, 122; O'Sullivan 1947, 28–30; Patterson 1992; Williams 1990, 48–52; Williams, G 1998.

NEATH ABBEY, Neath Port Talbot, Llandaff, SS 738973

Neath Abbey was founded by Richard de Granville, constable to Earl Robert of Gloucester (d 1147), and one of the second generation of Norman conquistadors in Glamorgan.[1] By the mid-1120s, the earl had established the western frontier of his authority on the banks of the River Neath. Richard de Granville had pushed further into the Welsh territories beyond the river, carving out a lordship and throwing up an earth and timber castle on the west bank to consolidate his gains. About 1129, he chose to grant his Neath fee, together with other lands in Glamorgan and in Devon, to the Norman abbey of the Holy Trinity at Savigny.[2] Towards the end of Richard's charter, it was made clear the gifts were intended to endow a new monastery. It had been some six years since Savigny had established its first daughter house in Britain, but now the prospect of de Granville's patronage was sufficient to encourage the despatch of a new colony. Under the first abbot, Richard (d 1145), corporate conventual life is said to have begun at Neath on 25 October 1130.[3] In 1147, along with all other houses of the Savigniac congregation, Neath was absorbed into the Cistercian order (figs 18 and 19).[4]

At the heart of Richard de Granville's endowment was a considerable area of undeveloped land, described as 'all the waste which lies between the waters of the Neath, Tawe, Clydach and Pwll Cynan'.[5] Estimates vary as to its precise extent, though the gift may have comprised up to 26sq km of country.[6] Within sixty years, the abbey had extended its holdings to the point where the community controlled property as far afield as Devon and Somerset, and across the lordships of Gower and Glamorgan.[7] In Gower, for example, the monks held land at Paviland and Loughor, and in Glamorgan there were granges at Sker, St Mary Hill (Gelligarn), Marcross and Monknash. In Somerset, their property lay in the vill of Exford, at Watchet and at Hornblotton. Cowley has argued that despite the extent of the estate, the lands were too scattered for efficient management.[8]

Indeed, such was the precarious position in which the community found itself in the late 1190s that careful thought was given to moving the entire abbey to the site of its principal Somerset holding. Any hope of realizing this plan seems to have been abandoned following the foundation of Cleeve

Abbey in 1197–8, barely 14.7km from Exford, despite fierce protests lodged with the General Chapter not only by Neath, but also by Forde Abbey.[9] Instead, therefore, the Neath monks began a concerted effort to expand and develop their properties nearer home. Before 1250, for instance, they had obtained possession of the fee of Walterston in Gower in exchange for the Somerset holding at Hornblotton.[10] At much the same time, the abbey was extending and improving its granges in the Vale of Glamorgan, and also acquiring lands in the Welsh lordship of Afan. The expansion into this last area led to a series of bitterly fought and costly disputes with the neighbouring Cistercian community at Margam, disputes which continued well into the second half of the thirteenth century.[11]

The archaeological and architectural remains of Neath's granges in the county of Glamorgan have been studied by the RCAHMW.[12] At Monknash, in the south-west corner of the Vale of Glamorgan, there survives one of the finest monastic grange centres to be found anywhere in the British Isles. At the end of the thirteenth century, the arable estate at Monknash amounted to 10 carucates, something in excess of 324ha. Today, apart from a series of superb earthworks and a dovecote, there are the remains of a vast eleven-bay barn, measuring some 64.4m in length.[13] There are also extensive earthworks to be seen at the site of nearby Marcross grange.[14]

In terms of Neath's general thirteenth-century history, in 1207 the monks are known to have received several charters of confirmation from King John.[15] In 1224 one of the abbey's houses was attacked and burnt by Morgan Gam, his rebels destroying more than 400 sheep, killing four servants and wounding one of the lay brothers.[16] In the middle years of the century, some significant misdemeanour led to the excommunication of Abbot Robert by William de Burgh, bishop of Llandaff (1245–53), who even pressed the king to ensure the abbot's imprisonment.[17] Within a decade or so, the house was ruled by a man of rather more distinguished character, Adam of Carmarthen (c 1266–89).[18] His time at Neath was not entirely trouble free: in 1269 it was necessary to draw the General Chapter's attention to the 'frequent and rash audacity of certain lay brothers' at the house.[19] Yet there was sufficient stability within the community, and in the economy of the house, for Abbot Adam to initiate work on the complete reconstruction of the abbey church. In December 1284, with the building programme at its height, Neath was visited by Edward I (1272–1307). He presented the house with 'a very beautiful baldachin', perhaps a *baldacchino*, or canopy, intended for the high altar.[20]

Towards the end of the thirteenth century, Neath stood as one of the most financially secure monasteries in Wales. Its annual income in the papal taxation assessment of 1291 was given as £236 1s 5d.[21] At the time, it is estimated the monks were farming in excess of 2,024ha of arable, with nearly 5,000 sheep on their pastures.[22] Yet just two years before the compilation of the *Taxatio Ecclesiastica*, in 1289, Abbot Adam had been obliged to enter into a momentous exchange agreement with the abbey's then patron, Earl Gilbert de Clare (d 1295). By the terms of the agreement, Adam handed over very substantial tracts of land to the earl, in return for which he was to receive £100 of fixed annual rent from tenements in the boroughs of Neath, Cowbridge, Cardiff and Caerleon, and in the manors of Llanblethian and Llantwit Major.[23] There may have been a variety of reasons prompting such a step on the part of the abbey, not least the need to raise hard cash for the building programme in hand. In any case, at one stroke, Neath was henceforward to derive a considerable portion of its income from rentals rather than from direct exploitation.[24] A further important step in this direction was taken in 1322, when Abbot David first leased the manor of Exford.[25]

In an all too familiar Welsh pattern, the progressive abandonment of the grange economy was hastened by the catalogue of difficulties that the community faced over the fourteenth century and beyond. In 1316, during the rebellion of Llywelyn Bren, the monks were said to have been 'plundered of their goods ... their house devastated and ruined'.[26] To ease his monastery's plight, in 1336 Abbot William petitioned Edward III (1327–77) to confirm all earlier grants and privileges and to allow his house to appropriate the parish church of Neath itself.[27] By 1344 both Neath and the church at St Donats had indeed been appropriated.[28]

Any respite afforded by these new gains, however, must have proved short-lived. First, in 1348–50, came the devastation caused by the Black Death. Then, within sixty years, Wales was torn apart once again by the effects of the Glyn Dŵr uprising in the first decade of the fifteenth century. In the aftermath, as late as 1423, Neath was said to be still suffering grievously from indiscriminate pillaging: the abbey had been violated, robbed of its books, chalices and ornaments.[29]

On the long road to recovery, the initial steps seem to have been taken by the very able Thomas Franklin (1424–41). Abbot Thomas was undoubtedly a reformer of considerable stature, going on to become abbot of Margam (1441–60), and also carrying out duties on behalf of the General Chapter in Wales and further afield. He was eventually

commended by the pope for having repaired and restored Neath (and Margam), increasing the number of monks and ministers, and improving its worship and possessions.[30] Thereafter, Neath's new-found prosperity continued. In 1447 the community acquired a fresh source of income through the appropriation of the church of Llandeilo Talybont.[31] Further support came from Richard Neville, earl of Warwick (d 1471). As lord of Glamorgan, in 1468 he granted the house a long and important confirmation charter, listing all earlier grants back to the twelfth century.[32]

In the two or three decades before the suppression, Neath was decidedly one of the healthier Cistercian monasteries of Wales, both spiritually and financially. The position owed much to the qualities of its last abbot, Leyshon Thomas (c 1510–39).[33] A man of considerable learning, he not only worked hard to maintain the standing of his own house, but also became an influential figure within the Cistercian order at large. He was, for example, one of five abbots appointed by the General Chapter to visit the houses of England and Wales.[34] His eminent reputation for scholarship and hospitality encouraged a particularly glowing tribute from the poet Lewis Morgannwg: 'The convent of Neath, how much talked of in England! The lamp of France and Ireland! A school much resorted to by scholars ... In this compact retreat will be found the warmth of hospitality and welcome banquets'.[35]

In the *Valor Ecclesiasticus* of 1535, Neath's net annual income was given as £132 7s 7d,[36] yet it was spared from the first round of closures during the following year. In January 1537 Abbot Leyshon paid a heavy fine of £150 to prolong further the life of his house. Dearly bought, the delay was but temporary. In February 1539 the abbot and seven remaining monks finally surrendered the monastery to the king's visitors. Abbot Leyshon himself was described as having 'hitherto lived worshipfully and well'.[37] Around this time, John Leland wrote: 'It semid to me the fairest abbay of al Wales'.[38]

As with the Savigniac plantation at Basingwerk in north-east Wales, among the founder's initial gifts to Neath was the chapel of his castle, and it is possible that this provided the nucleus of the temporary accommodation occupied by the community over the earliest years.[39] It cannot have been too long, however, before permanent stone buildings were begun on an unencumbered site situated on the west bank of the River Clydach, just above its confluence with the Neath. Culverts drawn from the Clydach would have supplied the water to the monastic buildings. The church was sited at the highest point of the precinct, on a shelf of outcropping rock; the cloister ranges lay to the south, on slightly lower ground.[40] Important remains of the monastery survive (figs 175 and 176), together with those of a significant Elizabethan great house built over the south-east corner of the complex. In addition, part of the abbey's principal gatehouse (of the twelfth century and later) lies alongside the main roadway to the north west of the main site.[41] The buildings are all of a local grey-brown Pennant sandstone, with prominent dressings of white Sutton stone.

All trace of the assumed twelfth-century church has disappeared, though its position and scale must in some way be reflected in the surviving layout of the cloister and monastic buildings, as at Tintern. Lawrence Butler has proposed an outline plan for this church, one of broadly similar proportions to the aisleless Cistercian examples recorded at Tintern and Waverley (fig 38).[42] The earliest upstanding work to survive at Neath is the ten-bay west claustral range, thought to have been under construction from the 1170s, though it also incorporates features more likely to be of early thirteenth-century date, such as the Sutton stone lancets and the stiff-leaf capitals to some of the wall vault shafts. In fact, it is clear that the monks embarked on several major programmes of reconstruction, beginning in the first half of the thirteenth century and continuing through to the mid-fourteenth century. The chapter house, the monks' day room (fig 123) and the dormitory were almost entirely rebuilt in the second quarter of the thirteenth century. Among the new arrangements, the monks' latrine was now approached from the dormitory by way of a bridge at first-floor level.[43] At much the same time, the south range of the cloister was also completely transformed. The refectory was now set out in the preferred Cistercian form, at right angles to the cloister, with the warming house to the east and kitchen to the west.

Having completed the rebuilding of their claustral ranges, the monks began work on a brand new abbey church around 1280. To judge from features such as the tile pavements, the east processional doorway (figs 115, 116 and 118), and several surviving vault bosses (fig 117), the scheme extended into the early years of the fourteenth century. Cowley suggests it was the cost of the construction programme that may have been one of the principal reasons why Abbot Adam was drawn into the 1289 exchange agreement with Earl Gilbert de Clare. On the same day as the agreement, the earl granted the community 'all the timber necessary' for the building of the monastery and for the construction of one of its granges.[44] The new church was, in any case, built from east to west in such a way as to allow worship to continue in the Romanesque aisleless building

for as long as possible, in similar fashion to the near-contemporary scheme at Tintern. Again like Tintern, the nave elevations at Neath were of two storeys (fig 106), though here there were seven narrower and lower bays, compared to six at the Monmouthshire site.

Until they were lifted for conservation reasons in the late 1980s, the areas of *in situ* tile pavement at Neath represented the most extensive collection to be found at any Cistercian site in Wales. When the new abbey church was completed in the early fourteenth century, the floors of the monks' choir, the transepts and their chapels, and the whole eastern arm, seem to have been totally covered in elaborately patterned pavements, each containing a strong heraldic element. The unity of the scheme is emphasized by the fact that the tiles belong to a single style and fabric group, most recently dated by J M Lewis to *c* 1340.[45] The cloister walks may also have been tiled afresh in the mid-fourteenth century.

Towards the end of the Middle Ages, perhaps about 1500, one of Neath's last abbots began to adapt the southern parts of the dormitory and refectory ranges to serve as a comfortable suite of private accommodation.[46] A new block was raised to connect the dormitory with the latrine to the east, incorporating a projecting polygonal stair turret to provide improved access. A further block was added to the west of the dormitory, the accommodation extending into the south-east corner of the former monks' refectory. In all, this gave a continuous south-facing range of two and three storeys. The work of this period is most readily identified by the Bath stone used for window dressings.[47] The conversion as a whole clearly says a great deal about the enormous change to the Cistercian way of life. With fewer than ten monks in residence, the great communal chambers of earlier centuries, such as the refectory and the dormitory, were no longer seen as essential to maintain.

The new abbot's residence would certainly have been occupied by Leyshon Thomas, and it was here no doubt that he entertained his guests, including grateful bards such as Lewis Morgannwg. Of the buildings in Abbot Leyshon's times, the poet wrote:

the lead that roofs this abode – the dark blue canopy of the dwellings of the godly … Every colour is seen in the crystal windows … Here is the gold-adorned choir, the nave, the gilded tabernacle work, the pinnacles … a ceiling resplendent with kingly bearings … there is the white freestone … and the church walls of grey marble … The vast and lofty roof is like the sparkling heavens on

175 Neath Abbey: west front of church. Work on this second abbey church on the site began c 1280 and the whole was completed in the early fourteenth century. Above the west door and its vaulted porch, the facade was filled with a larger tracery window.

Photograph: *Royal Commission on the Ancient and Historical Monuments of Wales, Crown Copyright*

high … Never was there a fabric of mortal erection, nor roofed wall, nor vast habitation; never was there such a foundation nor splendid place.[48]

A bequest of £10 left by David Mathew in 1504 towards glazing the west window tells us that the church continued to receive attention during the early sixteenth century. Another bequest of £20, for a less specific purpose, was left by Sir Matthew Cradock in 1529.[49]

Following the suppression of Neath in 1539, the site of the abbey and the bulk of its former estates were first leased to Thomas Cromwell's nephew, Sir Richard Williams *alias* Cromwell (d 1545). In March 1542 Sir Richard was allowed to buy the properties outright for £731.[50] As late as 1547 the lead on the roofs was assessed at nearly two tons, and four bells were sent to Bristol to be melted down.[51] Before the end of the sixteenth century, the site of the former abbey had been purchased by Sir John Herbert

(d 1617), second secretary of state to Elizabeth I and James I.[52]

Although Sir Richard Williams had been born in Glamorgan, he established his main seat in Huntingdonshire. Having acquired the Benedictine nunnery of Hinchingbrooke in 1538, he began the conversion of the church and other buildings there for use as a house. From 1545 his son Henry undertook further significant works, changing the orientation of the emerging residence.[53] Given this interest in Hinchingbrooke, several authorities have claimed that neither Sir Richard nor his son undertook building of any scale at their south Wales property. Instead, it has been argued that the post-suppression mansion at Neath was begun by Sir John Herbert.[54] More recently, the RCAHMW has claimed that various features and details at Neath are sufficiently similar to those at Hinchingbrooke to suggest that it was indeed Sir Richard or his son Henry who began the principal programme of conversion, with a date of *c* 1560 given as a median point.[55] It is, however,

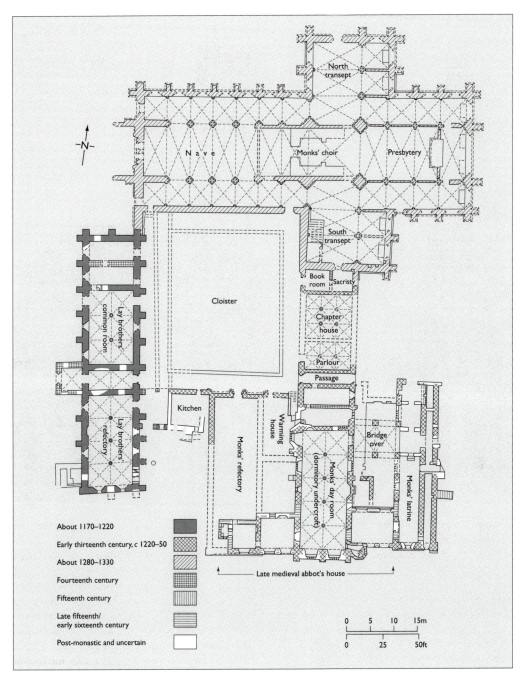

*176 Neath Abbey:
ground plan (after
Butler 1976a/
RCAHMW 1981/
Robinson 2006b, with
modifications).*

Drawing: *Pete
Lawrence, for Cadw*

North
transept

N a v e   Monks' choir   Presbytery

-N-

South
transept

Book
room   Sacristy

Chapter
house

Cloister

Parlour

Passage

Lay brothers'
common room

Kitchen

Warming
house

Bridge
over

Lay brothers'
refectory

Monks' refectory

Monks' day room
(dormitory undercroft)

Monks' latrine

Late medieval abbot's house

About 1170–1220

Early thirteenth century, c 1220–50

About 1280–1330

Fourteenth century

Fifteenth century

Late fifteenth/
early sixteenth century

Post-monastic and uncertain

0   5   10   15m

0   25   50ft

difficult to tie the characteristics of the mid-Tudor
house at Neath so closely to a single date. The work
was clearly carried out in more than one campaign,
and it remains likely that further improvements were
introduced by Herbert later in the century.

The house was raised over the entire south-east
corner of the site (fig 177), incorporating the
southern half of the monastic dormitory range and
the parallel latrine block, both of which had already
been transformed to create the abbot's residence

around 1500. A large new service wing was also
added to the north and east of the complex. The
completed mansion was of formidable scale, of two
storeys with attics. Much of the accommodation on
the ground floor consisted of barely altered monastic
spaces, with the main approach leading to the north
front. The former bridge structure between the
monks' dormitory and the latrine was used as a
porch recessed between the unequal halves of the
facade. The main rooms were on the first floor,

177 *Neath Abbey: reconstruction of Tudor house, from the north west. The house may have been begun by Sir Richard Williams (d 1545) or his son Henry. Later in the sixteenth century it became the property of Sir John Herbert (d 1617). Raised over the south-east corner of the former claustral buildings, the house incorporated the former monks' day room and the late medieval abbot's lodging.* Photograph: *Royal Commission on the Ancient and Historical Monuments of Wales, Crown Copyright*

266

leading off a central long gallery which spanned the house from east to west.[56] The church was not levelled completely, but must have been retained as some form of Gothic folly within a garden setting.

On Sir John Herbert's death, his Neath estate passed through his daughter to Sir William Doddington of Hampshire. Then, soon after 1654, it became the property of Sir Philip Hoby (d 1678). His widow, who died in 1699, was reputedly the last of the family to occupy the house.[57] Meanwhile, the ruinous church and other structures continued to be used as sources of building materials. An entry in the churchwardens' accounts for Neath parish in 1695, for example, records that twenty loads of stone were removed from the abbey to the church of St Thomas. Today, large areas of the upper stage of the west tower are faced with blocks of Sutton stone.[58]

In the first half of the eighteenth century, industry began to invade the abbey site. The processes associated with copper smelting and forging were first to appear, possibly as early as 1721. Smelting furnaces were built into the southern end of the west range, their chimneys blocking the lancet windows. Several authors have suggested the mansion had begun to fall into decay, now serving as tenements for the copper workers.[59] Yet if we are to accept the evidence of the Neath engraving by the brothers Buck, dated 1741, the Tudor house remained occupied and complete, its roofs intact and chimneys smoking. Moreover, when seen by Henry Wyndham on one of his tours of Wales in 1774–7, the 'Abbot's house' was in a tolerable state of preservation.[60] Nevertheless, the Buck engraving also shows that by the mid-eighteenth century the abbey church had already been reduced to much like the condition seen today. And, as the century progressed, further industrialization took its toll. Neath Abbey ironworks expanded into ruins, with the monastic kitchen now used as a foundry and the cloister filled with furnace ash.[61] As antiquarian concern grew, in 1848–9 the Neath Philosophical Institution effected some repairs to the vault and the windows of the monks' day room.[62] But at the end of the nineteenth century, Prebendary Mackenzie Walcott described the once proud abbey thus: 'Neglected Neath, once the ornament of a lovely vale, looms up through the dense veil of smoke, like the skeleton of a stranded ship crumbling piecemeal to decay under the influence of almost perpetual rain'.[63]

Exploratory excavations on the site were first undertaken in 1833, when the Revd Henry Hey Knight exposed areas at the east end of the church, principally to gather information on the tile pavements.[64] Further diggings and investigations were synthesized in a volume published by the Neath Philosophical Institution, with descriptions by Mr Knight and plates by Egbert Moxham, the account including a plan by J Jenkins.[65] This early work was reviewed and expanded by T S Sutton,[66] and then by Walter de Gray Birch.[67] Much fuller clearance excavations were carried out under the direction of Glen Taylor between 1924 and 1934. Up to 4,000 tons of debris was removed from the church alone. In places, an overburden of material up to 5.2m deep was removed. The work was brought to a close after Taylor's death in 1935, and the only published account of the findings was produced by C Stanley Thomas and Frank E Taylor.[68] A very large quantity of loose stonework derived from these excavations, now lying overgrown along the eastern margins of the site, remains to be investigated.

In 1944 the abbey was placed in the guardianship of the State, and five years later the ruins were given over outright. Programmes of fresh clearance and conservation followed (fig 14).[69] An official guide was prepared by Butler, currently supplemented by the Cadw official guide.[70] As outlined above, an extensive account of the Tudor house was published by the RCAHMW.[71] Most recently, in 2001, a watching brief carried out during the laying of a pipe trench in the area of the monastic cemetery recorded two burials.[72]

The church and main cloister buildings, an area of about 1ha, along with the abbey gatehouse, are together scheduled as an ancient monument (GM6). The boundary of the scheduled area represents but a small part of the entire medieval precinct.

BIBLIOGRAPHY
Architectural: Birch 1902, 89–121; Butler 1973, 1976a and 1984; [Jones] 1920; Knight and Moxham 1848; Lewis 1999, 240–5; Milne 2001a and 2001b; Newman 1995, 463–71; RCAHMW 1981, 78–89; Robinson 1998, 149–51; Robinson 2002b; Robinson 2006b; Sutton 1887; Thomas and Taylor 1938; *Archaeol Cambrensis*, **100**, 1948–9, 268–9; *Archaeol Cambrensis*, **101**, 1950–1, 79, 115; *Archaeol Cambrensis*, **106**, 1957, 106.
Historical: Birch 1902; Butler 1999b; Cowley 1967a and 1967b; Foster 1950; Francis 1845; Knowles and Hadcock 1971, 113, 122; Lewis 1887; Ormrod 1988–9; O'Sullivan 1947, 27–8; Wilcox 1990; Williams 1990, 53–6; Williams, G 1974.

STRATA FLORIDA ABBEY, Ceredigion, St Davids, SN 746657

Strata Florida Abbey was founded on 1 June 1164, almost certainly by the Norman constable of Cardigan and lord of the commote of Pennardd, Robert fitz

Stephen.[1] The founding colony of monks, which had been drawn from Whitland, was first settled on the banks of the Fflur brook, at a site known today as *yr hen fynachlog*, 'the old monastery'.[2] In the following year, however, Cardigan was seized by Rhys ap Gruffudd (d 1197). Robert fitz Stephen was captured in the process, though the Lord Rhys – as he is generally known – happily assumed the patronage of the infant community in the 'Vale of Flowers'.[3] Indeed, as Rhys himself proclaimed in a charter of 1184, he 'loved and cherished' Strata Florida.[4] Strengthened by his enthusiastic support and generous gifts, the monks moved in time to a new site on the south bank of the River Teifi, about 2.4km to the north east. Within a very few years, Strata Florida was in a position to send out daughter colonies of its own, first to Llantarnam in 1179, and then to the temporary site of Aberconwy, at Rhedynog Felen, in 1186 (fig 19). In addition, the monks of Strata Florida had oversight of the Cistercian nunnery at Llanllŷr, also established and endowed by the Lord Rhys.[5]

The nucleus of the community's estates lay in the landlocked uplands around the monastery itself. Here, Rhys had granted the monks vast tracts of open countryside ideally suited to large-scale sheep ranching.[6] As Gerald of Wales noted, Strata Florida 'was in the course of time enriched far more abundantly with oxen, studs of horses, herds of cattle and flocks of sheep, and the riches they produced, than all the houses of the same order throughout Wales'.[7] The leading pastoral granges were Blaenaeron, Cwmteuddwr, Cwmystwyth, Hafodwen, Mefenydd and Pennardd (the home grange), the last two properties being easily in excess of 2,024ha each. The need for land suitable for arable cultivation led the monks to expand their holdings into other areas, both in river valleys and on the coast. In the Severn valley they held the grange of Abermiwl, and on the Wye they had another at Aberdihonw. A further string of valuable granges lay on the fringes of Cardigan Bay, including Anhuniog, Morfa Bychan and Morfa Mawr. In all, by the end of the thirteenth century, Strata Florida's lands were organized around some fifteen grange centres.[8] And yet, from the outset, these were less the self-contained farms of the ideal Cistercian model than the hamlets of a still dependent peasantry, 'transferred by charter from secular to monastic lordship'.[9]

Throughout its history, the abbey's community remained as Welsh as the land in which it dwelt. Its first loyalty was to its patrons, the Deheubarth dynasty of princes. Although the Lord Rhys himself chose to be buried in the cathedral at St Davids,[10] many of his descendants were interred in the church and chapter house at Strata Florida. Having taken the

Cistercian habit, his brother, Cadell ap Gruffudd, was buried at the monastery as early as 1175. Rhys's son, Gruffudd, was laid to rest there in 1201, joined by his wife Matilda de Braose in 1210. In all, no fewer than nine more princes of the dynasty were buried at Strata Florida (mainly in the chapter house) over the next century.[11] It is not surprising, therefore, that the abbey community contributed substantially to maintaining a record of the Lord Rhys's lineage by composing major historical works. From about 1175 onwards, the Strata Florida monks kept annals which were in turn used for a lost Latin chronicle compiled in the abbey in the late thirteenth century, itself forming the basis of the Welsh *Brut y Tywysogyon* ('Chronicle of the Princes'). In sum, the monks of Strata Florida became significant custodians of native cultural traditions.[12]

Following the Lord Rhys's charter of 1184, work progressed on the construction of the abbey church and monastic buildings at the permanent Teifi site. As it happens, a key event is recorded in the Welsh chronicle for the year 1201: 'the community of Strata Florida went to the new church on the eve of Whit Sunday, after it had been nobly and handsomely built'.[13] However, little more than a decade later, the abbot and convent found themselves on the wrong side of King John (1199–1216). They were now partisans of Llywelyn ab Iorwerth (d 1240), the Gwynedd prince whose authority had begun to expand across native Wales as a whole. As King John's patience with Llywelyn grew thin, he turned against a number of the Welsh Cistercian houses, at least those seen as supporters of an insubordinate prince.[14] In 1212, the king ordered one of his henchmen to 'destroy the Abbey of Strata Florida, which harbours our enemies … in so far as you are able'.[15] It may only have been his own growing domestic difficulties which prevented John from carrying through the threat. Nevertheless, the abbey was fined up to £800, a crippling debt which was still being paid off in 1253.[16] Meanwhile, despite the disapproval of the English Crown, Strata Florida's support for Llywelyn ab Iorwerth continued.[17] In 1220, for example, a royal officer noted that the abbot was 'in the power' of the prince.[18] Of much greater significance, in October 1238, Llywelyn summoned 'all the princes of Wales' to a great assembly at Strata Florida. This was a momentous occasion, with a united federation of princes swearing allegiance to Llywelyn's heir, Dafydd (d 1246). For the age, it was a remarkable symbol of unified statehood. Furthermore, the location chosen for the event speaks volumes of the position the Cistercians now occupied in Welsh public life.[19]

Although the heavy fine imposed on Strata Florida by King John must surely have curbed over-ambitious building programmes, the greater part of the church and main claustral ranges may already have been complete. In any case, in 1255 the community purchased its 'great bell', which was presumably hung in the crossing tower. It was consecrated by Richard, bishop of Bangor (1236–67).[20] Later in the century, war and misfortune exacted a heavy toll on the monastery. First, it seems clear that Strata Florida suffered a degree of destruction during the Welsh wars of Edward I, in 1276–7 and 1282–3. Towards the close of 1284, the abbey received £78 by way of compensation for the damage wreaked during the second campaign.[21] But very much worse was to come. According to the chronicler at the Benedictine abbey of Chester, within twelve days of Christmas 1284 the church at Strata Florida was devastated by fire, though the Welsh annals place the event in 1286.[22] 'The fire and lightning struck the belfry', wrote the Chester monk, 'and burned the whole of it with the bells … and then devoured the whole church, which was completely covered with lead as far as the walls, except the presbytery … This happened in the night'. Next, as if the community had not suffered enough, it was caught up in a regional revolt sparked off by the Welsh uprising of 1294–5, during which the abbey was put to flames by a royalist force. In 1300, in granting permission for the abbot and convent 'to construct afresh, and rebuild their house', King Edward claimed the action had been 'contrary to our wishes'.[23]

In the *Taxatio Ecclesiastica* of 1291, Strata Florida's net annual income was assessed at £98 6s 9d.[24] At the time, the monks may have been farming over 2,430ha of arable, but their entire estate could have been anything up to five times larger.[25] Thereafter, although concrete evidence is obscure, the community increasingly abandoned the early Cistercian ideals of grange farming. By the 1330s, given that former grange lands had definitely been leased out to dependent tenants, tithes must have been assuming a growing importance in the abbey's economy.[26] The Black Death of 1348–50 can only have hastened the process. For all this, Strata Florida may have experienced a period of relative peace, if not prosperity, in the second half of the fourteenth century, due largely to the qualities of Abbot Llywelyn Vaughan (1344–80).[27]

Strata Florida's resolute Welshness brought it into further difficulty in the early fifteenth century. At the outbreak of the Owain Glyn Dŵr revolt, the abbot seems to have enlisted in the rebel cause. In 1401–2, Henry IV (1399–1413) took full possession of the abbey, temporarily ousting the monks. The chronicler Adam Usk paints a vivid picture of the occupation. Even the monastery of Strata Florida suffered, he wrote, when the king himself stayed at the site: 'its church and choir, right up to the high altar, was converted into a stable, and was completely stripped of its plate'.[28] In the wake of these events, and with fears of a permanent dispersion of the community, a Crown commission was appointed to administer the monastery's affairs for a period of two years.[29] Still the abbey's problems were not at an end. In the course of the revolt, in 1407, a force of 480 English troops was billeted at Strata Florida, to 'guard and defend it from the malice of the rebels'. As late as 1415, a garrison of 120 was again imposed on the community.[30]

To add to the abbey's ongoing misery, during the second quarter of the fifteenth century there occurred a series of internal disruptions brought about by weak, even corrupt, leadership. To begin with, in the Lent of 1428 – as a later allegation records – John ap Rhys, abbot of the daughter house of Aberconwy (now located at Maenan), came to Strata Florida with a body of armed men. Acting like a brigand, ap Rhys apparently occupied his mother house for a period of forty days, disrupting divine service, and eventually carrying away vestments, books, silver and livestock, together valued at £1,200.[31] Then, within a few years, Abbot Rhys (c 1436–41) became head of the abbey. While he had his strengths, as noted below, his ambitions may have overstretched the resources of the house. Rhys seems to have ended his days as a debtor in the prison at Carmarthen Castle.[32] In his stead, the prior and convent elected William Morris to the abbacy.[33] He had barely taken office when the troublesome John ap Rhys arrived once more on the scene. On the basis of a deception, ap Rhys managed to evict William and get him imprisoned at Aberystwyth. Eventually, the whole sorry episode came before the king, who decided that neither party should govern the house. The abbots of Margam (Thomas Franklin) and Whitland (David ap Rhys) were appointed keepers until the situation could be satisfactorily resolved.[34] In 1444 Abbot Morgan ap Rhys was elected – he was to rule Strata Florida with much greater stability for a period of over forty years.

The precise impact of all this disruption on the abbey buildings is difficult to determine, though the effects should certainly not be underestimated. In 1442 it remained convenient for the monks to blame much of the sorry state of their house on 'Owain Glyn Dŵr and his company'. So spoiled was the abbey, they claimed, 'the walls of the church excepted … it is not probable that the same can be repaired without the king's aid'.[35] In fact, before this time, the ill-fated Abbot Rhys had already laboured to improve matters, and in the later fifteenth century Abbot Morgan ap Rhys was praised by the native bards for his work as a builder, as well as for his spirituality and his hospitality.[36] At the close of the century, the house was ruled for a while by that most able of late Welsh Cistercian abbots, Dafydd ab Owain (*c* 1496–1500).[37]

In the early sixteenth century, Strata Florida was headed for a while by Richard Dorston (*c* 1509–13). His presence is a little surprising, for he had formerly been an abbot of Dore (1496–1500), and was deposed from there for 'inordinate Rule and governance'.[38] The last abbot of Strata Florida was Richard Talley (1516–39), whose long rule was marred near the end by the imprisonment of one of his monks, who was involved with an attempt to strike false coinage.[39] In the *Valor Ecclesiasticus* of 1535, the annual income of the house was given as £118 7s 3d.[40] It should have been suppressed in the following year, but Abbot Richard made a last-ditch effort to preserve monastic life, offering a fine, effectively a bribe, of £66 for Strata Florida's survival. The reprieve lasted less than three years: the house was finally surrendered to the king's visitors in February 1539.[41]

The temporary site occupied by the founding colony of monks in 1164 was somewhere on the banks of the Fflur brook, probably to the south of Old Abbey Farm. Its position is marked as *hen fynachlog*, 'the old monastery', on early maps, though to date no modern archaeological tool has been used to test the validity of the various assertions.[42] In the late 1890s, Stephen Williams inspected the site and felt confident that considerable foundations 'yet remain'. He reported hearsay evidence to the effect that within living memory fragments of the walls were still to be seen above ground. From the tenant of Old Abbey Farm, Williams ascertained that the church had been about 38.4m long by 12.8m wide. It stood on rising ground, he noted, with the claustral buildings located on the north side.[43]

In his great charter of 1184, the Lord Rhys proclaimed that he had 'begun to build the venerable monastery called Strata Florida, and after building it have loved and cherished it'.[44] This suggests that plans for the transfer of the community to a new site alongside the Teifi had been finalized, and that work on the stone buildings there was already well in hand. Today, the principal remains are those of a large 'Bernardine' church, featuring three chapels to each transept (figs 178 and 179). The nave piers were carried on low, continuous walls, broken only in the east and west end bays. The west door, originally of

178 Strata Florida Abbey: the church, looking west from the presbytery, during the excavations of 1887–90. At the centre of the presbytery (right) there is a large heap of vault rib fragments bearing a distinctive 'domino' or pellet motif. The collapsed west crossing arch appears in mid-view, with the nave and west door beyond.

Photograph: *National Library of Wales*

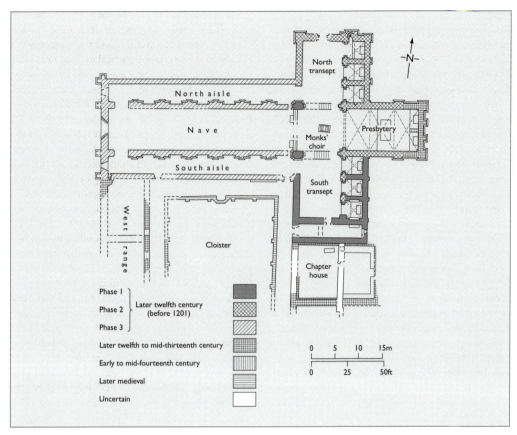

179 Strata Florida
Abbey: ground plan
(after Radford 1949a/
Robinson and Platt
1998, with
modifications).

Drawing: *Pete
Lawrence, for Cadw*

six continuous round-headed orders (fig 73), is particularly striking. To the south, there are traces of the cloister, the chapter house and the west range. The farmhouse of Abbey Farm appears to sit over at least part of the south range, and may incorporate medieval masonry.[45] There is much variety in the building materials. In addition to local rubble and poor freestone, an oolitic limestone used widely for dressings probably originated in the Cotswolds or the Bath area; purple Caerbwdy came from the coast near St Davids; and certain finer sandstones may have been brought from the Forest of Dean.[46]

It has been widely assumed that the reference in *Brut y Tywysogyon* to the monks entering their new church in 1201 implies the consecration of the east end. The nave, it is generally suggested, was completed over the following couple of decades.[47] A case can definitely be made, however, to argue that the church stood largely complete by 1201. In the process of construction, the original 'Bernardine' scheme was modified, the presbytery raised and extended and an unusual rib vault inserted. It seems, on stylistic grounds, that alterations to the chapter house were carried out in the 1220s. Here, the surviving evidence may reflect a rather wider programme of works on the monastic buildings. The significance of the

purchase of the 'great bell' in 1255 cannot be overlooked, though the church must surely have been complete for some time before this date.[48]

The disastrous fire of 1284 or 1286, coupled with the damage inflicted by royal forces at the time of the Welsh revolt in 1294–5, must inevitably have led to an extensive programme of reconstruction. Specifically, in his licence granted to Strata Florida in 1300, Edward I gave the monks permission to 'construct afresh, and rebuild their house'.[49] According to the Chester chronicler, the presbytery had been the only area to escape the fire of the 1280s, possibly by virtue of the stone vault over the area.[50] It so happens that lead from the roofs ran into the groined arches above the webs of the vault, and during the excavations of the late 1880s a large mass of material retaining its molten shape was discovered in the debris.[51] Overall, the abbey church itself was not so badly damaged that it required comprehensive rebuilding. Among the most prominent changes during the fourteenth century, the church was reroofed in stone rather than lead; painted glass in the windows may have been replaced by plain lights; and walls which once carried brightly coloured decoration were now whitewashed.[52] There were also various changes to the liturgical arrangements, including a probable reduction in the size of the monks' choir, with the enclosing screen walls positioned accordingly. It may have been at this time, too, that the chapter house was refashioned on a smaller scale.[53]

Not everything undertaken was of a remedial nature. Before the fires, the floors throughout much of the abbey church were paved with slabs of local slate, but in the first half of the fourteenth century the choir, transepts and the six transept chapels were all covered in decorative pavements comprised of relief, counter-relief and line-impressed tiles. At the same time, the presbytery floor was raised by two steps above the level of the crossing, and was again paved with the same tiles. Several thousand whole or fragmentary tiles were uncovered in the various nineteenth-century excavations (fig 178), with samples widely dispersed. Even so, very many do remain on display at the site.[54]

The troubles of the early fifteenth century would almost certainly have had further significant impact on the abbey buildings at Strata Florida. In spite of hyperbole, frequently the stock in trade of monastic petitioners and chroniclers, Adam Usk's reference to the church being used as a stable in 1401–2 must have had some foundation in fact. Four decades on, the monks continued to complain that their house had been so damaged by the Glyn Dŵr war, 'the walls of the church excepted', it could not easily be repaired.[55] Nevertheless, repairs and refurbishment were indeed in hand – at least, that is, according to the verse of grateful bards. Guto'r Glyn alludes to the various attempts made by Abbot Rhys (c 1436–41) to improve the buildings. According to Guto ap Siencyn, Rhys laid plans for work on the refectory, and built another fine room 'with glass windows' and 'with flowery ornament'.[56] Moreover, if we are to believe Dafydd Nanmor, the reputation of Abbot Morgan ap Rhys (1444–86) as a restorer extended to Cîteaux itself. Dafydd wrote of fine carvings in the transepts, with 'oak trees between them and the east, a myriad in number, on stone arches'. He was perhaps referring to elaborate oak screens. He also tells us of Morgan's work in restoring the choir, with ten new windows (of which half the cost went in glass), and an oak roof covered with 'heavy lead'. Dafydd was further impressed by the 'great belfry, lime dressed, big and white', with a cock on top of it.[57] Few traces of these works survive in the ruins, though certain minor modifications to the presbytery can be recognized. Of greater note, the cloister arcades were certainly comprehensively rebuilt in the fifteenth century.[58]

When the abbey was seen by John Leland in the late 1530s, he described it thus:

The chirch of Strateflerc is larg, side ilid and

crosse ilid. By is a large cloyster, the fratry and infirmitori be now mere ruines … The base court or camp afore the abbay is veri fair and large. The fundation of the body of the chirch was made to have been 60 foote lengger then it is now.[59]

If this account is taken at face value, some of the great communal chambers, the monks' refectory and the infirmary, were already in decay, possibly since the troubles of the fifteenth century. Leland's account might also lead us to conclude that the community had retreated to the east end of the church, raising the possibility that several of the nave bays had been abandoned.

Soon after the suppression of Strata Florida, Sir Richard Devereux (d 1547) was appointed receiver-general of the abbey's lands and his father, Lord Ferrers (d 1559), was made steward. Shortly before he died, Devereux secured a lease on the estates, and the greater part of these passed to his heirs, the earls of Essex.[60] The abbey's three bells were sold to the nearby parish of Caron, and the lead was stripped from the roofs and moved to Aberystwyth. As late as 1555 there were still 'eleven score sows' of it at Aberystwyth, estimated to be around 500kg.[61] By 1567 the site of the abbey itself had been acquired by John Stedman (d 1613). In the late seventeenth century it was perhaps Richard Stedman (d 1702/3) who built or rebuilt the house which can be seen in the Buck brothers' engraving of 1741 (fig 3) and which still stands over parts of the former claustral buildings.[62] In 1744 Richard Stedman junior died without heir; the house (together with the ruins of the abbey church) passed to his brother-in-law, Thomas Powell (d 1752) of Nanteos.

The earliest recorded excavations on the site were undertaken in 1847, in order to reveal something of the foundations to members of the newly formed Cambrian Archaeological Association during their first annual meeting held at Aberystwyth.[63] This initial exploration was followed in 1887–90 by several seasons of major clearance and excavation by Stephen Williams, during which most of the church, part of the chapter house, and the immediately adjacent areas were explored (figs 178 and 180).[64] Forty years afterwards, in 1931, the site was taken into the care of the State. Fresh clearance must have taken place (fig 181), and within four years an official guide had been produced by Ralegh Radford.[65] After the war, further clearance and consolidation were undertaken, and a revised edition of Radford's guide was published.[66] In 1966, in laying paths at the west front, foundations were found extending 'the line of the side walls and aisles of the church'.[67]

More recently, there has been a fresh programme of investigations looking, in particular, at the great mass of loose architectural detail excavated by Williams. This work, commissioned by Cadw, has led to refinements of earlier interpretations, as well as recovering much evidence for the superstructure of the church and chapter house facade. The full publication of the results, along with several accompanying studies, is forthcoming.[68] In summary form, the material is presented in the current Cadw guidebook.[69] There are, too, plans for a much wider investigation of Strata Florida within its vast landscape setting, the lead taken by David Austin.[70]

The immediate environs of the abbey church and cloister are scheduled as an ancient monument (CD1), with around 0.65ha covered. This is but a small fragment of the former monastic precinct, and does not even include prominent surviving earthworks to the south east. Abbey Farmhouse, built or rebuilt in the late seventeenth century, over part of the former south range, is a Grade II listed building (record number 9914).

180 Strata Florida Abbey: sculpted stone head of a monk, thirteenth century. The piece was found during the excavation of the abbey ruins by Stephen Williams in 1887–90.

Photograph: *Cadw, Crown Copyright*

181 Strata Florida Abbey: one of the south transept chapels, with loose ex situ stonework and tiles. Following the transfer of Strata Florida into the care of the State in 1931, the Office of Works began the first round of clearance and consolidation. The floors of the south transept chapels were relaid, with random patterns of early fourteenth-century tiles recovered from the wider abbey site. Photograph: *Cadw, Crown Copyright*

BIBLIOGRAPHY

Architectural: Knowles and St Joseph 1952, 116–17; Lewis 1999, 253–9; Radford 1935 and 1949a; Roberts 1848a; Robinson 1998, 176–9; Robinson and Platt 1998; Smith and Thomas 1977; Williams 1887, 1888, 1889a, 1889b, 1889c, 1889d, 1890c and 1891; *Archaeol Cambrensis*, **2**, 1847, 361–3; *Archaeol Cambrensis*, **101**, 1950–1, 80, 116; *Archaeol Cambrensis*, **106**, 1957, 107; *Archaeol Wales*, **6**, 1966, no. 46.

Historical: B[anks] 1880; Bowen 1950–1; Davies 1945–6; Jones 1931; Knowles and Hadcock 1971, 114, 126; O'Sullivan 1947, 11–14; Pierce 1950–1; Roberts 1848a and 1848b; Williams 1889a; Williams 1990, 56–9; Willis-Bund 1889.

STRATA MARCELLA ABBEY, Powys, St Asaph, SJ 251104

The abbey of Strata Marcella (or Ystryd Marchell) was founded in 1170 as a daughter house of Whitland (fig 19).[1] There is some suggestion that the initial site of the monastery may have been closer to Welshpool, and that the community moved to its final location in 1172, although the evidence is far from conclusive.[2] The founding patron was certainly Owain Cyfeiliog, prince of southern Powys, a great warrior lord who was also one of the most distinguished poets of his generation. In old age, Owain retired to the monastery he had established. He died there in the habit of a Cistercian monk in 1197, and was buried close to the site of the high altar.[3]

In addition to Owain's initial gifts, his son Gwenwynwyn (d 1216) proved a liberal benefactor of the house. Meanwhile, the monks made a number of purchases and small exchanges of land in an attempt to improve and consolidate their overall estate.[4] A great deal of Strata Marcella's early grange property was eventually organized into two extensive manors. One of these, known as Tir-y-Mynach, lay in the immediate Severn valley area. Predominantly an arable holding, in 1291 it contained up to 534ha of ploughland, with much of this consolidated as part of the home grange. The other manor was centred around Talerddig, north west of Carno, in the uplands of western Powys, in this case a chiefly pastoral property. The monks also held estates in the more distant uplands of Merioneth.[5]

The early success and expansion of Strata Marcella was such that in 1200–1 it was able to send out a colony to occupy the new foundation at Valle Crucis. In addition, the abbey was to have oversight of the Cistercian nunnery at Llanllugan, established perhaps sometime between 1170 and 1190.[6]

In the late thirteenth century, Strata Marcella was one of the Cistercian abbeys of north and central Wales that undoubtedly suffered damage and losses as a result of Edward I's campaign of 1282–3. Of the five houses which received partial compensation in 1284, Strata Marcella was given £43, the smallest figure awarded.[7] Less than ten years later, although the calculations may not have been entirely accurate, the annual income of the abbey's landed property was assessed at the comparatively minor sum of £19 7s 2d.[8]

By the late 1320s Strata Marcella's fortunes had definitely changed for the worse. The then lord of Powys, John Charlton (d 1353), seems to have openly opposed the community,[9] and it was probably in 1328 that he wrote to Edward III, claiming that the house was 'almost annihilated; for there were wont to be there sixty monks, and now there are but eight'.[10] In August 1328 the king wrote to the abbot of Clairvaux, informing him that Strata Marcella was the subject of an inquiry. His letter alleged that the abbot and monks had abandoned the observance of religion, and 'were leading a fearfully dissolute life, by irreparably wasting the effects of the monastery'. They had been removed, the king stated, and English monks put in their place. Finally, Edward requested that the rights of visitation should pass from Whitland to the abbot of Buildwas in neighbouring Shropshire, in whose house 'exists wholesome discipline and strict adherence to monastic rules'.[11] The matter dragged on, with the king writing twice more to Clairvaux, first in 1329 and again in 1330. Most telling is the content of Edward's letter of 1330, in which it is disclosed that unlawful assemblies were being held at the abbey, 'to excite contentions and hatred between the English and the Welsh'.[12] The Strata Marcella community, meanwhile, felt aggrieved and eventually launched a counter-petition in which Charlton himself was accused of wholly unreasonable behaviour.[13] Just how long monks from Buildwas were present is unclear, though the English house does not appear to have exercised long-term rights of visitation.[14]

Relations with the Charlton family eventually improved, and it was Lewis Charlton, bishop of Hereford (1361–9), who bequeathed Strata Marcella twenty marks towards the fabric of the abbey church.[15] In 1420, following the Glyn Dŵr revolt, the monks were granted a charter of confirmation by Edward Charlton. New privileges were also included, on account of 'the destruction and injury made by the Welsh rebels both to the church and the monastery and its holdings by plunder and by fire'.[16]

In the last quarter of the fifteenth century, Dafydd ab Owain was for a time abbot of the house.[17]

Later involved with building at Strata Florida and at Maenan, Dafydd may also have been responsible for new works at Strata Marcella. He was certainly praised by a number of Welsh bards during his time at the abbey. William Egwad, for example, wrote: 'What abbot is equal to Dafydd? ... in Latin, golden-tongued ... [a] most accomplished speaker'. And it was that master poet, Tudur Aled (d 1526), who produced this mouth-watering description of Dafydd's rich hospitality:

> In Dafydd's hall ... the tables bent beneath the weight of great masses of prime venison, wild game, and sea fish, with all manner of vegetables and fruits, including oranges and grapes. And exotic wines that washed it all down! – wines from Germany ... the vintages of the fragrant vineyards of Burgundy. All these and the home-brewed cider, mead, and bragget, too.[18]

The last abbot of Strata Marcella was John ap Rhys (1527–36), an illegitimate son of Robert ap Rhys, who was in turn close to Cardinal Wolsey. Though there are signs of favouritism in his election, John may well have been a sound choice. He seems to have found a small community, perhaps only three in number, and a monastery apparently already 'to a large extent in a state of ruin'. In an attempt to improve matters, early in his abbacy, perhaps in 1528, John was able to issue an indulgence, listing a series of privileges granted by the pope and Wolsey to all those who 'extended helping hands' towards the monastery of Strata Marcella.[19] Seven years afterwards, in 1535, the annual income of the house was assessed at a modest £64 14s 2d.[20] The suppression came in the spring of the following year, when there were no more than four monks at the house.[21]

Strata Marcella was situated close to the west bank of the River Severn.[22] Today, apart from a few fragments of loose *ex situ* masonry, no trace of the abbey buildings can be seen above ground. This said, prominent earthworks mark the position of the church and cloister (fig 77). They also indicate the locations of some of the main trenches dug during the limited programme of excavations overseen by Stephen Williams in 1890.[23] In fact, virtually all that is known of the scale and chronology of the complex is derived from these early excavations. Even though very little evidence was recovered for the precise form of the presbytery and transepts, the plan of 1890 shows a church designed along typically 'Bernardine' lines (fig 182). If the church was indeed completed to the scale shown in the Williams plan, with a nave of eleven bays, the total length would have extended to almost 83.2m, exceptionally large in a Welsh context.

On the basis of the plan, together with the drawings and written account provided by Williams, it may be suggested that work on the construction of the church began soon after the foundation.[24] It is also clear that it must have continued well into the thirteenth century. A number of the carved motifs indicate that the masons involved were familiar with the near-contemporary works at Strata Florida. Even

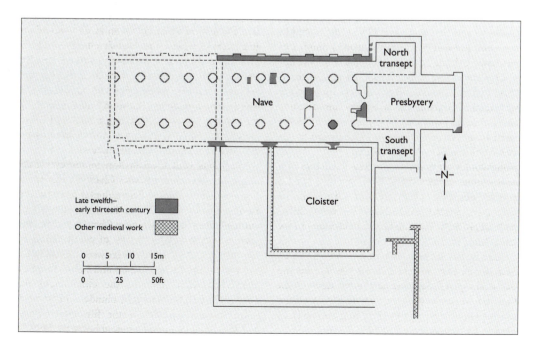

Late twelfth–early thirteenth century

Other medieval work

0 5 10 15m

0 25 50ft

North transept

Nave

Presbytery

South transept

Cloister

–N–

182 Strata Marcella Abbey: ground plan (after [Jones] and Williams 1891/ Arnold 1992, with modifications).

Drawing: *Pete Lawrence, for Cadw*

so, the Strata Marcella scheme shows significant advances, particularly in terms of a more complex nave pier form. Here, the piers were of a multi-shafted composition (fig 44). They stood on bases with a fine red sandstone casing, filled with a core of local rubble.[25]

Williams suggested that his excavations had located the pulpitum, marking the entrance to the monks' choir from the west. Its position, almost one full bay into the nave, was indicated by the early thirteenth-century base mouldings of the south side of the doorway.[26] At the east end of the crossing, there may have been four steps up into the presbytery, the floor level of which stood approximately 0.41m higher.[27] Most of the tile pavements encountered during the excavation were found in the presbytery and in the area of the north transept.[28]

From the findings of the 1890 excavation, there is little to suggest major rebuilding work after the mid-thirteenth century. The report does, however, mention the discovery of a large number of worked stones in the area of the crossing. A good deal of this material was found to be carved with a distinctive wave moulding, probably of early fourteenth-century date, which Williams thought must derive from the 'piers of the tower'.[29] In addition, the tiles known from the presbytery and north transept date from the early fourteenth century.[30] This evidence apart, there are rather stronger indications that the church may have been reduced in scale at some point. For Williams, it was the ravages of the Glyn Dŵr rebellion in the early fifteenth century that left the community unable to restore the entire building. He proposed that the monks were instead obliged to drastically shorten their nave, cutting off the eight western bays. In support of this theory, he pointed to the recovery of the northern jamb of a doorway set between the second pair of free-standing nave piers. The mouldings showed distinct signs of reuse, which for Williams suggested the possibility that this had once been the west doorway, now repositioned.[31] Most of the excavated stonework throughout the church was found to be limewashed.[32]

In 1990, to mark the centenary of the first investigation, the Powysland Club commissioned a geophysical survey of the site.[33] Using the results of this survey, together with map and air-photographic evidence, Christopher Arnold has reviewed the archaeology of the site as a whole. In a very useful exercise, he first attempts to plot the areas that were excavated in 1890. Arnold goes on to point out the lack of any convincing stratigraphic approach in the Victorian work, throwing considerable doubt on the interpretations based on the various discoveries.[34] In sum, in his reinterpretation, Arnold proposes that the completed church extended to no more than about 61m. Rather than seeing a reduction in the later Middle Ages, he suggests that the four western bays of the nave could represent an attempt to enlarge an already quite ambitious scheme. Without further excavation, however, it is virtually impossible to reach any firm conclusions. Nevertheless, the proposals would seem to fit better with what evidence is available on the layout of the cloister.

Although little work was done on the cloister in 1890, it does seem to have been located on the south side of the nave. In the area of the chapter house, Williams thought they had found traces of a vaulted roof, though no rib pieces were located.[35] Also, the excavations uncovered one or two fragments of Geometrical tracery which was apparently not grooved for glass. This could have belonged to a late thirteenth-century cloister arcade.[36] Other than this, David Williams mentions the possible location of the main abbey gatehouse.[37]

As noted above, even before the suppression, Abbot John claimed in his indulgence of about 1528 that Strata Marcella was already 'to a large extent in a state of ruin'.[38] The site seems to have been purchased by Edward Grey, Lord Powis (d 1551), in advance of the official closure.[39] On taking possession in that year, he complained to Cromwell that there was not a monk remaining at the site, and that 'they had rifled all that was moveable, and left him only a mass of walls in decay'.[40]

Within ten years, the site had been further plundered by Nicholas Purcell, who appears to have been a Crown tenant of the abbey.[41] At an inquiry of 1547, Purcell was accused of having disposed of a vast quantity of material from the former abbey, including a number of specific items.[42] He was said to have sold three bells to the parish of Chirk for £20, and to have obtained a further 20 marks for the organs from the parishioners of St Mary's in Shrewsbury. It was claimed that Purcell's servant, by his order, 'took certain gutters of lead and other spouts and conduits', which were then sold to repair the castle of Oswestry. Purcell was also said to have 'sold and delivered as much stone as made a whole steeple at the town of Montgomery and also a chimney to four fires', and further sold 'to Matthew, merchant of Welshpool, four bays of one house of the late abbey … with a crosschamber at the end covered with shingles with two chimneys of stones'.[43] Another of Purcell's servants removed 'all the glass that were in eight or nine great windows' of the abbey church and other buildings, together with their lead. Finally, the inquiry was told that the church and other plate and vestments were carried away, wasted and consumed by Purcell.[44]

The site was not entirely deserted, and in the seventeenth and eighteenth centuries it was occupied by a farm, referred to in 1634 as 'Streetmarshall Farme' and later known as Abbey Farm.[45] From a plan of 1780, the farm buildings were clearly arranged around three sides of a courtyard, perhaps representing the former monastic cloister. Arnold suggests it is the east side which is missing, which may in turn explain the failure to locate much in this area during the excavations of 1890.[46] The farm had in any case entirely disappeared by this time, with Williams's labour force encountering a substantial covering of debris across the site, in places up to 2.7m deep.[47]

Among the *ex situ* material which seems to have come from Strata Marcella, one of the most significant items now serves as the font in the parish church of All Saints, Buttington.[48] It dates from perhaps *c* 1220–30, and must have originated as a substantial capital, decorated with three rows of curling stiff-leaf foliage. If it is indeed derived from a free-standing pier, the chapter house must certainly be considered as a possible source. Richard Haslam has also suggested that the fine south doorway at St Mary's, Llanfair Caereinion, may have come from the abbey site.[49] However, as Williams has said, there is nothing to support traditions that the chancel roofs at St Aelhaiarn's, Guilsfield, or St Mary's, Welshpool, came from Strata Marcella.[50] Other material from the abbey may be found in the collections of the Powysland Museum, Welshpool.

An arbitrary area of the abbey precinct, including the church and cloister and amounting to about 3.95ha, is scheduled as an ancient monument (MG120).

BIBLIOGRAPHY
Architectural: Arnold 1992; Haslam 1979, 197–8; [Jones] and Williams 1891; Knowles and St Joseph 1952, 118–19; Lewis 1999, 259; Robinson 1998, 179–80; Williams 1992; Williams 1892.
Historical: Davies 1949–50; Jones *et al* 1947–8; Jones 1871–3; Jones [*et al*] 1877; Knowles and Hadcock 1971, 114, 126; O'Sullivan 1947, 14–16; Owen 1919; Thomas 1997; Williams 1976c; Williams 1990, 59–61.

TINTERN ABBEY, Monmouthshire, Llandaff, ST 532998

Situated on the lower reaches of the River Wye, surrounded by a tree-covered landscape of perfectly wild natural beauty, Tintern Abbey has been a focus of admiration and wonderment for well over two hundred years. Writing in the 1770s, that indefatigable early tourist, the Revd William Gilpin (1724–1804), informed his readers that the 'noble ruin' of the abbey would be the 'most beautiful and picturesque' view they could expect to encounter anywhere on the celebrated Wye valley tour. 'Everything around breathes an air so calm', he wrote, 'so sequestered from the commerce of life, that it is easy to conceive, a man of warm imagination, in monkish times, might have been allured by such a scene to become an inhabitant of it'.[1] A few decades later, at the turn of the eighteenth century, William Coxe (d 1828) was another to heap praise on the picturesque beauty of the surviving ruins, in spite of attendant crowds of 'importunate beggars'. In particular, Coxe felt the abbey church should be regarded as 'an excellent specimen of gothic architecture in its greatest purity'.[2] In the years since the Romantic era, Tintern has won even greater fame, as much for its association with one of the finest poems in the English language, as for the importance and quality of its architecture.[3] Today it stands as one of the best-known monastic sites in the entire British Isles.

Tintern was founded by Walter fitz Richard de Clare (d 1138), the Anglo-Norman lord of Chepstow, on 9 May 1131.[4] It was the first Cistercian landfall in Wales, colonized by monks who had been sent out from the abbey of L'Aumône in north-central France (figs 17 and 19).[5] Moreover, it stood in the very vanguard of the Cistercian settlement of Britain as a whole, preceded only by Bishop William Giffard's foundation some three years earlier at Waverley in Surrey.[6] Yet despite this significant early foothold in the south-eastern March, Tintern was to play no further role in the white monk colonization of Wales. Its only daughter houses were at Kingswood in Gloucestershire, founded in 1139, and at Tintern Parva in Ireland, established in 1201–3.[7]

At the beginning of the twelfth century, the heavily wooded slopes of the lower River Wye would have been comparatively remote, meeting most of the criteria expected by the Cistercian authorities for the siting of a new abbey. Not that the area was entirely without an existing population in the 1130s. For example, part of Walter de Clare's endowment to his new community included important property at Porthcaseg, situated just to the south of the abbey itself. Lands here had earlier belonged to the church of Llandaff, and had probably been worked long before the foundation.[8] That apart, among Walter's other early gifts to Tintern was land at Modesgate, Penterry and Wilcrick.[9] Interestingly, it appears the grants at Penterry and Wilcrick were very soon exchanged. Instead, the monks were given property at Merthyrgeryn on the Monmouthshire levels, together with a major estate at Woolaston across the Wye in Gloucestershire.[10] A confirmation of their holding at Trelleck was granted by Richard 'Strongbow' de Clare (d 1176), and in 1223–4 William Marshal the younger, earl of Pembroke (1219–31), gave them valuable new estates at Rogerstone and at Estavarney (Monkswood) near Usk.[11]

In addition to these major gifts, the land-hungry Tintern monks of the twelfth and early thirteenth centuries worked hard to extend and improve their overall estate. Smaller benefactions, exchanges, assarts of woodland and occasional purchases all formed part of the ongoing process.[12] In this way, wherever possible, properties were consolidated into the self-contained granges preferred by the early Cistercians. Eventually, Tintern was able to establish at least twelve granges, situated on both sides of the River Wye: Estavarney, Merthyrgeryn, Moor, Rogerstone, Ruding, Secular Firmary and Trelleck lay in today's Monmouthshire; Aluredeston (Alvington), Ashwell, Brockweir, Modesgate and Woolaston were all in Gloucestershire. One further aspect of Tintern's landed estate worth noting is the community's interest in maintaining a balanced agricultural economy. The granges at Trelleck and Rogerstone, for example, served as important arable centres, whereas at Moor the monks may have placed a greater emphasis on pastoralism.

During its formative early years, the Tintern community was led by at least one man with considerable strength of character. It seems that Abbot Henry (c 1148–57) had spent his youth making a 'lucrative profession of brigandage'. Having been moved to repentance, and taking the Cistercian habit, he developed an intense spirituality, 'conspicuous at the altar for the abundance of his tears'. Henry is said to have met both the pope and St Bernard, and he certainly went on to become abbot of Waverley.[13] In contrast, Abbot William's rule at Tintern (c 1169–88) may have been less happy. For a time, the house was in dispute with its sister at Waverley, and William's career ended abruptly in 1188 when he resigned after meeting visitors sent by the General Chapter.[14] He was succeeded by Eudo, previously abbot of Kingswood and earlier prior of Waverley.[15]

In 1189 the lordship of Chepstow and patronage of Tintern passed to William Marshal, the future earl of Pembroke (1199–1219). It was Marshal who established the abbey's daughter colony at Tintern Parva in County Wexford, occupied by 1203.[16] His son, William the younger, was particularly generous in the fullness of his confirmation of all earlier grants to the Welsh house. Moreover, in 1223–4, he was to offer further significant contributions of his own. In return, the monks were to maintain a lamp burning at the tomb of his mother, Isabel, countess of Pembroke.[17] The burial of Isabel Marshal at Tintern in 1220, presumably somewhere within the abbey church, was by no means the first such arrangement. Later, her sons Walter and Anselm were laid to rest in the monastery in 1245, and her daughter Matilda – whose body was carried into the church by her four sons – was buried there in 1248 (fig 183).[18]

Around this very time, the community was engaged in an extensive programme of rebuilding, with efforts focused on the principal claustral ranges. Indeed, the grants made by William Marshal the younger in the early 1220s were perhaps earmarked to support this no doubt costly scheme. In any case, as construction progressed the monks were blessed with another leader of note. Abbot Ralph (c 1232–45), says the Waverley annalist, was 'a man gifted in no small way with sobriety of habits, and splendour of wisdom'. Ralph is known to have carried out a number of Crown and Cistercian duties, later becoming head of Dunkeswell and, finally, serving as abbot of Waverley.[19] There is less information on his immediate successors at Tintern, though by 1267 the house was headed by Abbot John (c 1267–77), the man who appears to have taken the decision to begin work on a brand new abbey church.[20]

Some idea of the relative wealth Tintern had achieved by the close of the thirteenth century comes from the *Taxatio Ecclesiastica* of 1291. The total annual income of the house was assessed at £145 3s 0d,[21] a figure that might be seen as comparatively modest by the standards of some English houses and one that was comfortably exceeded in Wales at both Margam and Neath. Nevertheless, the Tintern monks were farming well over 1,214ha of arable land on the Welsh side of the Wye alone. In addition, there were some 3,264 sheep on their pastures, and it is clear from the list of wool-producing monasteries held by the Italian merchant Francesco Balducci Pegolotti that the Tintern fleeces were of the very finest quality.[22]

Meanwhile, in 1245–6, through the Marshal heiress Matilda (d 1248), the lordship of Chepstow had passed into the hands of the Bigod family, earls of Norfolk. Matilda's grandson, Roger Bigod, fifth earl of Norfolk (1270–1306), chose to invest heavily in the rebuilding of Chepstow Castle, creating new suites of lavish accommodation.[23] Even though the question is somewhat vexed, he eventually took a keen interest in the fortunes of the Tintern community. The first signs of his effective support seem to be represented by a grant of the church at Halvergate in Norfolk, which is to be dated no later

183 *Tintern Abbey: effigy of knight, c 1240–50, with other sepulchral fragments. It is tempting to link the principal effigy, or possibly the second head (lower left), with the burial in the church of two successive earls of Pembroke, Walter and Anselm Marshal, both of whom died in 1245.*

Photograph: *Royal Commission on the Ancient and Historical Monuments of Wales, Crown Copyright*

than 1290 and possibly rather earlier.[24] However, for proof positive of the earl's benevolence we must wait until the turn of the century. Now elderly, in poor health and still without child, Bigod was in fact forced to barter with the king over the future of his estates. In 1302, with but few exceptions, he effectively surrendered his estates and titles to Edward I.[25] Later that year Bigod also began setting aside certain insurances for the afterlife, choosing to grant the abbot and monks of Tintern 'all his manor of Acle … and the advowson of the church there'.[26] Situated more than 320km away in Norfolk, this was a particularly generous gift, amounting to the abbey's single most profitable asset and accounting for up to one quarter of its annual income by the sixteenth century. In a further charter, Earl Roger granted the monks the manor of Aluredeston (Alvington), Gloucestershire, in exchange for their property at Plateland in Monmouthshire. And, for a fee, he also gave them additional lands at Modesgate.[27] So great was Roger Bigod's munificence that for later observers – notably the traveller and antiquary William Worcestre (writing in the 1470s) – he was considered the abbey's founder.[28] In 1535, the year before Tintern's suppression, the monks were still distributing alms to the poor five times a year for the repose of his soul.[29]

Presumably through good relations with the earl of Norfolk, the abbot who had negotiated the acquisition of the manor of Acle was Ralph, whose first appearance in the records occurs in 1294.[30] Abbot Ralph was certainly a man in royal favour, and it is perhaps a measure of his character that he received no fewer than five summonses to Parliament between 1295 and 1305.[31] He was succeeded by the efficient and businesslike Hugh le Wyke (1305–20).[32] Perhaps driven by the need to fund ongoing building works, Abbot Hugh sought every opportunity to squeeze estate profitability, notably at Acle.[33] He also had the foresight to dispatch one of his monks on the long journey to Carlisle to secure royal approval of the abbey's lands and charters. At no little cost, Tintern's grants and privileges were confirmed by the dying Edward I in March and June 1307.[34] The abbots known to have followed Hugh le Wyke over the fourteenth century are Walter of Hereford (c 1320–7), Roger de Camme (occurs 1330–1), Walter (occurs 1333), Gilbert (occurs 1340–2), John (occurs 1349–75) and John Wysbech (1387–1407).[35]

In terms of the economy of the house, the beginning of the fourteenth century had seen the Tintern community reach a zenith in its fortunes. Apart from the very valuable tithes from the church of Lydd in Kent, first acquired in 1326–7,[36] Tintern made very few significant additions to its property

after this time. Yet as the century progressed, several episodes hint at weaknesses in management and monastic discipline. In 1330–4, for example, there was a dispute concerning the abbey's fisheries on the Wye. Weirs had been raised to such an extent that they were restricting the passage of river traffic to the town and castle at Monmouth, but the monks refused to co-operate and even assaulted officials sent to lower the weirs.[37] A few years later, in 1340, Tintern acknowledged a debt of some £174 owed to an Italian merchant of Lucca.[38]

Of much greater significance was the current of widespread economic change creeping into the agricultural affairs of the abbey at this time.[39] Tintern was by no means exceptional, with Cistercian houses everywhere being forced to abandon the ideals of grange farming, moving ever closer to the manorial system. More and more monastic land was leased out in return for regular fixed cash rents. Falling numbers of lay brothers and rises in wage prices for hired labour accelerated the process. Then, in the spring of 1349, the Black Death struck Wales. Although direct evidence is lacking, the pestilence must surely have compounded the difficulties Tintern was experiencing with labour shortages. The general trend across the abbey's estates is perhaps best summed up by the circumstances on its Merthyrgeryn holding. In 1291 this property on the edge of the Monmouthshire levels still seems to have been managed by lay brothers. By 1387–8, however, a detailed bailiff's account reveals the grange had been leased out almost entirely to tenants.[40] In the meantime, in spite of the Black Death, at the abbey itself a sizeable community was maintained through to the end of the fourteenth century. In 1395 there were fourteen monks led by Abbot John Wysbech.[41]

Yet the community was clearly experiencing significant financial difficulties in the early 1400s. In part, at least, this was due to the damaging effects of the Welsh uprising under Owain Glyn Dŵr. In 1401–2, for example, in petitioning Henry IV (1399–1413) for financial relief, Abbot John of Wysbech referred to his 'poor house of Tintern'.[42] In 1406, writing to the bishop of Hereford, the king noted that much of the abbey's property 'had been destroyed and consumed by the Welsh rebels', and as much was acknowledged once again in the following year.[43] Pilgrim offerings may have offered one source of cash relief. The monks claimed to possess a miraculous image of the Virgin which, despite attempts, could not be removed from a chapel outside the west door of the abbey church. In 1414, it was said 'a very great multitude [already] resort to the chapel', but now the pope granted an indulgence to all those who visited on certain feast days, 'and give alms'.[44]

Over the course of the fifteenth century, the reins of real financial control across the abbey's estates passed ever more into the hands of a lay steward.[45] In the 1450s Sir William Herbert of Raglan was serving in this role. In 1468 Edward IV created Herbert earl of Pembroke. Yet within a year, it was Abbot Thomas Colston (c 1460–86) who received the earl's body for burial within the abbey church following his execution after the battle of Edgecote (fig 184). In his will, Herbert had made provision for the construction of his funerary monument, offering any surplus in the endowment 'to build new cloisters' at Tintern.[46] His wife, Anne Devereux, was buried with him on her death in 1486. The herald, William Fellow, saw the grand tomb in 1531, noting that it lay 'in ye quiere before ye high aulter'.[47] Later in the century Herbert's eldest son, William Herbert, earl of Huntingdon (1479–91), and his wife, Mary Woodville (d 1481), were also buried at Tintern, as was Sir Walter Herbert (d 1507) and Sir George Herbert.[48]

The monks had by this time long played host to elderly corrodians, with the first record of such an inmate dating back to the early fourteenth century.[49]

It was never an obligation to be shouldered lightly, with suitable accommodation just one consideration to be taken into account. From 1521, for example, John Owain and his wife were occupying a chamber 'called "the candlehouse" above the great door next to the church'. They received a gallon of better beer a day, together with a portion of meat or fish equivalent to that eaten by one of the monks.[50]

The last abbot of Tintern was Richard Wyche, who took up office in 1521,[51] when the signs of impending calamity for the monasteries were already close at hand. Locally, in fact, Tintern's overbearing stewards, the earls of Worcester, were taking more than just a watchful interest in estate matters. Wyche sought to curb their ambitions, eventually bringing a list of grievances – for having been 'vexed and wronged' – before the influential court of the Star Chamber.[52] However, the die was very soon cast at the national level. In the *Valor Ecclesiasticus* of 1535, Tintern's net annual income was assessed at £192 1s 4d, still small by the standards of many English abbeys, but sufficient to rank it as the wealthiest of the Welsh religious houses.[53] In March 1536 one of

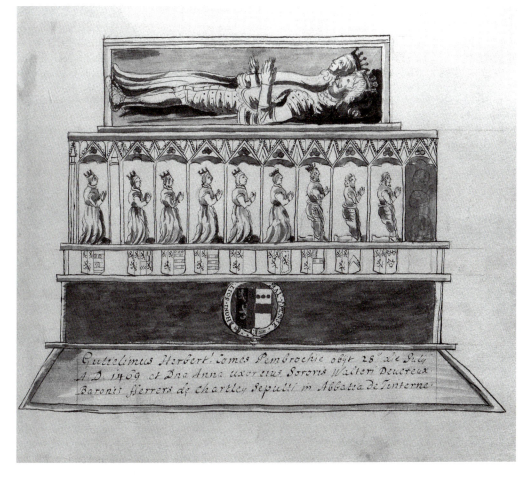

184 Tintern Abbey: drawing of the tomb of William Herbert, earl of Pembroke (d 1469), late seventeenth century. Herbert was buried at Tintern, in accordance with his will, following his death at the battle of Edgecote. In 1531 the tomb was seen by the herald William Fellow, who noted that it lay in the choir before the high altar.

Photograph: *Central Library, Cardiff*

the Crown's visitors in Wales, Dr John Vaughan, wrote to Thomas Cromwell with hearsay evidence, 'by the common people', that Tintern was a house 'greatly abused'.[54] Tintern was surrendered to the king's visitors on 3 September 1536 by Abbot Wyche and the twelve remaining choir monks. There were some thirty-five monastic servants also in residence at the time.[55]

Tintern was sited on the broad west bank of the lower Wye, immediately below a great sweeping meander in the course of the river and close to the point where the Angidy tumbles from its restricted valley into the parent waters. At least one spring, located on Butcher's Hill west of the abbey, was tapped and fed through stone-lined water channels to feed the monastic complex. The Angidy probably supplied the principal drainage flow, its course again being detected as stone-lined channels running beneath the main claustral ranges, from west to east.[56] It was presumably the natural topography which dictated the arrangement whereby the monastic buildings were positioned, from the first, to the north of the abbey church. The surviving ruins at Tintern are extensive (figs 185 and 186). They include virtually the entire late thirteenth-century abbey church, much of the three main claustral ranges, the lower courses of the monks' infirmary and the adjacent abbot's residence, together with guest accommodation, a watergate, the gatehouse chapel and sections of the precinct wall.[57]

Although few indications of the earliest masonry buildings can be readily identified above ground, much can be gleaned from observations made during the conservation works of the early twentieth century.[58] In particular, traces of an austere Romanesque Cistercian church (Tintern I), surely begun within a decade or so of the foundation, was in part recovered by Harold Brakspear in 1904–8, though his proposals – notably with regard to its length and the scale of the transepts – were modified in the light of further investigations of about 1919–20.[59] Aisleless throughout, the church measured around 52.7m in length (figs 35 and 38). Fragments of the contemporary cloister buildings survive in part encased within the walls of later phases, or are known as foundations from trenchings made around 1901–8. The east range was just over 30m long and approximately 8.8m wide internally. The whole was unvaulted. On the ground floor, adjoining the north transept, the chapter house was contained within the width of the range. Further north, the main body of the range may have served as part day room and part warming house. The entire first floor was presumably occupied as the choir monks' dormitory. In the adjacent north range, the monks' refectory was

apparently set out on an east–west axis. Less is known of the initial arrangements in the west range. The sum total of evidence is by no means great, but the layout as reconstructed adds considerably to our knowledge of the mission phase of Cistercian settlement in Britain.[60] Moreover, these early structures are important in that they determined much in the pattern of all subsequent building programmes at Tintern.

Even before the close of the twelfth century, the increasing size of the abbey community led to the need for a northwards extension of the east range and the building of a new latrine block.[61] Plans for a far more comprehensive reorganization of all three principal cloister ranges followed almost immediately, with a major programme of construction extending through to the middle years of the thirteenth century. As noted above, the generous grants made to the community by William Marshal the younger in 1223–4 may have been intended to support the programme.[62] The most prominent indications of the scale and quality of this phase of rebuilding are to be seen in the expanded and now vaulted chapter house (figs 136, 146 and 147) and in the large new refectory set out on a north–south alignment (fig 152). The warming house also belongs to this phase of construction, as does the kitchen, and the insertion of a substantial rib vault in the dormitory undercroft. At much the same time, the abbot seems to have acquired his own distinct block of accommodation. With these works complete, it was perhaps in the 1250s or 1260s that attention switched to the cloister alleys. Elegant new arcades were built to a particularly unusual design, based on two rows of trefoil-headed arches set out in a staggered, or syncopated, pattern.[63] At about the same time, a large infirmary hall was raised on the east side of the complex.[64]

It was presumably Abbot John (c 1267–77) who took the momentous decision to embark on the complete rebuilding of the abbey church in 1269.[65] The sources for the initial design of this new building may be traced, ultimately, to Henry III's rebuilding of Westminster Abbey, from 1245. The principal regional exemplar, however, was probably the north transept at Hereford Cathedral (fig 107), raised c 1255–68. According to the testimony of the fifteenth-century traveller and antiquary William Worcestre, the east end of this new church (Tintern II) was sufficiently advanced by 1288 for the monks to take possession of the presbytery and choir, celebrating the first mass at the high altar.[66] Work on the nave continued to the end of the thirteenth century, when Roger Bigod may have rescued a building programme somewhat in the doldrums, though the whole must have been sufficiently advanced by August 1301 to allow for a prestigious ceremony of dedication. Having requested this ceremony himself,[67] it seems very likely that Bigod was in attendance.[68] Thereafter, the abbey community was engaged with specific elements of furnishing and fitting out of the church well into the fourteenth century. For example, an arcaded porch was added directly outside the west door, probably in the 1320s and, before the end of that decade, a magnificent pulpitum was placed across the east end of the nave at the entrance to the monks' choir (fig 110).[69] Although the floors in the presbytery, choir and transepts may have been covered with tile pavements before the end of the thirteenth century, the tiling recorded from certain areas of the nave must represent a rather later scheme of fitting out.[70] Lastly, there are references from as late as 1340–52 to 'the Keeper of the Work of the church of Tintern'.[71]

Of the building programmes known to have been carried out elsewhere in the monastic complex during the later Middle Ages, one of the most prominent involved various additions and improvements to the abbot's residence. In particular, about 1330–45, an imposing new hall was built above a cellared undercroft on the north-east side of the site, probably with direct access to a landing stage on the river (fig 128). A private chapel was housed on the upper floor of an adjacent two-storey block. In the fifteenth century various additions and alterations were made to the infirmary complex. The aisles of the once open infirmary hall were divided up by partition walls and large new kitchens were introduced to the north, where they might also serve the abbot's residence.[72]

In 1478 Tintern was visited by William Worcestre, who recorded a number of details pertaining to the architecture of the abbey, including various dimensions.[73] It is difficult to know quite what to make of a marginally later record (1490), which notes that Tintern was 'threatened in ruin in its walls, roofs, houses and granges [by] the passage of years and [by] negligence and incompetence'.[74] One last documentary source, the record of a visit by the herald, William Fellow, just five years before the suppression, not only provides us with details of various tomb locations, but also mentions 'a Chappell of St John Babtyste on the north syde of the churche' and a 'chapell of Mary Magdaleyne' on the south side 'of ye sayde monastery'.[75]

The entire precinct at Tintern may have covered up to 11ha, much if not all of it enclosed by a stone wall (fig 128).[76] The wall was broken by at least two outer gateways, one of which stood on the river frontage. There is a record of the abbey's 'great gate'

from 1536, when the monks referred to their 'porter and keeper of our gaol'.[77] The great gate may survive in part as St Anne's, a private house just inside the line of the precinct wall. On the north side of the house there are traces of a thirteenth-century vaulted gate hall. St Anne's also incorporates the remains of a gatehouse chapel. West of the abbey church, the guest house area of the inner court ranges in date from perhaps the late twelfth to the fifteenth centuries.[78]

At the suppression in 1536, the lead on the roofs of the abbey was valued at £124. A contemporary inventory of remaining ecclesiastical goods records a total of 13.3kg (469 ounces) of silver and gilt plate.[79] In March 1537 the site of the monastery and most of its former border possessions were granted to Henry Somerset, second earl of Worcester (d 1549).[80] With important castles at Raglan and Chepstow, Somerset had no desire to convert any part of Tintern to a significant domestic residence, though interestingly several letters he sent to Cromwell in the second half of 1537 were dated at the site.[81] As late as 1541, the king's plumbers were being paid to melt down lead at the abbey. Later still, in 1545–6, Somerset was still expected to pay £217 for lead and bells from Tintern.[82] In any case, the earl and his successor soon chose to lease out tenements and parcels of land in and around the former monastic buildings. By 1568 part of the site was apparently leased to Lady Eleanor Somerset, a dependent member of the family.[83] For the poorer tenants, makeshift homes raised amid the more adaptable cloister chambers had to suffice. Any suitable structure across the precinct area as a whole was probably seen as ripe for conversion to a cottage.[84]

From the 1560s new industrial opportunities at Tintern encouraged yet further tenant occupation. Archaeological excavations west of the abbey church have shown that non-ferrous metalworking began through Cistercian enterprise in the later Middle Ages.[85] From 1566, however, a thriving industrial complex emerged, based on new raw materials. The production of iron wire was attracted to the site by the potential for water power from the adjacent Angidy brook and by plentiful supplies of timber to provide furnace charcoal. The earliest furnace, known as the Laytons, was situated just outside the former monastic precinct, where the Angidy feeds into the Wye. By the end of the seventeenth century another furnace had come into blast and a new forge was in production higher up the Angidy valley. In all, furnaces, forges, mill-leats, ponds and all the associated industrial processes had transformed the abbey environs.[86]

By 1732, when the Buck brothers published their engraving of Tintern (fig 4), it is clear that the north

185 Tintern Abbey: the church, looking west from the presbytery. The presbytery and transept arcades (foreground and left) were more elaborate than those of the nave (in distance). Here the piers featured detached and belted shafts, and the arch mouldings were considerably richer. The eastern crossing arch (top of view) was reset during the conservation works of the early twentieth century. Photograph: Cadw, Crown Copyright

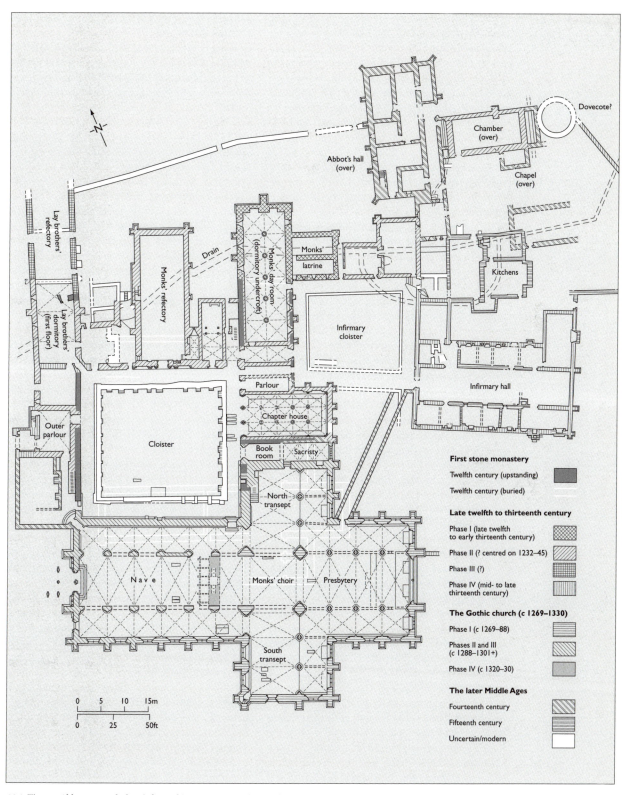

186 *Tintern Abbey: ground plan (after Robinson 2002a, with modifications).* Drawing: *Pete Lawrence, for Cadw*

arcade in the nave had already collapsed. Although a somewhat stylistic record, the Buck view reveals the abbey church much as we see it today.[87] The ruins were at this time largely neglected and overgrown, used by villagers as a fives court, with the body of the church a place to play quoits.[88] Yet, within a few decades, the wooded slopes of the Wye were to became a magnet for droves of 'Romantic' tourists, with Tintern acknowledged as the jewel and highlight of the tour.[89]

From an account recorded later in the eighteenth century, it seems it must have been Charles Somerset (1705–56), fourth duke of Beaufort, who first took a new pride in the ruins. Sometime before his death, the duke appears to have initiated steps to curb the neglect at Tintern. We are told that about the year 1756, 'or nearly that period', upwards of a hundred workmen were engaged by the estate steward to clear the interior of the church, said to have been 'choked up with rubbish, several feet above the present surface'.[90] Alas, some of the 'rubbish' was thrown into the river. The ground was levelled and turfed; fragments of fallen masonry were heaped in ornamental piles around the piers of the nave and presbytery arcades. An attempt was made to protect the good works from vandalism, with locking doors hung at the west front and iron gates used to close off the other principal entry points. However, none of these actions can be explained in terms of a modern concept of conservation. Nor can it be said that the clearance was work motivated by a search for antiquarian knowledge, though 'expectations were formed of finding some valuable reliques belonging to the Abbey'. Such growing pride in the Gothic ruins was, nevertheless, to anticipate the abbey's appeal to an ever-increasing body of visitors arriving in the Wye valley in the later eighteenth century.

Perhaps the most influential of these early tourists was the Revd William Gilpin, who made his Wye river voyage in 1770. It was to be twelve years before he published his acclaimed guidebook, *Observations on the River Wye*, though when it did appear it became an immediate best-seller.[91] Gilpin noted, for example, the effects of the Beaufort improvements to the interior of the church: 'the whole is reduced to one level; cleared of rubbish; and covered with neat turf, closely shorn; and interrupted with nothing'. He was aware, too, of the contrasting scenes of desolation and poverty surrounding the ruins. Referring to the 'wretchedness of the inhabitants', Gilpin noted that they 'occupy little huts, raised among the ruins of the monastery; and seem to have no employment, but begging'.[92] In any case, travellers were soon flocking to the Wye valley in ever greater numbers. From 1793 the local tourist

industry was given a further boost when the outbreak of war with France prevented journeys to favoured wild landscapes abroad, such as those of Switzerland or the Rhine. Instead, as the Monmouth author and bookseller Charles Heath observed, the Wye was 'honoured with a very large share of Public Notice'.[93] Among the best-known visitors of the 1790s were Turner (fig 1), Wordsworth and Coleridge.[94]

As the new century dawned, the burgeoning tourist appeal of Tintern Abbey showed no sign of waning.[95] Crowds of beggars and would-be guides descended on every boat landing at the ruins.[96] Charles Heath could barely keep pace with the demand for his popular guide, producing eleven editions by 1828.[97] A new road, unfortunately cutting through the medieval precinct, was built in the early 1820s and brought with it a new generation of tourists. Writers of the time continued to heap praise on the beauty of the abbey church, but could scarce avoid mentioning the homes of the unfortunate local inhabitants. Like Gilpin and Coxe before them, the early Victorians were disturbed by the surrounding squalor. W H Thomas, for example, wrote of his disappointment at seeing the abbey 'encumbered on every side with unpicturesque cottages and pigsties, rudely built with the consecrated stones of the violated ruin'.[98] With the completion of the Wye Valley Railway in 1876, Tintern became yet more accessible.

Among the earliest signs of a more inquisitive antiquarian interest, we might note the collection of drawings of 1801 by John Carter.[99] Two more superb sets of drawings were produced in the 1840s, the first published by Joseph Potter in 1847, to be followed a year later by the work of Edmund Sharpe.[100] Sadly, however, before any notable written account of the abbey's architecture had appeared, the remains of the pulpitum were stripped out from the nave. The surviving fragments had survived the levelling works of the 1750s and the base remained in position through to the second half of the nineteenth century, when it was captured in several early photographs.[101] Its relevance to the ritual arrangements of the church had been lost, however, and its presence confounded those who wished for an uninterrupted vista along the full length of the building. The pulpitum was removed, without record, probably before 1880.[102] Ironically, this was just before a pioneer study of the ruins was published by the London architect Thomas Blashill (1850–1905). His work might be said to have established the foundations for our current understanding of the development of the abbey complex.[103]

In 1901 Tintern was recognized as a monument of national importance. The abbey was purchased by the Crown from the ninth duke of Beaufort, via the Office of Woods, for the sum of £15,000. The ruins were in a particularly fragile condition, far more so than the authorities initially recognized. From 1901 through to 1913–14, the Office of Woods engaged F W Waller (1846–1933) to supervise the necessary repair and maintenance.[104] Works to the church were of paramount importance, but the domestic buildings around the cloister were also to receive attention.[105] During this period, very limited excavation was conducted by the Corsham architect and antiquary Harold Brakspear (1870–1934),[106] who was also engaged to prepare a ground plan of the abbey. He spent two weeks taking measurements on site, using a gang of labourers put at his disposal to 'excavate' in one or two places.[107]

In 1913–14 responsibility for the conservation of Tintern Abbey passed to the Office of Works. At this time concern was mounting over the safety of the surviving south arcade of the nave. It was thought to be in danger of imminent collapse, and timber shoring had been erected by Waller as an emergency measure. After much debate, reported at length in the architectural press, major structural repairs were undertaken, beginning with the construction of a lattice girder roof over the south aisle. Then, in an enormous – if not breathtaking – operation, with vast temporary brick supports, each of the piers of the arcade had to be dismantled. They were hollowed out to accommodate steel stanchions, which continue to support the great weight of the wall above. In time, as the conservation programme moved forward, the whole appearance of the abbey was transformed. The ivy, so beloved of the early tourists, but which had caused so much decay to the stonework, had to be removed. The post-monastic encroachments were cleared away, and more of the abbey buildings were uncovered and displayed. As a whole, this round of conservation was complete by about 1928.[108]

In the following decades, more of the monastic buildings on the north-east side of the site were uncovered and consolidated for display. Gradually, through to the 1960s, it was possible to add the outline of the infirmary kitchens and the abbot's accommodation to the overall ground plan. The guest house area of the inner court was excavated in 1979–81.[109] In 1997 a small excavation was carried out in the nave to confirm the position of the pulpitum, and there has been a recent archaeological evaluation in advance of a floodlighting scheme.[110] Meanwhile, a major new phase of conservation work on the fabric of the abbey was begun in 1999.

The first official guidebook to Tintern was published by Harold Brakspear and Morton Evans,

going into a second edition in 1910.[111] This was replaced by a further Brakspear guide, which in turn passed through several more editions, with minor modifications to the interpretation.[112] After the war, it was not until 1956 that a totally new guide was produced by Oswin Craster.[113] This was superseded by the initial Cadw guidebook in 1986, now in its fourth edition.[114]

The abbey church, principal monastic buildings and an area of the inner court to the west, are together scheduled as an ancient monument (MM102). A total of about 3.2ha is covered. The watergate has recently been scheduled independently (MM265), and all identified surviving stretches of precinct wall are also so protected (MM157). St Anne's, the house which incorporates the gatehouse chapel, is listed as Grade II (record number 2051).

BIBLIOGRAPHY

Architectural: Baylis 1902–4; Blashill 1878 and 1881–2; Blockley 1997a, 1997b and 1998a; [Brakspear] 1904; Brakspear 1919; Brakspear and Evans 1910; Courtney 1989; Courtney and Gray 1991; Craster 1956; Gardner 1929; Harrison 1997c; Harrison *et al* 1998; Harvey 1922 and 1924; Heath 1793; Hemp 1938; Henderson 1935; Howell 2000; Knowles and St Joseph 1952, 122–3; Lewis 1996; Lewis 1999, 260–1; Newman 2000, 536–57; [Paul] 1898a; Peers 1922; Potter 1847; Robinson 1995a, 1996a and 1997; Robinson 1998, 186–91; Robinson 2002a and 2004; Schlee 2000a and 2000b; Sharpe 1848; Wood 1912; Woof and Hebron 1998; *Archaeol Cambrensis*, 6th ser, **10**, 1910, 485; *Archaeol Cambrensis*, 6th ser, **13**, 1913, 451.

Historical: Blashill 1886; Bradney 1904–32, II, pt 2, 255–63; Harrison 2000; Knowles and Hadcock 1971, 114, 127; O'Sullivan 1947, 38–40; Taylor 1869; Williams 1965–8a; Williams 1976a, 94–146; Williams 1990, 61–4; Williams 1999; Wood 1902–4, 1908 and 1909.

VALLE CRUCIS ABBEY, Denbighshire, St Asaph, SJ 204442

The truly delightful and no less engaging ruins of Valle Crucis Abbey lie just a few kilometres outside the eisteddfod town of Llangollen, at the foot of the very aptly named Horseshoe Pass. In the Middle Ages, this was the commote of Iâl (Yale), a district at the heart of the old Welsh kingdom of Powys.[1] The abbey's founder, encouraged by the abbots of Whitland, Strata Florida, Strata Marcella and Cwmhir, was Madog ap Gruffudd (d 1236), prince of northern Powys.[2] According to the native Welsh chronicle, *Brut y Tywysogyon*, the monastery of Valle Crucis was 'built' in the year 1200.[3] Official Cistercian records, however, date the beginning of conventual life to 28 January 1201.[4] The new house was in any case colonized by a community of monks sent out from Strata Marcella. The Latin name, Valle Crucis ('Valley of the Cross'), is derived from the nearby Pillar of Eliseg, a ninth-century memorial high cross with an inscription recording the ancestry and glories of the kings of Powys.[5] For much of the medieval period, however, Valle Crucis was also known as *Abbatia de Llangwest*, from the original Welsh name for the site, Llanegwestl.[6] Indeed, to ensure the seclusion demanded by the Cistercian authorities, it was necessary for the founder to move at least some of the existing inhabitants of Llanegwestl, making alternative provision for them elsewhere in his lordship.[7]

In addition to the grants offered through his foundation charter, Madog ap Gruffudd bestowed further gifts and privileges upon the early community.[8] On his death in 1236, the prince was buried in the abbey he had founded.[9] In the same year, Madog's son, Gruffudd Maelor (d 1269), confirmed all the gifts and liberties which had been conferred on the house by his father.[10] In all, the Valle Crucis community's landed estates remained centred around Llanegwestl itself.[11] The monks had access to extensive grazing lands for their flocks and herds on the granges of Mwstwr, Hafodyrabad and Buddugre'r Abad. At the more distant lowland 'manor' of Halghton on the Dee, and at Stansty Abbot and Wrexham Abbot, they held larger areas of arable, water meadows and woodland.[12] Yet despite these various agricultural assets, land was not in itself the mainstay of the Valle Crucis economy. The community's real wealth was derived from the tithes of a number of surrounding parishes, including Chirk, Llangollen, Ruabon and Wrexham. Initially granted to help bolster the income of the house in its early decades, by the end of the Middle Ages these appropriated churches were accounting for up to three-quarters of the abbey's entire revenue.[13]

The General Chapter was quick to impose its authority on the early community, reprimanding the abbot within just a year or two of the foundation for not regularly celebrating mass.[14] Three decades later, in 1234, the abbot of Valle Crucis was again in trouble with the General Chapter, this time for allowing women to enter the precincts of the house.[15]

Politically, the community remained loyal to the native Welsh princes, especially the dynasty of northern Powys. This said, for much of the thirteenth century, real political power and authority

lay in neighbouring Gwynedd. Effectively, then, the monks of Valle Crucis were allied at first to Llywelyn ab Iorwerth (d 1240) and then to his grandson, Llywelyn ap Gruffudd (d 1282). In 1274 the abbot was one of several Cistercian heads in Wales who wrote to the pope defending the reputation of Llywelyn ap Gruffudd as a 'protector ... of our Order', countering charges which had been laid against him by Anian, bishop of St Asaph (1268–93).[16] It was perhaps in gratitude that Llywelyn loaned Valle Crucis a total of £40, allowing Abbot Madog (*c* 1275–84) to journey to Rome on the business of his house.[17]

The community's ongoing support for Llywelyn ap Gruffudd was to result in considerable misfortune during the two Welsh wars of Edward I, in 1276–7 and 1282–3.[18] The abbey's estates proved a natural target for the invading English forces, with Valle Crucis one of several Cistercian houses in north and west Wales suffering substantial damage to their property at this time. Moreover, there is good reason to suggest that the impact of the wars extended to the fabric of the monastery itself. His conquest over, Edward sought to make amends with the white monks. In December 1283, for example, he may well have seen war-damaged Valle Crucis at first hand; he certainly made the abbey a gift of £26 13s 4d.[19] Late in 1284, as part of a wider round of payments made in compensation for the impact of the second war, Valle Crucis was awarded £160, by far the largest sum given to any of the Welsh Cistercian houses.[20] Edward I was at Valle Crucis once again in July 1295, resulting in 'oblations of the King at the great altar'.[21]

Some indication of the relative wealth of the abbey at the end of the thirteenth century comes from the *Taxatio Ecclesiastica* of 1291. Here we find evidence to support the view that the wars had taken a heavy toll on the community's landholdings, now valued at just £14 14s 8d.[22] If the figures can be accepted, they suggest the Valle Crucis estates were among the poorest in Wales. However, with the addition of tithes, known to have been appropriated by this time, the total assessment for the house was some £91.

The opening of the fourteenth century was a satisfactory time for the monks of Valle Crucis. For example, they continued to find favour with the princes of northern Powys: the founder's great-grandson was buried before the high altar in 1306 (fig 187).[23] It is worth remembering, too, that the community had become thoroughly involved in Welsh literary activity. Importantly, it seems that the continuation of the native chronicle, *Brut y Tywysogyon*, for the years 1282–1332 was compiled at Valle Crucis.[24] Of equal note, the house maintained its international links with the Cistercian authorities. In spite of a general prohibition on travel abroad, the abbot is known to have attended the General Chapter in 1309.[25] Furthermore, a certain amount of building work was undertaken in the time of Abbot Adam (c 1330–44).[26] Inevitably, however, the community must have faced new difficulties in the wake of the Black Death (1348–50). As elsewhere, it is reasonable to assume that the impact of the plague hastened the abbey's move towards the adoption of an increasingly *rentier* economy.[27] In any event, worse was to follow during the Owain Glyn Dŵr uprising of the early fifteenth century. Although there is no direct record of any destruction at Valle Crucis, the community may well have been caught in the crossfire between the opposing armies.[28] It was left to Robert of Lancaster, bishop of St Asaph (1410–33), who was also allowed to hold the abbacy of Valle Crucis *in commendam*, to restore the house.[29] His term as abbot was extended in 1419, on account of the fact he had both 'repaired the monastery on its destruction by fire', as well as restoring his cathedral.[30]

Under three very notable abbots who ruled the house in the later fifteenth and early sixteenth centuries, Valle Crucis saw a marked revival in its fortunes. The abbots in question, Siôn ap Rhisiart (c 1455–61), Dafydd ab Ieuan (c 1480–1503) and Siôn Llwyd (c 1503–27), earned for themselves considerable reputations as scholars, bardic patrons, collectors of Welsh literary manuscripts and builders.[31] As such, they gave their abbey greater standing in north-east Wales than it had enjoyed for quite some time. It was in the roles of patronage and the provision of bountiful hospitality, however, that these men really excelled. As Glanmor Williams wrote of Siôn ap Rhisiart, comparing his reputation with the white monk ideals of the twelfth century: 'anything less like those bread-and-water-loving ascetics than this *bon vivant* whose "wines and viands made a heaven of earth" it would be hard to find'.[32]

Siôn ap Rhisiart and his successor, Dafydd ab Ieuan, were the chief patrons of the poets Guto'r Glyn and Gutun Owain. Concerning Abbot Dafydd, for example, Guto'r wrote: 'Of Valle Crucis Abbot good, Whose full-stocked tables ever groan, With wine and meat, free as your own'.[33] In another poem dedicated to Dafydd, Guto'r refers to features of the monastery itself. He calls it 'the palace of Peter' and mentions Dafydd's work: 'he gilt and foliated the images, the choir, the chalices, and books'.[34] In very much the same vein, one of Gutun Owain's eulogies in praise of Dafydd runs: 'A place where gold is freely current is the monastery, and its choir excels that of Sarum, and rich are the carvings of the leaves, and of

187 *Valle Crucis Abbey: grave slab of Madog ap Gruffudd, great-grandson of the abbey's founder. He was buried before the high altar in 1306. The slab was found in this position during clearance work by the Ministry of Works in 1956.*

Photograph: *Cadw, Crown Copyright*

the statues'. The same poem goes on to refer to the abbot's fine dwelling house, 'with its skilfully wrought roof'.[35] What makes this body of work of particular interest is the fact that Guto'r Glyn and Gutun Owain were the leading poets of their generation, to whom many of the finest homes of Wales offered an open door. They had probably seen more buildings than most, but the abbots of Valle Crucis 'ranked as high as any on their list of builders of enterprise and good taste'.[36]

The last of the three abbots of this outstanding era was Siôn Llwyd, who won great praise from that master poet of the early sixteenth century, Tudur Aled (d 1526).[37] It is a mark of Abbot Siôn's standing that he was appointed to the commission nominated to compile the Welsh pedigree of Henry VII (1485–1509). In 1518 he was described as 'the king's chaplain and doctor of both laws'.[38]

Unfortunately for Valle Crucis, Siôn Llwyd's

eventual successor was a man of quite different character.[39] Robert Salusbury (1528–35) hailed from an avaricious local gentry family.[40] Youthful and aggressive, Salusbury's poor reputation – to say nothing of his criminal record – was already too well known to the community. On his election to the abbacy, five of the seven monks then in residence promptly left for other monasteries.[41] In the sad chain of events leading to Salusbury's eventual downfall, he also dragged the hitherto good reputation of Valle Crucis into the gutter. In February 1534, at a visitation headed by Abbot Leyshon Thomas of Neath, Abbot Salusbury was accused of various 'crymys and excessys'.[42] The following year, when the king's commissioners, John Vaughan and Adam Becansaw, came to Valle Crucis, they lost no time in having Salusbury arrested for his part in highway robbery.[43] Vaughan and Becansaw noted that there were six monks at the house, but that none was fit to serve as abbot 'as the house is in so much debt and decay'.[44]

One last abbot was installed at Valle Crucis – John Deram, a monk of St Mary Graces in London and probably a Cromwell favourite.[45] In any event, monastic life at the house had very little time left to run. In the *Valor Ecclesiasticus* of 1535, the net income of Valle Crucis was assessed at £188 8s 0d, of which some three-quarters was derived from spiritualities.[46] The final surrender by Abbot Deram and his six monks seems to have occurred between the autumn of 1536 and January 1537.[47]

Valle Crucis Abbey was carefully located in an otherwise narrow and generally steep-sided valley, flanked by the slopes of Coed Hyrddyn and Fron Fawr. The church and monastic buildings were positioned on the west bank of the small but swift-flowing stream, the Nant Eglwyseg, which itself runs south into the nearby River Dee. No trace of a precinct wall survives, though some of the features of the medieval topography can be interpolated from post-suppression sources.[48] Abbey Farm, to the north west of the church and close to the main road, might well represent the site of a gatehouse, or perhaps the home grange. There is a small, but well-built, conduit head at the top of the slope adjacent to the farm, representing one of the points from which fresh water was distributed to the monastic buildings.[49] Much of the thirteenth-century abbey church survives, together with considerable remains of the east range of cloister buildings. Foundations of the south and west ranges have also been excavated and consolidated for display.[50]

At a time when a number of established Cistercian houses in both the north and south of England were adopting radical new designs for their churches, the infant community at Valle Crucis remained faithful to the 'Bernardine' plan (figs 188 and 189). The scheme was for a deliberately modest building, with a short vaulted presbytery, transepts with two eastern chapels and a nave of just five bays. The construction programme must have been initiated soon after the foundation, with work at the east end well advanced by about 1225–30, to judge from the sculptural detailing. It seems likely that by the mid-thirteenth century considerable progress would also have been made on the nave (fig 190). For Roland Paul, the fabric sequence was to be understood in two principal phases: the presbytery, transepts and the south wall of the nave representing phase one; the nave piers and remaining walls following with no great gap in phase two.[51] Ralegh Radford, on the other hand, chose to see the entire ground plan established in a single phase.[52] Either way, before the overall scheme was complete, an undocumented but drastic fire swept through the monastery, staining the lower courses of stonework in the church a deep, rose-red colour and leaving archaeological traces of its impact in the southern and western claustral ranges.[53] Further damage is to be inferred from the compensation payments made to the community in the 1280s, following Edward I's Welsh wars.

In the wake of these episodes, the original design of the church was slightly modified, and in due course the entire building was completed. Among the earliest changes were those made to the west front, especially the insertion of the central doorway with its foliate capitals and richly moulded arch. The upper part of the presbytery also belongs to this second stage of building, as does the remarkable buttress arrangement to its east facade (fig 119). Furthermore, it was presumably the early fire which created a weakness in the south-west crossing pier, necessitating its rebuilding and the introduction of a massive supporting wall in the adjacent bay of the nave arcade. There is greater uncertainty surrounding the chronology of the principal windows in the west front, where each of the two-light openings was surmounted by a cusped circle, the whole being framed within an enclosing arch which appears both inside and out. The composition might belong to the third quarter of the thirteenth century, though it is possible the work followed the Edwardian war damage. Early fourteenth-century tiles are known from the site, indicating a phase of furnishing and fitting out (fig 191).[54] A rare inscription on the west gable of the nave reveals that further reconstruction must have taken place around 1330–44 (fig 121).[55]

The principal cloister ranges, which lay to the

south of the church, were initially raised as part of the early building campaigns. The best survival of this work is the barrel-vaulted sacristy adjoining the south transept. The foundations of a mid-thirteenth-century refectory, orientated north–south, have also been excavated.[56] Stylistic evidence suggests that the east range was almost entirely rebuilt in the mid-fourteenth century (fig 125), with the chapter house standing as the most prominent survival of this extensive programme of work (fig 150).[57] Radford, however, felt that the dating should remain open to question,[58] particularly given the belief that Valle Crucis suffered damage during the Welsh uprising of the early fifteenth century. We must bear in mind the claims made by Abbot Robert of Lancaster in 1419 that he had been responsible for repairs to the monastery, 'on its destruction by fire'.[59]

Confirmation that the bardic tributes of the later fifteenth and early sixteenth centuries were not mere poetic exaggerations is provided by additional architectural evidence in the east range.[60] It was probably during the time of Dafydd ab Ieuan (c 1480–1503) that the northern half of the monks' dormitory was converted to serve as a comfortable suite of accommodation for the abbot himself. His hall appears to have been contained within the main range, though a camera or private apartment was fashioned in an extension sitting over the eastern part of the sacristy (figs 125 and 157). As a yet more drastic indication of the changes to communal Cistercian life, the scheme may even have involved the removal of at least the east cloister arcade.

Following the suppression, in July 1537 the Valle Crucis estates were acquired on a lease of twenty-one years by the Yorkshireman Sir William Pickering (d 1542).[61] The property passed to his son, Sir William Pickering II (d 1574), who in 1551–2 was granted a further lease of sixty-six years.[62] The Pickering heiress, Hester, was married to Edward Wootton (d 1625) of Boughton Malherbe in Kent. Lord Wootton, as he became in 1603, acquired yet a further lease from James I,[63] and was in turn succeeded by his son, Thomas (d 1630). Thomas's widow, Mary, lost the Valle Crucis estate about 1651, possibly as a result of sequestration or confiscation.[64] It was later purchased by John Trevor, and in time became part of the Coed Helen estate.[65]

The east range of monastic buildings, including the abbot's residence, was retained by the Pickerings for use as a tenant farm. Other structures were pressed into agricultural use, with the refectory perhaps serving as a barn. A large quantity of lead, valued at over £16, was still at the site in 1546.[66] Meanwhile, both the abbey and the newly converted house had become targets for the local gentry,

envious of the Pickering lease. Between 1542 and 1544 Edward Almer seems to have made several raids on the site, taking away stone and glass for use in his own mansion at Pant Iocyn. About 1584 a number of local inhabitants were accused of making severe depredations to the 'mansion house' of Valle Crucis and pulling down the 'great and high stone walls'. The resident around this time was Edward Davies.[67] In 1606, Lord Wootton had a detailed survey made of the estate. The abbey tenant was now Richard Matthews, who occupied the 'dwellinge house' and also held 'one dovehouse, one barne [and] one garden'. He was still in possession of the property in 1623.[68] It is difficult to say how long the house remained occupied thereafter, though it may have been abandoned in the later seventeenth century. The 1742 print by the brothers Buck certainly shows a roofless building.[69] Just how much faith should be placed in this topographical evidence is a moot point, though in any case the former east range was again occupied before 1800, as shown for example in a view by Paul Sandby (fig 5), and continued to serve as a farmhouse through into the nineteenth century. Valle Crucis, meanwhile, became one of the key stopping points for tourists in search of the picturesque in north Wales, publicized by influential writers such as William Gilpin and John Byng.[70]

Various details were recorded in a collection of early nineteenth-century drawings by John Chessell Buckler (d 1894),[71] but the first significant antiquarian interest in Valle Crucis is to be traced to a paper published in 1846 by the Revd John Williams (Ab Ithel), appearing in the journal of the newly formed Cambrian Archaeological Association.[72] Williams described the Cistercian setting as a 'home of peace and happiness – a paradise for restored man'. He went on: 'In the midst of these hallowed precincts the rubbish is heaped up to a great height … and ash-trees grow luxuriantly upon the mounds, adding to the picturesque effect of the ruin'.[73] This is perhaps just the condition in which the site was seen and planned by the Revd John Parker about 1850 (fig 8).[74] Williams further informs us that the 'abbot's house' remained tenanted to a farmer, but, he wrote, 'a lady resides close behind the abbey church, which may be said to be her special custody, and she shows it to visitors'.[75]

Archaeological investigations of the ruins began in 1851–2, with the work directed by Viscount Dungannon and Watkin Wynne. From the brief report on the year-long clearance programme, it seems that 'earth and rubbish to the depth of four feet from the west door to the east end' were removed. In the process, 'a very large quantity of hewn stones were discovered … some of them

188 *Valle Crucis Abbey: crossing and presbytery, looking east. Begun in the early thirteenth century, the 'Bernardine' church was designed with a regularized crossing from the outset. The south-west crossing pier may have been weakened during a disastrous fire in the mid-thirteenth century, necessitating its rebuilding and strengthening. The pulpitum was probably moved to its position between the two western crossing piers in the early fourteenth century. A fragment can be seen to the right, with a nave altar in front.* Photograph: *Cadw, Crown Copyright*

elaborately carved'. In addition, four 'monumental tombstones were discovered in the chancel'.[76] Capitals were left piled up against the wall of the south aisle and a commemorative tablet placed on the same wall. Eleven years later, an anonymous correspondent, signing himself 'A Traveller', was harshly critical of the work, which he felt had been done 'in a rather "botchy" manner'. This same writer was also fearful of the impact of mass tourism, bemoaning the 'excursion trains' arriving at Llangollen from the 'manufacturing districts' of England, which then 'vomit forth their miscellaneous crowds upon the abbey'.[77]

In 1872 the west front of the abbey church was restored under the direction of Sir Gilbert Scott (d 1878).[78] Further excavation (or rather clearance) and

restoration were carried out towards the end of the nineteenth century under the direction of the Revd H T Owen, who occupied the position of warden of the abbey.[79] It was at this time that much of the cloister and west range were cleared for the first time. Meanwhile, the upstanding buildings were discussed in some detail by E P Loftus Brock,[80] and then with much greater authority by Harold Hughes.[81] The abbey was taken into the care of the State in 1950 and a new round of consolidation was initiated. As 'part of a policy to improve the appearance and understanding of the ruins', the west and south cloister ranges, hitherto still covered with farm walls and accumulated debris, were excavated in 1970.[82] Further archaeological evaluation and minor excavation was carried out to the west of the abbey

292

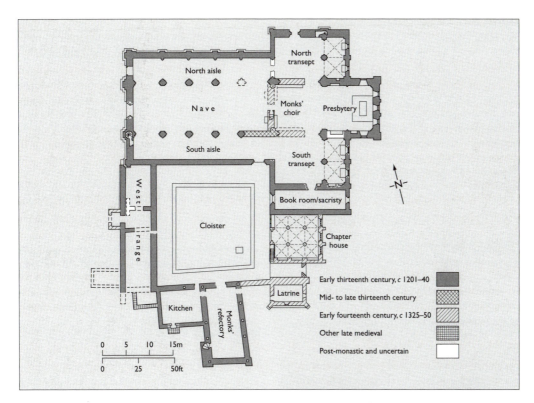

189 *Valle Crucis Abbey: ground plan (after Radford 1953/Evans 1995, with modifications).*

Drawing: *Pete Lawrence, for Cadw*

church in 1993–4 in connection with the construction of a new visitor centre.[83] The official guide was published by Ralegh Radford,[84] since supplemented by the Cadw guidebook.[85]

An area of some 1.9ha, including the church, the principal cloister ranges and a fragment of the monastic precinct, is scheduled as an ancient monument (DE3). The site also features in the register of landscapes, parks and gardens in Wales (Grade II), chiefly on account of the eighteenth-century summerhouse aligned on a substantial pond on the east side of the church and monastic buildings.[86]

BIBLIOGRAPHY

Architectural: Brock 1878a; Butler 1976b; Dungannon 1852; Evans 1995; Gresham 1968, 254–5; Holme 1929; Hubbard 1986, 292–7; Hughes 1894 and 1895a; [Hughes] 1935; Jones 1866; [Kernan and Whittle] 1995, 264–5; Knowles and St Joseph 1952, 110–11; Lewis 1999, 262; Lovegrove 1936; Owen 1895; [Paul] 1899a; Price 1952; Radford 1953; RCAHMCW 1914, 161–5; Robinson 1998, 194–7; Silvester 2001; Thomas 1993 and 1994; Williams (*Ab Ithel*) 1846; *Archaeol Cambrensis*, **101**, 1950–1, 116; *Archaeol Cambrensis*, **106**, 1957, 107.

Historical: Knowles and Hadcock 1971, 114, 127; Jones 1866; O'Sullivan 1947, 18–19; Pratt 1997; Price 1952; Williams 1990, 64–6; Williams (*Ab Ithel*) 1846.

190 *Valle Crucis Abbey: sculpted capitals, east processional doorway, first half of the thirteenth century.* Photograph: *Cadw, Crown Copyright*

WHITLAND ABBEY, Carmarthenshire, St Davids, SN 208182

Whitland was one of just four Cistercian houses in England and Wales directly colonized from St Bernard's Clairvaux (figs 17 and 19).[1] Its foundation can almost certainly be attributed to the first Norman bishop of St Davids, Bernard (1115–48), a former royal servant foisted on the see by Henry I. The evidence suggests that he brought the initial community of monks to south-west Wales in 1140.[2] By 1144 they were probably settled on diocesan land at Little Trefgarn north of Haverfordwest.[3] Several years after Bernard's death, however, perhaps about 1151 (if not earlier), the community moved to a more suitable site at Whitland, where land within the Norman lordship of St Clears had been granted by a Devon man named John of Torrington.[4]

In the late 1160s, as Rhys ap Gruffudd began to consolidate his hold over the kingdom of Deheubarth, he willingly assumed the mantle of Whitland's patron.[5] The prince's liberal endowments, later confirmed by King John, undoubtedly did much to ensure the early community's economic well being.[6] Indeed, in the mid-fifteenth century, it was claimed that the early monastery was 'so richly endowed' it was able to support a hundred monks in addition to servants.[7] Some confirmation of the twelfth-century abbey's numerical strength comes from the fact it was able to colonize three daughter houses in the heart of Wales by 1176, at Strata Florida, Strata Marcella and Cwmhir. Two more colonies were later sent to Ireland, to Comber and Tracton (figs 17 and 19).[8]

In the early years of the thirteenth century, Whitland was ruled for a while by Abbot Cadwgan (1203–15). The *Cronica de Wallia*, which may in any case have originated at Whitland, describes him as 'an extraordinarily eloquent and wise man'.[9] Gerald of Wales thought rather differently, preferring to see him as ambitious and cunning.[10] Cadwgan had earlier been a monk at Strata Florida, and in 1215 was promoted to the see of Bangor. In 1236 he retired to Dore Abbey.[11] In his time at Whitland, it is possible he was responsible for certain modifications to the east end of the abbey church.

Whitland's landed estates, held mainly in the modern counties of Carmarthenshire and Ceredigion, were divided more or less evenly between areas of upland pasture and lowland holdings more suited to arable cultivation. By the late thirteenth century, these estates were worked from up to seventeen grange centres.[12] The three largest arable granges at the time averaged around four and a half carucates each, perhaps 162 to 202ha, but on the basis of the *Taxatio Ecclesiastica* of 1291, the abbey was farming over 2,025ha of arable in total, with at least 1,100 sheep on its pastures.[13] The value of the house at this time was assessed at a modest £43 15s 4d.[14] In time, estates were consolidated, and those at Castell Cossam and Rhuddlan Defi eventually accounted for nearly half the abbey's income from landed property.

The comparatively low valuation recorded for Whitland in 1291 may reflect damage inflicted on its estates during the Welsh wars of Edward I.[15] In fact, although an inquiry had rightfully assessed that the figure for compensation should be £260, the abbot was still suing for payment in the reign of Edward II (1307–27).[16] Suspicions of a house which had long connived to promote the Welsh cause found open expression during the Owain Glyn Dŵr uprising of the early fifteenth century, when the abbot of Whitland was accused of being 'a rebel'.[17] To some degree, it may have been the lasting effects of the rebellion which contributed to an ongoing period of economic difficulty for the community. By 1440 Abbot David (1433–43) was claiming that Whitland was 'so diminished by ravages of sword and fire' that the revenues of his 'monastery, houses, buildings and barns' were insufficient to support himself and eight monks.[18]

In the *Valor Ecclesiasticus* of 1535, Whitland's net annual income was assessed at £135 3s 6d.[19] And, although the house was suppressed in the wake of the 1536 Act,[20] it was formally re-founded 'by virtue of the king's restitution' on 25 April 1537. It seems that

191 Valle Crucis Abbey: counter-relief tile, first half of the fourteenth century. The design depicts a man standing between two trees, probably in costume of c 1340 or later. He may be admiring himself in a mirror, or perhaps holds a cadge, the ring on which hawks were carried during hunting. Tiles of similar design and date are known from Strata Florida and Strata Marcella.

Photograph: National Museums & Galleries of Wales

Abbot William was obliged to put up the enormous sum of £400 for this privilege.[21] As a result, when visited by John Leland around this very time, he noted 'Ty Gwyn ar Tav [Whitland], Barnardines, still stondeth'.[22] The brief respite lasted less than two years, and Whitland Abbey was finally surrendered on 12 February 1539, by which time there were just five monks in residence.[23]

Considering the uncertainty surrounding the initial location of the abbey, it is hardly surprising that nothing is known of any temporary structures raised by the founding colony over the first decade (c 1140–51). As for the permanent buildings, these were set up on the broad east bank of the south-flowing Colomendy brook, just above its confluence with the Afon Gronw, itself a major tributary of the Afon Tâf.[24] The surviving remains include the recently excavated footings of the abbey church, together with fragments of the northern end of the west range (fig 192).

The church, which must have been well advanced within a decade or two of the community's arrival on this site, was of the classic 'Bernardine' plan. It featured a short square-ended presbytery, two chapels to each transept and an eight-bay nave. The nave, at least, must have been of a very similar scale and appearance to that at Margam, with piers of virtually identical plan (fig 44). Likewise, the east end seems to have been designed with an unsegregated crossing. From the evidence of the plan alone, this twelfth-century structure remained largely unaltered throughout the abbey's history. In the early thirteenth century, however, various modifications were made in the area of the crossing, with walls introduced to close off the transepts. Moreover, loose architectural fragments suggest that a rib vault, with a 'domino' motif similar to that identified at Strata Florida, may have been inserted in the presbytery. In this context, it is worth considering the possibility that the instigator of this work may have been Abbot

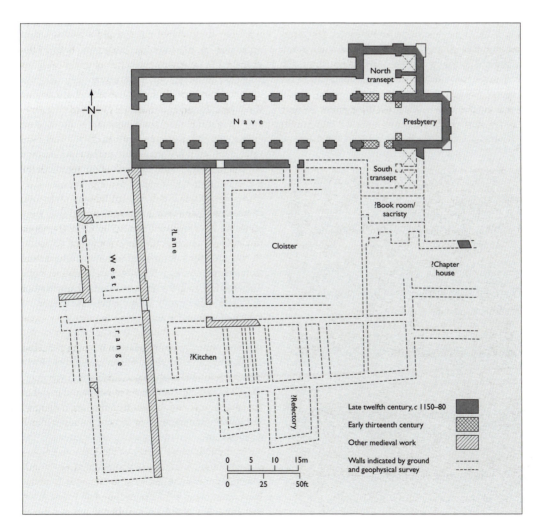

192 *Whitland Abbey: ground plan (after Ludlow 2002, with modifications).*

Drawing: *Pete Lawrence, for Cadw*

Cadwgan (1203–15), who had come to Whitland from Strata Florida. Matching the detail of these architectural developments to the chronologies of tile pavements is difficult, but it is also tempting to associate a known early grouping with the wider programme of modifications.[25]

In the late thirteenth century the Deheubarth prince, Maredudd ap Rhys Gryg (d 1271), was buried 'on the steps in front of the altar'.[26] Fragments of tile pavements found in the south-west corner of the presbytery and on the north side of the crossing suggest a new phase of refurbishment in the late thirteenth or early fourteenth century (fig 193).[27] An area of thick stone flagging uncovered in the north transept during the recent excavations may have been lain during the later Middle Ages and was possibly associated with a timber screen dividing the transept in two.[28]

The cloister was situated to the south of the church. Here, apart from the standing fragments of the west range, a recent geophysical survey has confirmed the general disposition of the buildings (fig 192). In the area of the south range, the results suggest that a north–south refectory may have replaced a primary east–west arrangement. To the east, the survey indicates that the eventual plan of the chapter house extended beyond the width of the range proper, and to the west there seems to have been a wide lay brothers' lane, beyond which are the surviving traces of the range itself. In the extensive

assemblage of dressed stone fragments recovered from the excavations, there is a sizeable quantity of material described as 'Perpendicular in style'. Some of this material could well have come from a late rebuilding of the cloister arcades.[29]

Following the final suppression, in 1545 the abbey demesne was acquired on lease by Dr John Vaughan of Narbeth, one of the royal commissioners who had been appointed by Cromwell to look into the affairs of the Welsh religious houses in 1535–6.[30] For a while at least, Vaughan may have settled at the abbey site, occupying the 'manor house of Whitland'.[31] Despite this, many of the former monastery buildings were soon subject to unlicensed plunder. The chief culprits seem to have been John Vaughan himself, together with several other prominent locals, notably Sir John Perrot (d 1592), along with Richard Vaughan and his son Richard Vaughan the younger. A special commission was set up in 1581 to investigate 'the spoilation of Whytland Abbey'. The inquest was told of the wholesale removal of iron, lead gutters, glass, timber, statuary and even the effigy of the 'late abott' of the house. Only the 'grett chamber and two little other chambers' were spared, as they were under lock and key. Perrot's agents was particularly busy 'digging and hewinge out of the free stones' and carrying them away for his conversion of Laugharne Castle.[32]

Clearly, the abbey buildings must already have been much reduced when, in 1636, an ironworks was established at Whitland by the industrialist George Mynne (d 1648).[33] Making ready use of the monastic water engineering, as well as the supply of building stone, Mynne was licensed to cut timber for charcoal and to erect 'two forges and one ffurnace'. The work seems to have followed somewhat varied fortunes, but by the late eighteenth century it was in the hands of the Morgan family, great Carmarthenshire ironmasters. In 1825 the Morgan heiress married The Hon Henry Yelverton, who acquired Whitland in 1836 and subsequently built the present mansion to the south east of the main abbey buildings.

The earliest investigation of the monastic remains was apparently undertaken in the later 1830s, after the property had been acquired by Henry Yelverton. In 1837 it was reported in the *Gentleman's Magazine* that 'the bases of several clustered pillars of the church were revealed', along with 'foundations of extensive buildings, as of cloisters or monastic cells, a doorway and several architectural fragments, the style of which was decidedly of the 12th century'.[34] A drawing of 1838, by Charles Norris, seems to record something of these excavations (fig 49).[35] Thirty years later, the Revd William Thomas pointed out that the walls of the abbey church 'are still to be

193 Whitland Abbey: relief tile, second half of the thirteenth century. In a frieze set between two concentric circles, the design incorporates shields of arms alternating with animals. At the centre is an Agnus Dei motif. The precise spot from which the tile was recovered is unknown.

Photograph: *National Museums & Galleries of Wales*

seen'.[36] The RCAHMCW account of 1917 added little of substance. Greater clarity emerged after the investigation and planning of the site by Alfred Clapham in the early 1920s.[37] With local interest growing, excavations were undertaken in 1926 by the Carmarthen-based architect Ernest Collier. Unfortunately the work was never published in full, with only brief interim reports appearing.[38] Almost all Collier's work was focused on the abbey church. He cut trenches across the nave and north transept, and seems to have 'cleared' the presbytery.[39]

Nothing more was done at Whitland until an earthwork survey was carried out by Terry James in the late 1970s. His work revealed details of the precinct topography and drew attention to the post-monastic industrial history of the site.[40] In the mid-1990s, in advance of a scheme to consolidate and landscape the ruins for public display, evaluation and clearance excavations were undertaken by the Dyfed Archaeological Trust.[41] Again, this work focused on the abbey church and was of necessity of a rather superficial nature. It was largely restricted to Collier's trenches, with the excavators working down to a level suitable for display, without disturbing the underlying archaeology.[42] Programmes of geophysical

survey, topographical survey and standing building recording were carried out in 1999 to supplement the results of the excavations.[43] The whole has been brought together for publication by Neil Ludlow.[44]

In the Colomendy valley to the north of the site, there are extensive earthworks defining elements of the precinct, including watercourses, fishponds and several dams. Further fishponds have been identified to the west of the abbey. The precise site of the later forge or forges has yet to be identified.[45]

The site of the church and cloister is scheduled as an ancient monument (CM14), with some 1.4ha covered, but the area takes in very little of the surrounding precinct.

BIBLIOGRAPHY

Architectural: Clapham 1921, 205–8; [Collier] 1925–6; Collier 1927; Crane 1995; *GM* 1839; James 1978; James 2000, 58–9; Lewis 1999, 262–3; Ludlow 2000, 2001 and 2002; RCAHMCW 1917, 151–3; Richard 1935–9, 346–7, 364–8; Robinson 1998, 204–5; Schlee and Wilson 1999.
Historical: Knowles and Hadcock 1971, 115, 128; Ludlow 2002; O'Sullivan 1947, 8–10; Williams 1990, 66–8.

NOTES

PREFACE

1 In this context, the scholar who has laboured most heroically on our behalf is Father Chrysogonus Waddell, a monk of Gethsemani Abbey. His three seminal studies, *Narrative and Legislative Texts from Early Cîteaux* (1999; henceforth *Narrative Texts*), *Cistercian Lay Brothers: Twelfth-Century Usages with Related Texts* (2000; henceforth *Lay Brothers*) and *Twelfth-Century Statutes from the Cistercian General Chapter* (2002; henceforth *Statutes*) are now essential sources.

2 Almost half a century ago, Marcel Aubert asked whether 'a school of Cistercian architecture' can ever be said to have existed in reality (Aubert 1958). Of course, we cannot overlook the occasional twelfth-century reference to the raising of wooden buildings 'according to the form of the order' (Fergusson 1983, 76; 1984a, 24), or the reprimands for later buildings put up in stone 'against the form of the order', as at Longpont in Picardie in 1192 (*Statutes*, 244; Norton 1986, 338). On the other hand, discussion of the influence of St Bernard of Clairvaux (d 1153) on the twelfth-century Cistercian architectural aesthetic, and the notion of a distinct 'Bernardine' creation, has all but gone away on the wind. Nevertheless, the debate concerning ideals is a wide one and remains implicit in almost every architectural work on the Cistercians. For a recent European overview, see Kinder 1997.

3 For the fourteen sites (thirteen in modern Wales and one in Herefordshire), see catalogue entries.

4 The *Vita Prima* is the most authoritative of the four twelfth-century lives of St Bernard. It was composed by three men writing successively: William of St Thierry (d 1148), Arnold (or Ernald) of Bonneval and Geoffrey of Auxerre, abbot of Clairvaux (1161–5). The full text is to be found in Migne 1844–64, CLXXXV, cols 225–368. There is a vast literature on the *Vita Prima*, but for a concise and masterly overview, see Brooke 1986, 18–22, and the fuller insight given in Bredero 1996, 23–140. For an introduction and extracts, see Matarasso 1993, 19–41. On the importance of a careful reading for the significance of the building programme at Clairvaux, see Gajewski 2004, 71–2. For St Bernard himself, see the summary in Farmer 1992, 51–2, and (more significantly) Bredero 1996, together with the various papers in Sommerfeldt 1992 and in Pressouyre and Kinder 1992.

5 Clairvaux, which lay in the diocese of Langres (and is now in the French department of Aube), was founded as the fourth daughter of Cîteaux in 1115. St Bernard was appointed as the first abbot, and remained there until his death in 1153. On the location and what survives, see Peugniez 2001, 120–3. For the present state of published knowledge, see the collection of essays brought together in Leroux 1991, with much summarized in Kinder 1996b. A further set of short essays appears in Selle 1998. See also Schlink 1970, 91, 108–16, 138–41; Dimier 1974; Fergusson 1994.

6 The passage appears in Migne 1844–64, CLXXXV, cols 284–5. For various translations, see Braunfels 1972, 243–4 (largely followed here); Webb and Walker 1960, 86–8; Brooke 1986, 21. We might remember Bernard's harsh criticisms of excesses in monastic art and architecture in his celebrated *Apologia* of *c* 1125, on which more is said below (*see* chapter 1), but see Rudolph 1990.

7 Migne 1844–64, CLXXXV, col 285. This, at least, has been the orthodox view accepted by many scholars. In sum, it was Clairvaux I (the *monasterium vetus* as it has been called since the eighteenth century) which was the complex regarded as too small by Bernard's advisers. Work on Clairvaux II began *c* 1135 (or perhaps 1133), under the patronage of Count Theobald of Blois (d 1152). The new church was consecrated ten years later: Aubert 1947, I, 64; Kinder 1996b, 371; Frankl 2000, 93.

8 This is all too clear from Kinder 1991.

9 It was Dom Nicolas Milley who called the original settlement to the west of the later complex the *monasterium vetus*. For copies of his principal drawings, see Aubert 1947, I, 3, 9, 11; Kinder 1991; Pressouyre and Kinder 1992, 216–17. The principal source for plans of Clairvaux I, II and III (as known) is Dimier 1949–67, I, plans 82–84. For differing views on the fabric of the *monasterium vetus*, see Schaefer 1982, 4–8; Kinder 1991, 206–8; Coppack 2004, 39.

10 Untermann (1984, 618–24) has suggested (without much evidence) that the start date for Clairvaux II should be pushed back to the 1120s. Dr Alexandra Kennedy [Gajewski] argues convincingly for the 1130s, but challenges Bonneval's account. Using a range of pictorial and documentary evidence, she concludes that the building so familiar to us from the 1708 drawings cannot be a church of the 1130s, and that it represents an entirely new rebuild, begun *c* 1148–53. If true, then she assumes a church of rather more modest scale may have been constructed in the 1130s: Kennedy [Gajewski] 1996, 131–65. For similar views, see also Schlink 1970, 108–19, 138–41; Henriet 2001, 275–8. There are also closely worded summaries of these arguments in Frankl 2000, 317–18, notes 51A, 55.

11 The plan form has been dubbed 'Bernardine', primarily based on the arguments in Esser 1953 and 1954; Hahn 1957, 84–124. The views of these authors on uniformity are explored further below (*see* chapter 5).

12 There were eighty-six Cistercian monasteries in Britain: sixty-two in England, thirteen in Wales and eleven in Scotland. Another thirty-three houses were established in Ireland, and there was one abbey on the Isle of Man. These figures do not include temporary or aborted foundations, nor do they take account of the nunneries identified as Cistercian. For England and Wales, see Knowles and Hadcock 1971, 110–28; for Scotland, Fawcett 1994, 132–9; for Ireland, Stalley 1987, 239–50. See also the catalogue in Robinson 1998, 63–205 (authored by Glyn Coppack, Richard Fawcett and David Robinson, hereafter referred to under the editor's name).

13 The only other recent attempt to assess the Welsh material as a whole is Butler 1994, though one should not overlook Williams 2001, 99–125.

14 For much of what follows, see Davies 1987, 3–23.

15 Talbot 1967, 261–2.

INTRODUCTION
DESPOILMENT AND REDISCOVERY

1 The official instructions to the king's commissioners were that they should 'pull down to the ground all the walls of the churches, stepulls, cloysters, fraterys, dorters, chapter howsys and the rest … leaving only houses necessary for a farmer': *Let Pap Henry VIII*, 11, 105.

2 For the process in general, see Knowles 1948–59, III, 383–8; Fergusson 1984a, 157–60; Williams, G 1997, 95–6; Coppack 1998, 124–31; also Aston 1973. For a summary of events at the Welsh Cistercian houses, see Williams 2001, 88–92. For one example of a sale of goods (at Dore), see Williams 1970–8b, and for a case study (Tintern), see Courtney and Gray 1991, 145–9.

3 With the exception, of course, of those maintained in whole (eg, Tewkesbury, Sherborne) or in part (eg, Malmesbury, Pershore) for parochial worship, or those converted to serve as new cathedrals (eg, St Peter's, Gloucester, St Augustine's, Bristol).

4 What is known of the sequence of events at individual sites is outlined in the catalogue entries. As yet, no historian has attempted to look in detail at the overall pattern of post-suppression usage at Welsh monastic sites.

5 See, for example, Andrews 1989, 94–105; Woof and Hebron 1998, 103–78; Robinson 2002a, 21–3.

6 We might also include the church at Aberconwy, converted for parish worship in the late thirteenth century, even if transformed almost beyond recognition.

7 RCAHMW 1981, 78–89.

8 Moore and Moore 1974; RCAHMW 1981, 323–31.

9 James 2000, 58–9.

10 A new house was built at the site in the 1650s: Butler 1987.

11 Bradney 1904–32, III, pt 2, 227–8; Newman 2000, 336.

12 Robinson and Platt 1998, 23, 43.

13 Pratt 1997, 39–49.

14 Smith 2001, 447, 469–71.

15 Williams 1992, 82–3.

16 Williams 2001, 89.

17 Owen 1917, 74–82.

18 On which, see Haslam 1979, 140–2; Radford 1982, 70–3.

19 Owen 1919, 29–31.

20 Owen 1935, 360–3. For the full inquiry, see PRO, E178/3349.

21 Williams 2001, 90.

22 Woof and Hebron 1998, 132. I know of only one earlier view of Tintern, an engraving of the west front, *c* 1710–18: Bodleian Library, Gough Maps 44, fol 59.

23 The Buck views of these abbeys were published in 1741–2. For early antiquarianism and Cistercian sites, see Fergusson 1984a, 160–2.

24 On which, see Courtney and Gray 1991, 150–3; Coates 1992.

25 Williams 1995, 1–2; Robinson 2002a, 21–2; and catalogue entry.

26 For Cistercian sites and the Romantic movement in England, see Fergusson 1984a, 162–4. For the Wye valley, Andrews 1989, 84–107.

27 For Fountains, see Coppack 2003, 132–9; for Furness, Dade-Robertson 2000, 11–40; for Roche, Fergusson 1984a, 162.

28 See the many examples in Woof and Hebron 1998, 103–80.

29 Andrews 1989, 118–19.

30 Derrick Pratt has catalogued no fewer than eighty-eight different engravings of Valle Crucis: Pratt 1997, 67 n 17.

31 RCAHMW 1981, 324–5; [Whittle] 2000, 102–13.

32 For general background on what follows, see Williams 1995; Williams 2001, 285–92.

33 For Carter's work, see BL, Add. MS 29938, fols 131v–153 (Tintern); BL, Add. MS 29940, fols 62–81 (Margam). For Buckler's drawings, see BL, Add. MS 27763, fols 75–156; BL, Add. MS 36402, fols 31–35, 40–42 (Dore); BL, Add. MS 36417, fols 24–25, 46–50 (Valle Crucis). Buckler seems to have collected material for a projected volume on 'Cistercian Architecture'. It can be found as three volumes at BL, Add. MS 27763–27765. See also the observations in Fergusson and Harrison 1999, 190–1, 252 nn 8–9.

34 The only record of this work is that provided in [Rees] 1849, 244–55.

35 GM 1839, 597; James 1978, 72.

36 For Strata Florida, see *Archaeol Cambrensis*, 2, 1847, 361; for Valle Crucis, Dungannon 1852.

37 Potter 1847; Sharpe 1848. Potter's volume of plates, also featuring Buildwas Abbey in Shropshire, is reckoned to be the earliest set of measured drawings of Cistercian buildings to be published in this country: Fergusson 1984a, 91 n 2. The wider study by Edmund Sharpe (1874–7) was a further landmark around this time.

38 For Tintern, see Blashill 1881–2; for Strata Florida, Williams 1889a and 1889b; for Strata Marcella, [Jones] and Williams 1891; for Cwmhir, Williams 1890a; for Valle Crucis, Hughes 1894 and 1895b. For a general assessment of those investigations in Wales up until this time, see Williams 1995, 3–14; and for the work of the energetic Stephen Williams at Cwmhir, Strata Florida and Strata Marcella, see Williams 1992, 72–84. On Ireland in this period, see Stalley 1987, 4–5.

39 Between them, the two men investigated Beaulieu (Hope and Brakspear 1906), Byland, Forde, Fountains (Hope 1900a), Furness (Hope 1900b), Hailes (Brakspear 1901), Jervaulx (Hope and Brakspear 1911), Kirkstall (Hope and Bilson 1907), Louth Park, Pipewell, Rievaulx, Sibton, Stanley (Brakspear 1906–7) and Waverley (Brakspear 1905). Additional sources for the publication of these excavations will be found in Fergusson 1984a, 117–48, *passim*; Robinson 1998, 81–175, *passim*.

40 The paper in question, Bilson 1909, reused much of the material first covered by the architect in his contribution to Hope and Bilson 1907, 73–141. His transformation of the insular focus in scholarship is a point made in Fergusson 1984a, xxiii.

41 For some account of the background to guardianship in Wales around this time, see Taylor 1946b. Meanwhile, in Scotland, it is only at Dundrennan Abbey, in State care since 1840, that the Crown works pre-date those at Tintern. For the context of the initial Tintern conservation programme, see Robinson 1997; Robinson 2002a, 25.

42 In Scotland, apart from Dundrennan, five more Cistercian abbeys were taken into State care between 1913 and 1933: information from Dr Richard Fawcett.

43 Dr C A Ralegh Radford (1900–98) played a not insignificant role during this period, and was responsible for three of the official guidebooks to Welsh Cistercian sites: Radford 1935, 1946 and 1953.

44 Much the same conclusion is reached on the English and Scottish abbeys: Fergusson 1984a, xxiii; Dr Richard Fawcett, pers comm. For a detailed account of the approach at Rievaulx, with much in common with that at Tintern, see Fergusson and Harrison 1999, 195–211.

45 On France, see Aubert 1947, since supplemented, for example, by Bruzelius 1979; Dimier 1982; Bruzelius 1990.

46 On Germany, see Eydoux 1952, supplemented by Elm 1980–2 (which includes a piece on architecture: Schröder 1980–2); Nicolai 1990 and 1993; Seeger 1997; for Italy, Fraccaro de Longhi 1958, supplemented by Negri 1981; for Switzerland, Bucher 1957; and for Spain, Eydoux 1954; Valle Pérez 1982 and 1994. For views on the impact of Italian Cistercian architecture on a group of Polish abbeys, see Bialoskorska 1965.

47 Hahn 1957. Among those works which have appeared more recently, and which look at the European evidence generally, see especially Van der Meer 1965; Dimier 1971; Braunfels 1972, 67–110; Pressouyre and Kinder 1992; Tobin 1995; Kinder 1997; Leroux-Dhuys 1998; Williams 1998, 174–257; Rüffer 1999.

48 See, in general, Butler 1982a; for a general overview of archaeological work on monastic sites in France during this period, Bonde and Maines 1988.

49 For summaries and additional sources, see Fergusson 1984a, 114–15, 130, 136–8; Robinson 1998, 73–4, 132–3, 156–7; on Kirkstall, see also Moorhouse and Wrathmell 1987.

50 Butler was perhaps the only scholar looking at Cistercian archaeology and architecture in Wales with fresh eyes at this time. Apart from those excavations in north Wales, he produced an essay which placed the two Glamorganshire houses in their regional context and also published the official guidebook to Neath. See Butler 1964, 1971, 1976a and 1976b; Butler and Evans 1980.

51 On which, see Rahtz and Hirst 1976; Hirst *et al* 1983.

52 Fergusson 1984a.

53 Norton and Park 1986.

54 Stalley 1987. Professor Stalley also contributed a paper on the Cistercian churches of Ireland to the Norton and Park volume: Stalley 1986.

55 For Fountains, see Coppack 2003 (first published 1993); for Rievaulx, Fergusson and Harrison 1999.

56 The two recent overviews are Coppack 1998; Robinson 1998. For an interesting conceptual view on the use of 'space' within a group of the Yorkshire monasteries, see Cassidy-Welch 2001.

57 Coomans 2000.

58 In addition, it is clear from the work of 1977–84 at Sawley Abbey in Lancashire, for example, that archaeological excavation has a great deal more to contribute to our understanding, particularly of early timber buildings. The Sawley project also gave the opportunity for combining the results of excavation with detailed structural examination on one of the smaller English sites, leading to the claim that it is 'the most informative second-tier house yet examined': Coppack *et al* 2002 (with the quote at 101); Coppack 1998, 28–31.

59 This remark (equally applicable to the Scottish houses) is merely an observation, not a criticism. Furthermore, in thinking of material relevant to the present study, Dore Abbey has to be noted as the great exception. It was covered at length by Fergusson (1984a, 94–100) and features throughout Norton and Park 1986. Also in the latter volume, the first church at Tintern is discussed in the essay on early architecture, and there is some coverage of both Wales and Scotland in the chapter on the later Middle Ages: see Coldstream 1986; Halsey 1986.

60 Butler 1994, 4. See also Butler 1999a.

61 Stalley 2002, 13–17. There is much in the corpus of work by the late Professor Lawrence Hoey, for example, which runs counter to such an approach.

CHAPTER 1

THE CISTERCIANS AND THEIR SETTLEMENT OF WALES

1 For general accounts of the origins of the order, and its subsequent history, see Lekai 1977; Pacaut 1993; Bolton 1996; Burton 1998; Williams 1998; Lawrence 2001, 172–98; Brooke 2003, 166–94. For ideas on the development of Cistercian culture and its role in general ecclesiastical reform, see Newman 1996. A useful list of works published on the order up to the late 1960s will be found in Donkin 1969.

2 The use of the simple name, *Novum Monasterium*, remained current until *c* 1119: *Narrative Texts*, 400 n 8.

3 Knowles first published his masterpiece, *The Monastic Order*, in 1940. In the second edition, he allowed much that he had written on the early Cistercians to stand: Knowles 1963a, 198–200, 208–19 (though see also his footnote, 752–3). Other authors have begun their introduction to the Cistercians by referring to Knowles (eg, Fergusson 1984a, 3; Holdsworth 1986a, 40). I make no apology for doing so here.

4 Knowles quoted the second edition: Mahn 1951, 41 (the original is in French). See also *Narrative Texts*, 199.

5 Knowles 1963a, 752.

6 Hitherto, David Knowles tackled the issue himself, in Knowles 1963b (a work since criticized); the first modern edition of the important early Cistercian texts appeared as Bouton and Van Damme 1974 (reprinted 1985); an extremely useful review of the arguments was presented in Holdsworth 1986a; and the discussions of the early documents were again advanced in Auberger 1986, 327–92. Professor Christopher Brooke has given reasons why he feels all attempts to plot the history of the Cistercian constitution through the early documents are likely to founder: Brooke 2003, 9.

7 This point is made in Cassidy-Welch 2001, 13–14. See, for example, Lekai 1977; Elder 1998, 219–36 (essay by Lekai).

8 For just two examples of the myth of uniformity, see Auberger 1986; Waddell 1994.

9 The three volumes (*see* Preface n 1) supersede all earlier editions of the material. The major omission at this stage is a fresh edition of the Cistercian customary, the *Ecclesiastica Officia*, for which see currently the two editions noted in the bibliography under this title.

10 For the statutes after 1200, we are still dependent upon Canivez's edition of 1933–41 (*Statuta*). In this volume, for the twelfth-century statutes I provide the reference to both editions, though Waddell's must now take precedence.

11 Berman 2000.

12 The two key responses are: McGuire 2000; Waddell 2000. They point to the positive contributions of the volume, though both identify fundamental flaws.

13 For the Rule itself, see McCann 1976; on its adoption and success, Knowles 1963a, 3–15; Lawrence 2001, 18–38, 54 106, *passim*; Brooke 2003, 52–85.

14 Braunfels 1972, 234–5; Lawrence 2001, 74–5.

15 Lackner 1972; Braunfels 1972, 47–66; Bouchard 1987 and 1990; Lawrence 2001, 83–106; Brooke 2003, 62–5. For a summary of the congregation's architectural achievements, see Conant 1993, 185–221.

16 For these two Tuscan congregations of monks, see Leyser 1984, 29–33; Lawrence 2001, 149–51; for the founders, Farmer 1992, 262–3, 422. On the desert fathers, see Lawrence 2001, 1–17.

17 In general, see Knowles 1963a, 191–207; Burton 1994, 63–84; Lawrence 2001, 146–71; Aston 2001.

18 Quoted in Lawrence 2001, 149.

19 The source for much that follows is the corpus of narrative and legislative texts for early Cîteaux: *Narrative Texts*, 399–440, *passim*; see also Elder 1998. For Robert, see Auberger 1986, 77–80; Farmer 1992, 419; Van Damme 1999. For arguments on the extent of the eremitical element in early Cistercian ideal, see Leclercq 1965; Leyser 1984, 18–96, *passim*. Wider issues with regard to the actual founding of the Cistercian order are raised in McGuire 1995.

20 *Narrative Texts (Exordium Parvum)*, 419, 430. The number of monks Robert took with him varies according to the early sources (twenty-one is often quoted): *Narrative Texts*, 400 n 7. For further views of the 'intent' of the first Cistercians, see Leclercq 1969.

21 *Narrative Texts (Exordium Cistercii)*, 400; *(Exordium Parvum)*, 421. The monks originally settled at La Forgeotte, and a year or so later moved about 1.4km to the south: Auberger 1986, 91–4, 116–24. The site was initially given to them by Raynard, viscount of Beaune, supported by Odo I, duke of Burgundy (1078–1102): Bouchard 1987.

22 For the location and a summary of what survives, see Peugniez 2001, 49–51. For a recent overview of Cîteaux and its buildings, see the collection of essays in Plouvier and Saint-Denis 1998. See also Plouvier 1994; Kinder 1996a. Numerous drawings of the buildings were made in the seventeenth and eighteenth centuries, that is, before their destruction in the years after 1791: see Gras 1982; Plouvier and Saint-Denis 1998, 380–90. Early descriptive sources also survive, with much of interest recorded at the time of the General Chapter of 1667: see Chabeuf 1883–4.

23 *Narrative Texts*, 422–8. For Alberic, see Farmer 1992, 11–12; Van Damme 1999.

24 *Narrative Texts (Exordium Parvum)*, 438–9. For Stephen's abbacy, see in particular Newman 1997; Farmer 1992, 442–3; Bolton 1996, 348–9; Elder 1998, 47–123; Burton 1998, 9–13; Van Damme 1999. Waddell confirms the belief that much of the early Cistercian narrative and legislative literature was written, at least in its primitive form, by Stephen Harding, by 1119: *Narrative Texts*, 137–68, *passim*.

25 There is still much of basic value on these two 'elder daughters' in King 1954, 106–47 (La Ferté), 148–206 (Pontigny). For locations, Peugniez 2001, 61–2, 69–72.

26 On the number of followers who came with Bernard, and on his date of entry, see *Narrative Texts*, 403 n 9. See also Williams 1998, 3–7.

27 King 1954, 207–328 (Clairvaux), 329–87 (Morimond). For locations, Peugniez 2001, 120–3, 139–40.

28 The literature on St Bernard, and his role in the creation of the Cistercian identity, is vast, but see Knowles 1963a, 217–19; Lekai 1977, 33–51; Holdsworth 1986b and 1990; Rudolph 1990; Pressouyre and Kinder 1992; Sommerfeldt 1992; Bredero 1996; France 1998a, 26–49.

29 For his main body of correspondence, see *Bernard Letters*.

30 Of course, the expansion was by no means entirely due to St Bernard's influence, but see Bredero 1996, 248–75. On the growth of the order, with statistics, see Van der Meer 1965; Cocheril 1966; Vongrey and Hervay 1967; Donkin 1967; Cocheril 1976; Donkin 1978, 21–31; Locatelli 1992; Williams 1998, 12–21.

31 On this important topic, see Williams 1998, 21–5. Professor Berman (2000, 106–48, *passim*) has suggested that the incorporation of existing abbeys was the main method by which the Cistercians expanded through to the 1160s. This is unlikely to become an accepted view, though she is at least correct to emphasize the degree to which the process was underplayed in the past.

32 For the site, see Gardelles 1979; Peugniez 2001, 20–2. The link with

Pontigny was subsequently tenuous.

33 For Savigny and the merger, see Laveille 1896–9, III, 7–17; Knowles 1963a, 249–51; Hill 1968, 80–115; Suydam 1976; Poulle 1994; Burton 1994, 64, 67–9; and now, importantly, Holdsworth 2004; for Obazine, Barrière 1977; for the sites, Peugniez 2001, 219–23, 315–16. Although the mergers of 1147 are questioned in Berman 2000, 142–8, several scholars have assembled more than enough evidence to reassert the case for their approval by the Cistercian General Chapter held at Cîteaux in that year.

34 *William of Malmesbury*, I, 576–85, *passim*; Elder 1998, 51–6.

35 *Orderic Vitalis*, IV, 311–27.

36 Waddell now argues for two recoverable early recensions: one, dating to *c* 1136–7, comprised the *Exordium Cistercii*, the *Summa Cartae Caritatis* and the *Capitula*; the second, of *c* 1147 (which included updated and edited material), comprised the *Exordium Parvum*, the *Cartae Caritatis Prior* and the *Instituta*. After 1152, the *Cartae Caritatis Prior* was replaced by the *Cartae Caritatis Posterior*. See *Narrative Texts*, 133–88.

37 On the dating of the two documents, see the summary conclusions in *Narrative Texts*, 230–1, 273.

38 *William of Malmesbury*, I, 581; Elder 1998, 53–4, and also 128–44 (essay by Waddell).

39 In the final recension it comprised 121 chapters: *Ecclesiastica Officia* (1). For a brief discussion of early white monk life based on the observances, see Lackner 1978.

40 For the most recent views, see *Narrative Texts*, 167–75, 299–318. In both cases the statutes are likely to include material dating back to the early years of the New Monastery. See also Waddell 1993.

41 On what follows, see the very useful summary in Fergusson 1984a, 5–22; see also Auberger 1992. In due course, probably towards 1147, a distinct chapter summarizing the essential elements of the Cistercian philosophy was written into the *Exordium Parvum* as chapter XV. It deals with matters such as clothing, diet, the location of abbeys, appropriate property and the employment of lay brothers: *Narrative Texts*, 434–5 (and notes by Waddell, 415, 436–7).

42 *Narrative Texts (Instituta I)*, 458: 'places removed from human habitation'.

43 *Narrative Texts (Capitula XI)*, 409; *(Instituta IV)*, 459. For a comment on their white habits, see *Orderic Vitalis*, IV, 311, 325. On the Cistercian habit and its general development, see France 1998a, 72–98.

44 *Narrative Texts (Instituta XIV, XXIV)*, 462, 466.

45 *Narrative Texts (Instituta X, XX)*, 460, 464; but on this point in general, Rudolph 1987.

46 *Narrative Texts (Instituta LXXV)*, 489.

47 *Narrative Texts (Instituta XII, XXX)*, 461, 468.

48 *Narrative Texts (Cartae Caritatis Prior)*, 445–6.

49 For Cistercian liturgy, see Lekai 1977, 248–60; Williams 1998, 228–33.

50 *Narrative Texts (Instituta IX)*, 460.

51 For recent debate on how soon the Cistercians defined themselves as distinctive in their economy, see, for example, Berman 1986; Bouchard 1991, *passim*; Waddell 1994. There is an admirable summary in Burton 1999, 217–18. For an earlier, but balanced, account of the order's approach, see Lekai 1977, 282–333.

52 On the lay brothers, see Lekai 1977, 334–46; Williams 1998, 79–88.

53 The earliest recoverable recension may possibly date from the 1130s, though a fuller version can probably be assigned to the period around 1147: *Lay Brothers*.

54 But see Waddell's comment: *Lay Brothers*, 165 nn 3–4.

55 For a general overview, see Williams 1998, 276–95. See also

Donnelly 1954; Donkin 1978, 51–67; Pressouyre 1994.

56 See, for instance, the guidance for their *horarium*: *Lay Brothers*, 168–75.

57 For this well-known reference of 1157 (or 1158), see Norton 1986, 328, appearing in *Statuta*, I, 61. There is a reassessment of the context for the statute in *Statutes*, 70, 579.

58 Holdsworth 1986a, 55.

59 On this and what follows, see Fergusson 1984a, 11–14.

60 For attempts to define spiritual ideals in Cistercian architecture see, for example, Bucher 1957, 274–6; Bucher 1960–1.

61 For a full account and review of its significance, see Rudolph 1990. Transcripts of the key sections on art and architecture will also be found in: Migne 1844–64, CLXXXII, cols 914–16; Braunfels 1972, 241–2; Matarasso 1993, 55–7.

62 Stalley 1987, 2.

63 For this section, see Knowles 1963a, 227–66; Burton 1986; Burton 1994, 69–77; Burton 1998, 14–25. I am grateful to Dr Burton for allowing me to see her forthcoming paper, 'Homines sanctitatis eximiae, religionis consummatae: the Cistercians in England and Wales'.

64 *Annales Monastici*, II, 221; Knowles and Hadcock 1971, 127–8. For L'Aumône, see Cuissard 1881–4.

65 Knowles and Hadcock 1971, 119. On subsequent Savigniac foundations in England, see Guilloreau 1909–10.

66 On the Cistercian settlement of Yorkshire, see Burton 1999, 98–124.

67 *Bernard Letters*, 141–2.

68 Knowles and Hadcock 1971, 124; Fergusson and Harrison 1999, 37–8.

69 Knowles and Hadcock 1971, 119; Burton 1999, 103–7; Coppack 2003, 19–21.

70 Norton and Park 1986, 396–7; Fergusson and Harrison 1999, 43; Coppack 2003, 27–9.

71 Knowles and Hadcock 1971, 116.

72 Gwynn and Hadcock 1970, 139–40; Stalley 1987, 12.

73 *Narrative Texts* (*Instituta* LXXXVI), 492–3.

74 Hill 1968, 80–115; Norton and Park 1986, 400.

75 Knowles and Hadcock 1971, 112–28, *passim*; Robinson 1998, 64–205, *passim*.

76 On the course of foundation and subsequent patronage, see Cowley 1977, 20–8; Williams 2001, 3–18. Further detail on the history of individual houses is given in the catalogue; in this section sources and references are kept to a minimum.

77 Catalogue entry; Janauschek 1877, 10, 19; O'Sullivan 1947, 38–9; Knowles and Hadcock 1971, 127; Williams 1976a, 94–146; Cowley 1977, 21; Williams 2001, 6–7.

78 Ward 1981, 440.

79 Gwynn and Hadcock 1970, 142–3; Knowles and Hadcock 1971, 121. The foundation of its first colony within eight years is of interest, especially in the light of the General Chapter statute instructing that abbeys had to house sixty professed monks before contemplating a daughter house: *Narrative Texts* (*Instituta* XXXVII), 472.

80 Cowley 1977, 17–21, 28–31.

81 Catalogue entry; Janauschek 1877, 98; Laveille 1896–9, II, 170–6; O'Sullivan 1947, 27–8; Knowles and Hadcock 1971, 122; Cowley 1977, 21; Williams 2001, 7.

82 Catalogue entry; Janauschek 1877, 99; Laveille 1896–9, II, 189–92; O'Sullivan 1947, 25, 27; Leach 1960, 34–40; Knowles and Hadcock 1971, 115; Williams 1981a; Williams 2001, 7.

83 Catalogue entry; Janauschek 1877, 61–2; Lloyd 1939, II, 593–4; O'Sullivan 1947, 8; Knowles and Hadcock 1971, 128; Cowley 1977, 22; Pryce 1996, 155–6, 159; Williams 2001, 5–6.

84 Catalogue entry; Janauschek 1877, 107; O'Sullivan 1947, 28–9; Knowles and Hadcock 1971, 122; Cowley 1977, 22–3; Evans 1996; Williams 2001, 7.

85 RCAHMW 1976, 16, 18–68, *passim*.

86 Janauschek 1877, 92–3; Knowles and Hadcock 1971, 115; Williams 1976a, 1–57; Shoesmith and Richardson 1997.

87 Donkin 1978, 29; Williams 1998, 15–16.

88 Cowley 1977, 23–4; RCAHMW 1982, 295–6; Williams 2001, 4.

89 *Mon Ang*, V, 555; *Episcopal Acts*, I, 276.

90 Williams 2001, 4–5. Gerald of Wales blamed the greed of Abbot Adam I of Dore for the failure: *Gerald of Wales*, IV, 206.

91 Janauschek 1877, 229; O'Sullivan 1947, 33–4; Knowles and Hadcock 1971, 120; Williams 1976a, 59–75; Cowley 1977, 27–8; Harrison 1998; Williams 2001, 7.

92 The monks settled at Darnhall in 1274, moving to Vale Royal in 1281: Thompson 1962, 183–4; Brown, Colvin and Taylor 1963, 248–9; Knowles and Hadcock 1971, 118, 127; Denton 1992.

93 On Rhys, see Davies 1987, 217–27. On his ecclesiastical patronage, see Pryce 1996.

94 Pryce 1996, 157–9.

95 Catalogue entry; Janauschek 1877, 151; O'Sullivan 1947, 11–12; Knowles and Hadcock 1971, 126; Cowley 1977, 25–6; Pryce 1996, 157–62, *passim*; Williams 2001, 6.

96 Catalogue entry; Janauschek 1877, 159–60; O'Sullivan 1947, 14–15; Knowles and Hadcock 1971, 126; Williams 1976c; Thomas 1997; Williams 2001, 6.

97 The reasons for rejecting a foundation date of 1143, which appear in some of the literature, are given in the catalogue entry. See also Janauschek 1877, 74–5; O'Sullivan 1947, 10; Knowles and Hadcock 1971, 115; Williams 1976b; Cowley 1977, 25, 26; Williams 2001, 6.

98 Gwynn and Hadcock 1970, 130, 143–4; Stalley 1987, 243, 249–50. For what little survives at Tracton, see Power 1994, 240–1.

99 This does not include the two houses of nuns (Llanllŷr and Llanllugan, *see* fig 18), founded *c* 1180 under the care of Strata Florida and Strata Marcella: Williams 1975.

100 Catalogue entry; Janauschek 1877, 190, 298 (though the date of foundation there seems incorrect); O'Sullivan 1947, 35–6; Knowles and Hadcock 1971, 121; Williams 1976a, 77–93; Cowley 1977, 26–7; Williams 2001, 6.

101 Catalogue entry; Janauschek 1877, 186–7; O'Sullivan 1947, 17; Hays 1963, 4–7; Knowles and Hadcock 1971, 118; Smith 1999, 102; Williams 2001, 6.

102 Maenan catalogue entry; Hays 1963, 57–77.

103 For the recent suggestions, see catalogue entries on Cymer and Cwmhir, and especially Smith 1999; Smith and Butler 2001, 297–317. See also Janauschek 1877, 204; Knowles and Hadcock 1971, 118; Williams 1981b; Williams 2001, 6; O'Sullivan 1947, 16.

104 Catalogue entry; Janauschek 1877, 205; Knowles and Hadcock 1971, 127; Williams 2001, 6; O'Sullivan 1947, 18; Price 1952, 13–22.

105 In particular, see O'Sullivan 1947; Cowley 1977; Williams 1984 and 2001.

106 Davies 1987, 196–201, with the quote at 197.

107 *Cal Pat Rolls*, 1436–41, 380. As late as 1336, Margam was able to support up to thirty-eight monks and forty lay brothers: Cowley 1977, 51. John Leland claimed that Cwmhir had been intended for sixty monks: *Leland*, 52. In general, see Williams 2001, 126–7.

108 Williams 2001, 127–30.

109 On which, see Williams 2001, 131–4.

110 See Cowley 1977, 139–64, *passim*; Williams 1997a, 18–22 (on the Dore library); Williams 2001, 134–6.

111 Gerald resented having to sell his books, and blamed the monk

Cadwgan, who went on to become bishop of Bangor: *Gerald of Wales*, IV, 161–7.

112 Hays 1963, 141–2.

113 Cowley 1977, 148; Davies 1987, 201. For a chronicling tradition at Tintern, see Harrison 2000.

114 See Williams, G 1976, 249–522, *passim*.

115 A very substantial body of work exists on the Welsh Cistercian economy, chiefly by Dr David Williams. See, in particular, Williams 1990 and Williams 2001, 166–284. See also the list of works on individual sites given in the bibliography.

116 Although dated, on the Cistercian grange in England, see Platt 1969; for a recent and wider contextual overview, Bond 2004. On the grange in Wales, see Williams 1984, II, 227–42; Williams 2001, 192–208.

117 The relevant early statues are those concerned with the siting of abbeys, the rejection of tithes and the formation of granges: *Narrative Texts* (*Instituta* I, V, IX), 458, 459, 460. For recent debate, see Berman 1986; Bouchard 1991; Waddell 1994.

118 See catalogue entries on these houses, and also Pierce 1950–1, 28–9; Cowley 1977, 71, 90–1.

119 For studies of individual granges, notable exceptions to this statement are the work on the Glamorgan estates of Margam and Neath abbeys, in RCAHMW 1982, 251–97, and the investigations of Tintern's holdings at Merthyrgeryn and Woolaston: Parks and Webster 1974; Fulford *et al* 1992. Professor David Austin of the University of Lampeter has been looking at the Strata Florida landscape in new and imaginative ways.

120 Summaries and further references are given in the site catalogue.

121 Catalogue entries; Williams 2001, 17, 26, 27.

122 Catalogue entry; Evans 1995, 10, 16.

123 Full details in catalogue entry; Robinson and Platt 1998, 17, 31.

124 On the wars, see Davies 1987, 333–88; Prestwich 1997, 170–232.

125 On the episode in general, see Hays 1963, 75–7; Hays 1971, 118–21; Williams, G 1976, 43–4; Williams 2001, 35–7. There is a strong suggestion that Whitland ought to have been included in the group receiving compensation, but that for some reason it forfeited its right: Cowley 1977, 214–15.

126 The known individual valuations are given in each of the catalogue entries. For comments on usage, see Cowley 1977, 92–6; Robinson 1980, I, 110–20. For a recent review, see Denton 1993. See also Williams 2001, 166–7.

127 From the same source: Furness £176; Jervaulx £200; Fountains £356, as given in Knowles and Hadcock 1971, 115–28, *passim*.

128 For a recent overview of late medieval monastic life, challenging earlier assumptions, see Clark 2002a.

129 For the historical background, see Williams 2001, 35–98.

130 Donnelly 1949.

131 For a particularly good analysis of the south Wales estates, see Cowley 1977, 229–67, *passim*. See also Williams, G 1976, 114–77.

132 *Statuta*, III, 525. On this period, see Knowles 1948–59, II, 125–9; Burton 1998, 30–2; Williams 2001, 50–1, 159–60.

133 On the uprising, see Davies 1995. For a summary of the impact on the Welsh Cistercians, see Williams 2001, 52–5.

134 Williams, G 1976, 212–45.

135 *Cal Pap Let*, VI, 282.

136 Jones 1873, 354–5.

137 Catalogue entry; *Cal Pat Rolls*, 1441–6, 95.

138 See Williams, G 1976, 249–70, 347–62; Williams 2001, 55–75.

139 Williams, G 1974, 86–7; Williams 2001, 72–3. On the Cistercians in England and Wales in general at this time, Knowles 1948–59, III, 28–38.

140 Williams 1976a, 110–11.

141 Catalogue entry; Price 1952, 262–3; Pratt 1997, 28–33.

142 Catalogue entries for Cwmhir, Cymer, Dore; Williams 2001, 66, 77.

143 On the course of events leading to the suppression, and on the process itself, see Knowles 1948–59, III, 141–417; Youings 1971. For Wales, see Williams, G 1997, 19–131; for the Welsh Cistercians, Williams 2001, 76–98.

144 Catalogue entries, all derived from *Valor Ecclesiasticus*, IV, *passim*. Fountains was the largest house in England at the time, with a valuation of £1,115. Other interesting figures, relative to the scale of the monastery complex, are: Furness (£805), Byland (£238), Jervaulx (£234), Waverley (£174), Cleeve (£155) and Buildwas (£110).

145 In summary, see Williams, G 1976, 562.

146 Youings 1971, 155–9.

147 For the mechanics of the process, see Williams 2001, 84–6.

148 For one record of the fines, see *Let Pap Henry VIII*, 13, II, 177; Williams, G 1997, 88; Williams 2001, 86.

149 Williams, G 1997, 88–9.

Chapter 2
Church Building in Wales Before the Cistercians

1 There is little by way of a general background synthesis, but see Radford 1963; Butler 1971; Haslam 1979; Hubbard 1986; Newman 1995 and 2000; Edwards 1996; Thurlby 1999; Lloyd *et al* 2004.

2 Davies 1987, 187. The exception appears to be the church in the Anglo-Saxon tradition at Presteigne in Powys: Edwards 1996, 52. One might also mention the pre-1120 church at Llandaff described in the *Book of Llandaff* (on which more is said below). For a summary of the archaeology of pre-Conquest belief in Wales, see Arnold and Davies 2000, 180–94.

3 On which, see Knowles 1963a, 31–82; Burton 1994, 1–18; Aston 2000, 67–73.

4 For further background, see Cowley 1977, 1–8; Davies 1987, 172–9; and the collection of essays in Edwards and Lane 1992.

5 The pre-Norman ecclesiastical establishment excavated at Burry Holms on the Gower peninsula cannot have been typical: RCAHMW 1976, 14–15. For a dated but useful review of the 'Celtic' monasteries of north Wales, see Johns 1960 and 1962. See also Radford 1963, 355–6.

6 Fortunately, the Welsh material can now be seen in the context of a fresh overview of Norman England: Fernie 2000.

7 For additional historical background, see Cowley 1977, 9–39; Davies 1987, 179–210. See also *Episcopal Acts*, I, 38–76. For a visual introduction to the twelfth-century changes, see Lord 2003, 54–85.

8 *Episcopal Acts*, I, 76–145; Davies 1987, 179–80. The location of the cathedrals and diocesan boundaries appear in fig 18.

9 *St Davids Acta*, 2–4; Davies 1919; *Episcopal Acts*, I, 133–44.

10 *Episcopal Acts*, I, 238.

11 Radford 1962, 9; Cowley 1977, 19–20.

12 Cowley 1977, 32–3; James 1985.

13 *Annales Cambriæ*, 39; *Episcopal Acts*, I, 251. See also Lovegrove 1926, 254, 261–2; Evans and Worsley 1981, 13. Jones and Freeman (1856, 139–40), however, were cautious of accepting the 'dedicatio' as proof of a brand-new building. In a new account of St Davids, Professor Stalley (2002, 18) reminds us of the possible influence the pre-existing church may have had on the design and layout of the later twelfth-century cathedral. For the most recent overview on St Davids (by Roger Stalley), see Lloyd *et al* 2004, 386–414.

14 For views on likely artistic rivalry with Llandaff in the 1120s and 1130s, see Draper 1999, 105–6; with the points underlined by the episcopal aspirations at Llandaff at this time: Davies 1999, 33–5. See further the important account of the rivalry between the two sees and the metropolitan claims for St Davids, in *Episcopal Acts*, I, 145–208.

15 The background is given in *Episcopal Acts*, I, 76–91.

16 *Episcopal Acts*, II, 437–43.

17 A single Norman capital is known from the site, and the church seems to have been entirely rebuilt in the wake of Edward I's second Welsh war (1282–3), under Bishop Anian II (d 1293) and his successor Llywelyn de Bromfield (1293–1314). The wave-moulded nave piers, for example, seem to fit with a number of late thirteenth- and early fourteenth-century buildings in the north-west midlands and north Wales, derived in some degree from that pool of masons assembled for King Edward's castle-building programme of the 1280s: Maddison 1978, 94 (where there is some comment on St Asaph).

18 Davies 1987, 30–1.

19 *Episcopal Acts*, I, 78–97.

20 Hervey went on to become the first bishop of Ely (1109–31), where he must have overseen the completion of the work on the nave and the beginning of the west front. In general, see Fernie 2000, 124–8; Maddison 2000, 25–35.

21 *Episcopal Acts*, I, 99; Radford 1949b, 258; Davies 1987, 44. It seems possible that David was a Welshman.

22 For the cathedral fabric in general, see Hughes 1901, 1902 and 1904; RCAHMW 1960, 1–9. For a summary of the findings on the Romanesque structure, see RCAHMW 1960, 3. For earlier accounts, Hughes 1901, 183–5; Radford 1949b, 257–9.

23 The cathedral was heavily restored by Sir George Gilbert Scott *c* 1866–75, with the work completed by Henry Barber. Several opportunities for excavation appear to have presented themselves, with the findings noted in two reports and summarized in Hughes 1901. In 1946, Ralegh Radford excavated the east termination of the south transept, discovering the apsed projection: Radford 1949b, 257–9.

24 There is conflicting evidence over the form of the nave, though Radford argued that it was aisleless and created a model for the rebuilding of other native *clas* churches in north Wales: Radford 1949b, 258–9; Radford 1963, 358–9.

25 Jones 1910, 155–7.

26 Most recently, it is suggested that the eastern arm of St Werburgh's was begun under the patronage of Earl Hugh *c* 1090 and may have been some way towards completion by 1092. St John's may have been started *c* 1100: Gem 2000; Fernie 2000, 166–8. On the Chester connections, see also Lord 2003, 62–3.

27 Urban was described as such in a petition seeking confirmation of his election: *Episcopal Acts*, II, 613. The diocese was known as Glamorgan until the middle years of his episcopate. On Urban's career in general, see *Episcopal Acts*, I, 125–8; *Llandaff Acta*, xi–xii, xxvii–xxxvii; Cowley and Williams 1971, 87–94. Most recently, for an overview of Norman Llandaff, see Davies 2003. For the cathedral in general, see Willis 1718 and Birch 1912, with further sources given in Thompson 1925.

28 *Episcopal Acts*, I, 147–90; Cowley and Williams 1971, 92–3.

29 The *Book of Llandaff* was almost certainly compiled in the 1120s. This reference to the early church is quoted in *Episcopal Acts*, II, 617–18; Lovegrove 1929, 75–6; Cowley and Williams 1971, 91; Butler 1971, 382. For a brief recent overview of the *Book of Llandaff* as an historical source, see Davies 2003, 1–6, and *passim*.

30 *Cartae Glamorgancia*, I, 46; *Episcopal Acts*, II, 618.

31 The *Book of Llandaff* is the source: *Episcopal Acts*, II, 618; Lovegrove 1929, 76; Cowley and Williams 1971, 91.

32 For new insights into Urban's aspirations for his see, with a suggestion that the patronage of the new building was connected with Robert, earl of Gloucester (d 1147), see Davies 1999.

33 For the cathedral fabric in general, see Freeman 1850a and 1850b; James 1929; Lovegrove 1929; North 1957; Butler 1971, 383–4, 387–8, 391; Newman 1995, 239–55. Malcolm Thurlby and Richard Plant have been kind enough to discuss their thinking on Llandaff with me.

34 On the three-apse plan, see Clapham 1934, 46; also Hearn 1971, 200–1. For Hereford, where the single presbytery arch is heavily restored, Thurlby 1995b, 16–19; Fernie 2000, 167–9. The arrangement might also be compared with that at St John's in Chester: Gem 2000, 40, 42–3.

35 On the suggestion of flanking towers, see Freeman 1850b, 66–8 (where they are considered to have been part of the early Gothic fabric); Lovegrove 1929, 89–90. Such towers may well have existed in the west country at Hereford and Exeter, and perhaps at St John's in Chester; they also occurred more widely across Norman England: RCHME 1931, 92–3; Thurlby 1995b, 19; Fernie 2000, 169–71; Gem 2000, 40; Morris 2000, 207.

36 For early views on the scale of Urban's church, see Freeman 1850b, 47–60. See also Lovegrove 1929, 80–1; Newman 1995, 247–8.

37 For the west country Romanesque context in general, see Fernie 2000, 152–76.

38 On the decorative similarities between Old Sarum and Llandaff, see Stalley 1971, 73. Interestingly, Bishop Roger's choir at Sarum was one of a number of early twelfth-century English examples ending with an ambulatory and three-apse plan, a more complex but not wholly unrelated arrangement to that which is suggested for Llandaff. For the detail, see RCHME 1980, 17–21; also Hearn 1971, 188–92.

39 For Hereford, see Thurlby 1995b, 20; on Malmesbury, Brakspear 1912–13, 413; Wilson 1978, 81–2, 88 (arguing for an ultimate Cluniac source); Robinson and Lea 2002, 25–35. For further views on the pedigree of paterae in the west country, see Thurlby 1995c, 115–19; Clapham (1934, 129–30) felt that the Llandaff examples were too elaborate for a building of the 1120s.

40 Stalley 1971, 76–7. For Leonard Stanley, see Verey and Brooks 1999, 444–5. They occur much closer to Llandaff, at Ewenny Priory, on which see further below.

41 For background, see in particular Cowley 1977, 9–17; in addition, Graham 1929; Davies 1987, 180–1, 196; Coplestone-Crow 1998.

42 Cowley 1977, 15–16, drawing on *Cartae Glamorgancia*, VI, 2265–6, and *Episcopal Acts*, II, 644. See also Davies 1943–4, 135–6; Nicholl 1936, 79–80. For confirmation of Maurice's gifts by Robert, earl of Gloucester, see *Gloucester Charters*, 73–4, 87–8. On the priory in general, see Turbervill 1901; Orrin 1988, 145–60; Newman 1995, 343–7.

43 J Conway Davies published a valuable collection of records relating to the priory, though he perhaps tended to overcomplicate the foundation sequence: Davies 1943–4, 120–2.

44 Radford 1952, 7–16. His phased view of Ewenny's development is followed, cautiously, in Butler 1971, 381–2.

45 As early as 1897, Harold Brakspear produced a ground plan showing a single Norman phase, reproduced in Turbervill 1901, facing 3. W St Clair Baddeley saw no reason to attribute any part of the Norman church to a date later than 1115–20: Baddeley 1913, 9.

46 In particular, Thurlby (1988) argues for a date of 1116–26 for the

entire building. Earlier, in his assessment of the links between Ewenny and Cormac's chapel at Cashel (Tipperary), Stalley (1981, 63, 80) had concluded that a pre-1134 date was likely. Halsey (1986, 72) also suggested a pre-1141 date. Newman (1995, 343) remains cautious. I see nothing too contradictory in the building of a cruciform church of this scale for a significant dependent cell, though perhaps the monastic buildings were expanded post-1141.

47 Cormeilles had been founded by William fitz Osbern himself c 1060: Graham 1929, 102–3; Knowles 1963a, 701; Cowley 1977, 9. Nothing of significance of the abbey fabric survives.

48 On the fabric of the church, see Freeman 1851; Lynam 1905; Clapham 1934, 56–7; Newman 2000, 164–7. There is additional archaeological context in Shoesmith 1991, 36–82, 164–70. I have profited greatly from my discussions on Chepstow with Malcolm Thurlby, who is to publish a fresh account of the building.

49 The eastern arm is conjecturally reconstructed by Shoesmith (1991, 164) with an apsidal presbytery flanked by shorter aisles also finished with apses, in the manner, say, of the late twelfth-century priory at Castle Acre.

50 This becomes more apparent from an illustration of the east end of Chepstow in 1838, where we see the columns on the former crossing piers rising to scalloped capitals with prominent neck-rings, as at St John's: Ormerod 1861, pl IX. There are difficulties over relative chronologies here, with the crossing at St John's now dated to the second quarter of the twelfth century and certainly begun no earlier than c 1100: Gem 2000, 38–41.

51 The Chepstow nave piers are most unusual in a west country Romanesque context, where cylindrical forms were by far the most common. One of the few exceptions was to be found in the ground floor of the bishop's chapel at Hereford (now lost), generally thought to have been built by Bishop Robert of Lorraine (1079–95): Fernie 2000, 233–6.

52 Interestingly, the southern triforium openings bear a resemblance to those at Bernay Abbey (Eure), some 29km south east of Chepstow's mother house at Cormeilles. I am grateful to Malcolm Thurlby for this observation.

53 As noted in Lynam 1905, 274–5; Wilson 1985, 82 n 96.

54 That is in the manner of the presbytery at Hereford Cathedral, as reconstructed by Gilbert Scott: Morris 2000, 209, fig 56. In a speculative reconstruction drawing first published in 1911, the transverse arches are shown sitting on vault responds comprised of half-columns backing on to dosserets: Shoesmith 1991, pl 1. Regardless of their precise form, the responds would certainly have added rhythm to the bay articulation along the nave.

55 Describing the features of the church at the time of a proposed restoration of 1837, George Ormerod noted: 'the roofs of the side aisles and nave as shewn by fragments, had been vaulted with arches of tufa placed between ribs of oolite': Ormerod 1861, 82. In this context, see the discussion of the early vaults at Gloucester in Wilson 1985, 60–6.

56 Interestingly, Fernie (2000, 266) accepts Chepstow as one of the very few fully vaulted churches known from Norman Britain.

57 For which, see Thurlby 1995b; Fernie 2000, 160–5, 168–9.

58 Graham 1929, 103–4; Knowles and Hadcock 1971, 71; Cowley 1977, 14. See, further, Martindale 1992 for the dependencies of St Florent in England.

59 Thurlby 1999, 129–31; Newman 2000, 395–7; Williams and Kissack 2001, 41–53.

60 Brecon was founded as a cell of Battle Abbey in East Sussex: Cowley 1977, 13–14; RCAHMW 1994, 9–11.

61 Abergavenny was a dependency of St Vincent, Le Mans (Sarthe):

Graham 1929, 104; Cowley 1977, 13; Robinson 1993b; Newman 2000, 92–3.

62 Kidwelly was founded by Roger, bishop of Salisbury (1102–39), as a cell of Sherborne Abbey (Dorset): Knowles and Hadcock 1971, 86; Williams, G 1991.

63 Pembroke was founded c 1098 by Arnulf of Montgomery, earl of Pembroke, as a daughter of St Martin at Sées (Orne): Episcopal Acts, I, 235; Thomas 1962; Cowley 1977, 270; Lloyd et al 2004, 296–7. The fabric at this site is discussed further in this volume (see chapter 4).

64 On the two foundations, see Cowley 1977, 30–3; and for context, Robinson 1980. A church of St John the Baptist at Llanthony was dedicated by Bishop Urban of Llandaff in 1108: Episcopal Acts, II, 615. Excavations at the site in 1978–9 may have recovered traces of an early twelfth-century church, though the evidence is inconclusive: see Evans 1983–8, 2–6, 51–2.

65 Coplestone-Crow 1998, 9–10. Mention might also be made of the later Cluniac cell at St Clears (Carmarthenshire), where the core fabric of the church is of twelfth-century date and there is a notable chancel arch.

66 Cowley 1977, 19–20.

67 Radford 1962; Lloyd et al 2004, 432–5.

68 For Penmon, see RCAHMW 1937, 119–21; Thurlby 2002, 252; for Tywyn, RCAHMW 1921, 170–1 (where the work is dated 1150–1200); Radford 1963, 358–9; Lord 2003, 61 (where a date in the 1140s is suggested).

69 Morgan 1885; [Caröe] 1933; Knight 1993; Newman 2000, 422–3, 426–8.

70 Jones 1910, 154–5; Radford 1963, 357; Davies 1987, 187–8; Lord 2003, 62.

CHAPTER 3
ABBEY SITES AND TEMPORARY BUILDINGS

1 Narrative Texts (Exordium Cistercii), 400. The description is borrowed from Deuteronomy 32:10.

2 Narrative Texts (Instituta I), 458; Statutes, 512.

3 Referring to the founders of Cîteaux, the author of the amplified Exordium Parvum (compiled towards 1147) wrote: 'because those holy men knew that blessed Benedict had built his monasteries not in cities, nor walled settlements or villages, but in places removed from populated areas, they promised to follow his example': Narrative Texts, 435. For this regulation explored in the context of the senior houses, see Auberger 1986, 87–108.

4 Ailred of Rievaulx's Speculum Caritatis, quoted in Knowles 1963a, 220–1.

5 Narrative Texts (Instituta XXXIII), 469. A Burgundian league is estimated to have been approximately 4km.

6 There are currently two published studies looking at factors influencing the siting of the Welsh abbeys: Butler 1982b; Williams 2001, 9–15. In a new account exploring the location and siting of more than sixty Cistercian houses in Wales and the west of England, James Bond systematically examines the influence of the following: patronage; the proximity of castles; the local settlement pattern; communications; earlier religious communities; the proximity of religious houses of other orders; the proximity of other Cistercian houses; previous land use; relief and altitude; water requirements; and access to building materials. I am grateful to Mr Bond for allowing me to see his paper in advance of publication. For the nature of Cistercian sites in general, see Kinder 1997, 79–111; Williams 1998, 172–93.

7 Donkin 1978, 31.

8 *Narrative Texts* (*Instituta* XXXVII), 472.

9 *Narrative Texts* (*Cartae Caritatis Prior*), 442.

10 As a very good example of such a procedure, we might note the land offered to Buildwas for the foundation of a daughter house (at Dunbrody) in County Wexford in 1171–2. A lay brother named Alan was sent to Ireland to inspect the site. In the event, his report was unfavourable and Dunbrody was in the end established as a daughter house of St Mary's Abbey, Dublin: Gwynn and Hadcock 1970, 131–2; Stalley 1987, 35–7.

11 *Narrative Texts* (*Instituta* XXX), 468, and n 2.

12 Catalogue entry on Cymer; *Statutes*, 415–16, 428–9 (though not Madog ap Gruffudd as identified there).

13 *Statuta*, I, 481; catalogue entry on Grace Dieu.

14 *Statuta*, II, 11, 19, 27, 43; Harrison 1998.

15 As estimated in Williams 1998, 181–4. The apparent early site change at Cîteaux itself seems often to be overlooked. Within a year or so of the settlement, the monks moved from La Forgeotte about 1.4km to the south: Auberger 1986, 91–4; Plouvier 1994, 68; Kinder 1996a, 354; Plouvier 1998, 141.

16 Donkin 1978, 31–6, 179–80. For Ireland, see Stalley 1987, 34–5. Of course, site changes were not only a feature of the Cistercian order. At least 10 per cent of the Augustinian communities in England and Wales, for example, are known to have transferred site: Robinson 1980, I, 76–85.

17 *Narrative Texts* (*Instituta* LXXXVI), 492.

18 Donkin 1978, 36.

19 For a general discussion, see Williams 2001, 11–15. There is no firm evidence to support an alleged move at Strata Marcella (from a site closer to Welshpool), and the suggestion that the community at Cwmhir was first located at Ty Faenor is here rejected. See catalogue entries on the relevant sites.

20 Catalogue entry; Leach 1960, 36–40. More is said on the temporary arrangements at Hên Blas later in this chapter.

21 See the catalogue entries on these sites.

22 Catalogue entry; Harrison 1998. On the decision to move, see *Statuta*, II, 155. The Cistercians at Grace Dieu may well have been unwitting victims of a pre-existing feud between John, lord of Monmouth, and the Welsh.

23 Catalogue entries on Aberconwy and Maenan; Hays 1963, 4–6, 57–77.

24 A research project seeking to address this has been under way at Poulton (Cheshire), the temporary site of Dieulacres (Staffordshire), since 1995: [Emery] 2002.

25 Catalogue entry; Williams 1889a, 21.

26 Catalogue entries on Dore and Margam; Cowley 1977, 23–4; Williams 2001, 4–5. Even if the sites could be positively identified, there is no guarantee that anything survives archaeologically.

27 *Cal Pap Let*, I, 131.

28 *Cal Pat Rolls*, 1441–6, 95.

29 *Bernard Letters*, 156.

30 Williams 2001, 260–2, 265–70.

31 Quoted in Burton 1998, 26. For further context, see Knowles 1963a, 674–7; Cowley 1977, 72–5. For a detailed Yorkshire case study, see Donkin 1978, 39–51, 181–4. Of course, one of the early statutes had made it clear: 'It is not proper to have housing outside the monastery gate, except for animals, because danger for souls can arise therefrom': *Narrative Texts* (*Instituta* XXI), 464.

32 As indicated in later grants: Price 1952, 260; Williams 2001, 10.

33 Quoted in Hays 1963, 64.

34 Hays 1963, 70.

35 Cowley 1977, 79–81.

36 RCAHMW 1991, 156–7.

37 In general, see Butler 1982b, 35; Williams 2001, 10. At least five of the Irish Cistercian abbeys lay on older religious sites: Stalley 1987, 38–9.

38 Williams 1976a, 94.

39 Shoesmith and Richardson 1997, 4.

40 For Neath, see RCAHMW 1976, 41.

41 Nash-Williams 1950, 146–54; RCAHMW 1976, 16, 37–62, *passim*. It is of further interest to note that the late medieval Cryke chapel overlooking the abbey site sits within a circular enclosure: Margam catalogue entry.

42 Fergusson and Harrison 1999.

43 In general, see Bond 2001; also Williams 2001, 118.

44 Williams 1998, 194–6; Williams 2001, 102–4.

45 *Cal Close Rolls*, 1234–7, 44; 1237–42, 185; 1253–4, 11.

46 *Cartae Glamorgancia*, V, 1684–5. The new abbey church had probably been under construction from *c* 1280.

47 See, for example, the catalogue entries on Basingwerk, Neath, Strata Florida and Valle Crucis.

48 Smith 2001, 447, 469–71; Smith and Suggett 2002, 58–62.

49 Davies 1992.

50 *Narrative Texts* (*Capitula* IX), 408; (*Instituta* XII), 461; and notes at 167–75. For an earlier translation, see Lekai 1977, 448.

51 See, in general, Bilson 1909, 198; Schaefer 1982; Fergusson 1983; Fergusson 1984a, 23–5; Halsey 1986, 65–7; Coppack 1998, 23–31; Coppack 2004, 46–42.

52 *Narrative Texts* (*Exordium Parvum*), 421. A pre-existing chapel may have been used for the earliest services: *Narrative Texts*, 401, note; Lekai 1977, 14; Auberger 1986, 91–4.

53 *Narrative Texts* (*Exordium Parvum*), 421. See also Guignard 1878, 63; Lekai 1977, 452.

54 Manrique 1642–56, I, 10, quoted in Schaefer 1982, 2, and n 8. See also Guignard 1878, 61–75; King 1954, 5–6.

55 There is much confusion (and disagreement) in the literature about the early sequence of construction at Clairvaux. The main sources are Fowler 1907; Aubert 1947, I, 13–15; Jeulin 1954; King 1954, 211–13; Schaefer 1982, 4–8; Kinder 1991, 206–9; Kinder 1996b, 371; Coppack 2004, 39.

56 Manrique 1642–56, I, 80, quoted in Schaefer 1982, 4, and n 20; Fergusson 1983, 81. Jeulin (1954, 325) refers to 'a modest chapel and fragile wooden huts'.

57 In 1517 the site was seen and described by the queen of Sicily: Didron 1845, 236–7. In 1667 the visitor was Dom Joseph Méglinger (a monk of Wettingen, in Switzerland), who was attending a meeting of the General Chapter: Migne 1844–64, CLXXXV, cols 1608–9. Both accounts are quoted in Schaefer 1982, 5, with fuller summaries of the visits given in King 1954, 293–8, 304–8.

58 For Nicolas Milley's 1708 illustrations, see Pressouyre and Kinder 1992, 216–17. There are various reproductions in Aubert 1947, I, 3, 11; Kinder 1991, 207–8; Schaefer 1982, 6–7; Leroux-Dhuys 1998, 38.

59 As given in Dimier 1949–67, I, plan 82.

60 Schaefer 1982, 7–8.

61 Fergusson 1983, 81; Gilyard-Beer and Coppack 1986, 175; Coppack 1998, 23–5. More recently, see Coppack *et al* 2002, 103; Coppack 2003, 22–4.

62 Kinder 1991, 206–8; Kinder 1996b, 371. Indeed, stone buildings were assumed by Bilson 1909, 201; Aubert 1947, I, 13–15; Jeulin 1954, 326. Following Kinder, Coppack suggests in his most recent analysis that the historical evidence has been conflated. He now believes the wooden building raised by the monks on their arrival at Clairvaux in 1115 remained standing, to be described by Manrique in 1642. On the other hand, the *monasterium vetus* – described by

the queen of Sicily in 1517 and drawn by Milley in 1708 – was always of stone: Coppack 2004, 39.

63 For what is known, see King 1954, 106–7, 148–50, 329–30; Kinder 1980 (Pontigny); Schaefer 1982, 3–4, 7–8.

64 *Orderic Vitalis*, IV, 327.

65 Fergusson 1983, 76; Fergusson 1984a, 24; Coppack *et al* 2002, 102.

66 *Fountains Memorials*, 46–7; Gilyard-Beer and Coppack 1986, 174–5; Coppack 2004, 37.

67 Adam was the most active in the field, setting out Kirkstead (1139), Woburn (1145) and Vaudey (1147), and apparently replacing the founder's layout at Meaux (1151). Robert became the founding abbot of Newminster (1138) and set out the buildings there. We might add to the list Alexander, the first abbot of Kirkstall (1147–82), who is credited with setting out the buildings on the final site. For all this, see Fergusson 1983, 80–6; Coppack 1998, 25–6; Coppack *et al* 2002, 102–3. See also Halsey 1986, 66–8. For summary accounts of the abbeys, see Fergusson 1984a, 130–55, *passim*; Robinson 1998, 132–205, *passim*.

68 Fergusson 1983, 78. For summary accounts of these two houses, see Fergusson 1984a, 133–6, 150–1; Robinson 1998, 141–3, 184–5.

69 Fergusson 1983, 79; Fergusson 1984a, 24.

70 Quoted in Fergusson 1983, 79. See also Coppack 2004, 37–8.

71 Fergusson 1983, 80; Coppack 1998, 26.

72 The evidence is summarized in Coppack 1998, 27–31. For Fountains, see Gilyard-Beer and Coppack 1986, 151–4, 174–5; Coppack 2003, 21–6; Coppack 2004, 38–40; for Bordesley, Hirst *et al* 1983, 29–30; for Sawley, Coppack *et al* 2002, 30–45, 101–5; Coppack 2004, 40–2. Mention might also be made of the substantial timber building found east of the east range at Kirkstall in Yorkshire, interpreted as the initial infirmary hall: Moorhouse and Wrathmell 1987, 51–6.

73 Coppack 2001, 323–6; Coppack *et al* 2002, 30–45. Building 'A' could have served for the lay brothers; 'C' might easily have been a guest hall; 'E' was the most substantial and could have been of two storeys.

74 Tintern (1131) as a daughter of L'Aumône; Dore (1147) from Morimond; Whitland (1140) and Margam (1147) from Clairvaux. In addition there were the Savigniac houses established at Basingwerk (1131) and Neath (1130), discussed below.

75 *Narrative Texts* (*Capitula* IX), 408, as detailed above at the beginning of this section.

76 On the Margam endowment ceremony, see Cowley 1977, 23; Cowley 1998, 10–11; Robinson 1998, 138.

77 *Episcopal Acts*, I, 276.

78 The Benedictines at Monmouth seem to have occupied the church of St Cadog near the castle while their own church was under construction: Williams and Kissack 2001, 10.

79 Leach 1960, 36–40; Taylor 1971. This is followed in Robinson 1996b.

80 In this case, the suggestion is partly based on the fluid nature of the political situation on the western border of the lordship of Glamorgan at the time of the foundation: see RCAHMW 1991, 156–7; Robinson 2002b.

81 Butler 1976b, 115–16; Butler 1982a, 90.

82 Williams 1889a, 21–3. See also Robinson and Platt 1998, 25.

83 Catalogue entry; Robinson and Platt 1998, 24–9; Robinson 1998, 176–9.

CHAPTER 4
THE EARLIEST STONE CHURCHES

1 The absentees are Grace Dieu, on which nothing at all is known, and Llantarnam, where the limited excavations reported in Mein and Lewis 1990–1 remain unpublished. There is, however, a speculative sketch plan available of Llantarnam, published in Williams 2001, 288, fig 127.

2 As given in Dimier 1949–67, I, plan 78.

3 See, most recently, Plouvier 1994, 68, 72; Plouvier 1998, 130, 141–2. See also *Narrative Texts*, 403, and n 9; Bilson 1909, 200–1, 201 n 1; King 1954, 6; Schaefer 1982, 2–3; Fergusson 1984a, 27. See, further, Bonde and Maines 1987, in which comparisons are made with the first church of the Premonstratensians at Prémontré (Aisne); and, in this context, Plouvier 1990, 513–22, *passim*.

4 Frankl (2000, 93) was prepared to accept that this church could have been covered with a tunnel vault.

5 For the opposing views, see in summary Schaefer 1982, 4–8; Kinder 1991, 206–9; Coppack 2004, 39. The posited church of the 1130s is discussed below in chapter 5.

6 The form of the church was discussed in Bilson 1909, 201; Aubert 1947, I, 153. It is covered fully in Kinder 1980 and 1982. Dr Kinder argues for a small rectangular structure, not apsidal as appearing in Dimier 1949–67, I, plan 235.

7 The buildings are lost, with no reliable archaeological information of which I am aware. For the site, see Peugniez 2001, 108.

8 Indeed, in considering the early transition from temporary accommodation to stone buildings, we might remember the observations made by Gerald of Wales in the 1180s: 'settle the Cistercians in some barren retreat which is hidden away in an overgrown forest', he said, '[and] a year or two later you will find splendid churches there and fine monastic buildings' (Thorpe 1978, 106).

9 That is according to the statute of *c* 1113–19: *Narrative Texts* (*Capitula* IX), 408.

10 On this and what follows on the first stone church at Tintern, see Robinson 1996a; Robinson 1998, 188; Robinson 2002a, 27–9. Further general background and context will be found in Fergusson 1984a, 25–9; Halsey 1986, 69–75.

11 On which, see Fergusson 1984a, 129–30; Robinson 1998, 130.

12 His first attempt at the plan was published as [Brakspear] 1904.

13 It remains a common misconception that Tintern I was excavated by Harold Brakspear. In fact, he merely took advantage of being on hand to follow the progress of the early clearance and consolidation by the Office of Woods in 1901–13. True, a section of the south wall of the church was exposed for a visit by the Royal Archaeological Institute in 1904, for which meeting Brakspear produced a draft plan. In 1907–8, however, he was commissioned by the department to produce a comprehensive ground plan of the site, in which he depicted a slightly modified outline to the first church. The correspondence relating to this work can be found in PRO, Work 14/76. The original of his plan, drawn at '8 feet to the inch', is held with the Tintern archive at Cadw. The outline of Tintern I was further refined by the Office of Works, under the direction of Charles Peers, following 'probing' and minor diggings in 1919–20, on which see Peers 1922; Hemp 1938.

14 The western termination of the nave is determined by a chamfered plinth, found in the probings of 1919–20, and interpreted as the base of a south-west angle buttress: Robinson 1996a, 38. It is now displayed beneath a grille (*see* fig 35, 3).

15 Pointed barrel vaults are generally acknowledged as one of the more consistent features in early Cistercian architecture, representing a clear debt to Burgundian prototypes. The structural form was established with the building of the great abbey church, known as Cluny III (Saône-et-Loire), between 1088 and *c* 1130, for which see Conant 1993, 203–4. Regardless of any Burgundian connection,

Clapham (1934, 79) suggested the Tintern presbytery may have been vaulted. See further Halsey 1986, 72–3. A useful local comparison may be made, for example, with the barrel vaults covering the transept chapels at Ewenny, possibly by c 1126, based on an already well-established west country tradition.

16 The reconstruction of Tintern I by Terry Ball (1990, modified 1995), reproduced in Robinson 1995a, 28, shows an open timber roof over the nave. It is just as likely that this was boarded to imitate a stone barrel vault, as shown in Robinson 2002a, 28, and reproduced here (see fig 36). Timber barrel vaults were, it seems, to become popular with the Cistercians in the north of England, with examples likely at Byland, Fountains, Kirkstall and Rievaulx: Hearn and Thurlby 1997; Harrison 2002, 159; Coppack 2003, 51.

17 For the site in general see Butler 1976a; Newman 1995, 463–9; for the proposed early church, Butler 1984.

18 There is, for example, a proposal for a slightly alternate alignment in an addendum to Butler's article: Butler 1984, 150–1.

19 Noted in Malone 1984, 51; Fergusson 1984a, 95 n 16; O'Callaghan 1995, 97.

20 The existence of a pre-1170s layout is implicit in Harrison and Thurlby 1997, 47–9, though this should be read in conjunction with Harrison 1997b, 115–20.

21 The unevenness of the lateral walls in the north transept chapels would fit with the notion of barrel vaults having been removed, but the evidence is not conclusive.

22 Harrison and Thurlby 1997, 51.

23 Radford proposed a construction date of c 1176–95. For him, the aisleless nave must have stood in the position of the south aisle of the thirteenth-century church (fig 25): Radford 1982, 61–7. More recently, Butler (2004, 120–1) has put forward two alternative (but highly speculative) suggestions for the possible position of an early church.

24 For the suggestion of a foundation date in 1143, see Lloyd 1939, II, 594; Cowley 1977, 25. This is rejected in favour of 1176 in Remfry 1994, 1; Smith 1999, 101–2. See also Brooksby 1970, and catalogue entry for further details.

25 Whitland and its daughters at Strata Florida and Strata Marcella are looked at below in chapters 4 and 5, but in summary the details are given in figs 25 and 26.

26 Hirst et al 1983, 214–16; Fergusson 1984a, 25–9; Coppack 1998, 32–6. In France the form is known as 'nef unique': Kinder 1997, 164–8. One early French example of comparable scale is that partially known from Ourscamp (Oise), though here the presbytery featured an apsidal east end: Dimier 1949–67, I, plan 218. But see also Bruzelius 1981, 30, and n 13.

27 Brakspear 1905, 9, 18–20; Fergusson 1984a, 25–7; Halsey 1986, 70–1.

28 On the basis of surviving evidence from the south transept, the chapels may have had plain barrel vaults springing from moulded string courses: Brakspear 1905, 19.

29 Gilyard-Beer and Coppack 1986; Coppack 2003, 29–32.

30 See, most recently, Coppack 2003, 29; Coppack 2004, 43–4. For a contrasting interpretation of the evidence, in which a much larger aisled nave is suggested, see Fergusson and Harrison 1999, 48–51; Harrison 2002, 160, and n 61. See also Rüffer 2002.

31 It should date to the later 1130s: Fergusson and Harrison 1999, 46–8.

32 Gilyard-Beer and Coppack 1986, 180–1; France 1992, 194–8.

33 These are examined below in chapter 5.

34 Coppack 2001, 326–8; Coppack et al 2002, 45–9, 105–6.

35 Butler 1988 and 2002.

36 For the date of Grey and context, see Stalley 1987, 55, 93–5, 245;

more recently, Harrison 2002. Professor Stalley wonders whether the late dates of the churches at Bective, Dunbrody and Tintern Parva (relative to their foundations) suggest that earlier examples of the primitive form might lie buried: Stalley 1987, 45.

37 For Saddell (founded c 1207) and Culross (founded 1217/18), see Fawcett 1994, 65–6; Robinson 1998, 93, 169. Again, at the Scottish churches of Balmerino and Deer, the naves may originally have been unaisled.

38 For a survey of 'minor cruciform' churches across England and Wales, mostly of aisleless form, see Thurlby 2002.

39 See, for example, Fergusson 1984a, 28; Halsey 1986, 69–73; Franklin 1989, 47–9; Greene 1989, 84–7; Thurlby 2002, 251–2; Harrison 2002, 161; Coppack 2003, 30; Franklin 2004. For Kenilworth (founded c 1125) see Carey-Hill 1927; for Kirkham (c 1122), Coppack et al 1995, 63–70, 131–3; for Norton (1134), Greene 1989, 80–4; for Portchester (by 1128), Baker and Borg 1977, 105–20. For further context, see Robinson 1980.

40 Although there have been excavations at both sites, the work has not been sufficiently extensive to prove matters conclusively. For Carmarthen (founded c 1125–30), see James 1985; for Llanthony (c 1103–18), Evans 1980 and 1983–8.

41 In general, see Clapham 1923. Also, for a useful summary of Augustinian churches in Ireland, where in general terms variant forms of aisleless plans were retained over a longer period, see O'Keeffe 1999, 107–45, passim.

42 There are difficulties in leaping to the conclusion (as some have done) that the Augustinians were themselves the source, especially given the fragmentary nature of the congregation at this time. As with so much else during this early phase, the absence of firm dating evidence makes it almost impossible to be sure in which direction the influences were moving in any particular region at any one time.

43 [Taylor] 1938; Thomas 1962; Lloyd et al 2004, 296–7.

44 Episcopal Acts, I, 235; Cowley 1977, 270.

45 The date of the vault has become controversial. Lloyd et al (2004, 296–7), who in any case suggest a mid-thirteenth-century date for the nave as a whole, see it as an addition to the original fabric. The south transept became the base of a late medieval tower; the north transept is lost.

46 Although the nave at Pembroke may well provide the best impression available for the likely appearance of the first stone church at Tintern, it is too much of a leap of faith to link its barrel vaults to Burgundian inspiration. This is particularly true when we examine the regional context. Manorbier, for example, is another twelfth-century Pembrokeshire church with extensive stone vaulting, dated to the thirteenth century in Lloyd et al 2004, 274–5. And there is a marked south-westerly emphasis in the distribution of early stone vaulting in Wales generally, both in secular and ecclesiastical buildings: see Smith 1988, 372–4, 688–91. As outlined in more detail in a later chapter, the Premonstratensian church at Talley (founded 1184–9) also featured pointed barrel vaults of stone construction: Robinson and Platt 1998, 36–40.

Chapter 5
The Arrival of the 'Bernardine' Plan

1 For summaries of the three, see Bilson 1909, 210–17; Aubert 1947, I, 182–3, 191–3, 213–14; Hahn 1957, 108–10, 118–24; Dimier 1982, 46–7, 264–5, 299–301; Fergusson 1984a, 38, 52–3; Leroux-Dhuys 1998, 172–7, 296–8; Frankl 2000, 93–8, and nn 48E–59A. As to the two remaining senior French mother houses, Morimond is explored

in chapter 7, while the details of La Ferté are almost entirely lost, though a plan of 1680 survives, for which see Aubert 1947, I, 113, 180; Hirst *et al* 1983, 210.

2   For the most recent views, see Plouvier 1994, 68, 72–4; Kinder 1996a, 355; Plouvier 1998, 132, 142–4; Frankl 2000, 93 n 50.

3   For the corpus of illustrations, see Gras 1982; Plouvier and Saint-Denis 1998, 380–96. As many as eleven exploratory excavations were made on the site of the church between 1959 and 1964, though, sadly, a full report has not yet been published: Kinder 1996a, 356.

4   As shown, for example, in Dimier 1949–67, I, plan 79; Hahn 1957, 123.

5   As in Frankl 2000, 93.

6   The account appears in Migne 1844–64, CLXXXV, cols 284–5. For translations, see Webb and Walker 1960, 86–8; Braunfels 1972, 243–4; Brooke 1986, 21.

7   For the sources and explanation, see Aubert 1947, I, 64; Kinder 1991, 209–19; Fergusson 1994, 88; Kinder 1996b, 371; Gajewski 2004, 78.

8   As given in Dimier 1949–67, I, plan 83; Hahn 1957, 121.

9   See, in particular, Schlink 1970, 138–41; Untermann 1984, 618–24. Schlink argues that the church depicted in the 1708 illustrations is far too stylistically advanced to be a building of the 1130s, and that it must represent an entire reconstruction, probably begun in the early 1150s. For Stuart Harrison (who has shown me his notes for a forthcoming analysis) it is the scale of the church shown by Milley, both in elevation and in plan (figs 16, 34, 39 and 41), which stretches belief in comparison to the known Cistercian buildings of the 1130s and 1140s.

10   For the full review, see Kennedy [Gajewski] 1996, 131–65. In reaffirming the 1130s transfer from the *monasterium vetus*, she disputes the view put forward by Untermann (1984, 618–24) that the rebuilding may have taken place as early as the 1120s (followed in Nussbaum 2000, 30). Gajewski believes that the contradictory evidence of the *Vita Prima* suggests a start date for the new church of either 1132–3 or 1136–7, though she accepts that it was completed by *c* 1145: Kennedy [Gajewski] 1996, 133–60.

11   Fontenay is explored further below but in sum see, most recently, Bourgeois 2000; Auberger 2001.

12   Using a range of pictorial evidence, and not just the 1708 Milley illustrations, Gajewski argues that the chevet at the east end, seen by others as an addition of the 1150s and representing Clairvaux III (*see* fig 34), is actually part of a single build with the transepts and nave: Kennedy [Gajewski] 1996, 159–65. Her arguments are summarized in Frankl 2000, 317, nn 51A–51B. This same view was proposed in Schlink 1970, 138–41, and is given fresh support in Henriet 2001, 275–8, *passim*.

13   It is, for example, worth bearing in mind that although the precise relative chronologies between Clairvaux and Cîteaux may continue to evade us, the church thought to have been built at the mother house in the 1140s (Cîteaux II) was itself of considerable size (*see* fig 34). Again, at Foigny (Aisne), founded as a daughter house of Clairvaux in 1121, a church of comparable scale and form was begun no later than 1150–60: Dimier 1960; Dimier 1982, 48–9; Peugniez 2001, 365–6.

14   For which, see Kinder 1984.

15   Historically, the most widely accepted date for the construction of the church at Pontigny has been *c* 1150. Fontaine (1928, 7), for example, believed work began at the east end in 1150. Aubert (1947, I, 187; 1959) suggested the construction programme was initiated between 1140 and 1160, again at the east end, with the nave following on in 1160–70. Hahn (1957, 108–10) likewise suggested

1140–70 as the bracket range. Dimier (1982, 299–301) gives 1140–60 for the church as a whole. And Branner (1960, 16–17, 163) argued for a start date of *c* 1145 at the east end, with the nave completed soon after 1155.

16   Kinder 1992. See also Frankl 2000, 95–6.

17   Kennedy [Gajewski] 1996, 103–24.

18   Given that Guichard, the second abbot of Pontigny, came from Cîteaux in 1136, there seems a strong chance that the design of the transepts was influenced by the new work at the mother house: Kinder 1982, 84; Wilson 1992, 24.

19   There has been considerable debate about whether the nave ribs are afterthoughts to the original design. The point cannot be conclusively resolved: Kennedy [Gajewski] 1996, 115; Frankl 2000, 95–6.

20   On the basis of his excavations at Himmerod (founded 1135), Clairvaux's second daughter house in Germany, Esser became convinced that Bernard had exercised a direct influence on architectural planning. See, in particular, Esser 1953 and 1954. His views are considered to be rather excessive today. See also Eydoux 1953.

21   In fact, it was Hahn who produced the fullest analysis of the 'Bernardine' church concept: Hahn 1957, 84–128. For a summary of Eberbach, with good illustrations, see Dimier 1971, 103–7, pls 17–32. The house became Cistercian in 1135. The church is dated by Dimier to *c* 1170–86; Nussbaum (2000, 30, and n 81) gives 1140–50.

22   Hahn 1957, 66–82, 314–39. For Hahn, the system of modular proportions was a key element in the transmission of the ideal Cistercian plan over long distances. For a more recent discussion of Hahn's theory related to Bordesley Abbey, see Hirst *et al* 1983, 208–29; for its application to the Cistercian churches of Ireland, Stalley 1987, 68–75.

23   For his views on the 'Bernardine' plan, see Bucher 1957, 184–90 (with an English summary of the book's content at 273–80); see also Bucher 1960–1. For a summary of Bonmont, with illustrations, see Dimier 1971, 75–9, pls 11–16.

24   Otto Von Simson, for example, was in no doubt that Bernard 'took an active part in developing the design of Cistercian architecture'. He was another who saw proportion as a guiding principle in the planning of the Clairvaux family of churches: Von Simson 1956, 47–50.

25   For just one example of a work pointing to the contrasting evidence from plans alone, see Dimier 1987a. In looking at the evidence from the Irish abbeys, Stalley (1994) has shown the need for caution. For Wales, Butler (1994) seems prepared to accept that Bernard may have exercised at least some influence. See also Leroux 1991, 243–4.

26   For general background, see Hirst *et al* 1983, 208–22; Fergusson 1984a, 13, 34–8; Coldstream 1998, 40–1.

27   Of course, in reconstructing the plan of Clairvaux II based on Milley's illustrations of 1708, we now have to bear in mind the fresh doubt thrown over the date of the church depicted: Kennedy [Gajewski] 1996, 131–65.

28   For Aubert (1947, I, 97–8) there was no question that Geoffrey d'Ainai was one of the order's leading architectural masters of the time. Peter Fergusson seems prepared to allow for this possibility, based on the evidence available on Geoffrey's role: Fergusson 1983, 80–4; Fergusson 1984a, 13, 169. Halsey (1986, 67–8), however, questions whether he was really someone who designed and built Cistercian churches, a view expressed in Stalley 1994, 15. For Geoffrey's earlier role in the north of England (chiefly associated with laying out temporary buildings), see Fergusson 1984a, 39–40; Gilyard-Beer and Coppack 1986, 149, 174–5; Fergusson and

Harrison 1999, 54–5; Coppack *et al* 2002, 102–3.

29 Aubert 1947, I, 97; King 1954, 237. In 1138, Achard was despatched to Himmerod in Germany to advise on building there, the connection which allowed Esser to develop his 'Bernardine' theories: Esser 1953; Hahn 1957, 80, 252–3.

30 As Kinder has pointed out, it is clear from Dom Milley's illustrations of 1708 that the church depicted must have featured a three-storey internal elevation and cannot have been barrel-vaulted like many of the known 'Bernardine' examples. She likens it to the church at La Bénisson-Dieu (Loire), founded in 1138, in which small openings into the aisle roofs were placed between the arcade and the clerestory: Kinder 1991, 210–11. See also Kennedy [Gajewski] 1996, 148–50. For La Bénisson-Dieu, see Chauvin 1998, 16–17; Peugniez 2001, 447–9. In an earlier review of the evidence, Aubert suggested two possibilities: on the one hand, it may be that the *c* 1135 building was planned to have two storeys and to feature barrel vaults over the main vessel, but that this was never finished and rib vaults were introduced later; or it may be that the original barrel vault over the nave was rebuilt with a clerestory in the 1150s to match the new reconstructed presbytery (Clairvaux III): Aubert 1947, I, 182–3; see also Fergusson 1984a, 52–3.

31 There is a considerable literature on this highly celebrated site. In general, see Aubert 1928; Aubert 1947, I, 114, 157–8, 346–7; Hahn 1957, 97–103; Fergusson 1970, 211–12; Dimier 1982, 66–72, pls 1–15; Stalley 1987, 77–8; Leroux-Dhuys 1998, 188–95; Chauvin 1998, 60–3. The most recent guidebook (in English) is Boutevin 1996. However, it is fair to say that the chronology and the sequence of construction at Fontenay are probably less well understood than common assertions in the literature might imply. It has recently been argued that a date in the 1130s is more likely for the church: Kennedy [Gajewski] 1996, 88–102. For the two most recent studies of Fontenay, both of considerable importance, see Bourgeois 2000; Auberger 2001.

32 On the significance of light, see Fergusson 1984a, 13; Cassidy-Welch 2001, 98–100.

33 Hanno Hahn termed this arrangement 'Hohenstaffelung'. However, the Fontenay form varies from the eventual arrangement seen in the transept roofs at Clairvaux, where they were set at the same height as that over the nave (*see* fig 16).

34 On the absence of crossing towers in the order's early churches, see Fergusson 1970. For a re-evaluation of the earliest evidence for Cistercian towers in Britain and Ireland, see Harrison 2004.

35 Stalley 1987, 77.

36 Quite apart from any discussion of its 'Bernardine' precedence, it might also be remembered that the repertoire of components seen in this one Cistercian church were all present in similar form within general Burgundian ecclesiastical architecture of the early twelfth century. See, for example, the views in Kennedy [Gajewski] 1996, 39–50, 95–7.

37 As noted already in this chapter, there is debate concerning the original elevations and vaulting arrangements in Clairvaux II, now further complicated by the arguments that the church seen in the 1708 Milley illustrations is not that begun *c* 1135.

38 On the 'Bernardine' plan in England and Ireland, see Hahn 1957, 203–14.

39 Knowles and Hadcock 1971, 124; Fergusson and Harrison 1999, 37–8.

40 As noted in chapter 4, the evidence come from a geophysical survey. See Fergusson and Harrison 1999, 46–7. In planning his first stone monastery at Rievaulx, it seems that Abbot William may well have been assisted by Geoffrey d'Ainai: Gilyard-Beer and Coppack 1986,

174; Fergusson and Harrison 1999, 54–5.

41 Fergusson and Harrison 1999, 48–50, 54–5. The authors suggest that it was this phase of building that may have been influenced by Geoffrey d'Ainai.

42 Robinson 1998, 144–8; Fawcett and Oram 2004.

43 Fawcett 1994, 33–4; Fergusson and Harrison 1999, 48–51; Fawcett 2002, 29; Fawcett and Oram 2004, 76–86.

44 On the church and its debt to Vauclair, see Coppack 2003, 33–9. On Vauclair (itself a first-generation daughter house of Clairvaux, founded in 1134), see Courtois 1972 and 1982; Peugniez 2001, 371–2; on the arguments for the Rievaulx connection, Fergusson and Harrison 1999, 48–51, 54–5.

45 Archbishop Malachy stayed at Clairvaux on a journey to Rome in 1140 and established a remarkable bond of friendship with St Bernard: Gwynn and Hadcock 1970, 139–40; Stalley 1987, 248.

46 *Bernard Letters*, 454–5.

47 For the church, see Stalley 1980; Stalley 1987, 56–8, 81–2. For a note of caution on Robert's role, see Stalley 1994, 15–16.

48 Stalley 1987, 68–71.

49 Some authorities prefer 1146 as the date of foundation: Knowles and Hadcock 1971, 116; Robinson 1998, 73–4.

50 Tester 1973.

51 Hirst *et al* 1983, 219–20; Fergusson 1984a, 114–15.

52 For Abbot Thomas, see Knowles *et al* 2001, 128.

53 A presbytery of similar proportions, dating to *c* 1150, is known from Bordesley, where a barrel vault is suggested: Hirst *et al* 1983, 231–8.

54 On Ailred and his building campaigns, see Fergusson and Harrison 1999, 59–150, *passim*.

55 Fergusson and Harrison 1999, 69–91. For earlier views on the church, see Fergusson 1984a, 33–8; Halsey 1986, 77–80.

56 Coppack 2003, 43–54.

57 For Margam generally, see catalogue entry; David 1929; Butler 1971, *passim*; Robinson 1993a; Newman 1995, 424–9; Evans 1996, 21–36; Robinson 1998, 138–41.

58 For the main restoration schemes of 1805–9 and 1872–3, see Adams 1984; Evans 1996, 26–7, 137–9.

59 Regionally, the basic form of the Margam piers goes back to those in the lower floor of the episcopal palace chapel at Hereford, assumed to have been built by Bishop Robert of Lorraine (Lotharingia) (1079–95) and drawn by William Stukeley (1687–1765) before its loss in 1737. On the pedigree of the Hereford chapel itself, see Fernie 2000, 234, where the Stukeley drawings are reproduced. Round-headed arcades with plain, square orders are earlier found in the west of England on cylindrical piers at Great Malvern (after 1085) and at St John's, Chester (*c* 1125–50), both with three orders; and at Leominster (after 1125), with two: Thurlby 1995b, 23–4; Fernie 2000, *passim*; Gem 2000, *passim*. St Woolos, Newport (*c* 1140) has two-order arcades of similar form, again on cylindrical piers (*see* fig 30), but the overall form at Chepstow is closer to that found at Margam (*see* fig 29).

60 The wall shafts which rise on the second pair of nave piers (from the east) appear to have been introduced during one of the nineteenth-century phases of restoration. At first, the restored high roof was built of lath and plaster; it was replaced in 1872–3 with the panelled work that survives today: Adams 1984, 62–6.

61 The existing roof cuts across the heads of the two outer west front windows (*see* fig 42). The pitch of the pre-restoration roof, and the jambs of a gable window, appear in illustrations by John Carter: BL, Add. MS 29940, fols 63–64, with fol 63 reproduced in Birch 1897, 89. Wooden barrel vaults are suggested for the near-contemporary naves at Fountains and at Rievaulx: Fergusson and Harrison 1999,

69–81; Coppack 2003, 51.

62 As noted earlier, groin vaults may have covered both the aisles and the main vessel in the nave at Benedictine Chepstow.

63 Though the shaft-rings and the scalloped capitals may well have been reworked during the restoration of 1805–9, their original character is confirmed by a number of antiquarian drawings. Particularly valuable in this regard is Carter's detailed illustration of 1803: BL, Add. MS 29940, fol 64. The 'gorged' rolls that appear in the window mouldings are notable. They occur in similar chronological contexts (c 1170–80) at, for example, Augustinian Keynsham (on which more is said in chapter 6) and in the surviving east claustral range at Combe Abbey (Warwickshire).

64 As proposed for, say, the west front at Rievaulx: Fergusson and Harrison 1999, 75. At Buildwas, however, in a nave under way by c 1160–5 (see fig 58), there were tiered lancets in the west front gable: Fergusson 1984a, 92–4; Robinson 2002c, 10–11.

65 At Trois-Fontaines (Clairvaux's first daughter house, founded in 1118), the lower two registers are very similar to Margam; there appears to have been a rose window in the gable. For the site, see Dimier 1965; Erlande-Brandenburg 1977; Peugniez 2001, 133–4. The west front is illustrated in Fergusson 1984a, pl 15.

66 Fergusson and Harrison 1999, 69–81.

67 *Annales Monastici*, I, 20; Birch 1897, 59. It is of interest, too, that Bishop William extended his general protection to the abbey around this time: *Llandaff Acta*, 35–6.

68 To suggest a date closer to 1190 would not only push the features of the Margam west front rather later than some of the comparative motifs in advanced west country early Gothic, but would also imply a rather extended nave campaign, during which the piers would definitely have become long outmoded.

69 The doorway was located in a stable to the west of the abbey in 1840 and taken down. For the context, see Orrin 1988, 346; Newman 1995, 551; Evans 1996, 34.

70 Newman (1995, 551) describes this as a 'shuttlecock' motif. See also Stalley 2002, 25.

71 For the 1920s excavations, see [Collier] 1925–6; Collier 1927. The more recent programme of work is published in Ludlow 2002. See also Clapham 1921, 205–8; Robinson 1998, 204–5; James 2000, 58–9; Ludlow 2001.

72 This is the sequence of events as broadly accepted: see catalogue entry; Lloyd 1939, II, 593–4; Cowley 1977, 22; Pryce 1996, 155–6, 159.

73 The eight-bay naves at Margam and Whitland might be compared with those of similar scale at, for example, Bordesley, Dundrennan, Kirkstall and Roche in Britain; Baltinglass, Boyle and Mellifont in Ireland; Fontenay and Noirlac in France; and Chiaravalle Milanese in Italy. Smaller 'Bernardine' naves with seven or even fewer bays are not uncommon, and larger examples such as Rievaulx (nine bays), Dore (ten) and Fountains (eleven) might readily be cited. Some of these sites are illustrated here (see fig 41); for others, see Bilson 1909; Dimier 1971 and 1982; Stalley 1987; Robinson 1998, 64–205. For the fullest corpus of Cistercian plans, see Dimier 1949–67.

74 The northern piers have survived rather better than those to the south. A mason's mark identified on the first pier of the south arcade is of almost identical design to one on the north-east presbytery buttress: Ludlow 2002, 55, 57.

75 He describes it as 'a small nook column about 18 inches long, with dowels': [Collier] 1925–6, 64.

76 Cardiff City Library, Charles Norris Drawings, vol 17, fol 572.

77 The return wall, which can be seen surviving to three courses in the foreground of the drawing, is puzzling. But the only other obvious location to try and place a doorway of such elaboration (if that is indeed what it is) is the chapter house facade.

78 The south transept remains unexcavated, though there is no reason to assume its form was other than that seen in its northern counterpart.

79 Various clues as to the superstructure of Whitland are to be gleaned both from the freshly excavated *ex situ* stonework from the site and from those fragments which lie scattered around in adjacent buildings (especially at the house, Whitland Abbey). There are, for example, one or two vault ribs of a similar profile to those known from the transept chapels at the marginally later church of Strata Florida, on which more is said in chapter 6. Yet more intriguing is the discovery at Whitland of at least one fragment of 'domino' pattern vault rib, used extensively in the presbytery at Strata Florida in a remodelling thought to date to around the turn of the twelfth century. If the conclusions drawn on that site are correct, then the Whitland fragment suggests that a remodelling also took place here. This would not, however, preclude the notion of an earlier stone barrel vault over the presbytery. I have benefited greatly from discussions on these points with Stuart Harrison.

80 Staircases are found in just this position at Dundrennan and Roche, for example.

81 In liturgical terms, the steps from the nave into the crossing must have coincided in broad terms with the eastern end of the monks' choir stalls. Meanwhile, the topography also seems to have dictated a stepping up from the south transept into the crossing, and from the crossing into the north transept: Ludlow 2002, 54–5.

82 Collier 1927, 242; [Collier] 1925–6, 64.

83 The likely Fontenay-style appearance of the church is suggested in Robinson 1993a, 57; Robinson 1998, 204; Robinson and Platt 1998, 27. This is now the line followed in the report on recent archaeological investigations at the site: Ludlow 2002, 59–63.

84 The chapels were most likely laid out in the same fashion as those at Whitland. Butler (1994, 5), however, suggests they may have taken the *en échelon* form known at Fountains [and Rievaulx].

85 For Fontenay, see n 31 above. For Noirlac, see Aubert 1931; Crozet 1931; Aubert 1947, I, 119, 166–7, 270; Dimier 1982, 255–60, pls 99–108; Chauvin 1998, 88–91.

86 For Fountains, see Coppack 2003, 33–54; for Rievaulx, with a case made both for Abbot William's church (c 1140) and Abbot Ailred's (begun soon after 1147), including general comment, Fergusson and Harrison 1999, 48–51, 73–81, *passim*; for Melrose, Fawcett 1994, 33–4; Fawcett 2002, 29; Fawcett and Oram 2004, 80–4. Further observations on the gradual adoption of crossing towers will be found in Fergusson 1970, a work now considerably updated by Harrison 2004.

87 Stalley 1986, 120–4; Stalley 1987, 79–83.

88 Bonmont became Cistercian in 1131, and the church appears to have been largely finished by the early 1140s: Bucher 1957, 59–114; Dimier 1971, 75–9, pls 11–16; Peugniez 2001, 499–500.

89 For Boquen (founded in 1137), see Aubert 1947, I, 172–3, 233, 273; Dimier 1982, 53; Chauvin 1998, 22–3; Peugniez 2001, 82–3.

90 For L'Escaladieu (consecrated in 1160), see Aubert 1947, I, 165–6, 235; Dimier 1982, 75–9, pls 16–23; Chauvin 1998, 52–3; Peugniez 2001, 270–2.

91 For Melleray (founded in 1145, with the church consecrated in 1183), see Dimier 1982, 50; Chauvin 1998, 84–5; Peugniez 2001, 336–7.

92 For Vauclair (where the layout of the church is attributed to Geoffrey d'Ainai in 1140), see Courtois 1972 and 1982; Chauvin 1998, 138–9.

93 For Amelungsborn (begun soon after 1135), see Hahn 1957, 236–41; Frankl 2000, 95, 317 n 53.

94 Belonging to the Morimond affiliation, Maulbronn was founded in 1139. The church was begun *c* 1147 and consecrated in 1178: see Hahn 1957, 244–7; Knapp 1997, 31–66.

95 Alvastra was founded in 1143 and the church consecrated in 1185: see Swartling 1967; Dimier 1971, 30–1; France 1992, 29–30, 194.

96 Monasteranenagh, founded in 1148, with its church built *c* 1170–1210, is one of the better examples of desolate Cistercian design in Ireland: Stalley 1987, 104–5, 248–9.

97 For the most recent views, see Kennedy [Gajewski] 1996, *passim*.

98 Bony 1983, 512–13 n 14.

99 Bucher 1957, 278.

100 The phrase 'stripped austerity' is borrowed from Fergusson (1984a, 38). For an older view, see Bucher 1960–1. See also Stalley 1987, 79; Fergusson and Harrison 1999, 78–81; and for another perspective, Cassidy-Welch 2001, 91–103.

101 Halsey 1986, 77–85.

102 On this and what follows generally on the architectural context for Rievaulx, see Fergusson and Harrison 1999, 69–81.

103 Founded in 1138, Tre Fontane was another daughter house of Clairvaux. Its first abbot, Bernard Paganelli, a disciple of St Bernard, was to become Pope Eugenius III (1145–53): Fergusson and Harrison 1999, 62–3, 81. Construction work on the church was apparently begun in 1140, and cannot have progressed too far by the time of Ailred's visit in 1142. For a full account of recent investigations coupled with the restoration of this important Roman church, see Romanini 1994.

104 For this oft-quoted site, see Aubert 1947, I, 178–9; Labbé 1948–52; Picquenard 1961; Blanchot 1985; Chauvin 1998, 42–3. The similarity to Margam is noted in Stalley 1987, 83. For a recent reassessment of the significance of Clairmont, see Gajewski 2003, 160–3.

105 Unlike Margam and Whitland, there is no respond on the aisle side of the piers (*see* fig 43).

106 Stalley 1987, 79.

107 As noted earlier, it would be wrong to overlook entirely the regional Anglo-Norman antecedents for some of the structural elements.

108 This point has been made by many scholars, but see, in particular, Fergusson 1984a, 38; Fergusson and Harrison 1999, 80–1; Stalley 1987, 79.

CHAPTER 6
THE TRANSITION TO REGIONAL GOTHIC FORMS

1 Dr Christopher Wilson informs us that although the image was initially created by the German scholar Carl Schnaase in 1856, the precise formula 'missionaires de l'art gothique' first appeared in an essay of 1859 by M le baron F de Roisin: Wilson 1986, 86. For Schnaase, incidentally, there was no question of a wholesale transmission of French Gothic into areas east of the Rhine, but rather a merging of new elements with indigenous forms. For a fresh account of these developments in Germany, see Nussbaum 2000, 15–48.

2 Branner 1960, 14, 17. As Wilson points out, however, plain walling was to be a very prominent feature in Mendicant Gothic churches of the thirteenth century, used there as a demonstration of authority: Wilson 1986, n 1. See also Frankl 2000, 96.

3 Kennedy [Gajewski] 1996, 121–2.

4 The date is proposed in Musso 1991, 195–7.

5 For the Fontenay chapter house, see Aubert 1947, II, 62–3; Branner 1960, 18, 141–2; Kennedy [Gajewski] 1996, 90–4; Auberger 2001, 97–100. Schlink's date of 1160 is surely too late: Schlink 1970, 95 n 259. Some clustered piers of comparable proportions also survive for a demolished claustral building at Pontigny, noted in Wilson 1986, 98–9.

6 He referred to 'missionaries of French art': Bilson 1909, 197.

7 Aubert wrote of 'missionnaires du gothique': Aubert 1947, I, 248.

8 Wilson 1986. See also Wilson 1992, 44–5, 72–7.

9 Stalley 1986, 124–32; Stalley 1987, 92–103.

10 See, for example, Pérez 1994, 34, 43. A number of other relevant works by the author are cited there.

11 The literature on this subject is of course vast. Among the more accessible and scholarly overviews, see Bony 1983, 5–243; Wilson 1992, 13–90; Frankl 2000, 68–103. Among the older works on the theme, one should not overlook Bilson 1898–9.

12 The church is now situated in what are the northern suburbs of Paris, in the department of Seine-St-Denis.

13 Bony 1983, 117. See also Frankl 2000, 67, 309. On Abbot Suger and a fresh review of St-Denis, see Grant 1998, especially 28–31, 238–74. For Wilson, the splendour of early Gothic St-Denis is of 'a chaste and cerebral kind … unlikely to have raised any Cistercian hackles': Wilson 1992, 44. Indeed, Grant argues that a bond of genuine affection was eventually established between Suger and Bernard of Clairvaux, and she makes the point that Bernard was almost certainly present at the consecration of the new work in 1144: Grant 1998, 150–4.

14 For background, see Bony 1983, 45–155; Wilson 1992, 24–60; Erlande-Brandenburg and Mérel-Brandenburg 1995, 239–72; Grant 1998, 271–4.

15 A key general work of reference remains Enlart 1895. On early Gothic in Picardy, see most recently Sandron 2001. The significance of the Premonstratensian contribution is noted in Fergusson 1975, 175; Fergusson 1984a, 68; Wilson 1986, 101–5. Full bibliographies on the houses of this order can be found in Ardura 1993.

16 Noted in Fergusson 1975, 174; Wilson 1986, 92–3, 100–1. On attendance at the General Chapter, with a useful map of approximate routes, see Williams 1998, 33–41.

17 The church was dismantled in the late eighteenth century. For what is known, see Aubert 1947, I, 287; Dimier 1960; Dimier 1982, 48–9; Clark 1984, 170–2; Peugniez 2001, 365–6.

18 The nave seems to have had a three-storey elevation: Aubert 1947, I, 19–20, 219–20 (with an engraving showing traceried windows of a much later date); Fergusson 1975, 174; Peugniez 2001, 302–3.

19 For what is known of the site, see Aubert 1947, I, 225–6; Baron 1958 and 1960; Peugniez 2001, 291–6. On the General Chapter's concern, see *Statutes*, 247.

20 Interestingly, the late Professor Lawrence Hoey made the point that Gothic architecture in northern Britain 'develops independently of the rest of the country': Hoey 1987, 249.

21 Wilson 1992, 72. For a general review, see Draper 1986.

22 For a range of views on Cistercian early Gothic in Britain and on its place in the development of the new style in the north of England see, in particular, Fergusson 1984a, 54–90; Wilson 1986; also Thurlby 2000. There is a very useful summary in Coldstream 1998, 44–9. For more on definitions and on other complexities in the argument, see Thurlby 1994.

23 On Kirkstall in general, see Hope and Bilson 1907, 10–27, 83–140; Fergusson 1984a, 48–53; Thurlby 1995a; Robinson 1998, 132–4.

24 In an early paper, Fergusson (1970, 217–18) suggested that the tower was added to the design of Kirkstall as part of a revised

campaign of construction, initiated after a brief hiatus. It has since been argued that the tower was part of the original scheme: Thurlby 1995a, 65–6; Harrison 2004, 129–31. Meanwhile, in considering the progressive nature of Kirkstall in general, it is important not to overlook the work in the nave at its mother house, Fountains. Apparently under construction as late as the 1160s, it shows none of the progressive traits associated with northern French Gothic. For the date of the work, see Robinson 1998, 113; Coppack 2003, 43–52. Stylistically, however, one would have to argue that Fountains is the earlier building. For fresh views on the likelihood of an early tower at Fountains, see Harrison 2004, 126–9.

25 Halsey (1986, 83) supports Bilson's view that the church at Kirkstall was built in a period of about fifteen years: Hope and Bilson 1907, 84 n 2. The chapter house piers may date from c 1160–5. One of them (west) is a squat version of those in the nave; the other (east) has a cylindrical core surrounded by eight detached shafts: Hope and Bilson 1907, 29–30. For further context, see Hoey 1986, 49.

26 As defined by Hoey, clustered piers are essentially round piers scalloped into shafted profiles. The shafts can then differ in size, shape and number, but there is usually symmetry in both cardinal and diagonal directions around an imaginary core: Hoey 1987, 250 n 32.

27 Fergusson 1984a, 50. The church of Great Paxton is sometimes cited as an example of their early use in England, illustrated in Webb 1956, pls 13 and 20.

28 In general, see Héliot 1968 (which excludes Cistercian examples). On the Benedictine nunnery of Berteaucourt-les-Dames, see Enlart 1895, 72–87; on Dommartin, Enlart 1895, 104–22; Pontroué 1973; Fergusson 1975, 175; Wilson 1986, 101–3; Hoey 1987, 251 n 41; Ardura 1993, 220–6; on Selincourt, Wilson 1986, 103–4; Hoey 1987, 251 n 40; Ardura 1993, 499–505.

29 As in the chapter house at Fontenay (c 1150–5) and in a lost building at Pontigny: Fergusson 1975, 163–4; Wilson 1986, 98–9.

30 The lost buildings at Clairmarais, Foigny and Vauclair come to mind. See Fergusson 1979; Fergusson 1984a, 50, 68; Wilson 1986, 100–5. Cautiously, Hoey (1987, 251) noted that clustered piers were 'never popular in French Gothic'.

31 That is to say, Kirkstall may not be the earliest building in the north of England to feature clustered piers.

32 Although both buildings featured clustered piers, Wilson (1992, 73) has argued for Cistercian precedence. To explain the features of Roger's choir at York, he states it can be affirmed that at least one northern Cistercian church must have been built in the Gothic style by the late 1150s. Nevertheless, it is as well to be aware that the literature on the archbishop's patronage at Ripon and York is now considerable. The consensus view, despite the loss of much of York, is that both buildings were highly significant in the early dissemination of French Gothic in northern Britain. Gee (1977, 121–5) argued that York was in hand by 1160 and may have been complete by c 1175, whereas Ripon was incomplete at the archbishop's death. Fergusson (1984a, 54, 66, 85–7) dated York to c 1165–75 and Ripon to c 1175–80. Wilson (1986, 88–98, passim) argues that York was begun in the late 1150s and completed by 1166, and that Ripon is also a work of the 1160s. Thurlby (1994) seems to concur with Wilson's views on the dating of York. For an independent account of the French influences on Roger's work at Ripon, see Hearn 1983. In the most recent overview of the building, Harrison and Barker (1999, 72–6) favour a construction date starting in the 1170s and suggest that building might have continued for some time after his death in 1181.

33 Apart from its crypt, the York choir was lost in a rebuilding of the minster's eastern arm in the late fourteenth century. For the latest published views, see Thurlby 2000, together with the summary in Brown 2003, 4–9. A new investigation of Archbishop Roger's work at York Minster is being carried out by Christopher Norton and Stuart Harrison.

34 The structural remains at Furness are particularly complex, with considerable difference of opinion over the various building programmes. An early Savigniac church (c 1127–47) appears to have been replaced in piecemeal fashion by one of 'Bernardine' plan from the mid-twelfth century onwards. In the new church, both the transepts and the nave featured three-storey elevations. The nave piers alternated between cylindrical and clustered forms. The aisles were rib-vaulted, but there was no high vault. The historic accounts are: Brakspear 1900; Hope 1900b, 227–9, 244–9. Fergusson (1984a, 55–60) has suggested that Furness was the first English Cistercian church in the new Gothic style. He dated the nave to c 1160–5 and thought the transepts must be later. Wilson (1986, 110–12) has also advanced claims for the primacy of Furness in the formation of northern Gothic. He too sees the nave as the earliest work in the rebuilt church, cautiously suggesting a date in the 1150s. He goes on to say: 'The Furness [nave] master's knowledge of Picard architecture of c 1150 was so detailed as to suggest he had obtained it at first hand.' More recently, Harrison and Wood (1998, 4–9) have advanced the view that the transepts are in fact the earliest sections of the rebuilt church (but give no approximate date). The nave, they claim, is later than hitherto assumed, constructed in a deliberately outmoded style to harmonize with the transepts. This opinion is based on an archaeological analysis of the building, though the results await full publication.

35 Bearing in mind the content of the previous note, in his discussion of the design and dating of all four churches, Wilson (1986, 106–16) concluded that the nave at Furness and the church at Kirkstead are the best contenders for an early link (c 1150s) between the emerging French Gothic style and its northern English counterpart. He sees Roche (with a generally accepted date of c 1170–80) as a post-York development, and interprets Byland (begun around 1170) as a close copy of Ripon with an emphasis upon English elements of detail. See further Fergusson 1971; Fergusson 1984a, 54–83.

36 As observed above (n 24), there have been different views about the potentially earlier examples of towers at Fountains and Kirkstall, the cases summarized in Harrison 2004, 126–31. The tower scheme at Furness was, it appears, inherited from the pre-1147 Savigniac church: Fergusson 1984a, 55–6; Wilson 1986, 110–11. See also Harrison 2004, 134.

37 At Roche and Furness the three-storey elevations were raised on 'Bernardine' plans.

38 For illustrations of pier profiles at Roche (north transept and nave), Furness (transept) and Byland (south transept), see Bilson 1909, 244. The nave at Kirkstead also appears to have featured clustered piers, some with keeled shafts. In turn, the work at this site was clearly connected in some way to nearby Vaudey Abbey (where there were definitely clustered pier forms), and is also very likely to have influenced the design of the Benedictine abbey at Bardney, located just a few kilometres to the north west. For Vaudey, see Fergusson 1984a, 152; Robinson 1998, 197–8. For Bardney, Brakspear 1922. The Bardney connections are examined in Wilson 1986, 108–9, and for a fresh survey of the design sources for Bardney, see Alexander 2004. Meanwhile, clustered piers were also to spread, for example, to the transepts at Dundrennan in Scotland (c 1175–85): Fergusson 1984a, 66–7; Fawcett 1994, 45–7. They appeared too in Ireland, in the transepts at Inch (c 1200),

presumably via its mother house at Furness: Stalley 1987, 95.

39 Rib vaults existed in the presbytery and nave aisles at Kirkstall, though these were derived from Anglo-Norman Romanesque precedents: Hope and Bilson 1907, 117–23; Bilson 1909, 222–41, *passim*; Thurlby 1995a, 68.

40 For an interesting assessment of the historical and geographical contexts, see Grant 1991, *passim*, especially 117, 125–6.

41 Effectively, the general context for early Gothic architecture in the west country was first set out in Brakspear 1931. Although old, the regional summary by Webb (1956, 87–95) remains useful. More recently, see Wilson 1978; Fergusson 1984a, 91–100; Malone 1984 (based on the author's unpublished PhD thesis: Malone 1973); Hoey 1987, 259–62 (in which he states: 'The early Gothic architecture of the west stands apart from the rest of the country'); Wilson 1992, 77–82; Thurlby 1995c, 115–32; Malone 2004.

42 On Buildwas, see Thompson 1937; Fergusson 1984a, 91–4; Robinson 1998, 78–80; Robinson 2002c.

43 On Bordesley and the regional connections of the form, see Walsh 1994.

44 For Cleeve, see Gilyard-Beer 1990, 13–15. We might also remember the columnar piers, apparently based on west country models, in use notably at Baltinglass (*c* 1160–70) and Boyle (*c* 1175–80) in Ireland: Stalley 1987, 84–92.

45 The lower parts of the east processional doorway survive *in situ*, and in the west range there is a fine late twelfth-century doorway of 'West Country School' type (as defined in Brakspear 1931, 6–7). The *ex situ* vault rib fragments might well be of *c* 1160–70 date. See Crawley-Boevey 1920; Fergusson 1984a, 124–5; Watkins 1985, facing 120, facing 224; Robinson 1998, 108–9; Verey and Brooks 2002, 364–6.

46 A fire of 1212 may have seriously damaged the twelfth-century 'Bernardine' church, after which it was rebuilt in the early thirteenth century. See Brakspear 1906–7, 499–504; Fergusson 1984a, 147–8; Robinson 1998, 173–5.

47 Virtually nothing is known of this potentially very significant site. See Fergusson 1984a, 129–30; Robinson 1998, 130; Verey and Brooks 2002, 559–60.

48 Fergusson 1984a, 92–3. As in the aisles at Kirkstall (as well as Benedictine Malmesbury), the transverse arches of the ribs are pointed, whereas the diagonals are semicircular.

49 Wilson 1978, 83–5; Wilson 1992, 77–8. His views are endorsed in Thurlby 1995c, 117, 120. Keynsham is a particularly interesting site, with the late twelfth-century church there having a rib-vaulted aisleless nave. The foundation charter has been dated as early as 1166/7: *Gloucester Charters*, 99–100. An 1169 reference in the annals of Cardiff records that 'the church of Keynsham was begun' in that year, though the formal beginning of conventual life should be dated to 1172–3: Vincent 1993. At the time of writing, the best that is available on the important excavations at the site is Lowe 1987. Nevertheless, the material has been assessed for a forthcoming account by Malcolm Thurlby and Stuart Harrison, to be published in a forthcoming volume of *Somerset Archaeol Natur Hist*. Elsewhere, another partially excavated building which might be of interest in this general context is the Cluniac priory at Monkton Farley in Wiltshire, a Lewes dependency. On the basis of the published plans, the design of the western crossing piers seems to have retained outmoded Romanesque characteristics, combining them with rather more progressive early Gothic features: see Brakspear 1922–3, 240–3; Brakspear 1931, pl x.

50 For the familial connections, see Vincent 1993, 98–105, *passim*. On the sources of the work and its character, see Wilson 1978; Wilson 1992, 77–9; also Barker 1994, 47–53. Grant (1991, 121) suggests that Worcester owes not a little to precepts established in Normandy, arguing that the same source was responsible for a more general impetus into early Gothic in the west country. See also Grant 2005.

51 On the date of the work, see the discussion in Malone 2004, 351–3. The collegiate church of St Andrew at Wells was to achieve full cathedral status in the early thirteenth century: Rodwell 2001, I, 2–3, 127–60.

52 Wilson 1992, 78–82. For fuller accounts of Wells, see Bilson 1928; Harvey 1982; Colchester 1987; for a fresh investigation of possible Cistercian influences on the building, Malone 2004.

53 Thurlby 1995c, 164–5. The great church at Glastonbury, begun in 1185, adopts a somewhat different vocabulary: Brakspear 1931; Thurlby 1995c, 157.

54 The observation on the architectural links between St Davids and Worcester is made in Wilson 1978, 89 n 40; Wilson 1992, 78. The connection was earlier noted by Lovegrove (1929, *passim*), and St Davids was included as an outlying example by Brakspear (1931) in his west country group. However, as Draper (1999, 112–13) points out, the common links with Worcester are of a general nature, with no hint that the St Davids designer was fully aware of what was going on there. A full reassessment of the architectural significance of St Davids is now presented in Stalley 2002; Lloyd *et al* 2004, 386–414 (also by Stalley). The church is discussed later in this chapter in relation to Cistercian developments at Strata Florida.

55 Llanthony was one of the buildings included by Brakspear (1931) in his key west country group. On the site generally, see Gardner 1915 and 1916; Lovegrove 1942–3; Newman 2000, 342–7; on the widely accepted date for the east end, Lovegrove 1946–7, 68; Craster 1963; Evans 1983–8, 52–3. Yet Lovegrove (who is followed by others) was inclined to feel that the work had to be later than the Worcester west bays. The fact is that the fresh endowments which are assumed to have driven the building began to flow from as early as 1171. Meanwhile, we must also take into account the challenge made to such early dates on historical grounds by John Rhodes. In his published note, Rhodes proposes a start date for the work as late as *c* 1198: Rhodes 1990. In a communication to me (June 1992), he revises this to 1189, suggesting that construction continued through to 1217 or later.

56 Despite its scale and importance, Dore was not discussed by Brakspear in his account of the 'West Country School of Masons': Brakspear 1931.

57 For background on Dore, see catalogue entry; Williams 1976a, 1–57; Shoesmith and Richardson 1997. Very little is known of the early twelfth-century buildings at Morimond itself. The church, considered further in chapter 7, was rebuilt to an enlarged plan sometime after *c* 1155.

58 For important accounts of Dore, see RCHME 1931, 1–6 (where it is suggested the first rebuilding began *c* 1180); Fergusson 1984a, 94–100 (suggesting *c* 1170); Malone 1984 (*c* 1175); O'Callaghan 1995 (1170–80s); Harrison and Thurlby 1997 (*c* 1175). All dating suggestions are based on stylistic evidence.

59 The evidence is inconclusive, but this earlier scheme is likely to have been the posited first church.

60 These inner chapels were sacrificed in the later rebuilding of the presbytery, becoming part of the ambulatory aisle (fig 25). The southern arch has a moulded outer order.

61 Harrison and Thurlby (1997, 49, 50) argue that these shaft groups belong to the 'Bernardine' phase of the presbytery. The crocket capitals and angled abaci differ from the later forms further east. Also, on both sides, the shaft group does not course with the jambs

of the adjacent bay, but clearly there must have been at least one more intended bay in the original scheme. In fact, Paul (1904, 120–1) thought the 'Bernardine' presbytery was of three bays, its length echoed in the subsequent rebuilding. Fergusson (1984a, 95) preferred two; Harrison and Thurlby (1997, 48–9) say the available evidence does not allow for certainty either way.

62 The former line of these roofs is preserved as hood mouldings beneath the later roofing arrangement over the chapels: O'Callaghan 1995, 97; Harrison and Thurlby 1997, 47.

63 As noted in chapter 4, this could also have been the case in the pre-'Bernardine' church. The form is known in the 'Bernardine' churches at Fountains and Rievaulx, and occurs very locally in the last quarter of the twelfth century at Augustinian Llanthony, on which see Lovegrove 1946–7; Evans 1983–8.

64 As noted in O'Callaghan 1995, 97; Harrison and Thurlby 1997, 47–8. The need for upper choir entrances in this position arose when the monks' choir stalls extended across the full width of the crossing. A similar arrangement is known, for example, from Fountains: Coppack 2003, 53.

65 Malone (1984) opted for an especially complex structural history across the transepts, based on differences in rib, base and arcade profiles. Her sequence swings back and forth between both sides of the building. Fergusson (1984a) takes a similar line. However, there are grounds for accepting a more logical sequence from north to south, with the presbytery included, as argued in O'Callaghan 1995, 96–8; Harrison and Thurlby 1997, 49–52.

66 Solid walls between chapels are found in the west of England, for example at Bordesley (c 1150) and at Buildwas (no later than c 1160): Hirst et al 1983, 212–47, passim; Robinson 2002c, 9. In the north of England, they were abandoned in rebuilt transepts at Furness (perhaps c 1150–70) and at Roche (c 1170–80): Fergusson 1984a, 56–67.

67 Originally, the chapels in the north transept may have been designed with barrel vaults in mind, in which case the corbel-supported ribs were perhaps an afterthought: O'Callaghan 1995, 97. The geometry of the ribs was similar to that in the nave aisles at Malmesbury and in the chapter house at Buildwas (fig 60).

68 In detail, although there are five principal shafts in each group, a smaller set-back shaft separates the centre triplet from the outer pair.

69 Harrison and Thurlby 1997, 50–1 (where tufa is mentioned as another possibility). O'Callaghan (1995, 102–3) also suggested timber vaults, though he argues that the transept examples were introduced only in the subsequent rebuilding of the east end. See also Hearn and Thurlby 1997.

70 Fergusson (1970, 218) certainly thought that the Dore crossing carried a tower, but this has recently been challenged in Harrison 2004, 134. The evidence is by no means conclusive, with Harrison accepting the possibility of a timber tower. For an east–west section drawing through the crossing, see Blashill 1885, facing 366. At Bordesley, it is thought that the period one church was begun about 1150, though the lantern may have been introduced towards the end of the scheme: Hirst et al 1983, frontispiece, 244–6. For Buildwas, see Fergusson 1984a, 92–3; Robinson 2002c, 8; Harrison 2004, 132.

71 Bony 1949, 11 n 4.

72 Chars is dated to c 1165–70 and Le Bourg-Dun to c 1170. For an insightful review of the surviving Cistercian material in Normandy, see Grant 1988. The church at Mortemer was virtually complete by 1163, though the east end was rebuilt 1174–9: Gallagher 1982; Peugniez 2001, 324–5.

73 Malone 1984, 50.

74 Fergusson 1984a, 96, pl 116.

75 Noted in Hoey 1987, 259.

76 O'Callaghan 1995.

77 Harrison and Thurlby 1997, 49–52, 61–2. However, whilst west country precedents may well account for the assemblage of features found at Dore, this surely does not preclude the underlying wave of change lapping at the shores of England. Meanwhile, Lindy Grant is another to point out that north-eastern France is probably the source, for example, of 'the fussy elaborations, the gouges and fillets' which distinguish English arch mouldings: Grant 1991, 114–15. Such features were certainly to become characteristic of Welsh Cistercian buildings over the next half-century. Dr Grant's new work (Grant 2005) has appeared too late for its content to be taken into account here, though it includes much of interest on the architectural links between Normandy and England in this period.

78 To follow the sequence of his work see, in particular, Paul 1893, 1896, 1898b, 1904, 1927 and 1931. See also catalogue entry for further details.

79 For his ten-bay plan, see Paul 1927, facing 269; and again (with revisions) in Paul 1931, facing 500. This is the basis of the revised plan published by the RCHME, appearing in RCHME 1934, facing 226. See also Harrison 1997a, 73–5.

80 Harrison and Thurlby (1997, 53) suggest the ten bays were always intended.

81 It has sometimes been suggested that the elevation may have included a false triforium, in the manner of those at Llanthony, Pershore and St Davids: Shoesmith 1979–81, 262, and n 12; Fergusson 1984a, 97–8. This is rejected by O'Callaghan (1995, 101), and yet more convincingly in Harrison and Thurlby 1997, 53–6.

82 The colour of the stone, and the block size, is of more concern to O'Callaghan (1995, 99), who wonders – given all the evidence – if the arcades were raised at marginally different points. This does seem to have been the case at Buildwas, and was related to the need to progress the monastic buildings to one side.

83 The in situ capitals are illustrated in Blashill 1885, facing 368. The ex situ example is illustrated in Paul 1896, 298.

84 Illustrated in Paul 1896, 298. Only one of these can now be traced, its geometry and mouldings fitting with the in situ evidence: Harrison and Thurlby 1997, 54.

85 A single springer survives, corbelled off the wall adjoining the south-west crossing pier.

86 On the vaults, see Harrison and Thurlby 1997, 55–6, together with the slightly contradictory views in Harrison 1997a, 73. On the bosses, in summary see Alexander and Binski 1987, 233. Harrison, with advice from Richard Morris, notes that the ribs of the later bosses seem to use an early thirteenth-century profile. It is just possible they were cut to match the profile of existing springers.

87 On the site in general, see catalogue entry; Robinson and Platt 1998.

88 Following exploratory diggings in 1848 (Roberts 1848a, 130–1), Strata Florida was excavated by Stephen Williams in 1887–90: see, in particular, Williams 1887, 1889a, 1889b and 1890c. The site was further 'cleared' by the Office of Works in the 1930s and 1940s.

89 St Davids is considered further below, but on the late twelfth-century rebuilding, see Stalley 2002.

90 The original site and early buildings were considered in chapter 3. On the historical context for the foundation, see Cowley 1977, 25–6; Pryce 1996, 158–61.

91 Mon Ang, V, 632; Williams 1889a, appendix, x.

92 A very large quantity of ex situ stonework survives at the site. The principal contribution to the forthcoming site review (commissioned by Cadw) is an analysis of this stonework by Stuart

Harrison, work which has added considerably to our understanding of the abbey church and monastic ranges. The main conclusions are summarized in Robinson and Platt 1998. I am especially indebted to Stuart Harrison for sharing his ideas on the buildings with me in advance of publication.

93 As it happens, Strata Florida is the white monk church in Wales that corresponds most closely to the ideal formula proposed by Hahn (1957) in his modular scheme. Several commentators have drawn attention to the similarity of the completed Strata Florida plan and that of the later (*c* 1204 to 1235–40) Graiguenamanagh in Ireland, on which see Stalley 1987, 72–3, 99–103. Stalley points out that although some features of the Graiguenamanagh plan are consistent with the proportional system discussed by Hahn, others are not.

94 The capital in question is illustrated in Williams 1889a, facing 220, no. 22; Williams 1889b, facing 34, no. 22.

95 Stalley 1987, 180–3, with the Strata Florida capital illustrated as fig 56.

96 Illustrated in Williams 1889a, facing 220, nos 18, 21, 23; Williams 1889b, facing 34, nos 18, 21, 23.

97 Caerbwdy was quarried on the coast just to the south east of St Davids (Caerfai Bay and Caerbwdy Bay), and was used extensively in St Davids Cathedral.

98 Williams (1889a, facing 210, 213–15) illustrated five different profiles, and other related fragments have been found in the recent work.

99 These bosses are illustrated in Williams 1889a, facing 213, nos 24–7, 29. Williams thought they formed the central boss, but they are not articulated for ribs.

100 It is difficult to judge just how much this reflects the chronology at Strata Florida, and how much it is merely reflective of conservative (Burgundian) design.

101 The pointed form of the transept arcades was determined by Williams (1889a, 213, and illustrated facing 209), with the details broadly confirmed by the recent site work.

102 These observations on the upper levels are based on the work of Stuart Harrison.

103 There is nothing, for example, in the profile design of the east, north and south crossing arches which contradicts such a suggestion. The profiles are given in Williams 1889a, facing 210, the details of which are again confirmed by the recent investigations.

104 *Brut*, 81; *Brut (RBH)*, 183: 'that had been built with fine workmanship'.

105 On the evidence for the abandonment of the Fontenay-style arrangement, see Robinson and Platt 1998, 26–8; Harrison 2004, 131–2. A large quantity of the rib fragments from the extended presbytery was located by Williams (1889a, 209, and illustrated facing 202), though he ascribed them to the 'great east window'. The identification of the pieces as rib fragments was made by Stuart Harrison. Unlike the proposal for the 'Bernardine' phase at Dore, there is no indication of any bay articulation in the lower sections of the extended presbytery walls.

106 Williams 1889a, 210, illustrated facing 210.

107 There are illustrations of some in Williams 1889a, facing 210. Hoey (1986, 60) makes the point that compared to some areas of Britain, pier alternation in the west was not that common.

108 On regional pier types, see Hoey 1986, *passim*; Hoey 1987, *passim*. In passing, it should be noted that large fasciculated piers, featuring keeled shafts (like those at, say, Byland and Roche) are all but unknown from late twelfth-century contexts in the west of England. This said, much larger forms do appear in the nave of the Cluniac house at Wenlock, usually dated *c* 1220–60: Cranage 1921–2,

108–13. More intriguing, however, are the 'crossing' piers (of apparently *c* 1200) in the parish church at Llantwit Major, no great distance from Margam or Neath. They are not entirely convincing, but certainly bear major keeled shafts. For the church in general, see Halliday 1900 and 1905; Orrin 1988, 239–58; Newman 1995, 406–8.

109 For a discussion of the use of the *pilier cantonné* at St Davids, see Stalley 2002, 29–30.

110 Of course, screen walls set between piers in Cistercian churches were more common than can now be demonstrated. They are known, for instance, at twelfth-century Byland (Harrison 1990), Fountains (Coppack 2003, 52–3) and Rievaulx (Fergusson and Harrison 1999, 76); at thirteenth-century Tintern (Robinson 2002a, 40–4); and at late twelfth-century Baltinglass and Jerpoint in Ireland (Stalley 1987, 86), but they seldom provided a continuous base for a reduced arcade.

111 Williams 1889a, facing 222. The form is remarkably similar to the north-west respond capital in the presbytery at St Davids, illustrated in Lovegrove 1929, 275; Evans and Worsley 1981, 100.

112 Illustrated in Williams 1889a, facing 209, with their distribution noted on his plan, facing 182.

113 The suggestion is made, apart from other considerations, on the basis of the many diverse *ex situ* fragments which cannot readily be placed in the lower part of the church elevations. For a brief overview of the form in general, see Engel 1998; and on its appearance at St Davids, Draper 1999, 112; Stalley 2002, 34–6 (with a note of caution on earlier interpretations of the form at this site). On its occurrence at Christ Church Cathedral in Dublin, and the west country links, see Stalley 1981, 72–4. And for wider context, see Bony 1983, 373, 524 n 19, where the appearance of the form in the west nave bays at the Cistercian church of Vaux-de-Cernay (Yvelines) is mentioned as a probability. For this site, see Dimier 1982, 51; Chauvin 1998, 140–1; Peugniez 2001, 177–8.

114 For timber vaults at Dore, Llanthony and elsewhere, see Hearn and Thurlby 1997, especially 51–2. There is much debate over whether the vaults planned in the nave at St Davids were of stone or timber, and whether, in any case, they were ever completed: Stalley 2002, 36–9.

115 The ends of the hood moulding terminate in a triskelion motif that may well come direct from a long-standing native tradition. The inner order of the doorway was lost, presumably when the rere-arch was introduced as remedial work in the nineteenth century: see Williams, 1889a, 193–4.

116 Coldstream 1998, 56.

117 For a summary of the abbey church at Tewkesbury (begun *c* 1087 and completed *c* 1123) with an illustration of the arch, see Fernie 2000, 160–5. The west front was presumably one of the last parts of the church to go up.

118 The appearance of innovative elements at several of the Welsh Cistercian sites is one of the points made in the introduction to this volume. Here at Strata Florida, although this is clearly emphasized by the west door, we cannot but wonder about the 'audience' for the considerable architectural variety seen in the design of the entire church. The potential influence of the Deheubarth royal court is certainly not to be ruled out.

119 Williams 1889a, 202–3, facing 202, no. 52; Williams 1889b, 31.

120 The St Mary's, Shrewsbury, example is illustrated in Brakspear 1931, pl IIa. At St Davids the work appears around the north door, illustrated in Evans and Worsley 1981, 71. As noted in chapter 5, the porch doorway now at St Brides-super-Ely may well have come from Margam Abbey, increasing the interest of this example. For Christ Church, Dublin, see Stalley 1979, 114–15. See also Stalley

2002, 25, and n 44, where it is suggested that the motif may be derived from manuscript illumination, as in the canon tables of the Winchcombe Gospels (c 1130–40): Trinity College Dublin, MS 53.

121 For Deheubarth under the Lord Rhys, see Davies 1987, 217–24; Turvey 2002, 105–9. His church patronage is well covered in Pryce 1996.

122 The entry in the native chronicle for the year 1182 reads: '*Ecclesia Menevensis diruitur et de novo inchoatur*': *Annales Cambriæ*, **55**; *Episcopal Acts*, I, 289.

123 *St Davids Acta*, 7–8; *Annales Cambriæ*, **61**; Knowles *et al* 2001, 122.

124 This was during his tour around the country with Gerald of Wales: Thorpe 1978, 169.

125 Turvey 1996–7 and 1998–9.

126 One of the key problems is the extent to which, in the new scheme, work on the nave preceded that of the eastern arm. On previous attempts to sort out the chronological and sequential uncertainties, see Jones and Freeman 1856, 48–178; Lovegrove 1922; Lovegrove 1929. For a thorough and far more convincing review, see Stalley 2002; and further, Lloyd *et al* 2004, 386–407. There is a good set of early (1815) drawings of the cathedral by John Buckler: BL, Add. MS 36397, fols 38–74. I have further benefited from much profitable discussion on the architectural links between Strata Florida and St Davids with Malcolm Thurlby and Stuart Harrison.

127 For the collapse of the tower, see *Annales Cambriæ*, 75; *Episcopal Acts*, I, 349; Jones and Freeman 1856, 146.

128 A second disaster came in 1248 when an 'earthquake' was said to have destroyed 'a great part' of the building: *Annales Cambriæ*, 87; *Episcopal Acts*, I, 379. It is more difficult to assess what the damage may have been at this time, but see Stalley 2002, 19–20.

129 In the cathedral, the west choir/presbytery responds take the form of two large half-shafts with a cluster of three much smaller shafts at the centre (Lovegrove 1929, 274, fig 5). This is close to the full-form quatrefoil from the nave at Strata Florida (fig 44). Similarly, as noted above, the *pilier cantonné* used in the cathedral again finds close comparison at the Cistercian church (fig 44). There is an earlier west country example of this form at the Benedictine priory church of St James, Bristol.

130 Stalley (2002, 21) identifies eleven different types of chevron in the nave arcades at the cathedral.

131 On the use of alternate bands of Caerbwdy and cream limestone in the crossing arches at Strata Florida, see Williams 1889a, 211.

132 The west bay is of a different design: Stalley 2002, 21.

133 As Stalley (2002, 30–1) points out, the sumptuous approach adopted by the cathedral master was in marked contrast to, say, the 'smooth linearity' of the contemporary work at Wells. Yet it was much in line with the taste displayed by the Benedictines of Glastonbury in their new Lady Chapel (c 1184–9), or that in the church of the Augustinians at Keynsham (after c 1169).

134 Draper 1999, *passim*; Stalley 2002, *passim*.

135 Draper 1999, 108–9.

136 Pryce 1996, *passim*. For more on the relationship between Rhys and Bishop Peter, and on Rhys's burial in the cathedral, see Turvey 1996–7 and 1998–9.

137 Pryce 1996, 157–9.

138 Noted in Ludlow 2002, 63. Without further discovery and analysis, it is difficult to speculate further on just what this fragment may represent at Whitland.

139 The quote is taken from *Cronica de Wallia*, 35. On Cadwgan in general, see Cowley 1977, 122–3; Williams 2001, 20.

140 For Talley in general, see Williams 1897; O'Neil 1941; Robinson and Platt 1998, 25–41.

141 St-Jean at Amiens does not survive, though see Sartre 1971–2; Ardura 1993, 69–74.

142 Between 1192 and 1202, Abbot Peter of Whitland attempted to lay claim to Talley, seizing its estates and coming close to complete appropriation. See Cowley 1977, 73–4.

143 For the excavations of 1890, see [Jones] and Williams 1891; Williams 1892; for further background, Arnold 1992; Robinson 1998, 179–80.

144 Butler (1994, 5–6) suggests the transept chapels may have been arranged *en échelon*, but there are no solid indications to support this view.

145 [Jones] and Williams 1891, 168–9.

146 Arnold 1992; catalogue entry.

147 For the suggestion, see Haslam 1979, 127–8, 198. A comparable doorway is to be seen at Valle Crucis.

148 This point is part underlined by the fact that six masons' marks were common to both sites. These are illustrated in Williams 1889a, 218–19; [Jones] and Williams 1891, pl 17.

149 [Jones] and Williams 1891, pls 12 and 13.

150 [Jones] and Williams 1891, 166–7, pls 2, 4 and 10.

151 This is evidenced in the collections from the site at the Powysland Museum, Welshpool.

152 On the foundation, and particularly on the important political aspects behind the patronage of Cwmhir, see Remfry 1994; Smith 1999, 101–5; Smith and Butler 2001. For the buildings, see Williams 1890a and 1894–5; Haslam 1979; Radford 1982; Robinson 1998, 94–6; Jones 2000b. My appreciation of the building is the better for the discussions I had some years ago with Eleanor Schärer, then an undergraduate at the University of Warwick.

153 Radford 1982, 61–7. This was discussed above (*see* chapter 4).

154 Radford 1982, 69–74. To support his view that the construction programme moved from west to east, Radford argued that similar patterns of development occurred at two other Cistercian sites in north Wales, Aberconwy and Cymer. In fact, all three suggestions now seem highly implausible, as argued in this volume and (independently) in Butler 2004.

155 Williams 1894–5; for the capitals, see pl 6d and 6e (without neck-rings), also pl 7 (that with a grasping hand); for the vault boss, see pl 5, no. 7. See also the description of the Strata Florida transept chapels above.

156 The survey was carried out in 1998 by M J Noel of Geoquest Associates on behalf of Cadw. Butler (2004, 120–1) appears to favour a position for the twelfth-century presbytery to the south of the later church. For my own part, much as I would like to keep an open mind, I remain convinced that the thirteenth-century nave was aligned to an existing building and was not part of a new church begun from scratch.

157 Brooksby 1970; Radford 1982, 67.

158 In the past, it has been suggested that Devannor was the site of an aborted early foundation (1143), superseded by Cwmhir: RCAHMCW 1913, 6–7. The Fowler family acquired the abbey estate in 1565, building a new seat at Devannor c 1670. For further details, see the Cwmhir catalogue entry.

159 Smith 1999, 101–5; Smith and Butler 2001, 297–303.

160 In one version of the native chronicle, it is recorded that in 1198 'the community of Cwmhir went to reside at Cymer': *Brut (RBH)*, 180–1. For a fuller account, see the catalogue entry on Cymer.

161 For the charter, see Charles 1970. See also Remfry 1994, 2, 7; Smith and Butler 2001, 300–1.

162 For background, see Williams 1976a, 77–93; Cowley 1977, 26–7.

163 The new site might be expected to have been occupied within a

164 On the post-suppression site, see Bradney 1904–32, III, pt 2, 225–8; Mahoney [1979], 157–83; [Whittle] 1994, 80–2; Newman 2000, 336–8.

165 Mein and Lewis 1990–1, 101. The excavations remain unpublished at the time of writing.

166 This appears in Williams 2001, 288.

167 Mein's plan shows the west bay of the nave arcades as solid, in an arrangement not unlike late thirteenth-century Neath. The overall proportions of the building do not look especially 'Bernardine', and the possibility of a relatively late move to this site should not be ignored. The church is known to have been damaged by fire in the late fourteenth century: Williams 1976a, 83–4.

168 For background, see Hays 1963, 4–6; catalogue entry on Aberconwy.

169 Hughes 1895b.

170 RCAHMW 1956, 41–3. This point is underlined in Radford 1982, 71–2.

171 Butler 1964, 111–15.

172 As it happens, in a fresh assessment of all the evidence, Butler now agrees that a church of 'Bernardine' plan is to be expected: Butler 2004, 119–20. The nave at Strata Florida measures approximately 40.1m long, to be compared with the 41m here at Aberconwy. For more on the events of 1282–3, see catalogue entries on Aberconwy and Maenan.

173 On the possible context for the foundation and for patronage of the house by the Welsh princes, see Smith 1999; Smith and Butler 2001, 297–317. See also Williams 1981b; Pryce 2001, 275–8; and catalogue entry for further details.

174 On the buildings, see in general Brock 1878b; RCAHMCW 1921, 96–7; Radford 1946; Robinson 1995b; Robinson 1998, 97–8; Smith and Butler 2001, 317–21.

175 As early as 1241, certain difficulties encountered at the house led to a General Chapter instruction for the dispersal of the monks: *Statuta*, II, 238. In 1284, the community received £80 by way of compensation for war damages: *Littere Wallie*, 96–7.

176 A 'Bernardine' layout for the original church is now suggested in Smith and Butler 2001, 322; Butler 2004, 116–17.

177 There is one fragment of chevron (?reused) on the inner right (south) jamb of the central lancet. The overall arrangement was not unlike that at, say, Grey in Ireland, for which see Harrison 2002, 117–24.

178 Butler has recently argued this feature shows no sign of insertion into the wall, suggesting that the remodelling of the east end must have taken place at an early date: Smith and Butler 2001, 320; Butler 2004, 117–18. See also Brock 1878b, 466.

179 In this sense, Cymer might be compared with Corcomore, Abbeyknockmoy and Monasteranenagh, for which see Stalley 1987, 103–9.

180 See Smith and Butler 2001, 320.

181 In all, there is evidence for six clerestory windows at either side of the building, all with deeply splayed sills.

182 Basingwerk (fig 83) is the obvious Welsh example in the next section. Also, at Boyle Abbey in Ireland the arcades (*c* 1180) featured octagonal capitals: Stalley 1987, 87–92.

183 On the foundation and history of the house, see Jones 1933; Williams 1981a.

184 For Henry's charter, see *Mon Ang*, V, 262–3. See also catalogue entry for further details on the site change.

185 Hunter 1840, 51–2; Robinson 2002c, 26–7.

186 Reported by Arnold Taylor in Leach 1960, 37. The existence of an earlier church may be inferred, for example, from the alignment of the cloister and the east range of monastic buildings.

187 For the Basingwerk buildings in general, see Hodkinson 1905; RCAHMCW 1912, 40–1; Taylor 1971; Robinson 1996b.

188 It is not entirely clear whether the chapels were separated by solid walls or not.

189 As noted in RCAHMCW 1912, 40.

190 Hodkinson 1905, pls C and F. See also RCAHMCW 1912, figs 31 and 32.

191 Apart from the nave arcade at Cymer, Hulton Abbey in Staffordshire, founded 1218–20, may be considered as a broad regional parallel for Basingwerk. Here, too, the builders made late use of the 'Bernardine' plan, and the nave piers were most probably of octagonal form with arches of chamfered orders: see Robinson 1998, 127. I am grateful to Richard Morris (Warwick) for showing me his account of the architecture of Hulton before its publication: now Morris 2005, 74–6.

192 Fergusson 1984a, 92–4; Robinson 2002c, 12–13.

193 For the history of Valle Crucis in general, see Price 1952.

194 On the buildings in general, see Brock 1878a; Hughes 1894 and 1895a; RCAHMCW 1914, 161–5; Lovegrove 1936; Price 1952, 83–135; Radford 1953; Evans 1995.

195 There have been different views concerning the phasing of the crossing piers. Roland Paul, for example, thought the two eastern piers came first, with those to the west of marginally later date. He noted that the south-west pier was then largely rebuilt, following some 'failure of the masonry': [Paul] 1899a. Harold Hughes, on the other hand, argued that the piers were of a single phase, though again he observed that the south-west pier was subsequently rebuilt: Hughes 1894, 176–9. This is the view followed in Radford 1953; Evans 1995.

196 For which, see Hope and Brakspear 1909, 290, and pl III. It was Lawrence Hoey who first put this suggestion to me.

197 It is difficult to be certain how much original thirteenth-century work survives in the transepts. Hughes (1894, 175, 178) thought the features were all contemporary, whereas Radford (1953, 14–15) suggested the south transept chapels were of slightly later date, thus explaining the differences in the form of the lancets and the vault ribs. Looking at the south transept, one wonders how much restoration might have taken place in the nineteenth century.

198 The outer wall of the south aisle has been much rebuilt, and the details of these triple-shaft responds can only really be seen in the north aisle. For the form of the responds, see Price 1952, 103.

199 This is not to suggest that everything seen in the sculptural detailing was entirely new. Of no real surprise, there were evidently links to Strata Marcella and other houses in the family. The broad leaves with pointed tips on the crossing capital illustrated by Hughes (1894, 270), for example, are close to those of the Strata Florida nave pier capitals. Likewise, the stiff-leaf capitals of the south processional doorway at Valle Crucis might be compared to one illustrated by [Jones] and Williams (1891, pl 13, no. 4) from Strata Marcella (reproduced here as fig 78).

200 The fire is undocumented, but is evidenced in the rose-red staining of the lower courses of stonework in the church, and from archaeological investigations in the south and west cloister ranges: Hughes 1894, 182–3; Hughes 1895a, 5–6; Butler 1976b, 92–6. Lovegrove (1936, 7–14) suggested that two different 'schools' of craftsmanship were involved with the construction. He attributed the work before the fire to English (west country) influence, positing the idea that a purely Welsh school of masons became responsible for the later programme.

201 The later thirteenth- and fourteenth-century works at Valle Crucis are considered further in chapter 7.

202 This is not to overlook the transformation of the Dore and Margam presbyteries in the late twelfth and early thirteenth centuries, the details of which are more appropriately examined in chapter 7.

203 For the nave in general, see Williams 1894–5, 85–98; RCAHMCW 1913, 3–7; Radford 1982, 69–74. Recently, Butler has put forward a proposal that the early thirteenth-century rebuilding at Cwmhir began with a six-bay aisled presbytery and transepts: Butler 2004, 121–2. He is looking to solve some of the problematic issues surrounding the building history at the site, but his argument is surely not sustainable.

204 Reported in [Rees] 1849, 245.

205 Described in [Rees] 1849, 246. One of the jambs of the western doorway is illustrated in Williams 1894–5, 95, pl 3.

206 [Rees] 1849, 246. Williams (1894–5, 95) doubted whether such a door ever existed. See also Radford 1982, 72.

207 Hamer 1873, 172–5; RCAHMCW 1911, 114; Haslam 1979, 140–2. Dr Radford suggested that the material was removed from the east bay of the north arcade: Radford 1982, 70–3. There is also a suggestion that the south doorway at Llanidloes comes from Cwmhir: Williams 1894–5, 89; Haslam 1979, 140.

208 Hamer (1873, 172–5) considered they have been reduced by 4 feet (1.2m).

209 Illustrated in Williams 1894–5, pls 2 and 11. See also the comments in Radford 1982, 72.

210 Illustrated in Williams 1894–5, pls 9–11. See also Haslam 1979, 141; Radford 1982, 71.

211 The profile given by Williams (1894–5, 91) is not accurate, and there is a better version in Hamer 1873.

212 Radford (1982, 73) attempts to link this variation to the original liturgical arrangements in the church at Cwmhir.

213 The elevation reconstructed here (fig 83) cannot be guaranteed, especially in terms of the upper stage (discussed further below).

214 The details are illustrated in Williams 1894–5, pl 4.

215 On the west country background in general, there is still much of value in Brakspear 1931. For further context, see Webb 1956, 87–94; Stalley 1981, *passim*; Hoey 1987, 259–62; Stalley and Thurlby 1989, *passim*; Thurlby 1993, *passim*; Thurlby 1996, 164–81.

216 The shafts on the Wells piers were arranged around a stepped core; at Glastonbury the triple-shaft groups appear on the cardinal angles of an otherwise traditional compound pier: illustrated in Brakspear 1931, pl X. For Wells in general, see Bilson 1928; Harvey 1982; Colchester 1987. For further details on Wells and Glastonbury, see Malone 1973, 130–87.

217 Williams 1894–5, 91–2. Llandaff is one of the key buildings in Brakspear's west country school. It was designed, he felt, by the master of the great church at Glastonbury, or by one of his immediate pupils: Brakspear 1931, 16. The extent of the comparisons to be drawn between the two buildings certainly suggests a very close connection.

218 In general, see Lovegrove 1929; Malone 1973, 198–201; Newman 1995, 244–7; Thurlby 1996, 178–9.

219 Hoey 1987, 261–2.

220 The Dore presbytery is discussed in chapter 7. For Hereford, see Harvey 1974, 133–4; Morris 2000, 210–13, 237; for Pershore, Stalley and Thurlby 1989; Thurlby 1996, 164–81; for St Mary's, Haverfordwest, Lloyd *et al* 2004, 210–12; for Llanthony, Lovegrove 1946–7; Newman 2000, 338–47; for Lichfield, Thurlby 1993. Very little is known of Chirbury in Shropshire (begun *c* 1195), where a compound pier with triple-shaft groups lies exposed in the

parish churchyard.

221 Haslam 1979, 141.

222 Radford 1982, 71.

223 On which, see Brakspear 1933.

224 The sequence of events proposed by Smith is of particular interest in this context, particularly the notion that Mortimer's charter was intended to encourage the exiled community back to Cwmhir: Smith 1999, 101–5; Smith and Butler 2001, 297–303.

225 *Roger of Wendover*, III, 11–12; *Matthew Paris*, III, 203.

226 For connections to the Pershore choir, see Stalley and Thurlby 1989, 365–9; Thurlby 1996, 165–81. Brakspear (1931, 17) regarded Pershore and Llanidloes (Cwmhir) as representing 'the survival of the traditions' of his west country school into the second quarter of the thirteenth century.

227 Morris 1990, 169–75.

228 For interesting comment around this point, see Stalley 1981, 72–3.

CHAPTER 7
THE WELSH CISTERCIAN CHURCH TRANSFORMED

1 For an early, but still very valuable, account of the two models, see Bilson 1909, 210–20. More recently, see Coldstream 1986, 142–8.

2 The source, dating from 1178, mentions the donation of funds by King William I of Sicily in 1154 for the building of the new abbey church (*ad aedificationem novae basilicae Clarevallensis*): Migne 1844–64, CLXXXV, col 1341; Aubert 1947, I, 183; Fergusson 1994, 88; Gajewski 2004, 78. For Bernard's canonization and general context, see the relevant essays in Pressouyre and Kinder 1992; Fergusson 1994; Fergusson and Harrison 1999, 166–9.

3 Aubert 1947, I, 212–13; Esser 1953; Hahn 1957, 119–22. For a new and thought-provoking contextual discussion, see Gajewski 2004, 72–7.

4 See, for example, Schlink 1970, 108–19, 138–41; Untermann 1984, 618–24; Kinder 1991, 215; Henriet 2001, 275–7.

5 Her arguments for a single church are covered in chapter 5, above. For the motives behind the new building, see Kennedy [Gajewski] 1996, 161–5; Gajewski 2004, 78–9. See also the summary in Frankl 2000, 317–18 n 55. Gajewski accepts, however, that on Bernard's death the new chevet was immediately conceived as the appropriate mausoleum for his saintly body.

6 The date of the consecration was recorded in the *Chronicon Clarevallense* (1147–92): Migne 1844–64, CLXXXV, col 1248; Aubert 1947, I, 183; Dimier 1974, 309; Henriet 2001, 277–8. On the form of the building, see Hahn 1957, 119–22; Fergusson 1984a, 52–3; Kinder 1991; Fergusson 1994; Kinder 1996b. On the possible design sources, see Dimier 1957. For Schlink (1970, 110–15), the general form of the exterior could be seen as a simplified version of Cluny III. Others have pointed to the hemicycle at Premonstratensian Dommartin (*c* 1153–63) as of potential significance, though the chronologies of the two buildings are very close. For this church, see Enlart 1895, 104–22, and for discussions of its significance, Fergusson 1994, 90–3; Wilson 1986, 101–2.

7 On the Pontigny east arm, see Fontaine 1928, 44–52 (*c* 1180–1200); Aubert 1947, I, 213–14 (*c* 1185–1205/10); Bruzelius 1982 (1186–1210); Dimier 1982, 299–304 (*c* 1185–1205); Kennedy [Gajewski] 1996, 269–79 (*c* 1180–1200).

8 Aubert 1947, I, 216–17; Dimier 1957, 30–1. The site was excavated in the 1930s, but the published detail is rather superficial: Buhot 1940–2. See also Grant 1988, 132–7; Grant 2005, 117, 154–5.

9 For which, in summary, see Bilson 1909, 219–20; Dimier 1957;

Jansen 1984, 78–80, 104 n 15. Bruzelius (1982) points to the wider influence of the new Pontigny east end among certain houses of its filiation.

10 For the date and the form of Cîteaux III, see Bilson 1909, 215–17; Aubert 1947, I, 191–2; Hahn 1957, 122–3; Schlink 1970, 91–2; Dimier 1982, 47; Plouvier 1994, 69, 72; Kinder 1996a, 355; Plouvier 1998, 132, 142–3. Further context will also be found in Hearn 1971, 203–6.

11 Based on his excavations at the site in the 1950s, Henri-Paul Eydoux at first argued that the rectangular eastern arm at Morimond should be dated as early as c 1155–70: Eydoux 1956 and 1958. In a more recent work he revises his views, suggesting the transepts and nave were of the 1160s, and were initially attached to a Fontenay-style presbytery. The eastern arm was then replaced, he says, about 1230 by the building known from excavation: Eydoux 1982. For various qualifications, see Fergusson 1984a, 76–8. In the most recent review of the evidence, Gajewski argues for a date in the second half of the twelfth century, and probably before Cîteaux: Kennedy [Gajewski] 1996, 196–209. A summary of the argument appears in Frankl 2000, 318 n 59a.

12 For two sets of stimulating ideas on this theme, see Kennedy [Gajewski] 1996, 211–21; Fergusson and Harrison 1999, 163–74.

13 For background on Byland's long-drawn-out process of foundation, begun in 1134, see Robinson 1998, 81–3; Burton 1999, 110–12. By 1147 the community was settled at Stocking, remaining there until the final site was ready for full occupation in 1177. The cloister ranges had been started in the mid-1150s, though the permanent church was probably the last item to be put in hand. If it was begun in the 1170s, the design would have anticipated that at Cîteaux, but there is an ongoing debate over relative chronologies. In the most detailed account of Byland in print, Fergusson (1984a, 72–82) dates the first phase of the major church programme to c 1170–7, suggesting that building progressed through to the west front by c 1190. This account updates the author's earlier views appearing in Fergusson 1975. Fergusson's chronology is followed, though refined, in Harrison 1986 and 1990. The evidence can, however, be manipulated to make a case for somewhat later phasing, especially given the possibility that the monks actually occupied a church of temporary character on the final site. If Byland was indeed a close copy of Ripon, as accepted by Wilson (1986, 112–15; 1992, 76) and others, then the recent views on the date of the minster church (Harrison and Barker 1999, 72–6) have particular relevance here. For all this, it would be difficult to accept a start date for Byland too far into the 1180s.

14 Wilson 1992, 76. It was also, as Wilson and others have pointed out, the first Cistercian church to look familiarly English in style.

15 Strictly, the 'ambulatory aisle' at the east end was contained within the full-height elevation of the new presbytery, and it was the range of chapels which was housed in the one-storey extension: Bilson 1909, 214–15, 218; Fergusson 1984a, 73–5. On the need for additional chapel/altar space, see Williams 1998, 225; Fergusson and Harrison 1999, 164–6.

16 It is unfortunate that we know nothing of the buildings at L'Aumône (Waverley's mother house) at this time. Through it, though, Waverley of course belonged to the Cîteaux family. The dates given here represent the first phase in a complete rebuilding of the abbey church: Brakspear 1905, 20–34; Fergusson 1984a, 153–4.

17 For Meaux, see Fergusson 1984a, 133–6; Robinson 1998, 141–3; for Newbattle, Robinson 1998, 154–5; for Stratford Langthorne (still under construction in 1241), Coppack 1998, 71–2; Robinson 1998, 180–1; for Hailes I (c 1246–51), Brakspear 1901.

18 On Jervaulx, see Hope and Brakspear 1911, 310–11; Fergusson 1984a, 84–5.

19 The 'Englishness' of the design is emphasized in Coldstream 1986, 145; Coldstream 1998, 48. Fergusson and Harrison (1999, 169) suggest its widespread adoption in Britain is best explained in connection with specific traditions of liturgical arrangement.

20 Hoey 1995a; Fergusson and Harrison 1999, 151–74.

21 Hare 1993; Robinson 1998, 152–3.

22 On the excavated evidence for Stanley (early thirteenth century), see Brakspear 1906–7; for Pipewell (perhaps completed c 1311), Robinson 1998, 157; for Sawley (begun in the 1370s), Coppack 1998, 82–3; Coppack et al 2002, 106–7; for Whalley, Robinson 1998, 202–4. In addition to these various 'cliff' designs, we cannot entirely overlook the new eastern arm at Fountains (begun c 1205). Here, however, quite unlike any other Cistercian house, the work was to terminate as a single lofty transept – the so-called Nine Altars Chapel – a design imitated only at Durham Cathedral: Hope 1900a, 293–6; Coldstream 1998, 52–3; Coppack 2003, 71–8;. On the influence of the Fountains choir and related matters, see also Wilson 1991, 185–91.

23 The plan is reproduced, for example, in Aubert 1947, I, 195; Fergusson 1984a, 79; Leroux-Dhuys 1998, 53.

24 One of the earliest may have been at the royal house of Mortemer, the plan of which was conceived in the last quarter of the twelfth century: Gallagher 1982; Grant 1988, 115–16; also Dimier 1957. Thirteenth-century French examples of greater elaboration include Longpont (Aisne) and Royaumont (Val d'Oise), on which see Aubert 1947, I, 117, 121; Bruzelius 1979; Dimier 1982, 54–6.

25 For general context, see Coldstream 1986, 142–5. On Beaulieu, see Hope and Brakspear 1906, 147–51; Jansen 1984. For the connection, see Grant 1991, 122–4. Bonport had itself been founded by John's brother, Richard I, in 1190.

26 Both of these churches evoked King Henry III's Westminster. For Hailes II (c 1271–7), designed by the probably French Master Berengar, see Alexander and Binski 1987, 392 (no. 443); Coad 1993, 6–7, 18–19; Robinson 1998, 122, 124; for Edward I's Vale Royal (begun 1277), Thompson 1962; Brown et al 1963, 248–57; Robinson 1998, 192–3. The only other British example seems to have been Croxden in Staffordshire (a non-royal foundation), where the date of the east end has recently been pushed back to the late twelfth century: Hall 2003, I, 107–35; also Hoey 1993, 40–2; Robinson 1998, 91–2.

27 Adam was in office by 1186 and can be traced through to 1223: Knowles et al 2001, 126, 270; Smith and London 2001, 258. The course of his earlier career is unknown.

28 Gerald's antipathy towards Adam can in part be explained by the fact they were rivals for the vacant see of St Davids in 1198. For his account, see Gerald of Wales, I, 104; IV, 200–14 (especially 203).

29 Hillaby 1988–90, 231–3; Hillaby 1997c, 109–10.

30 Fergusson (1984a, 98) and Harrison and Thurlby (1997, 56–8) suggest c 1186 for the beginning of the scheme. Malone (1984, 51) and O'Callaghan (1995, 101) give c 1190. Coldstream (1986, 148–9) thought c 1200 more likely. For new thoughts on the context for the rectangular ambulatory form, see Malone 2004, 360–5.

31 Bilson 1909, 214–15; Fergusson 1984a, 98. The combined ambulatory and chapel arrangement is noted in Coldstream 1986, 142.

32 Fergusson 1984a, 98. A penance was imposed on Adam in 1199 for his lack of attendance at the General Chapter: Statuta, I, 238; Statutes, 433.

33 The arguments surrounding the dating of the work are noted above

34 (n 11). For the excavated plan, such as it is, see Eydoux 1956; reproduced in Fergusson 1984a, 77.

34 Donkin 1978, 28–9, fig 4; Williams 1998, 12–16, *passim*.

35 Noted in Frankl 2000, 318 n 59A. Among the best-known examples are Ebrach, Lilienfeld, Riddagshausen and Walkenried, for which see Nicolai 1988, 23–39; Nicolai 1990, 87–139; Nicolai 1993. For a brief account of Ebrach, with plan, see Dimier 1971, 37–8.

36 On the south side the outer order is moulded.

37 As implied, perhaps, in O'Callaghan 1995, 100–1.

38 O'Callaghan 1995, 102–3; Harrison and Thurlby 1997, 58–9.

39 As suggested in Fergusson 1984a, 98; Coldstream 1986, 148.

40 O'Callaghan 1995, 99–100; Harrison and Thurlby 1997, 61.

41 This is brought to light in Wilson 1999, 65, 75 n 53. For an illustration and brief discussion of the Lilienfeld ambulatory, see Nussbaum 2000, 38.

42 O'Callaghan 1995, 101–2.

43 Fergusson (1984a, 95) opts for about 1210, and O'Callaghan (1995, 102) feels the upper parts of the work must have been finished by 1220 'at the latest'.

44 Hillaby 1997c, 110–11.

45 Cowley 1977, 69–96, *passim*, 115; Cowley 1998.

46 The complete absence of documentary sources means we are entirely dependent upon stylistic details for the chronological phasing of the Margam work. In general, see David 1929; Robinson 1993a, 57–9; Newman 1995, 424–9; Robinson 1998, 140–1. In connection with the early thirteenth-century work, mention might be made of the occurrence of 'Peter the mason' (*Petro cementario*) as a witness to a contemporary Margam charter: *Cartae Glamorgancia*, VI, 2328. This reference was pointed out to me by Fred Cowley, who believes Peter must have been a person of note, probably involved in the abbey building programme.

47 *Annales Monastici*, I, 32; Knowles *et al* 2001, 137.

48 On what is known of Kirkstead, see Fergusson 1984a, 66; Wilson 1986, 108–10.

49 For more details, see catalogue entry. For Gilbert's abbacy and character, see Cowley 1977, 74, 123–5; Hillaby 1988–90, 224–6. For Gerald's account, see *Gerald of Wales*, IV, 129–43.

50 Smith and London 2001, 292. For more detail, see catalogue entry. John de la Warre was eventually to come out of retirement and serve as bishop of Llandaff (1254–6): *Llandaff Acta*, xvii; Cowley 1977, 191–2.

51 Evans 1996, 31. The bulk of the rib fragments which can be seen at the site come from the chapter house.

52 Wilson 1991, 188–9; Coppack 2003, 71–4. For a reconstructed elevation, see Fergusson and Harrison 1999, 174.

53 Fergusson and Harrison 1999, 151–74.

54 Although the base is sometimes thought to be a confection introduced during the late nineteenth-century restoration works at the site, its presence was noted by G T Clark in the 1860s: Clark 1867, 327. Whether it might be possible to say more in the future will depend on further detailed site survey, a thorough investigation of the loose stone fragments and archaeological excavation.

55 This said, the transept depth is not far out of step with layouts at Byland and Jervaulx, or for that matter with the near-contemporary refaced and modified work at Rievaulx.

56 The form of the windows matches that in the south aisle, but they appear to have been restored using Quarella sandstone, rather than the Sutton stone of the original work. Perhaps the most likely period for this phase of conservation is the late nineteenth to early twentieth century, when Emily Charlotte Talbot (d 1918) contributed so much to the upkeep of the abbey generally: Adams

1984, 65–7; Evans 1996, 139–40.

57 These are difficult to place in context. The lozenge core is surrounded by eight attached shafts set on the two-tier bases, which have non-water-holding detailing. Between the two levels of moulding, the shafts take on a polygonal form. Something akin to the individual base arrangement, though at a larger scale and not of polygonal form, existed in the chapter house at Tintern, on which see further below (ch 10); also Potter 1847, Tintern pl xxxix.

58 In both cases, there were five eastern chapels: three at the centre and one in each aisle.

59 There were five chapels in the Byland and Waverley aisles, and five again in the east half of the 'hall' extension at Dore.

60 For the Glastonbury crossing piers, see Brakspear 1931, pl x. On the general context, see Thurlby 1996, 174, 178. On the Llandaff west front, probably completed during the episcopate of Henry of Abergavenny (1193–1218) or his successor, William of Goldcliff (1219–29), see Lovegrove 1929, 81–2; Butler 1971, 387; Newman 1995, 245–6.

61 Stalley and Thurlby 1989, 355–63; Thurlby 1996, 165–79. The comparison would be even closer if the *en délit* shafts at Margam were originally polished or painted to effect the same contrasting manner seen in the rich Pershore design.

62 One very obvious and well-dated work where similar features (detached shafts with belts, moulded capitals and a heavily moulded hood) are combined is the Lady Chapel at Salisbury Cathedral, 1220–5.

63 Stalley and Thurlby (1989, 361 n 25) suggest broad resemblances to windows in Bishop Jocelyn's work in the episcopal palace at Wells (*c* 1230–40), and those of similar date inserted into the great tower at Chepstow Castle in Monmouthshire.

64 On Netley, see Jansen 1984, 81, 106 n 24; Hare 1993; Robinson 1998, 152–3; for Hailes in general, Coad 1993; Robinson 1998, 122–5. The form of the aisle windows at Hailes has been reconstructed from *ex situ* fragments by Richard Lea, to whom I am grateful for discussing this point with me.

65 The eastern arm at St Davids, for example, was largely rebuilt after the collapse of the central tower in 1220: Lovegrove 1926, 268–82; Stalley 2002, 19–20. At Llandaff, the Lady Chapel had been added to the east of the Norman presbytery *c* 1260–80: Butler 1971, 391; Newman 1995, 247.

66 The Dominicans were at Cardiff by 1242 and at Brecon before 1269. The Franciscans were established at Carmarthen *c* 1250 and at Cardiff before 1269: Knowles and Hadcock 1971, 215, 224. On what is known of the churches, see Clapham 1927, *passim*; Martin 1937, *passim*; James 1997.

67 On the emergence and development of the Decorated style in Britain, see Bony 1979; Wilson 1992, 178–88, 191–204; Coldstream 1994, especially 17–59.

68 In general terms, see Harrison *et al* 1998, *passim*; Newman 2000, 542–8; Robinson 2002a, 32–5, 40–7.

69 *Chronicle*, 272–83.

70 The transcript can be found as BL, Cotton Vesp. MS D XVII, fol 61. For additional detail, see Harrison *et al* 1998, 182–3; Harrison 2000, 94–6.

71 For Abbot John, see Smith and London 2001, 316, with a brief sketch of his career in Williams 1976a, 105–6.

72 See catalogue entry for further details. The first grant was that of the church of Halvergate in Norfolk, with the charter surviving as an *inspeximus* of 1307: *Cal Chart Rolls*, 1300–26, 99. The date of the original can be pushed back to at least 1290 on the basis of the witness list.

73 For the grant, see *Cal Chart Rolls*, 1300–26, 31; *Cal Pat Rolls*, 1301–7, 30; on Bigod's circumstances at the time, Morris 2003; see also Williams 1976a, 137–8; Cowley 1977, 266.

74 Harvey 1969, 60, 61; Harrison 2000, 93.

75 There are clearly differences to be observed in the character of the walling between the north and south walls of the nave. The consistently smaller blocks employed on the north side may well have come from the dismantled Romanesque church.

76 The higher sills are a puzzle, and cannot really be explained by a suggestion that a small chapel may have been located outside the aisle at this point. The plinth moulding, for example, runs through without a break. On the possible chapel, see Baylis 1902–4, 295 (footnote by J G Wood); Robinson 2002a, 35, 40.

77 The pattern here is complicated by the fact that a wall-passage runs behind the lower half of the 'window', which means the masons did not have the full wall thickness to play with. In the adjacent first bay (east) of the nave north aisle, and in the transept chapels, there is a third form of minor tracery, not unlike so-called Kentish style. If used cautiously, the reconstructions of the Tintern tracery in Potter (1847) and Sharpe (1848) provide useful records of the details.

78 Noted by Richard Morris in Harrison *et al* 1998, 245.

79 As noted, the construction period lasted for a minimum of thirty years, but there is no way of recovering the specific circumstances. On the complexities that might arise in such a building scheme, it is worth considering the contemporary (and perhaps not unrelated) works at Exeter Cathedral. There, even with a good set of building accounts, difficulties remain in attempting to recover the precise sequence in the overall programme: Jansen 1991. For instructive insights into the evolution of another thirteenth-century Cistercian church, at Villers-en-Brabant in Belgium, see Coomans 2000, 131–9.

80 Coldstream 1986, 151. On the high vault rib profile, Morris 1979, 17 (where it is suggested that stylistically it is a late thirteenth-century form).

81 Given the survival of the four gables at each arm of the church, it seems inconceivable that – had a tower existed – there would not be some trace of its presence. Antiquarian views of the church serve only to confirm this point. It was presumably the flèche which was mentioned as the 'belfry' by William Worcestre in 1470: Harvey 1969, 60–1.

82 Although, as we have observed, three-storey elevations had appeared in several northern houses in the late twelfth century, interest in them seems to have ebbed quite quickly. The obvious exception is Rievaulx's grand presbytery scheme of *c* 1220–30. For general background, see Coldstream 1986, 148–51; Fergusson and Harrison 1999, 169. In passing, it is of interest to note the suggestion that the initial design of the new presbytery at Exeter (under way *c* 1288–91), a building with definite architectural links to south Wales, may have been of two storeys: Jansen 1991, 46–7. A summary of the Exeter phasing will be found in Frankl 2000, 343 n 5. The links with south Wales are explored further in the context of Neath, below.

83 High vault shafts corbelled out at spandrel level, and associated with clustered piers, already had a considerable pedigree in British Gothic: Hoey 1987, 254–5.

84 It should be remembered that rose windows had been popular with the northern Cistercians in the late twelfth and early thirteenth centuries: Harrison 1995; Coppack 2003, 51, 74, 77.

85 On Westminster in general, see Binski 1995; on its debt to French Gothic and subsequent influence across Britain, Wilson 1987; Wilson 1992, 178–88. Westminster cannot, however, be regarded in isolation as the first English building to employ fully developed bar tracery. It shares this distinction with (at least) the Benedictine priory at Binham in Norfolk, where patterned tracery windows had been completed before 1244: Wilson 1987, 76–7; Coldstream 1994, 25. For another view on the context and early developments in England, see Bony 1979, 1–18.

86 For which, see Coldstream 1986, 150–1; Robinson 1998, 152–3.

87 For the principal regional responses to Westminster, see Wilson 1992, 183–8; Coldstream 1994, 27–35. Any concept of a regionally disseminated 'court style' during the second half of the thirteenth century, as considered by Bony (1979, 9–18), has to be qualified very carefully: Coldstream 1994, 186–91.

88 The north transept at Hereford was built by Bishop Peter of Aigueblanche (1240–68), a Savoyard who came to England with Henry III's queen, Eleanor of Provence. For further illustrations, see Harvey 1974, 145–6; Bony 1979, pls 18, 20 and 22; Coldstream 1994, 28; and for a recent discussion, Morris 2000, 214–18.

89 Incidentally, the cusps in the Tintern presbytery window (as elsewhere in the church) were cut from separate pieces of stone and inserted into channels in the tracery patterns. This feature occurred at Westminster and further afield in France and England. In the nineteenth century, Edmund Sharpe coined the term 'soffit cusps' to describe the form: Alexander 1996 (looking at the late thirteenth-century west window at Newstead Priory, Nottinghamshire).

90 For Lincoln, see Bony 1979, pl 32; Wilson 1992, 183–4; Coldstream 1994, 28–33, *passim*. Among the similarities, we might note the use of compact, bundled-shaft groups for mullions and rich mouldings to the inner head of the arches. As at Lincoln, the Tintern master also employed detached shaft groups on the inner splays.

91 The point is made in Coldstream 1986, 151; Coldstream 1994, 31–3; Coldstream 1998, 59. A similar case is made by Jansen (1991, 42) in her consideration of the eastern arm at Exeter Cathedral (*c* 1270–1310). Coldstream further suggests (1986, 140) that by this time there was a general love of window tracery among the Cistercians: just as Altenberg (entire church) and Eberbach (nave south aisle) reflected big Rhineland cathedrals, so Tintern followed London. For an overview on German Gothic of the period, see Nussbaum 2000, 49–85.

92 The 'New Work' at Old St Paul's was begun *c* 1258 and continued through to *c* 1310. It was from the 1270s that the cathedral took over from Westminster as the dominant London building project. For St Etheldreda's, see Bony 1979, pls 63–64 and 66–67. The east window in the chapel at Merton College, Oxford (*c* 1289–94) is another that bears stylistic kinship to St Etheldreda's, for which see Bony 1979, pl 72.

93 For what is known of Abbot Ralph's career, see Williams 1976a, 106; Harrison *et al* 1998, 185; Smith and London 2001, 316. See, further, catalogue entry.

94 This is the work attributed by Jansen (1991, 49) to the 'second master'. The Tintern connection is made by Richard Morris, in Harrison *et al* 1998, 244.

95 I am grateful to Richard Morris for discussing the Hereford and Tintern links with me. He has suggested that the Hereford masons did indeed go on to work at the abbey: Morris 2000, 215. At this point, we might note in passing that a Master Ralph (d 1292–3) was employed by Earl Roger Bigod at Chepstow Castle in the 1280s and early 1290s. For the only published detail on his career, see Harvey 1984, 239; Turner 2002, 14–17. However, a small collection of receivers' accounts at The National Archives (first identified by Dr A J Taylor in the 1950s) reveals that Tintern (at least as a location) was within the orbit of the activities controlled by Master Ralph. From

the same source, there is evidence that in 1282 he was working at Chipping Sodbury (*Solbir'*) for Thomas de Weyland, chief justice of Common Pleas under Edward I. For the original Tintern references, see PRO, SC6/921/24/2; SC6/921/26; and for Chipping Sodbury, PRO, SC6/921/23.

96 Richard Morris is confident that the designer of the Tintern features had worked previously on the palace chapel and great hall (*c* 1284–92): see Harrison *et al* 1998, 244; also Morris 1997, 47–8. For illustrations, see Bony 1979, pls 69–71.

97 Bigod was at Tintern's property at Modesgate the day before the ceremony, as evidenced by a charter he issued in favour of the community: *Cal Chart Rolls*, 1300–26, 106.

98 Although important evidence for screens has recently been brought to light at Dore: Harrison 1997a, 64–72.

99 On the discovery of the screen and its reconstruction, see Harrison *et al* 1998. Since that paper was written, all the *ex situ* fragments representing the pulpitum have been gathered together in one location on the site.

100 For Joy's career, see Harvey 1984, 164–5; Morris 1997, 45–51.

101 For the liturgy in early processions, see the *Ecclesiastica Officia* (1 and 2), chapter 17 (Palm Sunday), chapter 29 (Ascension Day), chapter 47 (Candlemas). For more on the theme in general, see Cassidy-Welch 2001, 59–60.

102 These points are discussed in more detail in Harrison *et al* 1998, 250–2. The same pattern of screen wall demolition, and the conversion of the nave to other uses, is recorded for much the same period at, for instance, Fountains, Hailes, Rievaulx and Waverley.

103 On the church in general, see Thomas and Taylor 1938; Butler 1976a; Newman 1995, 463–9; Robinson 1998, 149–51; Robinson 2002b.

104 As in Butler 1976a, 8, 13, followed by Newman 1995, 464.

105 Lewis 1887, 101; Birch 1902, 79–80.

106 Cowley 1977, 245–6. For the agreement, see *Cartae Glamorgancia*, V, 1677–9.

107 *Cartae Glamorgancia*, V, 1684–5.

108 Butler (1984, 147–8) has proposed a logical, if hypothetical, sequence of five stages.

109 Interestingly, this pattern of change is not unlike that observed in the south aisle and clerestory at Tintern.

110 The antecedents for the Neath porch were the Cistercian 'galilees' or 'paradises' of the twelfth century, on which see Aubert 1947, I, 364–5. Coldstream (1986, 151) makes the London connection, and the tracery is illustrated in Birch 1902, 94.

111 A point made in Morris 1997, 47–8.

112 The 1928 discovery of this boss, and its foliage-carved companion, is recorded in Thomas and Taylor 1938, 20. They came from clearance in the nave and presbytery, though the account is no more specific.

113 Butler 1973; Lewis 1999, 8, 240–5.

114 It is known that tilers often adopted tracery patterns in the design of their own products. Hence it is of more than marginal interest to note that several late thirteenth- to early fourteenth-century forms were depicted in the tile pavements laid at the east end of the church: see Lewis 1999, 34–5, 128.

115 We can expect spandrel-corbelled vault shafts, similar to those at Tintern.

116 For the Exeter presbytery, see Jansen 1991, 46–7.

117 Though they were removed in the late 1980s, the recorded areas of tile paving show that all the altars were surrounded by highly decorative tile pavements: see Lewis 1999, 240–5.

118 On the context, see Hays 1963, 54–77; Brown *et al* 1963, 337–41. See also Denton 1992.

119 *Littere Wallie*, 202–3; Hays 1963, 63.

120 Brown *et al* 1963, 339, 340; see catalogue entry on Maenan for further details.

121 Brown *et al* 1963, 340.

122 *Register Aberconwy*, 13.

123 For what is known of the buildings at Vale Royal, see Thompson 1962; Brown *et al* 1963, 248–57; Robinson 1998, 192–3. Dr John Maddison has pointed to a potential connection between the designer of the nave arcades at Tintern and the bases of the eastern crossing responds at Vale Royal Abbey (after 1277): Maddison 1978, 41.

124 Master Walter was responsible for the works at Vale Royal from 1278 until 1290: Harvey 1984, 136–7. For the architectural context in north Wales at this time, see Maddison 1978, 29–71.

125 A potential connection between Walter of Hereford and James of St George over the work at Maenan is suggested in Brown *et al* 1963, 339 n 7; in his account of Walter's career, Harvey (1984, 136–7) suggests the possibility he was sent to Maenan in 1284.

126 On which, see RCAHMW 1956, 1–2; Butler 1963; Butler and Evans 1980.

127 Butler and Evans 1980, 52.

128 Unlike the general trend in the thirteenth century, Sweetheart was in fact built on a 'Bernardine' plan. It is significant as one of the buildings introducing bar tracery window forms to Scotland: Fawcett 1994, 72–4; Robinson 1998, 181–4.

129 For these three, see Robinson 1998, 136–7, 144–8, 202–3. For further details on Melrose, see Fawcett and Oram 2004, 86–164.

130 These are too numerous to cite individually, but in general see Stalley 1987, 109–28; Coppack 1998, 79–93; Robinson 1998, 60–1, 64–205 *passim*.

131 This comes from a deed of 1307, in which there is reference to land formerly belonging to the '*magister fabrice nove ecclesie nostre*': see Birch 1897, 293.

132 Evans 1996, 91–2.

133 The references occur in 1340–52: Williams 1984, I, 133; Williams 2001, 99, quoting National Library of Wales, Badminton MS 1645, m 9; 1657, m 12d.

134 Harrison *et al* 1998 (251–2 for the removal of the screen walls).

135 The porch may have been built in the 1320s, just before, or contemporary with, the pulpitum. It was possibly the work of a Bristol designer: Harrison *et al* 1998, 187–8, 245.

136 Robinson 2002a, 35, 40.

137 On the wars and their context, see Davies 1987, 333–88; Prestwich 1997, 170–232.

138 For the fire, see Hughes 1894, 182–3; Hughes 1895a, 5–6; Butler 1976b, 92–6.

139 Williams 2001, 39–40.

140 *Littere Wallie*, 80–1, 90–1. For the context, see Williams, G 1976, 43–4.

141 For a description and good illustrations of the west front, see Hughes 1894, 263–7.

142 The inscription reads: +ADAM.ABBAS FECIT.HOC:OPVS: N.PACE/QVIESCAT:AME (Abbot Adam carried out this work; may he rest in peace. Amen). An Abbot Adam appears in documents *c* 1330–44: Price 1952, 148; Smith and London 2001, 318.

143 The sum awarded was £78: *Littere Wallie*, 60–1, 64.

144 For the quote, see *Chester Chronicle*, 114–17; and see catalogue entry for further details.

145 *Cal Pat Rolls*, 1292–1301, 499; Williams 1889a, 154, appendix, xlviii.

146 Williams 1889a, 182–229, *passim*; Robinson and Platt 1998, 31, 48–9.

147 Basingwerk received £100, Cymer £80 and Strata Marcella £43: *Littere Wallie*, 84, 96–7, 174.

148 Robinson 1995b; Smith and Butler 2001, 318, 321.

149 [Jones] and Williams 1891, 155, 169, pl 6, no. 1. For Williams, the form and scale of the mouldings was to be compared with the piers at Chester Cathedral.

150 Williams 1976a, 3.

151 Harrison and Thurlby 1997, 53–6; Harrison 1997a, 64–73.

152 RCHME 1931, 1; Williams 1976a, 3.

153 A fourteenth-century date is preferred in Pevsner 1963, 61–2; Coldstream 1986, 152, and n 61; Alexander and Binski 1987, 233.

154 Harrison and Thurlby 1997, 55–6. An early date is also given in Sledmere 1914, 55–6; RCHME 1931, 9.

155 For the context, see Williams, G 1976, *passim*. In passing, it may be noted that many of the fifteenth- and early sixteenth-century written sources imply a good deal of building in wood, including screens; some of the detail is picked up in a number of the site catalogue entries. By way of background on the craftsmanship in wood in late medieval Wales, see Crossley 1942–3; Lord 2003, 236–41.

156 Coldstream 1986, 159.

157 See catalogue entries on these sites for details, with similar descriptions surviving for Basingwerk, Strata Marcella and Valle Crucis.

158 Williams, G 1976, 356, 564.

159 Bradney 1904–32, III, pt 2, 226–7; Williams 1976a, 85–6.

CHAPTER 8
THE CLAUSTRAL LAYOUT

1 As noted, for example, in Dickinson 1961, 28; Brooke 2003, 6. For a new discussion of the Cistercian cloister as an imagined or abstract space, see Cassidy-Welch 2001, 47–71.

2 It is, for example, particularly significant that although the extensive corpus of Cistercian ground plans assembled by Anselme Dimier is invaluable for the abbey churches, it omits monastic buildings altogether: Dimier 1949–67.

3 Aubert 1947, II, 1–171.

4 Stalley 1987, 153–77.

5 Braunfels 1972, 94–109.

6 Kinder 1997, 129–38, 241–384. As a further quarry of information, see Williams 1998, 240–57. Many of the buildings cited in these sources are also illustrated in Van der Meer 1965.

7 Fergusson 1986.

8 The architectural reconstruction for this paper was undertaken by Stuart Harrison: Fergusson and Harrison 1994.

9 See Lillich 1998, and in particular the essays by Bell (1998) and Jansen (1998).

10 For a reasonably full bibliography of official guidebooks, see Robinson 1998. For relevant works by Brakspear and Hope, see the bibliography to this volume.

11 Fergusson and Harrison 1999.

12 Coomans 2000.

13 Others which deserve mention include Knapp (1997) on Maulbronn, and Bourgeois (2000) on Fontenay.

14 See Aubert 1947, II, facing 1; Dimier 1982, 39–41; also Braunfels 1972, 74–9; Lekai 1977, 265–7; still used is Leroux-Dhuys 1998, 52.

15 See, for instance, Coppack 1998, 79–93, *passim*; Coppack 2002.

16 The major exception is the chapter house, which is given no separate provision in the St Gall plan. For the Carolingian reforms, see Braunfels 1972, 27–46; Lawrence 2001, 66–82; on the emergence of the cloister, Horn 1973; Coppack 1990, 61–80; and (cautiously) Thompson 2001, 33–61; on the St Gall plan, Horn and Born 1979, with useful summaries in Braunfels 1972, 37–46; Conant 1993, 55–9; Stalley 1999, 184–8.

17 For general introductions to post-Conquest monastic planning in Britain, see Dickinson 1961; Gilyard-Beer 1976; Coppack 1990.

18 The initial arrangements at Clairvaux, as well as timber buildings, have both been discussed earlier in this volume, but in general see Schaefer 1982; Fergusson 1983; Fergusson 1984b; Coppack 1998, 23–31.

19 St Bernard's acceptance of the need to build on a grander scale at Clairvaux might be taken as the turning point: Webb and Walker 1960, 86–8; Braunfels 1972, 243–4.

20 On the arrangements in the east range in general, see Kinder 1997, 241–75; for France, Aubert 1947, II, 35–95; for specific case studies, Fergusson and Harrison 1999, 83–109 (Rievaulx); Coomans 2000, 305–45 (Villers); Hall 2003, I, 65–81 (Croxden); also Coomans 1998a.

21 For Basingwerk, see Taylor 1971, 6–7; Hubbard 1986, 353–4; Robinson 1996b; for Dore, Paul 1904, 124–5; Paul 1927, 274–5; RCHME 1931, 5–6; Hillaby 1988–90; Harrison 1997b, 113–24; for Margam, David 1929, 322–4; Robinson 1993a, 57–9; Newman 1995, 426–8; for Neath, Butler 1976a, 18–20; Newman 1995, 467–9; Robinson 2002b; for Strata Florida, Williams 1889a, 204–6; Radford 1949a; Robinson and Platt 1998, 53–5; for Tintern, Newman 2000, 550–1; Robinson 2002a, 50–4; Robinson 2004; for Valle Crucis, Hughes 1895a, 7–17; Radford 1953, 19–22; Hubbard 1986, 292–7; Evans 1995, 36–43.

22 For Cwmhir, see Williams 1894–5; Radford 1982, 61–6; for Cymer, Radford 1946; Robinson 1995b; Smith and Butler 2001, 318–21; for Strata Marcella, [Jones] and Williams 1891; Arnold 1992; for Whitland, Ludlow 2000 and 2001; Ludlow 2002, 67–74.

23 The various references to the sacristy in the order's customary all seem to imply direct access to the church, presumably via this doorway in the transept wall: *Ecclesiastica Officia* (1 and 2), chapters 23.21–3, 53.11–14.

24 For France, see Aubert 1947, II, 39–51; for Fontenay, Auberger 2001, 97.

25 In general, see Dimier 1971, *passim*. The book room and sacristy are often depicted in the fullest corpus of Cistercian ground plans: Dimier 1949–67.

26 Robinson 2002a, 50; Robinson 2004, 96, 117.

27 Coomans 2000, 333–5.

28 Her point is that the first room within the east range was initially used exclusively as the sacristy and was only later subdivided (by wood or stone): Kinder 1997, 241–4. On the chronological complexity which could occur, see the account of the structural history at Bordesley: Hirst *et al* 1983, 103–22. This includes a very useful collection of comparative drawings.

29 The space at Dore was also barrel-vaulted. When the east range at Valle Crucis was remodelled, probably in the mid-fourteenth century, a book cupboard with an elaborate screen facade was fashioned in the cloister wall of the chapter house (*see* fig 125): Evans 1995, 15, 36.

30 Newman 2000, 550; Robinson 2002a, 50.

31 On the chapter house in general, see Braunfels 1972, 98–102; Kinder 1997, 244–67.

32 By far the most common pattern, both on the Continent and across the British Isles.

33 For Fountains, see Hope 1900a, 342–5; Coppack and Gilyard-Beer

34 1993, 31–3; Coppack 2003, 57–8; for Furness, Hope 1900b, 260–2; Robinson 1998, 117–18.

34 The chapter house at Fontenay featured ribs as early as c 1150–5, and might be considered the prototype for the ideal form (*see* fig 54). On this example, see Aubert 1947, II, 62–3; Auberger 2001, 97–100.

35 The form is discussed in more detail in a later chapter. On the identity of the 'universal' type, see Wilson 1999, 60–2. See also Bonde *et al* 1990, 202–4.

36 Gardner 1976, 69 n 47.

37 A corpus of thumbnail plans can be found in Robinson 1998, 64–205, *passim*.

38 On the chapter house liturgy, see *Ecclesiastica Officia* (1 and 2), chapter 70.1–70.96.

39 As suggested, for example, in Hope 1900a, 345; Hope 1900b, 262–3; Brakspear 1905, 41; Hope and Bilson 1907 (all referring to the *auditorium juxta capitulum*); Hope and Brakspear 1906, 155; Gilyard-Beer 1976, 31.

40 For instance, it was the room in which he designated work assignments and handed out the necessary tools to the monks: *Ecclesiastica Officia* (1 and 2), chapter 75. See, further, Aubert 1947, II, 70–1; Braunfels 1972, 76; Kinder 1997, 268; Coomans 1998a, 125; Williams 1998, 243–4; Fergusson and Harrison 1999, 103. One of the most interesting recent considerations is that by Bonde and Maines 1997, especially 51–2.

41 The west doorway to the Basingwerk parlour still stood complete in 1800 (*see* fig 84). For Buildwas, see Robinson 2002c, 18–19; for Fountains, Hope 1900a, 345; Coppack and Gilyard-Beer 1993, 33; for Rievaulx, Fergusson and Harrison 1999, 103; for Roche, Fergusson 1990a, 18.

42 For Tintern, see Robinson 2002a, 52; for Neath, Butler 1976a, 18.

43 For Fountains, see Hope 1900a, 345–6; Coppack and Gilyard-Beer 1993, 34; for Rievaulx, Fergusson and Harrison 1999, 103–5; for Tintern, Robinson 2002a, 52; for Neath, Butler 1976a, 18. Something similar also occurred at Byland, where the stair was modified not long after its original construction. It remained in this position throughout the abbey's history: Harrison 1990, 13.

44 For Beaulieu, see Hope and Brakspear 1906, 157; for Buildwas, Robinson 2002c, 11, 20; for Fountains, Coppack and Gilyard-Beer 1993, 33, 39; for Hailes, Coad 1993; for Jervaulx, Hope and Brakspear 1911, 320, 323; for Netley, Robinson 1998, 152–3.

45 Taylor 1971, 7; Robinson 1996b.

46 Butler 1976a, 21. On the rebuilding in general, see catalogue entry for Neath.

47 On the rebuilding generally, see catalogue entry for Tintern; Harrison *et al* 1998, 181–2; Robinson 2002a, 29–31. For the day stair, see Craster 1956, 22; Newman 2000, 551; Robinson 2002a, 55. Above the head of the recessed archway from the cloister, there are a number of (?reused) carved fragments.

48 Coomans 1998a, 132–5 (Val-Saint-Lambert), 143–7; Coomans 2000, 339–40, 344 (Villers); Dimier 1971, 104–7, 205–7 (Eberbach and Casamari).

49 The stair, however, took a parallel course, climbing within the thickness of the wall: Hughes 1895a, 10–11; Evans 1995, 38–9.

50 At Cîteaux, Clairvaux and a number of other large European houses, the range was vaulted in three 'aisles'. For collections of plans showing many European examples, see Dimier 1971; Braunfels 1972, 78–92; Dimier 1982.

51 Having cited these examples, it would be wrong to give the impression there was a totally 'standard' arrangement to the termination of Cistercian east ranges. The topography at Rievaulx,

for instance, required a particular solution, with a two-storey undercroft. Unusually, at Buildwas and Byland (both Savigniac houses in origin), there were open arcades in the east wall of the range at this point, opening towards outer enclosures. For these and other British examples, see Robinson 1998, 64–205, *passim*; for Fountains, Hope 1900a, 346–7; Coppack and Gilyard-Beer 1993, 33–4; for Beaulieu, Hope and Brakspear 1906, 156; for Stanley, Brakspear 1906–7, 508–10; for Furness, Hope 1900b, 263–5; for Rievaulx, Fergusson and Harrison 1999, 105–7; for Byland, Harrison 1990; for Buildwas, Robinson 2002c.

52 The discovery of the hearth was made during the conservation works of the early twentieth century: Robinson 2004, 101.

53 Robinson 2002a, 27–8, 52–4.

54 Its preservation stems from its incorporation into the ground-floor arrangements of the post-suppression house over this part of the site: Butler 1976a, 19; RCAHMW 1981, 85–8; Robinson 2002b.

55 [Lovegrove] 1921, 404; Taylor 1971; Robinson 1996b.

56 David 1929, 324; Robinson 1993a, 59; Newman 1995, 428.

57 For the 1517 description, see Didron 1845, 231. For Stanley, see Brakspear 1906–7, 509–10. See also Aubert 1947, I, 119–22.

58 As in Aubert 1947, II, 74–85; Braunfels 1972, 76; Kinder 1997, 269–71; Coomans 1998a, 136–9; Jansen 1998, 65–6; Fergusson and Harrison 1999, 105–7; Auberger 2001, 107–10; Coppack 2003, 35, 58.

59 McCann 1976, chapter 48; *Ecclesiastica Officia* (1 and 2), chapter 75. For more on the Cistercian work ethic in this context, see Holdsworth 1973; Burton 1994, 164–5; Lawrence 2001, 175–6.

60 In general, see Aubert 1947, II, 85–95; Braunfels 1972, 103; Kinder 1997, 271–4; Jansen 1998; Williams 1998, 247–8.

61 McCann 1976, chapter 22. See also Harvey 1993, 130–2.

62 *Narrative Texts* (*Capitula* IX), 408, (*Instituta* XII), 461.

63 The measurement is derived from Milley's 1708 plan (*see* fig 39). The room was described by the queen of Sicily in 1517: Didron 1845, 228.

64 At both Eberbach and Poblet the cloister is situated north of the church. For Eberbach, see Dimier 1971, 107; Einsingbach 1986, 21–2; for Poblet, Dimier 1971, 133.

65 *Statutes*, 244; *Statuta*, I, 150. Bell (2004, 188–9) has suggested, albeit very tentatively, that the lack of accepted form in the Longpont dormitory *might* imply the occurrence of partitioned private chambers. He acknowledges that this would be a very early example of such a pattern. For the site, see Peugniez 2001, 366–9.

66 Braunfels (1972, 103) says they 'aspired everywhere' to do this.

67 Aubert 1947, II, 87–8; Dimier 1982, 139, 190. For more on Silvacane, see Molina 1999, 42–3. For the sites generally, see Peugniez 2001, 409–11, 413–16, 420–3.

68 For Le Val (c 1200–20), see Aubert 1947, II, 37–9, 90; Peugniez 2001, 187–8; for Eberbach (c 1240–60), Dimier 1971, pl 30; for Alcobaça, Dimier 1971, 129. Other examples are illustrated in Van der Meer 1965.

69 Aubert 1947, II, 89–90; Chauvin 1998, 28–9; Jansen 1998, 72; Peugniez 2001, 373–5.

70 For Bindon, see Robinson 1998, 71; for Buildwas, Robinson 2002c, 20; for Cleeve, Gilyard-Beer 1990; for the Irish sites, Stalley 1987, 55, 166–7.

71 Hodkinson 1905, 173; Taylor 1971; Robinson 1996b.

72 For Roche, see Fergusson 1990a, 14–19; for Fountains (where the dormitory also extended over the projecting chapter house), Hope 1900a, 345–54; Coppack and Gilyard-Beer 1993, 35–6; Coppack 2003, 58–9; for Forde, Robinson 1998, 110; for Rievaulx, Fergusson and Harrison 1999, 108; for Furness, Hope 1900b, 266–7.

73 Robinson 2002a, 54.

74 Butler 1976a, 19.

75 Robinson 1993a, 59; Evans 1996, 22–3.

76 Paul 1927, 274; Harrison and Thurlby 1997, 61; Harrison 1997b, 116.

77 Butler 1976a, 17. The night stair within the north transept at Tintern was rebuilt in 1905, during the early programme of conservation of the site: Robinson 2002a, 47.

78 Lekai 1977, 373–4. There is comparative material in Harvey 1993, 130–2; Jansen 1998, 78–9.

79 This is the figure given in Fergusson and Harrison 1999, 108.

80 On the Rule and appropriate decorum within the dormitory, see McCann 1976, chapter 22; Ecclesiastica Officia (1 and 2), chapter 72.13–25. See also William of Malmesbury, I, 581.

81 In general, see Lekai 1977, 373–4; Kinder 1997, 272–4; Jansen 1998, 74–6. On the attempts by the General Chapter to contain the trend, see Bell 2004.

82 Harvey 1993, 130.

83 Butler 1976b, 81, 95.

84 On the east range in general, see Hughes 1895a, 13–15; Radford 1953, 21–2; Evans 1995, 38–41. For more on dating, see Maddison 1978, 96–8.

85 A suggested reconstruction appears in Evans 1995, 38–9. The precise numbers in the community at this time cannot be determined, though the figure is unlikely to have exceeded fifteen. There were just seven monks at Valle Crucis at the time of the suppression: Pratt 1997, 38.

86 There were curtains at Benedictine Westminster, for instance, in the fourteenth and fifteenth centuries: Harvey 1993, 130–1. For traces of wooden partitions at Furness, see Hope 1900b, 267; at Fountains, Hope 1900a, 353.

87 In other words, not unlike the arrangement depicted in the St Gall plan: Braunfels 1972, 38–9; Horn and Born 1979; Conant 1993, 57. For other contextual background on monastic latrines, see Gilyard-Beer 1976, 30–1; Lillich 1982b; Coppack 1990, 97–9; Bond 2001, 104–5, 119–22; for Cistercian latrines in general, Aubert 1947, II, 94–5; Kinder 1997, 274–5; on decorum within the latrine, Ecclesiastica Officia (1 and 2), chapter 72.15–16.

88 These sites are introduced in Chauvin 1998, 52–3, 108–11; Peugniez 2001, 184–7, 270–2, 420–3. See also Aubert 1947, I, 121, 123.

89 For Cleeve, see Gilyard-Beer 1990, 22–3; for Fountains, Hope 1900a, 354–6; Coppack 2003, 57; for Hailes, Coad 1993, 11–12; for Jervaulx, Hope and Brakspear 1911, 323–4; for Rievaulx, Fergusson and Harrison 1999, 108–9, 117; for Roche, Fergusson 1990a, 19; for Sawley, Coppack et al 2002, 51–75, 107.

90 Robinson 2002a, 54.

91 Hughes 1895a, 12–13; Evans 1995, 43.

92 Butler 1976a, 20; RCAHMW 1981, 87–8.

93 For Byland (where it was a second-phase arrangement), see Harrison 1990, 14–15; for Furness, Hope 1900b, 267–8.

94 There have been different views on the way this now isolated fragment should be interpreted. David (1929, 324) and others thought it likely that it represented the infirmary, but there cannot really be much doubt it was in fact a bridge linkage in the manner of neighbouring Neath: Robinson 1993a, 59; Newman 1995, 428.

95 On the south (or north) range in general, see Kinder 1997, 277–87; for France, Aubert 1947, II, 97–119; for detailed case studies, Fergusson 1986 (on Rievaulx and Byland); Fergusson and Harrison 1999, 137–50 (Rievaulx); Coomans 2000, 347–91 (Villers).

96 For Basingwerk, see Taylor 1971, 7–8; Hubbard 1986, 354–5; Robinson 1996b; for Cymer, Radford 1946; Robinson 1995b; Smith

and Butler 2001, 318–21; for Dore, Paul 1904, 125; Harrison 1997b, 118–20; for Neath, Butler 1976a, 21; Newman 1995, 468; Robinson 2002b; for Tintern, Newman 2000, 551–3; Robinson 2002a, 55–8; for Valle Crucis, Hughes 1895a, 7; Radford 1953, 23; Butler 1976b; Hubbard 1986, 292–7; Evans 1995, 446–5; for Whitland, Ludlow 2000 and 2001; Ludlow 2002, 71–3.

97 See chapter 11.

98 This was stipulated in the key statute of c 1113–19: Narrative Texts (Capitula IX), 408 (Instituta XII), 461.

99 Gilyard-Beer and Coppack 1986, 174–5; Coppack 1998, 23–31; Coppack et al 2002, 101–5; Coppack 2003, 21–4.

100 In general, see Fergusson 1986, 161–6; Coppack 1998, 32–43.

101 Fergusson 1986, 171–2. The date is given as the 1140s in Fergusson and Harrison 1999, 147. We now have to bear in mind the new views on the date of the rebuildings at Clairvaux: Kennedy [Gajewski] 1996, 131–65. Musso (1991, 197) has dated the west range at Clairvaux to c 1140–60.

102 For Byland, see Fergusson 1986, 167–8; Harrison 1990, 18–20; for Fountains, Hope 1900a, 361–5; Coppack and Gilyard-Beer 1993, 43–4; Coppack 2003, 65–7; for Kirkstall, Hope and Bilson 1907, 46–9, 52–3; Fergusson 1986, 165–6; Moorhouse and Wrathmell 1987, 19–22, 45–7; for Rievaulx, Fergusson and Harrison 1999, 137, 140–6.

103 Aubert 1947, II, 114–16; Kinder 1997, 277–80.

104 According to Coppack and Gilyard-Beer (1993, 39), the fire was kept from 1 November until Good Friday. Knowles (1963, 466) says from 1 November onwards, according to the Benedictine Regularis Concordia.

105 An entire chapter of the order's customary was devoted to the procedure: Ecclesiastica Officia (1 and 2), chapter 90. See also Lekai 1977, 375; Cassidy-Welch 2001, 147–9; and the comparative evidence in Harvey 1993, 96–9.

106 Ecclesiastica Officia (1 and 2), chapter 72.6–8; Braunfels 1972, 76; Lekai 1977, 374–5; Williams 1998, 244; Fergusson and Harrison 1999, 147. The early post-Conquest Benedictines appear to have been shaved in the cloister: Lanfranc Constitutions, 136–9.

107 Though it is much restored: Aubert 1947, II, 115–16; Auberger 2001, 110–11.

108 Dimier 1971, 196–7.

109 For Byland, see Harrison 1990, 19; for Croxden, Hall 2003, I, 61; for Fountains (one of the best-surviving English examples), Hope 1900a, 356–61; Coppack and Gilyard-Beer 1993, 39–41; for Furness, Hope 1900b, 268; for Hailes, Coad 1993, 12–13; for Kirkstall, Hope and Bilson 1907, 43–5; for Rievaulx, Fergusson and Harrison 1999, 139–40; for Waverley, Brakspear 1905, 47–8.

110 Aubert 1947, II, 116; Peugniez 2001, 367.

111 Robinson 2002a, 29–31, 55–6.

112 For Dore, see Harrison 1997b, 117, 119; for Neath, Butler 1976a, 21; for Valle Crucis, Butler 1976b, 89–90, 94–5; Evans 1995, 44.

113 Taylor 1971, 7. For the argument to carry any serious weight, one must assume that the thirteenth-century fireplace was located in the west wall of the extension, lost when the whole was remodelled. See also Robinson 1996b.

114 Hope 1900a, 359–60; Coppack and Gilyard-Beer 1993, 40–1; Coppack 2003, 63–4.

115 Fergusson and Harrison 1999, 140.

116 For Byland, see Harrison 1990, 19; for Croxden, Hall 2003, I, 61.

117 Robinson 2002a, 56.

118 Aubert 1947, II, 117–99; Kinder 1997, 281–3; Williams 1998, 247.

119 McCann 1976, chapter 35. For the duties of the weekly helpers, see Ecclesiastica Officia (1 and 2), chapter 108.

120 Dimier 1971, 132–3, 150 (pl 42); Van der Meer 1965, pl 348; Erdmann 1994, 39; Peugniez 2001, 318–19.

121 For Villers, see Coomans 2000, 373–9, 389–90; for Byland, Harrison 1990, 20; for Fountains, Hope 1900a, 365–9; Coppack and Gilyard-Beer 1993, 44–5; Coppack 2003, 43.

122 For Basingwerk, see Taylor 1971, 8; for Tintern, Robinson 2002a, 58; for Valle Crucis, Butler 1976a, 87; Evans 1995, 45.

123 Braunfels 1972, 38–41; Horn and Born 1979.

124 A senior monk, the cellarer was effectively one of two deputies for the abbot: Knowles 1963a, 427–30 (with the quote at 430).

125 Gilyard-Beer 1976, 36–8.

126 Dickinson 1961, 38–40; Gilyard-Beer 1976, 38–40; Coppack 1990, 75–6; Thompson 2001, 65–92.

127 For the *conversi*, see Williams 1998, 79–88, and for their usages, *Lay Brothers*.

128 On the Cistercian west range in general, see Gilyard-Beer 1976, 50–1; Kinder 1997, 305–31; for France, Aubert 1947, II, 120–40; for Denmark, France 1998b, 2–13; for recent case studies, Fergusson and Harrison 1999, 50–8 (Rievaulx); McGee and Perkins 1998, 88–90 (Rufford); Coomans 2000, 393–428 (Villers); Hall 2003, I, 57–60 (Croxden).

129 The Rule of St Benedict had set out the qualities needed in a monk for the office of cellarer: McCann 1976, chapter 31. On his Cistercian duties, see *Ecclesiastica Officia* (1 and 2), chapter 117.

130 For which, see Aubert 1947, II, 130–1, 136–7; Musso 1991; Kinder 1996b, 372; Leroux-Dhuys 1998, 30, 176–7; Peugniez 2001, 120–3.

131 For Longuay and Noirlac, see Aubert 1947, II, 126–7, 131–2; Dimier 1982, 242 (pl 100), 258–9; Peugniez 2001, 96–9, 138; for Maulbronn, Knapp 1997, 70–4; for Chorin, Erdmann 1994; for Alcobaça, Kinder 1997, 306, 320–1.

132 See Hope 1900a, 371–83; Coppack and Gilyard-Beer 1993, 52–8; Coppack 2003, 37, 61–2.

133 Illustrated in Coppack and Gilyard-Beer 1993, 54–5; Robinson 1998, 111.

134 *Ecclesiastica Officia* (1 and 2), chapter 117.1; 117.28.

135 Hope 1900a, 383–5.

136 In general, see Robinson 1998, 64–205, *passim*. For Byland, Harrison 1990, 20–1; for Furness, Hope 1900b, 274–9; for Jervaulx, Hope and Brakspear 1911, 340–2; for Kirkstall, Hope and Bilson 1907, 54–9; for Waverley, Brakspear 1905, 52–7; for Melrose, Fawcett 1994, 106–7; Fawcett and Oram 2004, 192–7. At Jervaulx and Waverley the lay brothers' latrine projected westwards from the range, in much the same fashion as at Fountains. At Byland, on the other hand, it turned eastward, effectively enclosing a lay brothers' cloister.

137 For Beaulieu, see Hope and Brakspear 1906, 163–8; for Rufford, McGee and Perkins 1998, 88–90.

138 For Basingwerk, see Taylor 1971, 8; Robinson 1996b; for Dore, Paul 1904, 125; Harrison 1997b, 116–19; for Neath, Butler 1976a, 21–3; Newman 1995, 465–6; for Strata Florida, Radford 1949a; Robinson and Platt 1998, 55; for Valle Crucis, Butler 1976b, 81–6, 92–3; Evans 1995, 46–7; for Whitland, Ludlow 2000; Ludlow 2002, 66–9, 71.

139 There are further details in the catalogue entry. See also Thomas and Taylor 1938, 17; Butler 1976a, 21–3; Newman 1995, 465–6; Robinson 2002b.

140 Brakspear 1919; Craster 1956; Newman 2000, 553–4; Robinson 2002a, 28, 30, 59.

141 The extant features were noted by Williams (1889a, 224–5), but he made no attempt to excavate in this area. Nor, it seems, was the west range selected for 'clearance' as part of the early presentation programme: Radford 1949a; Robinson and Platt 1998, 55.

142 Further details on the recent programme of investigations are given in the Whitland catalogue entry. For the report, see Ludlow 2002, 64, 66–9. See also Clapham 1921, 207–8.

143 Butler 1976b, 81–6, 92–3; Evans 1995, 46–7.

144 Butler 1976b, 81–2. Another site where the west range was one of the earliest constructions is Byland. The sequence makes perfect sense if one assumes the lay brothers assisted in the subsequent construction programme: Fergusson 1984a, 69–75; Harrison 1990, 20–1; Robinson 1998, 81–2.

145 Based on the robbed-out remains, the excavation report refers to 'inner' and 'outer' south rooms: Butler 1976b, 83–4.

146 Butler 1976b, 84, 92–3.

147 Paul 1904, 118–19, 125; Paul 1927, 274; Paul 1931, 500.

148 Harrison 1997b, 116–19. To follow his argument, one also needs to look at the plan in Harrison and Thurlby 1997, 48.

149 Nothing was said to be visible in the early 1920s: [Lovegrove] 1921, 405. On the little uncovered since, see Taylor 1971, 8. The known arrangements bear some comparison with those at Buildwas, the house which assumed responsibility for Basingwerk in 1157, on which see Robinson 2002c, 22.

150 On timber-framing traditions in Wales, see Smith 1988, 74–83, 380–1.

151 Owen 1919, 29–31; and see catalogue entry for further details.

152 As suggested in Smith and Butler 2001, 319.

153 Aubert 1947, I, 53; II, 122–3. This is taken up by Kinder (1997, 311, 329) and by Coomans (2000, 399, 424). See also Braunfels 1972, 77–9.

154 Aubert 1947, II, facing 1; Dimier 1982, 39–41.

155 Aubert 1947, I, 11, 109; II, 122; Plouvier 1998, 138–9, 148 (Cîteaux); Musso 1991, 192 (Clairvaux).

156 Aubert 1947, I, 110, 115, 121; Braunfels 1972, 92; Dimier 1982, 55, 226, 252.

157 Dimier 1971, 197, 298.

158 In general, see Robinson 1998, *passim*. For Beaulieu, see Hope and Brakspear 1906, 163–8; for Boxley, Tester 1973; for Buildwas, Robinson 2002c, 22; for Byland (where the lane features a remarkable series of thirty-five niche seats on the east side), Harrison 1990, 20–1; for Rufford, McGee and Perkins 1998; for Sawley, Coppack *et al* 2002, 30, 70–1.

159 Stalley 1980, 312–13.

160 Butler 1976a, 18, 21–3; Robinson 2002b.

161 This is based on what we otherwise know about the width of the range. The short stretch of wall along the south-west side of the cloister might be the boundary of a lane, rather than the inner wall of the range itself (*see* fig 160): Taylor 1971; Robinson 1996b.

162 Robinson 2002a, 28–9.

163 For Clairmont, see Aubert 1947, I, 178–9; Labbé 1948–52; for Villers, Coomans 2000, 413, 427–8; for Eberbach, Dimier 1971, 104, 124.

164 For Kirkstall, see Hope and Bilson 1907, 58; for Stanley, Brakspear 1906–7, 512–13.

165 It is suggested by Harrison (1997a, 116–18) that the eventual Dore arrangement reflects an earlier cloister plan. The possibility of a broad lane at Whitland is noted in Clapham 1921, 206–7. Ludlow (2002, 71) wonders if, like Dore, this might again be a reflection of the initial claustral layout.

166 Hope 1900a, 381–2; Hope and Bilson 1907, 58.

167 Micklethwaite 1882.

168 Williams 1998, 249.

169 The cloister has been identified by geophysical survey: Coppack and Gilyard-Beer 1993, 10, 54; Coppack 2003, 56.

170 Fergusson and Harrison 1999, 56–8. For tensions between choir

171 In general, see Kinder 1997, 333–75. New discussions of the buildings to both the west and east of the cloister will be found in Hall 2003, I, 26–49, 83–106; Hall 2004. For France, see Aubert 1947, II, 141–59.

172 The infirmary complex and the abbot's lodging are considered in chapter 12.

173 On the monastic infirmary in general, see Dickinson 1961, 41–2; Gilyard-Beer 1976, 40–3; Coppack 1990, 76–8; Fernie 2000, 206–7.

174 For introductions to Cistercian infirmary architecture, see Braunfels 1972, 106, 108; Dimier 1987b; Bell 1998; Williams 1998, 250–2. New ideas are explored in Hall 2003, I, 95–106; Hall 2004. On Cistercian medicine, see Bell 1989.

175 The infirmary hall is No. 73 on Milley's southern view (*see* fig 16). See Braunfels 1972, 80–1; Dimier 1987b, 809, 811; Pressouyre and Kinder 1992, 78–9.

176 For an introduction to Dunes, see Peugniez 2001, 460–1; for the imaginary drawing of 1580 by Pierre Pourbus, Van der Meer 1965, figs 230–232; Braunfels 1972, 92–5; Pressouyre and Kinder 1992, 76; Coomans 2000, 193.

177 On abbatial accommodation in general, see Dickinson 1961, 38–42; Gilyard-Beer 1976, 38–40; Thompson 2001, 65–92; on the Cistercians, Ramey 1996; Williams 1998, 253.

178 *Ecclesiastica Officia* (1 and 2), chapter 110.6–11.

179 As Fergusson and Harrison (1999, 128–9) point out, this is the earliest example of the building type known in the entire order.

180 Hope 1900a, 335–6; Coppack and Gilyard-Beer 1993, 45–7; Coppack 2003, 59.

181 For Buildwas (one of the most substantial survivals), see Robinson 2002c, 23; for Byland (situated south east of the cloister), Harrison 1990, 18; for Furness, Hope 1900b, 290–7; for Jervaulx, Hope and Brakspear 1911, 332–4; for Kirkstall, Hope and Bilson 1907, 34–8; for Roche (located south east of the cloister), Fergusson 1990a, 23–4; for Waverley, Brakspear 1905, 70–1.

182 In general, see Kinder 1997, 356–60; for recent case studies, Fergusson and Harrison 1999, 128–35 (Rievaulx); Coomans 2000, 449–58 (Villers); Coppack 2003, 98–102 (Fountains); Hall 2003, I, 84–95 (Croxden).

183 For context, see Williams 1998, 249–50.

184 *Statuta*, I, 115.

185 In his south view, the relevant structures are Nos 50–53 (*see* fig 16); his plan shows them as Nos 45–48 (*see* fig 39). The plan and view are reproduced in Braunfels 1972, 80–1.

186 Coomans 2000, 413–16, 426–7. In France, traces of the lay brothers' infirmary have been identified at Fontmorigny (Cher) and Jouy (Seine-et-Marne): Aubert 1947, II, 140; Peugniez 2001, 94–5, 170–1.

187 For Fountains, see Hope 1900a, 385–7; Coppack and Gilyard-Beer 1993, 56–7; Coppack 2003, 60–2; for Jervaulx, Hope and Brakspear 1911, 343–4; for Waverley, Brakspear 1905, 56–7; for Roche, Fergusson 1990a, 22–3.

188 On the subject of monastic hospitality in general, see Rowell 2000; for the Cistercians, Lekai 1977, 380–1; Kinder 1997, 371–5; Williams 1998, 124–9; for France, Aubert 1947, II, 154–6.

189 McCann 1976, chapter 53. See also Knowles 1963a, 479–81.

190 *Narrative Texts* (*Capitula* IX), 408 (*Instituta* XII), 461. One of the early timber buildings excavated at Sawley Abbey has been interpreted as a guest hall: Coppack 1998, 30–1; Coppack *et al* 2002, 103–4.

191 On the role of the guest house monk, and on the arrangements for receiving guests (and of the gatekeeper's role in this regard), see *Ecclesiastica Officia* (1 and 2), chapters 87, 120.1–20.

192 Birch 1897, 62, 76, 81; Williams 2001, 146. See also Williams 1998, 125.

193 *Gerald of Wales*, VI, 43; Cowley 1977, 73, 207–8.

194 Robinson and Platt 1998, 43; Williams 2001, 21.

195 *Gerald of Wales*, VI, 68; Thorpe 1978, 127; Cowley 1977, 204.

196 Williams 1998, 125–7, which includes further examples of similar class distinction.

197 The principal (high-status) guest house and associated structures appear on the north-east side of the church. To the south east is what most often appears as the almonry: Braunfels 1972, 38–9; Horn and Born 1979. Robert Willis distinguished the one as the *hospitium* of distinguished guests and the other as the paupers' *hospitium*. His redrawing of the plan is reproduced in Thompson 2001, 40.

198 Though now see the relevant chapters in Rowell 2000.

199 It appears as No. 33 on Milley's plan of 1708 (*see* fig 39). For what survives, see Vilain 1998, 24–6.

200 For Fontenay, see Auberger 2001, 42, 131–2; for Quincy, Aubert 1947, II, 154–6; Peugniez 2001, 72–3.

201 For Silvacane, see Molina 1999, 19–21; for Vauclair, Courtois 1982, 327–8.

202 Coomans 2000, 459–74.

203 In general, see Hope 1900a, 388–93; Coppack and Gilyard-Beer 1993, 59–61; Coppack 2003, 59–60.

204 The layout of the building was recovered by geophysical survey in 1992: Coppack and Gilyard-Beer 1993, 60–1; Coppack 2003, 68–70.

205 Brakspear 1905, 75–7, 81–5.

206 Hope and Bilson 1907, 60–3; Wrathmell 1987; Moorhouse and Wrathmell 1987, 2–3; Coppack 1990, 104–5.

207 The numbers as a whole are in any case not large: Rowell 2000; Ramey 2004, 63.

208 Brown 1988, 69–75.

209 In a recent study of the Stoneleigh gatehouse/guest house complex, Ramey (2004) suggests the surviving guest house was erected between a late thirteenth-century guest building (now lost) and a new gatehouse, of *c* 1342–5. The older building may have served as a chamber block, the new structure as a hall. See also Robinson 1998, 175–6; Emery 2000, 421–2; Morris 2004, 35.

210 The unusual location of the guest house here was determined by the site topography: Hope 1900b, 238–9; Robinson 1998, 119.

211 For general background to Cistercian hospitality in Wales, and on the range of visitors, see Cowley 1977, 203–9, *passim*; Williams 2001, 143–6.

212 On the early clearance, see Robinson 1997, 44–7, 50; for the buildings, Courtney 1989; Robinson 2002a, 19.

213 Courtney (1989, 101, 124) goes so far as to describe it as a 'first-floor hall'. Mr James Wood, however, argued that it was a mill building, based on his investigations of historic watercourses around the site: Wood 1912, 16–17. The guest house interpretation is by no means certain, but it is difficult to ascribe another function to what looks (in origin at least) like a domestic building.

214 In essence, corrodians were people who sought security in their old age at a monastic house. They generally provided a cash gift or land endowment in return for their 'corrody', a certain bundle of privileges which included some form of accommodation. On this element within Cistercian communities, see Williams 1998, 122–3; Williams 2001, 141–3. On the arrangements at Benedictine Westminster (with useful context) see Harvey 1993, 179–209.

215 This theme is further examined in the context of abbatial accommodation in chapter 12. In general, see Williams, G 1976,

249–62, *passim*; Williams 2001, 145–6. Specific quotes and their sources will also be found in the appropriate catalogue entries.

216 Price 1952, 270.

217 Butler 1976a, 11.

218 Jones 1933, 176.

219 Radford (1946, 3) thought it likely that it was a guest house. The estimated felling date for the timber used in the roof of the building is 1441: Smith 2001, 447, 469–71; Smith and Suggett 2002, 58–62. Immediately to the south, there is a second domestic building, described by Smith (2001, 447) as sub-medieval in character. However, we cannot discount the possibility that this, too, may have been monastic in origin.

220 Radford 1953, 6, 8, 21–2; Evans 1995, 40–1.

221 Price 1952, 161–5; Pratt 1997, 10–11; Williams 2001, 145.

222 Taylor 1971, 7–8; Hubbard 1986, 355.

223 Hodkinson 1905, pls J–M. There are further photographs, taken in the late 1920s, in the Cadw archive on the site. See catalogue entry for Basingwerk for further detail.

224 On monastic precincts generally, see Dickinson 1961, 5–10; Gilyard-Beer 1976, 43–6; Coppack 1990, 100–28; Aston 2000, 107–14; Thompson 2001, 105–25. On the Cistercian precinct, Williams 1998, 199–209; Coppack 1998, 95–111; Williams 2001, 119–21. There is further useful context in Pressouyre 1994.

225 This said, however, it would be wrong to imagine a direct correlation between precinct size and wealth.

226 For more on this theme, see Cassidy-Welch 2001, 23–45. Rowell (2000, 42–3, 201–5) argues that although access to monastic precincts was managed via gatehouses, their architectural purpose was not merely one of restriction. She urges us to consider a more sophisticated vocabulary in terms of their position, varying functions and manning arrangements.

227 *Narrative Texts* (*Capitula IX*), 408 (*Instituta XII*), 461.

228 The importance of the gatehouse and its porter were first set out in the Rule of St Benedict: McCann 1976, chapter 66. For the duties of the Cistercian gatekeeper, see *Ecclesiastica Officia* (1 and 2), chapter 120. See also Kinder 1997, 371–5.

229 The full description appears in Migne 1844–64, CLXXXV, cols 569–74. The key passages are translated in Braunfels 1972, 245; Matarasso 1993, 287–92.

230 Migne 1844–64, CLXXXV, col 285. For translations, see Webb and Walker 1960, 88; Braunfels 1972, 244; Brooke 1986, 22.

231 Williams 1998, 199. For the full plan of the precinct at Clairvaux, see Aubert 1947, I, 9, 11; Vilain 1998, 18.

232 Aubert 1947, I, 7; Gras 1982; Plouvier 1998, 124–5.

233 All illustrated in Aubert 1947, I, 14, 17, 113, 126, 129, 132. There is a brief section on precinct walls in Aubert 1947, II, 141–3. For introductions to Le Val and Vauluisant, which have not been mentioned so far, see Peugniez 2001, 75–6, 187–8. On the precinct walls at Fontenay, see Auberger 2001, 139–41.

234 Van der Meer 1965, figs 230–232; Braunfels 1972, 92–4. For recent studies of two Continental precincts, see Coomans 2000, 505–42 (on Villers); Erdmann 1994, 48–51 (on Chorin). There are well-preserved German examples at Maulbronn (Knapp 1997, *passim*, plan at 193) and Bebenhausen (Pressouyre 1994, 471–81).

235 Coppack 1998, 105. The author argues that there is no indication of the English Cistercians having formalized their precincts before the last years of the twelfth century.

236 Coppack 1990, 100–3; Coppack 1998, 99–102; Fergusson and Harrison 1999, 175–86.

237 Coppack 1998, 105, 107.

238 Rahtz and Hirst 1976, 28–37; Astill 1993; Robinson 1998, 72; Aston

239 For Fountains, see Hope 1900a, 397–401; Coppack and Gilyard-Beer 1993, 12–13, 59–64; Coppack 1998, 102–5; Coppack 2003, 79, 81, 118–26; for Furness, Hope 1900b, 232–7.

240 Lengths of wall survive and its course is traceable elsewhere: Hope and Brakspear 1906, 140–7.

241 Coppack (1998, 105) suggests that in almost every case Cistercian precincts were larger than those of the Benedictines and Augustinians, averaging around 24.3ha compared to about 12.1ha.

242 Although Brakspear (1906–7, 496–8) suggested the Stanley precinct covered 9.7ha, this has been refined in a survey of the superb site earthworks by Graham Brown (1996), now of English Heritage. His work indicates a minimum of 11.3ha, with a possible extension to 15.7ha. See also Knowles and St Joseph 1952, 140–1; Aston 2000, 112–13.

243 Knowles and St Joseph 1952, 142–3; Gilyard-Beer 1990, 3–10.

244 Based on a survey by the former RCHME, quoted in Hall and Strachan 2001, 201; Hall 2001, 68–9. See also Knowles and St Joseph 1952, 126–7; Aston 2000, 111–13.

245 Tester 1973; Robinson 1998, 74.

246 This view goes back more than a century: see the bold claim made in the context of Waverley in Brakspear 1905, 15–16. The general point is made in Fergusson 1990b, 52, 55; Coppack 1998, 108. See also Morant 1995, 41–5; Williams 1998, 200–2.

247 For Beaulieu, see Hope and Brakspear 1906, 141–3, 145–7; for Byland, Harrison 1990, 21–3; for Cleeve, Gilyard-Beer 1990, 3–10; for Croxden, Hall 2003, I, 27–8; II, figs 15, 18; for Fountains, Hope 1900a, 400–1; Coppack and Gilyard-Beer 1993, 61–2; for Furness, Hope 1900b, 233–7; for Kirkstall, Hope and Bilson 1907, 8–10; for Roche, Fergusson 1990a, 3–7; for Tilty, Hall and Strachan 2001, 202.

248 Morant 1995, *passim*; Ramey 2004, 63.

249 The earliest examples may well have been of timber.

250 Fergusson 1990b.

251 For the outer court, see Coppack 1990, 100–28; Coppack 1998, 95–111; Williams 1998, 204–9.

252 As suggested in Fergusson 1990b, 56; Coppack 1998, 108.

253 Kinder 1997, 373–4; Williams 1998, 202–5. For France, Aubert 1947, II, 144–7.

254 Hall 2001; Hall 2003, I, 29–49.

255 See, for example, Hope 1900b, 236; Gilyard-Beer 1976, 46; Coppack 1998, 108.

256 Hall 2001, 64–90.

257 In general, see Robinson 1998, 89, 119, 125, 134, 148, 185, 186; for Kirkstead, Pevsner *et al* 1989, 418; Hall 2001, 68–74; for Furness, Hope 1900b, 234–6; for Hailes, Verey and Brooks 1999, 396–7.

258 For Beaulieu, see Hope and Brakspear 1906, 146–7; for Whalley, Robinson 1998, 204; Hall 2001, 88, 90. The Cleeve suggestion is made in Coppack 1998, 108.

259 Coppack 1990, 103–9; Coppack 1998, 108.

260 Coppack 1990, 109–25; Coppack 1998, 108–11.

261 Bond 2001, *passim*.

262 Coppack 1998, 97–111, *passim*; Fergusson and Harrison 1999, 186; Hall and Strachan 2001, 201.

263 Brakspear 1919; Robinson 2002a, 19.

264 Williams 1990, 20, 86, drawing on Ellis 1927, 1–7.

265 Stone 1997.

266 Ludlow 2002, 79–85; James 1978.

267 Some features were noted in Williams 1890b, 412–13. The more recent Cwmhir work is to be published in the near future. I am grateful to Dr Sian Rees for sharing the general conclusions with me. The recent work at Strata Florida has been led by Professor

David Austin, who has been kind enough to share his initial ideas with me.

268 Stone 1997, 127–31.

269 Both were comparatively wealthy houses with no shortage of local building stone. On Neath, see Butler 1976a, 13.

270 Birch 1897, 363; Williams 2001, 120.

271 Williams 1981a, 104, drawing on W[illiams] 1846, 111.

272 For another aerial view of the site, see Knowles and St Joseph 1952, 118–19. Williams questions whether walls were ever built here, or at neighbouring Valle Crucis: Williams 1998, 202; Williams 2001, 119.

273 Thorpe 1978, 127.

274 W[illiams] 1846, 106–7.

275 Birch 1897, 359. What appears to have been a medieval gatehouse, south east of the church, survived as part of the post-suppression house at Margam. It was destroyed in 1744: Moore and Moore 1974, 163–4; RCAHMW 1981, 323–4, 328; Evans 1996, 35.

276 For the original reference, see Coxe 1801, I, 115–16; Williams 2001, 120.

277 Williams 1976a, 100.

278 Williams 1984, I, 144; Robinson and Platt 1998, 43.

279 Williams 1976a, 64–6.

280 Morant 1995, 192. The gate features in many early prints of the site. See, for example, Woof and Hebron 1998, 113, 135, 172.

281 Wood 1912, 11–12; Newman 2000, 556–7. For an early illustration, see Williams 2001, pl XI-B.

282 The road is the A4230. See Butler 1976a, 27; Newman 1995, 471; Morant 1995, 189.

283 Newman 1995, 429; Evans 1996, 37–8. It is illustrated in Williams 2001, plate XI-A.

284 Gray 1903, 128–31. The window is of Sutton stone, unlike the sandstone dressings used for the east window. It may date from c 1300.

285 Evans 1996, 37.

286 Newman 2000, 556–7; Robinson 2002a, 19.

287 Williams 1984, I, 144. James Wood was surely mistaken to suggest the chapel was built in the second half of the fifteenth century. He thought it was intended as the burial place of William Herbert: Wood 1912, 15–16.

288 Williams 1984, I, 122.

289 James 1978; Ludlow 2002, 80, 85–8.

290 Stone 1997, 131–6.

291 Evans 1996, 21, 33. An estate map of 1814 shows the mill building, but not the present pond: [Whittle] 2000, 105, 107.

292 A probable mill pond is shown at this point in a 1764 estate map of the site: National Library of Wales, Badminton Maps, vol 2, no. 6; Courtney and Gray 1991, 146, 150; Robinson 1995a, 22; Robinson 2002a, 19.

293 Newman (2000, 336) seems content to accept a monastic origin. The view has been challenged by Mein in, for example, Mein and Lewis 1990–1, 101. Coppack (1998, 102) suggests that large barns are unusual features in Cistercian precincts.

294 *Leland*, 118.

Chapter 9
Cloisters and Cloister Arcades

1 See Stalley 1999, 182–4 (with the quote taken from 182); Stalley 1987, 51; Brooke 2003, 6–7. For a new general overview of the monastic cloister, see Schütz 2004.

2 Braunfels 1972, 41; Stalley 1999, 182.

3 On the matter of origins, see Braunfels 1972, 31–46, *passim*; Horn 1973; Brooke 1987; Thompson 2001, 33–61. For the derivation of the St Gall cloister itself, see Horn and Born 1979, I, 241–5.

4 That is in so far as one can judge from the surviving evidence, bearing in mind how little is known of Cistercian building before the middle years of the twelfth century. For France in general, see Aubert 1947, II, 1–33.

5 Fontaine 1928; Aubert 1947, I, 130–1; Dimier 1982, 299–304.

6 In general, see Robinson 1998, 80, 110, 145, 175.

7 As suggested in Mein and Lewis 1990–1, and depicted in Mein's sketch plan of the site, reproduced in Williams 2001, 288.

8 The need for an adequate supply of water to the claustral buildings is usually given as the key factor. On the positioning of the cloister at Aberconwy, see Butler 1964, 115–17; for Maenan, Butler and Evans 1980; Butler 1987.

9 Braunfels 1972, 97–8; Stalley 1999, 182.

10 Aubert 1947, II, 6–9; Bourgeois 2000; Auberger 2001, 87–95.

11 Stalley 1999, 182–3.

12 In general terms, the lack of a later replacement was not necessarily related to insufficient wealth or patronage: the decision to keep the original seems to have been a question of deliberate choice.

13 One important and quite remarkable exception is to be found in the cloister of the Cistercian nuns at Las Huelgas in Spain. Here, the miniature church facade carved on the face of one capital is taken to represent an intimate representation of the entry to the heavenly paradise. It is illustrated in Tobin 1995, 19. The subject has been explored by Dr Rose Walker.

14 On the *Apologia* in general, see Rudolph 1990.

15 Transcripts appear in Migne 1844–64, CLXXXII, col 916; Braunfels 1972, 242; Matarasso 1993, 57.

16 *Narrative Texts* (*Capitula XXVI*), 413 (*Instituta XX*), 464.

17 For a recent consideration of the theme, see Cassidy-Welch 2001, 47–8, 65–71. On the different usages of the words *claustra* and *claustrum* during the Middle Ages, Meyvaert 1973, 53–4; Brooke 2003, 7.

18 *Ecclesiastica Officia* (1 and 2), chapter 17 (Palm Sunday), chapter 29 (Ascension Day), chapter 47 (Candlemas). For more on the theme of processions, see Cassidy-Welch 2001, 58–61.

19 Cassidy-Welch 2001, 59–60.

20 *Ecclesiastica Officia* (1 and 2), chapter 55.

21 Cassidy-Welch 2001, 61.

22 See, for example, Butler 1982a, 93.

23 The details for the most part remain unpublished: Harrison 1997c, 74 n 1. I am grateful to Stuart Harrison for discussing his work on these northern cloisters with me. For Newminster (where a section of the arcade was reconstructed from fragments in the 1920s), see Fergusson 1984a, 137; Robinson 1998, 156; for Byland, Harrison 1990, 12; for Furness, Hope 1900b, 257 (where the date is given as early thirteenth century). There are also published details of the late twelfth-century cloister arcades at Kirkstall (Hope and Bilson 1907, 27–8, fig 21) and Jervaulx (Hope and Brakspear 1911, 315–16).

24 Fergusson and Harrison 1999, 137.

25 Despite the lean-to form of the outer roof, internally there may well have been a boarded arrangement to create the appearance of a barrel vault: information from Stuart Harrison and Glyn Coppack.

26 The whole arcade seems to have been painted white, with the capitals perhaps picked out in red: Coppack 1988, 8; Fergusson 1990a, 14–15. A section of the arcade, pieced together from fragments, is displayed in the site museum.

27 Hope 1900a, 339–40; Coppack 1988, 29; Coppack 2003, 68.

28 Brakspear 1905, 36.

29 This also seems to have been the case in Ireland: Stalley 1987, 153–4.

30 Clapham 1921, 208.

31 Williams 1889a, 206, facing 206, no. 2; Williams 1889b, 34, facing 32, no. 2.

32 Robinson 2002c, 11, 14.

33 The abbey church at Beaulieu was dedicated in 1246. On the construction and artistic links in general, see Jansen 1984; Grant 1991, 122–4; on the cloister, Hope and Brakspear 1906, 152.

34 Brakspear 1906–7, 506.

35 See chapter 7 for the church, and the Dore catalogue entry for further details; also Paul 1927; Hillaby 1988–90; O'Callaghan 1995; Harrison and Thurlby 1997; Harrison 1997b.

36 On Abbot Stephen, see Williams 1976a, 10–11; Williams 1997a, 24; Smith and London 2001, 258.

37 Harrison 1997b, 118. The footings in question appear on several of Paul's plans: Paul 1904 and 1927.

38 Harrison 1997a, 75–6; Harrison 1997b, 114, 116.

39 Mid-thirteenth-century cloister arcades carried on triple-shaft groups are known from the Augustinian priories of Norton in Cheshire and Haverfordwest in Pembrokeshire, though both were adorned with figure sculpture. For Norton, see Greene 1989, 111–18; for Haverfordwest, Rees 1999, 67–8; Lloyd et al 2004, 209.

40 See Robinson 2002a, 29–31, 50–60; Robinson 2004, 105–8; also catalogue entry for Tintern. The chapter house and the refectory are examined in chapters 10 and 11.

41 The investigations were carried out by Stuart Harrison on behalf of Cadw. The results are not yet published in full, but I am grateful to Mr Harrison for discussing his findings with me. Summary notes appear in Harrison 1997c, 69–71; Harrison et al 1998, 182; Robinson 2002a, 31, 48–9.

42 To date, only one moulded corner capital has been identified, though more possibilities for both capitals and bases appear in early photographs.

43 For which, see Harrison 1997c, 73, with further comment below.

44 Also used singly in the arcades, the ribs here featured triple rolls and fillets, with bead mouldings flanking the axial roll.

45 On which, see Grant 1991, 120–1 (where the form is described as 'contrapuntal'); Decaëns 1998, 60–4; Frankl 2000, 279, 366 n 34a.

46 Grant 1991, 120 n 34.

47 As suggested, for example, in Webb 1956, 58; Brooke 2003, 249–50.

48 Grant 1991, 120. On the Lincoln work, see Pevsner et al 1989, pl 20, 454; Wilson 1992, 162–3; Harrison 1997c, 68–9.

49 On which, see most recently Maddison 2000, 53–6, especially 55. As at Lincoln, the outer arches have trefoil heads, while the inner are pointed.

50 For Keynsham, see Knowles and Hadcock 1971, 161–2; for the syncopated arcade, smaller in scale than the known cloisters, see Harrison 1997c, 70–3.

51 For Monk Bretton, see Knowles and Hadcock 1971, 100; for the arcade, Harrison 1997c, 69, 70. Harrison draws a number of comparisons between the Monk Bretton and Tintern arcades.

52 Hall 2003, I, 56; II, figs A11–A17.

53 A point made by Richard Morris in correspondence of 1989–90, on the basis of an initial consideration of the fragments. The best parallels are with the chapter house detailing. For recent views on the date of this Salisbury work, see Brown 1999, 28–31.

54 On which, see Harrison et al 1998, 182–5; Robinson 2002a, 32–5; Tintern catalogue entry.

55 It is unclear if a set of larger springers, with foliate terminals to the mouldings, may be related to this infill work. They employed different jointing techniques, but the overall size of the arches and

the bay spacing remained unaltered: Harrison 1997c, 69.

56 Collation arrangements are discussed in more detail below, but for the existence of a porch at Fountains, see Coppack and Gilyard-Beer 1993, 30; Coppack 2003, 68.

57 Hayward 1973, 97. There is an illustration in Leroux-Dhuys 1998, 225.

58 Aubert 1947, II, 15–16, 18–20; Hayward 1973, 96–7; Dimier 1982, 259; Frankl 2000, 279.

59 The south walk at Maulbronn was begun around 1214–20. The work on the north, east and west arcades dates from after 1270: Knapp 1997, 79–82, 96–114, passim; Frankl 2000, 279.

60 The arcades at Hailes were in any case replaced in the late fifteenth century: Coad 1993, 7–8. For Netley, see Hare 1993, 210–11; Robinson 1998, 151–3.

61 [Jones] and Williams 1891, 173, pl 8. Given the nature of their sketch drawings, one must accept this as no more than a very tentative suggestion.

62 Clark 1867, 328; David 1929, 322–3; Robinson 1993a, 59; Newman 1995, 428–9; Evans 1996, 25.

63 BL, K. Top. XLVII, 44.3A.

64 Evans (1996, 25) mentions the occasional appearance of the outlines of the cloister walks during dry summers.

65 Robinson 1996b. Early guidebooks make no mention of these cloister arrangements.

66 The draughtsman behind the Office of Works reconstruction (1926) was probably mistaken in showing the colonnettes as free-standing above the base level (see fig 13), but it is unclear if any individual fragments were located.

67 Hughes 1894, 171–2, 274–5; Hughes 1895a, 6–7. He dated the work to the fifteenth century, but it is possibly earlier.

68 The footings of the low walls which had supported the south-east corner of the Valle Crucis arcade survived until 1963. They were removed in that year, and fragments of the arcade put in store: information from Lawrence Butler; also Butler 1976b, 86.

69 The earliest known Irish example was constructed c 1390–1400: Stalley 1987, 154–60.

70 Robinson 2002a, 62. There was also a late medieval covered arcade linking a doorway in the north aisle of the presbytery with the infirmary court and abbot's lodging.

71 Webb 1956, 155–7; Harvey 1974, 145, 251. For more on Gloucester, see Wilson 1992, 210–12.

72 Brakspear 1906–7, 506.

73 Walsh 1979. Professor Walsh also offers some confirmation of a late twelfth-century cloister arcade, including a 'double-scalloped capital and quadruple column [corner?] base'. These are illustrated in Rahtz and Hirst 1976, 142 (capital); Hirst et al 1983, 264 (base).

74 Walsh 1979, 47–8.

75 Harrison 1990, 12. Byland was unusual among the Yorkshire houses in this regard. Fountains, Kirkstall and Rievaulx, for instance, all seem to have retained their twelfth-century arcades through to the suppression.

76 Coad 1993, 7–8; Robinson 1998, 124–5; Verey and Brooks 1999, 398, 400.

77 RCHME 1952, 242; Fergusson 1984a, 125; Robinson 1998, 109–10.

78 The arrangements on the west and south sides were probably the same, but the evidence does not survive.

79 For early identification of these arrangements, see Radford 1935, 10; Radford 1949a. The new reconstruction given here is based on the work of Stuart Harrison. Too few mullions have survived to be sure of the full glazing arrangements. See also Robinson and Platt 1998, 52–4.

80 The suggestion is made in Ludlow 2002, 73, 76.

81 Williams 1984, I, 141, quoting National Library of Wales, Badminton MS 1575. At Croxden, the community had replaced the shingles on its cloister roofs in 1374: Hall 2003, I, 55.

82 There were at least two versions of Herbert's will: see the Tintern catalogue entry for further details, together with Wood 1907, 10; Wood 1912, 15 n 9; Robinson 2002a, 17, 23, 36–7.

83 We know, for example, from the comprehensive excavations at Bordesley that the floor of the presbytery in the abbey church itself was paved with no more than plain stone slabs up to about 1200: Hirst *et al* 1983, 28, 35–8. Excavations (1970) in the south-west corner of the cloister at Valle Crucis found no surviving trace of a floor or paving: Butler 1976b, 86.

84 For an important survey of early Cistercian tile pavements, see Norton and Park 1986, 228–55; on the Welsh material, Lewis 1999, 1–13.

85 Brakspear 1906–7, 506.

86 Thompson 1937, 15; Robinson 2002c, 14.

87 Lewis 1999, 236; Rees 1999, 66.

88 Lewis 1999, 227 (Basingwerk), 241, 245 (Neath).

89 It is worth mentioning that a rectangular cistern lies exposed in the south-east corner of the cloister at Valle Crucis. Excavations in 1970 confirmed it was fed by running water, which may well have served for garden use. On the excavation, see Butler 1976b, 86, 93. For general comment on gardens, see Fergusson and Harrison 1999, 65–6, and their reconstructions at 88–9, 134–5. The best-known Welsh monastic cloister garden is the recently excavated example at Haverfordwest: Rees 1999, 66–7.

90 See in general Braunfels 1972, 101, 103; Lillich 1982b; Grüger 1984; Kinder 1997, 135–8; Williams 1998, 246–7; Bond 2001, 115–16.

91 *Ecclesiastica Officia* (1 and 2), chapters 76.4–8, 108.15–16 (daily meals), chapter 108.32–43 (*mandatum*). A fuller account of the *mandatum* rite is given below in chapter 11, in the context of refectories.

92 Aubert 1947, II, 26; Braunfels 1972, 80; Plouvier 1998, 138, 145–6.

93 Aubert 1947, II, 26–31; Boutevin 1996, 60 (Fontenay).

94 Many of these are illustrated in Van der Meer 1965; Leroux-Dhuys 1998. See also Dimier 1971, *passim*; Grüger 1984, 207–8.

95 See, for example, Coppack 1990, 88, 90 (Kirkstall); Coppack 2003, 56 (Fountains). I am grateful to Stuart Harrison for discussing the general issue with me. For further context on free-standing *lavatoria* in England, Godfrey 1952.

96 Fawcett and Oram 2004, 175–6.

97 On which, see Fergusson 1986; also chapters 8 and 11.

98 Lillich (1982b, 140–1) goes so far as to suggest this recessed form may have been invented by the Cistercians to cope with the cold winters encountered in northern Britain.

99 Stalley 1980, 310–12, 348–50; Stalley 1987, 170–2. Professor Stalley argues that the Mellifont pavilion was of English inspiration, owing less to Cistercian preference for this form on the Continent. Another British example is known from Louth Park, Lincolnshire.

100 For general context, see Gilyard-Beer 1981; Kinder 1997, 133–4; France 1998a, 95; Williams 1998, 240–1.

101 McCann 1976, chapter 42.

102 For the Cistercian practice, see *Ecclesiastica Officia* (1 and 2), chapter 81.

103 As Gilyard-Beer (1981, 129) points out, benching alone cannot provide conclusive proof of a Collation alley.

104 Aubert 1947, II, 20–6; Gardelles 1979; France 1998a, 95; Peugniez 2001, 20–2.

105 Gilyard-Beer 1981, 129, 131; also Tester 1973, 156.

106 For Byland, see Gilyard-Beer 1981, 130; Harrison 1990, 12; for Cleeve, Gilyard-Beer 1981, 130; Gilyard-Beer 1990, 11; for Fountains, Coppack 2003, 68.

107 Fawcett and Oram 2004, 178.

108 Gilyard-Beer 1981, 130; Hamlin 1983; Stalley 1987, 160–2.

109 Robinson 2002a, 49. Gilyard-Beer's view (1981, 130) that the rectangular depression in the cloister opposite the position of the abbot's seat represents a projecting reader's bay is unconvincing. An undated photograph in the site archive held by Cadw shows that a trial trench was dug here at some point. From what can be seen, there are no strong indications of walls or foundations.

110 Robinson and Platt 1998, 52–3.

111 Ludlow 2000; Ludlow 2002, 73.

CHAPTER 10

THE CHAPTER HOUSE

1 Gardner 1976, 39. It was 'in chapter', too, that a Benedictine community was transformed into a deliberative body, one with certain customs and rights, whether in conjunction with or opposed to the abbot: Knowles 1963a, 412–13, 415. Guidance for the conduct of daily Benedictine chapter meetings was set out by Archbishop Lanfranc about 1077: *Lanfranc Constitutions*, 164–7.

2 Hélinand was a monk of Froidmont (Oise), for which see Aubert 1947, I, 75; Peugniez 2001, 377. For this passage from his *Epistola ad Galterum*, see Migne 1844–64, CCXII, col 758, quoted in Gardner 1976, 10; Fergusson and Harrison 1994, 238; Fergusson and Harrison 1999, 97; Cassidy-Welch 2001, 105.

3 *Ecclesiastica Officia* (1 and 2), chapter 70.

4 St Benedict had called for his Rule to be 'read aloud often to the community, so that no brother may excuse himself on the ground of ignorance': Gardner 1976, 11.

5 For the delivery of sermons during chapter, see *Ecclesiastica Officia* (1 and 2), chapter 67. The attendance of the *conversi* is implied in chapter XI of their usages: *Lay Brothers*, 183, and Waddell's notes at 184–5.

6 The Rule of St Benedict decreed that when anything important is to be done, the abbot should call together the whole community and explain what the business is: McCann 1976, chapter 3.

7 For general discussions on this theme, see Knowles 1963a, 637; Gardner 1976, 10–55; Lekai 1977, 365–6; Fergusson and Harrison 1994, 237–44; Fergusson and Harrison 1999, 97–8; Lawrence 2001, 110–11; Cassidy-Welch 2001, 105–32.

8 This is evident from several statutes passed by the General Chapter: *Statutes*, 88, 390. In general, see Williams 1998, 134, 242. See also Fergusson and Harrison 1994, 240–4.

9 See, for example, Branner 1960, 18, 141–2; Kennedy [Gajewski] 1996, 90–4.

10 Fergusson 1984a, 92–3; Robinson 2002c, 17–18.

11 For Basingwerk, see Brock 1878b, 472–3; Taylor 1971, 6; Robinson 1996b; for Margam, David 1929, 323–4; Robinson 1993a, 57–8; Newman 1995, 426–8; for Valle Crucis, Hughes 1895a, 7–16; Price 1952, 122–5; Radford 1953, 19–20; Maddison 1978, 96–8; Evans 1995, 36–7.

12 For Cymer, see Radford 1946, 5; for Dore, Hillaby 1988–90; Hillaby 1997c; Harrison 1997b, 120–4; for Neath, Butler 1976a, 18; Robinson 2002b; for Strata Florida, Williams 1889a, 204–6; Williams 1889b, 32–4; Radford 1949a; Robinson and Platt 1998, 54–5; for Tintern, Robinson 2002a, 51–2; Robinson 2004.

13 For Cwmhir, see Williams 1894–5, 95–7, pl 8; for Strata Marcella,

[Jones] and Williams 1891, 164 (where there is mention of traces of the chapter house vault), 186; for an interpretation based on the geophysical survey at Whitland, Ludlow 2002, 73.

14 The date range suggested here (on which there is more discussion below) coincides with the known rule of Abbot Gilbert, for which see Cowley 1977, 116–17, 123–5; Knowles *et al* 2001, 137; Williams 2001, 20, 161.

15 The two most important accounts of centrally planned chapter houses are Gardner 1976; Zukowsky 1977.

16 Margam is discussed alongside the neighbouring Cistercian polygonal chapter house at Dore in the general context of centrally planned designs in Hillaby 1988–90. A third definite British Cistercian example was built at Whalley after 1330: Robinson 1998, 203. For overviews of Cistercian chapter houses in general, see Braunfels 1972, 98–102; Kinder 1997, 244–67; for France, Aubert 1947, II, 51–70; for Germany, Eydoux 1952, 161–4; for Ireland, Stalley 1987, 162–6.

17 For which, see Braunfels 1972, 37–46; Horn and Born 1979. The place for the chapter gathering appears to have been the north walk of the cloister. For a general discussion of the chapter assembly and its location in the period *c* 750–1000, see Gardner 1976, 10–55.

18 The quote is taken from the *Gesta abbatum Fontanellensium*, quoted in Braunfels 1972, 236; Gardner 1976, 27, 48. For more on Ansegis and his abbey, see Braunfels 1972, 28–9, with a further comment at 58.

19 It was raised in the time of Abbot Odilo (994–1049): Braunfels 1972, 51, 54–8; Gardner 1976, 59–62.

20 In sum, see Gardner 1976, 56–68. For the northern French context, see Beck 1965–6.

21 For which, see Schaefer 1982; Coppack 1998, 23–31; and, in this context, Fergusson and Harrison 1994, 233–4.

22 *Narrative Texts* (*Capitula* IX), 408 (*Instituta* XII), 461.

23 As noted in chapter 8, there is little to see of the principal claustral ranges at either site, though early plans record the layouts: Aubert 1947, I, 11, 109. For more on Cîteaux, see Plouvier 1998; on Clairvaux, Musso 1991; Vilain 1998.

24 On the Cîteaux chapter house, see Aubert 1947, II, 63; Plouvier 1998, 76; on the number of monks, Lekai 1977, 50; Williams 1998, 35. The likely scale of the building is quoted in Coomans 1998b, 158. He compares its scale with the surviving chapter house at Vaucelles, estimated at approximately 335 square metres. For more on this site, see Chauvin 1998, 136–7; Peugniez 2001, 291–6.

25 Gardner 1976, 68–73.

26 The present two-bay arrangement represents a later medieval modification: Aubert 1947, II, 62–3; Branner 1960, 18, 141–2; Auberger 2001, 97–117.

27 For Noirlac, see Dimier 1982, 248 (pl 106), 259–60; for Pontigny, Fontaine 1928; Aubert 1947, I, 130–1; Braunfels 1972, 90; Dimier 1982, 304.

28 A point made, for example, in Gardner 1976, 69.

29 Christopher Wilson goes so far as to suggest that this was the 'universal' white monk type, though noting that 'typically' it was the six western bays which were contained within the range. He puts Fontenay forward as the prototype of the form: Wilson 1999, 60–2.

30 The idea of 'centrality' within the design has been linked to the liturgical use of the room, including matters such as discipline and the reception of novices: Bonde *et al* 1990, 202–4, 208 n 6.

31 Among the first group, it should be noted that at Vaucelles, Alcobaça, Heiligenkreuz and Val-Saint-Lambert the east range was three bays in width. In general, see Van der Meer 1965, *passim*; Dimier 1971, *passim*; Braunfels 1972, 74–110; Dimier 1982, *passim*.

On Val-Saint-Lambert (and the similar arrangement at Villers), see Coomans 1998a; Coomans 2000, 317–44. A notable early exception to these two broad forms may have been the chapter house at Cîteaux's elder daughter of La Ferté, which was apparently three bays wide by four deep, with the eastern bay projecting beyond the range: Aubert 1947, I, 113; Peugniez 2001, 61–2.

32 The general point is made in Fernie 2000, 201–3. See also Dickinson 1961, 31–2; Gilyard-Beer 1976, 31–4.

33 Brakspear 1905, 8–9; Coppack 1998, 32–5. For contemporary developments in Normandy, see Beck 1965–6.

34 Based on his excavations around 1900, Brakspear posited a twelfth-century chapter house measuring 9.8m east–west by 6.1m wide, separated (he believed) from the south transept by a 'narrow passage': Brakspear 1905, 8–9, 38. This is challenged by Coppack, who prefers to interpret the Waverley evidence along near-contemporary French (and English) lines: Coppack 1998, 32, 34.

35 Fergusson and Harrison 1994, 232–3; Fergusson and Harrison 1999, 87, 90, 94–5.

36 Hope 1900a, 345; Coppack and Gilyard-Beer 1993, 4–5, 34; Coppack 1998, 36–9; Coppack 2003, 33–5.

37 Hope and Brakspear 1911, 317; Robinson 1998, 129.

38 Fergusson and Harrison 1999, 94–5; Fawcett and Oram 2004, 182–3.

39 Much the same design was also used later at Dunbrody: Stalley 1980, 300–1; Stalley 1987, 55, 62, 164.

40 On the early conservation of the site, see Baylis 1902–4; Robinson 1997; on the consolidated chapter house, Robinson 2004, 96–8. The early plan appears in Potter 1847, Tintern pl i (*see* fig 9).

41 For Tintern's twelfth-century buildings in general, see Robinson 1996a; Robinson 2002a, 27–9. As suggested in discussing the twelfth-century church at Tintern (above, chapter 4), some confirmation of early growth and the achievement of a position of relative stability comes from the foundation of the daughter house at Kingswood in 1139: Knowles and Hadcock 1971, 121; Williams 1976a, 102.

42 Robinson 2004, 101–3.

43 This was not, however, the view held by Charles Peers. He claimed (1922, 9): 'Early in the 13th century a gradual rebuilding and enlargement of the cloister was undertaken, enough of the 12th century masonry being retained to show that the first chapter house was of the same size as that now existing'. In a subsequent reinterpretation, Brakspear (1929) determined that the entire eastwards extension dated to the early thirteenth century. Later, Brakspear (1934), followed by Craster (1956), altered the sequence to show a late twelfth-century extension, followed in the early thirteenth century by a further reworking, with the addition of buttresses and an internal vault. This last proposal seems most unlikely.

44 That is as shown on the plan in Robinson 2002a, 28.

45 This may still have allowed for a narrow chamber accommodating the day stair to the monks' dormitory immediately to the north, a detail retained in the later arrangements (fig 26): Robinson 2004, 117.

46 Effectively, such a tripartite division of the facade reflected the 'standard' internal arrangement of three north–south bays.

47 Taylor 1971, 6. The early programme of consolidation may have masked some of the original features. One wonders, for example, if the twelfth-century chapter house may not have extended to the south wall of the later parlour, in which case the existing doorway to this room may have been recycled.

48 Paul 1904, 124–5.

49 For which, see Birch 1897, 92; David 1929, 324; Robinson 1993a, 58. See also Hillaby 1988–90, 224. For what is known of Whitland, see Ludlow 2002, 73.

50 For accounts of Ailred's chapter house and its conceptual qualities, see Fergusson and Harrison 1994, 221–32, 235–45; Fergusson and Harrison 1999, 90–9.

51 For example, when the full community was gathered to hear a sermon on a major feast day: Fergusson and Harrison 1994, 238–40; Fergusson and Harrison 1999, 98–9. The authors also point to burial and commemorative archetypes for the form of the building, since it was to be the resting place of Rievaulx's founding abbot, William (d 1145).

52 A provision of a separate chapter house for the lay brothers was almost certainly very rare, if it occurred at all: Aubert 1947, I, 52 n 2. See also comments in *Lay Brothers*, 184 nn 2–4.

53 Hope 1900a, 342–5; Coppack and Gilyard-Beer 1993, 31–3; Coppack 2003, 57–8.

54 Gardner (1976, 72) suggested these bays were originally intended for the lay brothers. The northern and southern compartments of the westernmost bay were at some point partitioned off from the remainder to form book cupboards: Hope 1900a, 343; Coppack and Gilyard-Beer 1993, 32.

55 In Britain, as in France, Germany and Italy, a facade with a central doorway and flanking windows might be said to be the 'universal' Cistercian type.

56 For Vauclair, see Aubert 1947, II, 55–6; Courtois 1982; Peugniez 2001, 371–2. See also Fergusson and Harrison 1994, 249–50 n 39.

57 Hope and Bilson 1907, 29–30. The design was unusual, with paired entrance doorways and four square bays housed within the width of the range. The eastern half of the building was entirely rebuilt in the thirteenth century.

58 For Jervaulx, see Hope and Brakspear 1911, 317–18; Robinson 1998, 129; for Roche, Fergusson 1990a, 15, 18; Robinson 1998, 167.

59 For Buildwas, see Thompson 1937, 17–18; Gardner 1976, 70–1; Fergusson 1984a, 92–3; Robinson 2002c, 17–18; for Combe, Fergusson 1984a, 122; Robinson 1998, 89–90; for Forde, RCHME 1952, 240–1; Robinson 1998, 110; for Waverley, Brakspear 1905, 38–40; Robinson 1998, 201.

60 For the Margam chapter house in general, see Clark 1867, 329–31; Gamwell 1887, 11; Birch 1897, 92–9; David 1929, 323–4; Butler 1971, 388; Robinson 1993a, 57–8; Newman 1995, 426–8; Evans 1996, 22–5. The Dore building is discussed in Blashill 1885, 368; Paul 1893, 268–9; Paul 1896, 300; Paul 1904, 124–5; RCHME 1931, 6; Harrison 1997b, 120–4.

61 See, for instance, Paul 1893, 268–9; Zukowsky 1977, 6–7.

62 See, for instance, Stratford 1978, 51, 64 n 8. Several writers have wondered if the two buildings were designed by the same mason: Birch 1897, 94; Evans 1996, 23.

63 For his discussions of the two buildings, see Hillaby 1988–90, 222–7, 233–8; Hillaby 1997c. On Abbot Adam in general, see *Gerald of Wales*, I, 104; IV, 200–14; Williams 1976a, 8–9; Hillaby 1988–90, 227–31.

64 See Margam catalogue entry; Birch 1897, 96–7; Evans 1996, 24.

65 As noted in Hillaby 1997c, 106.

66 The engraving of 1780 is by Francis Chesham, from a painting by S H Grimm. See catalogue entry for further details. Parts of the ruins adjoining the chapter house were taken down by Thomas Mansel Talbot in 1788, and within five years two of the windows and 'the entire central column had given way'. For the fall of the vault, see Birch 1897, 96–7; Moore and Moore 1974, 163; Evans 1996, 24. In 1803, John Carter made a sketch of the central column

and reconstructed the plan of the vault from a drawing supplied to him: BL, Add. MS 29940, fol 72.

67 Birch 1897, 94.

68 Several commentators have referred to the opening in the lower wall beneath this window, but its purpose remains unexplained: Birch 1897, 94–5; Newman 1995, 428; Evans 1996, 24 (where it is suggested it was removed from another part of the abbey complex).

69 RCHME 1931, 6.

70 Illustrated in Paul 1893, 268.

71 Blashill 1883–5, 7; Blashill 1885, 368.

72 Paul 1893, 268–9.

73 Hillaby 1988–90; Hillaby 1997c; Harrison 1997b, 120–4.

74 Paul 1893, 268. All trace has since been lost: Hillaby 1988–90, 222.

75 Blashill 1885, 368. Subsequently, Roland Paul was to confuse the issue by publishing a plan of the base fragment with twelve shafts of the same size: Hillaby 1988–90, 222.

76 On this and the following points, see Harrison 1997b, 120–2 (which includes a reconstructed cross section of the building).

77 Although at Margam there do not appear to have been any bounding wall ribs.

78 It seems that Paul altered his views on the likely pier arrangement in the vestibule, though he eventually settled on two median piers on a north–south axis creating a six-bay plan: Paul 1927, facing 269; RCHME 1934, facing 226. See also Harrison 1997b, 122–3, where it is suggested that the two piers were of a similar form to those in the east ambulatory aisle (*see* fig 98).

79 Williams 1894–5, 95–7, pl 8. It is difficult to test this hypothesis without locating some of the capitals in question. Williams also speculated about a capital from Strata Marcella, reused as the font in nearby Buttington church, again wondering if this may have originated in the chapter house: [Jones] and Williams 1891, 186, pl 15.

80 A point made in Gardner 1976, 282. See also Stratford 1978, 51. For a list of thirty-four British chapter houses of circular and polygonal form, not all of them well substantiated, see Hillaby 1988–90, 244. See also Webb 1956, 61–3; Braunfels 1972, 168–71; Zukowsky 1977. In passing, we might remember that towards the end of the fourteenth century an octagonal chapter house was built at Cistercian Whalley: Robinson 1998, 203.

81 For which, see Gardner 1976, 117–43; Stratford 1978; Hillaby 1988–90, 236–7; Barker 1994, 36–41.

82 See, for example, Malone 1973, 72–9; Wilson 1978, 89 n 40; Harrison and Thurlby 1997, 49–62, *passim*.

83 Andrews 1931, 201–2; Gardner 1976, 115–17.

84 The Worcester chapter house is a very substantial building, some 17m in diameter and rib-vaulted. According to Andrews (1931, 201–2), the room at Pershore was about 11m across, with a flat ceiling allowing for the dormitory above.

85 This point is also made in Hillaby 1988–90, 238. For fountain pavilions, see above, chapter 9. The dates of those at Cîteaux and Clairvaux are unknown, though they may well have been of the mid- to late twelfth century.

86 Stalley 1980, 310–12, 349; Stalley 1987, 171–2.

87 There were certainly early historical connections between the abbeys of Mellifont and Margam, with the abbot of the Irish house witnessing at least one Margam charter: Birch 1897, 152. Later, in 1228, the abbot of Margam was involved in the mission to break up the so-called 'conspiracy of Mellifont': Stalley 1987, 17–20; Williams 2001, 163–4.

88 For full discussions of the iconography of centrally planned chapter houses, see Gardner 1976, 164–255; Zukowsky 1977. See also

Harvey 1974, 212–13; Stratford 1978, 51–5; Fergusson and Harrison 1994, 237; Fergusson and Harrison 1999, 97.

89 I hope to take this up in a separate study. Interestingly, having considered the possible iconography behind centrally planned chapter houses, Gardner felt the popularity of the later polygonal form was mostly owing to architectural development, particularly experiments in stone vaulting: Gardner 1976, 288–9.

90 As in Paul 1893, 268–9; Paul 1896, 300; Gardner 1976, 282, 291 nn 3 and 4; Zukowsky 1977, 6–7.

91 Stratford 1978, 64 n 8.

92 Hillaby 1988–90, 224–7, 232–3; Hillaby 1997c, 106–12.

93 For the general context, see Brakspear 1931; Webb 1956, 87–95; Wilson 1992, 77–83; Thurlby 1995c, 157–64. For Llanthony, see Newman 2000, 342–9; for Llandaff, Newman 1995, 244–7.

94 By far the most stimulating contextual ideas have been put forward by Christopher Wilson in his account of the origins of the stellar vaults in the crypt at Glasgow Cathedral. Here, we are reminded of the star-shaped vault pattern in the design of a chapter house in the portfolio (c 1235–40) of the Picard draughtsman, Villard de Honnecourt. The possibility that early thirteenth-century Cistercian chapter houses of square plan may also have been covered with stellar vaults argues in favour of the basic concept having originated somewhere within the order itself: Wilson 1999, *passim*.

95 In considering this phase of work, it is of interest to note the appearance of a *Petro cementario* (Peter the mason) as witness to a Margam charter of c 1202: *Cartae Glamorgancia*, VI, 2328. I am grateful to Fred Cowley for pointing me in the direction of this reference.

96 Knowles *et al* 2001, 137. The 'foreign visitors' almost certainly represent a delegation sent from Clairvaux.

97 *Annales Monastici*, I, 29–30.

98 *Gerald of Wales*, IV, 129–43. See also Cowley 1977, 116–17, 123–5.

99 *Annales Monastici*, I, 32; Birch 1897, 197.

100 For the church, see chapter 7. On his abbacy, see Williams 1976a, 8–9; Knowles *et al* 2001, 126, 270.

101 Hillaby 1988–90, 227–31.

102 As proposed in Harrison 1997b, 124; Robinson 1998, 104, 140.

103 For his abbacy, see Smith and London 2001, 258; for Gerald's comment, *Gerald of Wales*, IV, 194, 206.

104 On the late nineteenth-century excavation of the building, see Williams 1889a, 205–6, plan facing 182, and illustrations facing 206, 210; Williams 1889b, 33–4. Much the same plan of the chapter house was reproduced in Radford 1935.

105 The reconstruction of the early thirteenth-century chapter house facade is one element of the work on the site by Stuart Harrison, for which see catalogue entry. The triple-arched arrangement is based, in part, on the quantity of *ex situ* jamb stones recovered. For a summary of the findings, see Robinson and Platt 1998, 54–5. Interestingly, it seems very likely that the chapter house at Whitland (Strata Florida's mother house) was upgraded at much the same time. A large capital found in the nave of the church in 1994–5 (of stiff-leaf design and articulated for a cluster of four shafts) may well represent one of the jambs of the central doorway. The piece is illustrated (though not attributed) in Ludlow 2002, 74–5. It may be compared with the Strata Florida example illustrated in Williams 1889a, pl facing 206, no. 1.

106 The eastwards extension was located as part of the clearance of the site by the Office (later Ministry) of Works after 1931. It first appeared on an official ground plan in Radford 1949a.

107 Maelgwyn ap Rhys was not the first of the Deheubarth princes to be buried at Strata Florida, though his was the earliest specifically recorded interment in the chapter house: *Brut*, 102.

108 The known dates of subsequent burials range from 1235 to 1275: Robinson and Platt 1998, 55.

109 For which, see Robinson and Platt 1998, 16–17, 31–2; also catalogue entry.

110 Radford (1949a) certainly believed the reduction in the size of the building occurred in the fourteenth century. It is possible that any thirteenth-century stone vault was removed at the time, to be replaced by a timber ceiling.

111 Hughes 1895b, 166–7; RCAHMW 1956, 43 (where the features are dated to c 1235).

112 On which see Hays 1963, 56–71; also catalogue entry.

113 In general, see Brock 1878b, 472–3; Hodkinson 1905, 172; Taylor 1971, 6; Hubbard 1986, 353–4; Robinson 1996b.

114 The remodelled Waverley chapter house is dated c 1180–95: Brakspear 1905, 10, 38–40.

115 There can be little doubt that the Margam and Dore works would have drawn considerable attention in the region; it is reasonable to assume that the Waverley programme would also have been known to the Tintern community.

116 For the Marshal endowment, see *Cal Chart Rolls*, 1300–26, 104; *Mon Ang*, V, 267–9. On the thirteenth-century rebuilding in general, Harrison *et al* 1998, 181–2; Robinson 2002a, 29–31, 48–58.

117 Ralph went on from Tintern to become abbot of Dunkeswell (1245–52) and then Waverley (1252–66): *Annales Monastici*, II, 336, 345; Williams 1976a, 104–5; Smith and London 2001, 277, 316, 321.

118 For which, see Robinson 2004, 105–8, 120–9.

119 Potter 1847, Tintern pl xxxix.

120 The partitions at Fountains were of timber: Coppack and Gilyard-Beer 1993, 32; Coppack 2003, 58. At Furness, where the chapter house was rebuilt in the 1220s, the partitions were of stone: Hope 1900b, 260–2.

121 The lower sections of the four eastern piers remain *in situ*, whereas the positions of the four to west are marked by loose moulded stones: Robinson 2004, 97–8.

122 The stone in question currently sits as a loose piece marking the position of one of the western piers.

123 The reconstructions given here (figs 146 and 147) assume that all eight piers were of the same style, and that the capitals matched throughout. It is possible that the form of the more elaborate sub-base depicted by Potter (figs 148 and 149a) belongs with the eastern piers, and that the simpler profile (represented by the one surviving example) may have gone with the western bays.

124 These are currently to be found with other *ex situ* material on a terrace at the north side of the site.

125 Illustrated in Robinson 2004, 127.

126 Illustrated in Robinson 2004, 128.

127 The south window was blocked around 1300, following the reconstruction of the abbey church and the creation of a sacristy between the north transept and the eastern extension of the chapter house (fig 26).

128 For the refectory, see Potter 1847, Tintern pl xxxvii; Robinson 2002a, 57–8. The building is discussed below in chapter 11.

129 For Hereford, see Harvey 1974, 133–4; Morris 2000, 208–12; for Oxford, RCHME 1939, 46; Harvey 1974, 133; for Lacock, Pevsner and Cherry 1975, 286; for Brecon, RCAHMW 1994, 11, 23.

130 On the Neath work in general, see Butler 1976a, 18–21; Newman 1995, 467–8; Robinson 2002b. The former prior, Gervase, was appointed abbot in 1218, but nothing further is known of him: Smith and London 2001, 295.

131 On which, see Cowley 1967b; Cowley 1977, 76–7.

132 All trace of the building had been lost before the abbey was planned in 1846, for which see Birch 1902, 93. Nothing was uncovered in the extensive clearances of 1924–34: Thomas and Taylor 1938, 15.

133 The abbey ruins were given over to the State outright in that year. There are summaries of the conservation programme in *Archaeol Cambrensis*, *100*, 1948–9, 268–9; *101*, 1950–1, 79, 115; *106*, 1957, 106.

134 This is the interpretation given in the first official guide: Butler 1976a, 18, and ground plan.

135 As shown in the plan published in Sutton 1887.

136 For the Furness building, see Hope 1900b, 260–2; Robinson 1998, 117–18; for Dundrennan, Fawcett 1994, 99–100; Robinson 1998, 106; for Stanley, Brakspear 1906–7, 506–7. The chapter house at Cleeve was another to be extended in this way in the mid-thirteenth century, though here the vault ribs spanned the full width of the building, as at Waverley: Gilyard-Beer 1990, 17. On the other hand, at Hulton in Staffordshire (to take one example of an English abbey with comparatively modest endowments) the chapter house of *c* 1260–80 was a nine-bay (three by three) form comparable to the proportions of that built at Buildwas almost a century earlier. For an account of the Hulton building, see Morris 2005, 80–3.

137 Cassidy-Welch 2001, 111–16, 131.

138 In general, see Hughes 1895a, 7–9; Price 1952, 122–5; Radford 1953, 6, 19–20; Maddison 1978, 96–8; Evans 1995, 16–17, 36–7; Robinson 1998, 196–7.

139 Noted in Price 1952, 123. The sections are drawn in Hughes 1895a, facing 7.

140 The central window had been converted to a door during the abbey's use as farm buildings: Hughes 1895a, 9; Price 1952, 124.

141 Noted in Brock 1878a, 154–5; Maddison 1978, 96–8.

142 On which, see Morris 1978, 21–9. The form may have found popularity in Edward I's castle-building works in north Wales during the 1280s, spreading from there.

143 Price (1952, 122) suggested *c* 1315–50. But for Maddison (1978, 96–8), the detailing 'has a very primitive quality which makes a more precise dating than *c* 1320–1400 unwise'.

144 On the Glyn Dŵr revolt and the Welsh Cistercians in general, see Williams, G 1976, 212–45; Williams 2001, 52–5.

145 See Price 1952, 45–6; also Butler 1976b, 80; Williams 2001, 55. In the event, Robert of Lancaster held both offices *in commendam* until his death in 1433.

CHAPTER 11
THE MONKS' REFECTORY

1 On the monastic refectory in general, see Webb 1956, 64–5; Dickinson 1961, 34–5; Gilyard-Beer 1976, 35–6.

2 For the times of meals according to the Rule of St Benedict, see McCann 1976, chapter 41. See also Knowles 1963a, 714–15.

3 A point made in Hall 2003, I, 63. See also the discussions on first-floor refectories, with the suggestion that the cenacle (*cenaculum*), the room of the Last Supper, may have been a powerful model: Fergusson 1986, 174–7; Fergusson and Harrison 1999, 146–50.

4 For this tradition among houses of Italian mendicants, see Braunfels 1972, 145–51. See also Fergusson 1986, 175–6. A Cistercian example may be seen at Staffarda (Piedmont) in Italy.

5 Reading during the meal had been prescribed in the Rule of St Benedict: McCann 1976, chapter 38.

6 On Cistercian refectories in general, see Braunfels 1972, 103–7;

Fergusson 1986; Kinder 1997, 283–7; Williams 1998, 244–5. Many examples are illustrated in Van der Meer 1965, *passim*, and in Leroux-Dhuys 1998, *passim*. For France, see Aubert 1947, II, 97–114; for Ireland, Stalley 1987, 169–70.

7 *Ecclesiastica Officia* (1 and 2), chapters 76–7.

8 It was the prior who presided over the meal, whereas the abbot was to take his meals with guests in the guest house: *Ecclesiastica Officia* (1 and 2), chapters 110–11.

9 Psalm 51. For more on liturgy in the Cistercian refectory, and on food, see Lekai 1977, 368–73; Williams 1998, 245–6.

10 In general, for Basingwerk, see Hodkinson 1905, 173–4; Taylor 1971, 8; Robinson 1996b; for Cymer, Radford 1946; Robinson 1995b; Smith and Butler 2001, 319, 321; for Dore, Harrison 1997b, 116–20, *passim*; for Neath, Butler 1976a, 21; Newman 1995, 468; Robinson 2002b; for Tintern, Craster 1956, 24; Newman 2000, 552–3; Robinson 2002a, 57–8; for Valle Crucis, Butler 1976b, 88–9, 93–4; Evans 1995, 44–5; for Whitland, Ludlow 2000 and 2001; Ludlow 2002, 71–3.

11 For the kitchen and the warming house, *see* chapter 8.

12 Horn and Born 1979, I, 263–84; Braunfels 1972, 38–9.

13 On the emergence of these groups, see Burton 1994, 43–60, 98–100; Robinson 1980. The only modern overview of Augustinian buildings in England is Dickinson 1968. It is suggested by Fergusson and Harrison (1999, 148–9) that the Augustinian preference for a first-floor refectory was connected to the cenacle (*cenaculum*), the room in which the Last Supper took place. This building was entrusted to the canons after the capture of Jerusalem in 1099. For what remains, see Folda 1995, 469–71. Among the British Cistercians, there were first-floor refectories at Byland and Rievaulx, also linked by Fergusson and Harrison (1999, 149–50) to the cenacle model.

14 *Narrative Texts* (*Capitula* IX), 408 (*Instituta* XII), 461; noted above in chapter 3.

15 Gilyard-Beer and Coppack 1986, 174–5; Coppack 1998, 23–31; Coppack *et al* 2002, 101–5; Coppack 2003, 21–4.

16 For the general context, see Fergusson 1986, 161–8; Coppack 1998, 32–43; Fergusson and Harrison 1999, 146–50.

17 Brakspear 1905, 8–10, 49; Robinson 1998, 200.

18 For Byland, see Harrison 1990, 18–20; for Fountains, Hope and Bilson 1907, 52–3; Gilyard-Beer and Coppack 1986, 181–3; Coppack 2003, 33–9; for Furness, Hope 1900b, 269–70; for Kirkstall, Hope and Bilson 1907, 51–3; Moorhouse and Wrathmell 1987, 45–6; for Rievaulx, Fergusson and Harrison 1999, 48–9, 137–9. The same was probably true of Rievaulx's daughter at Melrose in Scotland: Fawcett and Oram 2004, 191–2.

19 Tester 1973; Robinson 1998, 74.

20 Brakspear and Evans 1910, 39; Robinson 2002a, 27–8. The footings of this refectory had been exposed as part of the early works programme in time for them to be indicated on Brakspear's ground plan of 1908: Robinson 1996a; Robinson 1997. See also Peers 1922, 9.

21 Fragments of the north wall may have been retained along the cloister side of the later southern range: Taylor 1971, 8.

22 As depicted on the plan in Harrison and Thurlby 1997, 48.

23 An excavation in the area of the south range in 1974–5 failed to identify any positive evidence for the monastic structures: Jones 1981.

24 As suggested in Fergusson 1986, 171–2. The date is given as the 1140s in Fergusson and Harrison 1999, 147. We now have to bear in mind the new views on the date of the rebuildings at Clairvaux: Kennedy [Gajewski] 1996, 131–65. Musso (1991, 197) dates the west

range at Clairvaux to *c* 1140–60.

25 See, for example, Hope 1900a, 363; Aubert 1947, I, 118; II, 97–100; Dickinson 1961, 34–5; Braunfels 1972, 76–7, 103–5; Gilyard-Beer 1976, 50.

26 Fergusson 1986, 170–1; Fergusson and Harrison 1999, 147–8. It might be noted, however, that at Kirkstall Abbey the kitchen and the warming house may already have connected with the south walk of the cloister in the mid-twelfth-century east–west layout of the south range: Hope and Bilson 1907, 51–3. Professor Fergusson also explores a possible iconographical interpretation for the realignment of Cistercian refectories, especially in relation to the two-storey refectory block at Rievaulx, suggesting a link to the cenacle (*cenaculum*): Fergusson and Harrison 1999, 148–50. Meanwhile, the buildings essential to the monastic life are effectively enumerated in the Cistercian processional route followed during the *benedictio acquae*, the blessing with holy water of all the principal rooms before high mass on Sundays: *Ecclesiastica Officia* (1 and 2), chapter 55.14–16.

27 The building itself is lost: Aubert 1947, II, 100; Auberger 2001, 112–15.

28 Aubert 1947, II, 99–100; Braunfels 1972, 90; Dimier 1982, 139–40, 181–2, 320–1; Stalley 1987, 58, 62, 87, 104, 169; Leroux-Dhuys 1998, 350–1; Molina 1999, 44–5.

29 This is the date given in Plouvier 1998, 148.

30 For the French sites, see Aubert 1947, II, 97–114; Dimier 1982, *passim*. General details of the locations appear in Peugniez 2001, *passim*. For Maulbronn (*c* 1213–40), see Knapp 1997, 81–6; for Villers (*c* 1210–40), Coomans 2000, 361–72; for Poblet, Dimier 1971, 132, 151 (pl 43); for Alcobaça, Dimier 1971, 291 (pl 130), 297; for Rueda, Soler 2004, 66–71.

31 Hope and Bilson 1907, 46–9, 51–3; Moorhouse and Wrathmell 1987, 19–22, 45–7; Fergusson and Harrison 1999, 146–7.

32 Fergusson (1986, 165–6, 170) drawing on the work of Hope and Bilson suggests an early 1150s date; Coppack (in Robinson 1998, 132–3) says about 1160.

33 Although this goes unrecognized in Fergusson 1986, 167, it has since been proposed in Harrison 1990, 19. I am grateful to Stuart Harrison for discussing his views on the site with me.

34 Hope 1900a, 361–5; Coppack and Gilyard-Beer 1993, 43–4; Coppack 2003, 64–7.

35 Fergusson 1986, 160–4; Fergusson and Harrison 1999, 137, 140–6.

36 Brakspear 1905, 49–51.

37 For Roche, see Fergusson 1990a, 19–20; for Jervaulx, Hope and Brakspear 1911, 339; for Sawley, Coppack *et al* 2002, 61–2, 108; for Bindon, where the date is less certain, Robinson 1998, 71.

38 For Beaulieu, Hope and Brakspear 1906, 159–62; Jansen 1984, 87–9; for Cleeve, Gilyard-Beer 1990, 23–7; for Hailes, Coad 1993, 13–15; for Melrose, Fawcett and Oram 2004, 191–2.

39 Robinson 1998, 75–6 (Buckfast), 93 (Culross), 164–5 (Robertsbridge), 173 (Sibton).

40 Gilyard-Beer 1990, 30–7.

41 As suggested for the reconstruction of the Rievaulx building, *c* 1200: Fergusson and Harrison 1999, 143.

42 See chapter 9.

43 Braunfels 1972, 101, 103; Lillich 1982b; Grüger 1984; Kinder 1997, 135–8; Bond 2001, 115–16.

44 Aubert 1947, II, 26; Braunfels 1972, 80; Plouvier 1998, 138, 145–6.

45 See, for example, Coppack 1990, 88, 90; Coppack 2003, 56.

46 Fawcett and Oram 2004, 175–6.

47 It has been suggested that the form was invented by the Cistercians to cope with the cold winters in northern Britain: Lillich

1982b, 140–1.

48 Bond 2001, 117–18.

49 The programme also included the chapter house. In general, see Harrison *et al* 1998, 181–2; Robinson 2002a, 29–32, 50–8; Robinson 2004, 105–8. See also above, chapters 9 and 10.

50 As noted in Brakspear and Evans 1910, 39; Brakspear 1929, 20. A similar sequence occurred at Fountains: Coppack 2003, 65–6.

51 For some of these details, see Potter 1847, Tintern pl xxxvii.

52 Examples of taps from Fountains and Kirkstall are illustrated in Coppack 1990, 92–3; Coppack 2003, 65.

53 See, in particular, Fergusson 1986, 178–80; Fergusson and Harrison 1999, 149. See also Lekai 1977, 374; Cassidy-Welch 2001, 61–2.

54 It has earlier been mentioned in the context of pavilion *lavatoria* in chapter 9.

55 McCann 1976, chapter 35. On its importance to early post-Conquest Benedictines in England, see *Lanfranc Constitutions*, 4–5, 52–8.

56 Lillich 1982b, 147.

57 *Ecclesiastica Officia* (1 and 2), chapter 108.32–43.

58 *Ecclesiastica Officia* (1 and 2), chapter 21. A further version of the rite for visiting guests was carried out by two members of the community who were chosen each week specifically for the purpose: *Ecclesiastica Officia* (1 and 2), chapter 107. This had been separately prescribed in the Rule of St Benedict: McCann 1976, chapter 53.

59 Hope 1900a, 361; Rochet 1998, 196; Fergusson and Harrison 1999, 149.

60 Newman 2000, 552–3; Robinson 2002a, 57–8.

61 As shown in plan in Potter 1847, Tintern pl xxxvii. On the west side, the sills of several windows would need to have been raised to clear the reader's pulpit (*see* fig 153).

62 As seen in the surviving third bay (northwards) on the east side (*see* fig 152). In the adjacent second bay there is now no indication of such oculi, nor are they shown in Potter 1847, Tintern pl xxxvii.

63 Again as shown in Potter 1847, Tintern pl xxxvii.

64 For the chapter house, see above, chapter 10; Robinson 2004, 107–8. Both designs might in some ways be seen as forerunners of Tintern's mid- to later thirteenth-century syncopated cloister arcade, for which *see* chapter 9.

65 The form of the pulpit shown in the reconstruction drawing (*see* fig 153) is modelled on the best British survival at Beaulieu: Hope and Brakspear 1906, 161. There are good examples (sometimes restored) at Royaumont in France (Peugniez 2001, 184–7), and Huerta and Rueda in Spain (Braunfels 1972, 106; Soler 2004, 67–71).

66 Similar, that is, to the reconstructed form at Rievaulx: Fergusson and Harrison 1999, 143.

67 The evidence is entirely stylistic. Very little is known of Neath's abbots in this period. In 1218, Gervase (who had been prior) was elected, and sometime between 1245 and 1253, Abbot Robert was jailed and excommunicated: Smith and London 2001, 295.

68 In general, see Butler 1976a, 21; Newman 1995, 468; Robinson 1997b.

69 A set of undated early photographs in Cadw's site archive on Neath show a square stone base at the centre of the doorway. Some of the detached shafts (of Blue Lias) are also shown in position in these views.

70 Butler 1976a, 21; RCAHMW 1981, 84–5.

71 For a speculative plan of the layout of the twelfth-century monastery (with an east–west refectory), see Harrison and Thurlby 1997, 48. On the Dore building programmes in general, see catalogue entry; RCHME 1931, 1–6; Shoesmith and Richardson

72 Paul 1904, 125.

73 In the Paul collection held by the Society of Antiquaries of London. See also Paul 1931.

74 Harrison 1997b, 118–20.

75 In general, see Butler 1976b, 88–9, 93–4; Evans 1995, 44–5; Robinson 1998, 196.

76 Butler 1976a, 93–4, fig 2.

77 The excavator suggests the position in which it was found is consistent with its having fallen from the south side of the refectory pulpit arch: Butler 1976a, 88, 112. The sandstone head is now in the National Museums & Galleries of Wales, Cardiff.

78 For the north Wales school of sculpture, see Gresham 1968, *passim*.

79 Butler 1976b, 112–14. See also Lewis and Williams 1976, 36.

80 Lord 2003, 98. The proposal is not entirely convincing. One might, for example, equally make a case for the head representing St Maurus (d 584), an important disciple of St Benedict at Monte Cassino and described by St Gregory the Great as a model of religious virtues. Interestingly, Valle Crucis is known to have possessed a fifteenth-century manuscript of the *Dialogues* of St Gregory: Lewis and Williams 1976, 18. For St Maurus, see Farmer 1992, 332.

81 In general, see Brock 1878b, 474; Hodkinson 1905, 173–4, pls G, H and I; RCAHMCW 1912, 40; [Lovegrove] 1921, 404; Taylor 1971, 8; Hubbard 1986, 354–5; Robinson 1996b; Robinson 1998, 67.

82 As noted in Taylor 1971, 8.

83 For the Rievaulx passage, see Fergusson and Harrison 1999, 87, 138.

84 For more on this reorganization, see Basingwerk catalogue entry and chapter 8.

85 Illustrations are reproduced in RCAHMCW 1912, figs 31 (the Buck engraving of 1742) and 32 (a view of 1800).

86 The blocking presumably dates from after the suppression of the house, when the room was doubtless put to other uses.

87 The Chester pulpit was dated by Harvey (1974, 203) to *c* 1260. The date of *c* 1290 given in Pevsner and Hubbard (1971, 147) is surely too late. For Brecon (usually dated to the mid-thirteenth century), see Clapham 1927, 92–5; Haslam 1979, 293–4.

88 A roof of seven bays is clearly depicted in the Buck engraving of 1742: RCAHMCW 1912, fig 31.

89 The geophysical evidence is summarized in Ludlow 2000 and 2001. It is presented more fully in Ludlow 2002, 71–3.

90 In general, see Radford 1946, 5; Robinson 1995b; Smith and Butler 2001, 319, 321.

91 *Leland*, 118; Robinson and Platt 1998, 32, 55–6.

92 On some of these later changes, see Coppack 1998, 79–93; Coppack 2002.

Chapter 12
Infirmary Provision and the Abbot's Accommodation

1 These were introduced in chapter 8.

2 Hall 2003, I, 83–106. I am very grateful to Dr Hall for showing me a draft of her paper entitled 'East of the cloister: infirmaries, abbots' lodgings, and other chambers' in advance of publication: now Hall 2004. Among the abbeys of Wales and the March, a good example of the sort of thing to which she refers is known from Dore. On his eventual retirement (partly enforced), Abbot Thomas Cleubery (*c* 1516–23) occupied a complex of three rooms called 'the new chamber', with an adjacent chapel, on the north side of the monastery: Williams 1976a, 26; Williams 1997a, 29.

3 Coppack 1990, 76–8; Coppack 1998, 87–93; Fergusson and Harrison 1999, 130–5; Coppack 2002, *passim*; Coppack 2003, 95–102. For further general thoughts, see Ramey 1996; Kinder 1997, 333–75, *passim*.

4 Bell 1998, 212–21.

5 Fergusson and Harrison 1999, 120–7.

6 McCann 1976, chapter 36.

7 Horn and Born 1979, I, 288–9, 302–28, 313–21; II, 175–88. See also Braunfels 1972, 37–46.

8 As pointed out in Fergusson and Harrison 1999, 121–2. See also Conant 1993, 185–21, *passim*.

9 For brief introductions to monastic infirmaries, see Dickinson 1961, 41–2; Gilyard-Beer 1976, 40–3; Coppack 1990, 76–8; Fernie 2000, 206–7.

10 *Narrative Texts* (*Capitula* IX), 408, (*Instituta* XII), 461.

11 *Ecclesiastica Officia* (1 and 2), chapters 91–3; 116. On Cistercian medicine, see also Lekai 1977, 375–7; Bell 1989; Cassidy-Welch 2001, 133–65; on the Cistercian infirmary in general, Dimier 1987b; Williams 1998, 250–2.

12 Fergusson and Harrison 1999, 110–27.

13 Fergusson and Harrison 1999, 247 n 21.

14 It appears as building No. 36, to the south east of the abbey church. In France, the infirmary hall is generally known as the *salle des morts*.

15 Plouvier 1994, 80–1; Plouvier 1998, 150–1 (with a plan and internal elevation of 1790). Marginally different dimensions are given in Lekai 1977, 375; Dimier 1987b, 807–8, 811.

16 The infirmary hall is No. 73 on Milley's southern view (*see* fig 16), and is to the south of No. 72 on his ground plan (*see* fig 39). See Braunfels 1972, 80–1; Dimier 1987b, 809, 811; Pressouyre and Kinder 1992, 78–9. On the fate of the buildings, see Vilain 1998, 29–31.

17 The drawing was mentioned in chapter 8, above. It is reproduced in Van der Meer 1965, figs 230–232; Braunfels 1972, 92–5; Pressouyre and Kinder 1992, 76; Coomans 2000, 193.

18 In general, see Braunfels 1972, 106, 108; Kinder 1997, 362–6. For Ourscamp (and other French material), see Peigné-Delacourt 1876; Aubert 1947, II, 150–3; for Eberbach, Eydoux 1952, 167; Dimier 1971, 107; Dimier 1987b, 810–13; for Maulbronn, Knapp 1997, 65–6, 92; for Fossanova, Dimier 1971, 196; Dimier 1987b, 812–13. For further context on infirmary buildings, see the account of the complex at Villers in Coomans 2000, 431–48.

19 Mention of most of the known structures will be found in Robinson 1998, 64–205, *passim*.

20 Brakspear 1905, 57–8.

21 The infirmary area was excavated in 1959–64, with the evidence reassessed in Moorhouse and Wrathmell 1987, 51–6. Despite the 1170s date preferred by some, Moorhouse and Wrathmell suggest the timber building could have been built as late as *c* 1200. In their account of Jervaulx Abbey, Hope and Brakspear (1911, 325) suggest wooden buildings are likely to have served the immediate needs at many sites.

22 Fergusson and Harrison 1999, 110–27.

23 The evidence is speculative, but it is suggested that the early stone infirmary dates from the time of Abbot Richard of Clairvaux (1150–70): Coppack and Gilyard-Beer 1993, 5–7, 48; Coppack 2003, 34, 59. Stuart Harrison informs me that he believes he has identified further evidence for the form of the initial Fountains structure.

24 Brakspear 1905, 58–64. Fergusson and Harrison (1999, 125–6) suggest the architectural sources for all these early north–south infirmary halls in England came from outside the Cistercian order.

25 Hope 1900a, 319–35; Coppack and Gilyard-Beer 1993, 48–51. The ruins lay buried until excavated by Richard Walbran in 1849–50: Hope 1900a, 321; Coppack 2003, 139–41.

26 Coppack 2003, 78–80.

27 For Beaulieu, see Hope and Brakspear 1906, 168–71; Dimier 1987b, 804–5; for Buildwas, Thompson 1937, 19; Robinson 2002c, 23; for Croxden (*c* 1242–68), Hall 2003, I, 95–8; Hall 2004, 209–11; for Jervaulx, Hope and Brakspear 1911, 325–32; for Kirkstall, Hope and Bilson 1907, 38–43; Moorhouse and Wrathmell 1987, 51–6. Hall (2003, I, 98) argues that the infirmary halls at Croxden and Beaulieu were two-storey structures.

28 Hope 1900a, 320 n 2; Fergusson 1984a, 131, 134. For the two abbots, see Smith and London 2001, 291, 293.

29 Hope 1900b, 281–90.

30 In general, see Brakspear 1934, 18–20; Craster 1956, 26–8; Newman 2000, 554; Robinson 2002a, 60–2.

31 Harvey 1969, 58–9.

32 Brakspear and Evans 1910, 42–3; Wood 1912, 19–27; Robinson 1996a, 36–7.

33 The correspondence and official files that allow for a partial reconstruction of events are noted in Robinson 1997.

34 I have found no record of this window in any other source on Tintern. In his account, Wood continued: 'It may be hoped that when the excavations are finished … this may be laid in order on the floor of the hall, so as to show permanently, as far as the fragments will allow, the construction of this window': Wood 1912, 20, 22.

35 Wood thought this room was the kitchen. He noted: 'There are in the floor arrangements for carrying off water which require explanation': Wood 1912, 22.

36 *Cal Chart Rolls*, 1300–26, 98; Wood 1912, 21.

37 Bell 1998, 221–30.

38 *Ecclesiastica Officia* (1 and 2), chapter 90.

39 Bell 1998, 230–1; Williams 1998, 252–3; Cassidy-Welch 2001, 147–60; Hall 2003, I, 99; Hall 2004, 208.

40 In sum, see Coppack 2002, 200–1. For Meaux, see Fergusson 1984a, 135.

41 *Statuta*, IV, 619–20; V, 53; Fergusson and Harrison 1999, 131–2.

42 Wood 1912, 21–2.

43 Commentators have always been suspicious, given that Worcestre's dimensions for the 'two' buildings are precisely the same: Harvey 1969, 58–9.

44 Wood 1912, 23–7. In fact, Waddell now suggests that the earliest evidence for a Cistercian infirmary chapel comes from a statute of 1191, connected to the abbey of Santes Creus: *Statutes*, 227.

45 Brakspear 1934, 20.

46 Price 1952, 134–5.

47 I am grateful to Professor David Austin for showing me a preliminary survey of these earthworks.

48 Paul 1927, 274; Paul 1931, 500; Stone 1997, 136–7.

49 Williams 1976a, 5; Hillaby 1997a, 44. This is of much interest in the context of the points made in Hall 2003, I, 89–107; Hall 2004, 206–7.

50 *Leland*, 118; Robinson and Platt 1998, 32, 56.

51 Williams 2001, 117.

52 *Ecclesiastica Officia* (1 and 2), chapter 110.6–11; McCann 1976, chapters 2, 22; Williams 1998, 72.

53 Aubert 1947, II, 90–1.

54 Newman 1996, 47–51.

55 For medieval Cistercian abbatial accommodation in general, see Ramey 1996; Kinder 1997, 356–60; Williams 1998, 253. For what little is known of the Irish buildings, see Stalley 1987, 173–4. See also the case study on Villers in Coomans 2000, 449–58.

56 See above, chapter 8. On abbatial accommodation in general, see Dickinson 1961, 38–42; Gilyard-Beer 1976, 38–40; Thompson 2001, 65–92. Also useful in this context is Emery 2000, *passim*.

57 Fergusson and Harrison 1999, 129.

58 As Fergusson and Harrison (1999, 128–9) point out, this is the earliest example of the building type known in the entire order. See also Fergusson 1998.

59 Hope 1900a, 335–6; Coppack and Gilyard-Beer 1993, 45–7; Coppack 2003, 34, 59.

60 As suggested in Hope 1900a, 336.

61 For Kirkstall, see Hope and Bilson 1907, 34–8; for Waverley, Brakspear 1905, 70–1.

62 For Croxden, see Hall 2003, I, 84–6. It is Hall who also argues for the identifications at Roche and Jervaulx: Hall 2003, I, 92–4; Hall 2004, 201, 204–5. At Roche, the building in question has in the past been identified either as the infirmary or as the infirmarer's lodging: Fergusson 1990a, 23–4. For the complex at Jervaulx, see Hope and Brakspear 1911, 325–34, *passim*.

63 For Buildwas, where a substantial hall and chamber block continues to survive, complete with a fourteenth-century arch-braced roof over one wing, see Emery 2000, 547 n 3; Robinson 2002c, 23; for Byland (situated south east of the cloister), Harrison 1990, 18; for Croxden (where a new abbot's lodging was built from 1335), Hall 2003, I, 86–9; for Furness (where it is believed the abbots adapted the first infirmary building), Hope 1900b, 290–7.

64 In general, see Coppack 2002, 202–5. On Fountains, see Coppack 2003, 99–102; on Rievaulx, Fergusson and Harrison 1999, 132–5.

65 Godfrey 1929; Sherwood and Pevsner 1974, 809–11.

66 For Sawley (unusual in its early date), see Coppack 2002, 206; Coppack *et al* 2002, 79–80, 108–9; for Rufford, McGee and Perkins 1998, 88–91; Robinson 1998, 168; for the elaborate work at Hailes, Coad 1993, 15–16, 21; for Stoneleigh, Morris 2004, 40–1.

67 RCHME 1952, 244–6; Robinson 1998, 110. The cloister was on the north side of the church at Forde, with the house projecting from the north-west corner.

68 In general, see Brakspear 1934, 20; Craster 1956, 28; Newman 2000, 554–6; Robinson 2002a, 63–4.

69 Until the early 1960s, parts of this area were covered with a post-medieval cottage and its garden: Robinson 1997, 49.

70 For the works at these three sites, see notes 59, 61–2, above.

71 Abbot Ralph has earlier been mentioned in connection with both the chapter house (chapter 10) and the refectory (chapter 11). For what is known, see *Annales Monastici*, II, 336, 345; Williams 1976a, 104–5; Smith and London 2001, 316; Robinson 2002a, 12, 30. The proposed dates of the programme on Tintern's north and east claustral ranges have recently been given fresh support in the context of the Marshal family's work at Chepstow Castle. Morris and Coldstream suggest there 'must have been exchanges of masons' between the two sites: in Turner *et al* 2004, 277.

72 For Fountains, see Hope 1900a, 329–30; for Kirkstall, Hope and Bilson 1907, 40; for Waverley, Brakspear 1905, 65–6.

73 For the visitation, see *Narrative Texts* (*Carta Caritatis Prior*), 445; Williams 1998, 41–3.

74 Hall 2003, I, 91–2; Hall 2004, 206.

75 The known abbots around this time were Roger de Camme, 1330–1, Walter, 1333, and Gilbert, 1340–2: Williams 1976a, 107–8; Smith and London 2001, 317. On the date of the works, see Harrison *et al* 1998, 188, 245–6. The works are also mentioned in Emery 2000, 693.

76 Smith and London 2001, 276; Hall 2003, I, 86–9.

77 For Bishop Henry's hall at St Davids (*c* 1335–40), see Emery 2000, 643–7; Lloyd *et al* 2004, 423–4; for the Worcester hall (*c* 1320–30),

Pevsner 1968, 309; Emery 2000, 461; for Haughmond (*c* 1325–46), Emery 2000, 545–7; for Berkeley (*c* 1340), Verey and Brooks 2002, 178–9; for Caerphilly (1320s), Newman 1995, 174–5.

78 For the works at Valle Crucis, *see* chapters 8 and 10, together with the catalogue entry; Maddison 1978, 96–8; Robinson 1998, 196–7.

79 For the general context, see in particular Williams, G 1976, 376–462, *passim*; also Williams 1984, I, 80–99, *passim*; Williams 2001, 62–75, *passim*.

80 Coldstream 1986, 159.

81 As noted in chapter 1.

82 On the rebellion and its impact, see Williams, G 1976, 212–45; Davies 1995; Williams 2001, 52–5. See also the various individual site catalogue entries.

83 *Cal Pap Let*, VI, 282. See also Margam catalogue entry.

84 Jones 1873, 354–5.

85 *Cal Pat Rolls*, 1441–6, 95. See also Strata Florida catalogue entry.

86 Williams, G 1976, 262; Smith and Thomas 1977, 14. For more on Rhys, see Strata Florida catalogue entry.

87 Williams, G 1976, 386; Smith and Thomas 1977, 14–15; Robinson and Platt 1998, 33.

88 There are earthworks to the south east of the east range, but there is no guarantee the abbot's lodging lay in this area during the late Middle Ages.

89 On his career in general, see Hays 1963, 137–8; Williams, G 1976, 386–7; Williams 2001, 71–2; for his time at Strata Marcella, Williams 1976c, 170–2.

90 Williams, G 1976, 382; Williams 1976c, 171–2.

91 Hays 1963, 138. A connection to Dafydd is not mentioned in Hubbard 1986, 300. The tower dates from *c* 1505–25, possibly the work of William Hort (or Hart): Harvey 1984, 131, 149.

92 Hays 1963, 156; Williams, G 1976, 387.

93 For which see Butler 1987.

94 Williams 1981b, 42–4; Pryce 2001, 284–5. See also Cymer catalogue entry.

95 Smith 2001, 447, 469–71; Smith and Suggett 2002, 58–62.

96 For further context, see Smith 1988, 37–71.

97 Suggett 1996, 28, 107, 109.

98 As noted in the Valle Crucis catalogue entry, in 1419 it was claimed Abbot Robert of Lancaster had 'repaired the monastery on its destruction by fire': *Cal Pap Let*, VII, 117, 177.

99 In general, see Price 1952, 46–8; Pratt 1997, 10–17; Williams 2001, 66–7, 72. Williams (2001, 298) gives the dates for Siôn ap Rhisiart as 1455–61. Williams, G (1976, 262) suggests he may have flourished *c* 1450–80.

100 Williams, G 1976, 263.

101 Price 1952, 278–9.

102 Williams, G 1976, 385.

103 Williams, G 1976, 380 1. For a translation of the full poem, see Price 1952, 269–71.

104 [Jones] 1846, 26.

105 Price 1952, 277–8. There is another translation of this poem in Williams (*Ab Ithel*) 1846.

106 This proposal was first made in Radford 1953, 6, 8. It is accepted in, for example, Williams, G 1976, 387–8; Evans 1995, 18, 40–1; Emery 2000, 694–5. Hughes (1895a, 13–16), on the other hand, felt the alterations were unlikely to pre-date the suppression.

107 Williams, G 1976, 562; Pratt 1997, 13.

108 The plain chamfered rere-arch of this doorway survives, although the outer face belongs to the post-suppression reworking of the building.

109 In closing on Valle Crucis, it is worth noting the details of a late corrody (1530) offered to John Howe. In return for his gift of £20,

he was to receive 'a suitably furnished decent chamber … with an adequate bed with sheets and other necessaries': Pratt 1997, 16. It reminds us, as Hall (2003, I, 89–95; 2004, 207–8) points out, that by the late Middle Ages domestic chambers of various kinds lay scattered across the precinct, sometimes near the main claustral complex.

110 In general, see Jones 1933, 175–6; Williams 1981a, 100; Williams 2001, 69.

111 Jones 1933, 176.

112 Jones 1933, 176; Williams 2001, 69.

113 W[illiams] 1846, 111.

114 For a very brief note of the works, see Davies 1924.

115 Taylor (1971, 7) saw this as the warming house, a view followed in Hubbard 1986, 354.

116 Taylor 1971, 7; Robinson 1996b; Emery 2000, 694–5. To the east of this block, there is a long rectangular range which may have served for the accommodation of guests, at least during the last decades of monastic life. This point was explored in more detail in chapter 8 and is also covered in the Basingwerk catalogue entry.

117 *Cartae Glamorgancia*, IV, 1500–1; Birch 1902, 136–7.

118 See, in general, Birch 1897, 340–8; Williams, G 1976, 258; Williams, G 1997, 77–8; Williams 2001, 55, 58.

119 Williams, G 1974, 86; Williams, G 1976, 395–6; Williams 2001, 72–3.

120 Birch 1902, 139–40; Williams, G 1976, 395; Butler 1976a, 10–11.

121 The work is entirely undocumented, and the stylistic detail is by no means open to a single interpretation. After 1468, apart from Leyshon Thomas, the only other abbot of Neath so far identified is John (*c* 1502–7): Williams 2001, 296.

122 See the brief account of the house in Butler 1976a, 23, with the dates and phasing modified in RCAHMW 1981, 78–89, *passim*. See also Newman 1995, 469; Emery 2000, 694–5; Robinson 2002b.

123 Williams, G 1976, 387.

124 Coppack 2002.

125 Robinson 2002a, 62.

126 Williams 1976a; Robinson 2002a, 64.

127 Price 1952, 184–92; Pratt 1997, 39–49; and catalogue entry.

128 Moore and Moore 1974; RCAHMW 1981, 323–31; Evans 1996, 35–6.

129 For Maenan, see Butler 1987; for Llantarnam, Newman 2000, 336–7; and catalogue entry.

Catalogue of Sites

Introduction

1 The only other work that seeks to provide a specific overview of the Welsh buildings is Butler 1994. The same author (Butler 1999a) explores common trends and highlights disparate developments in a study comparing the Cistercian abbeys of Wales with those in Yorkshire. Among his many contributions on the Welsh Cistercians, Williams (2001, 99–125) offers a useful summary of the 'conventual buildings'. The national survey by Coppack (1998) and those essays edited by Norton and Park (1986) also include material on the white monk buildings of Wales. Historical surveys are more numerous, but of particular note are: O'Sullivan 1947; Cowley 1977; Williams 1984, 1990 and 2001.

Aberconwy Abbey

1 The abbey's 'Register and Chronicle' survives in a fourteenth-century manuscript: BL, Harleian MS 3725. There are translations in

Lowe 1912–28, I, 448–58; Hays 1963, 146–50. For the foundation, see *Register Aberconwy*, 7; Janauschek 1877, 186–7, 298; Hays 1963, 4. Most authorities accept the 1186 date: see, for example, Lloyd 1939, II, 601; Knowles and Hadcock 1971, 118; Davies 1987, 197.

2 *Brut*, 73; *Brut (RBH)*, 169; *Brenhinedd*, 187.

3 Hays (1963, 6) thought the founder *may* have been Rhodri, but felt it was 'only speculation'. More recently, Smith (Smith and Butler 2001, 298) accepts that Rhodri was probably the first benefactor. Gresham (1982–3, 314–18) made a case to suggest that Rhodri and his brother, Dafydd (d 1203), made a joint invitation to the Cistercians at Strata Florida to found an abbey in Gwynedd. See also Insley 1999, 236–7.

4 For Gruffudd's grant, see *Register Aberconwy*, 7–8. See also Hays 1963, 6–9; Smith and Butler, 2001, 301–2.

5 We may infer this from an 1192 reference to the abbey of Aberconwy: *Statutes*, 248; *Statuta*, I, 152. Although Gerald of Wales refers to the Cistercian abbey at Conwy in the account of his 1188 tour, the passage is an addition of *c* 1197: see Thorpe 1978, 195 n 389. See, also, Lloyd 1939, II, 601 n 142; Hays 1963, 5–6; Insley 1999, 236.

6 The two charters do not survive as originals; each is known only in the form of an *inspeximus* of Edward III (1332). In the first charter (*Mon Ang*, V, 672–4) Llywelyn grants the abbey extensive lands throughout Gwynedd, together with a series of important rights and privileges. In the second charter (*Cal Chart Rolls*, 1327–41, 267–9), the prince confirmed and augmented the privileges. The endowments granted through the first charter are considered at some length in Gresham 1939, and Gresham 1982–3. The precise date of the charters has long been a matter of debate, with more recent scholarship also challenging the authenticity of the texts, suggesting they may have been drafted in a later period, perhaps in the era following King Edward I's conquest of Gwynedd: see Insley 1999; Insley 2003, 169–70. Nevertheless, Llywelyn's support for the monks at Aberconwy cannot be in doubt, and a charter of endowments (perhaps as early as 1199, or soon after) is certainly to be expected: Smith and Butler 2001, 301–4.

7 For the location and extent of the Aberconwy estates in general, see Gresham 1939; Hays 1963, 8–19; Williams 1990, 36–8; Williams 2001, 178.

8 Llywelyn ab Iorwerth spent his last hours at the abbey, having taken the habit of a Cistercian monk. The body of his son, Gruffudd, was brought back to Gwynedd in 1248, some four years after his death falling in an attempt to escape from the Tower of London. See *Annales Cambriæ*, 82–3; Hays 1963, 44–9, *passim*; Richards 1966, 35. Insley (1999, 237) suggests Aberconwy was 'perhaps one of the nearest things in native Wales to a "dynastic" monastery'.

9 Hays 1963, 52–3; Smith 1998, 221; Williams 2001, 31–2.

10 In fact, Llywelyn intended to give the monks both Llanbadrig and another royal chapel at Llanbeblig, though the grant for the latter seems to have fallen through: Hays 1963, 50, 116–17. For this period in the abbey's history in general, see Hays 1963, 52–60.

11 For the events at this time, see Hays 1963, 54–5; Davies 1987, 334–7; Smith 1998, 437–8.

12 Hays 1963, 61–77; Richards 1966, 37–8.

13 Williams (1990, 36) suggests the site was perhaps at SH 461574. The RCAHMW (1960, 223) records a house of 1673 at Rhedynog-Felen-Fawr (SH 460574). Gresham (1982–3, 312–13) put forward the intriguing possibility that the settling colony of monks occupied an earlier earthwork enclosure known by the name Dinas y Prif (SH 463577), for which see RCAHMW 1960, 224–5.

14 On the choice of site, see Gresham 1982–3, 314–15.

15 Butler (1964, 117) suggests the community may have had to use a spring at Ty Gwyn, about a quarter of a mile (0.37km) to the south west (mentioned in Lowe 1912–28, I), or that they tapped the more distant Perhey stream flowing off Conwy mountain.

16 Williams 1835, 75.

17 All of this is noted in Hughes 1895b. He suggested the reused stones in the south porch were of late twelfth-century date, and offered a restored profile of two orders featuring a roll to the otherwise flat soffit with flanking angle rolls. The scale of the arch represented by these stones might be more in keeping with a transept chapel arcade than a main nave arcade. Hughes also suggested the lowest courses of walling in the west front could be of late twelfth-century date: Hughes 1895b, 164.

18 RCAHMW 1956, 39–43. The survey modifies, but does not fundamentally challenge, the earlier work by Harold Hughes. Radford (1982, 71–2) compares Aberconwy with Cymer and Cwmhir, suggesting all three shared a development sequence in which the nave was built first. These views are questioned in the present study.

19 Butler 1964, 111–15.

20 Hughes 1937.

21 Fresh doubts are raised in Butler and Evans 1980, 51–2.

22 The plan at Cymer is generally thought to represent a compromise solution to building difficulties encountered by the community. The most telling feature is the way the east wall is simply butt-jointed to the side walls of the church.

23 In a new consideration of the evidence, this is also the conclusion reached by Butler, acknowledging that some other explanation is needed to account for the apparently early string course on the east face of the present chancel: Butler 2004, 119–20.

24 Hays 1963, 47; Williams 2001, 28. See, also, Williams 1835, 16–20; Lowe 1912–28, I, 178–80; Richards 1966, 41. The king appears to have arranged some small compensation payment in July of 1246, with a further award for damages following in 1251, in all totalling about £46: Hays 1963, 48–9. Butler and Evans (1980, 51–2) wonder about the possibility of this episode leading to the loss of the presbytery, and to the introduction of a blocking wall at the east end of the nave, thereby providing an explanation for the scale of the present church; but see also Butler 2004, 118–20.

25 The wall contains a pair of two-light windows of mid- to later thirteenth-century date, of which the eastern example is the better preserved. Hughes (1895b, 166) believed it was *in situ*, but the RCAHMW (1956, 41) suggests it is reused.

26 Hughes 1895b, 168–74; RCAHMW 1956, 39–43; Richards 1966, 42. On the legal arrangement involved in the conversion, see Brown *et al* 1963, 340 n 1.

27 RCAHMW 1956, 41. For the later history of the church in general, see Richards 1966, 42–53.

28 RCAHMW 1956, 39; Richards 1966, 53–4.

29 Rhys 1883, III, 120. Quoted in Hughes 1895b, 162; RCAHMW 1956, 39; Hays 1963, 9; Butler 1964, 115–16. Butler (2004, 119) now wonders whether the building was indeed Cistercian.

30 Rhys 1883, III, 120.

31 As Butler (1964, 116) notes, the door appears to have had a semicircular arched head, the jambs featuring three recessed orders. He wondered if the structure might form part of the infirmary block.

32 Williams 1835, 75.

33 Hughes 1895b, 166–8; RCAHMW 1956, 39, 43 (dated there to *c* 1235). As it stands, the west doorway is almost certainly reused, since it was clearly designed in origin without door jambs. The arch orders spring from leaf capitals without neck-rings.

Basingwerk Abbey

1 Janauschek's lists give a range of dates, beginning with 1131, then 1132, 1149, 1156 and 1159: Janauschek 1877, 99. As Knowles and Hadcock (1971, 115) pointed out, 1131 seems the most widely accepted year, as given in Lloyd 1939, II, 456; Hill 1968, 35; Davies 1987, 196. See also *Mon Ang*, V, 261; Laveille 1896–9, II, 190 (which suggests the community was settled on land given by William Peverell); Jones 1933, 170–2; O'Sullivan 1947, 25; Williams 1981a, 89–90.

2 For early Norman advances and Welsh resistance in this area, see Davies 1987, 24–55, *passim.*

3 For the merger and its context, see Knowles 1963a, 249–52; Hill 1968, 80–115; Burton 1994, 67–9. The date of the merger has recently been challenged by Berman (2000, 142–8), though her views have not won wide acceptance.

4 *Mon Ang*, V, 263; W[illiams] 1846, 103. The charter was confirmed by Edward III in 1328: *Cal Chart Rolls, 1327–41*, 225.

5 Taylor's identification was based, in part, on the apparently interchangeable use of 'Coleshill' and 'Basingwerk' in twelfth- and thirteenth-century documentation. See Leach 1960, 36–40. Hên Blas is located at SJ 222735.

6 Williams 1981a, 89–90; Williams 2001, 14. See also Donkin 1978, 179.

7 At least one source makes reference to the 'foundation' of Basingwerk in 1157: *Chester Chronicle*, 23. For Henry's charter, see *Mon Ang*, V, 262–3; W[illiams] 1846, 103. See also Jones 1933, 170–2; Leach 1960, 36.

8 Buildwas had been founded in 1135. Following merger with the Cistercians, it appears to have assumed growing status within Savigny's British family, acquiring oversight of St Mary's Abbey, Dublin, in 1156 and Basingwerk in 1157: Hunter 1840, 51–2; Gwynn and Hadcock 1970, 130–1; Robinson 2002c, 26–7.

9 *Gerald of Wales*, VI, 137.

10 For Basingwerk's lands and its economy in general, see Williams 1981a, 105–12; Williams 1990, 38–40; Williams 2001, 178. See also Owen 1919–20, 48–65.

11 Owen 1919–20, 59–60; Williams 1981a, 109.

12 Jones 1933, 172–3; Williams 1981a, 107–9. For the context surrounding the gifts to Basingwerk in Penllyn, see Pryce 2001, 274–5.

13 Of older origins, the chapel and holy well had been granted to the Benedictines at Chester in 1093. See Jones 1933, 171–2; David 1971; Williams 1981a, 99; Williams 2001, 147–8; and for Dafydd's charter, W[illiams] 1846, 107–8.

14 *Statuta*, II, 394; Williams 2001, 147. For the Winifred cult, see David 1971; Farmer 1992, 500; Gray 2000, 34–6.

15 Jones 1933, 174; Williams 1981a, 93.

16 *Littere Wallie*, 84; Hays 1963, 76.

17 *Cal Chart Rolls*, 1257–1300, 289–91.

18 The Glossop grant was made in 1290, and Holywell in 1292: *Cal Chart Rolls, 1257–1300*, 372, 423; Williams 1981a, 110–11.

19 *Taxatio Ecclesiastica*, 259, 262, 289; *Mon Ang*, V, 261–2; W[illiams] 1846, 109–10; O'Sullivan 1947, 27, and n 9. The figures for income from spiritualities are not available.

20 Cowley 1977, 222–3; Williams 1981a, 94–5.

21 Cowley 1977, 51 n 41.

22 Williams 1981a, 95–8; for a specific plea (1346), *Ancient Correspondence*, 185.

23 Williams 1978; Williams 1981a, 97–8; Williams 2001, 57–8.

24 In general, see David 1971; Williams 1981a, 99; Hubbard 1986, 32–4; Williams 2001, 147–8.

25 Jones 1933, 176.

26 Williams, G 1976, 430.

27 Jones 1933, 176; Williams 1981a, 100; Williams 2001, 69.

28 W[illiams] 1846, 111.

29 Owen 1919–20, *passim*; Jones 1933, 177; Williams 1981a, 101–2.

30 *Valor Ecclesiasticus*, IV, 437–8; *Mon Ang*, V, 263–4; W[illiams] 1846, 112–15; O'Sullivan 1947, 27, and n 10. See also the information on the suppression period accounts in Owen 1919–20, 48–60; Jones 1933, 176–7.

31 The precise date is not known: Williams 1981a, 102; Williams 2001, 86.

32 For the full account of the chapel, see Leach 1960, 25–60.

33 For the buildings in general, see, in particular, Hodkinson 1905; RCAHMCW 1912, 40–1; Taylor 1946a and 1971; Robinson 1996b; Robinson 1998, 66–7.

34 The range in question is illustrated by a series of photographs in Hodkinson's account of the site, when the area was tenanted for a tan yard. Hodkinson was clearly impressed by the scale of these structures, identifying them as 'undoubtedly cellarer's buildings, with, probably, guest-house over': Hodkinson 1905, 170, 174, pls J–M. Above a low stone-built ground storey, the upper floor was of conventional box-frame construction, with the roof featuring both arch-braced and crown-post trusses. The side wall frames included large braces, clearly intended for architectural display. The construction is certainly late medieval in origin (unless a reuse of timbers is to be considered). Further photographs, taken in the late 1920s, can be found in the site archive at Cadw. See, further, W[illiams] 1846, 101–2; RCAHMCW 1912, 40–1. Taylor (1971, 7–8) thought the range might have been erected after the suppression, possibly on the site of the infirmary. Hubbard (1986, 355) also says they are post-suppression in date.

35 [Taylor] 1947, 321–2.

36 See comments by Taylor in Leach 1960, 37.

37 Lewis 1999, 77, 183, 227.

38 Lewis 1999, 86–7, 215, 227. From early works records, there is evidence of tile flooring in parts of the church, the sacristy, and also the east and west cloister walks. In some cases, the covering was probably plain tiles of the fifteenth or early sixteenth centuries.

39 From early photographs, published in Hodkinson 1905 (and in the site archive with Cadw), the appearance of the timber-framing suggests the work may date before the end of the fifteenth century. The timbers were sampled for tree-ring dating in the early 1990s, but the results proved inconclusive. All the framing has since been removed from the site and is at present in storage.

40 For the initial lease, see *Let Pap Henry VIII*, 12, II, 470. In general, see W[illiams] 1846, 115–16; Taylor 1971, 3; Williams 1981a, 103; Williams 2001, 91.

41 Quoted in Hodkinson 1905, 174–5; RCAHMCW 1912, 41; Taylor 1971, 3. See also Williams 1981a, 103; Williams 2001, 91, 110. In Pevsner and Hubbard (1971, 151) a tradition that the camber-beam roof in the nave of St Mary Hill was brought from Basingwerk is rejected.

42 See RCAHMCW 1912, 41; Williams, G 1976, 439. Hubbard (1986, 337–8) accepts that the roof comes from elsewhere, but gives no evidence to support the tradition that it had belonged to Basingwerk. See, further, Lord 2003, 230–1. There are also traditions, generally not well supported, that the east window of Llanrhaiadr church, near Ruthin, and coloured glass at Llanasa, came from the abbey: W[illiams] 1846, 116; Hodkinson 1905, 174; Williams 1981a, 103.

43 Taylor 1971, 3; Williams 2001, 89.

44 Williams 1981a, 103.

45 As reported in W[illiams] 1846, 102.

46 W[illiams] 1846, 99–102.

47 Brock 1878b, 468–76; Hodkinson 1905; RCAHMCW 1912, 40–1.

48 Williams 2001, 288, quoting [Brock] 1891, 127.

49 See, for example, *Archaeol Cambrensis*, **1**, 1846, facing 334; Hodkinson 1905, pls B and C; RCAHMCW 1912, figs 31–33.

50 RCAHMCW 1912, figs 31–32.

51 [Lovegrove] 1921, 405.

52 Davies 1924.

53 Revised as Taylor 1946a; subsequent editions (including Taylor 1971) through to 1984.

54 Robinson 1996b; now revised as Robinson 2006a.

55 The survey was carried out by Geophysical Surveys of Bradford (Report 91/91) on behalf of Cadw.

56 Greenfield Valley Heritage Park is managed by the local authority.

Cwmhir Abbey

1 For the most recent views on the foundation, see Remfry 1994, 1; Smith and Butler 2001, 298. See also *Mon Ang*, V, 457; Lloyd 1939, II, 594, 600; O'Sullivan 1947, 10; Knowles and Hadcock 1971, 115; Williams 1976b, 73–4; Cowley 1977, 25–6.

2 On Rhys's support for the Cistercians and his early patronage of Whitland, see Pryce 1996, 156–61. See also Smith and Butler 2001, 298.

3 *Leland*, 52; O'Sullivan 1947, 10. Williams (1976b, 84–5) believes that we should not take the claim on the number of monks too seriously: even if correct, 'it would probably have referred to monks and lay brethren together'.

4 The date (22 July 1143) is given by Janauschek (1877, 74–5) and apparently derives from the late thirteenth-century 'Chronicle of the Abbey of St Werburgh, Chester': BL, Cotton Vesp. MS A, fol 33 (though this does not appear in the published edition of the source: *Chester Chronicle*). It is followed (and accepted), to a greater or lesser degree, in [Rees] 1849, 233–5; Williams 1894–5, 61; Day 1911, 13; RCAHMCW 1913, 3; Lloyd 1939, II, 594; O'Sullivan 1947, 10; Charles 1970, 70; Cowley 1977, 25; Radford 1982, 58–9.

5 Devannor (Ty Faenor) is at SO 07147106. For the suggestion, see RCAHMCW 1913, 6–7, repeated in Knowles and Hadcock 1971, 115. Williams (1976b, 74; 2001, 14–15) seems to prefer to leave the matter open; Brooksby (1970), in assessing a probable twelfth-century stone corbel found at Devannor, argues against the likelihood of an earlier (1143) monastery on the site.

6 Smith 1999, 102–4; Smith and Butler 2001, 299–301. See also Remfry 1994, 1–9.

7 *Brut*, 75.

8 The charter is transcribed in Charles 1970. See also Remfry 1994, 2, 7; Smith and Butler 2001, 299–300.

9 This point was made long ago in [Rees] 1849, 235–6. Now see Smith and Butler 2001, 300–1.

10 Smith 1999, 102–5; Smith and Butler 2001, 300–3. The settlement of Cwmhir monks at Cymer was noted in the Welsh chronicle: *Brut*, 79; *Brut (RBH)*, 180–1. See also the entry on Cymer in this catalogue.

11 Knowles *et al* 2001, 126. His death is noted in *Brut*, 72.

12 *Statutes*, 340; *Statuta*, I, 191; Knowles 1963a, 660; Williams 1976b, 78. Such problems with lay brothers were not peculiar to Cwmhir: Cowley 1977, 118–21.

13 *Cal Chart Rolls*, 1226–57, 155; *Mon Ang*, V, 459; [Rees] 1849, 236–7, 239; Williams 1976b, 79–80; O'Sullivan 1947, 10, and n 20; Remfry 1994, 1. There is a later *inspeximus* charter (1318) of Edward II: *Cal Pat Rolls*, 1317–21, 163.

14 For Cwmhir's lands in general, see Rowley-Morris 1893; Charles 1970, 70–2; Williams 1976b, 88–99; Williams 1990, 40–1; Percival 1993; Remfry 1994, 1–12; Williams 2001, 181.

15 Typically, there is considerable variation in the place-names given in both primary and secondary sources. For a summary attempt to identify locations at key dates, see Remfry 1994, 15–16. As for Golon, it was Cwmhir's most valuable property at the suppression, contributing up to a third of all recorded income.

16 The grange bordered the Wye, near its confluence with the Marteg: Charles 1970, 72; Percival 1993.

17 Williams 1976b, 89–91.

18 Williams 1976b, 9–2.

19 For this period in general, see Davies 1987, 236–51, 279.

20 Varying accounts of the event in question will be found in: [Rees] 1849, 237–9; Williams 1894–5, 72–7; Lloyd 1939, II, 668, 675–6; Williams 1976b, 77, 80; Cowley 1977, 212; Radford 1982, 60; Remfry 1994, 12; Williams 2001, 27.

21 'Sed abbas loci, ut ædificia sumptuosis valde laboribus constructa salvaret …': for the particulars, see *Matthew Paris*, III, 202–3. As for the grange in question, this has often been identified as Gwernegof. There is some confusion over another reference from Matthew Paris to the burning of a 'Cridia Abbey' in 1228: Williams 1894–5, 75; Lloyd 1939, II, 668; Williams 1976b, 77.

22 *Cal Close Rolls*, 1231–4, 547; *Cal Chart Rolls*, 1226–57, 155.

23 *Cal Close Rolls*, 1251–3, 143; *Cal Close Rolls*, 1253–4, 20; O'Sullivan 1947, 10; Williams 1976b, 98.

24 *Annales Cambriæ*, 80–1; [Rees] 1849, 239; Williams 1976b, 80.

25 On this episode, see O'Sullivan 1947, 67–8; Williams 2001, 30.

26 For Abbot Cadwgan, see Smith and London 2001, 258. For Llywelyn's death, and the burial of his body at Cwmhir, see Williams 1894–5, 78–83; Day 1911, 14–16; Williams 1976b, 80–1; Remfry 1994, 13; Smith 1998, 568; Williams 2001, 32.

27 *Taxatio Ecclesiastica*, 274, 276–7, 293; [Rees] 1849, 240, 258–9; Williams 1894–5, 69; O'Sullivan 1947, 11, and n 25; Cowley 1977, 274.

28 On this period in general, see Williams 1976b, 81.

29 Cowley 1977, 261.

30 Williams 1971b, 181; Williams 1976b, 85.

31 *Leland*, 52. See also the comments in: [Rees] 1849, 240; Williams 1894–5, 84; Day 1911, 16; O'Sullivan 1947, 108–9; Radford 1982, 60. Dunn (1967, 30–1) suggests 1401 or 1402 as the most likely dates. There is no reference to such an episode in Davies 1995.

32 But see Williams, G 1976, 230; Williams, G 1997, 75.

33 On this late period, see Williams 1976b, 82–4.

34 Williams 1976a, 26–7; Williams 1976b, 83–4; Williams 2001, 66, 77.

35 *Valor Ecclesiasticus*, IV, 407; *Mon Ang*, V, 459; [Rees] 1849, 241, 259; Williams 1894–5, 70; O'Sullivan 1947, 11, and n 26.

36 Williams 1976b, 89.

37 Williams 1976b, 86; Williams 2001, 86.

38 *Leland*, 52; [Rees] 1849, 256.

39 Brooksby 1970; also Radford 1982, 67. Lord (2003, 80–2, 98–9) links it tentatively to work seen on a group of fonts in Radnorshire/Breconshire.

40 Though he accepted an original foundation date of 1143, Radford believed the effective life of the monastery had begun in 1176: Radford 1982, especially 61–7, with his reconstruction at fig 3. In a recent review of Radford's conclusions, Butler (2004, 120–2) suggests

two possible alternatives for the arrangements and positioning of such an aisleless church. Although his ideas are imaginative, neither is wholly convincing (as he is prepared to acknowledge).

41 For Grey, see Stalley 1987, 55, 63, 93–5; for Culross and Saddell, Robinson 1998, 93–4, 169; for Rushen, Butler 2002. See also the general discussion in Harrison 2002, 160–1.

42 Clearance was initiated in the early 1820s and the findings communicated in [Rees] 1849, 244–9; the report reprinted in Williams 1894–5, 85–6; RCAHMCW 1913, 4–5. The failure to recover any trace of the east end led to the conclusion 'that the choir part of the church was never built': [Rees] 1849, 245. When the site was excavated by Stephen Williams in the 1890s, one of the objectives was 'to determine whether any part of the church eastward of the nave had been built': Williams 1894–5, 88. His work failed to provide a definitive answer.

43 For recent descriptions, see Radford 1982, 69–70; Jones 2000a and 2000b.

44 Williams 1894–5, 92–3; Davies 1992. Jones (2000b, 3) says the rubble core of the walls is fine-grained quartzite.

45 There can be absolutely no doubt this material came from Cwmhir: [Rees] 1849, 251–4; Williams 1894–5, 88–98; RCAHMCW 1911, 114; Haslam 1979, 140–1; Radford 1982, 70–3.

46 Hamer (1873, 172–5) was of the view that the piers could have been reduced by about 1.2m.

47 Radford 1982, 73.

48 No help is provided by what we know of the abbots of this period: Knowles et al 2001, 126; Smith and London 2001, 258.

49 Williams 1894–5, 91–2. For the Llandaff reference, see Freeman 1850b, 62–4.

50 See, most recently, Newman 1995, 244–7; also Thurlby 1996, 178–9.

51 In sum, the buildings are to be seen within the orbit of early Gothic developments in midland and south-west England and Wales. Since the work of Brakspear (1931), the term 'west country' continues to be applied, if loosely. Brakspear argued, for example, that square or polygonal abaci were a rather earlier characteristic in the regional 'school', with rounded forms tending to appear later.

52 Brakspear 1931, passim; Morris 2000, 210–13, 237. For Haverfordwest, see Lloyd et al 2004, 210–12.

53 Haslam 1979, 141.

54 Radford 1982, 71.

55 Butler (2004, 123) is the most recent student of Cwmhir to consider the possibility of Roger Mortimer's involvement. However, I cannot accept his highly speculative proposal that the early thirteenth-century rebuilding began with the construction of a six-bay aisled presbytery and transepts, in the manner of Byland and Dore. The focus of most of the Mortimer patronage seems to have been the house of Victorine canons at Wigmore in Herefordshire, perhaps settled in 1172, with the church dedicated in 1179: Knowles and Hadcock 1971, 144, 179; Brakspear 1933.

56 For Pershore, see Thurlby 1996, 165–81; for St Frideswide, Morris 1990.

57 Roger of Wendover, III, 11–12; Matthew Paris, III, 203. See also Radford 1982, 69; Williams 2001, 99.

58 Williams 1890a, 150–1; Williams 1894–5, 87.

59 The wall fragments he excavated are no longer visible. For comments on the cloister buildings, see Williams 1894–5, 90; Day 1911, 20–1.

60 Williams 1894–5, 90; Radford 1982, 66.

61 Williams 1894–5, 95–7, pl 8. If his reconstruction is correct, it would be difficult to place such an elaborate pier at some other point in the complex.

62 Blockley 1998b; Jones 2000a.

63 [Rees] 1849, 249; Radford 1982, 72.

64 The RCAHMCW (1913, 3) suggested 'the eastern limb and transepts utterly perished sometime during the 15th century … so that the east end of the nave was closed by a wall'.

65 Williams 1976b, 87; Williams 2001, 110.

66 Williams 1976b, 86–7; Williams 2001, 88.

67 Williams 1976b, 87. Elsewhere, it is said the abbey's possessions were leased to John Turner in 1538 for a term of twenty-one years, and that in 1546 the site of the monastery was granted to Walter Hendley and John Williams: [Rees] 1849, 241.

68 Hamer 1873, 172–5; RCAHMCW 1911, 114; [Lovegrove] 1932; Haslam 1979, 140–2; Radford 1982, 70–3.

69 Williams 1894–5, 89; Haslam 1979, 140.

70 For the claims, see, for example: [Rees] 1849, 254–5; Hamer 1873, 168, 172–5; [Lovegrove] 1932; Davies 1992.

71 Williams 1894–5, 89; Williams 1976b, 77; Radford 1982, 70 n 57. In fact, dendrochronology has now provided a felling date of 1537–8 for the timbers in the nave roof at Llanidloes: Lord 2003, 231, based on information from Richard Suggett.

72 [Rees] 1849, 242–3; Williams 1894–5, 84–5.

73 Day 1911, 18; Haslam 1979, 216–17; [Evans] 1999, 119.

74 Williams 1905, 135.

75 Newman 1965, 1966, and 1981; [Evans] 1999, 119.

76 On this and the associated gardens, see [Evans] 1999, 119–22. See also Haslam 1979, 216.

77 The full account appears as [Rees] 1849, 244–55. The section on the clearance work is reprinted in Williams 1894–5, 85–6; RCAHMCW 1913, 4–5.

78 [Rees] 1849, 244–5. Radford (1982, 61) seemed to take this observation seriously and compared the description to the bakehouse at Inch Abbey in Northern Ireland; for a plan of which, see Stalley 1987, 32.

79 Elsewhere, material from the abbey has been identified in the churches at Llanbadarn Fynydd, Llanddewi Ystradenni, Nantmel and, especially, Llanbister: Williams 1894–5, 86–7; Davies 1992; [Evans] 1999, 119. Also, it is said that 'several hundred tons of broken stone were taken away and used in improving roads in the neighbourhood': [Rees] 1849, 255.

80 Williams (2001, 110, pl v-A) raises the possibility that the scene represents the Assumption; rejected in Lord 2003, 188.

81 Williams 1890a; Williams 1894–5.

82 Jones 2000a and 2000b.

83 The work was carried out in 1998 by M J Noel of Geoquest Associates.

84 [Evans] 1999, 118–22.

Cymer Abbey

1 Statutes, 415–16, 428–9; Statuta, I, 230, 236. The founder appears simply as 'Grifini' in the 1198 statute and is described as prince of North Wales in 1199.

2 For the two most authoritative accounts of the foundation, see Smith 1999, 101–5 (reproduced with some modification in Smith and Butler 2001, 297–303), and Pryce 2001, 275–8. Smith argues that Gruffudd ap Cynan was probably the prince mainly responsible for settling this community in Gwynedd and identifies him as the 'Grifini' in the two statutes. Fr Chrysogonus Waddell (Statutes, 428–9) believes the prince is to be identified as Madog ap Gruffudd (d 1236) and the house in question is Valle Crucis. See also Mon Ang, V, 742; Lloyd 1939, II, 602; Knowles and Hadcock 1971, 118;

Williams 1981b, 38. Both versions of *Brut y Tywysogyon* give the year of settlement as 1198, whereas Janauschek's lists imply 1199: *Brut*, 79; *Brut (RBH)*, 180–1; Janauschek 1877, 204.

3 The charter survives as an *inspeximus* of 1323, for which see *Cal Chart Rolls, 1321–4*, 400. It is discussed in full, with a transcript, in Williams-Jones 1957–60. The version printed by Dugdale is from a slightly later confirmation. Mistakenly, it appears under the entry for Cymer's mother house, Cwmhir: *Mon Ang*, V, 458–9. For the political and military positions in north-west Wales at the time of the foundation, see Lloyd 1939, II, 588–9; Davies 1987, 236–41.

4 Smith 1999; Smith and Butler 2001, 297–317. The term 'apostolic gestation' is borrowed from Berman 2000, *passim*.

5 *Brut (RBH)*, 180–1. This varies from the Peniarth MS 20 version, which reads: 'a community from Cwmhir went to reside at Cymer in Nannau in Meirionnydd': *Brut*, 79.

6 Cwmhir's founder was Cadwallon ap Madog, chief lord of the *cantref* of Maelienydd. See the catalogue entry for Cwmhir.

7 Smith suggests that the charter granted to the community at Cwmhir in 1199 was intended to encourage the return of the monks: Smith and Butler 2001, 299–300, 303. For the charter, see Charles 1970.

8 Davies 1987, 236–51; Turvey 2002, 84–90.

9 Williams-Jones 1957–60, 54, 57. Llywelyn acknowledged the gifts of Gruffudd and Maredudd ap Cynan, as well as those of Gruffudd's son Hywel, and other unspecified benefactors.

10 On Cymer's lands in general, see Richards 1957–60, 246–9; Williams 1981b, 48–54; Gresham 1984 (discussing identifications and boundaries); Williams 1990, 41–3; Williams 2001, 180–1; Smith and Butler 2001, 305–8. For additional views on the early grants, see Pryce 2001, 276–9.

11 Griffith 1981–4.

12 Williams 1981b, 52; Smith and Butler 2001, 307–8.

13 Williams 1981b, 53–4; Smith and Butler 2001, 308.

14 *Statuta*, II, 238; Williams 1981b, 39.

15 Williams 1981b, 39–40; Smith 1998, 220–1; Smith and Butler 2001, 311–12; Pryce 2001, 282.

16 *Littere Wallie*, 32–3; Hays 1971, 131. For the suggestion that rather more may have lain behind this gesture of support, see Smith and Butler 2001, 312.

17 *Ancient Correspondence*, 27, 75, 85, 87; *Littere Wallie*, 32, 45; Williams-Jones 1957–60, 62–3.

18 Williams 1981b, 40; Smith and Butler 2001, 313.

19 The gift was made '*ad quedam opera sui monasterii perficienda*': Brown *et al* 1963, 340 n 4; Williams 1981b, 40.

20 *Littere Wallie*, 96–7. Williams 1981b, 40.

21 *Taxatio Ecclesiastica*, 292–3; O'Sullivan 1947, 17, and n 96. The figure of £11 (1)4s 4d given by [Jones] (1846, 456) and Williams-Jones (1957–60, 60) does not include any of the spiritualities then held by the house.

22 In 1379 the community numbered the abbot and four monks: Pryce 2001, 284. Williams (1981b, 36, 43) gives five in 1388; Williams, G (1976, 562) gives five in 1377–81. It is unknown how recent a decline this figure represents.

23 For what is known, see Williams 1981b, 42; Williams 2001, 52–5; Pryce 2001, 284. In 1412, English troops were posted at the abbey as part of the campaign to restore Crown authority in Merioneth: Davies 1995, 299–300.

24 In 1442–3, the abbacy was variously claimed by John ap Rhys and John Cobbe. See, in general, O'Sullivan 1947, 111; Williams-Jones 1957–60, 61; Williams 1981b, 42–4; Williams 2001, 56–7; Pryce 2001, 284–5.

25 *Cal Pat Rolls, 1441–6*, 151–2.

26 *Cal Pat Rolls, 1441–6*, 164. It is not entirely clear whether Richard Kirby was Cobbe's direct successor.

27 *Cal Pat Rolls, 1452–61*, 65; Pryce 2001, 285.

28 Jones 1937, 273; Williams 1981b, 45–6, 47; Smith and Butler 2001, 315–16; Pryce 2001, 286.

29 Williams 2001, 65–8. In 1537, Lewis ap Thomas (d 1561) was made bishop of Shrewsbury, then a suffragan appointment within the diocese of St Asaph: Williams 1981b, 46.

30 *Valor Ecclesiasticus*, IV, 426; *Mon Ang*, V, 743; [Jones] 1846, 456–8; O'Sullivan 1947, 17, and n 97.

31 Williams 1981b, 36, 47; Pryce 2001, 286. Williams, G (1976, 562) has ?four monks for 1534–6.

32 For the buildings in general, see Radford 1946 (and subsequent editions); Robinson 1995b; Robinson 1998, 97–8; Smith and Butler 2001, 317–25; Smith 2001, 447, 469–71.

33 Williams 1981b, 37. Lawrence Butler (Smith and Butler 2001, 317) suggests the carved features are of Cefn-y-fedw sandstone.

34 Brock (1878b, 467) thought there were sufficient traces of four of the windows on the south side to show that they were of two lights each.

35 As suggested in Radford 1946: Radford 1982, 71–2.

36 This is the view expressed in Smith and Butler 2001, 313, 320.

37 Suggett 1996, 28, 107, 109; Smith 2001, 447, 469–71; Smith and Suggett 2002, 58–62.

38 For several very minor bequests towards the maintenance of the abbey's fabric after this date, see Pryce 2001, 286.

39 Williams 1981b, 47; Smith and Butler 2001, 316.

40 For notes on the early descent, see [Jones] 1846, 459–60.

41 Ellis 1927, 1–7; Williams 1990, 20, 86.

42 [Jones] 1846, 446–50.

43 Brock 1878b, 463–7; with the observation on the east end given at 466.

44 RCAHMCW 1921, 96–7.

45 RCAHMCW 1921, 96, fig 93.

46 Radford 1946.

47 Robinson 1995b.

48 For these two accounts, see Smith and Butler 2001, 317–25; Butler 2004, 116–18.

49 Much as in the early paper by Brock (1878b, 466), Butler's argument rests on the view that there is no sign of these features having been inserted into an earlier wall: Smith and Butler 2001, 320; Butler 2004, 117–18.

50 Basingwerk is one obvious example. In Ireland, the arcades at Boyle (*c* 1180) include octagonal capitals (Stalley 1987, 87–92); at Hulton Abbey in Staffordshire the somewhat later thirteenth-century arcades had the same combination of octagonal piers and double-chamfered arches: Robinson 1998, 127. I am grateful to Richard Morris for showing me his account of the architecture and worked stones at Hulton in advance of publication: Morris 2005, 75–8.

DORE ABBEY

1 About 1283, Bishop Thomas Bek (1280–93) of St Davids went so far as to claim jurisdiction over Dore, 'saving the rights of the monks', asserting that the abbey lay in the parish of Ewyas Harold, itself in the Welsh diocese until 1847. The claim was resisted by Bishop Richard Swinfield of Hereford (1282–1317): Williams 1976a, 1, 3; Williams 1997a, 17.

2 It was a plea of poverty which drove the request: *Statuta*, III, 210;

Cowley 1977, 235.

3 Talbot 1967, 261–2; Williams, G 1976, 398.

4 *Mon Ang*, V, 552; Janauschek 1877, 92–3; Knowles and Hadcock 1971, 112, 115; Williams 1976a, 1–3; Williams 1997a, 15.

5 Morimond (Haute-Marne) was founded from Cîteaux in 1115: King 1954, 329–87; Peugniez 2001, 139–40. Its special province of settlement lay in central and eastern Europe, in the German-speaking lands and Poland. However, it also developed a network of filiations in Gascony and northern Spain: Donkin 1978, 21–9; Williams 1998, 12–25, *passim*. For challenging new views on Gascon and Spanish settlement, see Berman 2000, 136–42.

6 The location is given as approximately SO 084346: Williams 1990, 43; Williams 2001, 4–5.

7 Walter de Clifford's charter is given in *Mon Ang*, V, 555. See also *Episcopal Acts*, I, 276.

8 *Gerald of Wales*, IV, 206; Williams 1976a, 8–9; Williams 1997a, 15. The General Chapter had decreed in 1189 (to be repeated in 1204) that if a community failed to attract the complement of thirteen, it was to be given up altogether, or reduced to grange status: *Statuta*, I, 111, 295; *Statutes*, 155–6.

9 Williams 1976a, 59–61; Cowley 1977, 27–8; and see entry in this catalogue.

10 On the background and foundation of Vale Royal, see Thompson 1962, 183–4; Brown *et al* 1963, 248–9; Denton 1992; Robinson 1998, 192–3. Edward's choice of mother house reflected the kindnesses shown to him by the monks of Dore during his captivity at Hereford in 1265: Williams 1976a, 13–14; Williams 1997a, 16.

11 *Statuta*, III, 42–3.

12 *Mon Ang*, V, 709.

13 On Dore's lands and economy in general, see Williams 1976a, 32–50; Williams 1990, 43–4; Williams 1997a, 29–36; Williams 2001, 303.

14 Williams 1976a, 39; Williams 1997a, 30–1.

15 *Gerald of Wales*, IV, 186–96. Subsequently, both King John (1199–1216) and Henry III (1216–72) made the monks pay heavily for their holdings in Treville wood: Williams 1976a, 33; Hillaby 1988–90, 230–1. See also Donkin 1978, 132.

16 There had earlier been a hermitage on the site: Williams 1976a, 35–6; Williams 1997a, 29; Williams 2001, 201.

17 Williams 1976a, 37–9.

18 *Mon Ang*, V, 555–6 (Henry III); *Cal Chart Rolls*, 1327–41, 14–15 (Edward III).

19 Williams (1976a, 8–9) gives *c* 1186 to 1216; Hillaby (1988–90, 227–33) gives 1186 by 89 to 1215; Knowles *et al* (2001, 126, 270) refine to 1186 by 87; Smith and London (2001, 258) have his successor, Adam II, occurring in 1213.

20 *Gerald of Wales*, I, 104; IV, 200–14 (especially 203).

21 In 1199, a penance was imposed on Adam for not having attended the General Chapter meeting: *Statuta*, I, 238; *Statutes*, 433.

22 Adam's intellectual pursuits are explored in Hillaby 1988–90, 231–3; Hillaby 1997c, 109–10. For Gilbert, see *Gerald of Wales*, IV, 129–43.

23 *Gerald of Wales*, IV, 194, 206; Smith and London 2001, 258. Of additional interest, in his time (1217), it was reported to the General Chapter that at Dore (and Tintern) the office was sung in three-part and four-part voice, 'in the manner of seculars': *Statuta*, I, 472.

24 For what is known, see Williams 1976a, 10–11; Williams 1997a, 24.

25 Cowley 1977, 122–3; Williams 2001, 20.

26 *Statuta*, II, 206.

27 For his reputation, see Talbot 1959; for the library at Dore, Williams 1997a, 18–23.

28 For the period generally, see Williams 1976a, 11–14; Williams 1997a,

24–5; for some of the disputes, *Episcopal Acts*, I, 402–4. Smith and London (2001, 258–9) seem less certain Henry was in office before 1263.

29 Paul 1927, 271; RCHME 1931, 1; Williams 1976a, 3.

30 *Statuta*, III, 118.

31 *Taxatio Ecclesiastica*, 159, 172, 174, 274, 278, 283, 284. Williams (1976a, 45) gives £94 gross. See also *Mon Ang*, V, 552.

32 Williams 1976a, 49–50. Dore was said to have sixteen sacks of wool normally available for export in Pegolotti's list of about 1300: Donkin 1978, 81.

33 *Cal Close Rolls*, 1288–96, 447.

34 Williams 1976a, 40–2; Williams 1997a, 31–2.

35 In general, see Williams 1976a, 42–5; Williams 1997a, 32–3; Hillaby 1997b, 99–101.

36 There is no mention of Dore's appropriation in Verey and Brooks 1999, 331–2.

37 *Cal Pap Let*, III, 167. For the church, see Pevsner *et al* 1989, 798.

38 Talbot 1943; Williams 1976a, 15–18; Williams 1997a, 25–6; Smith and London 2001, 259.

39 *Cal Close Rolls*, 1318–23, 404. For the context, see Stalley 1987, 22; Williams 2001, 164.

40 Williams 1997a, 26, quoting *Cal Pat Rolls*, 1330–4, 513; *Cal Close Rolls*, 1333–7, 370.

41 The record of the gift, with its date, is noted in the annals of Dore: Williams 1965–8b, 88–9; Williams 1976a, 15; Williams 1997a, 22. For an interesting suggestion on how de Grandson came by the relic, see Hillaby 1997b, 97–8. The excitement and interest raised by the relic could well have attracted additional funds for ongoing or new building works.

42 The exact cause of the dispute and the reason for the election of a monk of St Mary Graces are unknown: Williams 1976a, 18–21; Williams 1997a, 26–7.

43 In 1403, Bykeleswade's abbacy ended in disgrace. He was eventually charged with a felony: *Cal Pat Rolls*, 1401–5, 438.

44. *Cal Pat Rolls*, 1405–8, 65.

45 Williams 1976a, 21–6; Williams 1997a, 27–9.

46 *Cal Pat Rolls*, 1452–61, 48.

47 Blashill 1883–5, 9, quoting BL, Harleian MS 6158, fol 151. This did not prevent Dorston going on to be abbot of Strata Florida in *c* 1509–13: Williams 2001, 69–70.

48 Williams 1965–8b, 98; Williams 1976a, 26; Williams 1997a, 29.

49 Williams 1976a, 26–7; Williams 1997a, 29; Williams 2001, 66.

50 Williams 1976a, 27–8.

51 *Valor Ecclesiasticus*, III, 33; *Mon Ang*, V, 556.

52 Williams 1976a, 30–1; Williams 1997b, 149.

53 This is the conclusion drawn in the recent informative account of the precinct: Stone 1997, 127–31.

54 Blashill 1883–5, 1885 and 1901–2.

55 To follow the sequence, see, in particular, Paul 1893, 1896, 1898b, 1904, 1927 and 1931. On his death in 1935, Paul left his notes, plans and drawings to the Society of Antiquaries of London, where they are now held.

56 RCHME 1931, 1–9.

57 RCHME 1934, facing 226, 227.

58 Bony 1949, 11 n 4.

59 Pevsner 1963, 57–62.

60 Malone 1973, 44–59; Malone 1984, with the quote at 50.

61 Fergusson further states that nothing in the west of England prior to the transepts at Dore 'can be unambiguously identified as Early Gothic': Fergusson 1984a, 94–100, with the quotes at 96, 99.

62 O'Callaghan 1995, 103.

63 Harrison and Thurlby 1997, 49–52, 61–2.

64 Shoesmith and Richardson 1997.

65 As in *Narrative Texts* (*Capitula* IX), 408. There is no consensus as to how long such temporary wooden structures would have served at Dore.

66 This is mentioned as a possibility in Malone 1984, 51; the point is also made in Fergusson 1984a, 95 n 16; and in O'Callaghan 1995, 97.

67 The arguments are not perhaps articulated as clearly as one would like, though the existence of this pre-1170s layout is implicit in Harrison and Thurlby 1997, 47–8, with additional material in Harrison 1997b, 115–20.

68 The dates which have been given are: Pevsner (1963), *c* 1175–80; Malone (1984), *c* 1175; Fergusson (1984a), *c* 1170; Harrison and Thurlby (1997), *c* 1175.

69 Paul (1904, 120–1) suggested the twelfth-century presbytery is mirrored in the later rebuilding, but see Fergusson 1984a, 95; Harrison and Thurlby 1997, 48–9.

70 Malone (1984), in part followed by Fergusson (1984a), opted for an especially complex structural history across the transepts, based on differences in rib, base and arcade profiles. Her sequence swings back and fore between the two sides of the building. This is rejected, rightly in my view, by O'Callaghan (1995), and by Harrison and Thurlby (1997), who prefer a more logical sequence from north to south, with the presbytery included. As for solid walls between transept chapels, these are found in the west of England at Buildwas, no later than the 1160s: Robinson 2002c, 9.

71 Alongside Dore, the west bays in the nave at Worcester Cathedral (*see* fig 61) represent one of the first unequivocal early Gothic schemes in the west of England. The Worcester master also employed a grouping of five high vault shafts, though unlike Dore they formed part of a large compound pier. The broad comparison extends to the way in which the capitals of the three central shafts (at both sites) merge into one another, sharing a single abacus. For some aspects of the contextual background, see Hoey 1987, 259–62. On Worcester and its sources, see Wilson 1978; Wilson 1992, 77–8.

72 Harrison (2004, 134) has recently questioned whether a stone tower was ever built over the crossing. Paul originally thought the nave was of eleven bays. Then, in his excavations of 1895, he thought he had found the west front of a nine-bay nave. In 1905, further excavations revealed the northern end and south-west angle buttress of a 'later west front', together with 'the respond of the north arcade … and some interesting fragments of the west doorway': Paul 1893, 266, 267; Paul 1896, 299; Paul 1931. In Harrison and Thurlby (1997, 53) the view is that the ten bays were always intended, whereas Harrison (1997a, 73–5) reopens the question, given advice by Richard Morris on the likely date of the west window mouldings.

73 In Shoesmith (1979–81, 262, and n 12) and in Fergusson (1984a, 97–8) it is suggested the elevation may have included a false triforium, in the manner of Pershore or St Davids. This is rejected by O'Callaghan (1995, 98–9), and even more convincingly in Harrison and Thurlby (1997, 53–6).

74 Both Fergusson (1984a, 98) and Harrison and Thurlby (1997, 56–8) accept *c* 1186; Malone (1984, 51) has *c* 1190, as does O'Callaghan (1995, 101); Pevsner (1963, 57) and Coldstream (1986, 148–9) were inclined to suggest a later date, *c* 1200.

75 At Byland, however, the ambulatory aisle was contained within the full height of the building: see Fergusson 1984a, 69–75; Harrison 1990.

76 At Cîteaux, as at Dore, the ambulatory aisle was outside the main elevation. For Cîteaux III in general, see Aubert 1947, I, 190–3 (there

given as Cîteaux IV); Hahn 1957, 238–57, *passim*; Schlink 1970, 91–2; Plouvier 1998, 130–2. On the possible Dore connection, see Fergusson 1984a, 98.

77 The dating of Morimond continues to generate considerable debate. The site was first excavated in the 1950s, and dated by Eydoux (1956 and 1958) to *c* 1155–70; but see also Eydoux 1982. Nicolai (1988 and 1990) has added to the debate, though more recently he has suggested the work on the new presbytery was begun in the last decade of the twelfth century: Nicolai 1993, 190. In a further review of the evidence, Kennedy [Gajewski] (1996, 196–209) argues for a late twelfth-century date, and before Cîteaux III.

78 Fergusson (1984a, 95), for example, opts for about 1210, whereas O'Callaghan (1995, 102) says the upper parts of the work 'must have been nearing completion by 1220 at the latest'. Hillaby (1997, 110–11) argues very forcibly that the Interdict of 1208–13 would have broken any programme of construction, and for him Adam's contributions must have been complete by 1208.

79 Harrison 1997a, 64–73.

80 RCHME 1931, 1; Williams 1976a, 3.

81 A fourteenth-century date is preferred in: Pevsner 1963, 61–2; Coldstream 1986, 152, and n 61; Alexander and Binski 1987, 233. An earlier date is given in: Sledmere 1914, 55–6; RCHME 1931, 9; Harrison and Thurlby 1997, 55–6.

82 On the basis of the stylistic evidence, construction may well have run into the abbacy of Adam II (*c* 1213–27). For an account of the building, see Harrison 1997b, 120–4. For other views, Hillaby 1988–90, 222–38; Hillaby 1997c.

83 Harrison 1997a, 75–6.

84 See Paul 1931; Stone 1997. One of Paul's unpublished sketch plans at the Society of Antiquaries indicates the extent of the remains about 55m east of the dormitory range.

85 Williams 1976a, 5; Hillaby 1997a, 44.

86 For background, see Youings 1971, 107–8, 212–16. On the sales of goods, Williams 1970–8b; Williams 1976a, 31–2; Williams 1997b, 149–50.

87 Williams 1976a, 5, 31; Williams 1997b, 150; Shoesmith and Richardson 1997, 150.

88 On which, see Blashill 1901–2; Colvin 1946–8; Shoesmith and Richardson 1997, 163–72, 177–80.

89 Gibson 1727.

90 Buckler's material can be found in BL, Add. MS 27763, fols 75–156; BL, Add. MS 36402, fols 31–35, 40–42.

91 *Archaeol J*, **34**, 1877, 492.

92 Blashill 1882; Blashill 1885, 368; Hillaby 1997c, 104–5.

93 Paul 1893, 1896 and 1931.

94 Paul 1898b.

95 Hillaby 1997d.

96 Tyers and Boswijk 1998. Some of the timbers have been found to be reused material from the early thirteenth century; others date from the Scudamore restoration of the 1630s.

GRACE DIEU ABBEY

1 *Statuta*, I, 481.

2 A certain degree of procrastination on the part of investigating Cistercian abbots played some role in the delay, though – as subsequent events were to demonstrate – political unrest fuelled by the founder's ambition was probably the key factor. For the post-1217 references to the proposed house at the General Chapter, see

Statuta, II, 11, 19, 27, 43. On the foundation in general, see *Annales Monastici*, II, 302; Janauschek 1877, 229; Bradney 1904–32, II, pt 1, 122; Williams 1961–4, 85–7; Knowles and Hadcock 1971, 113, 120 (where the mother house is given, incorrectly, as Waverley); Williams 1976a, 59–61; Cowley 1977, 27–8; Harrison 1998; Williams 2001, 13–14. The house was actually named 'de Gratia Dei', 'of the Grace of God': Williams 1976a, 59. For lists of known abbots, see Williams 1976a, 147; Smith and London 2001, 283–4.

3   *Annales Monastici*, II, 312; Williams 1976a, 59–60; Cowley 1977, 28, 212–13; Harrison 1998, 26.

4   *Cal Close Rolls*, 1234–7, 44.

5   *Statuta*, II, 155; *Annales Monastici*, II, 317; *Episcopal Acts*, II, 713–14.

6   *Cal Close Rolls*, 1237–42, 185; 1253–4, 11.

7   The General Chapter certainly ordered the abbots of Thame (Oxfordshire) and Neath to inspect the site: *Statuta*, III, 161, 200–1; Cowley 1977, 230.

8   For Grace Dieu's lands in general, see Williams 1961–4, 90–4; Williams 1976a, 69–73; Williams 1990, 44–5. The estate at Stowe was originally the gift of Henry III: *Mon Ang*, V, 685–6.

9   *Cal Chart Rolls*, 1257–1300, 304. The property had been acquired from Henry III in 1227, on payment of £120. The 1267 'lease' was virtually a sale, as royal officials later recognized: Williams 1976a, 69; Cowley 1977, 263.

10 *Taxatio Ecclesiastica*, 172, 174, 281, 284. See also O'Sullivan 1947, 34, and n 15; Williams 1961–4, 99; Cowley 1977, 82, 272, 274.

11 The advowson of the church was acquired in 1291 (*Cal Pat Rolls*, 1281–92, 451), and it may have been appropriated soon afterwards: Williams 1976a, 61; Cowley 1977, 266.

12 *Cal Pat Rolls*, 1330–4, 523; *Cal Fine Rolls*, 1337–47, 65; Williams 1976a, 69–70; Cowley 1977, 263.

13 Williams 1976a, 62. The monks provided their own bread, wine and candles.

14 On this and what follows, see Williams 1976a, 62–3; Williams 2001, 56.

15 Williams 1976a, 62, quoting BL, Royal MS 12E, XIV, fol 23, but rejecting the 1351 date in favour of 1451. Smith and London (2001, 284) retain the 1351 date.

16 *Valor Ecclesiasticus*, IV, 361; *Mon Ang*, V, 686. See also O'Sullivan 1947, 34, and n 16; Williams 1961–4, 100.

17 Williams 1976a, 63–6.

18 Owen 1950, 196.

19 Bradney 1904–32, II, pt 1, 122–6; Williams 1961–4, 89; Williams 1976a, 66.

20 Williams 1961–4, 101–2; Williams 1976a, 64–6.

21 Williams 1961–4, 89; Williams 1976a, 66.

22 Parc Grace Dieu, built in 1588, is at SO 448127: Williams 2001, 91.

23 Grace Dieu is not, for example, mentioned in a comprehensive early eighteenth-century list of churches (both standing and in ruin) in the diocese of Llandaff: Williams 1976a, 66.

24 For the identification of the close, see Owen 1950, 191. Williams (1976a, 67; 1990, 44) has suggested it may have been near Abbey Cottage, approximately SO 447134, though this has been questioned recently: Mein 2000b. There is a map showing the relative locations in Williams 2001, 206.

25 *Leland*, 50.

26 Coxe 1801, II, 289. See also Bradney 1904–32, II, pt 1, 126–7.

27 Williams 1970–8a; Williams 1976a, 68.

28 Phillips and Hamilton 2000. The authors point to the need for a more comprehensive survey if there is to be a chance of improving the results.

29 The site is to the south east of Abbey Meadow, at SO 457125. From

the published description, it is a capital, which would have sat on a slender column some 0.45m in diameter: Mein 2000a.

LLANTARNAM ABBEY

1   *Brut*, 72; *Brut (RBH)*, 169. See also Lloyd 1939, II, 600; O'Sullivan 1947, 35–6; Williams 1965–8c, 131; Knowles and Hadcock 1971, 121; Williams 1976a, 77; Cowley 1977, 26–7. The date is preferred to the 1189 given in Janauschek 1877, 190, 298.

2   *Taxatio Ecclesiastica*, 281b. The point is made in Cowley 1977, 27; Williams 2001, 14; and is accepted in Donkin 1978, 180.

3   *Brenhinedd*, 185. As for the 1179 entries in *Brut y Tywysogyon*, one reads: 'And a community was started in the monastery of Caerleon, which is called Dewma' (*Brut (RBH)*, 169); the other records: 'And a community was set up at Nant-teyrnon near Caerleon, which is called Dewma' (*Brut*, 72). As David Williams (2001, 16) explains, 'Dewma' was the historic parish in which the first site lay, whereas 'Caerleon' was the name of the lordship. See also Mahoney [1979] 11–21.

4   As in *Mon Ang*, V, 727–8. See also O'Sullivan 1947, 35–6.

5   Williams 1965–8c, 131; Williams 1976a, 77. Williams (2001, 16) points out that Llantarnam is a likely corruption of Glan-teyrnon.

6   For the General Chapter decree, see *Statuta*, III, 115. See also Williams 1965–8c, 132; Williams 1976a, 77–8; Cowley 1977, 27; Williams 2001, 16.

7   On Llantarnam's lands in general, see Williams 1965–8c; Williams 1976a, 88–91; Williams 1990, 46–8; Williams 2001, 184–5; also, Bradney 1904–32, III, pt 2, 224–7; Mahoney [1979], 22–36, 91–114. The estimate of arable acreage in 1291 is given in Cowley 1977, 274. For a political dimension to the abbey's endowments, see Gray 1998.

8   *Taxatio Ecclesiastica*, 281, 284–5. See also O'Sullivan 1947, 36, and nn 38, 39; Williams 1965–8c, 144; Cowley 1977, 272.

9   *Ancient Petitions*, 286. For more on the background to the troubles, see Bradney 1904–32, III, pt 2, 225; Williams 1976a, 83; Cowley 1977, 252; for the Welsh rebellion, Davies 1987, 388.

10 Williams, G 1976, 492–3. See also Newman 1995, 507; Gray 1996; Gray 2000, 14–15; Williams 2001, 148–9.

11 *Valor Ecclesiasticus*, IV, 365; *Mon Ang*, V, 728. See also O'Sullivan 1947, 36, and n 41; Williams 1965–8c, 144.

12 Williams 1965–8c, 140; Williams 1976a, 87.

13 Wakeman 1848, 343; O'Sullivan 1947, 35.

14 Williams 1976a, 78; Williams 1990, 46; Williams 2001, 14. Pentrebach (ST 285921) stands in the former parish of Dewma, one of the names given to the early community.

15 Williams 1965–8c, 132; Williams 1976a, 78. For the General Chapter instruction, see *Statuta*, III, 111.

16 The chief exceptions in Britain were the moves from Poulton to Dieulacres (1158–1214) and Stanlaw to Whalley (1172–1296). See Donkin 1978, 31–6, 179–80, and, more generally, Williams 1998, 181–4.

17 Since 1946, the nineteenth-century house has been home to a convent of sisters of the order of St Joseph: Mahoney [1979].

18 Mein and Lewis 1990–1, 101. In addition, from records of the Cory family (owners of the house from 1895 to the 1940s), Mein believes he may have identified the probable site of the chapter house. During the work, various worn (*ex situ*) fragments of medieval floor tiles were recovered, representing groups of *c* 1250–1300 and of the late fifteenth or early sixteenth centuries: Mein and Lewis 1990–1, 102–3; Lewis 1999, 238.

19 Williams 2001, 288.

20 The west bay of the nave arcades is shown solid, in an arrangement not unlike Neath, though there the church is after about 1280. Were the community settled here soon after the foundation, it may be reasonable to look for a building of broadly 'Bernardine' proportions. If, however, the move took place about 1272, we should perhaps keep more of an open mind on the likely form of the church.

21 Bradney 1904–32, III, pt 2, 225; Williams 1965–8c, 138; Williams 1976a, 83–4.

22 Williams, G 1976, 356, 564.

23 A transcript of the relevant parts of Morgan's will is given in Bradney 1904–32, III, pt 2, 226–7. See also Williams 1965–8c, 139–40; Williams 1976a, 85–6; Williams, G 1976, 565.

24 Williams 1965–8c, 140; Williams 2001, 89.

25 Williams 1976a, 87–8.

26 Bradney 1904–32, III, pt 2, 227; Williams, G 1997, 98.

27 Bradney 1904–32, III, pt 2, 227–8; Allgood 1907; Williams 1976a, 78; Mahoney [1979], 157–83; [Whittle] 1994, 81; Newman 2000, 336.

28 Coxe 1801, I, 115–16. The 'Magna Porta' was presumably the great inner gatehouse into the precinct. It is interesting to speculate whether the 'stone cells, converted into stables' may have been one of the vaulted undercrofts of either the east or west claustral range. An engraving of the Morgan house, by the Revd John Gardnor (1793), was published in Williams 1796, facing 255. It can also be found at: National Library of Wales, MS 18940E. I am grateful to David Williams for these details. For a further small sketch of the house c 1820, see Bradney 1904–32, III, pt 2, 238.

29 [Whittle] 1994, 81–2; Newman 2000, 336–7. For the Blewitt period in general, see Bradney 1904–32, III, pt 2, 236–8.

30 Mein and Lewis 1990–1, 101.

31 [Whittle] 1994, 80–2.

MAENAN ABBEY

1 Brown et al 1963, 337–8; Hays 1963, 57–8.

2 For the war and its aftermath, see Davies 1987, 348–79; Prestwich 1997, 170–232.

3 Throughout the course of the transfer arrangements, the evidence seems to make it clear that the king intended Maenan to be a new royal foundation, to which the older abbey of the Gwynedd princes was to be united.

4 This point is made in both Brown et al 1963, 338–9 and in Hays 1963, 62–8.

5 Littere Wallie, 202. Vale Royal was King Edward's own foundation, established in 1274: Robinson 1998, 192–3.

6 Littere Wallie, 202–3; Brown et al 1963, 338–9; Hays 1963, 63.

7 Brown et al 1963, 339.

8 The evidence for the March visit is inferential: a payment is recorded for the shipping of the king's pavilions from Aberconwy to Maenan and back on 26–7 of that month. The evidence for the October visit is clear cut: Brown et al 1963, 339, 340. The purpose of the two visits (inauguration and dedication) is unquestioned in Butler and Evans 1980, 37 n 5.

9 The details are given in Hays 1963, 64–5. Pecham's letter to the king was written on 14 June 1284.

10 Cal Chart Rolls, 1257–1300, 279; Mon Ang, V, 674–5; Hays 1963, 70–3, 186–7. For a full discussion of the charter (and its various copies), together with an analysis of the extent of the grant itself, see Butler 1981.

11 Hays (1963, 78) points out that the name Aberllechog is occasionally found, as an alternative or ancient name for Maenan.

12 Littere Wallie, 95–6; Hays 1963, 76.

13 Taxatio Ecclesiastica, 289, 292, 294; O'Sullivan 1947, 18, and n 106.

14 For the later valuation, see Register Aberconwy, 8–9. For the full comparison of values, see Hays 1963, 103–19.

15 Hays 1963, 121–4; for the 1344 debt, Cal Close Rolls, 1343–6, 338, 351; for the general situation among the Welsh Cistercians at this time, Williams 2001, 39–61, passim.

16 Cal Pat Rolls, 1408–13, 141; Hays 1963, 130–2.

17 Ancient Petitions, 235. The episode is covered in Hays 1963, 132–3; Williams 2001, 57.

18 This was in the context of a pardon for payment of a subsidy to King Henry VI. The pardon was enrolled again in 1449, 'in consideration of the poverty of the abbey and the cost of building the same': Cal Pat Rolls, 1446–52, 227, 296.

19 Hays 1963, 137–9, 156–7; Williams 2001, 71–2.

20 Valor Ecclesiasticus, IV, 441–2; Mon Ang, V, 675; O'Sullivan 1947, 18, and n 107; Hays 1963, 161–76.

21 Hays 1963, 176–8; Williams 2001, 77–8.

22 Hays 1963, 179.

23 This point was made by the late Arnold Taylor: Taylor 1950, 440; see also Brown et al 1963, 340. For Master James's career in general, see Harvey 1984, 265–8.

24 A connection between James of St George and Walter of Hereford over the work at Maenan is suggested in Brown et al 1963, 339 n 7. Moreover, in his account of Master Walter's career, Harvey (1984, 136–7) notes the possibility that he was sent to Maenan (1284) to begin the new monastery.

25 Brown et al 1963, 340.

26 An undated payment of £7 8s 10d (probably of 1284–6) is recorded for this gift: Brown et al 1963, 340.

27 Register Aberconwy, 13.

28 The owner was Dr G H B Kenrick. For his findings, see RCAHMW 1956, 1; Butler and Evans 1980, 39, and n 11. A newel stair in the same position is known at the marginally earlier church at Netley, for which see Hare 1993; Robinson 1998, 152–3.

29 Butler 1963, 35–6.

30 In presenting their conclusion, the authors raise several remaining objections, notably the lack of any apparent buttressing along the outer face of the wall, something one would expect in vaulted (?) transept chapels of this period: Butler and Evans 1980, 47–50.

31 Minor excavations to the north east of the main site by Richard White in 1982 located nothing significant belonging to the abbey: White 1987.

32 Butler and Evans 1980, 52.

33 Hays 1963, 137–9, 156–7; Williams, G 1976, 386–7. There is no real clue in the bardic verse lauding these two abbots as to which elements of the buildings may have benefited from their attention. As at Valle Crucis, it may have been improved accommodation for the abbot himself, and perhaps his guests. The cloister arcades might also have been rebuilt in the late Middle Ages, to judge from fragments of masonry built into the Wynn house at Gwydir: RCAHMW 1956, 185–9.

34 Owen 1917, 74–82; Williams 2001, 90.

35 The RCAHMW (1956, 185–9) suggests that material from Maenan was used in several phases of the construction at Gwydir. As Butler and Evans (1980, 39) point out, John Wynn had been steward of the abbey's possessions in Caernarvonshire and was presumably ideally placed to take advantage of the suppression spoils. See also Hays 1963, 174–5.

36 It weighed almost 73kg: Owen 1897, 286.

37 For the most recent account, see Butler 1987, correcting one or two points of detail in Butler 1963 and Butler and Evans 1980. See also Butler 1981, 32 nn 21–2.

38 In Butler (1963, 30–1) it is said that the site finally passed to the Wynn family of Melai before the end of the sixteenth century. The source is Lowe 1912–28, I, 278–84, 286–7. Hays (1963, 180), presumably following Elias (1898, 40), says that in the reign of Elizabeth I (1558–1603) the site was granted to Ellis Wynn, who used part of the remains to build a house.

39 In 1963 this was at the Rapallo House Museum in Llandudno, whose collections have since passed to the newer Llandudno Museum.

40 Butler 1963, 30–1; Butler and Evans 1980, 39; Butler 1987, 171.

41 Rhys 1883, II, 305–6.

42 It was published in Lowe 1912–28, I, 279.

43 Butler 1987.

MARGAM ABBEY

1 The others were Rievaulx (1132), Whitland (1140) and Boxley (1143). Fountains was received into the Cistercian order (1133–4) as a daughter house of Clairvaux; in Ireland, Mellifont was also founded (1142) directly from Clairvaux: see Gwynn and Hadcock 1970, 139–40; Knowles and Hadcock 1971, 116, 119, 124, 128; Burton 1986; Burton 1999, 98–109.

2 For Earl Robert and Glamorgan, see *Gloucester Charters*, 3; Nicholl 1936, 1–14, *passim*; RCAHMW 1991, 14–17. As half-brother to the Empress Matilda, and a protagonist of her cause, Robert played a major role in the civil war of King Stephen's reign. As for Bernard of Clairvaux, given his somewhat poor relations with Stephen, his natural allegiance may have been for the empress and her supporters. His decision to send two colonies of monks to Wales in the 1140s – first to Whitland (1140) and then to Margam – could well have emerged through links with two of Matilda's most powerful supporters in the southern March, Bishop Bernard of St Davids and Robert of Gloucester himself. The case for such contact is made in Cowley 1977, 22–3; Cowley 1998, 9–11. For a cautious overview of St Bernard's known involvement with England, see Holdsworth 1986b. For fresh insights into the possible motivation for the foundation on the part of St Bernard, see Holdsworth 2004, 74–7.

3 The fact that St Bernard sent his own brother to Bristol to receive the endowment gift emphasizes the importance of Margam's foundation to Clairvaux. For the foundation in general, see *Annales Monastici*, I, 14; *Episcopal Acts*, II, 637; Janauschek 1877, 107, 292; Birch 1897, 13–15; Lloyd 1939, II, 440, 595; Knowles and Hadcock 1971, 113, 122.

4 Robert had died on 31 October. In his charter (*Gloucester Charters*, 114) he gave to Clairvaux 'totam terram que est inter Kenefeg et Avenam a cilio montium sicut predicte aque …'. See also *Cartae Glamorgancia*, IV, 1219–20; Cowley 1977, 71.

5 *Gloucester Charters*, 117–18; Griffiths 1988, 180 n 4; Cowley 1998, 12.

6 For example, *Gloucester Charters*, 121–3 (before 1183), 126–7 (1189–99), 130–43 (c 1214–16); *Episcopal Acts*, II, 658, 689–90.

7 Cowley 1977, 49–50; Cowley 1998, 13. For the list of known abbots, see Knowles *et al* 2001, 137; Smith and London 2001, 292.

8 See, in particular, Griffiths 1988.

9 For the episode in general, see Cowley 1977, 23–4; RCAHMW 1982, 295–6; Williams 2001, 4; also Gray 1903a, 144–9; for the grants,

Cartae Glamorgancia, I, 127–8, 148–9; II, 346–7; *Episcopal Acts*, II, 646–7. Birch (1897, 8–12) thought that Pendar had been the temporary home of the Margam community itself, an error repeated by Robert Patterson in *Gloucester Charters*, 114.

10 Williams 1976a, 82.

11 The name Conan suggests the abbot was either a Welshman or a Breton, either of which would be of interest. Gerald of Wales was later to look back with nostalgic affection to the days of his rule: Knowles 1963a, 659–60; Cowley 1977, 49, 125; Knowles *et al* 2001, 137.

12 *Statuta*, I, 123, 138; *Statutes*, 194, 222–3; Cowley 1977, 119–20.

13 *Statuta*, I, 324; O'Sullivan 1947, 98; Knowles 1963a, 660.

14 *Gerald of Wales*, IV, 141–2; Cowley 1977, 120–1; Cowley 1992, 7.

15 For Gilbert's office in general, see Cowley 1977, 123–5; Cowley 1992; both include insights into Gerald's character assessment of Gilbert. Incidentally, Gerald tells us Gilbert was of north-country origin.

16 *Cartae Glamorgancia*, II, 282–7; *Episcopal Acts*, II, 684–5; Birch 1897, 170–4.

17 For the full account, see *Gerald of Wales*, IV, 129–43.

18 For King John's charters, see *Cartae Glamorgancia*, I, 46–7; Clark 1868, 43; *Mon Ang*, V, 741; O'Sullivan 1947, 29. For his visits to the abbey, *Annales Monastici*, I, 29–30; Cowley 1977, 205; Hillaby 1988–90, 230–1. For John and the Cistercians, Knowles 1963a, 366–70.

19 *Annales Monastici*, I, 32; *Episcopal Acts*, II, 688; Birch 1897, 197; Knowles *et al* 2001, 137.

20 Smith and London 2001, 292; also Williams 2001, 19–20. John de la Warre was from a well-known Bristol family.

21 For the conspiracy, see Gwynn and Hadcock 1970, 139–40; Stalley 1987, 17–20.

22 Birch 1897, 219–22; Gwynn and Hadcock 1970, 123, 134–5, 140–1; Williams 2001, 163–4.

23 Birch 1897, 345.

24 *Llandaff Acta*, xvii; Birch 1897, 266; Cowley 1977, 191–2.

25 *Cal Chart Rolls*, 1226–57, 225; Birch 1897, 249.

26 For Margam's lands in general, see Nicholl 1936, 117–19; Cowley 1967a; Cowley 1977, 75–81; Williams 1990, 48–52; Evans 1996, 37–46; Williams 2001, 176, 184.

27 Cowley 1967b; Cowley 1977, 76–7, 125–6.

28 Cowley 1977, 79–81, 181–3; Cowley 1998, 14–15.

29 This is in part due to Margam's rich collection of charters and in part due to the work of scholars over a long period.

30 Clark 1867 and 1868; Birch 1897, *passim*; Gray 1903a, 1903b and 1905.

31 Cowley 1967a and 1967b; Cowley 1977, *passim*; RCAHMW 1982, 266–97; Williams 1990, 48–52; Evans 1996, 37–46.

32 Cowley (1977, 78) suggests thirteen, based on the *Taxatio Ecclesiastica* information of 1291. The RCAHMW (182, 266–97) lists about twenty-five sites, followed by Williams 2001, 184.

33 Gray 1903a, 121–44; Cowley 1963; RCAHMW 1982, 267–74, 276–7.

34 Cowley 1977, 80–1; RCAHMW 1982, 287–9; RCAHMW 1991, 157–9. Gerald of Wales was to provide testimony as to the common occurrence of such activity by the Welsh Cistercians: *Gerald of Wales*, IV, 177.

35 Cowley 1977, 82, 88, 272. Pegolotti's near-contemporary estimate for the abbey's wool clip was 25 sacks (with perhaps 240 fleeces to a sack): Donkin 1978, 81. We might bear in mind the serious scab epidemic which was said to have had a devastating effect on the Glamorgan sheep flocks in 1281: *Chronicle*, 281; Cowley 1977, 87.

36 *Taxatio Ecclesiastica*, 220, 238, 283–4; Clark 1867, 316–17; O'Sullivan 1947, 29, and n 35; Cowley 1977, 96, 274.

37 Cowley 1977, 248, drawing on *Chronicle*, 281; *Cartae Glamorgancia*, V, 1156.

38 It was, nevertheless, an agreement the General Chapter was at first content to approve: *Statuta*, III, 254.

39 Cowley 1977, 224–5, 248–9.

40 Cowley 1977, 249, drawing on *Cartae Glamorgancia*, V, 1155–9, and correcting Birch 1897, 299–300. See also Cowley and Williams 1971, 134.

41 *Cartae Glamorgancia*, IV, 1196–9; Birch 1897, 304–6 (incorrectly dated 1326); Williams 2001, 43.

42 Cowley and Williams 1971, 134–5; Cowley 1977, 250–1.

43 *Cartae Glamorgancia*, IV, 1199. The size of the community is quoted in Knowles and Hadcock 1971, 122.

44 This is the conclusion drawn in Cowley and Williams 1971, 134–5; Cowley 1977, 238–45, *passim*, 251–2, 262; Cowley 1998, 19–20.

45 *Cal Pat Rolls*, 1350–4, 109, 426–7; *Cartae Glamorgancia*, IV, 1290–1.

46 Birch 1897, 319–23; Cowley and Williams 1971, 143–4; Williams, G 1976, 164–5; Cowley 1977, 266–7; Evans 1996, 81–3; On Aberafan, see also *Ancient Petitions*, 305–6.

47 Cowley 1977, 95, drawing on *Cartae Glamorgancia*, IV, 1351, 1361. The figures were actually 400 marks sterling (1383) and 500 marks (1385).

48 *Cal Pap Let*, VI, 282; Williams, G 1976, 231; Evans 1996, 85.

49 Birch 1897, 342–3; Evans 1996, 85–6.

50 In general, see Birch 1897, 340–8; Williams, G 1976, 258; Evans 1996, 87–8; Williams 2001, 55, 58. Some authors appear to be mistaken in believing that he became abbot of Margam as early as *c* 1422–3.

51 *Cal Pap Let*, IX, 527–8.

52 Evans 1996, 90–1. See also Birch 1897, 348–50.

53 Williams, G 1976, 400–1; Evans 1996, 91–2.

54 Evans 1996, 91–2.

55 *Valor Ecclesiasticus*, IV, 351–2; Clark 1867, 321–2; O'Sullivan 1947, 29, and n 36.

56 Williams, G 1967, 95; Williams 2001, 85. Evans (1996, 98–9) is mistaken on the date of the suppression and on the number of monks at the house.

57 Nash-Williams 1950, 146–54; RCAHMW 1976, 16, 18–68, *passim*.

58 On the architecture of Margam in general, see Robinson 1993a, together with Robinson 1998, 138–41; also David 1929; Butler 1971, *passim*; Newman 1995, 424–9; Evans 1996, 21–36.

59 *Annales Monastici*, I, 20; Birch 1897, 59. Bishop William extended his general protection to the abbey: *Llandaff Acta*, 35–6.

60 David (1929, 323) suggests the masonry is reused. In Carter's ground plan of 1803 (*see* fig 7) the book room and sacristy are separated by an internal wall, with a doorway.

61 That is, in an arrangement similar to that proposed for Clairvaux's daughter houses at Rievaulx (*c* 1135–40) and Mellifont (1150s): Stalley 1980, 300–1; Fergusson and Harrison 1994, 217, 221.

62 In general, see Orrin 1988, 346; Newman 1995, 551; Evans 1996, 34.

63 In thinking about this phase of works, it is of interest to note the appearance of a 'Peter the mason' (*Petro cementario*) as a witness to an early thirteenth-century Margam charter: *Cartae Glamorgancia*, VI, 2328. Dr Cowley, who pointed this reference out to me, believes he was a person of note, very likely involved with the building programme.

64 The reference appears in a deed of 1307, where a parcel of land is noted as 'formerly belonging to the office of the master of the works of the new church' (*magister fabrice nove ecclesie nostre*): Birch 1897, 293. Gray (1903, 144) thought this new building might have been a replacement for the sand-covered parish church at Kenfig.

65 The plan is BL, K. Top. XLVII, 44.3A.

66 Evans 1996, 30–1; Lewis 1999, 239.

67 Evans 1996, 31.

68 *Mon Ang*, V, 741; Birch 1897, 312.

69 Williams 2001, 83, 117, quoting PRO, E315/100, fol 91; E315/92, fol 97d.

70 Williams, G 1967, 95; Evans 1996, 101; derived from PRO, LR6/151. As much as 90 tons of lead was melted down into 415 'sows' in 1539: Williams 2001, 89.

71 *Leland*, 51.

72 Evans 1996, 35.

73 Moore and Moore 1974, 163–4; RCAHMW 1981, 324–5, 328.

74 Evans 1996, 33. An estate map of 1814 shows the mill building, but the present pond is not in existence: [Whittle] 2000, 105, 107.

75 For the chapel, see Gray 1903a, 128–31; Newman 1995, 429; Evans 1996, 37–8; for general context and the use of such chapels, Hall 2001.

76 For the original lease, see *Let Pap Henry VIII*, 13, I, 578, 580; on Mansel's acquisitions in general, Clark 1867, 323–4; Birch 1897, 359–64; Williams, G 1967, 99–102; Evans 1996, 99–101.

77 Williams 2001, 88.

78 For the house and its development, see Moore and Moore 1974; RCAHMW 1981, 323–31; Newman 1995, 422, 429–31; Evans 1996, 35–6; [Whittle] 2000, 102–13; for the family succession, Evans 1996, 128–40.

79 The history of the paintings, with good reproductions of both views, is covered in Moore and Moore 1974. The accuracy of the southern view is confirmed in a 1684 sketch by Thomas Dineley, also reproduced in the 1974 paper.

80 Moore and Moore 1974, 155, 158; RCAHMW 1981, 324–5; Adams 1984, 61; Hughes 1998, 9.

81 RCAHMW 1981, 326–31; Newman 1995, 429–30; Hughes 1998; [Whittle] 2000, 109–11.

82 Newman 1995, 430–1. Tragically, the house was ravaged by fire in 1977; the work of restoration continues: Evans 1996, 156–7.

83 Williams 2001, 88. Details of the incumbents from 1542 to 1954 are given in Evans 1996, 104–13.

84 Adams 1984, 60–1; Evans 1996, 24.

85 Birch 1897, 95–6; Moore and Moore 1974, 163; Lewis and Williams 1976, 34–5; Evans 1996, 24.

86 Birch 1897, 96–7; Evans 1996, 24. In 1803, John Carter sketched the central column and reconstructed the plan of the vault from a drawing supplied to him: BL, Add. MS 29940, fol 72. Dr Cowley tells me (based on information from John Adams) that the central pillar was built up again in 1811.

87 Adams 1984, 60–1; Evans 1996, 26–7.

88 BL, Add. MS 29940, fols 62–81. His sketch of the west front and his ground plan are redrawn in Birch 1897, facing 82 and 89.

89 Adams 1984, 60–5; Evans 1996, 26–7.

90 Adams 1984, 65–6; Newman 1995, 425–6; Evans 1996, 28, 117, 137–9.

91 Adams 1984, 66–7; Evans 1996, 139–40; [Whittle] 2000, 104, 111. With regards to the monastic ruins, this may have been the period when the windows in the chapels of the south transept received attention (*see* fig 99). Various nineteenth-century engravings certainly show them in a much poorer state than they are in today. Some of the work appears to have been carried out by the Gloucester architect F W Waller (1846–1933), later employed by the Office of Works in the early conservation of Tintern. In a letter of November 1900 to the Office of Works, Waller mentioned that he had recently been engaged at Margam, where 'as little as possible

was done': Robinson 1997, 43.

92 Clark 1867, 324–34.

93 Prichard 1881; Gamwell 1887, 10–13. The account by Birch (1897, 82–101) is based largely on the work of G T Clark. It includes (facing 85) a plan of the chapter house drawn by Roland Paul, dated 1896. Paul had first planned the Margam chapter house in connection with his work at Dore: Paul 1893, 268. Birch's volume also includes a redrawing of a plan of c 1870 by Prebendary Mackenzie Walcott: BL, Add. MS 31380, fol 72.

94 David 1929; Butler 1971, 382, 388; Evans 1996, 21–36. The plan in Butler's account is inaccurate, showing seven rather than six twelfth-century bays in the surviving nave.

95 Robinson 1993a.

96 Evans 1996, 24–5, 30.

97 Jones 1981.

98 Evans 1996, 158.

99 Locock 2001a and 2001b. Little new interpretation has emerged from this work, though it does confirm the sensitivity of the archaeological deposits in the presbytery area.

100 [Whittle] 2000, 102–13.

NEATH ABBEY

1 On the background to the conquest, and on de Granville, see Nicholl 1936, 14–17; RCAHMW 1991, 14–16, 156–7.

2 The original foundation charter appeared at auction in 1990 and was purchased by the Glamorgan Archives Joint Committee. It is deposited as A/N 1 at the West Glamorgan Archive Service in Swansea: Wilcox 1990; Butler 1999b. A version was published by Dugdale in *Mon Ang*, V, 259. Slightly different transcriptions appear in *Cartae Glamorgancia*, I, 74–6; Francis 1845; Birch 1902, 30–3, 309–10.

3 Savigny had sent its first colony to Tulketh in Lancashire in 1124, the monks moving to Furness in 1127: Knowles and Hadcock 1971, 119, 127. For Neath's foundation, see *Annales Monastici*, I, 13; *Annales Cambriæ*, 39; Janauschek 1877, 98; Laveille 1896–9, II, 170–6; Lloyd 1939, II, 122; O'Sullivan 1947, 27; Cowley and Williams 1971, 97; Knowles and Hadcock 1971, 122; Butler 1976a, 5; Cowley 1977, 21; for Abbot Richard, Knowles *et al* 2001, 138, 272.

4 For the merger, see Knowles 1963a, 249–52; Hill 1968, 80–115; Burton 1994, 67–9. The date of the merger has recently been challenged by Berman (2000, 142–8), though her views have not won wide acceptance.

5 Birch (1902, 30–3, 309–10) identified the area with the Crymlyn Bog.

6 This figure is given in Cowley and Williams 1971, 97. Thomas and Taylor (1938, 7) and Butler (1976a, 5) give about/nearly 3,240ha; Williams (2001, 182) suggests about 2,590ha.

7 For Neath's lands in general, see Nicholl 1936, 107–17; Cowley 1967a; Cowley and Williams 1971, 97–8; Cowley 1977, 75–7; Williams 1990, 53–6.

8 Cowley 1977, 75–6.

9 *Statuta*, I, 217, 235–6; *Statutes*, 393, 427. For Cleeve, see Knowles and Hadcock 1971, 112, 117.

10 Cowley 1977, 76, derived from *Cartae Glamorgancia*, II, 570–2; see also Lewis 1887, 99–100.

11 Cowley 1967b; Cowley 1977, 76–7, 124–6.

12 RCAHMW 1982, 251–65.

13 The site is at SS 918706: RCAHMW 1982, 262–6; Williams 1990, 54; Williams 2001, 200.

14 Located at SS 926694: RCAHMW 1982, 258–60.

15 *Mon Ang*, V, 259–60; O'Sullivan 1947, 28. One of these had, in effect, to be bought by the abbey for a substantial sum: *Cartae Glamorgancia*, II, 309; Cowley 1977, 77.

16 Morgan Gam (or ab Owain) was lord of Afan: Lewis 1887, 100–1; Williams, G 1974, 75; Cowley 1977, 83.

17 *Llandaff Acta*, 78.

18 Butler 1976a, 8; Smith and London 2001, 295. The worn effigy of an ecclesiastic holding a church, located in the dormitory undercroft, is thought to be Adam's monument: Birch 1902; Newman 1995, 468.

19 *Statuta*, III, 72; Cowley 1977, 121.

20 Lewis 1887, 101; Birch 1902, 79–80; Williams, G 1974, 80.

21 *Taxatio Ecclesiastica*, 205, 277, 279, 282; O'Sullivan 1947, 28, and n 21; Cowley 1977, 96, 274.

22 Cowley 1977, 82, 88, 272.

23 *Cartae Glamorgancia*, V, 1677–9; Lewis 1887, 101–4, 113–15; Cowley 1977, 245–6.

24 For the general economic trend over the following century, see Williams, G 1974, 82–5.

25 Birch 1902, 123–4; Cowley 1977, 247–8.

26 *Cal Pat Rolls*, 1316–17, 263; Cowley 1977, 213.

27 *Ancient Petitions*, 404–5. For Edward's charter, see *Cal Chart Rolls*, 1327–41, 357; *Cartae Glamorgancia*, IV, 1200.

28 *Cal Pap Pet*, I, 40, 62; Cowley 1977, 266. See also *Cartae Glamorgancia*, IV, 1256–7.

29 *Cartae Glamorgancia*, IV, 1500–1; Birch 1902, 136–7; Williams, G 1974, 84.

30 *Cal Pap Let*, IX, 527–8. See, in general, Birch 1897, 340–8; Williams, G 1976, 258; Williams, G 1997, 77–8; Williams 2001, 55, 58. Some authors appear to be mistaken in believing that he became abbot of Margam as early as c 1422–3.

31 *Cal Pat Rolls*, 1446–52, 34; Williams 2001, 55.

32 *Cartae Glamorgancia*, V, 1677–90; Francis 1845; Lewis 1887, 88–9.

33 In general, see Williams, G 1974, 86–7; Williams, G 1976, 395–6; Butler 1976a, 10–11; Williams 2001, 72–3.

34 *Statuta*, VI, 540; Birch 1902, 142–3.

35 Williams, G 1976, 395; Birch 1902.

36 *Valor Ecclesiasticus*, IV, 351; *Mon Ang*, V, 260; O'Sullivan 1947, 28, and n 22.

37 For the fine, see *Let Pap Henry VIII*, 13, II, 177. In general, see Williams, G 1967, 95–6; Williams, G 1997, 88–9; Williams 2001, 79–80.

38 *Leland*, 51.

39 The location of Richard de Granville's castle at Neath is given as in or near the Roman fort, approximately SS 748978: RCAHMW 1991, 156–7. Interestingly, this point was made by Lewis 1887, 94–5. The RCAHMW suggests that the castle was dismantled by the monks, and may have gone by 1207 when King John confirmed to the abbey '*locum ubi castellum Ricardi de Granavilla quondam fuit*': *Cartae Glamorgancia*, II, 309.

40 Butler 1976a, 13.

41 The gatehouse is on the A4230 (SS 937975). For the buildings in general, see Thomas and Taylor 1938; Butler 1971, 389–90, 397; Butler 1976a; Newman 1995, 463–71; Robinson 2002b.

42 Butler 1984. His two key pieces of evidence are: a section of link wall at the north-west corner of the existing cloister; and the difference in alignment between the upper and lower courses of the south transept west wall. These allow him to fix the positions of the west front and the south transept of the twelfth-century church. But note the alternate alignment of the church proposed in an addendum to the article: Butler 1984, 150–1.

43 A parallel relationship between the dormitory and the latrine can also be seen at Savigniac Furness: Hope 1900b, 267–8; Robinson 1998, 116–19.

44 *Cartae Glamorgancia*, V, 1684–5; Birch 1902, 82; Cowley 1977, 246–7.

45 Lewis 1999, 29–40, 240–5. Butler (1973) suggested the donor could have been either Hugh de Audley, earl of Gloucester (1337–47), or Elizabeth de Clare in the years 1342 to 1348. See also Knight and Moxham 1848; Birch 1902, 97–110; Jones 1996.

46 After 1468, the only known abbots of Neath are John (c 1502–7) and Leyshon Thomas (c 1510–39): Williams 1971b and 1973; Williams 2001, 296.

47 Butler 1976a, 23; RCAHMW 1981, 78–89.

48 Birch 1902, 139.

49 Williams, G 1976, 356, 564–5; Williams 2001, 108.

50 *Let Pap Henry VIII*, 17, 106; [Jones] 1920, 379; Williams, G 1967, 101; Williams, G 1974, 89.

51 Butler 1976a, 12; Williams, G 1997, 95.

52 Williams, G 1974, 89; RCAHMW 1981, 78.

53 Howard 1987, 149–50, 155, 202.

54 Thomas and Taylor (1938, 9) were of the view that the Cromwell family did not in fact occupy the site, and that the house was built by Herbert after he had purchased the property from Francis Cromwell. This is further suggested in: Williams, G 1974, 89; Butler 1976a, 12.

55 RCAHMW 1981, 78–9, 84.

56 RCAHMW 1981, 84–9; Newman 1995, 469–71. For such monastic conversions in general, see Howard 1987, 136–62.

57 [Jones] 1920, 379; Thomas and Taylor 1938, 9; Williams, G 1974, 89; RCAHMW 1981, 78.

58 Thomas and Taylor 1938, 9. Newman (1995, 456) presumes the material came from Neath Castle.

59 Butler 1976a, 12, 26–7. Thomas and Taylor (1938, 9) state that in 1731 the abbey buildings were leased for fourteen years for the purpose of copper smelting.

60 The Buck engraving is reproduced in Williams, G 1974, pl 10. For Wyndham's tour account, see Birch 1902, 117.

61 Thomas and Taylor 1938, 9; Butler 1976a, 26–7. For the ironworks, see Newman 1995, 471–2.

62 [Jones] 1920, 375, 380.

63 BL, Add. MS 29720, fol 14; Birch 1902, 121.

64 Birch 1902, 98–9; [Jones] 1920, 380. The Revd Henry Hey Knight was rector of Neath at the time.

65 Knight and Moxham 1848; Birch 1902, 92–3.

66 Sutton 1887. This account included a plan by D Godfrey Thomas.

67 Birch 1902, 89–121.

68 Thomas and Taylor 1938, 19–22.

69 There are summary accounts of the early conservation work in: *Archaeol Cambrensis*, **100**, 1948–9, 268–9; *Archaeol Cambrensis*, **101**, 1950–1, 79, 115; *Archaeol Cambrensis*, **106**, 1957, 106.

70 Butler 1976a; Robinson 2002b (now revised as Robinson 2006b).

71 RCAHMW 1981, 78–89.

72 Milne 2001a and 2001b.

STRATA FLORIDA ABBEY

1 The precise date comes from official Cistercian lists: Janauschek 1877, 151, 295. The year is confirmed by the Welsh chronicle: *Brut*, 64; *Brenhinedd*, 169. The principal secondary sources are: Lloyd 1939, II, 597–8; O'Sullivan 1947, 11–12; Pierce 1950–1, 20; Knowles

and Hadcock 1971, 126; Cowley 1977, 25; Pryce 1996, 156; Robinson and Platt 1998, 10–11; Williams 2001, 6. See also Willis-Bund 1889.

2 The site is given by Williams (1990, 56) at approximately SN 717645.

3 The Welsh name for the site is Ystrad Fleur. For Rhys, and the political background in south-west Wales, see Davies 1987, 217–27.

4 Rhys's charter of 1184 is preserved in an important *inspeximus* and confirmation of Edward III (1336): *Cal Chart Rolls*, 1327–41, 382–6. There is a version of Rhys's charter appears in *Mon Ang*, V, 632–3. There is an English translation in Williams 1889a, appendix, x–xiii.

5 For Llantarnam and Aberconwy, see entries in this catalogue; for Llanllŷr, Williams 1975, 164; Pryce 1996, 161.

6 For Strata Florida's lands in general, see Owen 1935, 10–27; Bowen 1950–1; Pierce 1950–1, 27–31; Williams 1990, 56–9; Robinson and Platt 1998, 20–1; Williams 2001, 181.

7 *Gerald of Wales*, IV, 152.

8 Williams 2001, 181. Cowley (1977, 78) calculates twenty-three granges based on the information provided in the *Taxatio Ecclesiastica* of 1291.

9 Pierce 1950–1, 28–9; Cowley 1977, 90–1.

10 *Annales Cambriæ*, 60. This was probably Rhys's own wish, and intended to foster the contact of his dynasty with the shrine of the country's patron saint: Pryce 1996, 168.

11 *Brut, passim; Brut (RBH), passim*. The two lists given by Williams (1889a, 91–2, appendix, i–ii) contain inaccuracies. See also Davies 1987, 225; Robinson and Platt 1998, 55.

12 Cowley 1977, 148–9; Davies 1987, 201, 435; Pryce 1996, 163–5. We might also recall that in 1202 Gerald of Wales sought to pawn his prized collection of books to Strata Florida. In the end, the abbey bought them for its library outright. For a disgruntled Gerald, it was little more than theft: *Gerald of Wales*, IV, 161–7; Cowley 1977, 122; Williams 2001, 20–1.

13 *Brut*, 81; *Brut (RBH)*, 183: 'that had been built with fine workmanship'.

14 For the relationship between Llewelyn and John, see Davies 1987, 239–43, 292–7; for the king's attitude to the Welsh Cistercians, Hays 1963, 42–4; also, Cowley 1977, 210–12.

15 Williams 1889a, appendix, xx; Cowley 1977, 212; Williams 2001, 17, 26.

16 The fine may have been imposed before the threat of destruction. Cowley (1977, 212) gives the scale of the fine as 700 marks. Abbot Gruffudd made peace with King Henry III with respect to the debt in 1247–8: *Cal Close Rolls*, 1247–51, 8; Williams 1889a, appendix, ii. But instalments were still being repaid as late as 1253: *Cal Close Rolls*, 1251–3, 398.

17 The deposition of the abbot by the General Chapter in 1217 was probably related to such support: *Statuta*, I, 484.

18 Williams 2001, 26.

19 *Ancient Correspondence*, 30; *Annales Cambriæ*, 82.

20 *Brut*, 110; *Brut (RBH)*, 247; Robinson and Platt 1998, 16–17.

21 *Littere Wallie*, 60–1, 64; Williams 1889a, 152, appendix, xlviii–l; Cowley 1977, 214.

22 *Chester Chronicle*, 114–17; *Annales Cambriæ*, 109.

23 *Cal Pat Rolls*, 1292–1301, 499; *Mon Ang*, V, 633; Roberts 1848b, 193; Williams 1889a, 154, appendix, xlviii. There is an interesting sidelight on this episode in the Worcester annals: *Annales Monastici*, IV, 520.

24 *Taxatio Ecclesiastica*, 274, 276–7, 289, 291, 293; O'Sullivan 1947, 14, and n 61; Cowley 1977, 274.

25 Cowley 1977, 272; Robinson and Platt 1998, 20.

26 This is the conclusion drawn in Cowley 1977, 186–7, 259–60.

27 Williams, G 1976, 159; Williams 2001, 51–2; Smith and London 2001, 312. In 1380, it was Llywelyn who obtained a significant *inspeximus* and confirmation charter from Richard II: *Cal Pat Rolls*, 1377–81, 551.

28 *Adam Usk*, 144–5. On the Glyn Dŵr phase at the abbey in general, see Williams 1889a, 161–5; O'Sullivan 1947, 109; Williams 2001, 53–4.

29 *Ancient Petitions*, 363–4; *Cal Pat Rolls*, 1401–5, 61; Williams 1889a, appendix, lv.

30 In 1407 the garrison comprised 120 men-at-arms and 360 archers; in 1415 it was 40 men-at-arms and 80 archers: Williams 1889a, appendix, lvi.

31 The information comes from a petition addressed to Henry VI in 1442–3: *Ancient Petitions*, 235; Williams 1889a, appendix, xxxix–xli. On this particular incident, and on the period at Strata Florida in general, see Hays 1963, 132–3; Williams 2001, 55–7.

32 *Cal Pat Rolls*, 1441–6, 95–6; O'Sullivan 1947, 110; Williams, G 1976, 262.

33 *Cal Pat Rolls*, 1441–6, 151–2.

34 Williams 2001, 57. For a full transcript of Henry VI's resolution, see Williams 1889a, appendix, xli–xlvii. Before 1442, John ap Rhys had moved from Maenan to become abbot of Cymer, another house which seems to have suffered at his hands: *Ancient Petitions*, 503; *Cal Pat Rolls*, 1441–6, 164.

35 *Cal Pat Rolls*, 1441–6, 95.

36 Williams, G 1976, 262, 386; Smith and Thomas 1977, 14–15.

37 Williams, G 1976, 386–7; Williams 2001, 71–2.

38 Williams 2001, 69–70. For Dore, see Williams 1976a, 23.

39 Williams 1889a, appendix, lxxvii–lxxx; Williams 2001, 70.

40 *Valor Ecclesiasticus*, IV, 396; *Mon Ang*, V, 633; Roberts 1848b, 211–12; Williams 1889a, appendix, xc.

41 Williams, G 1997, 88–9; Williams 2001, 80. For the fine, see *Let Pap Henry VIII*, 13, II, 177.

42 According to the relevant first edition 6-inch OS sheet, the site is due south of Old Abbey Farm, at SN 717645, reproduced in Williams 2001, 15, fig 12. See also Robinson and Platt 1998, 25.

43 Williams 1889a, 21; Williams 1889e, 20–1. Incidentally, Williams persisted in the belief that the monastery on the Fflur had been founded by the Lord Rhys's grandfather, Rhys ap Tewdwr (d 1093).

44 *Mon Ang*, V, 632; Williams 1889a, appendix, x. On the buildings at Strata Florida in general, see Radford 1949a; Smith and Thomas 1977, 19–29; Robinson 1998, 176–9; Robinson and Platt 1998, 25–33, 43–56. The views are all modified in this volume.

45 For Abbey Farmhouse, see Smith 1998, 270.

46 Davies and Waters 1992.

47 For the 1201 reference, see *Brut*, 81. On chronologies see, for example, Radford 1949a; Smith and Thomas 1977, 19. In part, this conclusion is drawn from comparisons with the known chronology of St Davids Cathedral, on which see, most recently, Stalley 2002.

48 Robinson and Platt 1998, 30.

49 *Mon Ang*, V, 633; *Cal Pat Rolls*, 1292–1301, 499.

50 *Chester Chronicle*, 116–17. On the vault, see Robinson and Platt 1998, 50.

51 Reported in Williams 1889a, 153–4.

52 Williams 1889a, 182–229, *passim*; Williams 1889b, 24–48, *passim*; Williams 1890c, *passim*.

53 Robinson and Platt 1998, 31, 48–9, 54–5.

54 For the nineteenth-century tile discoveries, see in particular Williams 1889a, 225–7, and plates; Williams 1891. In his review of the Strata Florida tiles, J M Lewis assigns most of the material to his groups 51 and 61: Lewis 1999, 87–90, 98–101, 253–9.

55 *Adam Usk*, 144–5; *Cal Pat Rolls*, 1441–6, 95.

56 Williams, G 1976, 262; Smith and Thomas 1977, 14.

57 Williams, G 1976, 386; Smith and Thomas 1977, 14–15; Robinson and Platt 1998, 33.

58 Robinson and Platt 1998, 50–1, 52–3.

59 *Leland*, 118.

60 On this, and what follows, see Williams 1889a, 177–81, appendix, ci–cv; Robinson and Platt 1998, 23.

61 Williams 2001, 89.

62 Smith 1998, 270.

63 Clearance was carried out over the three days before the visit, so when the members arrived 'the pavement and walls were bare and ready for inspection': Williams 1889a, 182–3; note in *Archaeol Cambrensis*, **2**, 1847, 361; Roberts 1848a, 130–1.

64 See, in particular, Williams 1889a and 1890c. On the background to the work and the course of the excavations, see Williams 1992, 73–8. There was some early criticism by antiquaries of the methods employed in the excavations. Many of Williams's original notes, together with plans and other documentation, can be found as: National Library of Wales, Birmingham Corporation Waterworks, Box 3.

65 Radford 1935.

66 Radford 1949a. Reprinted in much the same form through to the 1980s. There are notes on some of the later clearance work in *Archaeol Cambrensis*, **101**, 1950–1, 80, 116; *Archaeol Cambrensis*, **106**, 1957, 107.

67 *Archaeol Wales* 1966, no. 46. It was suggested the nave was intended to run further west, or could this have been a galilee porch? This note is the only known reference to the find.

68 The principal contribution to the forthcoming site review is an analysis of the loose stonework by Stuart Harrison, work that adds significantly to our understanding of the abbey church and monastic ranges. Apart from my own contribution, other sections of the review will look at the tiles (J M Lewis), the wall paintings (David Park) and the grave markers (Mark Redknap).

69 Robinson and Platt 1998.

70 I am grateful to Professor Austin (University of Wales Lampeter) for sharing his ideas with me. A conference on the theme was held at Lampeter in September 2003.

STRATA MARCELLA ABBEY

1 *Mon Ang*, V, 636 note a; Janauschek 1877, 159–60; O'Sullivan 1947, 14–15; Knowles and Hadcock 1971, 114, 126; Williams 1976c, 155–7; Thomas 1997. The house was known to the Welsh as Ystrad Marchell.

2 Donkin 1978, 180. There appears to be a degree of confusion over this point, stemming in part from the thirteenth-century use of an alternative name for the house, 'Pool Abbey'. As Williams (1976c, 156–7) points out, various alternatives suggest themselves. One of the more intriguing, derived from an 1172 reference given by Janauschek (1877, 159–60), and concerning '*Pola, filia Stratae-Marcelli*', raises the possibility that Pool was a short-lived daughter house of Strata Marcella.

3 For Owain, see Davies 1987, 233; for comments by Gerald of Wales, Thorpe 1978, 202–3; on Owain's death, *Register Aberconwy*, 7; Hays 1963, 147; Williams 1976c, 161–2.

4 For the abbey's lands in general, see Williams 1976c, 182–91; Williams 1990, 59–61; Thomas 1997, *passim*, especially 112–28; Williams 2001, 179; also Jones 1871–3.

5 For the Merioneth grants in context, see Pryce 2001, 273–4, 279–81.

6 For Valle Crucis, see Knowles and Hadcock 1971, 114, 127; for Llanllugan, Williams 1975, 159; Williams 2001, 7–8.

7 *Littere Wallie*, 174; Hays 1963, 76; Williams 1976c, 164.

8 *Taxatio Ecclesiastica*, 289; O'Sullivan 1947, 16.

9 For this episode in general, see O'Sullivan 1947, 89–91; Williams 1976c, 166–9; Williams 2001, 43–4.

10 *Ancient Petitions*, 489–90. Williams (1976c, 160) wonders if the figure of sixty may have included lay brothers.

11 *Cal Close Rolls*, 1327–30, 410.

12 *Cal Close Rolls*, 1327–30, 566–7; *Cal Close Rolls*, 1330–3, 150 (from which the quote is taken).

13 *Ancient Petitions*, 411–12.

14 On the abbots of this period, see Smith and London 2001, 313.

15 The bequest was made at the time of the bishop's death: Williams 1976c, 169.

16 Jones 1873, 354–5; Jones [*et al*] 1877, 398–401; Williams 1976c, 169–70.

17 On Dafydd's career in general, see Williams, G 1976, 386–7; Williams 1976c, 170–1; Williams 2001, 71–2. His abbacy at Strata Marcella probably ran from 1485 to 1490.

18 For William Egwad, see Williams 1976c, 171; for Tudur Aled, Williams, G 1976, 382.

19 The claim that the abbey was in ruin appears in the indulgence. For a transcript of this early printed document, see Owen 1919, 7–13. See also Williams 2001, 68–9. It is illustrated in Lewis and Williams 1976, 29.

20 *Valor Ecclesiasticus*, IV, 449–50; *Mon Ang*, V, 638; O'Sullivan 1947, 16, and n 89.

21 The abbot seems to have ridden to London to surrender his monastery: Williams 2001, 86.

22 John Leland placed it 2 miles (2.9km) from Welshpool, 'hard on the farthar banke of Severne': *Leland*, 55.

23 For the report on the excavations, see [Jones] and Williams 1891; Williams 1892. In all, the investigations extended over forty-eight working days. Stephen Williams was certainly not present the whole of the time, with daily guidance in the hands of Morris Jones. For more on the background to the excavations, and on the discoveries made, see Jones and Williams 1890; Williams 1992, 78–84; also, Williams 1976c, 158–9.

24 See, for example, the fragment of an early (*c* 1170–90) trumpet-scalloped capital: [Jones] and Williams 1891, pl 12, no. 7.

25 The source of the red sandstone is thought to be the Grinshill of Shelvock quarries near Shrewsbury: [Jones] and Williams 1891, 166, 172.

26 [Jones] and Williams 1891, 167, 168, pl 4.

27 [Jones] and Williams 1891, 168–9.

28 [Jones] and Williams 1891, 169, 171, 188–95.

29 [Jones] and Williams 1891, 155, 169, pl 6, no. 1. For Williams, the form and scale of the mouldings was to be compared to the tower piers at Chester Cathedral. The material is mentioned in Haslam 1979, 37, 198.

30 Lewis 1999, 88–9, 98–9, 259. Lewis suggests that the deterioration of the stamp used in one of the tile forms indicates the pavements were laid later than those with the same pattern at Strata Florida and Valle Crucis.

31 [Jones] and Williams 1891, 167–8, pl 4. Williams did, however, allow for the possibility that the doorway could have served as the entrance to the lay brothers' choir.

32 It is suggested (without giving the evidence) that this was done 'probably at a late period, and after it had been damaged by fire':

[Jones] and Williams 1891, 158, 172.

33 The survey was carried out by Geophysical Surveys of Bradford, Report 90/75; Arnold 1992, 94.

34 Arnold 1992, 88–9.

35 [Jones] and Williams 1891, 164.

36 [Jones] and Williams 1891, 173, 181, pl 8.

37 Williams 1992, 83. He places it at SJ 24651045.

38 Owen 1919, 7.

39 In a letter to Cromwell, October 1536, Grey stated he had 'bargained and clearly bought of the late abbot and convent of Stratmarcell, the monastery there': Owen 1919, 20–1.

40 Jones [*et al*] 1877, 401–2; Williams 1976c, 176; Williams 2001, 83.

41 For Purcell's role in the abbey's affairs generally, see Williams 1976c, 176–9.

42 For a transcript of the inquiry proceedings, see Owen 1919, 29–31.

43 If this is a reference to a building from the abbey precinct itself, it clearly indicates that timber-framed structures formed part of the complex.

44 The episode is also cited in Williams 2001, 90; Williams, G 1997, 96.

45 See Williams 1992, 82–3; Williams 2001, 90, 92; both reproduce a 1780 plan of Abbey Farm. [Jones] and Williams (1891, 161) reported that the farm was occupied into the early nineteenth century. For early nineteenth-century observations on the layout and buildings of the farm, see Jones [*et al*] 1877, 402–4.

46 Arnold 1992, 90–2.

47 [Jones] and Williams 1891, *passim*.

48 [Jones] and Williams 1891, 162–3, 186–7, pl 15; Haslam 1979, 83, 198.

49 Haslam 1979, 127–8, 198. There is certainly a family resemblance between the sculpture seen in the capitals and material from Strata Marcella and Valle Crucis. The doorway in question is well illustrated by an engraving in *Archaeol Cambrensis*, 4th ser, **11**, 1880, facing 145.

50 Williams 1976c, 159; Haslam 1979, 105–6, 207–8.

Tintern Abbey

1 Gilpin 1782, 31–2. See also the commentaries on Gilpin in Andrews 1989, 86–94, *passim*; Woof and Hebron 1998, 137–40.

2 *Mon Ang*, V, 266–7; Coxe 1801, II, 352. For general accounts of Tintern, see Williams 1976a, 94–146; Robinson 2002a, 11–25.

3 William Wordsworth first visited Tintern in 1793. The finishing touches of his *Lines Written a Few Miles Above Tintern Abbey* were committed to memory on the homeward journey following his second Wye tour in 1798: Robinson 2002a, 23. For a recent commentary on the poem, and a full transcript, see Woof and Hebron 1998, 43–65.

4 The precise date is believed to mark the arrival of the colonizing community, as given in Janauschek 1877, 10, 19. The year is confirmed in *Annales Cambriæ*, 39. The principal secondary sources are: O'Sullivan 1947, 38; Knowles and Hadcock 1971, 114, 127; Williams 1976a, 94; Cowley 1977, 21. The terms of the original foundation charter can be determined only from later *inspeximus* charters: see, in particular, *Mon Ang*, V, 267–9 (a charter of William Marshal the younger, 1222); *Cal Chart Rolls*, 1300–26, 88–9, 96–100 (an *inspeximus* and confirmation of a sequence of charters by Edward I, March 1307); *Cal Chart Rolls*, 1300–26, 103–6 (a further *inspeximus* and confirmation of Edward I, June 1307). For Walter fitz Richard, see Wood 1908, 349–51; Wood 1910, 12.

5 L'Aumône lay in the diocese of Blois and is today in Loir-et-Cher. It

was founded in 1121 as a first-generation daughter of Cîteaux, and was widely known as 'Petit-Cîteaux': Cuissard 1881–4; Peugniez 2001, 108.

6 William Giffard, bishop of Winchester (1107–29), had brought the Cistercians to Waverley in 1128. It, too, had been settled from L'Aumône: *Annales Monastici*, II, 221; Janauschek 1877, 16–17, 286; Knowles 1963a, 230; Knowles and Hadcock 1971, 127–8. Walter de Clare's knowledge of the French abbey probably came through the bishop, his kinsman: Ward 1981, 440.

7 For Kingswood (founded by William of Berkeley), see Knowles and Hadcock 1971, 121; Robinson 1998, 130; for Tintern Parva (founded by William Marshal), *Statutes*, 435; Gwynn and Hadcock 1970, 142–3; Stalley 1987, 249.

8 Williams 1976a, 134; Cowley 1977, 71. For the initial grant, see *Cal Chart Rolls*, 1300–26, 88.

9 For Tintern's lands and its economy in general, see Williams 1965–8a; Williams 1976a, 113–40; Williams 1990, 61–4; Williams 2001, 185–6.

10 This can be picked up through confirmation charters: see *Cal Chart Rolls*, 1300–26, 96–8. For Woolaston (where it appears the monks again took on responsibility for existing serfs and tenants), see *VCH* 1972, 102–9, *passim*; Williams 1976a, 122–8.

11 *Cal Chart Rolls*, 1300–26, 103; *Mon Ang*, V, 267–9.

12 For example, in a charter granted by Walter Marshal, earl of Pembroke (1241–5), the monks were allowed to dyke areas of their grange at Moor on the Monmouthshire levels at will: *Cal Chart Rolls*, 1300–26, 104. As late as 1282, the abbey was fined the heavy sum of £112 for felling 81ha of royal forest at Woolaston without licence: *VCH* 1972, 103, 107.

13 Williams 1976a, 103; Williams 2001, 19. Knowles *et al* (2001, 145) appear less certain of his dates.

14 *Annales Monastici*, II, 245; Williams 1976a, 103.

15 Knowles *et al* 2001, 136, 145.

16 Williams 1976a, 103–4; Robinson 2002a, 12. Marshal was also responsible for the foundation of Graiguenamanagh in County Kilkenny a few years later. It was colonized by Stanley in Wiltshire, a further Cistercian house of which he was patron: Gwynn and Hadcock 1970, 133–4; Stalley 1987, 245.

17 *Cal Chart Rolls*, 1300–26, 104; Robinson 2002a, 12.

18 For these burials, see *Annales Cambriæ*, 86; Wood 1910, 16–17; Williams 1976a, 101–2; Harrison 2000, 95. A note of 1531, compiled by the herald William Fellow, records that Gilbert 'Strongbow', earl of Pembroke (d 1148), was buried in the chapter house, and Eve McMurrough, wife of Richard 'Strongbow' (d 1176), was buried in the abbey church: Siddons 1996, 38. It has also been claimed that the founder was buried at Tintern: Wood 1902–4; Bradney 1904–32, II, pt 2, 259. There is evidence of at least two military effigies at the site, of approximately the correct date for the two Marshal brothers (*see* fig 183), but the fragments are now very badly mutilated. For more on the sepulchral monuments known from Tintern, see Rodger 1911, *passim*; Williams 1976a, 101–2.

19 *Annales Monastici*, II, 336, 345; Williams 1976a, 104–5; Smith and London 2001, 277, 316, 321.

20 On the period, see Williams 1976a, 105–6; Smith and London 2001, 316. The first appearance of Abbot John is as a witness to a charter of 1267: *Cal Chart Rolls*, 1257–1300, 304. Of particular interest, we know that his duties for the king and for the Cistercian order would have given him opportunities to view the works at Westminster Abbey (1270), and also the new programmes in hand at both Netley (1273) and Waverley (1273, 1276): *Cal Close Rolls*, 1268–72, 285; Williams 1976a, 105–6. John appears to have resigned his office in

1277, probably on grounds of ill health: *Statuta*, III, 169, 171.

21 *Taxatio Ecclesiastica*, 161, 196, 281–2, 284; O'Sullivan 1947, 39, and n 77; Williams 1965–8a, 15–16; Cowley 1977, 274.

22 Williams 1976a, 120; Cowley 1977, 88.

23 For the Bigod period of lordship, see Wood 1910, 18–26; for his work at Chepstow, Turner 2002, 14–17.

24 The charter survives only as an *inspeximus* of 1307: *Cal Chart Rolls*, 1300–26, 99. The date of the original can be pushed back to at least 1290 on the basis of the witness list, and perhaps to before 1279, if the grant was made before the Statute of Mortmain came into effect. In 1307, the Tintern monks were allowed to retain the church, which had been 'wrongfully appropriated': *Cal Pat Rolls*, 1301–7, 530–1; Williams 1976a, 138; Cowley 1977, 266.

25 Bigod was much encumbered with debt throughout his career. On this and his relations with Edward I, see Wood 1910, 23–4; Prestwich 1997, 243, 413–14, 537–8. For the most recent views on the 1302 agreement between the earl and the king, see Morris 2003.

26 *Cal Chart Rolls*, 1300–26, 31; *Cal Pat Rolls*, 1301–7, 30; Williams 1976a, 137–8; Cowley 1977, 266.

27 *Cal Chart Rolls*, 1300–26, 31, 99–100; *VCH* 1972, 107–8.

28 *Mon Ang*, V, 266; Harvey 1969, 60, 61.

29 *Valor Ecclesiasticus*, IV, 370–1; Williams 1965–8a, 19.

30 Williams 1976a, 106; Smith and London 2001, 316.

31 Cowley 1977, 223; Williams 2001, 40–1.

32 Williams 1976a, 106; Harrison 2000, 89; Smith and London 2001, 316–17.

33 Cowley 1977, 255–6.

34 *Cal Chart Rolls*, 1300–26, 88–9, 96–100, 103–6; Harrison 2000, 89–90.

35 Williams 1976a, 107–8; Smith and London 2001, 317 (where it is suggested the John of 1349–75 may have been more than one man).

36 The church had earlier been held by the Italian abbey of Santa Maria de Gloria, in the diocese of Anagni. The grant of 1326–7 was initially for a period of five years: Churchill 1933, I, 54 n 3.

37 Williams 1976a, 139, quoting *Cal Close Rolls*, 1330–3, 370–1; *Cal Close Rolls*, 1333–7, 304–5. See also *Ancient Petitions*, 257–8.

38 *Cal Close Rolls*, 1339–41, 492. Building works still underway at the monastery might have been one of the reasons for mortgaging property, or even the future wool clip, in a bid to raise hard cash. But we must be careful of reading too much into this single record, since Tintern was one of numerous Cistercian houses recording debts owed to Italian merchants around this time: Cowley 1977, 231–2; Donkin 1978, 146–54, 195–8.

39 For a general discussion of the available evidence, see Cowley 1977, 253–9.

40 Williams 1976a, 128–32; Cowley 1977, 256–7. For summaries of the Merthyrgeryn bailiff's accounts for 1387–8 and 1388–9, see Williams 1965–8a, 20–4 (from National Library of Wales, Badminton MS 1571).

41 Williams 1976a, 96; Cowley 1977, 51, quoting BL, Add. MS 7488.

42 *Ancient Petitions*, 364–5 (also 239–43).

43 *Cal Pat Rolls*, 1405–8, 378; Williams 1976a, 108; Williams 2001, 54.

44 *Cal Pap Let*, VI, 452.

45 For the background, see Cowley 1977, 257–8; Williams 2001, 218; Robinson 2002a, 16–17.

46 For Herbert's period of lordship, see Wood 1910, 32–3. There are at least two versions of the earl's will. In the later version (known for longer), he gave 'a *c* tonne of [?] … to make the cloistre of Tyntarne', leading some authorities to suggest it was 100 tons of stone, wood, or lead: Wood 1907, 10. The earlier will states quite specifically: 'I bequeath all that salt I have at Chepstow to ye building of my tomb

... and the remainder of the same to build new cloisters'. The salt was presumably to be sold for the purposes: Wood 1912, 15 n 9; Williams, G 1976, 564.

47 Siddons 1996, 38. The tomb was illustrated in the seventeenth-century family chronicle, the *Herbertorum Prosapia*: Cardiff Central Library, MS 5.7; also, Bradney 1904–32, II, pt 2, 259.

48 According to William Fellow, the earl of Huntingdon's tomb was on the north side of the choir, his brother George lying in the same tomb. Sir Walter Herbert was said to lie in the chapel of St John the Baptist on the north side of the church: Siddons 1996, 38. However, the illustration of the earl of Huntingdon's tomb in the family chronicle shows Mary Woodville with her husband.

49 In general, see Williams 1976a, 99–100; Williams 2001, 141–3.

50 Williams 1976a, 100.

51 Robinson 2002a, 17–18.

52 Williams 1976b, 110–11. The earls in question were Charles Somerset (1514–26) and his son Henry Somerset (d 1549).

53 *Valor Ecclesiasticus*, IV, 370–1; *Mon Ang*, V, 272–3; Williams 1965–8a, 17–20.

54 *Let Pap Henry VIII*, 10, 160; Williams 1976a, 111; Williams, G 1997, 79.

55 Williams 1976a, 111–12.

56 A detailed investigation of the watercourses, using both topographical survey and historical sources, is much needed. For some account, not wholly reliable, see Wood 1912, 16–18; also Courtney 1989, *passim*.

57 The principal single source for the Tintern buildings is now Robinson 2002a, 27–64, with additional or complementary material in Brakspear 1919; Craster 1956; Courtney 1989; Newman 2000, 536–57; Robinson 2004.

58 Robinson 1996a and 1997; Robinson 2002a, 27–9.

59 [Brakspear] 1904; Brakspear 1929; Robinson 1996a.

60 On which, see in general, Fergusson 1984a, 23–9; Coppack 1998, 32–9.

61 Robinson 2002a, 29–30.

62 For the grants, see *Cal Chart Rolls*, 1300–26, 103; *Mon Ang*, V, 267–9. For the work, Robinson 2002a, 30–1, 50–60; Robinson 2004, 105–8.

63 Harrison 1997c, 69–71; Robinson 2002a, 31, 48–9.

64 Robinson 2002a, 31–2, 60–1.

65 Two independent sources provide us with the date for the beginning of the new church programme: Harrison *et al* 1998, 182–5; Robinson 2002a, 32–5.

66 Harvey 1969, 60, 61; Harrison 2000, 93.

67 A sixteenth-century transcript of a lost Tintern chronicle records for 1301: 'The new churche of Tintern abbay, 32 yeres in building, was finished by Roger Bygod, and at his request was halowed the.5. kalends of August': Harrison *et al* 1998, 183; Harrison 2000, 95. The source is Thomas Talbot's transcript, *Ex cronica de Tinterne*: BL, Cotton Vesp. MS D XVII, fol 61.

68 Bigod was at Modesgate, Tintern's property across the Wye on 4 August, where he put his seal to a charter in favour of the community: *Cal Chart Rolls*, 1300–26, 106.

69 Harrison *et al* 1998; Robinson 2002a, 44.

70 Lewis 1996; Lewis 1999, 260–1.

71 National Library of Wales, Badminton MS 1645, m 9; 1657, m 12d; Williams 2001, 99.

72 Robinson 2002a, 35–7.

73 Harvey 1969, 58–61; Harrison 2000, 91–3.

74 *Cal Pap Let*, XVI, 3–4.

75 Siddons 1996, 38.

76 Robinson 2002a, 19. In a footnote to his account of 'The Situation'

of the abbey, Charles Heath noted, 'Before the late improvements took place ... a Wall, of considerable height and strength, surrounded the Monastery, apparently erected to protect it from depredations of river floods. A large portion of this defence has been erased': Heath 1793, and later editions, unpaginated.

77 Williams 1976a, 100.

78 Courtney 1989.

79 Williams 1976a, 111–12; Courtney and Gray 1991, 145; Robinson 2002a, 18.

80 *Let Pap Henry VIII*, 12, I, 350–1.

81 The letters range from June to December: *Let Pap Henry VIII*, 12, II, 52–3, 189, 294, 358, 420. Williams (2001, 92) suggests he sometimes resided there, and so he must have occupied some suite of accommodation suitable to his rank, possibly a conversion of the abbot's hall or of some other convenient domestic block.

82 Williams 1976a, 112; Courtney and Gray 1991, 145.

83 Courtney and Gray 1991, 149, 155. The estates were now in the hands of William Somerset, third earl of Worcester (1549–89).

84 Courtney and Gray 1991, 155–6; Williams 2001, 92.

85 Courtney 1989.

86 For the development of the iron industry, see Bradney 1904–32, II, pt 2, 260–1; Courtney and Gray 1991, 150–3; Coates 1992; Newman 2000, 557–8.

87 For the Buck view, see Woof and Hebron 1998, 132.

88 Heath 1793, and later editions, unpaginated, under the section headed 'Stone Effigy'.

89 Andrews 1989, 94–105; Harrison *et al* 1998, 188–9; Woof and Hebron 1998, 103–80; Robinson 2002a, 21–3.

90 Heath 1793, and later editions, unpaginated. One of the duke's workmen was William Knowles of Chepstow, whose son provided the information published by Heath. If the date 1756 is correct, then one must assume it was the fourth duke who initiated the actions. His son, Henry Somerset (1744–1803), the fifth duke, was just twelve at the time. The moving spirit behind the work may have been Thomas Wright (d 1786), employed as architect and garden designer at Badminton from *c* 1746. I am grateful to Mrs M E Richards, archivist at Badminton (1995), for advice on this point.

91 Gilpin 1782; Woof and Hebron 1998, 137–40.

92 Gilpin 1782, 34–5.

93 Heath 1793, and later editions.

94 For some account of visitors around this time, see Taylor 1869, 45–56. There is an excellent contextual overview in Woof and Hebron 1998.

95 Robinson 2002a, 23–5.

96 See, for example, the account in Coxe 1801, II, 351–2.

97 Heath 1793, and editions through to 1828.

98 Thomas 1839, 22.

99 BL, Add. MS 29938, fols 131v–153.

100 The forty-six plates of drawings produced by the Lichfield architect and antiquary Joseph Potter remain an invaluable source for the architecture of Tintern: Potter 1847, Tintern pls i–xlvi. Tintern was also one of the sites measured in painstaking detail by Edmund Sharpe, engraved and published in his *Architectural Parallels*: Sharpe 1848.

101 Photographs of the screen in place are reproduced, for example, in Woof and Hebron 1998, 130; Robinson 2002a, 25.

102 Harrison *et al* 1998, 188–96.

103 Blashill 1881–2. See also Blashill 1878 and 1886.

104 F S Waller and F W Waller (father and son) served as resident architects to the dean and chapter of Gloucester Cathedral, based at College Green: Robinson 1997, 43–7. See also the notes in *Archaeol*

Cambrensis, 6th ser, **10**, 1910, 485; *Archaeol Cambrensis*, 6th ser, **13**, 1913, 451.

105 Baylis 1902–4.

106 [Brakspear] 1904. The clearance of the infirmary hall seems to have been conducted under Brakspear's supervision: Wood 1912, 19–28; PRO, Work 14/76, 14/77.

107 For the preparation of the plan, see Robinson 1996a.

108 Harvey 1922 and 1924; Robinson 1997, 47–8.

109 Courtney 1989; Robinson 1997, 48–50.

110 Blockley 1997b; Schlee 2000a and 2000b.

111 Brakspear and Evans 1910.

112 Brakspear 1919; with further editions in 1919, 1921 and 1929.

113 Craster 1956.

114 The first edition of the Cadw guidebook was published in 1986, replaced by Robinson 1995a, and now by Robinson 2002a.

VALLE CRUCIS ABBEY

1 For the territorial and political background (with a map), see Davies 1987, 227–36.

2 The foundation charter is contained within an *inspeximus* of Edward I, dated 25 April 1295: *Cal Chart Rolls*, 1257–1300, 457; *Mon Ang*, V, 637 (where it appears under the deeds of Strata Marcella); Jones 1866, 15–16; Price 1952, 243–4.

3 *Brut (RBH)*, 183; *Brut*, 81: 'In that year there was built a monastery in Iâl, which is called Llynegwestl'.

4 Janauschek 1877, 205. The principal secondary sources are Lloyd 1939, II, 602; Price 1952, 13–22, 41–2; Knowles and Hadcock 1971, 114, 127.

5 Price 1952, 8–9; Evans 1995, 50–2 (text by J K Knight).

6 As, for example, in *Brut y Tywysogyon*. Williams (*Ab Ithel*) 1846, 19; Lloyd 1939, II, 602; Williams 2001, 15.

7 As indicated in later grants: Price 1952, 260; Williams 2001, 10.

8 As indicated in *Cal Chart Rolls*, 1257–1300, 457–9; Jones 1866, 16–19; Price 1952, 33, 244–7.

9 Williams (*Ab Ithel*) 1846, 23; Price 1952, 15, 17; Radford 1953, 5; Williams 2001, 154. The decorated, but mutilated, fragment of a slab thought to represent his tomb was recovered from the choir, in front of the high altar: Gresham 1968, 65–7.

10 Jones 1866, 19–20; Price 1952, 247. He, too, was buried at Valle Crucis: *Brut*, 115; Price 1952, 17–18.

11 For the lands of Valle Crucis in general, see Price 1952, 57–82; Williams 1990, 64–6; Pratt 1997, *passim*; Williams 2001, 179, 313.

12 For the locations, see maps in Evans 1995, 6–7; Pratt 1997, 4.

13 O'Sullivan 1947, 55–7; Price 1952, 66–82; Pratt 1997, 12–13; Williams 2001, 274.

14 *Statuta*, I, 281; Price 1952, 42. On the General Chapter and discipline in England and Wales in general at this time, see Knowles 1963a, 654–61.

15 *Statuta*, II, 137.

16 O'Sullivan 1947, 67–8; Cowley 1977, 212; Williams 2001, 30.

17 Williams 2001, 32. For Madog, see Smith and London 2001, 318.

18 On the wars in general, see Davies 1987, 333–54; Prestwich 1997, 170–232; for the impact on the Cistercians, Williams 2001, 35–41.

19 Williams 2001, 39–40.

20 *Littere Wallie*, 80–1, 90–1; Hays 1963, 76; Cowley 1977, 214. Receipts exist for a total sum of £1,700 paid out by the Crown at this time. The Valle Crucis figure stands out as particularly large: Williams, G 1976, 43–4.

21 Williams 2001, 40.

22 *Taxatio Ecclesiastica*, 289; Williams (*Ab Ithel*) 1846, 24–5; O'Sullivan 1947, 18, and n 117.

23 Madog ap Gruffudd's superb monument, 'perhaps the finest in North Wales', was found in front of the high altar in 1956: Gresham 1968, 137–40.

24 Williams, G 1976, 24–5; Davies 1987, 200–1; Williams 2001, 135.

25 Cowley 1977, 128–9; Williams 2001, 159–60.

26 On Adam, see Smith and London 2001, 318. The building work is covered below.

27 We have no record of the direct impact of the Black Death on Valle Crucis, but in general, see Williams 2001, 50–2; on the lease of property, Pratt 1997, 7–12.

28 In general, see Williams, G 1976, 212–45; Williams 2001, 52–5.

29 He was appointed to the abbacy of Valle Crucis in 1409 and elevated to the see the following year.

30 Price 1952, 45–6; Williams, G 1976, 231. For the 1419 extension, see *Cal Pap Let*, VII, 117, 177.

31 The dates are as given in Williams 2001, 298. Williams, G (1976, 262) suggests Siôn Rhisiart (John ap Richard) may have flourished 1450–80. In general, Price 1952, 46–8; Pratt 1997, 13–17.

32 Williams, G 1976, 263. The 'heaven of earth' quote is from a work of Gutun Owen. See also Williams 2001, 58–9.

33 Price 1952, 270.

34 [Jones] 1846, 26.

35 Price 1952, 277–8. There is another translation of this work in [Jones] 1846, 27.

36 Williams, G 1976, 387.

37 [Jones] 1846, 27–8.

38 Williams 2001, 66.

39 On Llwyd's death in 1527, a James ab Ieuan may have ruled for a short period: Pratt 1997, 29.

40 In general, see O'Sullivan 1947, 117, 119–20; Price 1952, 48–9; Williams, G 1976, 390–1, 403; Pratt 1997, 28–33; Williams 2001, 67–8.

41 Pratt 1997, 30.

42 Price 1952, 262–3 (though not 1528 as given there); Pratt 1997, 31.

43 Vaughan and Becansaw were at Valle Crucis in August 1535. Salusbury had spent much of the previous year in Oxfordshire, heading a band of robbers: Price 1952, 263–4; Williams, G 1976, 403; Pratt 1997, 26.

44 *Let Pap Henry VIII*, 9, 244.

45 Williams 2001, 76–7. His name appears variously as Deram, Derham, Durham and Heron or Herne: Pratt 1997, 38–9.

46 *Valor Ecclesiasticus*, IV, 446–7; O'Sullivan 1947, 18, and n 118; Pratt 1997, 20–3.

47 Pratt 1997, 38; Williams 2001, 86.

48 Pratt 1997, 46–9.

49 Illustrated in Bond 2001, 92.

50 For general accounts of the surviving buildings, see Hughes 1894 and 1895a; [Hughes] 1935; Radford 1953, 10–23; Hubbard 1986, 292–7; Evans 1995, 15–47.

51 [Paul] 1899a.

52 Radford 1953.

53 Hughes 1894, 182–3; Hughes 1895a, 5–6; Butler 1976b, 92–6.

54 Lewis 1999, 262.

55 This is based on reasoned supposition that the Abbot Adam referred to in the inscription was the man of that name who ruled the house *c* 1330–44: Smith and London 2001, 318; Price 1952, 148.

56 Butler 1976b, 88–9.

57 See, in particular, Maddison 1978, 96–8; also, Hughes 1894, 272; Hughes 1895a, 7–16; [Hughes] 1935, 340; Price 1952, 122–5.

58 Radford 1953, 6, 19–20.

59 Price 1952, 45–6.

60 Radford 1953, 6, 8, 21–2; Williams, G 1976, 387–8; Evans 1995, 18, 40–1.

61 For the post-suppression period in general, see Price 1952, 184–92; Pratt 1997, 39–49.

62 Price 1952, 186; Pratt 1997, 43.

63 Price 1952, 255–7.

64 Pratt 1997, 44. She is named Margaret in some sources.

65 Williams (*Ab Ithel*) 1846, 31; Price 1952, 191–5. But see also [Kernan and Whittle] 1995, 265.

66 Pratt 1997, 40.

67 Pratt 1997, 40; Williams 2001, 90. The sum of the evidence is puzzling, since an engraving published by Humphrey Lhwyd (1584) seems to show the east range without a roof: Price 1952, 189.

68 Pratt 1997, 44–8.

69 Reproduced in Evans 1995, 19.

70 Andrews 1989, 118–19.

71 BL, Add. MS 36417, fols 24–25, 46–50.

72 Williams (*Ab Ithel*) 1846.

73 Williams (*Ab Ithel*) 1846, 17, 19.

74 Williams 1995, 11. Parker's plan can be found (with another of Strata Florida) at National Library of Wales, Maps and Prints, P 556 (Parker Drawings), II).

75 Williams (*Ab Ithel*) 1846, 31–2; Price 1952, 193–4. The lady was a Miss Lloyd (d 1880).

76 Dungannon 1852, 278; Price 1952, 200–1; Williams 2001, 287.

77 [Traveller] 1863, 68–9.

78 Brock 1878a, 152; Price 1952, 202; Radford 1953, 9.

79 Owen 1895; Price 1952, 202–4.

80 Brock 1878a.

81 Hughes 1894 and 1895a. There is also a much later account: [Hughes] 1935.

82 For the report on the work, see Butler 1976b.

83 Nothing by way of structural evidence was encountered, though several burials were identified: Silvester 2001.

84 Radford 1953.

85 Evans 1995.

86 [Kernan and Whittle] 1995, 264–5.

WHITLAND ABBEY

1 Margam (1147) was another of the group (see catalogue entry).

2 Janauschek (1877, 61–2) gives the official date of settlement as 16 September. The house is generally referred to as 'Albalanda' or 'Blanchland' in medieval sources. A brief outline of the accepted foundation sequence is given in Knowles and Hadcock 1971, 128. For Bishop Bernard, see *Episcopal Acts*, 133–44; *St Davids Acta*, 2–4.

3 The move to 'a place in Trefgarn in Deuglethef' (that is, in the *cantref* of Dau Gleddau) is given in *Annales Cambriæ*, 43. See also *Episcopal Acts*, I, 260. Most authorities accept a site near Little Trefgarn (approximately SM 962249), though Williams (1984, I, 7–8; 1990, 66; 2001, 5–6) casts doubt upon it, preferring the Trefgarn near Lampeter Velfrey (SN 153151), a little over 5.9km south west of Whitland itself. This is also the location favoured in RCAHMCW 1917, 152–3.

4 This is the sequence of events given in Lloyd 1939, II, 593–4. Cowley (1977, 22) follows Lloyd, and suggests that Bishop Bernard 'was on terms of familiarity' with Bishop William Giffard of Winchester (1107–29), who had settled the first colony of Cistercians in Britain (at Waverley in 1128), and with Archbishop Thurstan of York (1114–40), who played a very significant role in the order's expansion in the north of England. Most recently, the same sequence is accepted in Pryce 1996, 155–6. See also Richard 1935–9, 351–2.

5 The precise date of the prince's initial links remains unclear. The lordship of St Clears was not captured by Rhys in 1164–5, remaining independent within the new Deheubarth until 1189. However, a Welshman named Cynan (d 1176) was abbot of Whitland by 1166, and we know that one of Rhys's sons, Cadwaladr, was buried there in 1186. For the Lord Rhys and the political situation, see Davies 1987, 217–24; for his likely early patronage of Whitland, Pryce 1996, 157–9.

6 For the confirmation charter, see *Mon Ang*, V, 591.

7 *Cal Pat Rolls*, 1436–41, 380.

8 Strata Florida (1164), Strata Marcella (1170), Cwmhir (1176), Comber (1199) and Tracton (1224): see Gwynn and Hadcock 1970, 130, 143; Knowles and Hadcock 1971, 115, 126 (and this catalogue).

9 *Cronica de Wallia*, 35.

10 *Gerald of Wales*, IV, 161–7. Gerald bore a grudge, blaming Cadwgan in his time at Strata Florida for the theft (as he saw it) of his library of books.

11 Cowley 1977, 122–3; Williams 2001, 20.

12 On Whitland's lands in general, see Richard 1935–9, 351–2; Williams 1990, 66–8; also, Owen 1935, 53–67. Williams (2001, 182) gives eleven granges; Cowley (1977, 78) gives seventeen at the end of the thirteenth century.

13 Cowley 1977, 78–96, 272–5, *passim*. For the relative importance of livestock in general, see Donkin 1978, 67–102, especially 81.

14 *Taxatio Ecclesiastica*, 276; O'Sullivan 1947, 9, and n 15; Cowley 1977, 276.

15 For a summary of the Welsh wars of 1276–7 and 1282–3, see Davies 1987, 333–54; Prestwich 1997, 170–232. At least one authority (William Rees, note in *Ancient Petitions*, 42) believed Whitland was more likely to have suffered during the great Welsh revolt of 1294–5, for which see Davies 1987, 382–6.

16 *Ancient Petitions*, 42; O'Sullivan 1947, 75; Cowley 1977, 214–15; Williams 2001, 37.

17 Williams 2001, 53, quoting *Cal Pat Rolls*, 1401–5, 298.

18 *Cal Pat Rolls*, 1436–41, 380.

19 *Valor Ecclesiasticus*, IV, 407–8; *Mon Ang*, V, 592. See also O'Sullivan 1947, 9–10, and n 16.

20 For which, see Knowles 1948–59, III, 268–319; Youings 1971, 25–55.

21 For the fine, see *Let Pap Henry VIII*, 13, II, 177. In general, see Jones 1937, 270; Williams, G 1997, 88–9; Williams 2001, 76–80, 82.

22 *Leland*, 58.

23 Knowles and Hadcock 1971, 128; Williams 1984, I, 118–19.

24 In general, see [Collier] 1925–6; Ludlow 2002.

25 For the group, see Lewis 1999, 17, 107, 263.

26 *Brut*, 116. According to Richard (1935–9, 358) a male body was found 'during excavation' alongside that of a female, 'in front of the high altar'. No trace of these burials was found in the work of 1994–5.

27 Later tiles are also known from the site. In general, see Richard 1935–9, 364–8; Lewis 1999, 262–3; also Ludlow 2002, 76–8.

28 Ludlow 2002, 55.

29 Ludlow 2002, 76.

30 Williams, G 1997, 72–104; Williams 2001, 91. For general context, see Williams 2001, 76–90.

31 The 'manor house of Whitland' is described in a detailed survey of 1582, though its precise site is unconfirmed: Ludlow 2002, 48, 95–6.

However, James (2000, 58–9) suggests the gate and twenty-two chambers listed in the survey may have been arranged around the former west range.

32 For the full commission report, see PRO, E178/3349. I am grateful to Stephen Priestly for providing a transcript copy. See also Owen 1935, 360–3.

33 On these later phases, see James 1978; Ludlow 2002, 48–9.

34 GM 1839, 597.

35 Cardiff City Library, Charles Norris Drawings, vol 17, fol 572.

36 His account of 1868 is quoted in RCAHMCW 1917, 152. Certainly the dimensions recorded by Thomas are a close approximation of those recovered in the recent excavations.

37 RCAHMCW 1917, 152–3; Clapham 1921, 205–8. Clapham's plan was quite accurate, apart from the presbytery, which is shown too long.

38 [Collier] 1925–6; Collier 1927. Almost forty years before, Collier had taken measurements for Stephen Williams on the Strata Florida excavations: Williams 1992, 75; Williams 2001, 287.

39 The project seems to have run short of funds, with only limited further work carried out in 1928.

40 James 1978.

41 The work was directed by Pete Crane for the Dyfed Archaeological Trust (now Cambria Archaeology), in partnership with Chris Fenton-Thomas of the Department of Archaeology at Trinity College, Carmarthen.

42 The site lay under extensive spoil heaps from the 1926–8 excavations, one of which included a large quantity of *ex situ* architectural fragments, and another a considerable body of tile: Ludlow 2002, 49–53.

43 The geophysical survey was undertaken by Archaeophysica Ltd, the building recording by Cambria Archaeology and the topographical work by Landmark Surveys.

44 For interim reports, see Ludlow 2000 and 2001; also James 2000, 58–9. The full report is in Ludlow 2002.

45 James 1978; Ludlow 2002, 88–91.

ABBREVIATIONS AND BIBLIOGRAPHY

BL	British Library
PRO	Public Record Office (now The National Archives), Kew
RCAHMCW	Royal Commission on the Ancient and Historical Monuments and Constructions in Wales and Monmouthshire
RCAHMW	Royal Commission on the Ancient and Historical Monuments of Wales
RCHME	Royal Commission on the Historical Monuments of England

Adam Usk: Given-Wilson, C (ed) 1997. *The Chronicle of Adam Usk 1377–1421*, Oxford

Adams, D J 1981. 'Masons and their marks at Margam Abbey', *Trans Port Talbot Hist Soc*, **2** (3), 87–91

Adams, D J 1984. 'The restoration of Margam Abbey church in the 19th century', *Trans Port Talbot Hist Soc*, **3** (3), 60–7

Alexander, J S 1996. 'The thirteenth-century west front of Newstead Priory, Nottinghamshire', *Trans Thoroton Soc Nottinghamshire*, **100**, 55–60

Alexander, J S (ed) 1998. *Southwell and Nottinghamshire: Medieval Art, Architecture and Industry*, Brit Archaeol Ass Conference Trans, 21, London

Alexander, J S 2004. 'Bardney Abbey, Lincolnshire: Benedictine with a Cistercian flavour', in Kinder (ed) 2004, 301–11

Alexander, J and Binski, P (eds) 1987. *Age of Chivalry: Art in Plantagenet England 1200–1400*, London

Allgood, H G C 1907. *Llantarnam Abbey* [Cardiff], British Library Pamphlet, 10368.g.20

Ancient Correspondence: Edwards, J G (ed) 1935. *Calendar of Ancient Correspondence Concerning Wales*, Cardiff

Ancient Petitions: Rees, W (ed) 1975. *Calendar of Ancient Petitions Relating to Wales*, Cardiff

Andrews, F B 1931. 'Pershore Abbey, Worcestershire: report on the excavations on the site of the abbatial buildings and nave, 1929–30', *Birmingham Archaeol Soc Trans Proc*, **53**, 196–204

Andrews, M 1989. *The Search for the Picturesque: Landscape, Aesthetics and Tourism in Britain, 1760–1800*, Aldershot

Annales Cambriæ: Williams (*Ab Ithel*), J (ed) 1860. *Annales Cambriæ*, Rolls Ser, 20, London

Annales Monastici: Luard, H R (ed) 1864–9. *Annales Monastici*, 5 vols, Rolls Ser, 36, London

Ardura, B 1993. *Abbayes, prieurés et monastères de l'ordre de Prémontré en France des origines à nos jours: dictionnaire historique at bibliographique*, Nancy

Arnold, C J 1992. 'Strata Marcella: the archaeological investigations of 1890 and the results of a geophysical survey in 1990', *Montgomeryshire Collect*, **80**, 88–94

Arnold, C J and Davies, J L 2000. *Roman and Early Medieval Wales*, Stroud

Association bourgignonne des sociétés savantes 1954. *Mélanges saint Bernard. XXIVe Congrès de l'Association bourgignonne des sociétés savantes (8e Centenaire de la mort de saint Bernard), Dijon 1953*, Dijon

Astill, G G 1993. *A Medieval Industrial Complex and its Landscape: The Metalworking Watermills and Workshops of Bordesley Abbey*, CBA Res Rep, 92, London

Aston, M 1973. 'English ruins and English history: the Dissolution and the sense of the past', *J Warburg Courtauld Insts*, **36**, 231–55

Aston, M 2000. *Monasteries in the Landscape*, Stroud (first published 1993 as *Monasteries*, London)

Aston, M 2001. 'The expansion of the monastic orders of Europe from the eleventh century', in Keevill *et al* (eds) 2001, 9–36

Auberger, J-B, 1986. *L'unanimité cistercienne primitive, mythe ou réalité?*, Cîteaux: Commentaria cistercienses, studia et documenta, 3, Achel

Auberger, J-B, 1992. 'Esthétique et spiritualité cistercienne', in Pressouyre and Kinder (eds) 1992, 121–33

Auberger, J-B, 2001. *Mystère de Fontenay: La spiritualité de saint Bernard en majesté*, La Pierre-qui-Vire

Aubert, M 1928. 'Fontenay', *Congrès archéologique de France* (Dijon), **91**, 234–52

Aubert, M 1931. 'L'abbaye de Noirlac', *Congrès archéologique de France* (Bourges), **94**, 175–224

Aubert, M 1947. *L'architecture cistercienne en France*, 2nd edn, 2 vols, Paris

Aubert, M 1958. 'Existe-t-il une architecture cistercienne?', *Cahiers de civilisation médiévale*, **1**, 153–8

Aubert, M 1959. 'L'abbaye de Pontigny', *Congrès archéologique de France* (Auxerre), **116**, 163–8

Baddeley, [W] St C 1913. 'Ewenny Priory, or St Michael of Ogmore', *Archaeol Cambrensis*, 6th ser, **13**, 1–50

Badham, S 1999. 'Medieval minor effigial monuments in west and south Wales: an interim survey', *J Church Monuments Soc*, **14**, 6–34

Baker, D and Borg, A 1977. 'The outer bailey – the site of the priory', in *Excavations at Portchester Castle: Vol III, Medieval* (ed B Cunliffe), Rep Res Comm Soc Antiq London, 34, 97–120, London

B[anks], R W 1880. 'The grange of Cwmtoyddwr', *Archaeol Cambrensis*, 4th ser, **11**, 30–50

Banks, R W 1888. 'Notes to the account of Cwmhir Abbey, Radnorshire', *Archaeol Cambrensis*, 5th ser, **5**, 204–17

Bannister, A T 1902. *The History of Ewias Harold*, Hereford

Barker, P 1994. *A Short Architectural History of Worcester Cathedral*, Worcester

Baron, F 1958. 'Histoire architecturale de l'abbaye de Vaucelles', *Cîteaux*, **9**, 276–85

Baron, F 1960. 'Les églises de Vaucelles', *Cîteaux*, **11**, 196–208

Barrière, B 1977. *L'abbaye cistercienne d'Obazine en Bas-Limousin*, Tulle

Baylis, P 1902–4. 'Tintern Abbey', *Trans Woolhope Natur Fld Club*, 294–9

Bearman, R (ed) 2004. *Stoneleigh Abbey: The House, Its Owners, Its Lands*, Stoneleigh

Beck, B 1965–6. 'Recherches sur les salles capitulaires en Normandie, et notamment dans les diocèses d'Avranches, Bayeux et Coutances', *Bulletin de la société des antiquaires de Normandie*, **58**, 1–118

Bell, D N 1989. 'The English Cistercians and the practice of medicine', *Cîteaux*, **40**, 139–73

Bell, D N 1998. 'The siting and size of Cistercian infirmaries in England and Wales', in Lillich (ed) 1998, 211–37

Bell, D N 2004. 'Chambers, cells, and cubicles: the Cistercian General Chapter and the development of the private room', in Kinder (ed) 2004, 187–98

Berman, C H 1986. *Medieval Agriculture, the Southern French Countryside, and the Early Cistercians: A Study of Forty-three Monasteries*, Trans American Phil Soc, 76 (5), Philadelphia

Berman, C H 2000. *The Cistercian Evolution: The Invention of a Religious Order in Twelfth-century Europe*, Philadelphia

Bernard Letters: James, B S (ed) 1998. *The Letters of St Bernard of Clairvaux*, new edn, Stroud

Bialoskorska, K 1965. 'Polish Cistercian architecture and its contacts with Italy', *Gesta*, **4**, 14–22

Bilson, J 1898–9. 'The beginnings of Gothic architecture', *J Roy Inst Brit Architect*, 3rd ser, **6**, 259–326

Bilson, J 1909. 'The architecture of the Cistercians, with special reference to some of their earlier churches in England', *Archaeol J*, **66**, 185–280

Bilson, J 1928. 'Notes on the earlier architectural history of Wells Cathedral', *Archaeol J*, **85**, 23–68

Binski, P 1995. *Westminster Abbey and the Plantagenets: Kingship and the Representation of Power 1200–1400*, New Haven and London

Birch, W de G 1897. *A History of Margam Abbey*, London (reprinted 1997, Swansea)

Birch, W de G 1902. *A History of Neath Abbey*, Neath

Birch, W de G 1912. *Memorials of the See and Cathedral of Llandaff*, Neath

Blanchot, H 1985. *Clairmont*, La Pierre-qui-Vire

Blashill, T 1878. *Guide to Tintern Abbey*, Monmouth

Blashill, T 1881–2. 'The architectural history of Tintern Abbey', *Trans Bristol Gloucestershire Archaeol Soc*, **6**, 88–106

[Blashill, T] 1882. 'Abbey Dore', *Trans Woolhope Natur Fld Club*, 168

Blashill, T 1883–5. 'Abbeydore', *Trans Woolhope Natur Fld Club*, 5–10

Blashill, T 1885. 'The architectural history of Dore Abbey', *J Brit Archaeol Ass*, **41**, 363–71

Blashill, T 1886. 'Tintern Abbey', *Archaeol Cambrensis*, 5th ser, **3**, 241–52

Blashill, T 1901–2. 'The 17th century restoration of Dore Abbey church', *Trans Woolhope Natur Fld Club*, **17**, 184–9

Blockley, K 1997a. 'Tintern Abbey', *Archaeol Wales*, **37**, 102

Blockley, K 1997b. 'Pulpitum screen, Tintern Abbey, Monmouthshire: archaeological evaluation', Cambrian Archaeological Projects Rep (unpublished), 34, Llanidloes

Blockley, K 1998a. 'Tintern Abbey: Abbey Cottage', *Archaeol Wales*, **38**, 135

Blockley, K 1998b. 'Abbeycwmhir', *Archaeol Wales*, **38**, 140

Bolton, B M 1996. 'Cistercian order', in Turner (ed) 1996, 7, 346 53

Bond, J 2001. 'Monastic water management in Great Britain: a review', in Keevill *et al* (eds) 2001, 88–136

Bond, J 2004. *Monastic Landscapes*, Stroud

Bonde, S, Boyden, E and Maines, C 1990. 'Centrality and community: liturgy and gothic chapter room design at the Augustinian abbey of Saint-Jean-des-Vignes, Soissons', *Gesta*, **29**, 189–213

Bonde, S and Maines, C 1987. 'Note sur la fouille de l'église de saint Norbert à Prémontré: son importance pour la première architecture cistercienne', *Cîteaux*, **38**, 100–1

Bonde, S and Maines, C 1988. 'The archaeology of monasticism: a survey of recent work in France, 1970–87', *Speculum*, **63**, 794–825

Bonde, S and Maines, C 1997. 'A room of one's own: elite spaces in monasteries of the reform movement and an abbot's parlour at Augustinian Saint-Jean-des-Vignes, Soissons (France)', in *Religion and Belief in Medieval Europe: Papers of the Medieval Europe Brugge 1997 Conference 4* (eds G de Boe and F Verhaeghe), 43–53, Zellik

Bony, J 1949. 'French influences on the origins of English Gothic architecture', *J Warburg Courtauld Insts*, **12**, 1–15

Bony, J 1979. *The English Decorated Style: Gothic Architecture Transformed 1250–1350*, Oxford

Bony, J 1983. *French Gothic Architecture of the 12th and 13th Centuries*, Berkeley and London

Bouchard, C B 1987. *Sword, Mitre, and Cloister: Nobility and the Church in Burgundy, 980–1198*, Ithaca and London

Bouchard, C B 1990. 'Merovingian, Carolingian and Cluniac monasticism: reform and renewal in Burgundy', *J Eccles Hist*, **41**, 365–88

Bouchard, C B 1991. *Holy Entrepreneurs: Cistercians, Knights, and Economic Exchange in Twelfth-century Burgundy*, Ithaca and London

Bourgeois, P 2000. *Abbaye Notre Dame de Fontenay – Monument du patrimoine mondial: Architecture et histoire*, 2 vols, Bégrolles en Mauges

Boutevin, P 1996. *Fontenay Abbey*, 2nd edn, Moisenay

Bouton, J de la Croix and Van Damme, J B (eds) 1974. *Les plus anciens textes de Cîteaux*, Cîteaux: Commentaria cistercienses, studia et documenta, 2, Achel (reprinted 1985)

Bowen, E G 1950–1. 'The monastic economy of the Cistercians at Strata Florida', *Ceredigion*, **1**, 34–7

Bradney, J A 1904–32. *A History of Monmouthshire: From the Coming of the Normans into Wales Down to the Present Time*, 4 vols, London

Brakspear, H 1900. 'On the first church at Furness', *Trans Lancashire Cheshire Antiq Soc*, **18**, 70–87

Brakspear, H 1901. 'The church of Hayles Abbey', *Archaeol J*, **58**, 350–7

[Brakspear, H] 1904. 'Tintern Abbey', *Archaeol J*, **61**, 213–14

Brakspear, H 1905. *Waverley Abbey*, Surrey Archaeol Soc, Guildford

Brakspear, H 1906–7. 'The Cistercian abbey of Stanley, Wiltshire', *Archaeologia*, **60**, 493–516

Brakspear, H 1912–13. 'Malmesbury Abbey', *Archaeologia*, **64**, 399–436

Brakspear, H 1919. *Tintern Abbey, Monmouthshire*, 2nd edn, London

Brakspear, H 1922. 'Bardney Abbey', *Archaeol J*, **79**, 1–92

Brakspear, H 1922–3. 'Excavations at some Wiltshire monasteries', *Archaeologia*, **73**, 225–52

Brakspear, H 1929. *Tintern Abbey, Monmouthshire*, 2nd edn, London

Brakspear, H 1931. 'A west country school of masons', *Archaeologia*, **81**, 1–18

Brakspear, H 1933. 'Wigmore Abbey', *Archaeol J*, **90**, 26–51

Brakspear, H 1934. *Tintern Abbey, Monmouthshire*, London

Brakspear, H and Evans, M 1910. *Tintern Abbey, Monmouthshire*, 2nd edn, London

Branner, R 1960. *Burgundian Gothic Architecture*, London

Braunfels, W 1972. *Monasteries of Western Europe: The Architecture of the Orders*, London

Bredero, A H 1996. *Bernard of Clairvaux: Between Cult and History*, Edinburgh

Brenhinedd: Jones, T (ed) 1971. *Brenhinedd y Saesson or the Kings of the Saxons*, Cardiff

Brock, E P L 1878a. 'Valle Crucis Abbey', *J Brit Archaeol Ass*, **34**, 145–58

Brock, E P L 1878b. 'The Cistercian abbeys of Cymmer and Basingwerk, with notes on the holy wells of Wales', *J Brit Archaeol Ass*, **34**, 463–79

[Brock, E P L] 1891. 'Basingwerk Abbey', *Archaeol Cambrensis*, 5th ser, **8**, 127–34

Brooke, C 1986. 'St Bernard, the patrons and monastic planning', in Norton and Park (eds) 1986, 11–23

Brooke, C 1987. 'Reflections on the monastic cloister', in *Romanesque and Gothic: Essays for George Zarnecki*, 2 vols (ed N Stratford), I, 19–25, Woodbridge

Brooke, C 2003. *The Age of the Cloister: The Story of Monastic Life in the Middle Ages*, Stroud

Brooksby, H 1970. 'A twelfth-century relic of Abbey Cwm-hir?', *Archaeol Cambrensis*, **119**, 132–3

Brown, R A, Colvin, H M and Taylor, A J 1963. *The History of the Kings Works: The Middle Ages*, 2 vols, London

Brown, S 1999. *'Sumptuous and Richly Adorn'd': The Decoration of Salisbury Cathedral*, London

Brown, S 2003. *'Our Magnificent Fabrick': York Minster, An Architectural History c 1250–1500*, Swindon

Brown, S W 1988. 'Excavations and building recording at Buckfast Abbey, Devon', *Devon Archaeol Soc Proc*, **46**, 13–89

Brut: Jones, T (ed) 1952. *Brut y Tywysogyon or the Chronicle of the Princes: Peniarth MS 20 Version*, Cardiff

Brut (RBH): Jones, T (ed) 1955. *Brut y Tywysogyon or the Chronicle of the Princes: Red Book of Hergest Version*, Cardiff

Bruzelius, C A 1979. 'Cistercian high Gothic: the abbey church of Longpont and the architecture of the Cistercians in the early thirteenth century', *Analecta Cisterciensia*, **35**, 3–204

Bruzelius, C A 1981. 'The twelfth-century church at Ourscamp', *Speculum*, **56**, 28–40

Bruzelius, C A 1982. 'The transept of the abbey church of Châalis and the filiation of Pontigny', in Chauvin (ed) 1982–7, III, 6, 447–54

Bruzelius, C A 1990. *L'apogée de l'art gothique: l'église abbatiale de Longpont at l'architecture cistercienne au début du XIIIe siècle*, Cîteaux: Commentaria cistercienses, Textes et documents, 2, Achel

Bucher, F 1957. *Notre-Dame de Bonmont und die ersten Zisterzienserabteien der Schweiz*, Berne

Bucher, F 1960–1. 'Cistercian architectural purism', *Comparative Stud Society Hist*, **3**, 89–105

Buhot, J 1940–2. 'Les fouilles de l'église abbatiale de Savigny-le-Vieux', *Bulletin de la Société française de fouilles archéologiques*, **7**, 299–302

Burton, J 1986. 'The foundation of the British Cistercian houses', in Norton and Park (eds) 1986, 24–39

Burton, J 1994. *Monastic and Religious Orders in Britain, 1000–1300*, Cambridge

Burton, J 1998. 'The Cistercian adventure', in Robinson (ed) 1998, 7–33

Burton, J 1999. *The Monastic Order in Yorkshire, 1069–1215*, Cambridge

Butler, L A S 1963. 'An excavation at the Cistercian abbey of Aberconwy at Maenan, 1963', *Trans Caernarvonshire Hist Soc*, **24**, 28–37

Butler, L A S 1964. 'An excavation in the vicarage garden, Conway, 1961', *Archaeol Cambrensis*, **113**, 97–128

Butler, L A S 1971. 'Medieval ecclesiastical architecture in Glamorgan and Gower', in Pugh (ed) 1971, 379–415

Butler, L A S 1973. 'Medieval floor tiles at Neath Abbey', *Archaeol Cambrensis*, **122**, 154–8

Butler, L A S 1976a. *Neath Abbey*, London

Butler, L A S 1976b. 'Valle Crucis Abbey: an excavation in 1970', *Archaeol Cambrensis*, **125**, 80–126

Butler, L A S 1981. 'The boundaries of the abbey of Aberconwy at Maenan, Gwynedd', *Archaeol Cambrensis*, **130**, 19–35

Butler, L A S 1982a. 'The Cistercians in England and Wales: a survey of recent archaeological work 1960–1980', in Lillich (ed) 1982a, 88–101

Butler, L A S 1982b. 'The Cistercians in Wales: factors in the choice of sites', in Chauvin (ed) 1982–7, III, 5, 35–8

Butler, L A S 1984. 'Neath Abbey: the twelfth-century church', *Archaeol Cambrensis*, **133**, 147–51

Butler, L A S 1987. 'The Wynn mansion at the abbey, Maenan, Gwynedd (1538–1848)', *Archaeol Cambrensis*, **136**, 171–3

Butler, L A S 1988. 'The Cistercian abbey of St Mary of Rushen: excavations 1978–9', *J Brit Archaeol Ass*, **141**, 60–104

Butler, L A S 1994. 'Saint Bernard of Clairvaux and the Cistercian abbeys in Wales', *Arte Medievale*, 2nd ser, **8** (1), vol 2, 1–11

Butler, L A S 1999a. 'The Cistercians in Wales and Yorkshire', *Archaeol Cambrensis*, **148**, 1–21

Butler, L A S 1999b. 'The foundation charter of Neath Abbey, Glamorgan', *Archaeol Cambrensis*, **148**, 214–16

Butler, L A S 2002. 'The Cistercian abbey of St Mary of Rushen, Isle of Man: excavations on the east range, 1988–9', *J Brit Archaeol Ass*, **155**, 168–94

Butler, L A S 2004. 'The lost choir: what was built at three Cistercian abbey churches in Wales?', in Kinder (ed) 2004, 115–23

Butler, L A S and Evans, D H 1980. 'The Cistercian abbey of Aberconway at Maenan, Gwynedd: excavations in 1968', *Archaeol Cambrensis*, **129**, 37–63

Cal Chart Rolls: *Calendar of the Charter Rolls Preserved in the Public Record Office*, 6 vols, 1903–27, London

Cal Close Rolls: *Calendar of the Close Rolls Preserved in the Public Record Office*, 1896–in progress, London

Cal Fine Rolls: *Calendar of the Fine Rolls Preserved in the Public Record Office*, 1911–62, London

Cal Pap Let: Bliss, W H, Johnson, C, Twemlow, J A, Haren, M J and Fuller, A P (eds) 1893–in progress. *Calendar of Entries in the Papal Registers Relating to Great Britain and Ireland: Papal Letters*, London and Dublin

Cal Pap Pet: Bliss, W H (ed) 1896. *Calendar of Entries in the Papal Registers Relating to Great Britain and Ireland: Petitions to the Pope*, London

Cal Pat Rolls: *Calendar of the Patent Rolls Preserved in the Public Record Office*, 1891–in progress, London

Carey-Hill, E 1927. 'Kenilworth Abbey', *Trans Birmingham Archaeol Soc*, **52**, 184–227

[Caröe, W D] 1933. 'The church of St Woollos', *Archaeol Cambrensis*, **88**, 388–92

Cartae Glamorgancia: Clark, G T (ed) 1910. *Cartae et alia munimenta quae ad dominium de Glamorgancia pertinent*, 2nd edn, 6 vols, Cardiff

Cassidy-Welch, M 2001. *Monastic Spaces and their Meanings: Thirteenth-century English Cistercian Monasteries*, Medieval Church Studies, 1, Turnhout

Chabeuf, H 1883–4. 'Voyage d'un délégué au Chapitre général de Cîteaux en 1667', *Mémoires de l'Académie des sciences, arts et belles-lettres de Dijon*, 3rd ser, **8**, 169–405

Charles, B G 1970. 'An early charter of the abbey of Cwmhir', *Trans Radnorshire Soc*, **40**, 68–74

Chauvin, B (ed) 1982–7. *Mélanges à la mémoire du père Anselme Dimier*, 3 vols in 6, Arbois

Chauvin, B (ed) 1998. *Cîteaux en France: 64 sites à découvrir*, Dossiers d'archéologie, 234, Dijon

Chester Chronicle: Christie, R C (ed) 1887. *Annales Cestrienses; or Chronicle of the Abbey of S. Werburg, at Chester*, Rec Soc Lancashire Cheshire, 14, London

Chronicle: Anon (ed) 1862. 'Chronicle of the thirteenth century: MS Exchequer Domesday', *Archaeol Cambrensis*, 3rd ser, **8**, 272–83

Churchill, I J 1933. *Canterbury Administration: The Administrative Machinery of the Archbishopric of Canterbury Illustrated from Original Records*, 2 vols, London

Clapham, A W 1921. 'Three monastic houses of South Wales', *Archaeol Cambrensis*, **76**, 205–14

Clapham, A W 1923. 'The architecture of the Premonstratensians, with special reference to their buildings in England', *Archaeologia*, **73**, 117–46

Clapham, A W 1927. 'The architectural remains of the mendicant orders in Wales', *Archaeol J*, **84**, 88–104

Clapham, A W 1934. *English Romanesque Architecture: After the Conquest*, Oxford

Clark, G T 1867. 'Contribution towards a cartulary of Margam', *Archaeol Cambrensis*, 3rd ser, **13**, 311–34

Clark, G T 1868. 'Contribution towards a cartulary of Margam', *Archaeol Cambrensis*, 3rd ser, **14**, 24–59, 182–96, 345–82

Clark, J G 2002a. 'The religious orders in pre-Reformation England', in Clark (ed) 2002b, 3–33

Clark, J G (ed) 2002b. *The Religious Orders in Pre-Reformation England*, Studies in the History of Medieval Religion, 18, Woodbridge

Clark, W W 1984. 'Cistercian influences on Premonstratensian church planning: Saint-Martin at Laon', in Lillich (ed) 1984, 161–88

Coad, J G 1993. *Hailes Abbey, Gloucestershire*, 2nd edn, London

Coates, S D 1992. *The Water Powered Industries of the Lower Wye Valley*, Monmouth

Cocheril, M 1966. 'L'atlas de l'ordre cistercien', *Cîteaux*, **17**, 119–44

Cocheril, M 1976. *Dictionnaire des monastères cisterciens: cartes géographiques*, Documentation cistercienne, 18, Rochefort

Colchester, L S 1987. *The New Bell's Cathedral Guides: Wells Cathedral*, London

Coldstream, N 1986. 'Cistercian architecture from Beaulieu to the dissolution', in Norton and Park (eds) 1986, 139–59

Coldstream, N 1994. *The Decorated Style: Architecture and Ornament 1240–1360*, London

Coldstream, N 1998. 'The mark of eternity: the Cistercians as builders', in Robinson (ed) 1998, 35–61

[Collier, E V] 1925–6. 'Whitland Abbey excavations: interim report', *Trans Carmarthenshire Antiq Soc*, **19**, 63–5, 79–80

Collier, E V 1927. 'Whitland Abbey', *Bull Board Celtic Stud*, **3**, 242–3

Colvin, H M 1946–8. 'The restoration of Abbey Dore church in 1633–4', *Trans Woolhope Natur Fld Club*, **32**, 235–7

Conant, K J 1993. *Carolingian and Romanesque Architecture 800 to 1200*, 4th edn (1978), new impression, New Haven and London

Coomans, T 1998a. 'The east range of Val-Saint-Lambert (1233–4)', in Lillich (ed) 1998, 95–157

Coomans, T 1998b. 'L'accueil du chapitre général au Moyen Âge', in Plouvier and Saint-Denis (eds) 1998, 154–64

Coomans, T 2000. *L'abbaye de Villers-en-Brabant: Construction, configuration et signification d'une abbaye cistercienne gothique*, Cîteaux: Commentaria cistercienses, studia et documenta, 11, Brussels and Brecht

Coplestone-Crow, B 1998. 'The foundation of the priories of Bassaleg and Malpas in the twelfth century', *Monmouthshire Antiq*, **14**, 1–13

Coppack, G 1988. *Abbeys: Yorkshire's Monastic Heritage*, London

Coppack, G 1990. *Abbeys and Priories*, London

Coppack, G 1998. *The White Monks: The Cistercians in Britain 1128–1540*, Stroud

Coppack, G 2001. 'Sawley Abbey: an English Cistercian abbey on the edge of *stabilitas*', *Cîteaux*, **52**, 319–36

Coppack, G 2002. 'The planning of Cistercian monasteries in the later Middle Ages: the evidence from Fountains, Rievaulx, Sawley and Rushen', in Clark (ed) 2002b, 197–209

Coppack, G 2003. *Fountains Abbey: The Cistercians in Northern England*, Stroud (first published 1993 as *Fountains Abbey*, London)

Coppack, G 2004. '"According to the form of the order": the earliest Cistercian buildings in England and their context', in Kinder (ed) 2004, 35–45

Coppack, G and Gilyard-Beer, R 1993. *Fountains Abbey*, London

Coppack, G, Harrison, S and Hayfield, C 1995. 'Kirkham Priory: the architecture and archaeology of an Augustinian house', *J Brit Archaeol Ass*, **148**, 55–136

Coppack, G, Hayfield, C and Williams, R 2002. 'Sawley Abbey: the architecture and archaeology of a smaller Cistercian abbey', *J Brit Archaeol Ass*, **155**, 22–114

Coss, P R and Lloyd, S D (eds) 1991. *Thirteenth Century England* III, Woodbridge

Courtney, P 1989. 'Excavations in the outer precinct of Tintern Abbey', *Medieval Archaeol*, **33**, 99–143

Courtney, P and Gray, M 1991. 'Tintern Abbey after the Dissolution', *Bull Board Celtic Stud*, **38**, 145–58

Courtois, R 1972. 'La première église cistercienne (XIIᵉ siècle) et l'abbaye de Vauclair (Aisne)', *Archéologie médiévale*, **2**, 103–32

Courtois, R 1982. 'Quinze ans de fouilles à l'abbaye de Vauclair, bilan provisoire (1966–1981)', in Chauvin (ed) 1982–7, III, 5, 305–52

Cowley, F G 1963. 'The besanding of Theodoric's grange, Margam: some new evidence', *Archaeol Cambrensis*, **112**, 188–90

Cowley, F G 1967a. 'The Cistercian economy in Glamorgan', *Morgannwg*, **11**, 5–26

Cowley, F G 1967b. 'Neath versus Margam: some 13th century disputes', *Trans Port Talbot Hist Soc*, **1**, 7–14

Cowley, F G 1977. *The Monastic Order in South Wales, 1066–1349*, Cardiff

Cowley, F G 1992. *Gerald of Wales and Margam Abbey*, 2nd edn, Friends of Margam Abbey Annual Lecture 1982, Margam

Cowley, F G 1998. 'Margam Abbey, 1147–1349', *Morgannwg*, **42**, 8–22

Cowley, F G and Williams, G 1971. 'The church in medieval Glamorgan', in Pugh (ed) 1971, 87–166

Coxe, W 1801. *An Historical Tour in Monmouthshire*, 2 vols, London (new edn, 1995, Cardiff)

Cranage, D H S, 1921–2. 'The monastery of St Milburge at Much Wenlock, Shropshire', *Archaeologia*, **72**, 105–32

Crane, P 1995. 'Whitland Abbey', *Archaeol Wales*, **35**, 62

Craster, O E 1956. *Tintern Abbey*, London (9th impression 1977)

Craster, O E 1963. *Llanthony Priory*, London

Crawley-Boevey, F 1920. 'Flaxley Abbey', *Archaeol J*, **77**, 445–7

Cronica de Wallia: Jones, T (ed) 1946–8. 'The Cronica de Wallia and other documents from Exeter Library MS 3514', *Bull Board Celtic Stud*, **12**, 27–44

Crossley, F H 1942–3. 'An introduction to the study of screens and lofts in Wales and Monmouthshire with especial reference to their design, provenance and influence', *Archaeol Cambrensis*, **107**, 135–60

Crozet, R 1931. *L'abbaye de Noirlac et l'architecture cistercienne en Berry*, Paris

Cuissard, C 1881–4. 'L'abbaye de l'Aumône ou le Petit-Cîteaux, 1102–1776', *Bull Soc Dunoise*, **4**, 393–420

Dade-Robertson, C 2000. *Furness Abbey: Romance, Scholarship and Culture*, Lancaster

David, C 1971. *St Winefride's Well: A History and Guide*, Holywell

David, H E 1929. 'Margam Abbey, Glamorgan', *Archaeol Cambrensis*, **84**, 317–24

Davies, D R 1946. 'Abbey Cwmhir', *Trans Radnorshire Soc*, **16**, 33–42

[Davies, D S] 1934. 'Abbey Cwm Hir', *Trans Radnorshire Soc*, **4**, 55–61

Davies, E 1924. 'Preservation work at Basingwerk Abbey', *Archaeol Cambrensis*, **79**, 409–10

Davies, J 1992. *The Stones of Abbey Cwmhir*, Llandrindod Wells

Davies, J and Waters, R 1992. 'Strata Florida Abbey: geology of architectural fragments', British Geological Survey Rep (unpublished)

Davies, J C 1943–4. 'Ewenny Priory: some recently found records', *Nat Lib Wales J*, **3**, 107–37

Davies, J C 1945–6. 'A papal bull of privileges to the abbey of Ystrad Fflur', *Nat Lib Wales J*, **4**, 197–203

Davies, J C 1949–50. 'The records of the abbey of Ystrad Marchell – Strata Marcella documents', *Montgomeryshire Collect*, **51**, 3–22, 164–87

Davies, J R 1999. 'The Book of Llandaff: a twelfth-century perspective', in *Anglo-Norman Stud*, **21** (ed C Harper-Bill), Proc Battle Conference 1998, 31–46, Woodbridge

Davies, J R 2003. *The Book of Llandaff and the Norman Church in Wales*, Woodbridge

Davies, R R 1987. *Conquest, Coexistence and Change: Wales 1063–1415*, Oxford

Davies, R R 1995. *The Revolt of Owain Glyn Dŵr*, Oxford

Davies, W S 1919. 'Materials for the life of Bishop Bernard of St David's', *Archaeol Cambrensis*, 6th ser, **19**, 299–322

Day, E H 1911. 'The Cistercian abbey of Cwm Hir', *Archaeol Cambrensis*, 6th ser, **11**, 9–25

Decaëns, H 1998. *Mont-Saint-Michel, Manche*, Paris

Denton, J 1992. 'From the foundation of Vale Royal Abbey to the Statute of Carlisle: Edward I and ecclesiastical patronage', in *Thirteenth Century England IV* (eds P R Coss and S D Lloyd), 123–37, Woodbridge

Denton J H 1993. 'The valuation of the ecclesiastical benefices of England and Wales in 1291–2', *Hist Res*, **66**, 231–50

Dickinson, J C 1961. *Monastic Life in Medieval England*, London

Dickinson, J C 1968. 'The buildings of the English Austin canons after the Dissolution of the Monasteries', *J Brit Archaeol Assoc*, 3rd ser, **31**, 60–75

Didron, E (ed) 1845. 'Un grand monastère au XVIᵉ siècle', *Annales archéologiques*, **3**, 223–9

Dimier, A 1949–67. *Recueil de plans d'églises cisterciennes, 2 vols; supplément*, 2 vols, Paris

Dimier, A 1957. 'Origine des déambulatoires à chapelles rayonnantes non saillantes', *Bulletin monumental*, **115**, 23–33

Dimier, A 1960. 'L'église de l'abbaye de Foigny', *Bulletin monumental*, **118**, 191–205

Dimier, A 1965. 'Le plan de l'église cistercienne de Trois-Fontaines', *Bulletin monumental*, **123**, 103–16

Dimier, A 1971. *L'art cistercien: hors de France*, La Pierre-qui-Vire

Dimier, A 1974. 'En marge du centenaire bernardin: l'église de Clairvaux', *Cîteaux*, **25**, 309–14

Dimier, A 1982. *L'art cistercien: France*, 3rd edn, La Pierre-qui-Vire

Dimier, A 1987a. 'Églises cisterciennes sur plan bernardin et sur plan bénédictin', in Chauvin (ed) 1982–7, I, 2, 751–7

Dimier, A 1987b. 'Infirmeries cisterciennes', in Chauvin (ed) 1982–7, I, 2, 804–25

Donkin, R A 1967. 'The growth and distribution of the Cistercian order in medieval Europe', *Studia Monastica*, **9**, 275–86

Donkin, R A 1969. *A Check List of Printed Works Relating to the Cistercian Order as a Whole and to the Houses of the British Isles in Particular*, Documentation cistercienne, 2, Rochefort

Donkin, R A 1978. *The Cistercians: Studies in the Geography of Medieval England and Wales*, Toronto

Donnelly, J S 1949. *The Decline of the Medieval Cistercian Laybrotherhood*, New York

Donnelly, J S 1954. 'Changes in the grange economy of English and Welsh Cistercian abbeys', *Traditio*, **10**, 399–458

Draper, P 1986. 'Recherches récentes sur l'architecture dans les Îles britanniques à la fin de l'époque romane et au début du gothique', *Bulletin monumental*, **144**, 305–28

Draper, P 1999. 'St Davids Cathedral: provincial or metropolitan?', in *Pierre, lumière, couleur: Études d'histoire de l'art du Moyen Âge en*

l'honneur d'Anne Prache (eds F Joubert and D Sandron), Cultures et civilisations médiévales, 20, 103–16, Paris

Dungannon, Viscount 1852. 'On the recent excavations at Valle Crucis Abbey', *Archaeol Cambrensis*, new ser, **3**, 276–82

Dunn, E 1967. 'Owain Glyndŵr and Radnorshire', *Trans Radnorshire Soc*, **37**, 27–35

Ecclesiastica Officia (1): Choisselet, D and Vernet, P (eds) 1989. *Les 'Ecclesiastica Officia' cisterciens du XIIème siècle*, Documentation cistercienne, 22, Reiningue

Ecclesiastica Officia (2): Cawley, M (ed) 1998. *The Ancient Usages of the Cistercian Order (Ecclesiastica Officia)*, Guadalupe Abbey, Lafayette, Oreg.

Edwards, N 1996. 'Identifying the archaeology of the early church in Wales and Cornwall', in *Church Archaeology: Research Directions for the Future* (eds J Blair and C Pyrah), CBA Res Rep, 104, 49–62, York

Edwards, N and Lane, A (eds) 1992. *The Early Church in Wales and the West*, Oxford

Einsingbach, W 1986. *Kloster Eberbach*, Munich

Elder, E R (ed) 1998. *The New Monastery: Texts and Studies on the Early Cistercians*, Cistercian Fathers Ser, 60, Kalamazoo

Elias, T 1898. 'The history and associations of the abbeys and convents of the Vale of Conway and district', *J Brit Archaeol Ass*, new ser, **4**, 30–62

Ellis, T P 1927. 'Merioneth notes', *Y Cymmrodor*, **38**, 1–44

Elm, K (ed) 1980–2. *Die Zisterzienser: Ordensleben zwischen Ideal und Wirklichkeit*, Cologne and Bonn

Emery, A 2000. *Greater Medieval Houses of England and Wales, 1300–1500: Volume II, East Anglia, Central England and Wales*, Cambridge

[Emery, M] 2002. 'Poulton: the search for a lost Cistercian abbey', *Curr Archaeol*, **180**, 520–5

Engel, U 1998. 'Two-storeyed elevations: the choir of Southwell Minster and the west country', in Alexander (ed) 1998, 33–43

Enlart, C 1895. *Monuments religieux de l'architecture romane et de transition dans la région picarde: anciens diocèses d'Amiens et de Boulogne*, Amiens and Paris

Episcopal Acts: Davies, J C (ed) 1946–8. *Episcopal Acts and Cognate Documents Relating to the Welsh Dioceses 1066–1272*, 2 vols, Cardiff

Erdmann, W 1994. *Zisterzienser-Abtei Chorin*, Königstein im Taunus

Erlande-Brandenburg, A 1977. 'L'abbaye de Trois-Fontaines', *Congrès archéologique de France* (Champagne), **135**, 695–706

Erlande-Brandenburg, A and Mérel-Brandenburg, A-B 1995. *Histoire de l'architecture française: Du Moyen Age à la Renaissance*, Paris

Esser, K-H 1953. 'Über den Kirchenbau des Heiligen Bernhard von Clairvaux: eine unwissenschaftliche Untersuchung aufgrund der Ausgrabungen der romanischen Abteikirche Himmerod', *Archiv für mittelrheinische Kirchengeschichte*, **5**, 195–222

Esser, K-H 1954. 'Les fouilles à Himmerod et le plan bernardin', in Association bourguignonne des sociétés savantes 1954, 311–15

Evans, A L 1996. *Margam Abbey*, 2nd edn, Port Talbot (first published 1958)

[Evans, D] 1999. Cadw: Welsh Historic Monuments, *Register of Landscapes, Parks and Gardens of Special Historic Interest in Wales, Part 1, Parks and Gardens: Powys*, Cardiff

Evans, D H 1980. 'Excavations at Llanthony Priory Gwent, 1978', *Monmouthshire Antiq*, **4** (1–2), 5–43

Evans, D H 1983–8. 'Further excavation and fieldwork at Llanthony Priory, Gwent', *Monmouthshire Antiq*, **5**, 1–61

Evans, D H 1995. *Valle Crucis Abbey*, rev edn, Cardiff

Evans, W and Worsley, R 1981. *Eglwys Gadeiriol Tyddewi/St Davids Cathedral 1181–1981*, St Davids

Eydoux, H-P 1952. *L'architecture des églises cisterciennes d'Allemagne*, Travaux et mémoires des Instituts Français en Allemagne, 1, Paris

Eydoux, H-P 1953. 'Les fouilles de l'abbatiale d'Himmerod et la notion d'un "plan bernardin"', *Bulletin monumental*, **111**, 29–36

Eydoux, H-P 1954. 'L'abbatiale de Moreruela et l'architecture des églises cisterciennes d'Espagne', *Cîteaux in de Nederlanden*, **5**, 173–207

Eydoux, H-P 1956. 'L'église abbatiale de Morimond', *Bulletin monumental*, **114**, 253–66

Eydoux, H-P 1958. 'L'église abbatiale de Morimond', *Analecta Sacri Ordinis Cisterciensis*, **14**, 3–111

Eydoux, H-P 1982. 'À propos des fouilles de Morimond', in Chauvin (ed) 1982–7, III, 5, 353–5

Farmer, D H 1992. *The Oxford Dictionary of Saints*, 3rd edn, Oxford

Fawcett, R 1994. *Scottish Abbeys and Priories*, London

Fawcett, R 2002. S*cottish Medieval Churches: Architecture and Furnishings*, Stroud

Fawcett, R and Oram, R 2004. *Melrose Abbey*, Stroud

Fergusson, P 1970. 'Early Cistercian churches in Yorkshire and the problem of the Cistercian crossing tower', *J Soc Architect Hist*, **29**, 211–21

Fergusson, P 1971. 'Roche Abbey: the source and date of the eastern remains', *J Brit Archaeol Ass*, 3rd ser, **34**, 30–42

Fergusson, P 1975. 'The south transept elevation of Byland Abbey', *J Brit Archaeol Ass*, 3rd ser, **38**, 155–76

Fergusson, P 1979. 'Notes on two engraved Cistercian designs', *Speculum*, **54**, 1–17

Fergusson, P 1983. 'The first architecture of the Cistercians in England and the work of Abbot Adam of Meaux', *J Brit Archaeol Ass*, **136**, 74–86

Fergusson, P 1984a. *Architecture of Solitude: Cistercian Abbeys in Twelfth-century England*, Princeton

Fergusson, P 1984b. 'The builders of Cistercian monasteries in twelfth-century England', in Lillich (ed) 1984, 14–29

Fergusson, P 1986. 'The twelfth-century refectories at Rievaulx and Byland abbeys', in Norton and Park (eds) 1986, 160–80

Fergusson, P 1990a. *Roche Abbey*, London

Fergusson, P 1990b. '"Porta Patens Esto": notes on early Cistercian gatehouses in the north of England', in *Medieval Architecture and its Intellectual Context* (eds E Fernie and P Crossley), 47–59, London

Fergusson, P 1994. 'Programmatic factors in the east extension of Clairvaux', *Arte Medievale*, ser 2, **8** (1), vol 2, 87–101

Fergusson, P 1998. 'Aelred's abbatial residence at Rievaulx Abbey', in Lillich (ed) 1998, 41–56

Fergusson, P and Harrison, S 1994. 'The Rievaulx Abbey chapter house', *Antiq J*, **74**, 211–55

Fergusson, P and Harrison, S 1999. *Rievaulx Abbey: Community, Architecture, Memory*, New Haven and London

Fernie, E 2000. *The Architecture of Norman England*, Oxford

Folda, J 1995. *The Art of the Crusaders in the Holy Land 1098–1187*, Cambridge

Fontaine, G 1928. *Pontigny: abbaye cistercienne*, Paris

Foster, A G (ed) 1950. 'Two deeds relating to Neath Abbey', *South Wales and Monmouth Rec Soc Publ*, **2**, 201–6

Fountains Memorials: Walbran, J R (ed) 1863. *Memorials of the Abbey of St Mary of Fountains*, Surtees Soc, 42, Durham

Fowler, J T 1907. 'An old description of the site of the Cistercian abbey of Clairvaux', *Yorkshire Archaeol J*, **19**, 8–16

Fraccaro de Longhi, L 1958. *L'architettura delle chiese cistercensi italiane, con particolare riferimento ad un gruppo omogeneo dell'Italia settentrionale*, Milan

France, J 1992. *The Cistercians in Scandinavia*, Cistercian Stud Ser, 131, Kalamazoo

France, J 1998a. *The Cistercians in Medieval Art*, Stroud

France, J 1998b. 'The cellarer's domain – evidence from Denmark', in Lillich (ed) 1998, 1–39

Francis, G G 1845. *Original Charters and Materials for a History of Neath and its Abbey*, privately printed, Swansea

Frankl, P 2000. *Gothic Architecture*, rev edn by Paul Crossley, New Haven and London

Franklin, J A 1989. 'Bridlington Priory: an Augustinian church and cloister in the twelfth century', in *Medieval Art and Architecture in the East Riding of Yorkshire* (ed C Wilson), Brit Archaeol Ass Conference Trans, 9, 44–61, London

Franklin, J A 2004. 'Augustinian architecture in the twelfth century: the context for Carlisle Cathedral', in *Carlisle and Cumbria: Roman and Medieval Architecture, Art and Archaeology* (ed M McCarthy and D Weston), Brit Archaeol Ass Conference Trans, 27, 73–88, Leeds

Freeman, E A 1850a. 'Some remarks on the architecture of the cathedral church of Llandaff', *Archaeol Cambrensis*, new ser, **1**, 108–34

Freeman, E A 1850b. *Remarks on the Architecture of Llandaff Cathedral, with an Essay Towards the History of the Fabric*, London and Tenby

Freeman, E A 1851. 'Chepstow Priory church', *Archaeol Cambrensis*, new ser, **2**, 1–8

Fulford, M G, Rippon, S, Allen, J R L and Hillam, J 1992. 'The medieval quay at Woolaston Grange, Gloucestershire', *Trans Bristol Gloucestershire Archaeol Soc*, **110**, 101–27

Gallagher, P F 1982. 'The Cistercian church at Mortemer: a reassessment of its chronology and possible sources', in Lillich (ed) 1982a, 53–70

Gajewski, A 2003. 'Twelfth-century Cistercian architecture in greater Anjou', in *Anjou: Medieval Art, Architecture and Archaeology* (eds J McNeill and D Prigent), Brit Archaeol Ass Conference Trans, 26, 151–67, Leeds

Gajewski, A 2004. 'The architecture of the choir at Clairvaux Abbey: Saint Bernard and the Cistercian principle of conspicuous poverty', in Kinder (ed) 2004, 71–80

Gamwell, S C 1887. 'Margam Abbey', *Archaeol Cambrensis*, 5th ser, **4**, 1–13

Gardelles, J 1979. 'L'abbaye de Cadouin', *Congrès Archéologique de France* (Périgord Noir), **137**, 146–78

Gardner, I 1915. 'Llanthony Prima', *Archaeol Cambrensis*, 6th ser, **15**, 343–76

Gardner, I 1916. 'Llanthony Prima', *Archaeol Cambrensis*, 6th ser, **16**, 37–66

Gardner, I 1929. 'Tintern Abbey', *J Brit Archaeol Ass*, new ser, **35**, 54–5

Gardner, W S 1976. 'The role of central planning in English Romanesque chapter house design', unpublished PhD thesis, Princeton University

Gee, E A 1977. 'Architectural history until 1290', in *A History of York Minster* (eds G E Aylmer and R Cant), 110–48, Oxford

Gem, R 2000. 'Romanesque architecture in Chester c 1075 to 1117', in *Medieval Archaeology, Art and Architecture at Chester* (ed A Thacker), Brit Archaeol Ass Conference Trans, 22, 31–44, Leeds

Gerald of Wales: Brewer, J S (ed) 1861–91. *Giraldus Cambrensis Opera*, 8 vols, Rolls Ser, 21, London

Gibson, M 1727. *A View of the Ancient and Present States of the Churches of Door, Home-Lacy and Hempsted*, London

Gilpin, W 1782. *Observations on the River Wye*, London

Gilyard-Beer, R 1976. *Abbeys: An Illustrated Guide to the Abbeys of England and Wales*, 2nd edn, London

Gilyard-Beer, R 1981. 'Boxley Abbey and the *Pulpitum Collationis*', in *Collectanea Historica: Essays in Memory of Stuart Rigold* (ed A Detsicas), 123–31, Maidstone

Gilyard-Beer, R 1990. *Cleeve Abbey*, 2nd edn, London

Gilyard-Beer, R and Coppack, G 1986. 'Excavations at Fountains Abbey, North Yorkshire, 1979–80: the early development of the monastery', *Archaeologia*, **108**, 147–88

Gloucester Charters: Patterson, R B (ed) 1973. *Earldom of Gloucester Charters: The Charters and Scribes of the Earls and Countesses of Gloucester to A.D. 1217*, Oxford

GM 1839. 'Whitland Abbey', *Gentleman's Mag*, **109** (2), 595–8

Godfrey, W H 1929. 'The abbot's parlour, Thame Park', *Archaeol J*, **86**, 59–68

Godfrey, W H 1952. 'English cloister lavatories as independent structures', *Archaeol J*, **106** (supplement for 1949), 91–7

Graham, R 1929. 'Four alien priories in Monmouthshire', *J Brit Archaeol Ass*, new ser, **35**, 102–21

Grant, L 1988. 'The architecture of the early Savigniacs and Cistercians in Normandy', in *Anglo-Norman Stud*, 10 (ed R A Brown), Proc Battle Conference 1987, 111–43, Woodbridge

Grant, L 1991. 'Gothic architecture in southern England and the French connection in the early thirteenth century', in Coss and Lloyd (eds) 1991, 113–26

Grant, L 1998. *Abbot Suger of St-Denis: Church and State in Early Twelfth-century France*, London

Grant, L 2004. 'Savigny and its saints', in Kinder (ed) 2004, 109–14

Grant, L 2005. *Architecture and Society in Normandy, 1120–1270*, New Haven and London

Gras, P 1982. 'Vues et plans de l'ancien Cîteaux', in Chauvin (ed) 1982–7, III, 6, 549–75

Gray, M 1996. 'Penrhys: the archaeology of a pilgrimage', *Morgannwg*, **40**, 10–32

Gray, M 1998. 'The politics of Cistercian grange foundation and endowment in south-east Wales', *Annu Rep Medieval Sett Res Grp*, **13**, 20–4

Gray, M 2000. *Images of Piety: The Iconography of Traditional Religion in Late Medieval Wales*, BAR Brit Ser 316, Oxford

Gray, T 1903a. 'The hermitage of Theodoric, and the site of Pendar', *Archaeol Cambrensis*, 6th ser, **3**, 121–53

Gray, T 1903b. 'Notes on the granges of Margam Abbey', *J Brit Archaeol Ass*, new ser, **9**, 161–81

Gray, T 1905. 'Notes on the granges of Margam Abbey', *J Brit Archaeol Ass*, new ser, **11**, 11–29

Greene, J P 1989. *Norton Priory: The Archaeology of a Medieval Religious House*, Cambridge

Gresham, C A 1939. 'The Aberconwy charter', *Archaeol Cambrensis*, **94**, 123–62

Gresham, C A 1968. *Medieval Stone Carving in North Wales: Sepulchral Slabs and Effigies of the Thirteenth and Fourteenth Centuries*, Cardiff

Gresham, C A 1982–3. 'The Aberconwy charter; further consideration', *Bull Board Celtic Stud*, **30**, 311–47

Gresham, C A 1984. 'The Cymer Abbey charter', *Bull Board Celtic Stud*, **31**, 142–57

Griffith, M O 1981–4. 'Abereiddon and Esgaireiddon', *J Merioneth Hist Rec Soc*, **9**, 367–89

Griffiths, M 1988. 'Native society on the Anglo-Norman frontier: the evidence of the Margam charters', *Welsh Hist Rev*, **14**, 179–216

Grigson, G 1959. 'The abbey of the Long Vale', *Country Life*, **125**, 94–6

Grüger, H 1984. 'Cistercian fountain houses in central Europe', in Lillich (ed) 1984, 201–22

Guignard, P 1878. *Les monuments primitifs de la règle cistercienne*, Dijon

Guilloreau, L 1909–10. 'Les fondations anglaises de l'abbaye de Savigny', *Revue Mabillon*, **5**, 290–335

Gwynn, A and Hadcock, R N 1970. *Medieval Religious Houses: Ireland*, London (reprinted 1988, Blackrock)

Hahn, H 1957. *Die frühe Kirchenbaukunst der Zisterzienser: Untersuchungen zur Baugeschichte von Kloster Eberbach im Rheingau und ihren europäischen Analogien im 12. Jahrhundert*, Berlin

Hall, J 2001. 'English Cistercian gatehouse chapels', *Cîteaux*, **52**, 61–92

Hall, J 2003. 'Croxden Abbey: buildings and community', 2 vols, unpublished PhD thesis, University of York

Hall, J 2004. 'East of the cloister: infirmaries, abbots' lodgings, and other chambers', in Kinder (ed) 2004, 199–211

Hall, J and Strachan, D 2001. 'The precinct and buildings of Tilty Abbey', *Essex Archaeol Hist*, **32**, 198–208

Halliday, G E 1900. 'Llantwit Major church, Glamorganshire', *Archaeol Cambrensis*, 5th ser, **17**, 129–56

Halliday, G E 1905. 'Llantwit Major church, Glamorganshire', *Archaeol Cambrensis*, 6th ser, **5**, 242–50

Halsey, R 1986. 'The earliest architecture of the Cistercians in England', in Norton and Park (eds) 1986, 65–85

Hamer, E 1873. 'A parochial account of Llanidloes', *Montgomeryshire Collect*, **6**, 155–96

Hamlin, A 1983. 'Collation seats in Irish Cistercian houses: Grey Abbey, County Down and Graiguenamanagh, County Kilkenny', *Medieval Archaeol*, **27**, 156–7

Hare, J 1993. 'Netley Abbey: monastery, mansion and ruin', *Proc Hampshire Fld Club Archaeol Soc*, **49**, 207–27

Harrison, J 1998. 'The troubled foundation of Grace Dieu Abbey', *Monmouthshire Antiq*, **14**, 25–9

Harrison, J 2000. 'The Tintern Abbey chronicles', *Monmouthshire Antiq*, **16**, 84–98

Harrison, S 1986. 'The stonework of Byland Abbey', *Ryedale Historian*, **13**, 26–47

Harrison, S 1990. *Byland Abbey*, London

Harrison, S 1995. 'Kirkstall Abbey: the 12th-century tracery and rose window', in Hoey (ed) 1995b, 73–8

Harrison, S 1997a. 'The loose architectural detail', in Shoesmith and Richardson (eds) 1997, 63–76

Harrison, S 1997b. 'The cloistral ranges and a fresh look at the chapter house', in Shoesmith and Richardson (eds) 1997, 113–24

Harrison, S 1997c. 'A syncopated arcade from Keynsham Abbey', in Keen (ed) 1997, 68–74

Harrison, S 2002. 'Grey Abbey, County Down: a new architectural survey and assessment', *J Brit Archaeol Ass*, **155**, 115–67

Harrison, S 2004. '"I lift mine eyes": a re-evaluation of the tower in Cistercian architecture in Britain and Ireland', in Kinder (ed) 2004, 125–35

Harrison, S and Barker, P 1999. 'Ripon Minster: an archaeological analysis and reconstruction of the 12th-century church', *J Brit Archaeol Ass*, **152**, 49–78

Harrison, S, Morris, R K and Robinson, D M 1998. 'A fourteenth-century pulpitum screen at Tintern Abbey, Monmouthshire', *Antiq J*, **78**, 177–268

Harrison, S and Thurlby, M 1997. 'An architectural history', in Shoesmith and Richardson (eds) 1997, 45–62

Harrison, S and Wood, J 1998. *Furness Abbey*, London

Harvey, B 1993. *Living and Dying in England 1100–1540: The Monastic Experience*, Oxford

Harvey, J H (ed) 1969. *William Worcestre Itineraries*, Oxford

Harvey, J H 1974. *Cathedrals of England and Wales*, 3rd edn, London

Harvey, J H 1982. 'The building of Wells Cathedral, I: 1175–1307', in *Wells Cathedral: A History* (ed L S Colchester), 52–75, Shepton Mallet

Harvey, J H 1984. *English Mediaeval Architects: A Biographical Dictionary Down to 1550*, rev edn, Gloucester

Harvey, W 1922. 'Tintern Abbey', *The Builder*, **123**, 239–45

Harvey, W 1924. 'Tintern Abbey: a record of repairs executed since 1913 under the direction of H. M. Office of Works', *The Structural Engineer*, April, 152–9; May, 206–13; December, 394–9

Haslam, R 1979. *The Buildings of Wales: Powys*, Harmondsworth

Hays, R W 1963. *The History of the Abbey of Aberconway 1186–1537*, Cardiff

Hays, R W 1971. 'The Welsh monasteries and the Edwardian conquest', in *Studies in Medieval Cistercian History*, Cistercian Stud Ser, 13, 110–37, Spencer, Mass.

Hayward, J 1973. 'Glazed cloisters and their development in the houses of the Cistercian order', *Gesta*, **12**, 93–109

Hearn, M F 1971. 'The rectangular ambulatory in English mediaeval architecture', *J Soc Architect Hist*, **30**, 187–208

Hearn, M F 1983. 'Ripon Minster: the beginnings of the Gothic style in northern England', *Trans American Phil Soc*, **73** (6), 1–140

Hearn, M F and Thurlby, M 1997. 'Previously undetected wooden ribbed vaults in medieval Britain', *J Brit Archaeol Ass*, **150**, 48–58

Heath, C 1793. *Historical and Descriptive Accounts of the Ancient and Present State of Tintern Abbey, Monmouth* (11th edn, 1828), Monmouth

Héliot, P 1968. 'La nef de l'église de Pogny et les piles fasiculées dans l'architecture romane', *Mémoires de la Société d'agriculture, commerce, sciences et arts du département de la Marne*, **83**, 80–92

Hemp, W J 1938. 'Two burials at Tintern Abbey', *Archaeol Cambrensis*, **93**, 131–3

Henderson, A E 1935. *Tintern Abbey Then and Now*, London

Henriet, J 2001. 'L'abbatiale cistercienne de Cherlieu', in *La création architecturale en Franche-Comté au XIIᵉ siècle: du roman au gothique* (ed É Vergnole), 244–79, Besançon

Hill, B D 1968. *English Cistercian Monasteries and their Patrons in the Twelfth Century*, Urbana

Hillaby, J 1988–90. '"The House of Houses": the Cistercians of Dore and the origins of the polygonal chapter house', *Trans Woolhope Natur Fld Club*, **46**, 209–43

Hillaby, J 1997a. 'The buried evidence: the Opus Dei', in Shoesmith and Richardson (eds) 1997, 37–44

Hillaby, J 1997b. 'Cults, patrons and sepulture', in Shoesmith and Richardson (eds) 1997, 97–102

Hillaby, J 1997c. 'Superfluity and singularity', in Shoesmith and Richardson (eds) 1997, 103–12

Hillaby, J 1997d. 'The Paul restoration', in Shoesmith and Richardson (eds) 1997, 201–4

Hirst, S M, Walsh, D A and Wright, S M 1983. *Bordesley Abbey II: Second Report on Excavations at Bordesley Abbey, Redditch, Hereford-Worcestershire*, BAR Brit Ser 111, Oxford

Hodkinson, E 1905. 'Notes on the architecture of Basingwerk Abbey, Flintshire', *J Chester Archaeol Hist Soc*, **11**, 169–77

Hoey, L R 1986. 'Pier alternation in Early English Gothic architecture', *J Brit Archaeol Ass*, **139**, 45–67

Hoey, L R 1987. 'Piers versus vault shafts in early English Gothic architecture', *J Soc Architect Hist*, **46**, 241–64

Hoey, L R 1993. 'Croxden Abbey', in Maddison (ed) 1993, 36–49

Hoey, L R 1995a. 'The 13th-century choir and transepts of Rievaulx Abbey', in Hoey (ed) 1995b, 97–116

Hoey, L R (ed) 1995b. *Yorkshire Monasticism: Archaeology, Art and Architecture from the 7th to 16th Centuries*, Brit Archaeol Ass Conference Trans, 16, London

Holdsworth, C J 1973. 'The blessings of work: the Cistercian view', in *Sanctity and Secularity: The Church and the World* (ed D Baker), Stud Church Hist, 10, 59–76, Oxford

Holdsworth, C J 1986a. 'The chronology and character of early Cistercian legislation on art and architecture', in Norton and Park (eds) 1986, 40–55

Holdsworth, C J 1986b. 'St Bernard and England', in *Anglo-Norman Stud*, 8 (ed R A Brown), Proc Battle Conference 1985, 138–53, Woodbridge

Holdsworth, C J 1990. 'Saint Bernard: what kind of saint?', in *Monastic Studies: The Continuity of Tradition* (ed J Loades), 86–101, Bangor

Holdsworth, C J 2004. 'The affiliation of Savigny', in *Truth as Gift: Studies in Honor of John R Sommerfeldt* (eds M L Dutton, D M LaCorte and P Lockey), Cistercian Stud Ser, 204, 43–88, Kalamazoo

Holme, G G 1929. *Guide to Valle Crucis Abbey, Llangollen*, Llangollen

Hope, W H St J 1900a. 'Fountains Abbey', *Yorkshire Archaeol J*, **15**, 269–402

Hope, W H St J 1900b. 'The abbey of St Mary in Furness, Lancashire', *Trans Cumberland Westmorland Antiq Archaeol Soc*, 16, 221–301

Hope, W H St J and Bilson, J 1907. *Architectural Description of Kirkstall Abbey*, Thoresby Soc Publ, 16, Leeds

Hope, W H St J and Brakspear, H 1906. 'The Cistercian abbey of Beaulieu, in the county of Southampton', *Archaeol J*, **63**, 129–86

Hope, W H St J and Brakspear, H 1909. 'Haughmond Abbey, Shropshire', *Archaeol J*, **66**, 281–310

Hope, W H St J and Brakspear, H 1911. 'Jervaulx Abbey', *Yorkshire Archaeol J*, **21**, 303–44

Horn, W 1973. 'On the origins of the medieval cloister', *Gesta*, **12**, 13–52

Horn, W and Born, E 1979. *The Plan of St Gall: A Study of the Architecture and Economy of, and Life in a Paradigmatic Carolingian Monastery*, 3 vols, Berkeley

Howard, M 1987. *The Early Tudor Country House: Architecture and Politics 1490–1550*, London

Howell, J K 2000. 'Tintern Abbey', *Archaeol Wales*, **40**, 114

Hubbard, E 1986. *The Buildings of Wales: Clwyd*, Harmondsworth

Hughes, H 1894. 'Valle Crucis Abbey', *Archaeol Cambrensis*, 5th ser, **11**, 169–85, 257–75

Hughes, H 1895a. 'Valle Crucis Abbey', *Archaeol Cambrensis*, 5th ser, **12**, 5–17

Hughes, H 1895b. 'The architectural history of St Mary's Church, Conway', *Archaeol Cambrensis*, 5th ser, **12**, 161–79

Hughes, H 1901. 'The architectural history of the cathedral church of St Deiniol, Bangor', *Archaeol Cambrensis*, 6th ser, **1**, 179–204

Hughes, H 1902. 'The architectural history of the cathedral church of St Deiniol, Bangor', *Archaeol Cambrensis*, 6th ser, **2**, 261–76

Hughes, H 1904. 'The architectural history of the cathedral church of St Deiniol, Bangor', *Archaeol Cambrensis*, 6th ser, **4**, 17–32

[Hughes, H] 1935. 'Valle Crucis Abbey', *Archaeol Cambrensis*, **90**, 333–43

Hughes, H 1937. 'Conwy Parish Church', *Archaeol Cambrensis*, **92**, 370–2

Hughes, J V 1998. *Margam Castle*, new edn, Swansea

Hunter, J (ed) 1840. 'Documents relating to the subjugation of the houses of St Mary, Dublin, and of Basingwerk, to the house of Buildwas', in *Ecclesiastical Documents*, Camden Society, 8, 51–5, London

Insley, C 1999. 'Fact and fiction in thirteenth-century Gwynedd: the Aberconwy charters', *Studia Celtica*, **33**, 235–50

Insley, C 2003. 'The wilderness years of Llywelyn the Great', in Prestwich *et al* (eds) 2003, 163–73

James, J II 1929. *A History and Survey of the Cathedral Church of SS Peter, Paul, Dubritius, Teilo and Oudoceus, Llandaff*, rev edn, Cardiff (first published 1898)

James, T 1978. 'A survey of the fishponds, watercourses and other earthworks at the site of Whitland Abbey and iron forge', *Carmarthenshire Antiq*, **14**, 71–8

James, T 1985. 'Excavations at the Augustinian priory of St John and St Teulyddog, Carmarthen, 1979', *Archaeol Cambrensis*, **134**, 120–61

James, T 1997. 'Excavations at Carmarthen Greyfriars, 1983–1990', *Medieval Archaeol*, **41**, 100–94

James, T 2000. 'Carmarthenshire's religious houses: a review of recent archaeological work', *Carmarthenshire Antiq*, **36**, 58–70

Janauschek, L 1877. *Originum Cisterciensium*, I, Vienna

Jansen, V 1984. 'Architectural remains of King John's abbey, Beaulieu (Hampshire)', in Lillich (ed) 1984, 76–144

Jansen, V 1991. 'The design and building sequence of the eastern arm of Exeter Cathedral, *c* 1270–1310: a qualified study', in *Medieval Art and Architecture at Exeter Cathedral* (ed F Kelly), Brit Archaeol Ass Conference Trans, 11, 35–56, London

Jansen, V 1998. 'Architecture and community in medieval monastic dormitories', in Lillich (ed) 1998, 59–94

Jeulin, P 1954. 'Les transformations topographiques et architecturales de l'abbaye de Clairvaux', in Association bourgignonne des sociétés savantes 1954, 325–41

Johns, C N 1960. 'The Celtic monasteries of north Wales', *Caernarvonshire Hist Soc Trans*, **21**, 14–43

Johns, C N 1962. 'The Celtic monasteries of north Wales', *Caernarvonshire Hist Soc Trans*, **23**, 129–31

Jones, A (ed) 1910. *History of Gruffydd ap Cynan (1054–1137)*, Manchester

Jones, A 1933. 'Basingwerk Abbey', in *Historical Essays in Honour of James Tait* (eds J G Edwards, V H Galbraith and E F Jacob), 169–78, Manchester

Jones, A 1937. 'The estates of the Welsh abbeys at the Dissolution', *Archaeol Cambrensis*, **92**, 269–86

Jones, A L 1996. *Heraldry in Glamorgan: 7, The Medieval Heraldic Inlaid Paving Tiles of Neath Abbey*, Cowbridge

Jones, D 1981. 'Excavations at Margam Abbey, 1974–5', *Archaeol Cambrensis*, **130**, 59–69

Jones, E D, Davies, N G and Roberts, R F 1947–8. 'Five Strata Marcella charters', *Nat Lib Wales J*, **5**, 50–4

[Jones], H L 1846. 'Cymmer Abbey, Merionethshire', *Archaeol Cambrensis*, **1**, 445–60

Jones, H L and Williams, J 1846. 'Basingwerk Abbey', *Archaeol Cambrensis*, **1**, 97–116

Jones, M C 1866. *Valle Crucis Abbey: Its Origin and Foundation Charter*, London (also published as 'Valle Crucis Abbey: its origin and foundation charter', *Archaeol Cambrensis*, 3rd ser, **12**, 1866, 400–17)

Jones, M C 1871. 'The abbey of Ystrad Marchell, (Strata Marcella), or Pola', *Montgomeryshire Collect*, **4**, 1–34, 293–332

Jones, M C 1872. 'The abbey of Ystrad Marchell, (Strata Marcella), or Pola', *Montgomeryshire Collect*, **5**, 109–48

Jones, M C 1873. 'The abbey of Ystrad Marchell, (Strata Marcella), or Pola', *Montgomeryshire Collect*, **6**, 347–86

Jones, M C [*et al*] 1877. 'The abbey of Ystrad Marchell: supplemental information', *Montgomeryshire Collect*, **10**, 397–406

Jones, M C and Williams, S W 1890. 'Proposed excavations on the site of Strata Marcella Abbey', *Archaeol Cambrensis*, 5th ser, **7**, 247–9

[Jones, M C] and Williams, S W 1891. 'Excavations on the site of Strata Marcella Abbey' [with 'Report on excavations at Strata Marcella Abbey, near Welshpool'], *Montgomeryshire Collect*, **25**, 149–96.

Jones, N W 2000a. 'Cwmhir Abbey, Abbeycwmhir', *Archaeol Wales*, **40**, 124, 125–6

Jones, N W 2000b. 'Abbeycwmhir: re-survey of the ruins', Clwyd-Powys Archaeological Trust Rep (unpublished), 225.2, Welshpool

Jones, N W and Thomas, D 1997. 'Abbeycwmhir', *Archaeol Wales*, **37**, 106

Jones, R O 1931. 'Strata Florida Abbey', *J Cardiganshire Antiq Soc*, **8**, 25–37

Jones, W B and Freeman, E A 1856. *The History and Antiquities of Saint David's*, London and Tenby (reprinted 1998, Haverfordwest)

[Jones, W H] 1920. 'Neath Abbey', *Archaeol Cambrensis*, 6th ser, **20**, 374–80

Keen, L (ed) 1997. *'Almost the Richest City': Bristol in the Middle Ages*, Brit Archaeol Ass Conference Trans, 19, London

Keevill, G, Aston, M and Hall, T (eds) 2001. *Monastic Archaeology: Papers on the Study of Medieval Monasteries*, Oxford

Kennedy [Gajewski], A K M 1996. 'Gothic architecture in northern Burgundy in the 12th and early 13th centuries', unpublished PhD thesis, Courtauld Institute of Art, London

[Kernan, C and Whittle, E] 1995. Cadw: Welsh Historic Monuments, *Register of Landscapes, Parks and Gardens of Special Historic Interest in Wales, Part 1, Parks and Gardens: Clwyd*, Cardiff

Kinder, T N 1980. 'Some observations on the origins of Pontigny and its first church', *Cîteaux*, **31**, 9–19

Kinder, T N 1982. 'A note on the plan of the first church at Pontigny', in Chauvin (ed) 1982–7, III, 6, 601–8

Kinder, T N 1984. 'The original chevet of Pontigny's church', in Lillich (ed) 1984, 30–8

Kinder, T N 1991. 'Les églises mediévales de Clairvaux: probabilités et fiction', in Leroux (ed) 1991, 205–29

Kinder, T N 1992. 'Toward dating construction of the abbey church of Pontigny', *J Brit Archaeol Ass*, **145**, 77–88

Kinder, T N 1996a. 'Cîteaux Abbey', in Turner (ed) 1996, 7, 354–6

Kinder, T N 1996b. 'Clairvaux Abbey', in Turner (ed) 1996, 7, 371–3

Kinder, T N 1997. *L'Europe Cistercienne*, La Pierre-qui-Vire (translated edn, 2002, *Cistercian Europe: Architecture of Contemplation*, Cistercian Stud Ser, 191, Kalamazoo)

Kinder, T N (ed) 2004. *Perspectives for an Architecture of Solitude: Essays on Cistercians, Art and Architecture in Honour of Peter Fergusson*, Turnhout

King, A A 1954. *Cîteaux and Her Elder Daughters*, London

Knapp, U 1997. *Das Kloster Maulbronn: Geschichte und Baugeschichte*, Stuttgart

Knight, H H and Moxham, E 1848. *Specimens of Inlaid Tiles Heraldic and Geometrical from Neath Abbey Glamorganshire*, nd, but *c* 1848, Neath Philosophical Institution

Knight, J K 1993. 'Newport, St Gwynllyw's (St Woolos) Cathedral', in Pounds (ed) 1993, 60–2

Knowles, D 1948–59, *The Religious Orders in England*, 3 vols, Cambridge

Knowles, D 1963a. *The Monastic Order in England: A History of its Development from the Times of St Dunstan to the Fourth Lateran Council 940–1216*, 2nd edn, Cambridge

Knowles, D 1963b. 'The primitive Cistercian documents', in Knowles, D, *Great Historical Enterprises: Problems in Monastic History*, 197–222, London

Knowles, D, Brooke, C N L and London, V C M (eds) 2001. *The Heads of Religious Houses: England and Wales. I, 940–1216*, 2nd edn, Cambridge

Knowles, D and Hadcock, R N 1971. *Medieval Religious Houses: England and Wales*, 2nd edn, London

Knowles, D and St Joseph, J K S 1952. *Monastic Sites from the Air*, Cambridge

Labbé, Y 1948–52. 'L'abbaye cistercienne N.-D. de Clermont', *Bulletin de la commission historique et archéologique de la Mayenne*, **62**, 19–49

Lackner, B K 1972. *The Eleventh-century Background of Cîteaux*, Cistercian Stud Ser, 8, Washington

Lackner, B K 1978. 'Early Cistercian life as described in the *Ecclesiastica Officia*', in *Cistercian Ideals and Reality* (ed J R Sommerfeldt), Cistercian Stud Ser, 60, 62–79, Kalamazoo

Lanfranc Constitutions: Knowles, D and Brooke, C N L (eds) 2002. *The Monastic Constitutions of Lanfranc*, Oxford

Laveille, A (ed) 1896–9. *Histoire de la congrégation de Savigny par Dom Claude Auvry*, 3 vols, Société de l'histoire de Normandie, 30, Rouen and Paris

Lawrence, C H 2001. *Medieval Monasticism: Forms of Religious Life in Western Europe in the Middle Ages*, 3rd edn, Harlow

Lay Brothers: Waddell, C (ed) 2000. *Cistercian Lay Brothers: Twelfth-century Usages with Related Texts*, Cîteaux: Commentaria cistercienses, studia et documenta, 10, Brecht

Leach, G B 1960. 'Excavations at Hen Blas, Coleshill Fawr, near Flint – second report', *Flintshire Hist Soc Pubs*, **18**, 13–60

Leclercq, J 1965. 'L'érémitisme et les cisterciens', in *L'Eremitismo in occidente nei secoli XI e XII*, Miscellanea del Centro di Studi Medioevali, 4, 573–80, Milan

Leclercq, J 1969. 'The intentions of the founders of the Cistercian order', *Cistercian Stud*, **4**, 21–61

Lekai, L J 1977. *The Cistercians: Ideals and Reality*, Kent, Ohio

Leland: Smith, L T (ed) 1906. *The Itinerary in Wales of John Leland, in or About the Years 1536–1539*, London

Leroux, J-F (ed) 1991. *Histoire de Clairvaux: Actes du colloque de Bar-sur-Aube/Clairvaux 22 et 23 juin 1990*, Association renaissance de l'abbaye de Clairvaux, Bar-sur-Aube

Leroux-Dhuys, J-F 1998. *Cistercian Abbeys: History and Architecture*, Paris and Cologne

Let Pap Henry VIII: Brewer, J S, Gairdner, J and Brodie, R H (eds) 1862–1932. *Letters and Papers, Foreign and Domestic, of the Reign of Henry VIII Preserved in the Public Record Office, the British Museum and Elsewhere in England*, 23 vols in 38, London

Lewis, D 1887. 'Notes on the charters of Neath Abbey', *Archaeol Cambrensis*, 5th ser, **4**, 86–115

Lewis, J M 1996. 'Some Tintern Abbey floor tiles at St George's Chapel, Windsor', *Monmouthshire Antiq*, **12**, 40–5

Lewis, J M 1999. *The Medieval Tiles of Wales*, Cardiff

Lewis, J M and Williams, D H 1976. *The White Monks in Wales*, Cardiff

Leyser, H 1984. *Hermits and the New Monasticism: A Study of Religious Communities in Western Europe 1000–1150*, London

Lillich, M P (ed) 1982a. *Studies in Cistercian Art and Architecture: Volume One*, Cistercian Stud Ser, 66, Kalamazoo

Lillich, M P 1982b. 'Cleanliness with Godliness: a discussion of medieval monastic plumbing', in Chauvin (ed) 1982–7, III, 5, 123–49

Lillich, M P (ed) 1984. *Studies in Cistercian Art and Architecture: Volume Two*, Cistercian Stud Ser, 69, Kalamazoo

Lillich, M P (ed) 1987. *Studies in Cistercian Art and Architecture: Volume Three*, Cistercian Stud Ser, 89, Kalamazoo

Lillich, M P (ed) 1998. *Studies in Cistercian Art and Architecture: Volume Five*, Cistercian Stud Ser, 167, Kalamazoo

Littere Wallie: Edwards, J G 1940. *Littere Wallie Preserved in Liber A in the Public Record Office*, Cardiff

Llandaff Acta: Crouch, D (ed) 1988. *Llandaff Episcopal Acta 1140–1287*, Cardiff

Lloyd, J E 1939. *A History of Wales from the Earliest Times to the Edwardian Conquest*, 3rd edn, 2 vols, London

Lloyd, T, Orbach, J and Scourfield, R 2004. *The Buildings of Wales: Pembrokeshire*, New Haven and London

Locatelli, R 1992. 'L'expansion de l'ordre cistercien', in *Bernard de Clairvaux: Histoire, mentalités, spiritualité*, Sources chrétiennes, 380, 103–40, Paris

Locock, M 2001a. 'Margam Abbey', *Archaeol Wales*, **41**, 150–1

Locock, M 2001b. 'Margam Abbey (SAM Gm5), Neath Port Talbot: archaeological evaluation', Glamorgan-Gwent Archaeological Trust Rep (unpublished), 2001/031, Swansea

Lord, P 2003. *The Visual Culture of Wales: Medieval Vision*, Cardiff

[Lovegrove, E W] 1921. 'Basingwerk Abbey', *Archaeol Cambrensis*, **76**, 401–5

Lovegrove, E W 1922. 'St David's Cathedral', *Archaeol Cambrensis*, **77**, 360–82

Lovegrove, E W 1926. 'The cathedral church of St David's', *Archaeol J*, **83**, 254–83

Lovegrove, E W 1929. 'The cathedral church of Llandaff', *J Brit Archaeol Ass*, new ser, **35**, 75–101

[Lovegrove, E W] 1932. 'Llanidloes church', *Archaeol Cambrensis*, **87**, 434–5

Lovegrove, E W 1936. 'Valle Crucis Abbey; its position in monasticism: the men who built it', *Archaeol Cambrensis*, **91**, 1–14

Lovegrove, E W 1942–3. 'Llanthony Priory', *Archaeol Cambrensis*, **97**, 213–29

Lovegrove, E W 1946–7. 'Llanthony Priory, Monmouthshire', *Archaeol Cambrensis*, **99**, 64–77

Lowe, B J 1987. 'Keynsham Abbey: excavations 1961–1985', *Somerset Archaeol Natur Hist*, **131**, 81–156

Lowe, W B 1912–28. *The Heart of Northern Wales*, 2 vols, privately printed, Llanfairfechan

Ludlow, N D 2000. 'Whitland Abbey', *Archaeol Wales*, **40**, 102–3

Ludlow, N D 2001. 'Whitland Abbey', *Archaeol Wales*, **41**, 142–3

Ludlow, N D 2002. 'Whitland Abbey, Carmarthenshire: a Cistercian site re-examined, 1994–9', *Archaeol Cambrensis*, **151**, 41–108

Lynam, C 1905. 'Notes on the nave of Chepstow parish church', *Archaeol J*, **62**, 273–8

Maddison, J M 1978. 'Decorated architecture in the north-west Midlands: an investigation of the work of provincial masons and their sources', unpublished PhD thesis, Manchester

Maddison, J (ed) 1993. *Medieval Art and Architecture at Lichfield*, Brit Archaeol Ass Conference Trans, 13, Leeds

Maddison, J 2000. *Ely Cathedral: Design and Meaning*, Ely

Mahn, J-B 1951. *L'ordre cistercien et son gouvernement des origines au milieu du XIIIe*, 2nd edn, Paris

Mahoney, T A [1979]. *Llantarnam Abbey: 800 Years of History*, privately printed, Llantarnam

Malone, C M 1973. 'West English Gothic architecture 1175–1250', unpublished PhD thesis, University of California, Berkeley

Malone, C M 1984. 'Abbey Dore: English versus French design', in Lillich (ed) 1984, 50–75

Malone, C M 2004. 'Cistercian design in the choir and transept of Wells Cathedral', in Kinder (ed) 2004, 351–67

Manrique, A 1642–56. *Cisterciensium seu verius ecclesiasticorum annalium a conditio cistercio*, 4 vols, Lyons

Martin, A R 1937. *Franciscan Architecture in England*, Manchester

Martindale, J 1992. 'Monasteries and castles: the priories of St-Florent de Saumur in England after 1066', in *England in the Eleventh Century* (ed C Hicks), Harlaxton Medieval Stud, 2, 135–56, Stamford

Matarasso, P (ed) 1993. *The Cistercian World: Monastic Writings of the Twelfth Century*, London

Matthew Paris: Luard, H R (ed) 1872–83. *Matthæi Parisiensis Monachi Sancti Albani, Chronica Majora*, 7 vols, Rolls Ser, 57, London

McCann, J 1976. *The Rule of St Benedict*, London

McGee, C and Perkins, J 1998. 'A study of the Cistercian abbey at Rufford, Nottinghamshire', in Alexander (ed) 1998, 83–92

McGuire, B P 1995. 'Who founded the order of Cîteaux?', in *The Joy of Learning and the Love of God: Essays in Honour of Jean Leclercq* (ed E R Elder), Cistercian Stud Ser, 160, 389–414, Kalamazoo

McGuire, B P 2000. 'Charity and unanimity: the invention of the Cistercian order – a review article', *Cîteaux*, **51**, 285–97

Mein, A G 2000a. 'Hendre farm, Llangattock-Vibon-Avel', *Archaeol Wales*, **40**, 109–10

Mein, A G 2000b. 'Abbey Cottage, Llanvihangel-Ystern-Llewern', *Archaeol Wales*, **40**, 153

Mein, A G and Lewis, J M 1990–1. 'Floor tiles from Llantarnam Abbey, Gwent', *Medieval and Later Pottery in Wales*, **12**, 101–4

Meyvaert, P 1973. 'The medieval monastic claustrum', *Gesta*, **12**, 53–60

Micklethwaite, J T 1882. 'Of the Cistercian plan', *Yorkshire Archaeol J*, **7**, 239–58

Migne, J-P (ed) 1844–64. *Patrologiae Cursus Completus*, Series Latina, 221 vols, Paris

Milne, H 2001a. 'Neath Abbey', *Archaeol Wales*, **41**, 151

Milne, H 2001b. 'Neath Abbey, Glamorgan: archaeological watching brief', Cambrian Archaeological Projects Rep (unpublished), 177, Llanidloes

Molina, N 1999. *L'abbaye de Silvacane*, Paris

Mon Ang: Caley, J, Ellis, H and Bandinel, B (eds) 1817–30. William Dugdale, *Monasticon Anglicanum*, 6 vols in 8, London

Moore, P and Moore, D 1974. 'Two topographical paintings of the old house at Margam, Glamorgan', *Archaeol Cambrensis*, **123**, 155–69

Moorhouse, S and Wrathmell, S 1987. *Kirkstall Abbey Volume 1 – The 1950–64 Excavations: A Reassessment*, Yorkshire Archaeol, 1, Wakefield

Morant, R W 1995. *The Monastic Gatehouse and Other Types of Portal of Medieval Religious Houses*, Lewes

Morgan, F C 1973. *A Short Account of the Church of Abbey Dore*, 6th edn, Abbey Dore

Morgan, C O S 1885. 'St Woollos church, Newport, Monmouthshire', *Archaeol Cambrensis*, 5th ser, **2**, 279–91

Morris, M 2003. 'The "murder" of an English earldom? Roger IV Bigod and Edward I', in Prestwich *et al* (eds) 2003, 89–99

Morris, R K 1978. 'The development of later Gothic mouldings in England *c* 1250–1400, Part I', *Architect Hist*, **21**, 18–57

Morris, R K 1979. 'The development of later Gothic mouldings in England *c* 1250–1400, Part II', *Architect Hist*, **22**, 1–48

Morris, R K 1990. 'The Gothic mouldings of the Latin and Lady chapels', in *Saint Frideswide's Monastery at Oxford: Archaeological and Architectural Studies* (ed J Blair), 169–83, Gloucester

Morris, R K 1997. 'European prodigy or regional eccentric?: the rebuilding of St Augustine's abbey church, Bristol', in Keen (ed) 1997, 41–56

Morris, R K 2000. 'The architectural history of the medieval cathedral church', in *Hereford Cathedral: A History* (eds G Aylmer and J Tiller), 203–40, London

Morris, R K 2004. 'From monastery to country house: an architectural history of Stoneleigh Abbey 1156–*c* 1660', in Bearman (ed) 2004, 15–61

Morris, R K 2005. 'The architecture and worked stones', in *Excavations at Hulton Abbey, Staffordshire 1987–1994* (W D Klemperer and N Boothroyd), Soc Medieval Archaeol Monogr Ser, 21, 69–86, Leeds

Musso, J M 1991. 'La restauration du bâtiment des convers de l'abbaye de Clairvaux', in Leroux (ed) 1991, 191–203

Narrative Texts: Waddell, C (ed) 1999. *Narrative and Legislative Texts from Early Cîteaux*, Cîteaux: Commentaria cistercienses, studia et documenta, 9, Brecht

Nash-Williams, V E 1950. *The Early Christian Monuments of Wales*, Cardiff

Negri, D 1981. *Abbazie cistercensi in Italia*, Pistoia

Newman, C W (ed) 1965. 'Report on the Abbey Cwm Hir Estate 1822, by Layton Cooke', *Trans Radnorshire Soc*, **35**, 44–50

Newman, C W (ed) 1966. 'Report on the Abbey Cwm Hir Estate 1822, by Layton Cooke', *Trans Radnorshire Soc*, **36**, 56–9

Newman, C W (ed) 1981. 'Report on the Abbey Cwm Hir Estate 1822, by Layton Cooke', *Trans Radnorshire Soc*, **51**, 45–56

Newman, J 1995. *The Buildings of Wales: Glamorgan*, London

Newman, J 2000. *The Buildings of Wales: Gwent/Monmouthshire*, London

Newman, M G 1996. *The Boundaries of Charity: Cistercian Culture and Ecclesiastical Reform, 1098–1180*, Stanford

Newman, M G 1997. 'Stephen Harding and the creation of the Cistercian community', *Revue Bénédictine*, **107**, 307–29

Nicholl, L D 1936. *The Normans in Glamorgan, Gower and Kidweli*, Cardiff

Nicolai, B 1988. 'Lilienfield und Walkenried: Zur Genese und Bedeutung eines zisterziensischen Bautypus', *Wiener Jahrbuch für Kunstgeschichte*, **41**, 23–39, 163–72

Nicolai, B 1990. *Libido Aedificandi: Walkenried und die monumentale Kirchenbaukunst der Zisterzienser um 1200*, Quellen und Forschungen zur Braunschweigischen Geschichte, 28, Brunswick

Nicolai, B 1993. 'Morimond et l'architecture cistercienne en Allemagne', *Bulletin monumental*, **151**, 181–98

North, F J 1957. *The Stones of Llandaff Cathedral*, Cardiff

Norton, C 1986. 'Table of Cistercian legislation on art and architecture', in Norton and Park (eds) 1986, 315–93

Norton, C and Park, D (eds) 1986. *Cistercian Art and Architecture in the British Isles*, Cambridge

NRS 1829. ['Dore Abbey'], *Gentleman's Mag*, **99** (2), 497–8

Nussbaum, N 2000. *German Gothic Church Architecture*, New Haven and London (published in 1994 as *Deutsche Kirchenbaukunst der Gotik*, Darmstadt)

O'Callaghan, B 1995. 'An analysis of the architecture of the Cistercian church at Abbey Dore', in Whitehead (ed) 1995, 94–104

O'Keeffe, T 1999. *An Anglo-Norman Monastery: Bridgetown Priory and the Architecture of the Augustinian Canons Regular in Ireland*, Cork

O'Neil, B H 1941. 'Talley Abbey, Carmarthenshire', *Archaeol Cambrensis*, **96**, 69–91

Orderic Vitalis: Chibnall, M (ed) 1969–80. *The Ecclesiastical History of Orderic Vitalis*, 6 vols, Oxford

Ormerod, G 1861. *Strigulensia: Archæological Memoirs Relating to the Confluence of the Severn and the Wye*, London

Ormrod, W M 1988–9. 'Edward II at Neath Abbey, 1326', *Neath Antiq Soc Trans*, 107–12

Orrin, G R 1988. *Medieval Churches of the Vale of Glamorgan*, Cowbridge

O'Sullivan, J F 1947. *Cistercian Settlements in Wales and Monmouthshire, 1140–1540*, Fordham Univ Stud, Hist Ser, 2, New York

Owen, E 1897. 'The spoils of the Welsh religious houses', *Archaeol Cambrensis*, 5th ser, **14**, 285–92

Owen, E 1917. 'The fate of the structures of Conway Abbey and Bangor and Beaumaris friaries', *Y Cymmrodor*, **27**, 70–144

Owen, E 1919. 'Strata Marcella Abbey immediately before and after its dissolution', *Y Cymmrodor*, **29**, 1–32

Owen, E 1919–20. 'The monastery of Basingwerk at the period of its dissolution', *Flintshire Hist Soc J*, **7**, 47–89

Owen, E (ed) 1950. 'Documents relating to the dissolved monastery of Grace Dieu', *South Wales and Monmouth Rec Soc Publ*, **2**, 189–99

Owen, G D 1935. 'Some agrarian conditions and changes in southwest Wales in the sixteenth century', unpublished PhD thesis, University of Wales, Aberystwyth

Owen, T H 1895. 'Valle Crucis Abbey', *J British Archaeol Ass*, new ser, **1**, 299–302

Pacaut, M 1993. *Les moines blancs: Histoire de l'ordre de Cîteaux*, Paris

Parks, L N and Webster, P V 1974. 'Merthyrgeryn: a grange of Tintern', *Archaeol Cambrensis*, **123**, 140–54

Patterson, R B 1992. 'The author of the Margam Annals: early thirteenth century Margam Abbey's compleat scribe', in *Anglo-Norman Stud*, **14** (ed M Chibnall), Proc Battle Conference 1991, 197–210, Woodbridge

Paul, R W 1893. 'Abbey Dore', *The Builder*, **64**, 265–9

Paul, R W 1896. 'Abbey Dore', *The Builder*, **70**, 298–300

[Paul, R W] 1898a. 'Tintern Abbey', *The Builder*, **75**, 9–11

Paul, R W 1898b. *Dore Abbey, Herefordshire: A Short Account of its History and an Appeal for its Repair*, Hereford

[Paul, R W] 1899a. 'Valle Crucis', *The Builder*, **77**, 13–15

[Paul, R W] 1899b. '"Bosses", Abbey Dore', *The Builder*, **77**, 34

[Paul, R W] 1902a. 'Abbey Dore', *The Builder*, **82**, 307

[Paul, R W] 1902b. 'Abbey Dore church, Hereford', *The Builder*, **83**, 448

[Paul, R W] 1903. 'Abbey Dore, Hereford', *The Builder*, **84**, 15

Paul, R W 1904. 'The church and monastery of Abbey Dore, Herefordshire', *Trans Bristol Gloucestershire Archaeol Soc*, **27**, 117–26

Paul, R 1927. 'Abbey Dore church, Herefordshire', *Archaeol Cambrensis*, **82**, 269–75

Paul, R 1931. 'Abbey Dore church, Herefordshire', *The Builder*, **141**, 500

Peers, C R 1922. 'Tintern Abbey', *Trans Bristol Gloucestershire Archaeol Soc*, **44**, 8–11

Peigné-Delacourt, A 1876. *Histoire de l'abbaye de Notre Dame d'Ourscamp*, Amiens

Percival, D 1993. 'The boundary of the medieval grange of Dolhelfa', *Trans Radnorshire Soc*, **63**, 42–4

Pérez, J C V 1994. 'Las primeras construcciones de la orden del Císter en el reino de Léon', *Arte Medievale*, 2nd ser, **8** (1), vol 2, 21–41

Peugniez, B 2001. *Routier cistercien: Abbayes et sites, France, Belgique, Luxembourg, Suisse*, Moisenay

Pevsner, N 1963. *The Buildings of England: Herefordshire*, Harmondsworth

Pevsner, N 1968. *The Buildings of England: Worcestershire*, Harmondsworth

Pevsner, N and Cherry, B 1975. *The Buildings of England: Wiltshire*, 2nd edn, Harmondsworth

Pevsner, N and Hubbard, E 1971. *The Buildings of England: Cheshire*, Harmondsworth

Pevsner, N, Harris, J and Antram, N 1989. *The Buildings of England: Lincolnshire*, 2nd edn, London

Phillips, N and Hamilton, M 2000. 'Geophysical survey at Grace Dieu Abbey', *Monmouthshire Antiq*, **16**, 51–4

Picquenard, G 1961. 'Abbaye de Clermont', *Congrès archéologique de France* (Maine), **119**, 328–32

Pierce, T Jones 1950–1. 'Strata Florida Abbey', *Ceredigion*, **1**, 18–33

Platt, C 1969. *The Monastic Grange in Medieval England*, London

Plouvier, M 1990. 'L'abbaye de Prémontré (Aisne)', *Congrès archéologique de France* (Aisne Méridionale), **148**, 509–48

Plouvier, M 1994. 'L'abbaye de Cîteaux', *Congrès archéologique de France* (Côte d'Or: Dijon La Côte et le Val-de-Saône), **152**, 65–99

Plouvier, M 1998. 'L'abbaye médiévale: histoire et analyse critique', in Plouvier and Saint-Denis (eds) 1998, 123–53

Plouvier, M and Saint-Denis, A (eds) 1998. *Pour une histoire monumentale de l'abbaye de Cîteaux, 1098–1998*, Cîteaux: Commentaria cistercienses, studia et documenta, 8, Brecht and Dijon

Pontroué, P 1973. 'Quatres ans de recherches archéologiques à l'abbaye de Dommartin, *Bulletin de la Commission départementale des monuments historiques du Pas-de-Calais*, **9**, 266–80

Popper, G (ed) 1978. *Medieval Art and Architecture at Worcester Cathedral*, Brit Archaeol Ass Conference Trans, 1, London

Potter, J 1847. *Remains of Ancient Monastic Architecture in England: Represented in a Series of Views, Plans, Elevations, Sections and Details*, London

Poulle, B 1994. 'Savigny and England', in *England and Normandy in the Middle Ages* (eds D Bates and A Curry), 159–68, London

Pounds, N J G (ed) 1993. *The Cardiff Area: Proceedings of the 139th Summer Meeting of the Royal Archaeological Institute*, London

Power, D (ed) 1994. *Archaeological Inventory of County Cork: Volume 2, East and South Cork*, Dublin

Pratt, D 1997. *The Dissolution of Valle Crucis Abbey*, 2nd edn, Wrexham

Pressouyre, L (ed) 1994. *L'espace cistercien*, Paris

Pressouyre, L and Kinder, T N (eds) 1992. *Saint Bernard et le monde cistercien*, new edn, Paris

Prestwich, M 1997. *Edward I*, new edn, New Haven and London

Prestwich, M, Britnell, R and Frame, R (eds) 2003. *Thirteenth-century England IX*, Woodbridge

Price, G V 1952. *Valle Crucis Abbey*, Liverpool

Prichard, J 1881. 'Margam Abbey', *Cardiff Natur Soc Rep Trans*, **13**, 50–3

Pryce, H 1996. 'Yr eglwys yn oes yr Arglwydd Rhys', in *Yr Arglwydd Rhys* (eds N A Jones and H Pryce), 145–77, Cardiff

Pryce, H 2001. 'The medieval church', in Smith and Smith (eds) 2001, 254–96

Pugh, T B (ed) 1971. *Glamorgan County History, III, The Middle Ages*, Cardiff

Radford, C A R 1935. *Strata Florida Abbey*, London

Radford, C A R 1946. *Cymmer Abbey*, London (new impression, 1981)

Radford, C A R 1949a. *Strata Florida Abbey*, London

Radford, C A R 1949b. 'Bangor Cathedral in the twelfth and thirteenth century: recent discoveries', *Archaeol Cambrensis*, **100**, 256–61

Radford, C A R 1952. *Ewenny Priory*, London (6th impression, 1976)

Radford, C A R 1953. *Valle Crucis Abbey*, London (12th impression, 1976)

Radford, C A R 1962. *St Dogmael's Abbey*, London (7th impression, 1975)

Radford, C A R 1963. 'The native ecclesiastical architecture of Wales (c 1100–1285): the study of a regional style', in *Culture and Environment: Essays in Honour of Sir Cyril Fox* (eds I LL Foster and L Alcock), 355–72, London

Radford, C A R 1982. 'The Cistercian abbey of Cwmhir, Radnorshire', *Archaeol Cambrensis*, **131**, 58–76

Rahtz, P and Hirst, S 1976. *Bordesley Abbey, Redditch, Hereford–Worcestershire: First Report on Excavations 1969–1973*, BAR Brit Ser, 23, Oxford

Ramey, R L 1996. 'Abbots' lodgings of the Cistercian order in the late fifteenth and early sixteenth centuries', unpublished MA thesis, University of York

Ramey, R L 2004. 'An archaeology of hospitality: the Stoneleigh Abbey gatehouse', in Bearman (ed) 2004, 62–81

RCAHMCW 1911. *Montgomery*, Roy Comm Ancient Hist Monuments Constructions Wales Monmouthshire, Inventories, London

RCAHMCW 1912. *Flint*, Roy Comm Ancient Hist Monuments Constructions Wales Monmouthshire, Inventories, London

RCAHMCW 1913. *Radnor*, Roy Comm Ancient Hist Monuments Constructions Wales Monmouthshire, Inventories, London

RCAHMCW 1914. *Denbigh*, Roy Comm Ancient Hist Monuments Constructions Wales Monmouthshire, Inventories, London

RCAHMCW 1917. *Carmarthen*, Roy Comm Ancient Hist Monuments Constructions Wales Monmouthshire, Inventories, London

RCAHMCW 1921. *County of Merioneth*, Roy Comm Ancient Hist Monuments Constructions Wales Monmouthshire, Inventories, London

RCAHMW 1937. *Anglesey*, Roy Comm Ancient Hist Monuments Wales Monmouthshire, Inventories, London

RCAHMW 1956. *Caernarvonshire: 1, East*, Roy Comm Ancient Hist Monuments Wales Monmouthshire, Inventories, London

RCAHMW 1960. *Caernarvonshire: 2, Central*, Roy Comm Ancient Hist Monuments Wales Monmouthshire, Inventories, London

RCAHMW 1976. *Glamorgan: 1, Part 3, The Early Christian Period*, Roy Comm Ancient Hist Monuments Wales, Inventories, Cardiff

RCAHMW 1981. *Glamorgan: 4, Part 1, The Greater Houses*, Roy Comm Ancient Hist Monuments Wales, Inventories, Cardiff

RCAHMW 1982. *Glamorgan: 3, Part 2, Medieval Secular Monuments – Non-Defensive*, Roy Comm Ancient Hist Monuments Wales, Inventories, Cardiff

RCAHMW 1991. *Glamorgan: 3, Part 1a, The Early Castles*, Roy Comm Ancient Hist Monuments Wales, Inventories, Cardiff

RCAHMW 1994. *The Cathedral Church of St John the Evangelist, Brecon: An Architectural Study*, Roy Comm Ancient Hist Monuments Wales, Brecon

RCHME 1931. *Herefordshire: 1, South-West*, Roy Comm Hist Monuments Engl, Inventories, London

RCHME 1934. *Herefordshire: 3, North-West*, Roy Comm Hist Monuments Engl, Inventories, London

RCHME 1939. *City of Oxford*, Roy Comm Hist Monuments Engl, Inventories, London

RCHME 1952. *Dorset: 1, West*, Roy Comm Hist Monuments Engl, Inventories, London

RCHME 1980. *City of Salisbury: 1*, Roy Comm Hist Monuments Engl, Inventories, London

Rees, S 1999. 'The Augustinian priory', in *A History of the Town and County of Haverfordwest* (ed D Miles), 53–78, Llandysul

[Rees, W J] 1849. 'Account of Cwmhir Abbey, Radnorshire', *Archaeol Cambrensis*, **4**, 233–60 (republished in 1850 with a preface and corrections as Rees, W J *Account of Abbey Cwmhir*)

Register Aberconwy: Ellis, H (ed) 1847. 'The Register and Chronicle of the abbey of Aberconway', *Camden Miscellany*, 1, 1–23, London

Remfry, P M 1994. *A Political History of Abbey Cwmhir and its Patrons, 1176 to 1282*, Malvern Link

Rhodes, J 1990. 'The date of Llanthony Prima church', *Monmouthshire Antiq*, **6**, 59

Rhys, J (ed) 1883. *Tours in Wales, by Thomas Pennant, Esq*, 3 vols, Caernarvon

Richard, A J 1935–9. 'Castles, boroughs, and religious houses', in *A History of Carmarthenshire*, 2 vols (ed J E Lloyd), I, 269–370, Cardiff

Richards, G 1966. 'The church of St Mary and All Saints, Conway', *J Hist Soc Church Wales*, **16**, 28–60

Richards, R 1957–60. 'The Cistercians and Cymer Abbey', *J Merioneth Hist Rec Soc*, **3**, 223–49

Roberts, G 1848a. 'Strata Florida Abbey', *Archaeol Cambrensis*, **3**, 110–36

Roberts, G 1848b. 'Documents and charters connected with the history of Strata Florida Abbey', *Archaeol Cambrensis*, **3**, 191–213

Robinson, D M 1980. *The Geography of Augustinian Settlement in Medieval England and Wales*, 2 vols, BAR Brit Ser, 80, Oxford

Robinson, D M 1993a. 'Margam Abbey', in Pounds (ed) 1993, 54–60

Robinson, D M 1993b. 'The priory church of St Mary, Abergavenny', in Pounds (ed) 1993, 43–6

Robinson, D M 1995a. *Tintern Abbey*, 3rd edn, Cardiff

Robinson, D M 1995b. *Cymer Abbey*, rev edn, Cardiff

Robinson, D M 1996a. 'The twelfth-century church at Tintern Abbey', *Monmouthshire Antiq*, **12**, 35–9

Robinson, D M 1996b. *Basingwerk Abbey*, Cardiff

Robinson, D M 1997. 'The making of a monument: the Office of Works and its successors at Tintern Abbey', *Monmouthshire Antiq*, **13**, 43–56

Robinson, D M (ed) 1998. *The Cistercian Abbeys of Britain: Far from the Concourse of Men*, London (also published in 1998 as Cistercian Stud Ser, 179, Kalamazoo; new paperback edn 2002, London)

Robinson, D M 2002a. *Tintern Abbey*, 4th edn, Cardiff

Robinson, D M 2002b. *Neath Abbey*, 4th edn, Cardiff

Robinson, D M 2002c. *Buildwas Abbey*, London

Robinson, D M 2004. 'The chapter house at Tintern Abbey', *Monmouthshire Antiq*, **20**, 95–129

Robinson, D M 2006a. *Basingwerk Abbey*, 2nd edn, Cardiff

Robinson, D M 2006b. *Neath Abbey*, 5th edn, Cardiff

Robinson, D M and Lea, R 2002. 'Malmesbury Abbey: history, archaeology and architecture to illustrate the significance of the south aisle screen', Engl Heritage Historical Analysis and Research Team, Rep and Pap (unpublished), 61, London

Robinson, D M and Platt, C 1998. *Strata Florida Abbey – Talley Abbey*, 2nd edn, Cardiff

Rochet, A C 1998. 'The refectory wing of the Cistercian abbey of Vaux-de-Cernay', in Lillich (ed) 1998, 187–210

Rodger, J W 1911. 'The stone cross slabs of South Wales and Monmouthshire', *Trans Cardiff Natur Soc*, **44**, 24–64

Rodwell, W 2001. *Wells Cathedral: Excavations and Structural Studies 1978–93*, 2 vols, Engl Heritage Archaeol Rep, 21, London

Roger of Wendover: Hewlett, H G (ed) 1886–9. *Chronica Rogeri de Wendover*, 3 vols, Rolls Ser, 84, London

Romanini, A M 1994. '"Ratio fecit diversum": la riscoperta delle Tre Fontane a Roma chiave di lettura dell'arte bernardina', *Arte Medievale*, ser 2, **8** (1), vol 1, 1–78

Rowell, R 2000. 'The archaeology of later monastic hospitality', unpublished PhD thesis, University of York

Rowley-Morris, E 1893. 'Possessions of the abbot and convent of Cwmhir in Kerry', *Montgomeryshire Collect*, **27**, 81–91

Rudolph, C 1987. 'The "Principal Founders" and the early artistic legislation of Cîteaux', in Lillich (ed) 1987, 1–45

Rudolph, C 1990. *The 'Things of Greater Importance': Bernard of Clairvaux's* Apologia *and the Medieval Attitude Toward Art*, Philadelphia

Rüffer, J 1999. *Orbis Cisterciensis, Zur Geschichte der monastischen und ästhetischen Kultur im 12. Jahrhundert*, Berlin

Rüffer, J 2002. 'Fountains Abbeys frühe Klosterkirche(n) – zum Stand der Bauforschung', *Cîteaux*, **53**, 73–98

Sandron, D 2001. *Picardie gothique: autour de Laon et Soissons, L'architecture religieuse*, Paris

Sartre, J 1971–2. 'L'architecture de l'abbaye de Saint-Jean d'Amiens', *Bulletin de la Société des antiquaires de Picardie*, **54**, 398–405

Schaefer, J O 1982. 'The earliest churches of the Cistercian order', in Lillich (ed) 1982a, 1–12

Schlee, D 2000a. 'Tintern Abbey', *Archaeol Wales*, **40**, 114

Schlee, D 2000b. 'Archaeological evaluation in advance of the Tintern Abbey floodlighting scheme', Cambrian Archaeological Projects Rep (unpublished), 147, Llanidloes

Schlee, D and Wilson, H 1999. 'Whitland Abbey', *Archaeol Wales*, **39**, 109

Schlink, W 1970. *Zwischen Cluny und Clairvaux: Die Kathedrale von Langres und die burgundische Architektur des 12. Jahrhunderts*, Berlin

Schröder, U 1980–2. 'Architektur der Zisterzienser', in Elm (ed) 1980–2, 311–44

Schütz, B 2004. *Klöster: Kulturerbe Europas*, Munich

Seeger, U 1997. *Zisterzienser und Gotikrezeption: Die Bautätigkeit des Babenbergers Leopold VI in Lilienfeld und Klosterneuburg*, Munich and Berlin

Selle, X de la (ed) 1998. *L'Abbaye de Clairvaux*, La Vie en Champagne, 14, Troyes

Sharpe, E 1848. *Architectural Parallels*, London

Sharpe, E 1874–7. *The Architecture of the Cistercians*, 3 vols, London

Sherwood, J and Pevsner, N 1974. *The Buildings of England: Oxfordshire*, Harmondsworth

Shoesmith, R 1979–81. 'Survey work at Dore Abbey', *Trans Woolhope Natur Fld Club*, **43**, 254–66

Shoesmith, R 1991. *Excavations at Chepstow 1973–1974*, Cambrian Archaeol Monogr, 4, Bangor

Shoesmith, R and Richardson, R (eds) 1997. *A Definitive History of Dore Abbey*, Woonton

Siddons, M P (ed) 1996. *Visitations by the Heralds in Wales*, Pubs Harleian Soc, new ser, 14, London

Silvester, B 2001. 'Archaeological works at Valle Crucis Abbey, Denbighshire', *Archaeol Wales*, **41**, 87–92

Sledmere, E 1914. *Abbey Dore, Herefordshire: Its Building and Restoration*, Hereford

Smith, D M and London, V C M (eds) 2001. *The Heads of Religious Houses, England and Wales: II, 1216–1377*, Cambridge

Smith, J B 1998. *Llywelyn ap Gruffudd, Prince of Wales*, Cardiff

Smith, J B 1999. 'Cymer Abbey and the Welsh princes', *J Merioneth Hist Rec Soc*, **13** (2), 101–18

Smith, J B and Butler, L A S 2001. 'The Cistercian order: Cymer Abbey', in Smith and Smith (eds) 2001, 297–325

Smith, J B and Smith, L B (eds) 2001. *History of Merioneth, Volume II, The Middle Ages*, Cardiff

Smith, J B and Thomas, W G 1977. *Abaty Ystrad Fflur*, London

Smith, P 1988. *Houses of the Welsh Countryside: A Study in Historical Geography*, 2nd edn, London

Smith, P 1998. 'The domestic architecture of the county, I', in *Cardiganshire County History, Volume 3, Cardiganshire in Modern Times* (eds G H Jenkins and I G Jones), 232–88, Cardiff

Smith, P 2001. 'Houses *c* 1415–*c* 1642', in Smith and Smith (eds) 2001, 422–506

Smith, P and Suggett, R 2002. 'Themes and variations in Merioneth: an essay on vernacular houses for Ron Brunskill', *Trans Ancient Monuments Soc*, **46**, 55–82

Soler, J I 2004. *Real Monasterio de Nuestra Señora de Rueda*, Zaragoza

Sommerfeldt, J R (ed) 1978. *Cistercian Ideals and Reality*, Cistercian Stud Ser, 60, Kalamazoo

Sommerfeldt, J R (ed) 1992. *Bernardus Magister: Papers Celebrating the Nonacentenary of the Birth of St Bernard of Clairvaux*, Cistercian Stud Ser, 135, Kalamazoo

Stalley, R A 1971. 'A twelfth-century patron of architecture: a study of the buildings erected by Roger, bishop of Salisbury 1102–1139', *J British Archaeol Ass*, 3rd ser, **34**, 62–83

Stalley, R A 1979. 'The medieval sculpture of Christ Church Cathedral, Dublin', *Archaeologia*, **106**, 107–22

Stalley, R A 1980. 'Mellifont Abbey: a study of its architectural history', *Proc Roy Ir Acad C*, **80**, 263–354

Stalley, R A 1981. 'Three Irish buildings with West Country origins', in *Medieval Art and Architecture at Wells and Glastonbury* (eds N Coldstream and P Draper), Brit Archaeol Ass Conference Trans, 4, 62–80, London

Stalley, R A 1986. 'The architecture of the Cistercian churches of Ireland, 1142–1272', in Norton and Park (eds) 1986, 117–38

Stalley, R A 1987. *The Cistercian Monasteries of Ireland: An Account of the History, Art and Architecture of the White Monks in Ireland from 1142 to 1540*, London and New Haven

Stalley, R A 1994. 'Saint Bernard, his views on architecture and the Irish dimension', *Arte Medievale*, 2nd ser, **8** (1), vol 2, 13–20

Stalley, R A 1999. *Early Medieval Architecture*, Oxford

Stalley, R A 2002. 'The architecture of St Davids Cathedral: chronology, catastrophe and design', *Antiq J*, **82**, 13–45

Stalley, R A and Thurlby, M 1989. 'The early Gothic choir of Pershore Abbey', *J Soc Architect Hist*, **58**, 351–70

Statuta: Canivez, J-M (ed) 1933–41. *Statuta Capitulorum Generalium Ordinis Cisterciensis ab Anno 1116 ad Annum 1786*, 8 vols, Louvain

Statutes: Waddell, C (ed) 2002. *Twelfth-century Statutes from the Cistercian General Chapter*, Cîteaux: Commentaria cistercienses, studia et documenta, 12, Brecht

St Davids Acta: Barrow, J (ed) 1998. *St Davids Episcopal Acta 1085–1280*, Cardiff

Stone, R 1997. 'The monastic precinct', in Shoesmith and Richardson (eds) 1997, 125–38

Stratford, N 1978. 'Notes on the Norman chapterhouse at Worcester', in Popper (ed) 1978, 51–70

Suggett, R 1996. 'The chronology of late-medieval timber houses in Wales', *Vernacular Architect*, **27**, 28–35, 106–11

Sutton, T S 1887. 'Neath Abbey', *Archaeol Cambrensis*, 5th ser, **4**, 81–5

Suydam, M 1976. 'Origins of the Savignac order: Savigny's role within twelfth-century monastic reform', *Revue Bénédictine*, **86**, 94–108

Swartling, I 1967. 'Cistercian abbey churches in Sweden and the "Bernardine Plan"', in *Nordisk Medeltid, konsthistoriska studier tillägnade Armin Tuulse* (eds S Karling, E Lagerlöf and J Svanberg), Stockholm Stud Hist Art, 13, 193–8, Uppsala

Talbot, C H 1943. 'Richard Straddell, abbot of Dore 1305–46', *Downside Rev*, **61**, 11–20

Talbot, C H 1959. 'Cadogan of Bangor', *Cîteaux*, **9**, 18–40

Talbot, C H (ed) 1967. *Letters from the English Abbots to the Chapter at Cîteaux, 1442–1521*, Camden Series 4, 4, London

Tavener, N 1998. 'Margam Abbey Church Hall', *Archaeol Wales*, **38**, 139

Taxatio Ecclesiastica: Astle, T, Ayscough, S and Caley, J (eds) 1802. *Taxatio Ecclesiastica Angliae et Walliae auctoritate Papae Nicholai IV circa A.D. 1291*, London

[Taylor, A J] 1938. 'Monkton Priory', *Archaeol Cambrensis*, **93**, 299–300

Taylor, A J 1946a. *Basingwerk Abbey*, London

Taylor, A J 1946b. 'The greater monastic houses', in *A Hundred Years of Welsh Archaeology* (ed V E Nash-Williams), Cambrian Archaeol Ass, 140–7, Gloucester

[Taylor, A J] 1947. 'Basingwerk Abbey', *Archaeol Cambrensis*, **99**, 321–2

Taylor, A J 1950. 'Master James of St George', *Engl Hist Rev*, **65**, 433–57

Taylor, A J 1971. *Basingwerk Abbey*, London

Taylor, J 1869. *Tintern Abbey, and its Founders*, Bristol (reprinted 1994, Cwmbran)

Tester, P J 1973. 'Excavations at Boxley Abbey', *Archaeol Cantiana*, **88**, 129–58

Thomas, C S and Taylor, F E 1938. *Neath Abbey 1130–1938: A Short Guide to the Ruins taken from the Notes of the Late Glen A. Taylor*, Neath

Thomas, D 1993. 'Valle Crucis Abbey', *Archaeol Wales*, **33**, 73

Thomas, D 1994. 'Valle Crucis Abbey', *Archaeol Wales*, **34**, 64

Thomas, G C G (ed) 1997. *The Charters of the Abbey of Ystrad Marchell*, Aberystwyth

Thomas, W G 1962. 'Monkton priory church', *Archaeol J*, **119**, 344–5

Thomas, W H 1839. *Tinterne and its Vicinity*, London

Thompson, A H 1937. *Buildwas Abbey, Shropshire*, London

Thompson, F H 1962. 'Excavations at the Cistercian abbey of Vale Royal, Cheshire, 1958', *Antiq J*, **42**, 183–207

Thompson, H M 1925. 'Llandaff Cathedral: a bibliography raisonné', *Archaeol Cambrensis*, **80**, 392–404

Thompson, M 2001. *Cloister, Abbot and Precinct in Medieval Monasteries*, Stroud

Thorpe, L (ed) 1978. *Gerald of Wales: The Journey through Wales and the Description of Wales*, Harmondsworth

Thurlby, M 1988. 'The Romanesque priory church of St Michael at Ewenny', *J Soc Architect Hist*, **47**, 281–94

Thurlby, M 1993. 'The early Gothic transepts of Lichfield Cathedral', in Maddison (ed) 1993, 50–64

Thurlby, M 1994. 'St Andrews Cathedral-Priory and the beginnings of Gothic architecture in northern Britain', in *Medieval Art and Architecture in the Diocese of St Andrews* (ed J Higgitt), Brit Archaeol Ass Conference Trans, 14, 47–60, London

Thurlby, M 1995a. 'Some design aspects of Kirkstall Abbey', in Hoey (ed) 1995b, 62–72

Thurlby, M 1995b. 'Hereford Cathedral: the Romanesque fabric', in Whitehead (ed) 1995, 15–28

Thurlby, M 1995c. 'The Lady Chapel of Glastonbury Abbey', *Antiq J*, **75**, 107–70

Thurlby, M 1996. 'The abbey church, Pershore: an architectural history', *Trans Worcestershire Archaeol Soc*, 3rd ser, **15**, 146–209

Thurlby, M 1999. *The Herefordshire School of Romanesque Sculpture*, Woonton

Thurlby, M 2000. 'Roger of Pont l'Evêque, archbishop of York (1154–81), and French sources for the beginnings of Gothic in northern Britain', in *England and the Continent in the Middle Ages: Studies in Memory of Andrew Martindale* (ed J Mitchell), Harlaxton Medieval Stud, 8, 35–47, Stamford

Thurlby, M 2002. 'Minor cruciform churches in Norman England and Wales', in *Anglo-Norman Stud*, 24 (ed J Gillingham), Proc Battle Conference 2001, 239–76, Woodbridge

Tobin, S 1995. *The Cistercians: Monks and Monasteries of Europe*, London

[Traveller, A] 1863. 'Valle Crucis Abbey', *Archaeol Cambrensis*, 3rd ser, **9**, 68–72

Turbervill, J P 1901. *Ewenny Priory: Monastery and Fortress*, London

Turner, J (ed) 1996. *The Dictionary of Art*, 34 vols, London

Turner, R C 2002. *Chepstow Castle*, Cardiff

Turner, R C (with Allen, J R L, Coldstream, N, Jones-Jenkins, C, Morris, R K M and Priestly, S G) 2004. 'The great tower, Chepstow Castle, Wales', *Antiq J*, **84**, 223–318

Turvey, R 1996–7. 'The death and burial of an excommunicate prince: the Lord Rhys and the cathedral church of St Davids: Part One', *J Pembrokeshire Hist Soc*, **7**, 26–49

Turvey, R 1998–9. 'The death and burial of an excommunicate prince: the Lord Rhys and the cathedral church of St Davids: Part Two', *J Pembrokeshire Hist Soc*, **8**, 5–26

Turvey, R 2002. *The Welsh Princes: The Native Rulers of Wales 1063–1283*, Harlow

Tyers, I and Boswijk, G 1998. 'Tree-ring analysis of oak timbers from Dore Abbey, Abbey Dore, Herefordshire', Engl Heritage Ancient Monuments Laboratory Rep (unpublished), 18/98, London

Untermann, M 1984. *Kirchenbauten der Prämonstratenser: Untersuchungen zum Problem einer Ordensbaukunst im 12. Jahrhundert*, Veröffentlichung der Abteilung Architektur des Kunsthistorischen Instituts der Universität zu Köln, 29, Cologne

Valle Pérez, J C 1982. *La arquitectura cisterciense en Galicia*, 2 vols, La Coruña

Valle Pérez, J C 1994. 'Las primeras construcciónes de la orden del Císter en el Reino de León', *Arte Medievale*, ser 2, **8** (1), vol 2, 21–43

Valor Ecclesiasticus: Caley, J and Hunter, J (eds) 1810–34. *Valor Ecclesiasticus*, 6 vols, London

Van Damme, J-B 1999. *The Three Founders of Cîteaux*, Cistercian Stud Ser, 176, Kalamazoo

Van der Meer, F 1965. *Atlas de l'ordre cistercien*, Paris and Brussels

VCH 1972. *The Victoria History of the County of Gloucestershire*, 10, Oxford

Verey, D and Brooks, A 1999. *The Buildings of England. Gloucestershire 1: The Cotswolds*, 3rd edn, London

Verey, D and Brooks, A 2002. *The Buildings of England. Gloucestershire 2: The Vale and the Forest of Dean*, 3rd edn, New Haven and London

Vilain, G 1998. 'Clairvaux II et III: architecture et histoire', *La Vie en Champagne*, nouvelle série, **14**, 17–39

Vince, A 1997. 'The medieval floor tiles', in Shoesmith and Richardson (eds) 1997, 77–84

Vincent, N 1993. 'The early years of Keynsham Abbey', *Trans Bristol Gloucestershire Archaeol Soc*, **111**, 95–113

Vongrey, F and Hervay, F 1967. 'Notes critiques sur l'atlas de l'ordre cistercien', *Analecta Cisterciensia* (*Analecta Sacri Ordinis Cisterciensis*), **23**, 115–52

Von Simson, O 1956. *The Gothic Cathedral: The Origins of Gothic Architecture and the Medieval Concept of Order*, London

Waddell, C 1993. 'Towards a new provisional edition of the statutes of the Cistercian General Chapter, c 1119–1189', in *Studiosorum Speculum: Studies in Honor of Louis J. Lekai, O. Cist* (eds J R Sommerfeldt and F Swietek), Cistercian Stud Ser, 141, 384–418, Kalamazoo

Waddell, C 1994. 'The Cistercian institutions and their early evolution: granges, economy, lay brothers', in Pressouyre (ed) 1994, 27–38

Waddell, C 2000. 'The myth of Cistercian origins: C H Berman and the manuscript sources', *Cîteaux*, **51**, 299–386

Wakeman, T 1848. 'Caerleon', *Archaeol Cambrensis*, **3**, 328–44

Walsh, D A 1979. 'A rebuilt cloister at Bordesley Abbey', *J Brit Archaeol Ass*, **132**, 42–9

Walsh, D A 1994. 'Regionalism and localism in early Cistercian architecture in England', *Arte Medievale*, 2nd ser, **8** (1), vol 2, 103–11

Ward, J C 1981. 'Fashions in monastic endowment: the foundations of the Clare family, 1066–1314', *J Eccles Hist*, **32**, 427–51

Ward, M 1994. 'High St Conwy', *Archaeol Wales*, **34**, 62

Wathen, J 1792. ['Dore Abbey'], *Gentleman's Mag*, **62**, 395–6

Watkins, B 1985. *The Story of Flaxley Abbey and the Cistercian Monks in the Forest of Dean*, privately printed, Flaxley

Webb, G 1956. *Architecture in Britain: The Middle Ages*, Harmondsworth (2nd edn 1965, Harmondsworth)

Webb, G and Walker, A 1960. *St Bernard of Clairvaux: The Story of His Life as Recorded in the Vita Prima Bernardi*, London

White, R B 1987. 'Excavations at Maenan Abbey, 1982', *Archaeol Cambrensis*, **136**, 173–5

Whitehead, D (ed) 1995. *Medieval Art, Architecture and Archaeology at Hereford*, Brit Archaeol Ass Conference Trans, 15, London

[Whittle, E] 1994. Cadw: Welsh Historic Monuments, *Register of Landscapes, Parks and Gardens of Special Historic Interest in Wales, Part 1, Parks and Gardens: Gwent*, Cardiff

[Whittle, E] 2000. Cadw: Welsh Historic Monuments, *Register of Landscapes, Parks and Gardens of Special Historic Interest in Wales, Part 1, Parks and Gardens: Glamorgan*, Cardiff

Wilcox, M 1990. 'The foundation charter of Neath Abbey', *Annu Rep Glamorgan Archivist 1990*, 17–18

William of Malmesbury: Mynors, R A B, Thomson, R M and Winterbottom, M 1998–9. *William of Malmesbury: Gesta Regum Anglorum*, 2 vols, Oxford

Williams, D 1796. *The History of Monmouthshire*, London

Williams, D H 1961–4. 'Grace Dieu Abbey', *Monmouthshire Antiq*, **1**, 85–106

Williams, D H 1965–8a. 'Tintern Abbey: its economic history', *Monmouthshire Antiq*, **2**, 1–32

Williams, D H 1965–8b 'Abbey Dore', *Monmouthshire Antiq*, **2**, 65–104

Williams, D H 1965–8c 'Llantarnam Abbey', *Monmouthshire Antiq*, **2**, 131–48

Williams, D H 1970–8a. 'Grace Dieu Abbey: an exploratory excavation', *Monmouthshire Antiq*, **3**, 55–8

Williams, D H 1970–8b. 'Sale of goods at Dore Abbey', *Monmouthshire Antiq*, **3**, 192–5

Williams, D H 1971a. 'Grace Dieu Abbey', *Archaeol Wales*, **11**, 33

Williams, D H 1971b. 'Fasti Cistercienses Cambrenses', *Bull Board Celtic Stud*, **24**, 181–229

Williams, D H 1973. 'Fasti Cistercienses Cambrenses', *Bull Board Celtic Stud*, **25**, 156–7

Williams, D H 1975. 'Cistercian nunneries in medieval Wales', *Cîteaux*, **25**, 155–74

Williams, D H 1976a. *White Monks in Gwent and the Border*, Pontypool

Williams, D H 1976b. 'The White Monks in Powys I (Cwmhir)', *Cistercian Stud*, **11**, 73–101

Williams, D H 1976c. 'The White Monks in Powys II (Strata Marcella)', *Cistercian Stud*, **11**, 155–91

Williams, D H 1978. 'Abbatial disputes at Basingwerk', *Cîteaux*, **39**, 330–2

Williams, D H 1981a. 'Basingwerk Abbey', *Cîteaux*, **32**, 87–113

Williams, D H 1981b. 'The Cistercians in west Wales: I, Cymer Abbey (1198–1536/7)', *Archaeol Cambrensis*, **130**, 36–58

Williams, D H 1984. *The Welsh Cistercians*, 2nd edn, 2 vols, Caldey Island

Williams, D H 1990. *Atlas of Cistercian Lands in Wales*, Cardiff

Williams, D H 1992. 'An appreciation of the life and work of Stephen William Williams (1837–99)', *Montgomeryshire Collect*, **80**, 55–88

Williams, D H 1995. 'The exploration and excavation of Cistercian sites in Wales', *Archaeol Cambrensis*, **144**, 1–25

Williams, D H 1997a. 'The abbey of Dore', in Shoesmith and Richardson (eds) 1997, 15–36

Williams, D H 1997b. 'The Dissolution', in Shoesmith and Richardson (eds) 1997, 149–52

Williams, D H 1998. *The Cistercians in the Early Middle Ages*, Leominster

Williams, D H 1999. 'Rogerstone grange, St Arvan's', *Monmouthshire Antiq*, **15**, 22–32

Williams, D H 2001. *The Welsh Cistercians*, Leominster

Williams, D H and Jenkins, G 1970. 'Grace Dieu Abbey', *Archaeol Wales*, **10**, 25–6

Williams, D H and Kissack, K E (eds) 2001. *Monmouth Priory: A History of the Benedictine Priory of the Blessed Virgin Mary and St Florent at Monmouth*, Monmouth

Williams, G 1967. *Welsh Reformation Essays*, Cardiff

Williams, G 1974. 'Neath Abbey', in *Neath and District: A Symposium* (ed E Jenkins), 73–91, 2nd edn, Neath

Williams, G 1976. *The Welsh Church from Conquest to Reformation*, rev edn, Cardiff

Williams, G 1991. 'Kidwelly Priory', in *Sir Gâr: Studies in Carmarthenshire History* (ed H James), 189–204, Carmarthen

Williams, G 1997. *Wales and the Reformation*, Cardiff

Williams, G 1998. 'Margam Abbey, the later years and the Dissolution', *Morgannwg*, **42**, 23–35

W[illiams], H L J J 1846. 'Basingwerk Abbey', *Archaeol Cambrensis*, **1**, 97–116

Williams (*Ab Ithel*), J 1846. 'Valle Crucis Abbey', *Archaeol Cambrensis*, **1**, 17–32, 151–3, 279–80

Williams, J 1905. *A General History of the County of Radnor* (ed E Davies), Brecknock

Williams, R 1835. *The History and Antiquities of the Town of Aberconwy*, privately printed, Denbigh

Williams, S W 1887. 'Report on excavations at Strata Florida Abbey, Cardiganshire', *Archaeol Cambrensis*, 5th ser, **4**, 290–9

Williams, S W 1888. 'Report on the excavations in the abbey of Strata Florida', *Archaeol Cambrensis*, 5th ser, **5**, 262–4

Williams, S W 1889a. *The Cistercian Abbey of Strata Florida: Its History and an Account of the Recent Excavations Made on the Site*, London

Williams, S W 1889b. 'On further excavations at Strata Florida Abbey', *Archaeol Cambrensis*, 5th ser, **6**, 24–58

Williams, S W 1889c. 'Strata Florida Abbey', *Archaeol Cambrensis*, 5th ser, **6**, 187–9

Williams, S W 1889d. 'Strata Florida Abbey', *Archaeol Cambrensis*, 5th ser, **6**, 266–7

Williams, S W 1889e. 'Who was the founder of Strata Florida?', *Archaeol Cambrensis*, 5th ser, **6**, 19–23

Williams, S W 1890a. 'The abbey of Cwmhir, Radnorshire', *Archaeol Cambrensis*, 5th ser, **7**, 150–2

Williams, S W 1890b. 'The Cistercian abbey of Cwmhir, Radnorshire', *Montgomeryshire Collect*, **24**, 395–416

Williams, S W 1890c. 'Strata Florida Abbey: report upon further excavations', *Archaeol Cambrensis*, 5th ser, **7**, 253–6

Williams, S W 1891. 'Tile-pavements at Strata Florida Abbey', *Archaeol Cambrensis*, 5th ser, **8**, 303–5

Williams, S W 1892. 'The Cistercian abbey of Strata Marcella', *Archaeol Cambrensis*, 5th ser, **9**, 1–17

Williams, S W 1894–5. 'The Cistercian abbey of Cwmhir, Radnorshire', *Trans Hon Soc Cymmrodorion*, 61–98

Williams, S W 1897. 'Excavations at Talley Abbey', *Archaeol Cambrensis*, 5th ser, **14**, 229–47

Williams-Jones, K 1957–60. 'Llywelyn's charter to Cymer Abbey in 1209', *J Merioneth Hist Rec Soc*, **3**, 45–78

Willis, B 1718. *A Survey of the Cathedral-Church of Llandaff*, London

Willis-Bund, J W 1889. 'Who was the founder of Strata Florida?', *Archaeol Cambrensis*, 5th ser, **6**, 5–18

Wilson, C 1978. 'The sources of the late twelfth-century work at Worcester Cathedral', in Popper (ed) 1978, 80–90

Wilson, C 1985. 'Abbot Serlo's church at Gloucester (1089–1100): its place in Romanesque architecture', in *Medieval Architecture at Gloucester and Tewkesbury* (eds T A Heslop and V A Sekules), Brit Archaeol Ass Conference Trans, 7, 52–83, London

Wilson, C 1986. 'The Cistercians as "missionaries of Gothic" in northern England', in Norton and Park (eds) 1986, 86–116

Wilson, C 1987. 'The English response to French Gothic architecture, c 1200–1350', in Alexander and Binski (eds) 1987, 74–82

Wilson, C 1991. 'The early thirteenth-century architecture of Beverley Minster: cathedral splendours and Cistercian austerities', in Coss and Lloyd (eds) 1991, 181–95

Wilson, C 1992. *The Gothic Cathedral*, rev edn, London

Wilson, C 1999. 'The stellar vaults of Glasgow Cathedral's inner crypt and Villard de Honnecourt's chapter-house plan: a conundrum revisited', in *Medieval Art and Architecture in the Diocese of Glasgow* (ed R Fawcett), Brit Archaeol Ass Conference Trans, 23, 55–76, London

Wood, J G 1902–4. 'A short history of Tintern Abbey and the lordship of Striguil', *Trans Woolhope Natur Fld Club*, 300–11

Wood, J G 1907. 'William Herbert, earl of Pembroke: a sequel to the battle of Danesmoor', *The Antiquary*, **43**, 8–11

Wood, J G 1908. 'Tintern Abbey', *Archaeol Cambrensis*, 6th ser, **8**, 345–58

Wood, J G 1909. 'Tintern Abbey', *Archaeol Cambrensis*, 6th ser, **9**, 49–64

Wood, J G 1910. *The Lordship, Castle and Town of Chepstow, otherwise Striguil*, Monmouthshire Caerleon Antiq Ass, Newport

Wood, J G 1912. *Some Features of the Monastic Buildings Disclosed by Recent Excavations within the Precincts of Tintern Abbey*, Monmouthshire Caerleon Antiq Ass, Newport

Woof, R and Hebron, S 1998. *Towards Tintern Abbey: A Bicentenary Celebration of 'Lyrical Balads', 1798*, Grasmere

Wrathmell, S 1987. *Kirkstall Abbey, the Guest House: A Guide to the Medieval Buildings*, 2nd edn, Wakefield

Youings, J 1971. *The Dissolution of the Monasteries*, London

Zukowsky, J R 1977. 'The polygonal chapter house: architecture and society in Gothic Britain', unpublished PhD thesis, State University of New York, Binghamton

INDEX

Illustrations are denoted by page numbers in *italics*. The following abbreviations have been used in this index: d – died; n – note.